Interred With Their Bones

Bill Miner in Canada

1903–1907

INTERRED WITH
THEIR BONES

BILL MINER IN CANADA

1903–1907

PETER GRAUER

© 2006 by Peter Grauer
First Edition, First Printing
10 9 8 7 6 5 4 3 2 1

ISBN: 0-9739980-1-6
History, Canadian History,
British Columbia History

Editor: Sue Elliott
Maps: Lawrence Tyssen
Digital Image Capture: Kirsten Grauer
Companion Web site: Kirsten Grauer
Cover, Design and Typography: David DiFrancesco
Original Artwork: Ken Davis of Kamloops
                 Wilfred Wright of Lac La Hache

Typeset in Goudy Old Style

Printed and bound in Canada by
Houghton Boston
Saskatoon, Saskatchewan

PARTNERS
in
PUBLISHING

Partners In Publishing
Box 845
Kamloops, B.C. v2c 5m8
Canada
www.partnersinpublishing.ca

To Karen, Kirsten and Karl

"The evil that men do lives after them;
The good is oft interred with their bones."

WILLIAM SHAKESPEARE, "JULIUS CAESAR."

(3.2.79)

"Most train robbers ain't smart, which is a lucky thing for the
railroads," Call said. "Five smart train robbers could bust
every railroad in this country."

LARRY MCMURTRY, "STREETS OF LAREDO."

(SIMON AND SCHUSTER, 1993)

"In the memory of a girl, riding in search of wild birds, will linger the
image of three men sitting in calm air, a battered coffee pot aslant
on a piece of stone. A place that might still hold the mystery of shouts
and gunshot, the silenced cranes on the edge of water.
Where clouds passing over the bodies of the hills might contain
the smoke of their cooking fires."

THERESA KISHKAN, "SISTERS OF GRASS."

(GOOSE LANE EDITIONS, 2000)

ACKNOWLEDGEMENTS

MANY CONSIDER THE WRITING OF A BOOK such as this a solitary and lonely affair. At times, it is just that. The writer fears that he labours in vain, and that no one will either want to or be able to share the views and passions about the times and characters he so vividly sees in his own mind's eye. It is a lonely obsession, one that demands isolation and confinement. But that is only for a brief period at the end of the journey when the real work of writing has to be done. For the six years I have spent researching this volume, I can truthfully say that I have enjoyed every minute of it. The people that have assisted me so generously over those past years have made the journey one of revelation and given me an appreciation for our collective fascination for our past and what it means to us today.

When I first sat down to list those that assisted me in completing this work, I wanted to be sure that I didn't miss anyone. I owed so much to each one of them that I was obsessed with not leaving someone out. I wanted to recognize all that they had done for me, logistically and inspirationally, to help me accomplish my task. Perhaps the most critical assistance I received was spiritual and emotional. This enabled me to confront and overcome a period of adversity that seriously tested me. For that I will be forever grateful to those selfless and caring individuals. As I faithfully documented all those persons that I wanted to distinguish, the exercise started to remind me of those interminable Academy Awards litanies from grateful recipients. I started to wonder how a reader, one who should be so faithful as to read the author's dry acknowledgments section, would react to an endless list of unknown worthies familiar only to the writer. I decided to forego that list, as all of you individually know how much in your debt I am, and that I will carry that remembrance of you with me forever.

But there are some that must be recognized for their individual efforts in getting this book published. David DiFrancesco, of the Thompson Rivers University Digital Art and Design faculty, generously contributed many hours in the design of this book and its cover. My Westwold friend Sue Elliott applied her formidable editing and proof reading skills to make it look as though I know the basics of English grammar and composition. Sandi Pringle of Westwold tenaciously held to the pursuit of Paul Stevens' beginnings in the United States, and ferreted out additional intriguing information about this little-known individual. My old friend Larry Tyssen took his drafting pen in hand to show his free-hand drafting skills had not been forgotten by creating all the maps for this book. Don Klancher of Kamloops gave generously of his knowledge of all things relating to the R.C.M.P. to ensure the force was represented accurately, as well as access to his voluminous collection of source material. Ken Davis of Kamloops and Wilf Wright of Williams Lake artistically enhanced the legitimacy of this book with their moody sketches of the cabins of Jack Budd and Shorty Dunn. Our special friend Fiona Osborne diligently researched the Vancouver Archives and discovered new sources of information for the story of Bill Miner and his friends, and also found Maisie Campbell-Johnston. Don Keizer and the late Jack Montieth, both of Powell River, allowed me to vicariously follow along on their video quest for the real Bill Miner across southern British Columbia almost twenty years ago. Their audio-taped interviews with Albert McKay in Surrey when he was approaching 100 years of age proved to be an invaluable source of first-hand information about facets of Miner's character and his relationship with a young boy in the hills above Kamloops.

The staff at the British Columbia Archives and the Legislative Library in Victoria acted with a proud professionalism when extending to me so much assistance over so many visits. The staff at the Thompson Nicola Library system in downtown Kamloops and at the North Shore branch provided a watchful eye out for the stranger with the laptop huddled in the corner those many days over the years.

Of all the institutions I visited across the province, the one I have to single out for special thanks is the Kamloops Museum and Archives. Their patience, cheerfulness and knowledge were much appreciated.

Many of the small community archives throughout the southern interior, most staffed by volunteers, helped make this book possible. Their devotion to and love of the stories of their towns, their citizens and of the province made research a pleasure, and enhanced the task I had set myself. They are all professionals and are keeping the records of our past alive by producing events, brochures and books detailing the stories they all have to tell. Visits to and research done at Princeton, Hedley, Merritt, Enderby, Armstrong, Quesnel, Chilliwack, Mission, Revelstoke and Maple Ridge were rewarding and fruitful. The RCMP Museum and Archives in Regina was most helpful in providing primary source material not previously studied. Access to our nation's archives in Ottawa, unfortunately, had to remain a distant and tantalizing resource. It was inaccessible to this researcher due to its very remoteness in distance, difficulty of access and cost of travel.

Finally, none of this would have been possible without the love and support of two people. My daughter Kirsten was unwavering of her belief in the project and encouragement for my efforts, and her computer and graphics skills allowed me to focus on the task of writing. She worked long hours to skillfully prepare photographs and maps for publication, as well as creating the Bill Miner website, a continually evolving project. My wife Karen, always my greatest booster and most constructive critic, created an ideal environment for me to work in. It was her selfless, giving nature that provided the encouragement, research help and quiet confidence to allow me to complete a sometimes daunting task. I must have tried her patience daily as I used her for a sounding board when each chapter came close to completion. Her comments and contributions helped make this book more readable and interesting than I could have done on my own. I will always remember and appreciate her comforting and attentive presence during those grey winter days while I was closeted in my office with only a keyboard for my boon companion.

Kamloops, April 2006.

CONTENTS

PREFACE

IT WAS LATE JUNE IN 1975, and the summer sun hurt our eyes as it flashed through the windshield and bounced off the dusty dashboard. The sound of tires on washboard and of gravel and rock hitting the wheel wells kept conversation to a minimum. The smell of the dust leaking through unseen cracks and joints tightened in our nostrils. As the pickup made its leisurely way over twisting backroads somewhere south and east of Kamloops, he turned to me and said, "This is the spot where Bill Miner stashed the C.P.R. bonds that he stole from the Mission train robbery."

Toddy (Edward Cecil) Pratt, born in his family's log house in Barnhartvale in 1900, went on to explain to me that after the bumbled robbery of the C.P.R. train east of Kamloops in 1906, Miner knew that the chances were pretty good that he, Shorty Dunn and Louis Colquhoun wouldn't be able to evade capture. Toddy told of how Miner, on foot after their horses had wandered away, had to stash $80,000 in bearer bonds which he had kept close to him since the Mission robbery in 1904. He picked the tunnels of the coal mines located in the bush south and east of Kamloops as his place to hide them away. The reason he hadn't cashed them was that the authorities would have been able to trace the person cashing the bonds immediately. The bonds were estimated to have been worth up to $5,000,000 in 1970s dollars.

This was only the first of many Bill Miner anecdotes Toddy would pass on to me over the years. When driving past the British Columbia Wildlife Park east of Kamloops, he pointed into a ravine in the silt cliffs bordering the south side of the valley and explained that this was the place where Miner and his buddies made their escape from the Ducks train robbery. This didn't agree with the B.C. Ministry of Highways' "Stop of Interest" plaque that used to be mounted on the Trans Canada Highway shoulder. It was placed near what the locals call Miner's Rock, miles east of Ducks, now called Monte Creek.

Toddy spent his childhood in the Barnhartvale valley east of Kamloops in what was then known as Upper Campbell Creek. The lower end of the creek, near where it emptied into the South Thompson River, was known as Campbell Creek proper. It was a little ranching community with a post office and school. This was where the large family of pioneer Lewis Campbell had their ranch and where the Wildlife Park is now located. Toddy went to the little one room schoolhouse in the hills above the Campbell's ranch on Upper Campbell Creek. The school was built near the edge of the watercourse, and late one morning in early May of 1906 when Toddy was six and in the first grade, the teacher sent him down to the nearby stream. He was delegated to fetch the class's supply of buttermilk which was chilling in the fast-moving water. He told me that when he had pulled the buttermilk out of the creek, he was greeted by three men on horseback. It was Bill Miner, Shorty Dunn and Lewis Colquhoun. Miner asked Toddy if they might share some of his buttermilk. Toddy passed it to the three strangers, and when they had all had a drink, they passed it back to him. Miner patted him on the head, and the three riders rode off towards the east. It was only much later that he would learn who the three riders were. Toddy often repeated that story to me.

Philip Borsos' movie "The Grey Fox" was released in 1983. Richard Farnsworth, the bit actor in so many of Hollywood's westerns, played Miner, and his appearance was eerily similar to Mary Spencer's original photos of Miner taken in Kamloops in 1906. Toddy and my son and daughter eagerly attended the viewing in Kamloops. During the movie the whispered comment was made that the little Kamloops boy passing Bill Miner an orange when he was on his way to prison was in reality Toddy. Toddy was sitting beside us, watching the movie with close attention and a small grin on his face the entire time.

Toddy passed away in 1993, and those casual remarks on that hot day in June have stayed with me since. They have led me on a journey through intriguing restricted source material and enjoying the company and conversation of some of the province's original pioneers and landowners. I was able to explore sites unvisited and unidentified for many years and made the acquaintance of enthusiastic and knowledgeable amateur and professional historians. Most of Toddy's stories were proved to have considerable basis in fact after the research was done, or else contained at least some germs of the truth.

For over 100 years the story of Bill Miner and his exploits in B.C. have intrigued and entertained British Columbians and Canadians. Legends, half-truths and mythology have coloured the memories and histories of Miner's short presence in B.C. between his arrival as a fugitive from a train robbery in Oregon in 1903 and his flight as a fugitive from the B.C. Penitentiary to the U.S. in 1907. The amount of source material as well as anecdotes is profuse, but to date no one has assembled all of this primary and secondary source material into one definitive volume. This book is a modest attempt to do just that.

Many and varied persons have assisted in the preparation of this work; however, there are a select few that require separate and distinct identification.

William Fernie was the Kamloops based B.C. Provincial Police constable responsible, with his Indian trackers, for making it possible for the Royal North West Mounted Police to capture the train robbers. He was married and had three children. His son died at the early age of 21 years of meningitis, but his two daughters lived into the 21ST century. I had the privilege of making the acquaintance of Daphne and Mary Fernie and visiting them in Victoria, where they were spending their ninth decade. They both passed away within months of each other in 2005, but not before bestowing upon me many first-hand accounts of their father, their early life in Kamloops, and their undiminished fervour for life. Their example of how women in the early 20TH Century in the interior of B.C. could enjoy a rewarding, challenging and relatively liberated life was an inspiration to both my wife and me.

If it were not for the vision and dedication of Anthony Martin of Abbotsford, much of what this book has to say would not have been possible. Tony worked for Correctional Services Canada for 35 years, retiring in 1993. He started off at the B.C. Penitentiary in New Westminster in 1958 and always maintained an interest in history. The B.C. Pen closed in 1980, and Tony was involved in the shutdown. During the decommissioning process he was told by friends that a lot of important material was being thrown out in the dumpsters. So Tony arranged that anything that they thought was important was sidetracked and stored in the piggery where he could check it out. As a result of these rescue efforts, he attempted to jump-start the creation of a penitentiary museum in the west. There had been one in existence for many years in Kingston, Ontario, and requests had been made for the B.C. Penitentiary historical items to be sent there. However, Tony had and has very strong opinions that there should be a repository in the West for materials such as he had rescued from the closing of the B.C. Penitentiary. Unfortunately, the timing of his attempts to start a museum coincided with downsizing and budget cutting, and the museum didn't happen. In the end, Tony found himself salvaging a great deal of the material and storing it on his own premises. In addition, when others knew that he had become an unofficial custodian of penitentiary-related items and ephemera, further items were passed to him by other retired officers. Part of the original material rescued from the dumpster consisted of original glass plate negatives of convict mug shots, including those of the three Ducks train robbers.

Just recently, Tony generously donated his entire collection to the Thompson Rivers University in Kamloops for the research benefit of future students and professional historians. Prior to this, Tony allowed me access and copying privileges to his material related to the incarceration of Bill Miner, Shorty Dunn and Louis Colquhoun. The files on the inquiry into the escape of Miner from the B.C. Penitentiary were invaluable in determining actual events as they transpired and the roles individual guards, prison officials, police and government officials played.

Much has been written on the reasons for the perpetuation of the memory and exploits of a manipulative American bandit who spent most of his adult life behind the bars of San Quentin Prison in California. In British Columbia his memory lives on in song and poetry, on the Internet, in bars, pubs and cocktail lounges, with stage companies and reviews, and in books, movies and magazine articles. In my research and in making inquiries, persons I contacted were only too willing to share their memories of Miner as passed down to them by parents, relatives and the original pioneers who had interacted with him and his friends. Museums and archives throughout the interior of B.C. and in the Fraser Valley meticulously archived their Bill Miner stories and anecdotes in the usual Bill Miner vertical files. There they were ready and waiting for my eager review. Billy Miner nightspots are even found in such unlikely spots as Williams Lake where Bill Miner never set foot. It was not only his presence in any area that caused the legend to come alive, it was the story itself that has proved to be so intriguing. Beginning with Frank W. Anderson's Frontier books first published in 1968, and which have never been out of print, books and small histories of Miner have surfaced on a regular basis. The most comprehensive and accurate history on the complete life of Miner was done by Mark Dugan and John Boessenecker in the book "The Grey Fox," published in 1992. It dispelled the various assumptions as to Miner's birthplace and many other myths that had been perpetuated over the years and detailed his exploits across the breadth of the United States. However, only three chapters were devoted to British Columbia as the authors had limited access to original source material.

The respected Canadian historian Jack Granatstein tells us that our Canadian history has been killed by elitist university lecturers, professors and high school teachers. He suggests that they have perpetuated a legacy of dull and uninteresting tomes and articles dealing with obscure leftist dogma and events, and research into topics that, while providing value to other historical experts, bears little relevance or interest to the general public. With the exception of the popular historical books of best-selling writers like Pierre

Berton and well-received regional histories and stories authored by local writers, more generalized Canadian history exists in a rarified realm accessed only by the most devout readers. So what explains the fascination amongst the general public with Bill Miner and his life and times in Canada? Why has Frank Anderson's little book on Miner remained in print and why is it still selling steadily after almost forty years? Perhaps it is because it is part of our shared and common collective history of B.C. The story is over 100 years old now, so it can legitimately constitute a history. However, those same intellectual elitists would dismiss it as irrelevant as it is only "about dead white guys."

The phenomenon can perhaps be explained away by the utilization, more than forty years ago, of a more fundamental and riveting manner of communicating usually dull Canadian history. A more basic medium of knowledge distribution was employed and may account for our seeming obsession with the bandit who brought the Wild West of the American Frontier into our Canadian group memory. In 1962, and most likely earlier, the Grade V elementary school classes throughout B.C. and Western Canada were introduced to a new reader. Published by J.M. Dent and Sons (Canada) in their Canadian Heritage Reader series, the text-book "Under Canadian Skies" consisted of numerous large print stories for elementary pupils under group headings such as "Maritime Yarns" and "Neighbours to the South." In the section entitled "Long Arm of the Law" and in the company of Almighty Voice and Sherlock Holmes, we find "Robbery Under Arms," written by one Pamela Stephen. It is the story of Bill Miner, well and profusely hand-illustrated, and interestingly written with surprisingly little deviance from fact. This reader was used by every class in the public schools of British Columbia and other parts of Canada for many years. It is little wonder that the story of Bill Miner has entered into the collective consciousness of so many of those elementary students of British Columbia that grew up in the decades from the Fifties to the Seventies.

It is the intent of this book to shine the light of history on and to recognize some of those citizens of British Columbia who played a part in this story of the early years of the century, but have now been forgotten. They were the farmers, ranchers, city folk and miners, prospectors, cowboys and Chinese irrigation workers who quietly built the province. Many were touched in some way by the brash American desperado and his daring exploits. This book hopes to help in recognizing the contributions made by two police forces and the First Nations trackers during those eventful and formative years. The cities, towns and villages that made up the province, at the coast and in the heartland, even then were realizing some of their hopes and dreams for the future. One overriding theme that arises when reviewing the sources from that time is the optimism which most inhabitants of Canada's westernmost province had for their future. The hard work, self reliance and perseverance displayed by new immigrants and pioneers alike confronted and overcame the vagaries of weather, climate, freight rates and government. Government then was not a benevolent parent, but a slow moving, irritable monolith hunched at the southern tip of Vancouver Island or in distant Ottawa. Communication with constituents was normally through the medium of newspapers with biased, partisan agendas, the politicians themselves hampered by vast distances and irregular transportation. The committed, individualistic and motivated populace was left to get on with building the province, and in so doing provided us with the deeds and inspiration for a thousand stories.

The reader should be apprised of some clarifying notes. All conversations that take place within this work and that are delineated by quotation marks, are from actual conversations as reported by contemporary participants. No conversations have been made up, and consequently some of the speech will be somewhat unfamiliar to the ears of modern readers. Our speech has changed over 100 years, some words now have different meanings, some have been lost, and others have been added. Our language is a living thing that changes and evolves with time and cultural shifts. In those days 100 years ago, the broad American drawl was as familiar an accent as that of the many immigrants from the British Isles, and a sprinkle of Chinook jargon liberally spiced the language of all rural Canadians. Words or phrases in italics are those of the author.

Place names have also changed in the last 100 years. Ducks Station is now Monte Creek, Upper Campbell Creek is Barnhartvale, Grande Prairie is Westwold, Fish Lake is Salmon Lake, Little Fish Lake is Stevens Lake in the Monte Hills, the Kamloops to Grande Prairie Road is now Barnhartvale Road or, as old timers still call it, the Old Vernon Highway, and Summit Lake is now Monte Lake. The communities of Anderson Creek and Rockford now only exist in old directories, and the once bustling community of Nicola is but a pale shadow of its former self. Aspen Grove has only the concrete sign foundation of Dodds' old store to mark its brief time as a centre for mining and ranching activity in the district. Their time has passed, and sagebrush and bunchgrass have tried to cover the signs of their fleeting industry. A century ago their futures all seemed bright and heavy with optimism. For a short period of time during the first decade of the new century, the spotlight of a young nation would focus on these quiet little towns, prosperous farms and ranches, and industrious, hard-working people. The man who was to draw that spotlight first rode into the district of the Similkameen in October of 1903.

———•+•———

Interred With Their Bones

I

BILL MINER

IN THAT LATE FALL OF 1903, a lone rider on a fine horse slowly made his way over the Dewdney Trail between Hope and Princeton. The vine maples on the rock slides blazed with scarlet flames, and the poplars beside the creek-beds lit up the isolated country with a brilliant yellow flash against the dark green fir. The horseman wore a long, dark rider's coat and a flat-brimmed, four-cornered Stetson, under which he sported a grizzled cavalry moustache. The left side of his face was pockmarked and scarred. His eyes were a marked bright blue, and the skin on his face was brown and weathered, that of a man spending most of his time outdoors.[1][2]

Occasionally, when he drew up at the top of a rise or at the end of one of the few straight stretches, he twisted in the saddle and squinted into the distance behind him, as if he were watching for men on his trail. He favoured his mount and didn't press him. He let him pick his own way and stopped often to let him gain his wind back at the end of a long pull, or to get a short drink from one of the many creeks beside the trail. The rider concentrated on keeping to the middle two feet of the six foot wide trail as only that centre section would bear any type of load. He rode his horse easily with a loose rein and kept at a steady fast walk.

In those days, anyone having access to a post office, sheriff's office, police station or other official government facility throughout the western U.S. and British Columbia would have found this rider's face boldly displayed on Pinkerton wanted posters. The rider was Bill Miner, an outlaw from the western United States with a long history

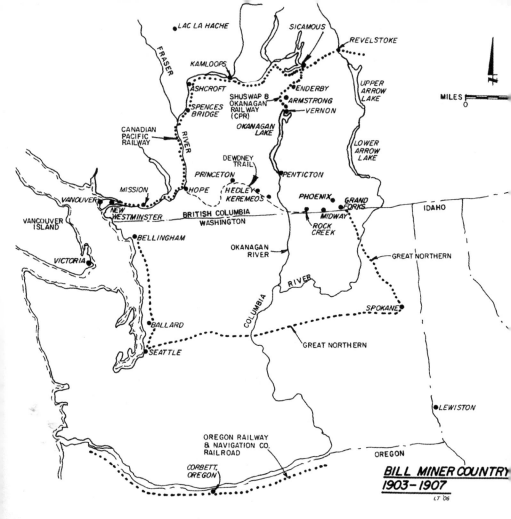

Bill Miner Country, 1903–1907.

of stagecoach and train robberies. His latest attempt at robbing the Oregon Railway and Navigation Company train on the 23RD of September in 1903 at Corbett, Oregon, had gone awfully wrong. His fellow robbers were captured, one was shot and badly wounded with a shotgun blast, and Miner himself had barely escaped. He hid out working in the oyster beds near Samish Flats in the San Juan Islands of northwest Washington State. He had worked in the beds shortly after being released from prison in 1901 and had become a well-liked superintendent on the job site. On October 1ST, he left the oyster beds to visit his sister in nearby Whatcom, south of Bellingham. It was there that his sister informed him that the law was closing in on him for that botched robbery near Corbett. His sister Mary Jane and her husband Louis Wellman had moved from Colorado Springs in Colorado and settled in Whatcom in 1903. Over the years, Mary Jane was and would continue to be visited by lawmen, Pinkerton detectives and newspaper reporters on a regular basis to determine whether she had any news of her brother's latest place of residence or of his latest caper. Miner knew that things were getting too hot for him in the States, and the Canadian border was only a few miles away. The Pinkerton investigation had determined that he was involved in the Corbett robbery, and reward posters of $1,300 for his arrest and conviction were distributed throughout the Northwest and in British Columbia.[34]

Bill Miner made his way across the border into British Columbia, Canada, where he was to spend an eventful four years making friends, working at ranches in the Nicola and Similkameen Valleys, rustling horses and robbing trains. He would devote considerable time to travelling throughout the Similkameen, Boundary, Nicola, Kamloops and Fraser Valley areas. He worked diligently at visiting and making favourable impressions on most of the Canadians he met, driving cattle and horses to auction, scouting out potential targets of opportunity, and generally enjoying this most peaceful part of His Majesty's Dominions. Also during this time he was to often return to the States via the Great Northern south of Phoenix, B.C., to Spokane, Washington, but his stay was always of short duration. He was to touch the lives of many ranchers, farmers and citizens during his sojourn in this new Canadian province, and the stories of his exploits in the vast and rugged southern interior and the Fraser Valley would last over 100 years. Those few years from 1903 to 1906 would prove to be some of the happiest of Bill's eventful life as he was a naturally gregarious man, enjoying the company of men, women and children alike. The good citizens of western Canada accepted him at face value, later expressing their admiration for his generosity, his professed piety and knowledge of the Bible, his genuine love of children, and his accomplished social graces such as dancing, fiddle playing and letter writing skills. His suaveness and garrulous manner would see him enter into the highest levels of society in the frontier life of the Similkameen. He would use his charms and reputation to convince the younger and more gullible members of society to join him in his lawless ways, convincing them that he knew what he was doing and that he had a wealth of successful experience. He neglected to advise these young men who hung on his every word of the thirty-three years of his life that had been spent in prison for being caught at his chosen avocation, the robbing of stagecoaches, the rustling of horses, and other petty crimes and misdemeanours. When Bill's time of freedom in Canada was eventually to end, those who knew him voiced their disappointment in him for betraying them, betraying their trusting ways and their support for him when he first arrived in their midst.

When Miner first crossed into Canada in the fall of 1903, he spent his days not far from the border on the north shore of the Fraser River near Haney, B.C. He spent a couple of weeks there living in a small cabin on the Andy Marx place. He practised his prison trade of cobbling shoes and fixed shoes for the nearby children for free.[5]

In tiny Port Haney, the then ten year old Ellen Paterson remembered seeing Bill Miner as a kindly old man.

"I remember Bill Miner. He used to sit beside the River Road and eat crowdy—a dish of rolled oats and water—for supper. As kids, we used to stand around and watch him eat. We weren't too afraid of strangers in those days. He looked like a simple sort of man—not odd —but not overly aggressive. He didn't look like the flamboyant bank-robber type. He used to push a bicycle around with his belongings tied on it. I don't think the bicycle had a chain—it may have. There weren't many bicycles around in those days. After we moved in the house on River Road (east of the brickyard), we found this same old bicycle lying beside the cow barn. It was the same one Bill Miner used to be seen with. Maybe he stayed in that old cow barn. He used to eat beside the road just west of the Carter house, east of Carr's Hill, but west of 7TH Avenue—near the old beaver dam."[6]

Miner had spent the last twenty years from December 1881 to June 1901 in San Quentin prison for robbing the Del Norte stage in Colorado. While he was in prison, three trans-continental railroads, including the Canadian Pacific, had successfully crossed Canada and the U.S. The day of the stagecoach was rapidly coming to an end, with the exception of those routes away from the railroads and their spur lines. In British Columbia not far north from where Miner made his way over the Dewdney Trail, the BX Express Company regularly ran stages between Ashcroft on the CPR mainline and Quesnel and Barkerville and the gold camps of the Cariboo to the north. Regularly scheduled stages ran from Kamloops to Vernon, and to Nicola, Aspen Grove and Princeton. Fred Revely ran a stage from Princeton to Hedley and to Spence's Bridge, and W.E. Wembley ran the stage from Hedley through Keremeos to Penticton.[7]

During those twenty years that Miner spent in San Quentin, Jesse James was shot by Bob Ford and Geronimo surrendered at Skeleton Canyon in Arizona. The melancholy dentist Doc Holiday died in Glenwood Springs, Colorado, and the Dalton Gang pulled off their abortive Coffeyville Raid. Sitting Bull was shot by one of his own people at the Standing Rock Reservation, and John Wesley Hardin, one of the last of the gunfighters and probably the most deadly, met his end with a bullet in the back of his head. In the British Empire, Queen Victoria died in January of 1901. In British Columbia, Boer War veterans, members of Lord Strathcona's Horse, were returning from South Africa to take up ranching, farming, government jobs and positions as constables with the B.C. Provincial Police force. The era of the lawless frontier of the American West was coming to an end, and communications and transportation were revolutionizing the way everyone was doing business. The telegraph was in constant use along the main lines of the railroads. By 1905 in the interior of the province telephone lines had been strung from tree to tree by the Dominion government between Kamloops, Nicola, Princeton and Hedley, Keremeos and Penticton.[8]

But time had not moved on for Bill Miner. Isolated from the mainstream of society in San Quentin for twenty years, and being

Princeton, 1906. GEORGE WINKLER FONDS, COURTESY OF B.C. ARCHIVES.

fixated on the challenges of day-to-day survival within a prison system that had not heard the word "rehabilitation," Miner's intellectual horizons were limited by the walls of the prison. His mind was in a time warp. He was still back in 1881 when the gunfight at the OK Corral had taken place, the McLean brothers were hung at New Westminster, Pat Garret had shot Billy the Kid, and Bill Miner was robbing the Del Norte stages in Colorado. Those were the days. In 1880 Bill was making the easy money and spending it just as freely in the pool halls and fandango parlours in California, and generally leading the good life. That is, he led the good life until the money ran out and he had to tap into his illegal sources again. When he got out of prison in 1901 after his twenty year stretch, he tried to go straight for a while, but collecting oysters in Puget Sound was not his idea of a proper job. It didn't fit the image he had of himself, and it didn't provide the cash he needed to fuel his desire for fine horses and fine, if loose, women, the latest in firearms, and some poker and pool money. So it was back to stealing the cash he needed. He joined up with some more experienced friends to pull off that train robbery in Corbett, Oregon, and barely escaped with his life. British Columbia, Canada, would now reap the benefits of the attentions of the amicable bandit from the States.

In late October of 1903, Miner packed up and left Haney. Communications with Washington State were a little too easy and newspapers on both sides of the border used each other's stories of crimes and criminals. Miner's world was shrinking.

He made his way over the Cascades on the Dewdney Trail and let his horse pick its way down the hill into the mining town of Princeton, nestled at the forks of the Tulameen and Similkameen Rivers. Miner was to learn that the isolation of the Princeton country would enable him to lead a life free from the threat of Pinkerton investigators and sheriff's posses and inquiring reporters. The trusting and friendly people of the Similkameen would accept the slight horseman with the American drawl readily and without qualms.

Princeton had originally been founded by rancher and mining promoter John Fall Allison in the early 1860s, and his widowed wife Susan Allison still ran the family ranch just east of the town. Mrs. Allison, a respected member of Princeton society and the mother of a respectable number of offspring, was to play more than a minor role in the story of Miner's sojourn in Princeton. That winter the two would meet under the most benign of circumstances.

In 1903 Princeton was on the cusp of a development boom. Mining speculation was running hot for copper and coal, and prospectors combed the surrounding creeks, rivers and mountains for gold and other minerals. Ranchers and farmers raised cattle, horses, hay, fruit trees and vegetables in the surrounding valley bottoms and hills. Railroad workers on the Great Northern Railway making its way up from the south and east fuelled the saloons and hotels on the main street, as well as the houses of the "soiled doves" on Angel Alley. Later changed by those citizens of a more reserved disposition to "Angela Avenue," the whorehouses and brothels along this street no doubt were greeted with a smile boding future patronage by Miner as he made his way through the bustling community. As he walked his mount down Bridge Street, he passed thriving businesses with railroad construction workers, miners, ranchers and farmers, as well as townsmen, milling about. Princeton consisted of an assay office, four general stores, three hotels, three sawmills, two butcher shops, a drug store, one newspaper, doctors, mining engineers, surveyors, and real estate and government offices. Miner pulled up to the town's livery stable, built by Bill Garrison in 1890, and boarded and stabled his horse. He introduced himself to Garrison as George Edwards, and that was to be the alias that Miner would go under throughout the time he was to spend in western Canada. Edwards and Garrison would form a friendship that lasted during the whole time he spent in the Princeton area.[9][10]

Miner noticed that Fred Revely's stagecoach, operating between Princeton and Otter Flats to the north and Hedley to the east, was also located in Garrison's barn. Princeton's wagon road connections with the outside world were to the north, 110 miles to Spence's Bridge, where one could catch the Canadian Pacific and its telegraph to all points east and west. To the east, a stagecoach took the traveller through Hedley and Keremeos to Penticton, then by lake steamer to Vernon, and finally by a branch railroad line to Sicamous Junction, where the CPR mainline could again be accessed. Kamloops was 132 miles by wagon road to the north through Tulameen, Aspen Grove and Nicola. The Dewdney Trail provided rudimentary wagon road access to mining towns like Phoenix and Midway east of Penticton, and the eastern environs of the state of Washington were a short ride south of Penticton and Rossland. Considerable traffic plied its way back and forth, east and west and north and south as the mines of the Similkameen, Boundary and Kootenay areas opened and closed and sprinkled their fickle fortunes indiscriminately upon workers, owners and the towns and infrastructure they supported. The Dewdney Trail west from Princeton was the only access into the Fraser Valley, Chilliwack, New Westminster and Vancouver, and it was inaccessible to wagon traffic. Periodically horses and cattle were driven to market and the auction at New Westminster using this trail.

CPR steamers and barges were loaded with cattle and horses at Hope for the journey downriver on the Fraser as the roads between Hope and points further west towards the Pacific were boggy and impassable for much of the year.

Through talking to Garrison and other residents, Miner soon determined which ranchers needed help with fencing, cattle and horse raising, and who the like-minded residents of the area were. It was through these connections that he would first meet Jack Budd.[11]

II

JACK BUDD

JACK BUDD, ANOTHER EX-PATRIOT AMERICAN on the run from a sheriff's posse, had a small horse ranch on Baldy Mountain about five miles from Princeton.

"He was known as an uncommunicative recluse of obscure work habits, who raised and sold a fine strain of animals, both horses and mules, but didn't make much other use of his 320-acre holdings. His cabin was in a wide gulch facing the Similkameen Valley. Barns, corrals and outbuildings were back of the cabin and the spread drew little attention from passers-by. The sides of the gap sloped upwards like wings and from its rims, outlined by cottonwoods, the view took off in all directions. As an observation lookout, it was a natural."[1]

Jack Budd was born John Charles Brian Budd in Texas on 19 January 1854 or 1857, depending upon the source. His parents were originally from Kentucky, and they had settled in Texas before the Civil War.[2][3] At the age of 41, and leaving a wife and daughter behind, Budd escaped into Canada in 1891 from somewhere in the northwest of the United States.[4][5]

"J.B. (Jack Budd) was being chased by the law and was slightly wounded but made it to his mother's house. The law was several hours later on catching up. The posse did not attack, shoot, or get too close. Jack Budd's mother was coaxed out of the house and spoken to by the 'LawBoss'. They knew Jack was in the house and informed her they would be back in 24 hours, if he was still inside they would burn the house down."[6]

Budd took them at their word and quickly made his way into

Jack Budd's cabin near Princeton. SKETCH BY KEN DAVIS, KAMLOOPS, 2006.

Canada. He was not to return to the United States for many decades.

Constable R. Hewat, the B.C. Provincial Police member in Princeton, had occasion to pen a description of Jack Budd in a report submitted to Provincial Police Superintendent Frederick Hussey in Victoria. In the time before fingerprints were used by police services, the Bertillon system of writing reports of skeletal and other bodily measurements and characteristics of persons of interest was used. The use of this system has resulted in remarkably detailed descriptions of criminals and suspects investigated by police and detective agencies. Jack Budd was described as being about fifty years of age in 1906, about 5 feet 8 inches tall and weighing about 150 pounds. He had a fair complexion, sandy light brown hair, and small blue eyes. When speaking he had a habit of squinting with one eye, or closing it completely, disconcerting all those with whom he was conversing if they were not on close terms with him. He had rather a long nose and a large mouth full of teeth in bad condition. He sported a long fair moustache, and when he removed the flat brimmed, grey fur, felt Stetson with the crown pinched into a four-cornered peak, it was apparent he was losing some of his hair at the front of his forehead. He had a broad American accent and was described as rather "free of manner," indicating a disposition uninclined to follow the rules of normal society. He smoked, was known to have a few drinks upon occasion, but picked his acquaintances with care. He always wore, even in the dead of summer, a long dark rider's coat, with at least one button at the top done up, and it was rumoured that hidden beneath its folds Budd always carried a .45 calibre Colt's revolver. Black knee length "top boots" completed this contemporary description of a man who was to spend almost 60 years in and around the Princeton area.[7][8][9]

Jack Budd's reputation in the Similkameen and Nicola Valley areas was not the best. He was described as a surly and uncommunicative individual who was not above preying on his fellow ranchers and farmers. Budd's friends also skirted the edge of the law, and they included Tom Arnold, Bob Tilton, Shorty Dunn and others who, from time to time, stayed in Budd's cabin with him and helped him with his horses and mules and in the intimidation of his neighbours.

Budd and his friends seemed particularly incensed with farmers who had fenced off large sections of land that formerly had been open range. The former Texan felt that all lands in the area should be open range and free for access by anyone. The Reith family had a farm next to Budd's, and Budd and his cohorts would periodically cut the Reith's south fences and let his mules and horses graze through the farmer's grain fields. Also, they would press their horses against the weaker sections of fence, and when they collapsed, they would ride indiscriminately through the grain, knocking it down and making it incapable of being properly harvested.[10]

In 1892, soon after he had crossed the border into Canada, Jack Budd was cowboying for the Douglas Lake Cattle Company. One of his fellow ranch hands was Bert Thomas, lately from Southampton, England. Thomas had got off the CPR train at Kamloops and made his way to visit his brother in Nicola. Thomas ended up working alongside Budd at Douglas Lake, and in Princeton the two of them would continue their acquaintance for over half a century.[11]

At Douglas Lake and the surrounding ranches and farms in the Nicola area, Budd was to admire the fine horse flesh and cattle being raised in the district and was suspected of helping himself to the fruits of the local ranchers' breeding labours without compensating them. Walter Clark, a B.C. Provincial Police Constable in Nicola, knew all about Jack Budd's rustling activities, but could never get enough evidence to prove it in court.

"There has been quite a few horses stolen from here and Aspen Grove and Jack Budd has been suspected of driving them away to the other side of the line or to the Coast and disposing of them … (He) does not bear the best of a reputation."[12]

As a result of both his legitimate and illegal activities around Douglas Lake and Nicola, Budd managed by 1898 to put enough of a stake together to go into a partnership with rancher George Aldous to build a saloon and hotel called the Tulameen in Princeton.[13] Unfortunately, within a few years it had burnt down. Budd then partnered up with Ed Pringle, and together they started a small livery stable in Princeton. It was most likely there that Miner, known for hanging around livery stables and talking about horses, first contacted Budd in the Similkameen country.[14][15]

It is probable that Miner and Budd did know each other previously. They both had a reputation of operating outside the law in the Pacific Northwest, and both had made their way into Canada just ahead of a posse. Miner was an inveterate letter writer and may have corresponded with Budd while he was in prison and after he had been released. A little known coincidence is the fact that in the late 1860s Miner had utilized the defence services of one James H. Budd in California. Miner was sentenced to three years in San Quentin for stealing horses. After the trial, Defence Attorney James Budd advised Miner that he would assist him in any way possible if he should require it. The defence attorney would later go on to become the governor of California, and in 1897, almost 30 years

The original road from Nicola Lake to Aspen Grove. PHOTO BY THE AUTHOR.

after representing Miner, Budd, now governor, met Miner in the San Quentin prison yard. Miner was serving his 25 years for robbing a stage in California and had had his good behaviour credits taken away due to his continued escape attempts. He petitioned the Governor on numerous occasions to have his credits restored, but the Governor left the decision up to the dedicated authority. Could the Governor and Jack Budd have been related? If so, it could answer many of the questions about the relationship between Budd and Miner.[16]

Budd's entrepreneurial aspirations also involved him in the mining speculation and prospecting sector around the Princeton area. Budd had copper mining claims in partnership with Alonzo Roberts and "Dad" Allen of Aspen Grove in the Aspen Grove Camp group of claims.[17]

This then was the man that Miner met up and partnered with in 1903 in Princeton. Neither Miner nor Budd was averse to skirting the fringes of the law and rustling horses for a few quick dollars. From essentially the same backgrounds in a more lawless society in the United States, they would act as partners and be seen to be so by their contemporaries around Princeton, Aspen Grove, Hedley and Nicola. Miner, as George Edwards, would be described by those who knew them both as a one-half partner in Budd's horse ranch and in his mining claims. Miner felt comfortable enough in the Princeton-Aspen Grove mining country that he would go on to take over a cabin close to Alonzo Roberts' place at Aspen Grove and near Missezula Lake. Budd and Miner both would be suspected of rustling horses and cattle, and their activities would be viewed as suspicious by those who were of a less generous nature. However, George Edwards, with considerable charm and a seemingly ready supply of cash and gold dust, managed to fool most of the people most of the time for a few years at least.[18] [19]

III

SIMILKAMEEN COUNTRY

DURING THE WINTER OF 1903–1904, George Edwards worked at odd jobs cowboying and doing regular farm work. He got to know many of the ranchers, farmers and residents of the Similkameen and Boundary country. He made the acquaintance of Susan Allison, the venerable widow of one of the original pioneers into the area, John Fall Allison. John Allison had died in 1897, and Susan Allison competently looked after the family's ranching and mining interests. She was a well-educated and progressive woman for her day, and entertained in her home poets, musicians, politicians and other people of interest. She and her husband had a large family, descendants of which today populate many areas of British Columbia. Her relationship with Edwards and his friends would prove to be critical for one of them in the not too distant future. Susan Allison's daughter Aurelia Angela Allison-McDiarmid remembers meeting the kindly gentleman George Edwards that winter.

"We first met Mr. Edwards one cold wintery day. Ambling up the snow drifted road came a large white mule. On his back was the fur clad figure of an old man, or so he seemed, what with the frost clinging to his drooping moustache. Alighting at the door, he came forward, hat in hand, bowing graciously, and said with a distinct southern accent, 'My name is Edwards, George Edwards, a friend of Mr. Jack Budd, who asked me to call, as I was passing this way.' As it was very cold, my mother asked him in for a cup of tea. Accepting gratefully, he chatted with my mother while my sister and I made tea. He spoke of current events and seemed to be well informed and well read. He said he was not staying long, but was returning in the spring to Mexico, where he had rich mines. Among other things, his father owned a large plantation in Georgia, but he had left home at sixteen, acquired a partner, and went prospecting, which he followed the greater part of his life, with rich rewards—the mines in Mexico being his latest. As we were quite young, he seemed old to us, judging him to be in his 60s, and of a kindly and courteous disposition. That winter he often stopped in for his cup of tea as he passed our home on the way to town, we also met him at dances and parties given in the private homes, where he seemed to be a welcome guest. Few old timers could say they had not danced with Mr. Edwards.

"On one occasion, he asked my mother if he might give Alice and I dancing lessons. Thinking to discourage him without giving undue offence, we explained that we had no music. He at once overcame that difficulty by saying 'But I can sing,' and he danced with first one, then the other, singing 'lightely, tightely, tightelty, tie' to the tune of 'Oh where, oh where has my little dog gone' while my mother, a dignified chaperone, sat very upright in her chair. It all seemed so ridiculous, it was hard to keep a serious face and the moment Mr. Edwards was gone, we gave way to gales of laughter, but we did learn to waltz! The old gentleman was quite proud of our achievements, and certainly had patience and a kind heart. I can say that the Mr. Edwards that we knew was a perfect gentleman and we really enjoyed his visits."[1]

Early in the spring of 1904, Edwards was introduced to the manager of the Douglas Lake Cattle Company, Joseph Greaves, by Jack Budd. Budd had worked at Douglas Lake previously and recommended his friend for a job at the now thriving cattle ranch. As George Edwards, he did fencing, cowhand work and general duties. During that time, irrigation of the hay fields was undertaken by the overland flood method. Former Chinese railway workers, now out of work as the CPR was completed, were ideal workers to run the flood irrigation at the ranch as they had been trained in China to irrigate vast fields of vegetables, grains and forage in just such a manner. This type of irrigation, utilized at all ranches and farms in B.C.'s interior at that time, was so labour intensive that the Chinese labourers and cooks outnumbered substantially the cowboys employed by the ranch.[2]

One morning Edwards was transporting a buckboard full of Chinese labourers out to the fields to irrigate the hay. The bed of the buckboard consisted of many loose boards, and all at once the team got away on him. The Chinese attempted to hold on by grasping the loose boards, but the bucking and swaying of the wagon made all their attempts to save themselves of little effect. By the time he had the horses settled down, two Chinese labourers were dead and a number of others were injured. Feelings ran high against Edwards on the part of the labourers, who were convinced that it was his intolerance of them that resulted in the death and injury to their fellows.[3]

Agitation against Edwards on the part of these labourers grew so heated that ranch manager Greaves had to ask Edwards to leave the ranch for his own safety. Edwards was paid off and made his way back over the hills from Douglas Lake to Budd's horse ranch.[4]

Edwards probably was not the most understanding of men towards Chinese workers, and almost certainly did not treat them as equals. In California when Edwards was growing up, the excess labour force posed by the Chinese workers left over from the completion of the American railroads drove the value of an individual American white worker's worth drastically down. The days of individual prospectors were over by the late 1850s and early 60s. Large corporations worked the claims, and the formerly independent prospectors and miners had to curtail their pride and work for wages at the behest of these large businesses with their water monitors and stamp mills. The role of the Chinese labourer was perceived to be the reason for the loss in individual freedom and choice for American workers, and racist feelings ran high in the camps and towns in California. Edwards was to import these prejudices with him into Canada, which also was not free of intolerance towards Chinese workers for the same reasons. Radical Canadian labour unions like the Wobblies (Industrial Workers of the World) and those making up the Vancouver Trades and Labour Council were pressing the Canadian provincial and federal politicians to restrict the immigration of Chinese, Japanese

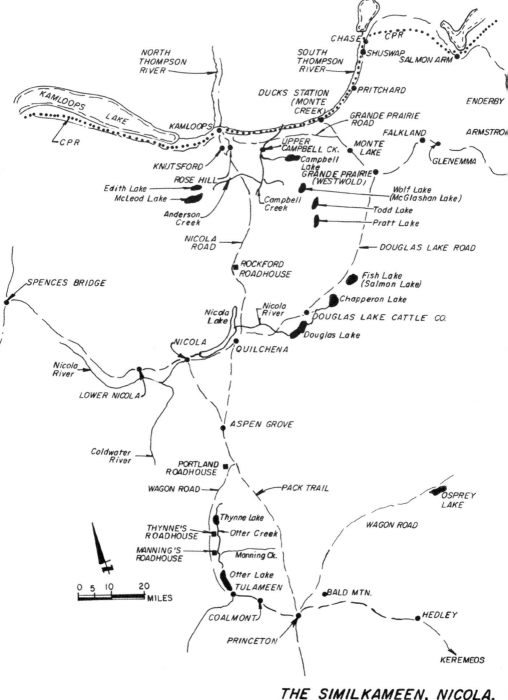

THE SIMILKAMEEN, NICOLA, AND KAMLOOPS DISTRICTS

LT '06

and east Asian workers into Canada by imposing a head tax and other restrictions.[5]

In interior cities, advertisements in local papers reflected the prejudices and concerns of some of the citizens. The Kamloops Inland Sentinel of Friday, the 13TH of January, 1905 ran the following advertisement:

"Business Locals"
"Patronize union white labour by leaving your laundry at
Dunc Brown's, agent for Cascade Laundry in Vancouver."[6]

It is probably not coincidence that Edwards' favourite hotel in Kamloops advertised a "white cook." Edwards would go on to exploit these racist and exclusionary feelings in Canada while he was here. At every opportunity he railed against big business in the form of the railroads and the large mining interests and advocated the benefits of socialism. While these anti-establishment feelings were most likely engendered by his early experiences in the mining camps of California, he was definitely not above stealing from rich and poor alike and enjoying the benefits to be obtained from those thefts.

Later that same spring of 1904, Edwards, rancher Bob Tilton and another cowboy who was a stranger rode into Quilchena, just north of Nicola, from Princeton. There Edwards met with Postmaster A. Jackson, posted letters and obtained stamps. The three riders finished their business and rode south towards Aspen Grove and Princeton. Jackson would see George Edwards many times over the next few years, riding between Princeton and Kamloops. Jackson learned that Edwards was a partner of Jack Budd, worked a horse ranch with him, and had mutual mining interests. Edwards would sometimes stay in the Quilchena and Nicola area for extended periods, and it was during one of those stays that he would break some horses for the Guichon ranch near Nicola.[7]

That same spring, Edwards, in company with Bob Tilton, a 26 year-old cowboy and sometime rancher, rode east to Phoenix. Phoenix was in the midst of a mining boom, and the easy money, poker and pool games and "soiled doves" that were an integral part of life in a mining town, attracted Edwards, and he wanted to see what other interests the area had to offer. Close to the American border, Phoenix and the Boundary country were filled with American miners and businessmen, as well as other immigrants of a more shady disposition. It was a town where George Edwards could do business. While there he made a number of friends, but before too long he and Tilton headed for the Armstrong and Spallumcheen country where Tilton's family lived.[8]

Bob Tilton's father Cyrus Tilton, had emigrated from Kansas into Washington Territory in a 27 wagon train. By 1891 the family was firmly entrenched in the north Okanagan area of Armstrong.[9] When Edwards and Tilton arrived in the early summer of 1904, they first went to work for a Jake Lawes doing some haying work at Lansdowne, close to the tiny community of Armstrong. Edwards hung around for a while and met Angus McKay and his family. Angus was married to Bob Tilton's sister Nellie, and Edwards would help them wallpaper their house that summer. Both the Tilton families and the McKay families would shortly move to the Rose Hill area to the south and above Kamloops, where Edwards would continue his relationship with them.

Soon it was time for Edwards to move on again. After helping him to get his first hay crop in, Edwards told Angus McKay that he and Bob Tilton were going to head south, where he was going to visit his sister in Washington. From there Edwards was going to proceed on to Mexico where he had some mining interests. Bob Tilton would accompany him as far as California, where Tilton had relatives.

Edwards was already planning his next robbery and making an alibi for any excess funds that he might display in the future.[10][11]

John Hatten Bromley was a successful rancher with a spread between Princeton and Hedley. He remembered that George Edwards "always acted the gentleman, dressed well and (rode) a good horse and (seemed) to have money to pay his way. Never knew him to work." Bromley had a very attractive daughter, Eliza, who was known as a competent cowgirl. She would often find herself at the Budd ranch checking for Bromley cattle as the Budd spread was not far from

Hedley circa 1906 with the Giant Mascot Mine buildings clinging to the sides of the mountain. George Winkler Fonds, Courtesy of B.C. Archives.

her father's. Budd's place was through a little canyon following a mountain trail. She loved to sit on the porch and speak with the two older Americans of their shared love of horses. The two men told her they were particular to horses that would run well, cover a lot of ground in a day, and had plenty of stamina. Budd and Edwards would often ask her in to sit down and have a meal with them. The meal usually consisted of sourdough pancakes and fried pork. She remembered that Edwards always had to stop before they ate to say grace. After she got to know the two men well, she would ride over for dinner on a frequent basis.[12][13]

Budd often told the young Eliza that he had a silver mine across the border in the States and that anytime he was short of cash he would head down there to get some more funds. Edwards, always trying to impress, took from his money belt and showed her the one and only one thousand dollar bill she would ever see in her life. Before he left on his many trips to the world beyond the mountains of the Similkameen, he always asked her whether he might pick up something she might like for when he returned. She would usually ask for candy or some such other modest item, but that obviously was not good enough for Mr. Edwards. One time when he came back from an extended trip, he brought her a beautiful set of silver-mounted spurs. Unfortunately Eliza was not to hold on to them long, as they were soon stolen from her.[14]

One day Eliza made her way over the hills to visit Budd and Edwards. She saw two of their better horses, Nell and Fancy, lying out full length in the dust of the corral. Dried sweat rings revealed they had been ridden hard just recently and were exhausted.

Young Eliza expressed her concern to Edwards and Budd. "What's happened to Nell and Fancy? They're all pooped!"

"Oh," Edwards replied, with a knowing smile, "If you had travelled as far as those horses last night you'd be tired too."[15]

Edwards, like Budd, explained his ready supply of funds to the pretty Eliza as the result of the proceeds from his rich copper mines in the U.S. Eliza retained fond memories of Edwards and would often dance with him at fêtes in Hedley and in Princeton. Long after Edwards had left the country, she would watch Jack Budd putter about his cabin and raise his horses and mules. She kept a lookout for any sign of the elusive Mr. Edwards. She was never to see him again.[16]

Other ladies also had the benefit of an acquaintance with the suave American mining entrepreneur, confusing them somewhat when he spouted socialist theory. "On one occasion, while driving with one of his feminine friends, Edwards talked political economy in a way that stamps him as a deep thinker as well as a deep schemer. He told her, 'I wish I had control of the air. I would dole it out to the rich and make them pay heavily for it too, but I'd let the poor have as much as they wanted.'"[17]

It was now time for Mr. Edwards to put his mind to more serious matters. Working for wages at Douglas Lake, breaking horses at the

Guichon Ranch, and doing general labour work at other ranches, supplemented by a discreet amount of horse rustling with his partner Budd, was not bringing in the cash that Bill needed to supplement the lifestyle he felt was his due and his inclination. He had kept his ear to the ground over the winter and listened to the conversations going on around him with regards to the movement of cash, gold bullion and other valuables. Often he would hitch his horse to the back of Garrison's livery wagon as Garrison plied his trade between Princeton and places like Hedley, Keremeos and Penticton. It was while enjoying the ride with Garrison that Edwards watched the single wagon from the Nickel Plate Mine above Hedley, escorted by heavily armed guards and Constable William Haines of Hedley, making its way to Penticton.

In 1904 an agreement was reached between the general manager of the Daly Reduction Company, M.K. Rodgers, and the B.C. Provincial Police. The company held interviews with Constable Haines in Hedley, and the results of these were forwarded to the constable's superiors. After a lengthy and convoluted communications process, negotiations were completed between Constable Haines and the company, Chief Constable Pearse in Kamloops and Superintendent F.S. Hussey in Victoria. The services of the Hedley constable were retained to assist in escorting the monthly production of two gold bars totalling 50 lbs. to Penticton. The Company agreed to compensate the personal expenses of Constable Haines as well as pay for a hired horse for the constable, its keep and fodder. In turn, Constable Haines on his return to Hedley could stop and make his calls in Keremeos and other points. It was noted in the correspondence that the road to be travelled was through rough and mountainous country, particularly between Keremeos and Penticton. The distance was 50 miles, and an additional concern was that the road was at times no farther than 20 miles from the American border and the desperados lurking there.[18]

At Penticton, under the responsibility of the Dominion Express Company, a CPR subsidiary, two gold bars were loaded on the steamer to Vernon, where the shipment took the branch line to

Sicamous Junction. Carefully loaded on the CPR express car, the gold bars made their way to the assay office in Seattle, Washington. Once a month the two gold bars rumbled through the hills to Penticton. Also, freight wagons with four-horse teams regularly hauled gold concentrate in 100 lb. cotton lined jute bags from Hedley to Penticton. There they were shipped by rail to the smelter at Tacoma, Washington. All of this activity was watched with a critical eye by the newcomer to the area.[19]

IV

THE MISSION ROBBERY

Continuing his scouting activities for likely revenue prospects in that summer of 1904, Miner returned to the Fraser Valley. He wanted to see what opportunities for a man of his specific entrepreneurial skills might be realized in the brash new society hacking its way out of the vast forests of the Lower Mainland. His reconnaissance found him riding his saddle horse from one end of the long verdant valley to the other. He visited Hope and Chilliwack and crossed by ferry to Mission on the other side of the river and the CPR Junction where the railway headed to the States. He travelled through Langley, New Westminster

First Avenue in Mission, B.C., with CPR mainline on the right and the Fraser River in the distance, circa 1907.
COURTESY OF MISSION MUSEUM AND ARCHIVES.

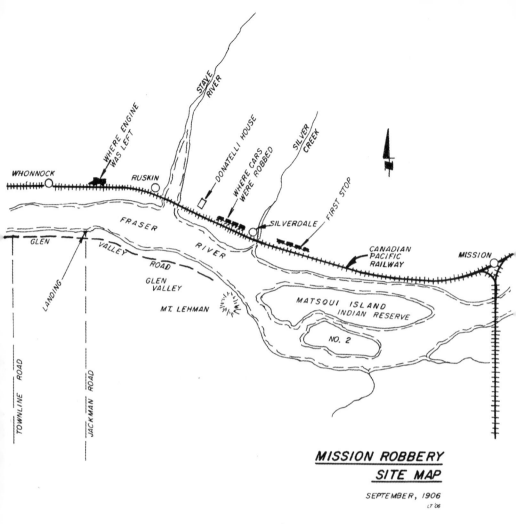

The Robbery west of Mission, 10 September 1904.

and Vancouver, all the while meeting people and watching for opportunities to utilize his particular preferences and inclination.

On some of his surveys along the CPR mainline, he would be joined by two unidentified associates, and together they familiarized themselves with the details of the people, communities and terrain of the Fraser Valley. Despite trying to keep a low profile, their activities did not go unnoticed.

The Solloways emigrated from England in 1870 to start a farm in the Mission area. They settled on a quarter section just north of the

Mission townsite, and not far from downtown. The CPR main line separated the community from the river, and the countryside along the railway right-of-way to the west and the east supported thriving small farms in the fertile alluvial soul. The Solloway family would remember vividly their great-great-grandfather Squire Solloway's visit with Miner and his friends.[1]

"In the month or few months before the train robbery, Bill and two of his helpers lived in a tent on the 'back' of the family property. They were very polite in their dealings with the Solloways. They'd knock at the back door to buy eggs, milk, butter and such from my great-great-grandmother, and apparently lived on the property."[2]

The Solloways were not the only ones to notice the mannerly trio. Amos Gibbard of Mission, then a young boy of eleven years, remembered the three strangers. The Gibbard quarter section was directly west of and adjacent to the Solloway property.[3]

"Miner and his two pals lived in Mission for almost a month before the robbery. I saw a lot of them since they lived in a tent right near us, almost where Harmon's Sawmill stands today. I remember they told my Dad they were looking for a place to set up a nursery, and I guess most folks believed them. They paid cash for everything and bought butter, milk and other food from the Solloway boys."

The young Gibbard watched as the three men wandered extensively around the Mission district and got to know the trails and the lay of the land throughout the whole area "better than anyone in Mission. They went by our place many a time. They were gentlemen and were kind. They weren't unclean and dirty, and I guess by acting politely they didn't raise any suspicion."[4]

Clarence McDonald, the clerk in the general store at Agassiz, received a visit from one of the mannerly campers in August. Miner came into his store and purchased a pair of cotton ladies stockings from him. Curiously, the mannerly elderly gentleman asked McDonald to get a pair of scissors. When the clerk handed him the scissors, Miner inexplicably proceeded to cut the feet out of them before he left.[5]

In the late summer, Miner made his way to Ashcroft to determine

The CPR bridge across the Fraser heading south to the U.S. from the Mission Junction, circa 1907.

the schedules for the gold shipments coming down from the Cariboo by stage and being loaded on the CPR express cars. On a Saturday afternoon early in late summer, he walked into the offices of the British Columbia Express Company and addressed the resident general manager Willis J. West. Posing as a dry-ground placer miner, he inquired about transportation to Barkerville, schedules of arrivals and departures, and general information. On the wall behind the agent was a Pinkerton wanted poster.

"The poster displayed a picture of a tough-looking westerner with long hair, dressed in a rough shirt, overalls, and high boots. No one would have associated this picture of the wanted criminal with the neat-looking dry-ground miner who was so industriously acquiring knowledge of travelling conditions in the Cariboo."

The poster advised that the Pinkertons would pay $2,500 for the apprehension, dead or alive, of one Bill Miner.[6]

Over the next few days he became a fixture around Ashcroft and slowly ingratiated himself with the BX Company station agent West. He managed to extract information about gold bullion shipments from the Bullion Pit Mine located near Likely. This mine was a large hydraulic operation associated with the Consolidated Cariboo Hydraulic Mining Co. and the South Fork Hydraulic and Mining Co. Miner was able to determine that the gold production from the Bullion Pit Mine was transported by stage to Ashcroft, where it was then loaded onto the CPR express car at the train station. He

Horse operated draw bridge mechanism on CPR bridge across Fraser, circa 1907. COURTESY OF MISSION MUSEUM AND ARCHIVES.

checked the schedules over the next few days and determined that the best day to hold up the CPR was on the 10TH of September, when the next stage from Likely came into Ashcroft. Unfortunately he didn't allow for changes in the hydraulic operation at the Bullion Mine due to low water flows towards the end of summer, nor for the fact that the Bullion stage route was only a branch of the BX's main stage line. Its next stage with Bullion gold aboard would not be for another week after that, so Miner's calculations would be critically off, with disappointing consequences. If Miner had been more careful in his assembly of information, he would have learned that the correct stage would have held gold totalling $60,000.[7]

The following Sunday Miner slipped into the side door of one of Ashcroft's three saloons. Normally closed on the Sabbath, for high rollers the doors were always open. At the poker table he saw Willis West from the BX Company and joined him and the others in a game of five-handed draw poker. After a few hours of good conversation and strong drinks to add to the enjoyment of the game, Miner managed to drop $200 to the skilled player from the BX office. Less than two years later, BX agent West would see photos of his fellow poker player plastered all over the front pages of Kamloops newspapers.[8]

By that September of 1904, there was hardly a town along the lower stretch of the Fraser River which Miner hadn't visited, where he was rumoured to have had a shack or cabin, or where he had camped in a tent over that long hot summer. His was a familiar face to residents in New Westminster, Chilliwack, Mission, Langley, Ladner and Haney. In the evenings that summer it would be remembered that he would hang around the Canadian Pacific Railway station at Agassiz, talk to the friendly telegraphers, and read any incoming messages. In doing so he knew all about train arrivals, departures, and the kind of cargo the various trains carried.[9]

He felt his plans were well set and he was confident in taking the bold steps into the next chapter in his varied and colourful career.

In the early evening of Saturday the 10TH of September in 1904, Bill Miner and two partners staked out their horses in the Gillis orchard near the hamlet of Mount Lehman, close to the shores of the Fraser River. To the north and across the river in the growing darkness was the little agricultural community of Silverdale on the main line of the CPR, just a few miles west of Mission City. The three men made their way on foot east to the CPR bridge at Mission Junction and crossed to the north side of the Fraser. This bridge had been built by the CPR in the late 19TH century to enable a branch line to connect with railroads and markets in the United States, and pedestrian traffic would regularly make its way across this only fixed crossing of the river before New Westminster.[10]

That evening, with fog rolling in and almost two hours late, the CPR's Transcontinental Express No. 1 passenger train pulled to a halt at the water tower near Mission, about 200 yards west of the station. At the throttle of engine No. 440 was engineer Nathaniel J. Scott and his fireman Harry Creelman. Back in the express car was the express messenger of the Dominion Express Company, Herbert

Mitchell, and CPR mail clerks W.M. Thorburn and W.F. Lough. The conductor of the passenger train was John Ward, and the head end and tail end brakemen were William Abbott and A.J. Buckley. The baggageman was Theo Michell. As water was being loaded into the tender, three masked figures made their way through the gloom and climbed onto the roof of the baggage car directly behind the engine and tender. After a few minutes, and with enough water to take them to Vancouver, Scott pushed the engine throttle forward and headed to Vancouver, where the schedule had demanded that they arrive by 7:45 P.M.[11][12]

Only a few minutes and about five miles out of Mission at 9:30 P.M., and close to the rail-side community of Silverdale, Scott and his fireman concentrated on their view of tracks in front of them, illuminated by the engine's powerful headlamp. Over the loud breathing sounds of the working steam engine and the banging of the steel wheels on the rail joints, they heard the sounds of coal rattling down the metal sides of the tender behind them. Scott felt a touch on his shoulder. He turned, and in the dim light of the engine cab, he saw they were confronted by a man with a handkerchief masking the lower part of his face. With a broad brimmed hat pulled down low on his forehead, only his eyes and nose were visible.

"I want you to stop the train," he said loudly, over the sounds of the rushing engine.

Thrusting a large pistol in front of him, the black clad figure advanced towards the train crew and held the weapon directly on the chest of engineer Scott. Behind him came two other masked men, also dressed in dark clothing and armed with a shotgun and a rifle. These two had their faces completely covered with sections of cotton women's stockings with holes cut out for their eyes, nose and mouth. Together they presented a sinister appearance. Quickly overcoming his surprise, and thinking that a joke or prank must be underway, Scott made a comment and reached forward to pull the mask down from the leader's face. The bandit reacted in a flash and shoved the large bore revolver directly under Scott's nose.

"It is no joke. Do what you are told and not a hair on your head will be hurt."

Scott quickly replied, "What do you want me to do? I am at your service."

Moving beside the engineer and keeping him covered with the pistol close to his head, he threatened, "You stop where I want you to, or I will shoot you dead."[13]

At the leader's command, Scott pulled back on the throttle and applying the brakes, brought the engine to a halt just west of the Silverdale crossing. Silence descended over the scene, broken only by the pant and huff of the idling engine and the creak of contracting metal. Ordering the two other dark figures to cover the train crew, the bandit leader searched Scott and Creelman for weapons, and Scott could easily detect the soft American drawl used by the leader. The bandit found Scott's gold railroad watch and some money and pocketed them.[14]

The robber straightened up, and coolly and slowly, and with much emphasis, turned to fireman Creelman and said to him, "You will now come with me. Don't try anything funny. Don't try to get away, or I'll shoot you down like a dog."[15]

It could plainly be seen by the two crew members that the leader of the bandits was an elderly man, the smallest and slightest of the trio, with a peculiarly wizened and weathered face visible above his bandana mask. Tufts of a grey cavalry style moustache bristled above the bandana. Now that the sounds of the travelling train were subdued, he reverted to a softer and easier tone of voice. It was noticed that he didn't issue more than a few words without accompanying them with oaths and curses, frequently threatening and warning the hapless crew with death if they disobeyed his commands. He did all the talking. He was "nervy to the point of bravado."

The other brace of outlaws said hardly a word. They were obviously under the leadership of the older man, and their movements were quick and nervous. The second man was about 30 years of age, 150 pounds and five feet nine inches in height. Round shouldered and of medium build, his dark hair stuck out above his stocking mask.

He wore dark blue overalls with spring buttons and brandished a 30.30 Winchester.

Peering out from his stocking mask, the third robber, about 24 years of age, was also five feet nine in height and with a medium to heavy build. Square shouldered and with a full face, he was observed to be clean shaven with a clear, fair complexion. He too had on a dark pair of old blue overalls, and he wielded a sinister looking shotgun, covering the train crew all the while.[16]

Creelman thought to himself that the leader was "about the nerviest man I ever saw." Even though he was masked, the fireman could discern the bright blue eyes above the handkerchief mask and the wrinkles and weathered lines around the visible parts of his face. Creelman watched closely, paying rapt attention so he could recognize as many features as possible. He saw the peculiar enlarged knuckle on the robber's right hand and the India ink tattoo at the base of his thumb, and he would before too long pass these descriptions on to investigators. Talk was sparse, but deadly serious, and the three bandits seemed to know just what they were about. They started to take charge of the situation immediately, anticipating each other's next moves without direction or discussion. It appeared to the train crew that they had probably done this type of work before and were well experienced.[17]

The robber chieftain and his partner, together with Creelman, got down off the engine and started making their way towards the back of the engine and tender. The leader took the fireman's shovel and threw it far into the dark brush beside the track. The robber with the shotgun was left to cover Engineer Scott, and at his feet lay a sack that was later found to contain dynamite. Again, the leader cautioned the fireman not to make any foolish moves or he would shoot him dead, and his pistol never wavered from the train workers walking in front of him.

Through the dark and the fog the only light to be seen other than the fireman's torch was a dim oil lamp shining from the Donatelli residence hard by the north side of the tracks. Mrs. Donatelli, watching with her children from an upstairs window, saw the train inexplicably come to a halt just outside their front door and quickly realized a robbery was in progress. She pulled her children back from the window and tucked them into their beds. She cautioned them to make no noise and to be still and not attract attention.[18]

The three picked their way through the gloom along the ballast beside the tracks and the silent resting cars. The quiet sounds of the resting engine behind them hissed and huffed in the night as the coal oil torch of the fireman dimly illuminated his way through the fog. The two robbers followed closely behind. They made their way carefully past the first five cars which were mail and express cars and a couple of deadheads. Windows opened in the cars above them and the heads of crew members leaned out, illuminated by the acetylene lanterns behind them. An express messenger and some others, including baggage man Theo Michell, called out, inquiring as to why the train had come to a stop.

The leader of the robbers responded, "I will blow your heads off if I see them out again."

With that the curious onlookers quickly retreated into their cars, and the robbers and the fireman arrived at the last of the five cars before the start of the passenger sections. Fireman Creelman saw in the distance the two lantern lights of the rear brakeman and conductor as they left the rear of the train to see what was going on, but the lights quickly disappeared back into the train.

One of those heads sticking out was Conductor John Ward of Vancouver. He had been alerted by the slowing of the train, and when it was stopped, he put his head out the window to see what the matter was. Seeing a man with a gun beside the rail bed, and assuming he was a hunter, Ward asked him why he had flagged the train and what he wanted. Upon being told to get his head back in the car, or have it blown off, he quickly retreated away from the window and made his way through the express and mail cars to the coaches. He quickly advised two CPR officials on board, engineering staff member H.B. Walkem and superintendent of CPR buildings Alex Wilson, of the violation occurring to their employer's train. Ward told the passengers closest to the head end that a holdup was in progress and to conceal their money and valuables. Unknown to the robbers, Ward then dispatched the rear brakeman on foot to make his way back to Mission City to report the robbery to the operator there. The operator was to notify Vancouver by telegraph of the robbery in progress and to request assistance. It was a distance of four miles, and the brakeman was to run most of the way.[19]

As the brakeman made his way to the end of the train, the news of a holdup in progress spread quickly amongst the passengers. One of the passengers was a provincial judge, Judge Bole of New Westminster. He was sitting together with an American acquaintance and also with W.H. Malkin, the well-known grocery distributor, "Jam King" and future Mayor of Vancouver. In great excitement the passengers began to conceal their valuables and barricaded the car doors. Judge Bole took his and his companions' watches and hid them in his grip, and they slipped their paper currency under the carpet of their first class Pullman car and in the cushions of the chairs they were sitting in.[20]

Robert Wilson, CPR Clerk of the Works and a passenger in one of the cars, would later vividly remember the details of the passengers' consternation. "Talk about queer hiding places, I saw more odd hiding places for valuables discovered in a few minutes than I ever thought was possible. As soon as the news of the holdup was communicated to the passengers, there was the greatest scramble I ever saw to hide money, watches and other valuables. The majority of the women passengers resorted to the usual hosiery receptacle for their jewelry and valuables, while the men stowed rolls of bills away in their shoes, hatbands and other unlikely places. For a while it was generally believed among the passengers that the robbers would go through the passengers as soon as they were finished with the express car."[21]

Several dropped their treasures down behind the passenger car heating pipes, hopefully out of sight.

Back in the Pullman with Malkin and their American friend, Bole stood and addressed the passengers in the first class car.

"Is there any gentleman present who has a weapon about him?"

There was no response.

The Judge drew a short-barreled, large calibre Smith and Wesson pistol from his pocket and, brandishing it aloft, he said, "Then I find that I am the only person here who is in a state to defend this car from those wretches. How many of you gentlemen are willing to stand by me and fight this gang (and) prevent them from entering this car?"

There was a rush of men to the Judge's side, reluctant to be identified as less than courageous under the scrutinizing gaze of the female passengers present.

"Good," he said, "we can give those fellows a surprise if this thing is managed coolly. Now, gentlemen, my plan of defence is this. First of all we shall send the porter back over the track with a lot of torpedoes to warn the freight train which we passed on the siding this side of Mission City, and which is likely to be down on us at any minute, and then we should not need any defence. So, Mr. Porter, you just run up the track and attend to this and we will be getting things ready here for the reception."

The porter courageously told the Judge that he would rather stand beside him "till he was riddled to pieces," but the Judge assured him that the placing of the torpedoes was by far the most valuable service he could render. Quickly, if reluctantly, the porter carefully ran well past the rear of the train in the dark, placed the torpedoes, and rushed back to the Pullman in time to assist in finishing off the defences. The Judge was acting as commander of his troops, directing his men to pile anything that was portable against the entrances at each end of the car. All valuables were hidden, the lights in the centre of the car put out, and all warily watched and listened for intruders. It was then starkly obvious that if the bandits were to find no valuables at all in the car, they would proceed to tear it apart, and perhaps even worse, so they retrieved some bills and change from their hidden stashes to placate the bandits and quickly turned the centre lights out again. The acetylene lamps in the corridors of the Pullman were left brilliantly lit illuminating the car entrances in a stark white light. The judge barricaded himself, revolver in hand, behind a heavy arm chair. The rest of the passengers concealed themselves as best they could. They were convinced that the robbers would quickly identify the Pullman car as the one most likely to hold "portly wads, costly chronometers, gold alberts and precious trinkets." The determined defenders patiently waited for the entrance of the unwitting robbers to their reception committee.[22]

In another of the cars, a man sat nervously holding a huge old cap and ball, large bore pistol in his lap, and warily keeping his eye on the car door. He was eventually persuaded to uncock his weapon as after 45 minutes it became obvious the robbers had no intention of entering the passenger cars.[23]

Dominion Express messenger Herbert Mitchell was looking out the door of express car No. 2026 when he heard one of the bandits tell the clerk looking out the window to pull his head back in or get it blown off. As the men approached Mitchell, they told him the same. As one of the bandits raised his hand toward him, Mitchell slammed the door. Thinking something serious was going on, he laid hold of his revolver and looked out the door on the other side, but nothing was seen. Temporarily satisfied that there was no cause for concern, Mitchell started back to work again at his desk, starkly lit by an acetylene lantern.

As the two robbers and the fireman marched along the rail bed, the bandit leader repeatedly threatened Creelman with death if he tried to do anything or attempt to escape. He directed Creelman to uncouple the passenger cars from the rest of the forward section of the train. As he did so, they heard the brakes set on all the cars behind them towards the tail end. With Creelman at gunpoint, the two robbers started the walk back to the engine. At the head end, when the fireman had uncoupled the train, the resulting whistle of escaping compressed air un-nerved the lone bandit at the head end covering Engineer Scott with the shotgun. He nervously accused the engineer of making signals, and Scott had to use all his powers of persuasion to assure him that the noise was a normal occurrence when uncoupling cars.

The two robbers and the fireman made their way back to the head end of the train. They climbed back aboard the engine's cab, and the

This is the only known photograph of the Mission robbery locomotive #440, wrecked at an unknown location. Courtesy of B.C. Archives.

leader directed the engineer to pull out, leaving the passenger cars stranded, their coal oil lanterns weakly glimmering and the acetylene lamps of the Pullman car shining brightly in the foggy dark, and with the occupants somewhat relieved. The barricades erected by the Judge and the other men were taken down, and the quiet murmurings of questions and rumours continued between the passengers through the dead hours of the night.

After proceeding west a mile or so, the bandit leader told Engineer Scott to stop the now five-car train once more. In front of the barrels of a pistol, a rifle and a shotgun, the engineer and fireman were ordered to accompany the robbers back along the rail bed to the express car, their way again lit by the feeble light of the fireman's torch. One of the robbers carried the sack full of dynamite. At the express car, Engineer Scott was abruptly ordered to tap on the express car door to get it opened. He did so, and after a couple of identifying questions from messenger Mitchell inside, the door was obediently opened by the unsuspecting employee.

While Scott and Creelman were covered by the shotgun, the masked leader with his pistol and the other bandit with the rifle leapt into the express car and confronted messenger Mitchell. They searched him thoroughly and took his .38 calibre Smith and Wesson revolver from him. The leader put it in his pocket.

"If you do what you are told, I won't harm a hair on your head. Where is the strongbox?" he barked.

The messenger quickly replied, "There isn't any strongbox."[24]

The leader then asked about a package consigned to Victoria, but Mitchell advised he had no knowledge of such a package.

The bandit leader turned to a safe sitting on the floor of the express car. He pointed out the car door with his free hand and said, "See there? My partner is carrying a sack of dynamite, and that is going to be used if the safe isn't opened pronto."

Mitchell, fearing the entire car would be blown to bits if the dynamite was employed, opened the safe. Little did he realize at the time that his employ with the Dominion Express Company, a subsidiary of the CPR, would soon come to an end as a result of acceding to the robbers' demands. In the safe were a package of gold dust worth $4,000 consigned to the U.S. assay office in Seattle, another package of gold dust worth $2,000 consigned to the Bank of British North America, and $914.37 in currency. The robber grabbed the contents of the safe, and in doing so, spread coins and change across the floor of the car.[25]

Again the bandit leader asked Mitchell about a package consigned to Victoria, and again Mitchell responded in ignorance of such a parcel.

From outside came the voice of engineer Scott, "Hurry up, you fellows, or I'll have to go back for more oil." Scott's coal oil torch was starting to run out.

The bandit leader laughed and grabbed the gold dust and cash, keeping the messenger covered with his pistol. Again he asked about the package consigned to Victoria, and again Mitchell denied any knowledge of it. As the bandit dropped down from the car, Mitchell was convinced that the robbers had expected something in the express car that was not there.[26]

The five men then proceeded to the mail car and confronted mail car clerks William Thorburn and W.F. Lough, quiet behind the locked door of the car. The clerks at first hesitated to open the door when the bandits hammered on it with their rifle butts and called for them to open up. When the desperados threatened to blow up the side of the mail car, the clerks relented and let the leader and one of the others in. The third man kept the head end crew covered. The clerks were searched for weapons, and though they had pistols available in the mail car, they pretended that they had none. They were instructed to hand over the registered mail bag and they did so. The two clerks heard the soft American drawl used by the bandit leader and noted the words used by him were "registered mail pouch." They remembered that this was the American manner of referring to the mail container, while in Canada it was referred to as a "sack." The leader and his partner then retreated from the car, uttering dire threats as to the clerks' continued good health if the robbers should be interfered with.[27]

After the robbers were satisfied that the express and mail cars had been sufficiently examined for any currency or gold dust, they and the engine crew back-tracked again to the front of the train. When they reached the rear of the engine tender, the leader directed Creelman to uncouple the cars from the locomotive and tender. They all then proceeded to climb back aboard, and the leader directed Scott to release the brakes and proceed west again, leaving another section of the hapless train behind.

"Go to the Whonnock mile-post and stop there, just in front of the church."

This and other statements made by the bandit leader intimated a sure knowledge of the country around this section of the Fraser Valley, the communities and crossroads, and the layout of the trails and roads throughout the area. As they proceeded along the CPR main line, the bandit leader engaged Scott in casual conversation, engendering a grudging admiration from the veteran engineer. The grizzled desperado, still masked by his bandana, reached into his pocket, withdrew Scott's gold railroad watch and the small amount of cash he had taken, and handed it back to him.

"That's alright, my boy," he said, in his soft drawl. "Put that back in your pocket, I don't want any man's money that works for wages."[28]

He then directed Scott to speed up the engine as they passed the little station of Ruskin at the confluence of the Stave River with the Fraser, and they soon reached the mile-post east of Whonnock, a good two miles from where they had left the express and mail cars and a mile east of the hamlet of Whonnock. The older bandit told Scott that this was the spot and to stop immediately.

When the engine and tender had come to a full stop close to the now-deserted church on Whonnock Road, the two bandits with the long guns descended from the engine, followed by the leader. He backed out of the cab, covering the engineer and fireman with the .38 Smith and Wesson revolver he had taken from Mitchell.

"Go back and get your train," the bandit leader ordered the train crew. He bade them a good night and jokingly cautioned them not to run into anything as they backed down the line towards Mission. The robbers stood calmly by the track, watching as the engine and tender vanished east into the mist and gloom, the powerful headlamp of the engine piercing the darkness until it backed around the first corner. This was the last the relieved train crew saw of the bandits. The three outlaws were standing on the ballast, lit up beside the tracks by the engine's light, the trees and brush beside the bank of the Fraser River behind them. It was as if it were a dream inspired from one of those penny dreadful pulp magazines full of fictional stories of the Old West. Not a shot had been fired, nor had anyone, train crew or passengers, been harmed. It was the CPR's first robbery in its history. However, it was not the first Canadian train robbery. In 1874 near Port Credit, Ontario, five thieves disguised as Ku Klux Klan members had robbed $45,000 from the Great Western Railway.[29]

Fireman Creelman soon uncovered a shovel missed by the bandits, had the steam worked up again, and the engineer and fireman sped back east to reassemble the two separated sections of their train.

They picked up the baggage, express and dead-headed cars, built up their air, then continued back to where they had left the stranded passengers. It was only then, when the passengers realized the train was again on its way to Vancouver and their trials were over, that they slowly abandoned their vigilance and let their spirits rise.[30]

V
PURSUIT AND INVESTIGATION

SATURDAY EVENING, 10 SEPTEMBER 1904

In Vancouver's Chinatown, some prominent members of the B.C. law enforcement community were sitting down in anticipation of an evening of fine oriental cuisine, drinks and good conversation. George Burns, the superintendent of the CPR police from Montreal, was visiting the west coast on a holiday. CPR superintendent of the Vancouver division, H.E. Beasley, and Mr. J.D. Townley were entertaining Mr. Burns in the company of Vancouver Chief of Police Samuel North and the local CPR police force's Special Service detective Inspector William McLeod. The unsuspecting McLeod was on the verge of entering into a trying relationship with a notorious American bandit which would stretch over the next half decade. He would follow in the footsteps of Bill Miner until the bandit finally left Canada far in the future, and after McLeod himself had changed his career. The intimate group was well into their banquet when word came from Beasley's office of a telegram sent by the operator at Mission advising him of the robbery at Silverdale. The officials, subdued but well-fed, made their way to Beasley's office at the CPR depot and there met B.C. Provincial Police Chief Constable Colin Campbell, who had also been notified of the event.[1]

Campbell had earlier telegraphed his superior, Superintendent H.S. Hussey in Victoria.

```
Canadian Pacific Railway Company's Telegraph
Vancouver B.C. Sept 10th 1904


Train No 1 four hours late held up six miles
west of Mission Junction
express and postoffice car robbed. Passengers
not molested. Robbers
ran engine and express car one mile east of
Whonnock. Whonnock got off
and supposed to have crossed fraser for the
south. Further particulars
later. Six thousand dollars express and
registered mail taken, train
ready to go here as soon as we can get men.


Colin S Campbell[2]
```

The telegraph and telephones in Beasley's office were soon clacking and humming with directions and orders. The provincial police in New Westminster, Mission, Abbotsford, Sumas and other points were advised about the possible direction taken by the robbers, and special constables were ordered to strategic locations, including along the American border.[3]

As soon as the crew of the ill-fated train pulled into Vancouver, they were summoned to Beasley's offices. They were interviewed and gave descriptions to the bank of law enforcement officials who confronted them. Adding to the official presence, and surely intimidating the train crew, were Superintendent Stewart of the Dominion Express Company, Mr. J. O. McLeod, the superintendent of the railway mail service, and Mr. F.E. Harrison, Assistant Postmaster.

SUNDAY, 11 SEPTEMBER 1904

By 2:00 A.M. Sunday, Superintendent Beasley and his party had left Vancouver on a special train to start the robbery investigation. The special train "only touched the high spots" on the rails as it made its way to the site of the robbery. Beasley was accompanied by Inspector McLeod of the CPR Special Service, Chief North of the Vancouver City Police and Chief Constable Campbell of the B.C. Provincial Police. The group also included Detective Scott, City Officers Hartney and Deptford, Provincial Officers Monroe and Smith and, fortunately for posterity, an enterprising Vancouver Province reporter.[4]

B.C. Provincial Police Constable A.W. Lane of Mission City was dispatched with three or four Special Constables on a commandeered engine south across the Fraser towards the international boundary line to possibly intercept the robbers there. Chief Constable Stanley Spain of New Westminster, also with Special Constables, was allocated the area south of the city to the American border, and other B.C. Provincial Police Constables in the Langley and Cloverdale areas were alerted by telegraph.

As Beasley's train made its way east to the robbery scene, Provincial Police Constable Smith and Vancouver police officer Hartney were let off at Whonnock, just a mile west of where the robbers abandoned the train. As dawn started to break they started making their way east on foot to possibly intercept the robbers if they had been careless enough to stay close to the scene of the crime.

The rest of the officers aboard Beasley's train proceeding to the scene of the holdup were nicely dozing when they ran into the warning torpedoes previously set out by the halted holdup train. The train was switched to an adjacent siding, just west of the Silverdale crossing and the spot where the robbers called the first halt to the train. Chief North from Vancouver would later describe the torpedoes going off to the Province reporter as if he were a Russian and the whole Japanese army was attacking him. This was a reference to the Russo-Japanese War which had been in all the papers in previous weeks.

At daybreak, and shrouded in the morning mist, the members of the investigating party accompanied Fireman Creelman as he described the holdup locations and the highlights of the activities at each location. Through his explanations, the investigators were able to put together a clear idea of the incident as it unfolded.

The first evidence found was the footprints of the rear brakeman in the sandy ballast of the rail bed in that spot. The footprints were only a few hours old and showed the brakeman moving at a rapid pace with very long steps as he made his way to Mission City on foot. He no doubt was spurred on with the realization of what was taking place toward the head end of the train, and it was his lantern Creelman saw disappear into the night.

At the spot where the robbery of the cars had taken place, numerous footprints were observed. Heavy brush bordered each side of the rail bed, and the spot was well screened from any potential witness observations. The nearest house was three-quarters of a mile away, and the robbery would have taken place well hidden in the mist and darkness. Creelman's lost shovel was found in the bush nearby as the detectives and police officers searched back and forth along the rail bed. Special Service Detective Inspector William McLeod hunted diligently for the sack of dynamite which was thought to have been thrown away by the robbers after the robbery, but no sign of it was found. No physical evidence was found that a robbery had taken place at this location just a few hours previously.

The investigators continued west, eager to get to the location where the robbers had vacated the engine. The mist was very heavy, obscuring the Fraser River to their left and making objects just a few yards away disappear.

Creelman pointed out where the robbers had jumped off the train and where the bandits had stood watching until the engine's headlight was out of sight. Tracks showed the three men had then walked west for two hundred yards just past where an Indian camp was located. Here the prints suddenly turned towards the grey Fraser River, silently gliding along beside the tracks. The footprints led along the riverbank continuing west, and it was obvious that some attempt had been made to confuse any trackers that might have been following. Provincial Police Constable Monroe, however, was able to keep the path the robbers had taken in view.

Ahead of them, Beasley's group of investigators soon spotted officers Smith and Hartney, previously dropped off on foot at Whonnock, standing close the water's edge. When the group met, the two officers pointed out where the footprints were grouped around where a boat appeared to have been tied up. The mark left by the prow of a boat was plainly visible in the soft, deep mud. One set of tracks indicated a man had pushed the boat off after his two companions had climbed aboard. The investigators checked up and down this north bank of the Fraser to ensure that the robber had not merely tried to throw pursuers off the scent by pretending to take to the river and cross to the other side. No further sign of the three bandits was found. The investigators peered across the broad width of the river through the rising mist and the brightening dawn at the far bank. Jackman Road could be seen leading down to a landing on the far shore. Mount Lehman rose above the flat floodplain to the east, and the American border was only eleven miles distant to the south.

As it was now 7:30 A.M., the robbers had a nine hour start. The pursuing police officers, representing the highest ranks of so many law enforcement entities, stood on the north shore of the Fraser that morning, probably only too aware that apprehension of the robbery perpetrators was now extremely unlikely. The robbers would have had plenty of time to make their way into the U.S., as that is where all felt that the robbers had come from. It was readily assumed by the investigators, perhaps smugly, that the robbers must have been American, as robbing trains in the States was a relatively common occurrence. In Canada it was a much rarer incident. It had happened only once before, in Ontario, and that had been carried out by American bandits also.[5]

Chief Constable Campbell composed another telegram to Hussey in Victoria, addressing it to the Superintendent's aid, Sergeant Murray. He sent it by rail to the nearest telegraph office.

```
Canadian Pacific Railway's Telegraph
Vancouver, B.C. Sept 11th 1904


Sargent Murray,
Victoria, B.C.
3 men in hold up of No 1. Description as
follows; 1st age 40 to 45 years
        Grayish hair 160 pounds 5 ft 9 in. medium
build high cheek bones, clothes between brown
and grey has 38 smith and wesson blue colour,
also big knuckle think on right hand. 2nd.
        Age about 30 weight 150 height 5 ft 9 in
slender build, round shouldered, dark clothes
and dark hair, rifle 30.30
        Blue overalls spring bottoms. 3rd, 5 ft
9 in medium build square-shouldered full
face, clean shaven, fair complexion  wore
old blue overalls age 24.


Colin S. Campbell.[6]
9:20AM
```

Continuing the investigations on the north side of the river, Chief Constable Campbell knocked on the door of the house of Albert Lee, the owner of the missing boat thought used by the escaping criminals. There was no response. The other members of the investigative team raised a hue and cry to wake up the residents. Inspector McLeod, who grew up on a farm, stated that surely they must be up at this time. However, it was some moments before the door finally opened and a confused and sleepy Mr. Lee stood in the doorway.

"Your rowboat!" stated Chief Constable Campbell, officiously.

"My rowboat, gentlemen, is tied up right over there," replied Mr. Lee, quickly taking in the officious looking group, and pointing through the trees to the river.

"It was there last night, but it has been stolen," triumphantly declared Chief Constable Campbell.

Mr. Lee, surrounded by rifle-toting police officers and detectives, walked down to the river, and it slowly became apparent to him that he was no longer in custody of his fishing skiff. He quickly informed the posse that it had been there when he went to bed the previous night and gave the officers a description of the fishing skiff. It was painted green inside and out, with the gunwale and a strip along the side painted black. Mr. Lee had used the boat to deliver mail to the Glen Valley and Mount Lehman communities directly across the river from Whonnock.[7]

Across that river and a bit downstream from the investigating officers and the irate Mr. Lee was the farm of Gilbert MacKay. McKay's property bordered the south shore of the Fraser River and was between Jackman and Town Line Roads. Just after daybreak that same morning, McKay strolled down to the riverbank in front of his property and found a sack of dynamite and a few fresh shotgun shells. He picked them up and would hold on to them until he heard about the robbery of the CPR train.[8][9]

Completing their investigations on the north shore of the river, Chief Constable Campbell and his search party began to make plans to cross the Fraser to continue their investigations. By later that Sunday morning the investigation and tracking of the robbers south of the Fraser were well underway. Robert Shortreed of Abbotsford with his posse scanned the Old Yale Road for tracks, found signs of three men, and backtracked them along Jackman Road to the banks of the Fraser. Feeling these were the men wanted for the robbery, they diligently followed up every track and lead. They were confident they were hot on the trail of the robbers. The muddy conditions made the tracks they were following, one of a person with hobnailed boots, easy to spot until they veered off into the brush on the Canadian side of the border. This was just north of Wiser Lake near Lynden, Washington, and it was here all signs of the robbers were lost. At three o'clock in the afternoon a length of fuse was found between the Fraser River and the Old Yale Road. As the robbers had carried dynamite, this, and the tracks of three men being followed, was felt to be a positive sign that the robbers had made their escape in that direction, heading towards the border.

Later that morning Gilbert McKay made his way up to one of the posses and passed over the sack of dynamite and the shotgun shells. It took all of the farmer's powers of persuasion to convince the police officers that he was a landowner that resided beside the Fraser opposite Whonnock and that he had found the items on the riverbank close to his home.[10]

Chief Constable Colin Campbell was now in charge of the entire investigation. With Constable Monroe he had crossed the river soon after finding Albert Lee's stolen boat abandoned several miles below Whonnock. It was surmised that it had drifted there after being abandoned by the robbers during their escape across the river. Constable Lane, Inspector McLeod, Detective Waddell, an ex-jailer named Grady and others were all strategically dispatched to aid in the investigation. Detectives, constables and volunteers patrolled the roads and farmlands throughout the area between the Fraser River and the American border, and between New Westminster and Sumas Lake.

MONDAY, 12 SEPTEMBER 1904

On the Monday following the robbery, the Vancouver Province and the New Westminster Columbian newspapers announced to the citizens of British Columbia news of the first robbery of a CPR train in Canada's history. The Province reporter who had accompanied the investigators gave detailed descriptions of the activities of the robbers on Saturday night and the police response the next day.

The description of the train robbers was featured in all the local papers and reflected the importance placed upon this forensic method of identification prior to the utilization of fingerprint technology. The physical attributes of the bandit leader given by the press were, with the exception of his age, very accurate. Although Miner was 58 years old at the time, he was described as about 40. Many were to make the same mistake about his age after future escapades.

The loot also warranted detailed investigation by reporters. The first statements issuing from the CPR and the Provincial Police to the press correctly indicated that the robbers had escaped with $7,000, chiefly in gold dust from the Cariboo. It was speculated that they were after gold from the Bullion Pit near Likely, a Consolidated Cariboo mine. The end of the season's cleanup at the mine was to later total $63,000, and this was thought to be the prize the thieves sought. The plans for shipment of this gold had been changed at the last moment, and the gold would eventually pass through unmolested a few days later. Another unconfirmed report stated that the train was supposed to have had on board a shipment of cash amounting to $274,000 from a bank in Winnipeg en route to a bank in Vancouver, but this was later denied by the authorities.[11]

The federal Post Office department speculated that no more than $50 in cash was obtained from the mail car in the nineteen letters taken by the bandits, and ironically for the thieves, many of the letters contained tax notices. CPR Inspector McLeod was quoted as saying that it was fortunate that the robbed train had been carrying only the lightest ever load of mail containing cash. Just the previous day the mail car had carried an amount substantially more than the $7,000 seized from the express car safe.[12]

Traditionally the registered mail sack stolen could have contained a considerable amount of valuables also, but this was never confirmed. It was this registered mail sack which was to be the source of considerable speculation after the robbery. It was later rumoured that the sack contained bearer bonds totalling, in most reports, $60,000 to $80,000 in 1904 dollars. The unconfirmed theft of these bearer bonds by Miner and his crew would echo down through the years until the present day. Miner, keeping abreast of the latest press reports, rumours and speculation, would himself attempt to perpetuate the confusion about the bonds and feed the press's insatiable desire for more news about his exploits. There is at present no primary documentary evidence for the existence of these bonds. The present CPR Archives will only note that any files associated with the robbery that would shed a light on the bonds' existence would have been in CPR

President Lord Shaughnessy's personal files which were destroyed soon after his death.[13]

Miner, when he felt it suited him and it was to his advantage, would brag about the amount he had realized from his efforts that dark night west of Mission. He would later smugly brag that he had obtained thirty to forty thousand from the safe of the express car. Continuing his practice of confusing the facts of his exploits and trying to throw his listener off the track, he claimed that he had gone through the whole amount in nine months as "he had a good many mouths to seal between the Fraser River and Montana."[14]

Monday's newspapers, the railway telegraph and the rudimentary phone lines in the interior of the province advised the good citizens of British Columbia, aspiring posse members and other civilians of the substantial rewards offered. The aggregate totalled $7,500, offered from the various offended parties. The CPR offered $1,000 for "information leading to the arrest and conviction" of the desperados. The Dominion Express Company and the CPR together offered $5,000 for "the arrest and conviction" of the guilty parties, with a proportional amount given for the arrest and conviction of any and every member of the gang. The British Columbia provincial government put up $1,500 for the "arrest and conviction" of the robbers, or $600 for the arrest and conviction of each and every member of the gang.[15]

While the published notices of reward did not call for the capture of the robbers "Dead or Alive" as was the wont of the American authorities under similar circumstances, the Province newspaper was in no doubt that the rewards would be paid whether or not a corpse or a live body was turned over. Canadian authorities prided themselves as being somewhat more delicate in spurring on the posses and lawmen in pursuit of suspected criminal perpetrators. The Province went on to speculate that if the robbers were found in the U.S., they would undoubtedly end up dead.[16]

Numerous erroneous reports circulated in the first days after the robbery that the perpetrators had been captured. Privately some of the police in charge of the pursuit felt that the robbers had made their way into the bush around Sumas and successfully escaped to the south across the border.

Superintendent James E. Dye of the Pinkerton Detective Agency in Seattle was in Vancouver by Monday, and five of his investigators followed him that evening to assist in the investigation. After collectively being taken aside and instructed by the senior management of the CPR as to the corporation's expectations, the detectives soon spread out in the company of provincial constables such as Stanley Spain of New Westminster and Otway Wilkie of Langley. Both the B.C. Provincial Police and the CPR often made use of private investigative agencies such as the Pinkertons. The Pinkertons soon had their touted "system" of hundreds of records being examined to determine common threads between the Mission robbery and other similar incidents. The Thiel Detective Agency out of Seattle, newly formed by an ex-Pinkerton detective, also assisted the Canadian police forces in their investigations of the Mission robbery.[17]

That afternoon, Western Division General Superintendent of the CPR Richard Marpole, Superintendent Beasley's superior in Vancouver, was interviewed by the Province, and he stated that every possible effort would be expended to capture the bandits. Marpole told reporters that the CPR was issuing a notice of reward for information leading to the arrest and conviction of the robbers and was eagerly awaiting results.[18]

TUESDAY, 13 SEPTEMBER 1904

As Tuesday dawned, the search for the robbers had gravitated to south of the U.S. border. It was estimated that as many as forty officers were in the field, with more being added as time progressed and more volunteers became available. Twenty ranchers were distributed throughout the posses, intent on acquiring the increasing rewards. American law enforcement officials assisted Chief Constable Campbell and other B.C. Provincial Police officers in their search for clues as to the whereabouts of the perpetrators. Bellingham, Lynden, Seattle and other points close to the Canadian border saw marshals, sheriffs and deputy sheriffs, police and ranchers combing the surrounding countryside and wooded areas for the thieves. A U.S. revenue cutter patrolled around Point Roberts and the mouth of the Fraser to thwart the robbers from stealing fishing boats in their attempt to escape. Cabins and logging roads, trails, ranches and farms were all diligently inspected for suspicious strangers.[19]

Information was soon passed on from the Pinkertons that indicated that the modus operandi followed by the leader of the robbers was the same used by the robber who had attempted to hold up the Oregon Railway and Navigation Company train in Corbett, Oregon, the previous year. The use of a boat, the description of the bandit, the method of boarding and taking control of the train, and the ready availability of dynamite were common to both robberies. The New Westminster Columbian came close to identifying the Mission Junction robber as Bill Miner, but not quite. They received an anonymous phone call from Bellingham which was somewhat confusedly transcribed. "One of the men (at the Mission robbery) was a miner whose family resides in Bellingham and who is known to have been implicated in a hold-up at Oregon, about a year ago."[20]

Bill Miner's sister Mary Jane Wellman and her husband were living on a homestead near what is now greater Bellingham, and his other sister Harriet was living near Bow, Washington. Their homes were watched and they were interviewed. The Seattle Pinkertons were well aware that Miner was on the loose again and were convinced he had made the attempted robbery at Corbett as well as successfully carrying out the robbery at Mission Junction in Canada.[21]

Chief Constable Campbell and other Provincial Police officers continued working the area south of the U.S. border around Lynden, Washington, and obtained scanty results. False arrests were made both in Canada and in the United States, but subsequent investigations led to the hapless individuals' release. Both Canadian and American authorities, including Sheriff Lukens of Whatcom County, were sweeping through the areas directly south of the border. An editorial was included in the Province newspaper pressing law enforcement to capture the train robbers quickly and to thwart the influx of

American desperados and train robbers into Canada. They are a "clever and alert gang of thieves who have superior knowledge of the transport from place to place of large sums of money or quantities of bullion."[22]

WEDNESDAY, 14 SEPTEMBER 1904

Faced with a cooling trail, Chief Constable Campbell pulled his five men and his twenty member civilian posse back up into Canada. They worked over the trails and roads south of the Fraser again, gradually moving south again towards the border. Campbell now became convinced that the holdup men had doubled back across the border and were now in the Fraser Valley again. That morning he sent Special Constable Wilson, Vancouver police officer Davies, and an undercover officer only known as J. Gault by rail up to Hope to watch the Dewdney Trail from Hope to Princeton, thinking perhaps that the bandits had made for the Nicola or Similkameen country and by that route would attempt to make their escape across the border. The Dewdney Trail branched off to the mining towns of Granite Creek and Princeton, and Constable Hugh Hunter in Princeton and Constable Haines in Hedley had been alerted and authorized to hire as many Special Constables as they should need. Long distance telephones located at Abbotsford and Nicola aided in communications, while the three officers placed themselves strategically along the trail to Princeton, keeping a lookout for suspicious strangers all along the way. All of the towns, mining camps and ranches of the interior cattle country had been alerted to the possibility of the bandits making their way into that sparsely settled country.[23]

As time progressed, the pursuers were becoming debilitated. Some had spent the last three nights under less than adequate conditions. The lucky members of one posse commandeered a large canvas tarp covering shingles in a mill and used it for shelter one night, but hot meals were universally non-existent. One CPR detective had hardly four hours sleep since the evening of the robbery. Exhaustion, lack of hot and nutritious food, wet and dirty clothes, no blankets, and the pressure of the chase turned some of the pursuers "gaunt and haggard."[24]

That evening the B.C. Provincial Police under Chief Constable Campbell, the CPR Special Service detectives under Inspector McLeod, and Pinkerton Superintendent Dye met in Aldergrove to re-think their investigation. The Pinkertons, well aware that Miner was the most logical suspect, released the information that they were almost certain the robbers had come out of Vancouver the day previous to the robbery. Armed with photos of Miner obtained from the San Quentin penitentiary in California, they no doubt made full use of these in their investigations.[25]

The Post Office department of the federal government released details on the mails stolen from the mail car. Only nineteen letters in all were taken, with $14 in registered mails and three tax notices from Calgary included. It was advised that a total of no more than $50 could have been obtained from the mail sacks. Again, no mention was made of any bearer bonds being included in the loot.

THURSDAY, 15 SEPTEMBER 1904

By September 15TH, investigators had a good idea who the bandit leader was. Inspector William McLeod stated from Bellingham that the robbers were known to law enforcement agencies, but he refused to identify them. Other sources told a Victoria Colonist reporter "they are clever crooks and are known in California." The New Westminster Columbian reporter went on to speculate that the leader of the Mission train robbers was "one Bill Morgan, alias E.A. Miner, alias old Bill Miner." The article notes, in error, that Bill Miner was a Canadian and summarized his criminal career. The detectives had information that he had made for the Fraser Valley after the attempted robbery of the Oregon Railway & Navigation Company train on 23 September 1903, and authorities had been watching for him in the Fraser Valley. The description of Bill Miner held by the detectives matched closely with that given by the fireman and engineer on the hijacked train.[26] [27]

By Saturday, the police were resigned to the fact that the robbers had successfully made their escape into the United States and over the Cascade Mountains.

B.C. Provincial Police Constable Monroe told the Province, "It looks to me as if their capture, if it does occur, will be merely an accident. They may be hiding in three different places or they may have left the country. It would take the entire Japanese army to find them, if they are cached away in that big district. Our particular hope now is that the size of the reward will tempt some of their pals to give them away. This is about the only way they will ever be taken. It would be different if the police knew for whom they were looking, but the descriptions are vague and the whole proposition is difficult."[28]

That day the federal government of Canada increased the reward by $5,000, making it a total of $12,500. This was a tidy sum for those times, but it was never to be collected.

The Vancouver Province had tried to keep public interest up in the days following the robbery by featuring detailed stories on the front page of each daily edition. One week after the robbery the Province printed its last front page article on the incident. With no additional hard facts to report, and having speculated endlessly on every rumour put forward, the paper stopped publishing daily references to the story. The confrontation between Russia and Japan reclaimed the front page.[29]

Chief Constable Campbell and his men continued their investigations long after media and public interest had died. Conscious of the critical gaze of CPR and government officials, the provincial police force expended all efforts in its attempt to reach a successful conclusion. The Pinkertons assured their major corporate client that they could be depended upon to pursue a spirited investigation, knowing with almost total surety the identity of the leader of the bandits. All hoped for a break in the case as time usually caused criminals to drop their guard and talk indiscreetly to their fellows.[30]

CPR president Thomas Shaughnessy assured apprehensive shippers that no efforts would be spared in bringing the criminals to justice. Shaughnessy was on his special train with cars the Cornwall and the York. Vice-President William Whyte in his special car the Manitoba was also in tow. Shaughnessy was nearly at the end of his inspection tour of the CPR main line and on his way with senior CPR officials to meet provincial politicians in Victoria. Superintendent Richard Marpole, also in his private car No.15, accompanied Canada's corporate elite. Superintendent Beasley of Vancouver was also accompanying the party as it prepared to embark on a CPR steamer to the province's capital. [31]

VI

THE GETAWAY

THE LITTLE FISHING SKIFF SILENTLY EMERGED from the fog and darkness surrounding the south bank of the Fraser River. With a whisper the prow of the boat pushed into the sand and the three passengers disembarked into the soft mud on the shore. They made their way to the landing at the end of Jackman Road and, carrying three bulky mail sacks and two long guns, went quickly and quietly south along the dirt wagon road. Aware of their surroundings and familiar with the layout of the land, they confidently made their way through the gloom. The sleeping farmhouses they passed were oblivious to their presence, with just the lonesome barking of distant dogs noting their passing. They did not take any care to cover their tracks and trudged straight through puddles and mud as they pushed their way through the quiet night air. At one obvious spot they dumped their sack of dynamite and a handful of shotgun shells. At another they dropped a length of fuse. They uncaringly left a clear trail, distinct and beckoning, until they were some eight miles from the river and closing on the American border. They suddenly veered to the east and entered a heavily timbered and brushy forest area where they took great care to ensure their tracks were covered. After trekking due east for a short time, they again changed direction and headed back north towards the Fraser. Taking old logging roads and trails scouted out in the days preceding the robbery, the bandits made good time.

At a sign and soft command from their slightly built leader, the quiet trio grouped around a large log lying on the forest floor under the towering cedars. Kneeling around the sacks, they emptied

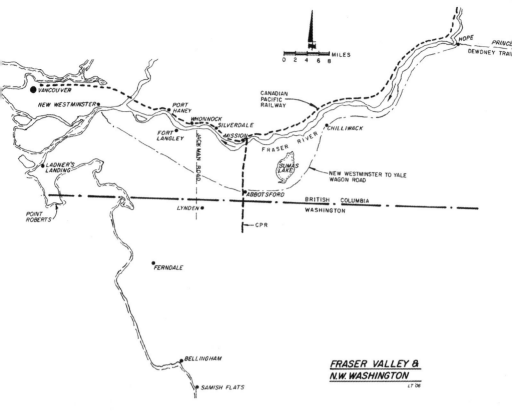

The Get-Away route of the Mission train robbers
and the district south of the Fraser River.

them onto the mossy ground. They did not light a fire for fear of exposure, but examined their ill-gotten gains by the feeble light of matches. They sorted through the contents and put some of the small but heavy bags, envelopes and papers back in the sacks. After considerable muted but heated and animated conversation, they dug a shallow hole and dumped a large amount of the remaining papers and envelopes into it, followed by the rifle and shotgun. Covering the hole again with soil, moss and dead branches, they shifted the packs onto their shoulders and set off, heading to the north in the direction of the Fraser River.[1]

With their lightened load they continued to make good time. Dawn was starting to break on the eastern horizon behind the mountains. They emerged from the heavy brush and intersected the

Boundary Commission Road as it headed northeast after crossing the border on its way to Matsqui. They followed the road until they came to Mount Lehman Road and followed it until they came to an abandoned homestead west of the hamlet of Mount Lehman. They were less than four miles east of Jackman Road, having almost completed a full circle since they had grounded their stolen boat on the south bank of the river. The pursuing lawmen at Whonnock had yet to cross the Fraser.[2]

In the abandoned house the three split their loot, and leaving the mail sacks behind, they made their way to the orchard near the Gillis farm, retrieved their patiently waiting horses, split up and went on their separate ways.[3]

The leader of the bandits confidently pushed his mount into a mile-eating trot as he made his way towards the sun rising over the eastern mountains. Veering to the south on roads and trails, he came to the New Westminster to Yale wagon road. Now in full daylight, he followed it, skirting the small community of Abbotsford. Making good time along the wagon road on the southern and eastern shore of Sumas Lake, he reached the farming community of Chilliwack later that day.[4]

Chilliwack was a busy little town in the heart of the fertile valley, separated from the south shore of the Fraser River by a newly built diking system. At the steamboat landing a mile from Chilliwack the steamers "Beaver," "Ramona," "Pheasant" and "Minto" tied up and smoked while quietly at rest. They all ran on regular schedules up and down the river and were the preferred mode of transport. The CPR monopoly's freight rates were considered onerous by all who wished to use them, and the local roads were often more of a quagmire than reliable transportation links. Over 600 people lived in Chilliwack proper, and the surrounding district contributed over 3,000 farmers, settlers and their families. The town was the centre of trade and commerce for that section of the Fraser Valley and looked forward to a bright future.[5]

Riding past the five corners and the road that led down to the boat landing, Bill Miner watched the bicycles busily wheeling back

STREET SCE
CHILLIWAC
190

Chilliwack in 1907 at the Five Corners on Yale Road East.
COURTESY OF CHILLIWACK MUSEUM AND HISTORICAL SOCIETY.

and forth on the main street. Wagons and teams and riders and pedestrians added to the busy Sunday scene as good folk made their way to and from the four local churches. A thin skein of dust rose into the air against the midday sun as the damp of the early morning burned off. Miner felt more and more comfortable as he slipped unnoticed, he thought, into the village close on the banks of the Fraser. As his horse relaxed and cooled down to a quiet walk down the main street, he failed to notice a man watching him closely from the side of the road. Jeff Harrison was the purser of the steamer "Minto" that plied its way between Harrison Mills and Chilliwack Landing. Harrison felt there was something suspicious about the lone rider, and filed away in his memory the bright blue eyes shaded under a white flat-brimmed Stetson and the distinctive face with its bristling moustaches. A few days later when Harrison was to see Edwards again, he would comment to the captain of the Minto, R.C. Menten, that he thought the older gentleman with the distinctive moustaches was one of the Mission robbers. He watched Edwards check his horse in at Rowat's "Chilliwack Livery" stable. R.G. Rowat's service was known as "nothing but first class," and George Edwards spent some time making sure his horse was looked after. Rowat remembered the elderly gentleman's horse as a "very fine, fast running horse; a tall black one."[6]

Sometime during that first day in Chilliwack, Edwards met with his friend Jack Budd. Together they had driven a small band of rustled horses over the Dewdney Trail from Princeton and sold them at auction in New Westminster shortly before the Mission robbery. Budd had arrived at Chilliwack the day before the Mission robbery and had put his horses up at Rowat's livery stable while waiting for his compatriot to show up. After spending some time together that day, Budd left Edwards for his horse ranch in the Similkameen. Provincial Police Constable A.W. Lane of Mission had also been in Chilliwack that day making inquiries about Budd, and things were getting a bit too warm for the recluse from the Similkameen. Budd did not want to have to face any uncomfortable questioning and quickly made his way back to the Princeton country, heading straight for his ranch and hoped for obscurity. Miner, however, was to continue as George Edwards to enjoy the sporting life in Chilliwack, constantly keeping his ears and eyes open for the latest news of the pursuit of the train robbers. The barbershop and poolroom "moccasin telegraph" and the Vancouver Province and the New Westminster Columbian newspapers would provide him with all the intelligence he needed to gauge the progress of the pursuit for the train robbers and how his own security was affected.[7]

It was also that first day that Edwards' cover in Chilliwack was close to being compromised. At 11:00 o'clock on Sunday morning, one of Edwards' partners in the Mission robbery rode into Chilliwack ahead of him. Commercial Hotel proprietor D.S. Dundas watched the stranger dismount in front of the hotel and hitch his horse to the rail in front. He checked into the hotel as "F.W. Hutchison of Greenwood, B.C.." Dressed in overalls, the stranger appeared to be highly agitated

St Thomas Church at the Five Corners in downtown Chilliwack, circa 1908. COURTESY OF CHILLIWACK MUSEUM AND HISTORICAL SOCIETY.

and acted in an extremely nervous manner. When it came time to pay the $1.50 for the room, Dundas saw gold nuggets and gold dust in the man's leather poke, along with gold coins. Waving a stub of a paint brush that didn't look as though it would hold any paint, the stranger told Dundas that he was a painter looking for work. Before he went up to his room, he borrowed a razor from a guest named Dixon and quickly went upstairs to shave. Soon the man came downstairs and onto the porch in front of the hotel, spending some time leaning against a pillar, nervously watching the scene on the main street. Dundas pointed him out to his friend G.C. Dolman and intimated to him that this was probably one of the Mission train robbers and that he was staying in Dundas' hotel. Dolman recognized the man as one he had seen in Vancouver five years previously hanging around the Palace Hotel. The stranger left Chilliwack early the next morning for parts unknown.[8]

The next day, Monday, and little more than 24 hours since the robbery, Harrison watched George Edwards confidently walk down the street to Al Chadsey's "Elite Barbershop." Advertising facial massages as a specialty, Chadsey would remember the genial elderly gentleman who sank into the barber's chair that day, reading the Vancouver Province as the towels were heated. He shaved the weathered and pocked face of the relaxing man who introduced himself as George Edwards. It was the first of many times he would cut the graying stubble from the face of the stranger he would learn only later was a famous bandit.[9]

Refreshed, Edwards strolled down the street and entered the premises and poolroom of proprietor E. Marriott. Edwards was to spend many of the following days in Chilliwack leisurely sitting at one of the card tables with his back to the wall, playing poker and being an all around "bon vivant." Marriott watched as the stranger kept a sharp watch on the door and anyone who entered through it. Free and easy with his money, the old gentleman often played opposite the same two men sitting in for the various hands. The two, known only as one Denny Pulford and the other as "Missouri Bill," seemed to have no fixed employment, and Missouri Bill in particular cultivated the old man's friendship with free and easy conversation and ready laughter. Unbeknownst to Edwards, or perhaps he did have an inkling, the two poker partners were in reality undercover CPR Special Service detectives sent up from Mission Junction by Inspector William McLeod. Charged with keeping an eye out for suspicious characters that could be suspects in the train robbery, the two secret agents were alternatively intrigued by and suspicious of the affable Edwards. Noticing his free-spending ways, they had singled him out as an individual worthy of further surveillance, and they spent considerable time keeping track of his whereabouts.[10]

Purser Harrison sat as a spectator to some of the games and watched Mr. Edwards shoot pool and play poker, joking with acquaintances and generally at ease and sure of himself in the company of his fellow sporting types. He often saw him walking on the streets of Chilliwack over the following days, casually passing provincial police constables, detectives and other robbery investigators with nary a turn.

Throughout the rest of the week, Edwards would continue in much the same manner. He would have his shaves at the Elite Barbershop, read his newspapers to keep up with the latest news on the hunt for the train robbers, and enjoy male company in the poolroom and around the card tables. He would make friends and re-establish contact with old ones. One such old friend he visited in the butcher shop opposite the drug store was William A. Nevard of Chilliwack. He was a well-known butcher in the area with a reputation for fairness and integrity. In the past, he had often travelled into the Similkameen to visit Budd and Edwards and other ranchers, buying beef and other livestock. He once purchased two mules from the friendly George Edwards, and Edwards and Budd had often driven cattle and horses down to Nevard at Chilliwack.[11][12]

G.C. Dolman was one of the new friends George Edwards would make in the area. Dolman had a stable in Chilliwack, and the two would talk about horses for hours, both being lovers of fine horse flesh. He remembered the tattoos Edwards had, one on the base of his thumb and one on his forearm.

During their long talks, Dolman saw Edwards with "... a lot of money, a big roll with a $1,000 bill on the outside, and a long buckskin sack in which he carried gold, mostly $20 gold pieces. I should say there was more than a pound of it."

Dolman noticed Edwards had a very sharp and cautious eye and watched everyone who came into the stable. He wore a heavy gold ring formed like a snake on his left hand.[13]

Another horse lover Edwards would cultivate was livery stable owner Reese. Reese and Edwards would drive around town in Reese's wagon and enjoy the sights. Reese, too, would see Edwards with a lot of money and "... with an automatic Colt's gun in his hand."

It was only at mid-week that the Chilliwack Progress gave any space to the Mission robbery. All of three paragraphs was allocated to it on the front page, the majority of the page being devoted to the upcoming fall fair and Council proceedings for a new wharf.[14]

By Friday the little municipality was all a-bustle with the excitement of the annual Chilliwack Exposition to be held the next week on the 21st to the 23rd of September. Athletic competitions including a baseball tournament, agricultural stock and produce displays, professional musical concerts on Wednesday and Thursday evenings, and horse races on Friday added to the festive occasion and the excitement. The local Chilliwack Progress lamented the fact that the provincial government had reduced the exposition grant from $860 to $248 and that the summer's drought had seen a reduction in the size of the root crops. It went on to assure its readers, however, that they shouldn't let these minor irritations deflect from the success of the best fall fair to be held in the Fraser Valley.[15]

The search for the train robbers was still underway, but the posses and officers were disenchanted and weary. The three detectives that had been sent up to watch the Dewdney Trail into the Similkameen and Granite Creek made their way back into town and checked in at the Harrison House. Detectives Wilson, Gault and Davies were satisfied to spend some time in the Chilliwack area and, if possible, take in the fair the next week. They passed the affable Mr. Edwards on the main street.[16]

J.E. Stevenson wanted to take in the Chilliwack Exposition also. Up in Princeton, he prepared his mount, securing his supplies behind his saddle. His friends told him that Jack Budd and George Edwards had driven a few horses over the Dewdney Trail some days before him, and he might just run into them. Stevenson made his way over the lonely trail and saw the tracks of the two riders and their horses ahead of him. He could tell by the signs that they had preceded him by a least a week, and he also saw the tracks of a single rider making his way back up from Hope. Budd had made good time and headed straight back to his ranch. Stevenson rode into Chilliwack on Sunday the 18TH and settled in to wait for the start of the fair. Recognizing Edwards from previous meetings in Princeton, Stevenson saw him in Chilliwack at the poolroom playing cards and generally living the good life. Stevenson would recollect that he saw Mr. Edwards around that time before the exposition, always with plenty of money. He also saw him sporting a .32 calibre Colt's automatic pistol, a deadly little firearm that hid nicely in a man's pocket. He met Missouri Bill, but did not really get to know who he was. Stevenson could see that he was one of Mr. Edwards' circle of friends.[17]

The steamers sailing out of Chilliwack started getting busy the day before the Exposition started, hauling passengers to Chilliwack from points both up and down the Fraser. On the 20TH, the steamer Ramona alone brought in thirty passengers from New Westminster. Again on the 22ND, the Ramona brought in special groups just for the horse races to be held on Friday. The musical concerts were a great success, and the fruits of the farmers' labours were most appreciated by the judges. The horse races were Mr. Edwards' favourite event. Along with Mr. Budd, he had entered a number of fleet horses in races in Princeton. He watched the Chilliwack entries closely. At the end of racing on Friday, the Ramona put on a special to get the racing aficionados back to New Westminster. Mr. Edwards prepared to leave that weekend for the Similkameen.

Riding his fine black horse at a walk as he left Chilliwack, Edwards passed a brand new automobile arriving from Bellingham across the border. As the lone rider left the town behind, local children and adults alike clustered around the noisy and smelly beast, expressing their amazement at the wonders of technology and wondering what the future had in store. Edwards kept his eyes on the horizon in front of him. He had a date to keep in Kamloops. The fall assizes started in early October and some of his friends would be attending a trial.[18]

That same weekend two teenage brothers were out grouse hunting near Mount Lehman and found themselves at an abandoned homestead. Inside the old house, they found three mailbags and turned them over to the authorities.[19]

—◆—

VII
THE GUNFIGHT AT MANNING'S

THE INCIDENT HAPPENED AT MANNING's roadhouse and saloon north of Tulameen. The Otter Valley Road was the main transportation link between Princeton, Tulameen, Aspen Grove and Nicola, and also to Kamloops and Spence's Bridge in the north. The town of Merritt did not yet exist. Along the way to these northern communities, roadhouses were built by entrepreneurs to service the travellers, stagecoaches, wagons and teams making their way through this mineral rich section of the Similkameen and Nicola areas. Some of the roadhouses still exist. Thynne's roadhouse near Thynne Lake, built by John Granville (Jack) Thynne in the 1890s, was frequently used by George Edwards on his trips back and forth to Nicola and Kamloops. The Portland Roadhouse on the site of the Portland Ranch near Aspen Grove still exists and also was used by Edwards. An obscure individual named Manning built a roadhouse and saloon near what is now called Manning Creek, four miles south of Thynne's. No sign of it is left. Only a few miles south of Thynne's, and between Thynne Lake and Otter Lake, this roadside hostel and tavern did not reach the class displayed by others along the route. It had developed a less than sterling reputation and was well known for the wild and wooly clientele it catered to. Needless to say, this was also a spot that George Edwards cultivated and where he met with friends to share drinks and a few games of cards.[1]

On 1 April 1904, April Fool's Day, a bunch of the boys from the ranches and mining camps surrounding Manning's were having a raucous time in the roadhouse. The Similkameen Star described it as "… a prolonged spree by a coterie of individuals known for their

Nicola Lake, B.C., circa 1904.
COURTESY OF NICOLA VALLEY MUSEUM AND ARCHIVES.

fine drinking qualities." Included in the group that Saturday was a man of diminutive stature, said to be a prospector, well-known for his argumentative and threatening ways. When drinking, he was known to quickly and often take offence, and would draw his large calibre Smith and Wesson revolver to settle any disputes to his satisfaction.

Described by a contemporary as "that little dark … gunman, the son of a Presbyterian minister in Nova Scotia," Smoky Chisholm would bully his way through many a fray until that day of reckoning in the saloon on the Otter Valley Road. That Saturday Chisholm was riding his cayuse Mowitch, known as a "chestnut streak of lightning." He dismounted in front of the premises and, after hitching his horse, entered the dark confines of the little roadhouse. George Edwards was there, along with a bunch of prospectors and hangers-on down from Granite Creek. With the cowboys from the surrounding ranches and others eager for a day of serious drinking was an unobtrusive miner named Steve Brooks. Saturday was always a day for prodigious imbibing and everyone present proceeded to do his best. Inevitably, Smoky Chisholm, now well into a full fledged drunk, was feeling particularly mean and nasty. He started to pick on the quiet miner Brooks, threatening him and pushing him across the floor. As the confrontation neared its climax, Chisholm drew his deadly Smith and Wesson and held it under Brooks' chin, all the while promising him a bullet for his troubles. Brooks, frightened, desperate and in fear of his life, lunged away from the startled Chisholm, grabbed a 44:40 Winchester carbine leaning against the wall, levered a shell into the chamber and fired from the hip at Smoky Chisholm from close range. It all happened in the blink of an eye. Down went the little gunman, writhing on the floor in pain. Brooks could only look on in anxiety and confusion. Chisholm had been hit in the upper part of his leg near the groin, and the bullet smashed into the long bone, fracturing it. Blood quickly spread darkly and thickly across the floor. His revolver now forgotten beside him, Chisholm swore and snarled and promised the now more frightened miner with the future retribution that would fall on his head. Brooks' friends hustled the shaken miner out the door, while others tended to the victim's wound.[2][3]

Suddenly sober, the partiers took measures that they knew would be in their own and the two antagonists' best interests. They knew that the law as practiced in His Majesty's Dominion was, while perhaps slow and plodding, inevitable and just. They sent for a doctor to attend to the wounds of Smoky Chisholm. A rider was dispatched to Princeton to phone the closest doctor, Dr. George Tuthill, in Nicola Lake to come down to attend the "bad man" Chisholm. The phone line, strung through trees and on poles, had just recently been completed through Nicola Lake to Princeton from Kamloops and would soon link up with Hedley and Penticton. At the same time in Princeton, Provincial Police Constable Hugh Hunter was advised of the incident, and he immediately set out for Manning's. Some of the partiers had loaded Chisholm into the bed of a wagon and were on their way to meet Dr. Tuthill, who in turn was on his way down from Nicola Lake, 50 miles to the north. Constable Hunter escorted Brooks to Nicola where the shooter was lodged in one of the two cells in the local courthouse.[4] [5]

Nicola Lake at that time was the hub of transportation, mining and ranching in the Nicola Valley south of Kamloops. It had the only courthouse and doctor in the area, as Princeton had yet to fulfill its potential as a rail centre as well as a mining and ranching community. Dr. Tuthill treated the now subdued and morose shootist Chisholm. After it was determined that he could do no more for the gunman locally, he was transported to the Royal Inland Hospital in Kamloops for further treatment to the serious wound to his leg. The good Dr. Tuthill would treat another bullet wound to the leg of a miscreant under different circumstances almost two years into the future. The unfortunate Brooks, confused and anxious, waited in his cell in the Nicola Lake courthouse for events to unfold.

The Similkameen Star in Princeton wrote of the victim and his shooter in somewhat cynical terms. "Smoky will now have the opportunity to smoke the pipe of peace and chew the cud of reflection, if not of repentance …. Brooks is almost sure to get short rations and no grog for a term."[6]

The valleys between Princeton and Kamloops buzzed with the news of the gunfight at Manning's. No sympathy was extended to Smoky Chisholm. The feelings throughout the district were leaning towards the plight of Steve Brooks, as Chisholm was known as a surly and cantankerous individual who probably deserved the large calibre bullet in his leg that was to leave him with a permanent limp. It was rumoured that Chisholm didn't want to prosecute and that he just wanted to escape across the border "into Uncle Sam's territory." He was only too aware of the level of disdain with which he was held by residents of the Similkameen and the Nicola.[7]

The early spring days of April passed slowly for Steven Brooks. In the Nicola Lake courthouse, Brooks' preliminary hearing was set for the first week of May, when a number of cases were to appear on the docket at the spring assizes to be held there. On April 30TH, Wentworth W. Wood, a Justice of the Peace in Kamloops, drove his buggy and team to Nicola Lake to preside over the preliminary hearing of Brooks to determine whether or not there was enough

Main Street of Nicola Lake, with Barwick's harness shop, circa 1904.
COURTESY OF NICOLA VALLEY MUSEUM AND ARCHIVES.

The Driard Hotel in downtown Nicola Lake.
COURTESY OF NICOLA VALLEY MUSEUM AND ARCHIVES.

evidence to go to trial. Accompanying him was Kamloops defence lawyer Alec Mcintyre. Mr. Mcintyre was assembling a recognized reputation for astute defence tactics and would be defending Brooks. He was the first of a long line of defence lawyers in Kamloops who would not endear themselves to law enforcement or the general populace. Although frowned upon by many of his peers in the justice system and those good citizens of a more law and order mien, he was a very effective advocate for those charged with crimes against His Majesty's good government. He would effectively represent Brooks over the next week's hearing.[8]

The end result of Rex vs. Brooks at Nicola Lake, complicated by the inability of Chisholm to appear against Brooks, was that the trial was adjourned and Brooks was released on bail of a moderate amount until the fall assizes in Kamloops in October. The disgruntled Magistrate Gillie commented "on the unsavoury character of Chisholm, condemning the reprehensible practice of men of his stamp carrying deadly weapons at all times and seasons." A temporarily grateful Brooks was released from the Nicola Lake courthouse, and with transportation arranged by his friends from Granite Creek, he made his way back to the Similkameen.[9]

Chisholm's recuperation progress was followed closely by the public and the press of Kamloops. In late August he was still on crutches, but making his way through the streets of the town. As his upper leg had been badly fractured by the bullet from the Winchester, recovery took much time, and he was to walk the rest of his life with a permanent limp. He was still residing in Royal Inland Hospital, "but is rapidly progressing towards recovery." By early September he was on the streets again. He wished through the press to "publicly acknowledge the skilful treatment and kindness ... received at the hands of both the medical and nursing staff of the hospital."[10]

In early October, George Edwards had interests in Kamloops and rode his tall black horse to the Tiltons' new place at Rose Hill. Living in the grasslands above the town, Cyrus Tilton and his clan had left the Armstrong country a year or so ago to try to make a success of dry land farming in the semi-arid desert country of Kamloops. Renewing

The Colonial Rooms, formerly the Colonial Hotel, Bill Miner's favourite hotel in Kamloops, circa 1925. Courtesy of Kamloops Museum and Archives.

old friendships with the Tiltons and the Angus McKays, who were also close by, Edwards stayed with them for a time, then made his way down into town and checked into his favourite hotel in Kamloops, the Colonial.[11]

The fall assizes in Kamloops started on Thursday, October 6TH. The indictment against Brooks was for "wounding with intent to do grievous bodily harm." When Rex vs. Brooks was called, defence lawyer Mcintyre requested an adjournment until the next day as his client Brooks was ill and under a doctor's care at the present time. The adjournment was granted, and the trial duly commenced the next day at 10:00 A.M. In the public gallery of the courtroom in Kamloops sat George Edwards, watching with interest the conduct of Attorney

Mcintyre. Edwards had friends from the Similkameen dispersed throughout the courtroom; some were in the dock, and some were witnesses or just trial observers. Respected Kamloops lawyer Frederick Fulton was the prosecutor for the Crown, and Judge Buff presided.[12]

The calling of witnesses occupied the morning, and front and centre was the uncomfortable William "Smoky" Chisholm. Mcintyre's presentation of the defense was not to deny the guilt of his client, but to stress in the strongest terms the right of self-defence. Hugh Hunter, the constable from Princeton, was called. So was one "Judge" Murphy, a local character who had been in attendance during the shooting. Jack Thynne from Thynne's roadhouse and ranch was also a witness.[13]

Mcintyre managed to effectively switch the roles of the former prosecution witnesses at Nicola Lake to defence witnesses, and he did not fail to dramatically emphasize this. Watched with interest by Edwards and his compatriots in the public gallery, Mcintyre stressed the good character of the accused and the wholly nefarious character of the Crown's chief witness, the wounded gunman, one William "Smoky" Chisholm. The defence and prosecutor's presentation to the jury was short, and at 8:00 P.M. the judge took an hour and ten minutes to carefully present an unbiased summary to the jury. The press felt that the judge weighed somewhat unfairly against the accused Brooks. At 9:15 P.M. the jury retired for about one and a half hours that evening, and when the trial was finally back in session, they brought in a verdict of not guilty. Brooks was immediately discharged. George Edwards was impressed with the conduct of defence attorney Mcintyre.[14][15]

The Kamloops Inland Sentinel, in its "Nicola Notes" section, stated that Steve Brooks and Smoky Chisholm returned "to their old shooting haunt" in the Similkameen, the best of friends.[16]

In November, George Edwards again returned to Chilliwack. He had enjoyed himself in September, meeting new friends and relaxing in the small town life of a thriving agricultural community. He would return a number of times that fall, finally leaving for Princeton for the winter shortly after Christmas. He came over the Dewdney

Trail early in November with eleven horses and was accompanied by George Aldous. George Aldous was almost six feet tall, about 30 years old with square shoulders, dark brown hair and a moustache. He lived with his wife Mary and son Howard on their ranch just outside Princeton. Aldous had been a partner with Jack Budd in the Tulameen Hotel in Princeton around 1898, but it had burned down and Aldous would invest with businessmen in other ventures around the Princeton area. He would raise horses on his ranch and buy and sell horses with Budd and Edwards, and he always found that they were fair and honest in their dealings. Edwards and Aldous loaded their horses onto a CPR steamer at Hope and boated them down the river to Chilliwack. They off-loaded them temporarily into a corral while they stabled their own personal horses, including Edwards' impressive black, in Rowat's Chilliwack Livery stable. They loaded the small herd of horses back onto a CPR steamer again for the trip down to Ladner's Landing and sold them there. They were not pleased with the freight rates that the CPR charged them per head of horses, and they hardly broke even on the deal. Edwards would remember that day in the future, planning on a time of reckoning. Coming back to Chilliwack, Edwards and Aldous checked into Mr. Dundas' Commercial Hotel, Edwards signing the register on the 13TH of November. Aldous stayed in Chilliwack a couple of days with Edwards, but soon left for the Similkameen and his family. Jack Budd came down and joined Edwards in the hotel on the 16TH. Together, Budd and Edwards would leave their horses stabled with Rowat for seven weeks, until after Christmas.[17]

Later in November, Edwards checked into the Dominion Hotel in Chilliwack and signed the register "Geo. Edwards, Nov. 27 1904, room 18." He was to remain in the hotel until after Christmas and became friendly with the wife of the owner and her young daughter. During quiet periods during the day, Edwards would show the little girl the tattoo of the dancing girl on his arm. The owner, Mr. McKenzie, knew Edwards well and remembered that he had introduced himself as a successful mining man. He saw him carrying "two big guns" in his pockets, and during the cold weather he always

McKenzie's Dominion Hotel in Chilliwack, circa 1907.
COURTESY OF CHILLIWACK MUSEUM AND HISTORICAL SOCIETY.

wore a long black fur coat and his typical white flat-brimmed Stetson. Mrs. McKenzie also saw Edwards' formidable pistols. She vividly remembered him squaring up his bill at one time during his stay, and he showed her a large roll of money and a $1,000 bill.[18]

"You hadn't ought to show your money. Someone will rob you," she cautioned him.

He reached into his coat pocket and pulled out one of his large pistols, holding it close to her so she could see its impressive size and the large load in the cylinders. "Not while I have this," he bragged.[19]

Hotel proprietor McKenzie became friendly with Edwards and went in together with him to order a case of hard liquor out of Vancouver. Each paid for half, and when it arrived on the steamer, they packed it over to Jeff Harrison's barn. Harrison was the purser who had seen Edwards arrive in Chilliwack back in September. Edwards and

McKenzie, Harrison and a select few others of Chilliwack's sporting types proceeded to tie on a fine drunk, and all viewed McKenzie and Edwards as superior and charitable gentlemen. McKenzie, away from his wife's control, must have been somewhat indiscreet during this drinking bout, asking questions of Edwards that were concerned with who he really was, where he was from and where he got his money. Edwards did not take this lightly and confronted the hotel owner the next day. He accused McKenzie of being an informant and of compromising Edwards' integrity. He threatened the hotel keeper and told him that he had told the others and would now tell him that he would not pick a physical fight with him, but would use his pistols to shoot him down like a dog. With that, Edwards pulled back his fur coat and placed his hands on his pistols. Mr. McKenzie quickly assured the irate Mr. Edwards that he needn't be afraid and convinced him that it would never happen again.[20]

During the time Edwards stayed in Chilliwack that fall and early winter, detectives, undercover agents and investigators of the Mission robbery continued to check in and out of the hotel, passing the successful mining promoter and greeting him respectfully. Mr. McKenzie's son Billy would often play cards at Marriott's poolroom with the elderly gentleman and saw him always sit with his back to the wall. He saw Edwards with two $1,000 bills in one game, and he carried these large bills in the watch pocket of his pants, secured with a safety pin.[21]

When he was settling his livery account with Rowat at the end of the month, he showed the livery owner a $1,000 bill and a number of $100s.

Rowat said to him, "You are a funny sort of a man, carrying all that money. Someone will go through you," meaning someone would run Edwards through with a knife to get his money.

Edwards smilingly replied, while throwing back his fur coat, "Not while I am carrying these," and put his hands on the two large pistols he was carrying on his hips at the time.[22]

Rowat remembered that Budd and Edwards left to head back to the Similkameen sometime in December. Besides their two horses, they led a red mule. Three days later they were back in town claiming the snow was too deep over the pass east of Hope. Rowat thought this was suspicious as he knew that the snow hadn't really started to come down yet and the trail was still bare. He would later surmise that they probably had determined that detectives or investigators were patrolling the trail and it was too risky to try to make their way through.[23]

On the 22ND of December, Edwards saw Missouri Bill check into the Commercial Hotel in Chilliwack. He remembered him from the days after the Mission robbery when he had played poker with him at Marriott's poolroom. In actuality, Missouri Bill was William L. Hodges, a CPR Special Service undercover detective continuing the investigation of the Mission robbery under the direction of Inspector McLeod in Vancouver. Edwards felt things uncomfortably warming up for him in Chilliwack. Budd and Edwards celebrated Christmas in the little town, and by the 6TH of January they had checked out and made their way to the Similkameen. Missouri Bill checked out the day after they had left.[24]

Soon after he was safely back in the Princeton area that winter, Edwards started spending considerable time in Hedley City, less than 30 miles from Princeton and the centre of mining life in that section of the Similkameen. The large population of miners ensured a plentiful supply of poker and pool players, "soiled doves," and parties and dances. There he played the role of the successful businessman and mining promoter, spending funds lavishly and generously. To anyone who asked, he innocently told them he had received his monies from a rich mine he and his friends had struck near Kamloops. As he entertained and mixed among the miners, merchants, prostitutes and citizens, he listened to the stories of the gold being mined at the Nickel Plate gold mine, how monthly shipments of two gold bricks worth $80,000 made their way over and through the hills to Penticton, then north by steamer and rail to Sicamous and the CPR. There it was shipped to the assay office in Seattle. He was to spend considerable time over the winter in the company of a young and vivacious Miss McNeil. Miss McNeil's career prior to meeting

Edwards was described by a contemporary as "chequered." Edwards had brought Miss McNeil back with him from a trip to Spokane. With her and his other male friends he was observed to spend, some thought, up to $20,000 over that winter on fine foods, lodging, liquor, cards, clothes, gifts and other staples necessary for a man of Edwards' refined tastes and expectations. For four consecutive nights Edwards was observed to lose over $4,000 each evening in poker games. By spring, he had retreated to Budd's cabin again, and Miss McNeil was employed as a waitress in one of Hedley's many hotels. She soon moved to Penticton where she was to live "a life of untrammeled freedom." Introduced to the high life by George Edwards, and now with an acquired taste for the luxuries money could buy, she would later feature in a sensational way in the Seattle papers.[25][26][27]

———◆———

VIII
ROSE HILL AND
ANDERSON CREEK

BRITISH COLUMBIA PROVINCIAL POLICE Superintendent Frederick Hussey received a letter in the mail from a prominent CPR official on the 13TH of January in 1905. It was from CPR Special Service Inspector William McLeod, and he was upset with how some of Hussey's men had been discussing with the press confidential matters pertaining to the investigation of the Mission robbery. In couched terms the private corporate police force official accused Chief Constable Stanley Spain in New Westminster of being indiscreet, and directed that Hussey should take steps to ensure this was stopped and that it did not happen again. Inspector McLeod expressed his disappointment that while secret and undercover investigations were still very much active and of a clandestine nature, they had been severely compromised by an irresponsible civil servant and the press. He pressed Superintendent Hussey to investigate the matter to determine the source of the leak.[1]

Enclosed with the letter were two recent newspaper clippings: one from the New Westminster Columbian and one from the Vancouver News Advertiser. In essence, they both summarized the progress of the Mission robbery investigation, the role the Pinkertons and the Dominion Secret Service were playing, and the fact that it had been correctly determined that the leader of the robbers had spent some time in New Westminster before the robbery. The articles went on to state the suspect was well known to secret service detectives, and authorities suspected, incorrectly as it turned out, that he had been in the "Hole in the Wall" in Montana [*sic*] over the past months. The American desperado Bill Miner was the obvious suspect for the caper, and law enforcement organizations were actively working on the apprehension of the elusive bandit.[2]

Meanwhile, up in the Similkameen country, the isolation and loneliness of the long winter was agreeably broken by the affable and generous George Edwards. With an ample source of funds, he continued to spend much time in Hedley, where things were still percolating at a higher temperature than Princeton and especially Aspen Grove. The little mining town on Twenty-Mile Creek was growing rapidly, and at the Nickel Plate gold mine the stamps in the stamp mill had started falling the previous spring in 1904. Relationships with the American towns over the line in Idaho and Washington states were strong, and on Labour Days a number of stages would come up with passengers from Loomis, Washington, to share in Hedley's festivities. Many of the miners and mining entrepreneurs in the Hedley area were American. The hotels were all operating at their maximum capacity, and the town boasted two general stores, a butcher shop and livery stables. Saturday nights in Hedley saw electric street lights add to the festive air, and houses of the well-to-do and the local Methodist church had interior electric lights shining into the darkness and reflecting off the snow. All the stores, including a new bank, jewelry and watch store, and gentlemen's clothing and haberdashery were fronted with fresh board sidewalks. That winter the Hedley Gazette newspaper started up with an editor who had a wry sense of humour and a cutting wit. While Fred Revely ran his stage between Princeton and Hedley, E.E. Webley ran his line between Hedley and Penticton in open coaches. Mr. Edwards looked with satisfaction at the pool halls, saloons and poker parlours that continued to cater to the more ribald tastes of the miners and others searching for a more exciting life, if just for a few hours. As a crowning touch, the last house on Ellis Street near Twenty Mile Creek boasted an enterprising whorehouse madam who imported three to four girls at a time, and more on special occasions. Mr. Edwards approved.[3] [4]

That winter in Hedley, Mr. Edwards hosted a number of dances in the new Fraternity Hall. He hired the Hedley Orchestra to play at these northern "fandangos" put on by the man whose youth had often been spent in the fandango parlours of San Francisco. He loved the intimacy of dancing with his arm around a woman and made sure he spent an equal time outside the hall, passing a bottle around with the husbands and brothers taking a break to cool off. Edwards always seemed to have enough money to pay for the orchestra and hall and was generous with all who attended. People came from miles around by horse and sleigh to take part in one of Edwards' soirees, bringing eats and delicacies and punch. He danced with all the ladies, young and old alike. He even got up to play the odd tune on the fiddle himself. Many of the women who attended these dances would remember years into the future the mannerly gentleman who asked them to dance, and would tell their children and grandchildren. They added to the legend. That February, Hedley's first telephone was installed in Love's Drug Store. It was directly connected to Princeton, Nicola Lake and Kamloops. In Kamloops, the Similkameen and the Nicola were connected via CPR's telegraph and trains with the rest of the world.[5]

By the end of March, telephone service had been completed between Kamloops, through Nicola, Princeton and Hedley, all the way to Penticton. Switchboards were being contemplated for Nicola Lake and Hedley City to enhance the efficiency of the line, and all the communities in between were now connected by copper wire.[6]

The little town of Nicola saw the first issue of its newspaper, the Nicola Herald, published on May 18TH, and the fledgling paper promised to bring news of the Nicola Valley to Aspen Grove, Coutlee, Lower Nicola, Quilchena and the district in general. Local interest was high when it was learned that CPR contractor activities at Spence's Bridge forecast the construction of a branch line from there to the cattle ranchers at Nicola Lake.[7][8]

A reflection of Nicola Lake's growing, if fleeting, importance, was the appointment of a Provincial Police constable responsible for the town and the surrounding area. Walter Clark, formerly a local mail carrier, was administered the Oath of Office and advised he was now to report via mail on a monthly basis to Chief Constable Burr in Ashcroft. He soon received via stage all the accoutrements needed by a rural constable in British Columbia, with the exception of a uniform or a horse. These he must supply himself. On the stage that day were one copy of the Provincial Police regulations, one Provincial Police badge, one Smith and Wesson revolver with holster, belt and cartridges, one rifle and cartridges, one baton, one pair of handcuffs, one pair of shackles, and 25 blank monthly police report forms. Later deliveries to Constable Clark included a lantern as he found it "very awkward getting along on dark nights without one" on the dark streets in Nicola Lake, and a necessary copy of the Criminal Code and amendments.

Constable Clark had received no prior formal training for his position and attained it through a vetting process of referrals and character checks. Most of the new constable's responsibilities involved alcohol offences and enforcing the Sunday Closing Act. This affected all the hotel barrooms and saloons in Nicola Lake and Quilchena, just a few miles up the road to Kamloops. The local temperance ladies and their compliant husbands were ever watchful for infractions and would eventually report perceived non-compliance to the unhappy Clark's superior in Ashcroft. Another of his responsibilities was to apprise himself of strangers passing through town and travellers who spent time in Nicola Lake. He had known Jack Budd for about eight years as Budd had spent considerable time in Nicola Lake when working for the Douglas Lake Ranch, and Budd was to apply for Canadian citizenship at the Nicola courthouse. Clark met George Edwards at Quilchena sometime later. He and the local ranchers suspected the two of being horse thieves that drove their rustled horses either across the border to the United States or down to the coast. Area ranchers had been experiencing considerable losses in their horse herds, and it was widely recognized that rustling was taking place on a large scale.

In May of 1905, Edwards started living at the Schisler Ranch on Bald Mountain, and when he was not on the road on one of his many trips, he helped out with ranching and farming chores. However, he didn't seem to like work much, and one time he paid for his board and room by buying the family a cow. James George Currie Schisler and his wife Emma had come with their children by covered wagon in 1900 from Phoenix to Princeton to start a life of ranching. Their daughter, twelve year old Millie, would remember Mr. Edwards with fondness. She described him as being a "kind gentleman" and a "wonderful person." At local social functions the young girl would dance with the kindly old man, and he often slipped two-bit pieces into her hand. Edwards always maintained that he obtained his money from his rich gold mine in Mexico. He explained away his frequent journeys from Princeton with a straight face by saying his financial affairs needed stabilization. One time before he left, he asked Emma Schisler to sew thousand dollar bills into the lining of his coat as he was afraid of being robbed. He bought boxes of oranges for the family, which were an expensive treat for those days, and when he wasn't out of town on his many business trips, the family noticed that he would often spend considerable time in Hedley.[9][10][11]

Millie's brother Fred inadvertently almost caused the demise of Mr. Edwards from heart failure. When he was eight years old, Fred was encouraged by his father to use his single shot .22 calibre rifle to shoot gophers and other varmints. Late one afternoon, while in the house and gazing out the front window, he saw a gopher in the distance on a hillside. He went and loaded his rifle and brought it back to the window. While he was fetching his trusty little firearm, the ranch crew had returned to the house, and the men were washing up on the broad front porch. One of the wash basins was located directly below the front porch window. Young Fred took aim at the gopher and fired. With a start Mr. Edwards, who was washing his face under the window, reared back with a look of shocked surprise on his face. Fred had shot his rifle directly over the man's head and caused him a severe sudden fright. There is no doubt that when the rifle was fired over his head, the normally unflappable Mr. Edwards must have immediately thought that an ambush or gunfight was underway and that his trail had been followed to the Similkameen.[12]

That spring saw Mr. Edwards on the road again. He started the first of many trips to Kamloops that year by stopping in at the McLeod Ranch on the Nicola Road. William McLeod and his brother John had settled in 1879 near the Cardew Hill a few miles south of Kamloops and became successful sheep ranchers. The fertile grasslands and high plateau meadows around Kamloops would see sheep raising continue to flourish as the century wore on. The McLeods established a summer camp at McLeod Lake, and they gradually moved into cattle as the years passed. Eventually John moved further east into the Campbell Creek Valley, while William married a local girl, Margaret Frisken. Together he and Margaret raised five sons and two daughters.[13]

When George Edwards came riding up that April of 1905, the grass was sprouting green and covering the hills all around the high country above Kamloops. It was evening, and the sun was close to the horizon in the west. The quaking aspens were leafing out and yellow-green in the evening light, and the smell of cottonwood buds and mud was in the air. Two of William McLeod's sons, fourteen year old William Jr. and sixteen year old Evander, watched the slight stranger in the broad brimmed four cornered white Stetson ride confidently into their yard. He was riding Jack Budd's bay horse "Bones," and the mount was sporting a fine new red leather saddle Edwards had recently acquired. He introduced himself to William McLeod Sr. as George Edwards, a mining promoter from Princeton, and told the McLeods that he was heading to Kamloops. He asked if he might have a bed for the night. Extending their hospitality, the McLeods welcomed the stranger to their home, as was the tradition in those days. Hospitality was extended to all travellers that passed by, with no fear that their trust would be betrayed.[14]

He was put up in the bunkhouse where young William had his bunk with his brother. By the light of the oil lamp, William McLeod and George Edwards talked far into the night. They talked of stories of the old west and frontier days in Canada and the U.S., and of outlaws and lawmen familiar to all. Young William showed Edwards a recent copy of the Vancouver Province speculating about the Mission robbery that had happened the previous September. The article stated that Bill Miner, the famous American train robber, had been the leader of the gang that had robbed the train at Mission and had humiliated the CPR, the Pinkertons and law enforcement ever since. The paper declared that the notorious Gates Brothers, who had just been killed in a shootout in California, were Bill Miner's partners the night they knocked over the train at Mission. Photos of the dead bandits were in the paper. Mr. Edwards went on to confidently assure young William that despite the best efforts of posses and police in British Columbia and Canada, Bill Miner was too clever a bandit to be caught by ordinary Canadians.[15]

After retiring to their bunks, Williams and Edwards continued the conversations about the Mission robbery. Edwards told William that the CPR deserved to be held up, and someone should do so again. He held the CPR in contempt and criticized the monopoly for hurting the small businessman and entrepreneur. He told the boy of the experiences he and his friend Jack Budd had had with the CPR and how the CPR had charged him and Budd exorbitant wharfage rates for a load of horses they had driven over the pass from Princeton to Chilliwack in the fall of 1904. There they had loaded the herd on a CPR steamer and shipped them down the Fraser to New Westminster. The rates the CPR charged them were so dear that they could not sell their horses for a decent profit. Despite the best efforts of Auctioneer Beatty from Vancouver at the New Westminster auction yards, Edwards and Budd were basically no further ahead after disposing of the animals. He went on to tell young McLeod how he had kept a nice small race mare that he fancied out of the auction for his own use. He had then ridden the mare to Bal Gondy's ranch near Ladner's Landing and visited for a time. He then rode the horse down to Blaine, Washington, for a while and in a day or two, via Gondy's ranch again, he rode the mare all the way back to Princeton. Blaine was only a few miles north of the area near Bellingham where Bill Miner's sister lived.[16][17]

At daylight the next morning, Edwards asked the senior McLeod if young William might guide him cross-country over the hills to the

Angus McKay place. Edwards claimed that McKay had two colts that he was thinking of buying. They both mounted up and William led Edwards northeast through the rolling spring grasslands. Skirting the few clumps of aspen, ponderosa pine and small lakes, the young rider led Edwards to within a few miles of the McKay place. Edwards bid William a warm farewell and left him with a dollar for his troubles. This was the first of many visits the affable American would make with the McLeods of Anderson Creek.[18]

Later that May George Edwards again rode the wagon road from Princeton through the Otter Lake valley, Aspen Grove, and Nicola to Kamloops. He attended another trial at the spring assizes in Kamloops, staying at the Colonial Hotel with its "white" cook. The trial was held in the same courthouse at the corner of Seymour Street and First Avenue as the Steve Brooks trial, and the courtroom was crowded with mining interests. This trial involved mining claims at the Sunset properties on Copper Mountain near Princeton, and Edwards' friend Jack Budd had some interest in the outcome through his own mining holdings. Emil Voight had brought his family into Canada from Switzerland at the turn of the century and established the "Voight's Camp" mining claims atop Wolf Creek Hill on Copper Mountain. Voight launched a court action against one "Groves et al", disputing title to the Olympia section of the Sunset properties, the site of one of B.C.'s largest and richest future copper mines. By 1905 the case had been in progress for some years, and the public was looking forward to a number of "nice points of law (to) be discussed by learned counsel." The trial commenced on Tuesday the 16TH, and by Friday the court rendered its verdict. The Court determined that the Olympia was a "bad claim" and found in favour of Voight. Costs were awarded to Groves; however, the judgment against him was dismissed.[19 20 21]

In early June some of the residents of Grande Prairie saw George Edwards riding alone about the country. Making no attempt to hide his actions, he greeted passersby respectfully and minded his own business. Herbert Guernsey saw him ride past his store, and Thomas Graham and Mrs. Tom Smith saw him ride by on the way to Ducks

Station, or, as it was to be called in the future, Monte Creek. Mr. Edwards was familiarizing himself with the country beside and south of the CPR main line.[22]

On the 20TH of July, George Edwards again visited the William McLeods, this time in the company of Bob Tilton, the twenty-seven year old son of Cyrus Tilton up on Rose Hill. Bob Tilton was a frequent traveller with Mr. Edwards and many of his friends from down in the Similkameen. Bob Tilton had a homestead near Princeton and had introduced Edwards to the Schislers. The two men were driving a small herd of eight horses to the Tilton ranch on Rose Hill, about four and one-half miles from Kamloops in the high plateau grasslands country near the McKays. At the invitation of the McLeods, the two riders stayed for dinner. Afterwards, they were soon on their way over the hills and through the meadows to the Tiltons' place. Both the Tiltons and the McKays had homesteaded in that high rolling hill country just a few miles above Kamloops. The wind blew fresh there, and the skies stretched on to mountains far in the distance. Just over the edge of the drop into the South Thompson valley they could see the smoke of Kamloops rising in the midday air. At night they could see the dim street lights burning on the main streets.

Edwards often stayed with the Tiltons over the years and enjoyed their hospitality. It was at this time too that Edwards renewed his acquaintance with the Angus McKay family. They also lived in the heart of the Rose Hill grasslands and were neighbours to the Tiltons. The quarter section owned by Cyrus Tilton was just to the southwest of that of Angus McKay.

During Christmas of 1903, before the McKay family had left Armstrong for Rose Hill, a package had come for twelve year old Bert McKay. The package was postmarked Spokane, Washington, and the young boy eagerly opened it to find a brand new .22 calibre repeating Winchester rifle. It was from family friend George Edwards. Since that time, Bert had honed his skills with the little rifle and had become a decent shot.[23]

George Edwards started visiting the McKay family again after they had moved to the Kamloops area in 1904. In the spring of 1905, Bert was looking after a captured coyote that his uncle Bob Tilton had tied up. Bert was having trouble keeping him supplied with meat. Edwards had showed up at the McKays' with a 32.40 rifle, and together with Bert, he went hunting squirrels for the coyote. Edwards told Bert that they had to hit the squirrels in the head with his rifle as if they didn't, there would not be enough meat left over for the coyote. Young Bert remembered Edwards as being an excellent shot, and they bagged enough squirrels and rabbits that day to keep the coyote going for a while.

Edwards and young McKay formed a friendship, and the older man would always visit Bert when he came to Kamloops or to visit the Tiltons. He once told Bert his opinions about the CPR. He said that the giant railroad was the biggest robber in the country. He told the boy that the CPR owned twenty miles on each side of the railway right-of-way and that they owned half of Vancouver.[24]

"He was a good shot. I saw him take a little bird out of the top of a big fir tree one time, he asked me to shoot first, but I knew I couldn't hit him, so I handed the gun to Edwards and he sat down on the side of the road, leaned against a bank, cocked his leg, rested the gun on his knee, and down came the bird from the top of the tree."

Bert McKay would often tell a story about his friend that he swore was not made up. "People don't believe this story, they think it was made up, but it was not."

That spring, young Bert was wandering the hills between the McKays and Tiltons with his .22 rifle that Edwards had sent him. He found himself above the Tiltons' place, and he made his way down to where he could see some men sitting around talking beside a newly constructed log building. When he got closer, he saw it was George Edwards and Bob Tilton.

"So I sat down alongside of them, and after a while Edwards said to me, 'Give me the rifle, please.' So I gave him the rifle, I didn't know what he was going to do with it. The building was about twelve feet away and was made of freshly cut logs and this was in the spring and it was quite warm and the sun was shining. Anyway (he) leaned back and took aim at something on the wall. I didn't know what it was, and he pulled the trigger. And then I could see there was something on the wall, so I got up and walked down there. And there was a fly, one of those great big blow flies, a big black fly and there was nothing but wings and legs left around the hole. After a few minutes, (Bob Tilton) reached across and he said, 'Give me that gun.' So I gave him the gun, and he took aim at another fly and there were wings and legs all around that hole. Those two men sat there I bet you, for an hour taking turn-abouts, waiting for a fly to alight on the end of the log. And they never missed very many."[25]

Bert remembered that Bob Tilton had won a prize for shooting in Armstrong some years before. He had made six bull's eyes out of seven in a long range shooting contest and had a reputation for being the best shot in the country.

It was that same summer that Edwards left Princeton to see his friends in Rose Hill above Kamloops again. He stopped overnight in Aspen Grove.

"Edwards had a race horse that had come from California. (It) had been cut in the wire, but healed up and was a lovely horse. And that night when he stayed at Aspen Grove the school teacher there wanted to go for a ride. But Edwards didn't want her to use his horse, because in those days the ladies all rode in a side-saddle. But Edwards said to me, 'How could I refuse her, I couldn't refuse.' So she went for the ride. But when they took the saddle off the hair was all rubbed off the front shoulder and Edwards was very put out about it. Well, when he came to our place he wanted to go to town to stay overnight, but he didn't want to ride his horse because it had this bad shoulder. So he asked me if I would walk to town with him, which was seven miles."

Late that afternoon, the young boy and the old man set off down the Rose Hill Road to Kamloops. In the distance in the valley below them, they could see the smoke from kitchen cooking fires and the lighting plant drifting to the east. The South Thompson River shone a glassy grey in the afternoon light, and the lowering sun made their eyes squint into the dust at their feet.

"We got in there just before supper time. We went down to the old Dominion Hotel and Edwards booked a room and then we had supper there. For supper Edwards noticed that on the menu they had fried oysters. So he told the waitress, 'Bring me fried oysters.' Then he asked me what I would have. Well, I didn't know, I had never seen an oyster. But then I said I'll have the same. And when the oysters came, I had never tasted them before and I ate one and got started on the second and then Edwards noticed I wasn't doing too well with the oysters. So he said, 'You don't like them, do you?' 'Well, I have never had them before,' I replied. So he called the waitress over and he told the waitress, he says, 'Bring this gentleman,' he says, 'roast beef.' And then Edwards said, 'Give me the oysters.' So I handed them acrosst and he had six and my four.[26]

"Well, that night we stayed in the hotel and we had room number seven and in the morning when we got up I was on the outside of the bed and when I reached down to put on my boots I noticed a bottle under the bed. So I reached down and got the bottle, and it was chuck full of whiskey and the cork had never been removed. So I said to Edwards, 'Look at this.' And he said, 'Give me that.' So I gave him the bottle and he pried out the cork, it was a cork in those days, and he tipped it up and tasted it very gingerly. Then he looked at me and said, 'This is good stuff.' So he took a little drink. He handed the bottle back to me and I put it down on the floor. Well, when we went to go we got as far as the door, and I said to him, 'Hey, you're forgetting the bottle.' And Edwards says, 'Oh no,' he says, 'We won't take the bottle. Whoever left it there will be back for it.' And he left the bottle behind.

"So we went down and had breakfast, and when breakfast was over he called the waitress over and he told her, 'If you go up to room number seven and look under the bed, you might see something that might interest you.' And I've always wondered to this day if that waitress went upstairs or not.

"After breakfast was over we went out on the street about nine in the morning, and Edwards says to me, 'I want to go to the bank, but it's too early.' So we walked up the street and as we went past the harness shop we stopped and looked in the window, and there was two or three saddles in there. One saddle was marked at fifty-five dollars. It was the best saddle in the shop. Edwards said to me, 'You haven't a very good saddle. Come on in and we'll have a look at that big saddle.' But I wouldn't go in. I told him, I said, 'My saddle is pretty good.' And I wasn't going to have him buy me a saddle. So then we walked up the street and then back and at that time it was 10 o'clock. The Commerce Bank was across the street so he says to me, 'I want to go over to the bank for a minute.' So we went over to the bank, and when we got to the door I stepped aside and Edwards said to me, 'No, no, come on in. I want you to come in.' To this day I don't know why he wanted me to go in there with him. So we went inside, and at that time of the morning there was only one person in the bank and that was the teller. And it was a young man. So Edwards walked up and he reached in his pocket and he pulled out a bill. He laid it on the counter and he asked the teller if he could cash it. And the teller took one look at it, and then he looked at Edwards, and he says, 'This is a one thousand dollar bill.' Edwards says, 'Yes.' So the teller says, 'I'll have to go see the manager.' So he went back into the manager's office, then came out after a little and says, 'Alright, we'll go good for it. What do you want for it?' And Edwards said, 'Give me seven one hundred dollar bills and the rest in small change.' And that's the story of the one thousand dollar bill. It's a true story. Every word that I said is the truth."[27]

After he had cashed the bill, Edwards and Bert started heading for home in the high hills to the southeast. They went up Victoria Street and started to pass by the Western Liquor Company. Edwards said to Bert, "Wait here a minute, I should get something." He went into the liquor store and emerged carrying a mickey of rye whiskey. Putting it in a coat pocket, he said to young McKay that he had wanted to pick up a bottle for the boys back at the ranch. Edwards and McKay slowly trudged back up into the hills above Kamloops.[28]

On Sunday, Mrs. McKay requested that Mr. Edwards accompany them to church. Services in those days in that part of the country were held in the homes of different farmers and ranchers living in the area. Edwards replied that no, he didn't want to go to services that Sunday. Mrs. McKay, however, wasn't about to be thwarted, and insisted that the visitor attend with their family. He couldn't get away from her demands without creating a stir, so he obliged her and went with the McKays to church.[29]

The service was held in the home of Thomas and Sarah Cooper, who lived on the half section to the northeast of the McKays. Rose Hill's first school was built and opened on the Cooper property that summer.

It was an intimate little gathering, with the local farming and ranching families from throughout the immediate area attending. One of the babies was fussing, so Miner took her on his knee to give the young wife some rest. Thomas Cooper took up the collection and was pleasantly surprised to see Angus McKay's elderly friend pull out a very large roll of bills and nonchalantly drop a one dollar bill in the collection plate. It was the first one dollar bill anyone had seen in the collection plate up in Rose Hill.[30][31]

That summer, too, a little town at the head of the Okanagan Valley was incorporated and granted municipal status. With that distinction came the posting of a Provincial Police Constable to be based in the fledgling agricultural and lumbering town of Enderby. Basil Gardom became Enderby's first police constable and received his .38 calibre Smith and Wesson revolver and holster from Superintendent Hussey on the 22ND of August. Within a year, Constable Gardom would be following in the footsteps of the notorious bandit Bill Miner.[32][33]

September found Edwards with a number of his friends across the border in northwest Washington State. There they obtained, whether legally or by other means is not known, 150 head of unbroken horses and herded them back into Canada at Blaine. The drovers found the unruly mavericks hard to handle and corralled them near Aldergrove. The corral was owned by a local farmer and his wife. The husband wasn't home, but Edwards managed to cajole the woman through charm and generosity into renting her corral to him. He paid her 50 cents a meal for each of his drovers and also bought her a ton of hay for her own use. Edwards then passed the word around the area, where he was well-known, that he needed some experienced riders to break some of the more undisciplined broncs. Albert Jordan and his brother presented themselves, and after some searching questions from the elderly leader of the drovers, they were hired. They were the sons of Joseph Jordan of Ladner who owned the livery stable and was also the local sheriff. The boys were in their mid-teenage years and were used to working around stock. Their father often had to leave them on their own to attend to law enforcement matters, and the boys soon learned to be independent and resourceful.[34]

Shortly after work started on breaking the horses, Edwards decided the corral was too small and moved the stock to a large fenced area near a deserted sawmill in Ladner. The Jordan boys worked hard for Edwards. At the end of most days they spat blood from the banging up their guts got from the spirited horses. They grew to respect the vast amount of knowledge Edwards had about horses and how to break and ride them. Unlike some horse breakers, Edwards would never allow the use of a whip during the breaking of the animals. In those days breaking horses was a job to be done in the fastest, most efficient manner possible. Time was a luxury that could not be spent indiscriminately on dumb animals, and breaking horses could be a cruel, dispassionate exercise. The horses were roped, they were choked down to their knees, and the saddle was strapped on and cinched tight. The rider then mounted the quivering brute, the holders let loose, and the wild ride began. The rider tried to stay on until the horse came to a standstill; exhausted. If the rider was bucked off, the whole procedure was repeated until the animal gave up.[35]

On some days during the work with the horses, Edwards would leave the men on their own and take the ferry across to New Westminster. He checked into the Lytton Hotel, and while there he tasted the wares that the prosperous dockside city had to offer. There he was recognized as a horse trader from the upper country by Police Chief McIntosh of New Westminster.[36]

When well into the job of taming the herd, Edwards took the elder brother Albert Jordan to a dance and cake social over at Point Roberts, just a few miles away but across the border on a peninsula in

Washington state. When it came time to auction off the baskets that the ladies had brought, Edwards ordered Albert to bid one dollar for the baskets, even though they were going at 50 cents each. Jordan, working at the behest of Edwards, bought eight baskets. The money was being used for the school, and the old man felt it was for a good cause. Edwards surreptitiously paid a small boy 50 cents to find out for him what was in the lady school teacher's basket, and ended up paying $18.50 for her basket when the bidding was finished.[37]

As the horse breaking was winding down, an unfortunate accident occurred. Albert's brother was bucked off by one of the broncs, and he crashed head first into a post. He suffered a concussion and was knocked unconscious. He remained in a coma for 48 hours, and his parents and the doctor feared that he might die. As the injured rider lay in his bed, his boss George Edwards sat by his bedside for the two days he remained comatose. He explained to the boy's father, Sheriff Joseph Jordan, that the boy had been hurt while working for him and that he wanted to see the boy through this bad time.[38]

It was during the time that his son was recuperating that Sheriff Jordan noticed the India ink tattoo at the base of Miner's thumb as he was washing up. It was the same tattoo described on a wanted poster from Oregon concerning a train robbery. Sheriff Jordan had the poster in his office and realized that the man in front of him was very possibly the American train robber Bill Miner. Sheriff Jordan was faced with a dilemma. He was impressed with the genuine concern the old man had for his injured son; however, Joseph Jordan was also the representative of the law in Ladner. After a great deal of agonized soul searching, he decided to temporarily ignore the facts and left Edwards to complete his horse breaking operations.[39]

Finally the brutal and dangerous job was done. Most of the broke horses were sold in the Fraser Valley, and the balance were driven up to Princeton by Edwards and his crew of drovers. The two Jordan brothers pleaded with their father to be allowed to go with the riders, but he adamantly refused. It was only much later that the two boys saw a wanted poster from Washington state after the robbery of the Great Northern. It displayed the face of their old friend George W.

Edwards. On the wanted poster he was known as Bill Miner and was described by the vengeful and frustrated Pinkertons as a notorious and vicious criminal and sodomite. A reward of $5,000 was offered, but it was never to be collected.[40]

In late September George W. Edwards was back in Princeton, but only for a short while. Ever restless and consumed with a wanderlust and an insatiable desire for the funds required to fuel the lifestyle to which he felt entitled, he had places to go and appointments to keep. He took leave of the Schislers and his friends in Princeton and travelled alone to Phoenix. After spending some time there, he caught the Great Northern down to Spokane in Washington state. A few days after Edwards entered the States, on October 2ND, the Great Northern Railway train was halted and robbed near Ballard in Washington. At 9:00 P.M., and in the dark, the Great Northern Overland passenger train engineer was confronted by an armed and masked gunman. He ordered the engineer to stop the train at a small fire burning beside the tracks. The bandits used dynamite to blow up the safe in the express car and fired warning shots to keep the passengers in their cars. It was rumoured by newspapers, but not confirmed by the railway, that at least three bandits got away with $36,000. The methods used by the bandits and the fact that one of them was called "Bill" by his partners led the press to believe Bill Miner had struck again. Newspapers identified the second thief as Miner's friend Jake Terry, but the Pinkertons and other law enforcement agencies would not publicly comment on the rumour.[41]

A short time after the robbery near Seattle, George Edwards crossed the border into Canada from Spokane and spent a week in Black's Hotel in Phoenix. There he would mix with old friends again and enjoy the good life that the wide open mining town had to offer. The new town's bordellos and saloons did a good business catering to the needs and whims of the miners and sporting types such as Edwards. A new acquaintance Edwards met up with was a good looking young man of 28 years, Lewis Colquhoun from Clifford, Ontario, northwest of Guelph. He was part of a highly respected land owning family who contributed greatly to the development of the area. Lewis was of above average intelligence and graduated from university as a school teacher. He taught school for a few years, but then received the devastating news that he had contracted the then fatal disease, tuberculosis. In that time, a diagnosis of "consumption" was a death sentence. While research and studies into vaccines and specific operations was progressing in Europe, the standard treatment prescribed for Colquhoun was to live in a drier climate. With his future now clear and shortened drastically, Lewis quit teaching and, leaving humid Ontario behind, travelled to British Columbia. He found work in the fall of 1904 in the dry border country of southeastern B.C. where mining in the mineral rich mountains and valleys and the building of railways to haul out the ore fuelled a burgeoning economy and employment was easy to obtain. Starting out working on the CPR telegraph line on Lake Slocan, he moved around that area from Rossland to Trail to Grand Forks and finally to Phoenix. He worked for the CPR, the Granby Mine, Hunter-Kendrick grocers, cattle and meat packing baron Pat Burns, and the Great Northern Railway at Rock Creek. He worked as a labourer installing cribbing on the Vancouver, Victoria and Eastern Railway bed, but his education naturally saw him gravitate to bookkeeping and time keeping positions. The progress of his disease caused symptoms to occur with increasing regularity, including the loss of weight and energy, with coughing, fever and night sweats. This affected his ability to hold down permanent positions and deprived him of motivation. His now fatalistic outlook on life and resignation to his destiny portrayed to others a shiftless, languid individual without the drive normal for a young man with his education and upbringing. His employers "universally gave him good character but say he lacked ambition and seemed to be lazy," although "he was an easy going young fellow." Despite his itinerant employment record, however, he always managed to pay his bills and ensured that those who got to know him remembered his honesty and integrity, if not his compulsion for promotion and success.[42 43 44]

Edwards would run into Colquhoun on two or three occasions during his stay in Phoenix that October. Colquhoun was working as a timekeeper on railway construction work at the time, and Edwards introduced himself to the young man as a stock-raiser and mining promoter basing his operations out of Princeton. Edwards invited Colquhoun to visit him anytime he was in the Similkameen country or Princeton. Colquhoun was impressed with the obvious success and easy camaraderie of the elderly gentleman with the soft drawl. He watched him spend his money freely on gambling, dancing, saloons and the many prostitutes that worked the mining camp at that time. Three weeks later in November, Edwards made another trip to Spokane, again staying a few days in Phoenix to enjoy the good life there. He again ran into Colquhoun and repeated his invitation to him, telling him "if he was to come to Princeton (he, Edwards) would be pleased to see him."[45][46]

The McLeods at Anderson Creek just outside Kamloops saw Mr. George W. Edwards, mounted on a fine sorrel horse and sitting in his fine red saddle, ride into their yard again that fall. Again he stayed overnight and regaled the McLeods with tales of his successful gold mine in Mexico, making sure they saw how much American money he had on him. Before he left for Kamloops the next morning, he left Evander McLeod with a five dollar bill. It was marked as being issued from the National Bank of Oklahoma. A week later he passed by again, this time on his way back to the Aspen Grove and Princeton country. He stopped only long enough to tell them he had spent some time in the Duck Range east of Kamloops and in the little communities of Ducks on Monte Creek and at Grande Prairie. The McLeods watched him ride off down the Nicola Road. They wouldn't see him again until May the next year. It was to be under entirely different circumstances.[47]

Back at the Schislers' ranch near Princeton, Miner settled into a calm routine, at least for a while. He spent time doing chores around the Schislers' and often went visiting into Princeton or to see his friend Jack Budd. That fall the prospector and trapper Shorty Dunn was hired by the Schislers to help in harvesting potatoes. There he met George Edwards and was impressed with the old fellow who seemed so knowledgeable about life and was so flush with cash. It was not long before Dunn was swept up in Edwards' rhetoric, and the two of them started to plan the next robbery of the CPR.[48 49]

In the early winter, Edwards left the Schislers to take up Jack Budd's trapper's cabin in the bush not far from Aspen Grove. There Edwards planned on spending the winter. The Schislers tried to dissuade him, telling him that Jack Budd was "an old skinflint, and would take him for everything he had."[50]

In Princeton, railroad surveys, right-of-way clearing and construction were coming closer to the small mining and ranching town from the direction of Keremeos. The administration of the B.C. Provincial Police in Victoria decided that Constable Hugh Hunter in Princeton now needed the assistance of another constable to monitor the additional men coming into town. As a result, Ronald Hewat of Princeton took the Oath of Office in front of Justice of the Peace F.W. Groves on November 9TH and assumed the duties of a full constable. Hewat had been attempting to become a member for over a year, but it had been decided that Constable Haines in Hedley could be utilized to pull up any slack that Hunter could not handle. There just was not enough work for an additional constable in Princeton at that time.[51 52]

Constable Hewat did not wait long before he contacted Superintendent Hussey in Victoria. In a letter dated the 13TH of December he wrote:

> "Dear Sir,
> I received from you by express on the 9th instance one Smith and Wesson revolver, a box of cartridges, also two padlocks for lock-up. I tried the revolver and found it alright. I can make a very good target with it. I will take good care of it and keep it oiled.
> I am your obedient servant,
> Ronald Hewat."[53]

Constable Hewat's handwriting was exquisite. His penmanship, command of the language, and the structure of his future reports revealed a well-educated man pleased with the responsibilities of his new position. Within six months the new constable would be severely taxed to maintain credibility in his new job.

Winter set in, and after he had completed a contract for breaking horses at the Guichon Ranch, George Edwards moved into the abandoned cabin that Jack Budd had taken over near Aspen Grove. It was close to Missezula Lake and not far from rancher Alonzo Roberts' place. There he would spend some time when not staying with the Schislers or making trips out to Princeton or Hedley to visit other friends and acquaintances. He also needed on a regular basis to take care of some of his other more personal needs not likely to be met in the bush surrounding Aspen Grove. Edwards and Budd had partnerships with the Aspen Grove prospector and rancher Roberts in a number of mineral claims around the area. Together with prospector and mining promoter J.P. "Dad" Allen, they had some "excellent showings" for "copper glances, chalco-pyrites and bornite."[54][55][56]

Over that winter Edwards would strike up a friendship with Roberts. Roberts described Edwards as a "likeable chap" who told him he had valuable producing mines in Argentina. Roberts remembered that he always had plenty of money on him, often displaying $10 and $20 gold pieces. Edwards was "decent ...", loved riding and hunting and rode a large black horse." He watched him eat opium pills on a regular basis and Edwards called them his "poppy root." When sitting around the stove that winter, Roberts saw that Edwards was a heavy pipe smoker and used "Black Strap tobacco."[57]

Edwards would often patronize the road house, store and post office in Aspen Grove owned by rancher William Alexander Dodds. Edwards made frequent purchases at Dodds' store, for which he always paid cash. Dodds remembered George Edwards and Jack Budd being suspected by the locals for being mixed up in some shady horse rustling business throughout the area, and noted that Edwards was often away; where to no one knew.[58]

Before the lakes froze up in the high country, Edwards rode onto the SX Ranch property near Corbett Lake a few miles from Dodds' store. Peter Marquart was soaking hides in little Mathew Lake on the

Thynne's Roadhouse, Otter Valley Road. PHOTO BY THE AUTHOR.

Portland Roadhouse on Otter Valley Road near Aspen Grove.
PHOTO BY THE AUTHOR.

ranch property in preparation for tanning. Marquart and Edwards were acquainted with each other, and the American had met the rancher's wife Marie and children Simon and Matilda. Peter Marquart was an accomplished horse breeder and stockman and would drive herds of fine horses down to Great Falls in Montana to sell to the American cavalry. He and Edwards had a common interest in talking about horses. That day Edwards asked if he might trade him some heavy bull hide so he could fix up a set of damaged stirrups in return for Edwards cobbling some shoes out of the tanned hides for the rancher's three oldest children. The rancher took him up on the offer, and his children would tell their own children one day about the old man who cobbled each of them a pair of shoes that winter.[59]

It was late fall in 1905 when a respected and well-known mining engineer with the distinctive name of Ronald C. Campbell-Johnston and his wife and daughter rode their horses into Aspen Grove. Assisting them with their pack train of baggage were Thompson Indians from the Cook's Ferry Band near Spence's Bridge. The Campbell-Johnstons had spent a few days in Spence's Bridge before they ventured south into the Nicola and Similkameen districts where the engineer was contracted to report on the coal prospects of the area. Railway construction camps were being set up to start the building of the branch line to Nicola Lake, and Spence's Bridge was wide open. The town was described by a contemporary as "a wild, hooting, tooting western camp; they say there was a shooting a week there." The daughter, Maisie Campbell-Johnston, would later write down her memories of the days she spent in this country. She greatly admired the mining men and prospectors, trappers and cowboys from all walks of life that were scattered to all points of the compass throughout the hills and valleys around her new home. Most of them she met at Dodds' store.[60]

"These men gathered on mail day at Dodds' when the mail stage came in. I can see Johnny Clapperton now, coming around the long stretch on the dead run, the old stage rocking from side to side. Johnny always came that way, the few passengers, generally a commercial traveller among them, would have a strained shaken

William Dodds' roadhouse at Aspen Grove in the 1920s.
COURTESY OF NICOLA VALLEY MUSEUM AND ARCHIVES.

William Dodds, his wife and child and an unknown friend.
COURTESY OF NICOLA VALLEY MUSEUM AND ARCHIVES.

look on their faces. Johnny, his horses steaming, would pull up with a flourish. He was a handsome, lean, dark cowpuncher, with tilted Stetson hat and high heeled boots." Maisie made friends with the gunman Smoky Chisholm and "Dad" Allan, the Indian fighter and scout for Wild Bill Hickok and friend of Mark Twain, and many others that she would remember with fondness years into the future.[61]

As the cold weather set in, the lonely little girl, miles away from other children, pined away in the house with just her mother for company. The only other women near by, white or native, were Mrs. Dodds, a Mrs. Brown and Julia Henshaw, the wife of the manager of the Golden Sovereign Mine. Going to visit Mr. Dodds and his wife at the store on a regular basis was one way of dissipating the boredom of the short days and long nights of winter. It was at Dodds' store that she met George Edwards. She described him as "quiet, well-educated, grizzled, with keen steel blue eyes, gentle and kindly of manner with women and children; a dead shot and a fine horseman." The older man and the young girl became fast friends. In the field beside Dodds' place, Edwards spent two days clearing a spot, then diverted a little stream to flow into the flattened area where the water soon froze solid in that high country. Every day that winter that the weather permitted, young Maisie was out skating on her little rink. "It was a kindly thoughtful act and helped to break the monotony of long dreary winter days."[62]

"We had many talks; one I remember particularly was on bigotry. It seems that (he) had two fine old grandmothers, both good Christian women, one was Roman Catholic and the other Protestant; they used to argue and fight over religion, sometimes not speaking for weeks, which worried him as a little boy because he loved both, and knew how kindly and sweet they were. So he said to me, 'Little 'un, ("Dad's" name for me), never let them make a bigot out of you; always be tolerant of the other fellow's religious views no matter what they are, so long as he prays, be thankful that he prays.'"[63]

Maisie, from the perspective of forty years, remembered Edwards and the others with a sweet nostalgia tinged with her own sometimes bitter life experiences. "These wild men of the mountains and plains were finer men with a greater sense of honour than many of our respected business men of today; at least, I would rather have them for pals. God rest their souls in peace."[64]

IX

Shorty Dunn

BILLY DUNN'S EARLY DAYS in the United States are somewhat hazy, but we do know that he was originally from Wisconsin and often referred to himself as a "Milwaukee Dutchman." Orphaned at an early age, he moved west and eventually made his way into Canada. No firm evidence exists for earlier brushes with law enforcement agencies in the States, and he always maintained that he was never in trouble prior to coming to Canada.

Going by the knowledge that we have now gained on Shorty Dunn and the examples of his art work and writings, he must have had a good rudimentary education from either his original parents, the orphanage-reform school he went to, or through the initiatives of the Dunn family that he says raised him. It was under the name William Dunn that he rode across the border into Canada in July of 1896.

One incident poignantly highlights Shorty Dunn's feelings about his childhood. In the Similkameen country in the early winter of 1905, Dunn was trapping at Osprey Lake in the company of Bob Tilton, as he was wont to do at times. His partner, skinning out a lynx up on a hill, heard Dunn singing a song in what Tilton later described as "a beautiful voice."

> *"If I knew those baby fingers*
> *Pressed against the window pane,*
> *Would be stiff and cold tomorrow*
> *Never to trouble us again,*
> *Would the bright eyes of our darling*

Catch the frown upon our brow,
Would the print of baby fingers
Pressed, vex us then as they do now."

Tilton asked Shorty how and where he had learned to sing so well, and Shorty replied, "I lost my parents when small and was raised in a religious institution and sang in the choir. One day I thought I had been badly treated and have never been too straight since."[1]

One source speculates that he had a reward on his head of $4,000 for killing a sheriff in Montana, but no confirmation on this has ever surfaced. Knowing his character as well as we now do, it is highly unlikely that he had acted in such a violent manner.[2]

One of Dunn's contemporaries gives a good description of him: "Dunn was a chunky sort of chap; rather dark. He was lively and talkative, and rather humorous. His outdoor life made him hardy, and he would go off into the mountains for months at a time alone. He was a good man with horses."[3]

Shorty Dunn was described by others as "chunky and rather dark," "short and stocky," "surly" and possessed of quite a temper.[4]

Arriving in Canada, he made his way straight up into the Cariboo country. Perhaps the rumours of the gold strike that year at Bonanza Creek near Dawson City in the Yukon pulled him north, but the Cariboo is where he stayed for the next five years. In the Cariboo country, he was to become acquainted with the ranchers and prospectors in the area around Lac La Hache and 115 Mile House, where he was well-liked by all those who made his acquaintance. He took up some land on Timothy Mountain near the lake, then abandoned it to live in a cabin on the Hamiltons' property.[5]

Later, Dunn built a cabin in a meadow eight miles east of John Wright's 132 Mile ranch. Today it is called the "Billy Dunn Meadow" by the old-timers, and even though the cabin burnt down in a forest fire in the 1930s, the memory of Dunn, his cabin and his exploits still live on in the area.

In 1948, local homesteader and rancher John Wright's grandson Wilf and his father Ernie left the ranch house early one morning to

Shorty Dunn's cabin near Lac La Hache, B.C., circa 1900.
SKETCH BY WILFRED WRIGHT, WILLIAMS LAKE, B.C.

look for some horses that had strayed. Leaving the 132 Mile House Ranch, they went southeast through Bucks Lake, Coyote Lake, by Wills Reservoir, east through Big Swale, Beaverdam Meadow and north through Goose Lake, Big Lake, Devil Meadow, and finally, as the moon was rising that evening, they came to Billy Dunn's Meadow.

Only the remains of the cabin were left. Wilf's father told him he remembered it was about 10 ft. x 12 ft. with a split pole roof topped with dirt. The cabin had burned in a forest fire in 1936, but "the old stove, coal oil cans, tin cans and bottles were scattered here and there through the moss." Some pieces of the log walls still stood, and some of the rails of the corral fence were still attached to the trees.

Wilf's father told him he remembered the cabin well, as "he had taken out a pre-emption on adjoining land in 1913." He went on to tell his son that Billy Dunn really was quite short, only about 5 feet 2 inches, if that. Shorty had worked at the 127 Mile ranch for Wilf's grandfather John Wright and his sons Will, Clem, Burt, Harry, Ernie (Wilf's father), and Fred. Ernie Wright was about eight years old when he first met Shorty Dunn at the ranch in about 1900. Dunn worked at many of the ranches in the area, including the 127 Mile, 130 Mile, 132 Mile and others along the San Jose River valley.[6]

Billy Dunn was well known and liked around Lac la Hache and 115 Mile House in those years at the end of the 19TH century. He was known as an excellent shot with both a rifle and a pistol and was an accomplished hunter and trapper. He surprised his new-found friends with his skills at creating poetry in the style of Robert Service and entertained their children with his cartooning prowess. He proved himself to be a skilled teamster and handler of horses. There is some indication that he may even have driven teams for the B.C. Express on the stages that passed through that country on the way to the gold fields at Williams and Antler Creeks. While he was a diligent prospector and explorer in good weather, in the winters he worked as a ranch hand for people like the Wrights and as a cowhand and bartender for the rancher and hotelier at 115 Mile House, Archie McKinley. The story is told that one day while Billy was tending the bar, a teamster by the name of "Big" Marten started acting up, and as many big men are prone to do, threw his weight around and intimidated the clientele. Well-known for being a mean drunk, and upon a supposed slight, Marten winged a glass bottle at Shorty behind the bar. Shorty dodged the missile, went into a swift crouch, and in a flash he had filled his fist with a pistol. Under the unwavering blank eye at the end of Shorty's revolver, "Big" Marten quickly deflated, and in the words of an observer, "weakened right down."[7]

In contrast, in 1896, Shorty Dunn took a pencil in his hand and wrote a poem for his friends.

How the School Ma'am Wrecked the Stage.[8]

I

As I sit and dream and ponder by my campfire warm and bright
Where the breeses sigh and whisper with the spirits of the night
I fain would tell this story—a tale of 'camouflage'
A queer tale is my story. How the schoolmaam wrecked the stage.

II

'Twas on a frosty morning. Over half a winter's snow
Came four fiery steeds a prancing from Ashcroft down below
The driver hale and happy sat a dreaming on the box
Of other days of gladsome times devoid of shoes or socks.

III

And as he reached the schoolhouse that nestled by the pike
A lady scattering snow outflew a shouting "Mike! Oh Mike!"
The horses then went 'bughouse' and the stage went upside down
The driver made a hasty dive and landed on his crown.

IV

The steeds sprang round the lady fair ne'er stopping for a mile
And in a snow drift four feet deep reposed the driver's smile
And soon the youthful schoolboys all with shovels gathered round
And dug-and dug—and then some more 'till the driver's map was found.

V

'Twas thus the schoolmaam hurriedly and without premeditation
Tipped o'er the stage from Ashcroft and caused such consternation
And as I dream and ponder with my pencil on this page
The gleeful Fairies whisper "How the schoolmaam wrecked the stage."

About 1901, Dunn heard about the rich mineral deposits in the Similkameen country and remembered the hospitable towns like Princeton he had passed through back in '96. The continual stories of the mining potential of this area that he heard from the travellers and miners passing through the Cariboo seemed to hold a brighter future for Shorty than the hills around the Cariboo country. The gold bearing streams in the hinterland around Barkerville were playing out,

Princeton sports club. Sitting on the board sidewalk at the right and in a straw boater is Shorty Dunn's faithful friend George Winkler. Seated at the far right is Provincial Police Constable Hugh Hunter, and with his dog at the left is William "Podunk" Davis, a famous local trapper. GEORGE WINKLER FONDS, COURTESY OF B.C. ARCHIVES.

and large corporations had taken over many of the original claims for hydraulic mining. He packed up and left the Cariboo country, but his short stay would be remembered when residents pondered future events. That year, on the cusp of the millennium, the short, dark 32 year old American rode down into the lively little mining town of Princeton, where his naturally affable personality and his sense of humour gained him friends and his prospecting prowess gained him future mining partners. In the same year that Billy Dunn rode into Princeton, Bill Miner walked through the gates of San Quentin Penitentiary in California after serving his twenty year stretch for stage robbery.

One such partner who was to stick by Shorty through periods of great adversity was the then Princeton resident George Winkler. Well-educated and having a healthy generosity of spirit, Winkler was also a prospector and miner, and in the coming years would stake Billy Dunn on many of his prospecting trips through the Similkameen and Ashnola valleys. He became one of Dunn's best and oldest friends. M.K. Rogers, who was associated with the rich Nickel Plate Mine in Hedley, was also a partner with Dunn in many mining properties in the Ashnola country. South of Hedley and Keremeos and towards the American border, the area was rumoured to have rich copper deposits.[9][10]

Many in the mining industry recognized Shorty Dunn's prospecting skills. American T.E Wood, a mining owner and promoter, also was a partner with Dunn on some of his claims. He bankrolled and supported him on many expeditions into the mountains of the Similkameen. Wood was the owner of the Emma Mine in Aspen, Colorado, and was the manager of a mine near Wardner, Idaho, for the St. Paul and Idaho Mining and Milling Company.

During most of the spring, summer and fall of each year, Dunn would usually be found in the far reaches of the mountains and rivers in the border country, far from civilization and the company of others. He enjoyed the testing of his character and skills that trapping, hunting and prospecting presented to him. In the winters he would come into town and work at various jobs throughout the area. He worked as a clerk in A.L. White's hardware store, was a ranch hand and farm hand on the Currie Schisler homestead, worked in a Princeton sawmill, and broke horses for local ranchers.

Soon after he arrived, he made the acquaintance of the venerable lady who was the wife of the original settler into the Vermillion Forks, or Princeton, country. Susan Louisa Allison was the founding matriarch of not only a large family, but also for the new settlers moving in around Princeton. Still resident today in the collective eye of the town's history, hers was a character of unbridled energy and enthusiasm, coupled with a true regard for the First Nations families around her as well as the citizens, farmers and ranchers of this section of the Similkameen. George Winkler remembers when he first met Mrs. Allison and Shorty Dunn.

"Mrs. Allison, sister-in-law of ex-Governor Dewdney and the first white woman in the Similkameen Valley, resided at Princeton when I was there. This white-haired old lady was a motherly soul, and besides raising a large family of her own, she had a heart big enough for the folks around there who had no homes of their own. She used to invite us to a dance at her place each Friday night, and it was at one of these affairs that I first met Shorty Dunn. He was working for Mrs. Allison at the time, and the night I first saw him he recited (poetry)! I got to know him pretty well after that."[11]

Billy Dunn did indeed have an artistic bent. Not only could he compose and recite poetry, but he was also an accomplished cartoonist and artist. He honed his artists' skills sketching on birch bark during those long and solitary hours in front of a fire, in his mining camps and on his trap lines, far from the studios of more city oriented artists in both distance and ambience.

George Winkler was quoted in a contemporary Victoria Colonist article: "Years ago I grubstaked him when he went trapping alone in the Ashnola Range. He got hurt and blood poisoning set in. For six weeks he was laid up at his camp, and during that time he used to exercise his cartooning faculty by drawing on chips with a charcoal stick. In the spring thaw Dunn dragged himself out over the snow to civilization. As a result of his misfortune, he had a poor catch for the winter, but he wanted to give me the whole thing. I refused it, and later he gave me a pony."[12]

In the memories of families in the Similkameen, Shorty Dunn's talents are still remembered. Mention is made that he was a very accomplished artist and that some of his paintings hang today in a ranch house near Keremeos.[13]

Future B.C. Provincial Police Deputy Commissioner Cecil Clark described Dunn as "… no common or garden (variety) crook. In fact, for a one time cow poke and packer, he was well read and something of a philosopher and poet to boot."[14]

In 1903 he took Mrs. Allison up on her offer to partner on shares of her ranch, but after a couple of years he decided that the ranching life was not for him. He found himself spending most of his days dreaming of being in the bush pursuing some vision of riches and enjoying the solitude, quiet and challenge of the wilderness.[15]

In the summer of 1904, Dunn had a contract for fencing with the local Indians at Twenty Mile Creek near Hedley and did quite a bit of work with them.[16]

In the early fall of 1905, young Millie Schisler remembered Billy Dunn working on the farm of her father, Currie Schisler. Dunn was in the potato patch, hoeing out the fall crop of spuds. An older man, erect, with a tanned face, impressive moustaches, twinkling blue eyes and a friendly manner, introduced himself to Billy as George Edwards. He had been living on the Schisler place and doing odd jobs for most of the year and had told the Schislers he had made some good returns from his gold mines in Mexico. He was living life to the fullest in the saloons and at the dances and private parties held in the Otter Valley, Nicola Lake, Hedley and Princeton. He worked alongside Dunn in the potato patch for a day or so, and as they worked, Edwards regaled the impressionable fellow American with tales of the frontier West across the border and deeds of derring-do.[17]

Shorty Dunn was later to admit that this was when George Edwards started discussing plans with him for holding up another train in British Columbia; the CPR at Kamloops.[18]

Another resident of the Similkameen described Dunn in somewhat less flattering terms, perhaps tempered by Dunn's future travails. She described him as "an easily influenced little man with a short fuse and a nervous trigger finger." He was "of medium build, square faced, dark haired and had a nervous unpredictable temper. Easily led he was the antithesis of Miner."[19]

That winter of 1905–1906, Dunn worked for Mrs. Allison at her ranch, and when the weather was good, he checked his traplines near Osprey Lake. In the late winter he worked for a month in a sawmill in Princeton. As the snow melted into spring, he would be found spending more time at Jack Budd's cabin in earnest conversation with Mr. Edwards.[20]

X

KAMLOOPS COUNTRY

KAMLOOPS IN 1906 was on the brink of change. Incorporation as a city had happened in 1893, and as the millennium changed the aspirations of the little town nestled on the banks of the Thompson River were rising. With a resident population of 1,596 souls in 1904, the once frontier town that supplied the needs of the surrounding ranches and farms was entering the modern era. It was fuelled by the economic generator of the Canadian Pacific railway that for past twenty years had exerted its influence, for good and bad, upon the local populace. Plans were afoot for a second railway to come through Kamloops from the north, and fruit-lands on the north shore of the Thompson were under development. Mining speculation for copper and coal was rife throughout the community, and almost every government worker, businessman or aspiring entrepreneur described himself as a prospector, mining consultant, mine manager or mine owner. In the Iron Mask Mine to the west of the city, sixty to eighty men were working, and plans were underway to develop a smelter beside the CPR's main line and a tramway to feed it with ore. In the past year, 3,720 tons of ore had been shipped to smelters in the Kootenays. Optimism ran high that the future would bring considerable prosperity to Kamloops. No inkling was felt of the calamity of the First World War that would temporarily halt that journey towards growth and development. Vague newspaper headlines of the war between Japan and Russia did not portend that fearful march towards death and destruction that was to take place across the seas in a few short years.[1]

Despite these visible signs of graduation into the twentieth century,

Mary Spencer photo, Kamloops looking east from the vicinity of the Old Nicola Wagon Road, circa 1906.
COURTESY OF KAMLOOPS MUSEUM AND ARCHIVES.

the roots of Kamloops were still very much solidly entrenched in the frontier Christian values of the rural ranching, farming, forestry and mining communities. These highly individualistic entrepreneurs sometimes felt they were but the pawns of the eastern metropolises and the CPR and its restrictive freight rates. It was more difficult for them to perceive that their lot was enhanced by their ability, through that same transportation giant, to efficiently export the fruits of their labours. Metal ores, cattle, lumber and produce flowed via rail to the growing markets to the east in Central Canada and to the south through the CPR's Mission Junction connection, and on to growing markets of the American neighbour. The port of Vancouver took these products across oceans to the Orient and other distant shores.

Some of Kamloops' more prominent citizens maintained a vital contact with the more metropolitan areas of B.C. Frederick Fulton, QC, had been a member of the B.C. Legislature since 1900 and had acted as Attorney General and Chief Commissioner of Lands and Works since 1905. A highly influential and respected politician, Fulton would leave a legacy for integrity and citizenship years after he had passed from the scene. In 1906 in his position as Attorney General, he would function as Crown Prosecutor in the Grand Jury inquiry into one of Western Canada's most notorious incidents.

Hewitt Bostock had been a gentleman rancher near Kamloops since 1888. In 1894 he started the Province newspaper in Vancouver, and after acquiring the local Kamloops Standard in 1896, he felt he had enough impetus and influence to run successfully for federal office in 1896. By 1904 he had been appointed to the Canadian Senate in Ottawa. The Vancouver Province that he had founded would provide detailed and sometimes controversial coverage of those 1906 incidents that involved Fulton.[2]

Chinese workers, who would play only a minor role in our story, were numerous in Kamloops since the completion of the CPR. Some took positions with local ranches and farms as cooks and domestic labour. The 1901 Census identifies a surprising number employed as flood irrigation workers in the hay fields of interior ranches. Taking up jobs in Kamloops in the service industry and as labourers, they largely kept to themselves in West Kamloops' Chinatown. There they would, amongst other things, indulge in their fondness for gambling, and they built tunnels from building to building to escape from the odd police raids.[3]

Opium selling was a legitimate trade requiring a business licence, and laundry and restaurant services were a mainstay of the Chinese economy. The agitation by labour unions in Vancouver and other metropolitan areas to limit the influx of Chinese immigrants was well underway. The Vancouver Trades and Labour Council, Industrial Workers of the World, the Tailors Union, the Cooks and Waiters Union, Hotel and Restaurant Employees Union, the Typographical Union and the Socialist Party of Canada all continued to pressure politicians to initiate methods to restrict Asian immigration into British Columbia.[4]

The Kamloops Indian Band lands were located directly across the South Thompson River from the town of Kamloops. The Chief of the Kamloops Indian Band during that first decade of the 20TH Century was Petit Louis, who had come into his position in 1855.

Petit Louis, progressive and respected, would continue as Chief until his death in 1915. Land claims in 1906 were at the top of the agenda, and representatives of interior bands were on their way to Ottawa to present their cases. An industrial school had been built in Kamloops in 1889; however, the progressive degradation of the local Shuswap culture had not yet been recognized. The members of the various Shuswap bands played an important economic role in the development of the southern interior. They supplied vital labour components to the ranching, lumbering and agricultural enterprises throughout the Thompson and Okanagan areas. Many of the traditions of former days were still intact, and most adults still spoke the Secwepemc language. Local relations between the First Nations peoples and the newcomers, particularly those on the ranches and in the rural areas, were still marked with a mutual respect for one another. Communications with the whites in Kamloops and surrounding ranches took place in the Chinook trading language assisted by universal sign language. Most whites of the day were quite conversant in Chinook Jargon, and some even spoke rudimentary Shuswap. Both Indians and whites subscribed to the Kamloops WaWa, a newsletter written in shorthand and in the Chinook Jargon. Kamloops served as the trade and commerce centre for the bands surrounding the town and also as a social meeting centre. There was considerable social interaction between the various bands of the Secwepemc peoples. This would result in members of at least three interior branches of the Shuswap nation being recruited by Kamloops members of the B.C. Provincial Police force to assist in tracking lawbreakers, amongst them the perpetrators of the future train holdup of the CPR. Law enforcement agencies throughout British Columbia had utilized the superior hunting and tracking skills of First Nations members in apprehending lawbreakers since first contact. The role played by these Shuswap trackers would prove to be of critical import in May of 1906.

In 1906, the mayor of Kamloops was Marshall Pollock Gordon, also Justice of the Peace and owner of a local furniture store, and there were five aldermen. As Justice of the Peace, Gordon would preside

*Kamloops Mayor M.P. Gordon (left) and his family at their home
at 205 Lorne Street in Kamloops, circa 1906.*
Courtesy of Kamloops Museum and Archives.

over the Grand Jury inquiry into the Ducks robbery. The City Clerk
had to post a $2,500 bond ensuring his honesty before being hired for
$1,000 a year. The Clerk had to rely on the generosity of friends to
meet the financial obligations required. On the 1906 council was one
of the first black aldermen to serve on a municipal council in Canada,
John Freemont Smith.

Council meetings were held regularly on Thursday evenings
in a building at the corner of First Avenue and Seymour Streets.
Originally a provincial government building, it was purchased by the
city from the senior government for $800, and the City shared offices
with the Provincial Government. Trials were often held during the
day in the same room as Council held its meetings. In May 1906, that
room would be taxed to the fullest during a trial whose implications
would reverberate down through the years. The city would stay in

Kamloops City Council at a municipal meeting in the Kamloops Courthouse, 1902. At far left is Alderman John Freemont Smith, and Mayor Marshal P. Gordon sits at his desk.

COURTESY OF KAMLOOPS MUSEUM AND ARCHIVES.

that wooden building for the next fifty-nine years.

Kamloops prided itself on the number of electric street lights, still rather dim, that were energized by the coal-fired powerhouse at the corner of Lorne Street and First Avenue. Fed by three tons of coal per day brought in by rail from New Westminster, the Royal Inland Hospital, the Provincial Men's Home and the Kamloops Gaol, all south of the town, were now connected to the power grid and sported new electric lights. Some of the more affluent citizens had table lamps powered by electricity. The two local papers, the Kamloops Standard and the Inland Sentinel, were still printed on presses run by water power.

Septic tanks were the recommended method of sewage disposal for those that could afford it; however, outdoor privies were still the rule for most dwellings. Photos of Kamloops in 1906 show those same

The Kamloops Club on McIntosh Street, circa 1899. Rear row standing, far left, City Clerk J.J. Carment, and at far right, Gold Commissioner and Government Agent George C. Tunstall. Seated on the steps in the front row, second from the right, is Constable William Fernie.

privies well back from the rear door of Kamloops homes, next to the wood shed. Septic tanks were pumped by hand into horse drawn tanks and dumped in a refuse ground just west of the City. The town foreman, at $75 per week, was responsible for Streets, Waterworks, Scavenger and Cemetery. The local volunteer fire department shared the use of the City's team of horses with the town works department, who utilized it for a myriad of uses, including drawing the local street grader and the water tank mounted on a wagon to damp down the dusty City streets on hot summer days.[5]

Bicycles were the preferred mode of transport within the confines of the City, and the automobile was still a distant rarity. Saddle horses and horse and buggy or wagon were the accepted means of local transportation, while those travellers without conveyances could avail themselves of regular stage connections to the Nicola

On left, Chief Constable E.T.W. Pearse and Frederick Fulton in front of Kamloops Courthouse and Council Chambers, on the occasion of Queen Victoria's Diamond Jubilee. COURTESY OF KAMLOOPS MUSEUM AND ARCHIVES.

Valley, the Similkameen and the Okanagan. The CPR's passenger service connected all the major cities in Canada to Kamloops, and steamers plied the waters of the Thompson system to points east, west and north. All City sidewalks were wooden and had to be maintained by the merchant or resident whose property they fronted. The CPR telegraph kept the local newspapers and residents abreast of the latest happenings in the outside world, and the telephone line had recently been strung south through trees and on poles between Kamloops, Nicola, Princeton, Hedley and Penticton. Plans to install a telephone switchboard at Nicola Lake were in the works.

The B.C. Provincial Police, formed in 1858 to ensure adherence to the laws of the British Empire during the gold rush, was responsible for law enforcement outside city boundaries. The force had been successful in enforcing law and order during difficult times and was well-regarded in law enforcement circles, with many of their recent recruits obtained from the veterans of Lord Strathcona's Horse and the South African Boer War. Uniforms were not provided, and horses and tack had to be supplied by the officers themselves. The force did supply their constables with .38 calibre five shot Smith and Wesson revolvers complete with cartridges and holster. A rifle and cartridges, baton, handcuffs, shackles, copies of the Criminal Code and the Indian Act with applicable amendments, and blank official Provincial Police forms were sent out on demand.[67]

The Chief Constable of the British Columbia Provincial Police in Kamloops, working out of the combined government building and City Hall, was Ernest T. W. Pearse, assisted by Boer War veteran Constable William Fernie. Pearse's district responsibilities included Hedley, with Constable Haines reporting to him, and Princeton, with Constable Hugh Hunter reporting. All the areas in between were Pearse's jurisdiction, with the inexplicable exception of Nicola, where Constable Walter Clark reported to Chief Constable Burr in Ashcroft.[8]

Like many of the prominent members of Kamloops' business community, Pearse was to hold quite a number of official provincial government positions, sometimes as many as four at the same time. Only the Chief Constable's position would have enabled a man to support a family, and these appointments were used to supplement other incomes. A certain degree of political nepotism was also involved. In 1906 Pearse was the Mining Recorder for the province and Chief Auditor for the City, as well as Chief Constable for the provincial police. He had been a licence inspector and tax collector in the past. His numerous brothers had settled in the Grande Prairie and Falkland areas, starting successful and profitable farms and ranches. In May of 1906, Pearse would act as the commanding officer of the future posses, special constables and searchers working out of Kamloops.

Provincial Police Constable William Lewis Fernie was to play one of the most important roles in the events of May 1906. He was born

Mary Spencer photo, B.C. Provincial Police Constable William Fernie.

COURTESY OF KAMLOOPS MUSEUM AND ARCHIVES.

in Cheshire, England, in 1870 to middle class parents and where his father was a medical doctor. Young Fernie also graduated from the medical school at Victoria University in Manchester. However, he didn't fancy the life of a doctor that his parents had picked out for him, but rather that of the cowboys he had read about in books as a young man. At the age of 18 he left England for Canada and worked as a cowboy at the Gang Ranch for a few years. By 1898 he had pre-empted a ranch of 320 acres up the North Thompson River from Kamloops, but there he soon determined that the life of a farmer was not for him.

He became an expert rifle shot, hunter and rider, a skilled and avid fly fisherman, and a lover of fine horses. He was a formative member of the Kamloops polo club and was a strong competitor. When Robert Service was in Kamloops working in the local Bank of Commerce, Fernie set him up with a horse and equipment so that Service could take part in the game. By contemporary accounts, Service was not an accomplished player, but he did leave the legacy of a love of poetry with Fernie, who further developed his own writing skills. Over the years, Fernie would avidly read Wordsworth and Service and was to continue to try his hand with the elusive muse. By some accounts he was a skilled poet, but only one of his attempts survives. It was penned upon his leaving the Cariboo, that place where so much poetry seems to have been generated over the years. Fernie's poem was written close to the time that Shorty Dunn penned his own paean to the Cariboo in 1896. In less than a decade the two poets would meet face to face under less than poetic circumstances.

Goodbye to Cariboo

Farewell to far Chilcotin and goodbye to Tatla Lake.
The thoroughfare that Waddington was not allowed to make
And hunters out at Bowron Lake, who dares the grizzlies' fang,
And trappers at Chilanko Forks, and cowboys at "The Gang".
Keep in at dark, good people, or, all breathing fire and smoke
You'll see Limpy's sixteen oxen, each couple with their yoke,
Don't speed around dark curves at night, or you may meet and spill;
Steve Tingley with his coach and four, tooling to Barkerville;
And the clanging bells you hear are, with ghostly manteaued load,
The packtrain of Old Cataline, strung out along the road.
If at Barkerville's old graveyard you cast a friendly glance
You'll see tombs of men from Germany, from England and from France,
From Denmark, Norway, Sweden and from Alsace and Lorraine;
From Austria and Hungary, from Portugal and Spain.
All men of different languages, by God's will once dispersed—
Surely the camp at Barkerville was Babylon reversed.
Here Judge Begbie gave his "dictum"—"Killers will surely rue,
For those who slay in this northland, there will be hanging too,"
If miners covet all the gold, they'll take the people true
For gold is in the hearts of those who toil in Cariboo.
Good-bye! Good folks of Cariboo, I leave you with a sigh,
My heart aches as I say it, but, "Klahowya" and "Goodbye";
Farewell now to the "Mountain" drear, I'll never traverse more
And struggle to "The Hundred Mile," or south to "Seventy-four."
For each of us the time's arrived, to go a different way,
I leave you, and I love you—that is all that I can say;
I'll never meet more friendly folk, wherever I may dwell.
Good-bye! Goodbye! Old Cariboo! Klahowya and Farewell.
Where careless of the winter and comparatively few
The kindest-hearted people dwell—the folks of Cariboo. [9]

He was described by his contemporaries as a modest and unassuming man, one who held back from the centre of attention and remained in the background, often missing the recognition due him. He was described by a contemporary as "the finest man I have ever met."

During that period of time in Canada's history, the country was still very closely tied to England, Scotland and Ireland, and the preponderance of the population of the province was of British extraction. In 1900 Britain became involved in the Boer War in South Africa. Like many young Canadians of his day, Fernie, with his good friend from Grande Prairie, William Ingram, joined the Lord Strathcona's Horse as cavalry troopers and served in that conflict during the period 1900 to 1901. Fernie was to lose his friend Ingram in that conflict in circumstances that would affect him for the rest of his life and leave him with a healthy skepticism for unbridled authority.[10]

Upon his return to Kamloops in 1901, he joined the Rocky Mountain Rangers under the command of the warden of the Kamloops Gaol, Captain John Vicars. Always the cavalry man, he assisted Senator Bostock in forming the 31ST B.C. Light Horse Regiment. Fernie sank himself with delight into the life he had made for himself in Kamloops. Sometimes thought of as stern and quiet, he was a man of many talents. He immersed himself in the challenges of his job and in the outdoor life in the surrounding hills, ranges and lakes. He was an avid and varied sportsman and participated as long as he was able in activities such as polo, tennis, fly-fishing and deer hunting. Like George Edwards in Princeton, he played the ukulele. He had a close relationship with the local First Nations peoples and, while working with them, honed his own increasingly skilled tracking, hunting and shooting skills. They taught him patience, persistence and focus. He became fluent in the Chinook trading language and picked up a smattering of the Shuswap tongue. He developed an affection for and a lifelong friendship with a number of the skilled trackers with whom he would solve so many future cases. His work as a Police Constable took him throughout the interior of B.C., and he became familiar with many of the farmers, ranchers, Indians and miners in the area. In September of 1905, the 35 year old Fernie married 26 year old Mary Isabel Lyle of Kamloops.[11][12]

The Kamloops Police Chief was Neil McGill, and the Criminal Code and other statutes as well as municipal bylaws were enforced by him and the Kamloops police force, consisting of a day and a night constable. Bylaws enforced included a speed limit of six miles per hour, no filth, ashes or rubble to be thrown into city streets, the discharge of firearms was banned within city limits and the City Pound regulations were to be enforced.[13]

Constable Frederick Hussey in the 1890s in his Provincial Police offices in the Kamloops Courthouse.
COURTESY OF KAMLOOPS MUSEUM AND ARCHIVES.

The Kamloops City Pound would be the unwitting source for the unlikely beginning to the story of the Ducks train robbery.

May 8th, 1906, in Kamloops was unseasonably hot. The Kamloops public works' water wagon, drawn by the team shared with the fire department, was watering down the dusty streets. At the edge of town, a small herd of 150 steers and heifers from the Campbell Ranch east of town was wandering through the residential section, munching on the fresh green grass growing on the shoulders of the roads. With the aid of local townsmen, the herd was corralled in the city's pound facilities at the west end of town, and word was sent out to the ranch that the cattle could be retrieved upon the payment of a fine of $30. The patriarch of the ranch, Lewis Campbell, called his son Walter to the ranch house and gave him $30 to rescue his cattle from the grip of the city bureaucracy. Walter assembled his best hands, some of them relatives by marriage, and at about 6:00 P.M., they mounted up and started to town. Lou Fox, Alvy Shaeffer and George Hughes smiled to themselves as Walter led them straight to the Montreal Hotel, where they proceeded to drink up $30 worth of fine whiskey. Thirty dollars bought a lot of drinks in those days, and by the time the funds ran out, it was dark outside and all the cowboys looked as though they "had been ridden hard and put away wet." Walter had bought each of the boys a fat bottle of whiskey, and they left the bar, mounted their ever-patient horses sleeping at the hitch outside the hotel, and made their way to where the cattle were impounded in the city's corrals.

Together the intoxicated cowboys roped the posts at the edge of the corral and pulled the log fence down. The herd, missing its home range, immediately filed through the opening, and together, cattle, horses and inebriated riders quietly made their way out of Kamloops. In the dark and aided by a bright spring moon, the drive made its way up the Hudson's Bay Gulch and took the road east of town to the Campbell Ranch, the cowboys sipping at their bottles and feeling satisfied and smug with life.

In the moonlight, the herd and riders plodded along the wagon road with the CPR railway tracks between them and the South Thompson River. It was after midnight when only a few miles from the ranch, they saw train #97 with a full head of steam pounding its way to Kamloops. It was remarked that the passenger train was late, and the cowboys wondered what had delayed it. They tucked the cattle into a corral close to the bunkhouse and stabled their horses. In their impatience to get to the comfort of their bunks, they neglected to rub down their heated horses. They dumped their saddles beside the stable door, and Alvy Shaeffer, in his eagerness to put his head on a pillow, even neglected to take his saddle off his unfortunate mount. Walter Campbell made his way to his mother's house further up the creek, and the rest of the boys dropped into their beds in the bunkhouse.[14][15]

XI

PREPARATIONS

THE YEAR OF 1906 DID NOT DAWN WELL for the citizens of British Columbia. A tragedy of startling proportions took place near midnight on a barren and rocky shore on Monday, the 22ND of January. That night the steamer S.S. Valencia en route from San Francisco to Seattle ran aground on the west coast of Vancouver Island. Over the next days, 117 passengers and crew lost their lives through the incompetence and lack of compassion on the part of many potential rescuers. The shock of the tragedy, its lurid aftermath and the inquiries following consumed the press and its readers for weeks after the event. Newspapers in all the interior towns in B.C. maintained coverage for their readers through the reporters of the major dailies in Vancouver, New Westminster and Victoria. The anguish of grief-stricken relatives would fill the files of the Provincial Police in Victoria and echo down through the years as the writer researched the events to soon take place in Kamloops.[1]

In Phoenix, Lewis Colquhoun was working as bookkeeper and timekeeper for the Brooklyn Mine. The progress of his tuberculosis continued, and he was forced to terminate his employment with the mine. Sometime in the late winter of 1906, a Dr. Gordon in Phoenix performed an operation on Colquhoun that was probably associated with his tuberculosis. Surgery was sometimes undertaken in the chest area of patients to try to relieve some of the symptoms of the advancing illness.[2]

After Colquhoun had recuperated, he took the Great Northern down to Spokane in March. Spokane, with its smelters and transportation links, was a burgeoning mining town growing quickly

Phoenix townsite, 1905. COURTESY OF B.C. ARCHIVES.

in the heart of eastern Washington state. The silver, lead, zinc, copper and gold mines of the American Pacific Northwest, as well as the West and East Kootenays of British Columbia, shipped their ore to Spokane smelters by rail and river steamer. All the amenities of a big city were available there, including skilled doctors knowledgeable about the latest treatments for tuberculosis. Colquhoun spent two days in Spokane and consulted with a specialist who had an office on the city's main street.[3]

During his time there, he visited a gun shop in the city's business district. He bought an Iver-Johnson revolver, planning to do some hunting when he got back to Canada. He took the train back across the border, stopping off at Midway for a couple of days. Remembering the invitation extended by the kindly gentleman from Princeton, Colquhoun made his fateful decision to take Royer's stage to Penticton, the Wembley stage to Hedley, and finally the Revely stage to that small town at the fork of the Similkameen and Tulameen Rivers.[4][5]

In February, as the days became milder and the roads more passable, Edwards had paid another of his many visits to Kamloops.

After stopping to visit the Tiltons and the McKays on Rose Hill, he made his way down into Kamloops from the high country on the steep mountain trail. As usual, he again stayed at Adolphe LaPointe's Colonial Hotel, and his friend Angus McKay saw him spending lots of money there. Kamloops residents admired the fine $300 race horse he was riding, with the distinctive red leather saddle.[6]

It was in February that George Edwards, planning for a busy summer in Princeton, and to ensure appreciative female companionship for the coming months, penned a letter to "soiled dove" Edna Moore in Phoenix.

> *Princeton, Feb 22nd 06*
> *My Dear Edner.*
> *Saturday I received your note and I think about that time you got a letter from me as I had writen in answer to your letter and had run that Party about the House as I told you there were too Girls here then but one of them has gon back to Hadley for there is nothing doing here but I think times will be quite lively in the Spring when the men get to working on the RR.*
> *When you come up here you want to take the stage at Phonix for Hadley. you will get to Hadley the next Night and the next day you come to Princeton to make connections you will have to leave Phonix Monday eve its twice as far to come around by Spencers Brige and I think it will cost more. the fare Phonix to Hadley is 17 Dollars and from Hadley to Princeton 3 more it will cost about 25 to get here but I wouldn't advise you to come ontill Spring we are quite a snowstorm here to Day. how is evie getting along give her my best regards*
> *I don't know of any News so good by for this time. Write soon to your true Friend*
> *George W. Edwards*[7]

Edwards' letter reveals at least a basic education, probably provided by his mother, an ex-school teacher. His handwriting is very legible, and his occasional misspellings revealed in this and others of his letters probably reflect his American pronunciation of some common

Canadian words.

Edna Moore and George Edwards were obviously acquainted enough to exchange letters with each other. He and Edna, and probably Evie, had partied together at a house on Angel Avenue the previous year in Princeton. After the busy summer season, two other girls had stayed in Princeton for a while, but one went back to Hedley where business with the Nickel Plate miners was more lucrative. Princeton winters in those early years before the railroads and the large mines had arrived must have been a bit dull. Edwards consoles her and entices her to come back to Princeton in 1906 as the Great Northern Railway tracks are advancing and clearing and right-of-way crews are busy working towards Princeton. He gives her detailed directions as to how to get to Princeton, and the costs and time required to get there from Phoenix. Unfortunately Edna, similar to many of the other girls in her trade, led a rather itinerant life, and would pull up stakes and move to other locations as the whim struck. Opportunities abounded in the Kootenays and the Boundary country with the mining operations and railway construction at their peak. Also, the riches of the metropolis of Spokane beckoned from just south of the border, reached easily on a branch line of the Great Northern.

Edna Moore never did pick up George Edwards' letter at the Phoenix post office, and he received it back in the local mail that spring stamped as "Unclaimed" with instructions to "Return to Writer."

Edwards' penchant for ladies of easy virtue was well known and had started in his late teens in the bordellos and fandango parlours of San Francisco. The male dominated frontier towns of B.C.'s rugged interior did not present many targets of female opportunity for eligible bachelors. The lifestyle Edwards set for himself did not enable him to practice extended periods of courtship with the few women available and the possible sexual favours that might bring. His demand for instant gratification in all areas required that he purchase the objects of his desires. This necessitated a ready and ample source of funds, and he would utilize the quickest means possible to acquire those funds. The letter he wrote to "Edner" reveals a man not just content with paying for the sexual services of women, but also exposes the not uncommon need for some men to form a bond with prostitutes. This bond would sometimes lead to becoming a part-time purveyor of business to the girls, as well as a trusted and respected companion who was not stingy with his money and who would probably often receive sexual favours and preferred treatment for his troubles. Contrary to what the Pinkertons would have had everyone believe, he had a true and obvious love of female companionship. As many of the men in that area and time would do, he resorted to those "ladies of easy virtue" to be found in the whorehouses and bordellos that followed mining camps and railway construction. Edwards' dalliances and close relationships with prostitutes did not affect his mannerisms or actions with the more respectable women of the communities he lived in or visited. Indeed, it probably contributed to the relaxed and gentile manner with which these relationships were characterized.

In early March Edwards sent a letter to his fifteen year old friend Bert McKay, living with his family in Rose Hill above Kamloops. Edwards must have been a conscientious letter writer for any to have survived into the twenty-first century. He obviously wanted to keep in contact with his friends from near and far through the mails. The following letter, written while plans for the train robbery at Ducks were well underway, reflects again his true regard for children and his modest efforts to guide them on the proper path of life.

> Princeton, March 4th, 06
> Friend Bert,
>   I just received your letter and you may be sure I was more than glad to heare from you. now my Boy you mus go to school and learn all you can I am glad you have such a good teacher and I will be sure to bring her some candy if she is a good girl and (illegible). I had a fine time when down below and am thinking of going down again before long but will come and see you before I go. At present I am feeling fine I did have a very severe attack of Lagrippe I tell you its pritty tuff. Bob (Tilton) is up 5 mile crick (north of Princeton)

trapping with a young man by the name of Dunn they are doing very well. The weather here is nice and pleasant in fact we have had a very pleasant winter very little snow and not very cold. I am glad you are all enjoying good health and getting along so finly.

I suppose Elmer and Edgar (Bert McKay's brothers) are getting along finly now. Bertie you must write whenever you can and give your Mama & Papa my best regards and best wishes and also the Children tell them to be good all they can and I will bring them a little something nice. I am sure the teacher will help all she can and i wont forget her candy too. I don't know of any news so good by for this time

and believe me your true friend

George W. Edwards[8]

Late that winter, about mid-March, Jack Budd was also looking after items that needed to be done before spring. In Aspen Grove he made a large cash purchase of around 10 lbs. of "Giant Powder" dynamite from W.A. Dodds at his store. Dodds wrapped the bundle of dynamite in old newspapers and remembered the incident as he had not as a rule sold much blasting powder to the local mining sector. The old newspaper was a copy of the Kamloops Sentinel of November 1905, with a mailing label on it to Dodd's store. Directly Budd left Dodd's store, he headed back to his ranch on Bald Mountain. Along with his some-time partner J.E. Rowlands, Budd did some necessary assessment work on their claim 13 miles below Princeton on the Similkameen River. He didn't return to his ranch until late March.[9]

On 21 March Shorty Dunn walked into his friend Charles Thomas' store in Princeton and bought two boxes of semi-automatic pistol cartridges. That spring his friend George Edwards had bought himself a 9mm Luger semi-automatic pistol and gave it to Dunn to use. These firearms, the latest in advanced weaponry, were being actively marketed in Canada and the U.S. and were available in mail-order catalogues to any who wished to purchase them. The rapid rate of fire achievable by these deadly pistols appealed to prospectors and hunters alike. That spring Albert Oelrich's wife Sara was home alone in the ranch house at One Mile Creek about eight miles north of Princeton when she heard a fusillade of rapid fire shots not far away, but in the dense brush. She could tell from the sound of the discharges that they were not a large calibre rifle, but probably from a pistol. Not hearing any more shots, she dismissed the incident and went about her chores. Later she recognized Shorty Dunn coming up to the house to greet her. She asked him about the shots she had heard earlier. Dunn told her that he had been camping not far from Oelrich's house and was trying out his new automatic pistol by shooting at grouse. He showed her the nine cartridges the pistol carried and explained the way it operated. He showed her that unlike other pistols she had seen, it had no cylinder and ejected each shell as it was fired. He showed her how the spent casing ejected out of the top of the breech automatically and how the weapon cocked itself each time it was fired. Lugers were a revolutionary handgun, and once the pistol was fired the first time, it would fire as fast as the shooter could pull the trigger.[10][11]

Near the middle of March the stagecoach pulled into Princeton, and Lewis Colquhoun disembarked. Depositing his large trunk in the Princeton Hotel, he checked in and stayed at the hotel for a couple of days. The bartender heard him inquire about where George Edwards lived. He spent those first days walking up and down the main street of the small town. One day he walked by the front windows of the local barber shop as George Edwards was lying back in the chair having a shave. When some of the other waiting customers made a comment about a young stranger walking by the front of the shop, Edwards swung around in the barber's chair. He immediately recognized Colquhoun from his visits to Phoenix and, after his shave was done, followed him to the Princeton Hotel. He asked Colquhoun what he had come out for, and the young man answered that he wanted to do some prospecting and some hunting. So Edwards asked him out to Budd's ranch to stay a while. They set off up the dusty wagon road, Colquhoun walking and Edwards riding his tall black horse. When they arrived at Budd's, Colquhoun was greeted and accepted by the part-time prospectors, the young and unmarried townsmen, and the general good old boys who haunted Budd's place.

Edwards took Budd's buckboard into town and loaded up Colquhoun's trunk at the Princeton Hotel. On the way back out of town, Edwards greeted Provincial Police Constable Hugh Hunter as he went about his business. Colquhoun would stay at Budd's for a good two weeks, helping Edwards with the chores about the horse ranch and meeting some of the locals such as Tom Arnold, the shifty-eyed sometime prospector, Deafie the barber, and one Guy Main Price. Shortly after Colquhoun arrived, the diminutive Shorty Dunn pulled in from a trapping expedition and was introduced to the former school teacher. Budd and all his friends were amusingly aware that Colquhoun's manner of speaking betrayed an advanced level of education. Also, it was immediately plain to all of them that he spoke the King's English with a pure eastern Canadian accent, and not in the American drawl that was heard so prevalently around Budd's cabin and indeed the whole southern Boundary country.[12]

Colquhoun heard from the others around Budd's ranch about the prospecting, trapping and hunting prowess of Shorty Dunn. He was told Shorty was a dead shot, that his hunting skills were without parallel in the area, and that he held a number of valuable mining claims in his name below Hedley and the Ashnola River. Others told Colquhoun that Dunn was known as a skilled teamster in the Cariboo and as a competent bronco buster in Princeton. Colquhoun cultivated the bushman, and when he felt that they had established a rapport, he asked Dunn whether he might be allowed to go hunting with him and do a bit of prospecting. To Colquhoun's disappointment, Dunn was non-committal and left on a trapping expedition without giving him an answer.

It was about this time that Constable Hugh Hunter, holder of so many government responsibilities in Princeton, saw Shorty Dunn step into his office. Dunn told him he was interested in making some extra money and wanted to know how much the bounty was for coyotes. Dunn was planning to put the new semi-automatic Luger to good use. After a short conversation Dunn left, and Hunter later saw him hanging around town having a few drinks.[13]

At the end of March, Dunn came back to Budd's ranch and at the beginning of his stay spent considerable time conferring with Edwards. Finally he approached Colquhoun and told him that he would agree to take the ex-school teacher along with him on a prospecting, trapping and hunting expedition to the north. Dunn borrowed a pack horse from Neil McFadden, a local carpenter in Princeton. Dunn had used the same horse as a pack horse over the winter. He told McFadden that he would need the horse for about three weeks to go on a prospecting trip north of Aspen Grove. The horse was branded with a block M on the right shoulder and had a white face and one white hind leg. He had a shaggy mane and was known to be a little mean if he was allowed to get away with things.[14][15]

The first week in April, Dunn and Colquhoun left Budd's ranch on foot, leading Dunn's horse and the one borrowed from McFadden. Both horses were loaded down with supplies. Edwards told them he would catch up with them in a couple of weeks. The two of them reached Dunn's camping spot near Aspen Grove, set up their tent and put the horses out in a makeshift corral. The next days were spent climbing around in the hills, prospecting and hunting. Colquhoun had plenty of opportunity to test out his new Iver-Johnson revolver. Dunn showed Colquhoun his new semi-automatic Luger, which he kept in a shoulder holster, and took the opportunity to get acquainted with its firing characteristics. He kept a lookout for the arrival of Edwards.[16]

Back in Princeton, Budd and Edwards were kept busy preparing for the trip planned with Dunn into the Kamloops country. On the 5TH of April, Edwards was in Charles Thomas' store in Princeton stocking up on camping supplies and food. Among his purchases were a brand new shovel and a pristine gold pan. Both he and Budd kept a company account at this store. On the 12TH of April, Budd was in Thomas' store by himself and purchased goods including a box of .22 cartridges and a box of .32 calibre Smokeless ammunition. Edwards owned two .32 calibre Colt's semi-automatic pocket pistols.[17]

On April 15TH, Alexander McKenzie of the McKenzie Ranch at One Mile Creek about thirteen miles north from Princeton spotted Edwards and Budd riding north together. They were mounted on two saddle horses and led two pack horses full of supplies. Edwards was sporting his distinctive red leather saddle. That day they stopped overnight at the Christopher Burkstead ranch about one mile north of McKenzie's. After unloading their horses and covering the supplies with a tarp, they were given a hot meal and a spot to sleep. The next morning they thanked Burkstead for his hospitality. Upon Burkstead's request, Budd agreed to come back in a few days to castrate some animals, but the rancher was to receive a letter from Budd later the next week advising him he could not come. Edwards and Budd headed north with their two pack horses on the rudimentary trails towards Aspen Grove.[18]

Early in the morning of April 18TH, a major earthquake hit San Francisco, with devastating fires killing 500 people and destroying 3,000 acres in the centre of the city.[19]

Soon after news of the earthquake made its way into all the small towns and hamlets in B.C.'s interior, T.J. Clemitson was outside his home in Grande Prairie. The spring weather was sunny and temperatures were steadily climbing. He could feel the sun's heat even at 7:00 in the morning. The rancher looked out onto the Vernon to Kamloops wagon road from his place about one mile below Herbert Guernsey's store. He saw George Edwards and Shorty Dunn riding by, travelling north towards Summit Lake. They had no one else with them, as their pack horse had been left back in their camp with Colquhoun. The trio had been camped at Batchelor's Meadows a few miles south of Grande Prairie on the Douglas Lake road for the past week.

At the meeting of the Kamloops City Council on the evening of Thursday the 19TH of April, a little more spark than normal was realized when an irate delegation appeared before Council to deliver complaints. It seemed that one Mr. Bell, a dairyman within the city limits, had allowed his resident bull, engorged with the passions of spring, to service his herd of dairy cows in full public view.[20]

On the 24TH of April, Edwards, Dunn and Colquhoun moved their camp in closer to Kamloops. In the remote hills south of Summit (Monte) Lake, homesteader Paul Stevens' wife Margaret paused from her late morning chores to watch Shorty Dunn ride into the yard of their modest farm. Isolated from any close neighbours, the Stevens had a rudimentary stump farm far from travelled wagon roads or main trails. Near Little Fish Lake, their place was about twenty miles south and east of Campbell's Crossing, located on the CPR main line. As she watched Dunn ride in, she saw he was mounted on a bay horse with a white face and one white hind leg. The horse had a fine red leather saddle on it. He approached her, greeted her and inquired about the trail he was following that went directly past her place. She told him that the trail would take him to Summit Lake, and there he could either go north and west to Kamloops or east to Grande Prairie. He told her he was a prospector and because he was not feeling well, needed to ride out to see a doctor. He thanked her for saving him a long ride, and she watched horse and rider make their way down the hill towards Summit Lake.[21]

In the evening of the 26TH of April, the regular Thursday meeting of the Kamloops City Council was again held. In a building shared with the Provincial Government as a courthouse, the business was mundane but necessary. Dairyman Bell, he with the passionate bovine, showed up at council and denied the occurrences vividly detailed at the last meeting, and that was the end of the matter, at least for that year. The next year Mr. Bell was to appear before Council on the same complaint. Spring temperatures had been rising that day, and the day's heat in the poorly insulated building had yet to be replaced by the cool of the evening. The rising spring temperatures reminded Mayor Gordon and his five member council to institute the annual sprinkling restrictions allowing irrigation only between 5 and 9 A.M., and 3 to 9 P.M. Tenders were opened for expansion of the water system, meeting the increasing needs of the little town. In the Kamloops Standard newspaper that day, it was noted that a major development of tree fruit orchards was underway on the north shore of the Thompson River, and CPR surveyors were in Nicola laying out for the construction of the branch line down from Spence's Bridge. The first electric table lamps were advertised for sale in local papers.[22 23]

Paul Stevens, whose wife Maggie had just met Shorty Dunn, had less than an enviable reputation in Kamloops. Even though he had married into the respected Todd and Pratt families, merchants and the local Kamloops police force were aware he was an individual to watch. He was a squatter miles back in the Monte Hills south of Summit Lake who had never applied for a pre-emption and just managed to scrape out an existence in the bush far removed from other contact. Deemed untrustworthy and lazy, he was denied credit at all establishments in Kamloops. He was chronically short of cash as his stock raising abilities in the heavily forested hills above Monte Lake were barely adequate. It was noted by a contemporary source that "Connection with bad characters and doubtful antecedent is against him." Stevens was originally from Idaho, and when he came into Canada is not known. However, that he had a connection with the fellow American train robber Bill Miner is almost certain.

Shortly after Edwards and his partners came into the Kamloops area, Paul Stevens made his way into Kamloops with his wagon and team. It was mid-morning and the mud of spring had mostly dried up. He drove a two-horse team past the stockyard and into the heart of town. On the north side of the CPR main line and opposite the station, he stopped in front of Samuel Brooks', General Merchant, small grocery store. Brooks recognized Stevens' face but did not know his name. He didn't normally get patronized by the ranching or farming trade, but he had seen him drive by the odd time. Stevens went on to order a pair of men's shoes and two pairs of women's shoes, all of the best quality, Ames and Holden from Montreal. Overalls, coffee, baking powder, and other groceries and incidentals made up an order totalling $19.50. This was a substantial outlay of cash when one considered that the same amount would purchase an oak bedroom suite complete with washstand, bedstead and bureau. Brooks clearly remembered the tea that was purchased. It was Tetley's #2 India and Ceylon in a half pound, 25 cent package. It was tightly wrapped in tin foil, with the trade mark label pasted on the surface of the foil. The label consisted of an elephant's head, with trunk erect and two packages of tea suspended from it marked "Ceylon." On the lower edge of the green label in bold black type was "London, England." Brooks would within a month be called on to describe the packaging in minute detail.[24][25]

After the goods were assembled, Stevens pulled out a number of small bills, and with a flourish, laid a total of $20 on the counter. Brooks thought it extremely strange that Stevens should have made such a large purchase from him when he had never dealt at the store previously. Brooks offered Stevens the 40 cents in change; however, Stevens refused it, saying, "Oh, keep the change and give me some candy."[26]

Stevens gathered up the groceries which had been bagged in jute sacks and made his way out to his wagon. As he pushed his way through the door, it was held open for him by Neil McGill, the Kamloops Chief of Police, on his way in to visit with Brooks. As Stevens mounted his wagon, Brooks asked the Chief who the man was. McGill replied that it was Paul Stevens from up in the hills above Summit Lake and that "he had a bad reputation among the merchants in town and it would not be advisable to allow him credit." Stevens turned his wagon around and headed east towards the upper Campbell Creek country where George Edwards and his two partners were camped.[27]

The first and most important camp that Edwards and his partners set up in the Kamloops area was three to four miles due south of the CPR main line along side the main stage road from Kamloops to Vernon. Located a few miles east of the Upper Campbell Creek community of what would later be called Barnhartvale, it was at the fork of the road that led down to Ducks Station on the CPR main line, and about three-quarters of a mile west of the large ranch owned by Albert Duck at Holmwood. This ranch was also used as a stage stop to change horses on the way to and from Grande Prairie and the Okanagan. There Edwards and his partners had set up their wall tent, and on a nearby hillside they staked out their three horses on long leads to graze. The locals noted that the trail down to the Campbell Ranch and the CPR main line where Campbell Creek flowed into the South Thompson River became well-worn during the time the

The Duck's Holmwood Ranch.
COURTESY OF KAMLOOPS MUSEUM AND ARCHIVES.

strangers camped beside Robbins Creek.[28]

On the last Sunday of April, the weather was the warmest it had reached that spring, and the day was as quiet and still and satisfying as only a sunny warm day in spring can be in the cattle country around Kamloops. May was fast approaching, and the calves were soaking up the sun as their mothers feasted on the lush green grass sprouting in the pastures. Albert Duck's wife Edith looked out her window at the cattle in the fields below her large log house at the Holmwood Ranch and savoured the smell of the fresh grass and cottonwood buds, the mud and the cattle as it floated softly in through the open windows. Her five children, Mona, Doris, Rupert, Wilfred and Arthur, were busy outside and called her attention to the arrival of a stranger riding along the stage road to Kamloops. She saw a grizzled elderly man on a roan pinto tie up at the fence below her house. He made his way up the hill and greeted her on the front porch. Edith called her husband Albert down from upstairs to deal with the stranger. He introduced himself to Albert as George Edwards and asked if he might have a wash and if he could purchase some groceries. As her husband and the American with the soft drawl were talking, Edith saw two men, whom she later was to learn were Colquhoun and Dunn, walking west towards Kamloops and leading a dark pack horse. Edwards asked the Ducks for some lard, tobacco, rice, two dozen boiled eggs and two bottles of milk. Albert Duck commented to the stranger that they didn't keep a store, and inquired from what direction he had come. The old man swept

Albert and Edith Duck. Courtesy of Val and Sandi Pringle, Westwold.

his arm to the east and said he and his partners had come from that direction. Duck replied that if that were so he would have passed stores in Grande Prairie that would have been able to meet his needs. Edwards replied that they had been in the mountains for some time and had not travelled near Grande Prairie. When Duck agreed to supply the stranger, Edwards asked if he might buy both smoking and chewing tobacco. Mr. Duck gave Edwards one plug of his own smoking tobacco, and Mrs. Duck started to collect the other items. Edwards removed his coat and hat and washed up at the basin on the front porch. Edith had her stove hot and ready for the noontime meal for her family and the two ranch hands, and she quickly boiled water and cooked the eggs. As he waited for her to put the items together, they talked of the latest news and what had brought the stranger to the Kamloops area. Edwards told the Ducks that he was a prospector and had been in the mountains with his partners for about six weeks. They asked him if he had heard about the San Francisco earthquake eleven days previously. Albert was surprised to learn that Edwards

*Albert Duck leaning against the wagon, and Walter Homfray
at the reins, near Ducks, B.C.*

knew nothing about it and seemed quite concerned. Albert gave him copies of the Victoria Colonist newspaper detailing the disaster for him to take away. Edwards thanked them for their generosity and paid $1.75 for the groceries and tobacco. When he left heading west towards his camp, Mrs. Duck noticed it was close to twelve noon.[29][30][31]

George Butler, who lived at Grande Prairie, and Cecil Russell were the two hired hands that worked for Albert Duck at the Holmwood Ranch. They were riding back from the west to the main ranch house to have their dinner. It was close to noon when they passed the fork of the road where it branched down to Ducks Station. There they saw Dunn and Colquhoun in their camp, tending a campfire and getting ready for their noon meal. Close by the camp they saw two dark bays staked out. They continued on their way and soon saw a rider on a white faced horse with white spots, coming towards them from the direction of the ranch house. It was Edwards, and he was carrying a bottle of milk in each hand. As they passed, Edwards greeted them, raised the two bottles of milk in a salute, and joked, "This is not whiskey, boys."[32]

That same afternoon at around 2:30, rancher H.B. Taite was out in his fields attempting to fix a broken irrigation flume. He was worried that he was going to lose too much water to the break and hoped he could hire some men to get the work done as soon as possible. Taking a break from the heat he stepped into the shade of a nearby ponderosa pine and saw three men and two horses coming down the road towards him. Edwards was wearing his wide brimmed Stetson and again was riding the roan pinto. Taite noticed the pinto was shod all round. Shorty Dunn, wearing a black Stetson and carrying a Winchester over his shoulder, was leading McFadden's bay with a pack on it. Taite did not see any other firearms. Colquhoun was wearing a sweater and a type of derby hat. Edwards greeted the rancher and asked how far it was to Kamloops. Edwards then asked about any camping spots between Taite's ranch and Kamloops. Taite told him there were probably some good spots nearer to Campbell Creek where it crossed the Vernon to Kamloops road. Edwards ventured to Taite that they had been prospecting around Grande Prairie. Taite, being knowledgeable about that country, questioned them as to where and who was working out in that area, but they could not give him any satisfactory answers. Taite was of the opinion that Edwards was being evasive about what they were doing in the Kamloops country and thought to himself that they had never been in the Grande Prairie area prospecting. Edwards make some comments about getting some milk, but did not press it further. Taite asked the three men if they were interested in doing some work for him and helping to fix the flume, but Edwards, who seemed to be the spokesman for the other two, turned him down, pleading prior commitments. The three men and their horses left the unfortunate Taite behind and continued towards Kamloops. Further down the road, ranchers William Buse and Hickson watched them make their way past their holdings and observed the strangers in their various camps throughout the area during the early part of that May.[33]

The little community of Ducks, later to be called Monte Creek, was a station and water stop on the CPR main line eighteen miles east of Kamloops. It was in the heart of the Kamloops ranching and cattle country, and 180 people lived in the immediate area. Senator Bostock's store supplied the settlers and ranchers with groceries and news, and the Wednesday and Saturday stage to Grande Prairie, twenty miles to the south, stopped outside its long front porch. William Plumm was the CPR's station agent and telegrapher at Ducks, as well as being Postmaster and Justice of the Peace. He had not only his wife Mary and daughters Violet and Ivy to be responsible for, but also his wife's mother and father lived with them in the little station agent's house. The camp of Edwards and his partners near the Holmwood ranch to the south was an easy ride downhill just two and one-half miles to the Ducks station. Plumm's days at the telegraph were broken by welcome visits from the elderly prospector from the Similkameen who had so many good stories to tell. George Edwards carefully watched the trains as they passed by Plumm's little station office and listened to Plumm interpret the telegraph as it busily clacked away, announcing CPR business. In conversations with the unsuspecting CPR employee, he made himself familiar with the schedules and makeup of the trains heading west towards Vancouver. Edwards paid particular attention to the daily first class passenger train #97, the Imperial Limited, from the east. It usually stopped for water at the Ducks water tower at exactly 23:09 hours railway time. It was the only one, heading east or west, that passed by Ducks in the darkest part of the night.[34][35][36]

On the 30TH of April, ex-army man Captain George Graves and Kamloops livery stable owner Montgomery were in a rig driving over the Kamloops to Vernon road on their way to Grande Prairie. Pulling up the draw beside the small creek etched deep into the silt soils, they were leaving the South Thompson Valley behind and breaking out into the fertile Upper Campbell Creek valley, not far from the Todd and Pratt farms. The day was a bit cooler than the previous day, but they still had to stop and cool the horses at the top of the pull. They continued on, and when they were about two miles west of the crossing of Upper Campbell Creek, they saw two riders approaching from the east. It was George Edwards and Shorty Dunn heading into Kamloops. Colquhoun had been left to take care of the camp. Edwards greeted the two on their wagon, commenting that the day was indeed hot and dusty. The travellers then continued on their ways.[37]

By the 3RD of May the activities of the three campers near Holmwood had become more active. Mrs. Samuel Bice saw the three trudging the roads around her farm near Upper Campbell Creek. She remembered the oldest one greeted her warmly. Mrs. Barnes at the Upper Campbell Creek Post Office saw two of them that same day and one, the eldest, asked her for some milk. She told him she had none available at the time, but referred them to her neighbours, the Buses. William Buse and his wife Annie owned the Hidden Vale Ranch. With their son William, they ranched in a fertile little valley not far east of Upper Campbell Creek. A small pothole lake would later take their name. Edwards and Dunn walked onto their place that day and asked if they might buy some milk. Annie Buse noticed that the older man with the grizzled moustaches wore a heavy gold ring with snake heads on his left hand and carried an expensive gold watch. She later described Shorty Dunn as a short "dark swarthy man (who) looked almost like a Mexican (and) had a slouch hat down over his eyes and had several weeks growth of beard on his chin." Edwards was very talkative and engaged her in agreeable conversation for some while, asking her about the names of the different ranges in the hills to the south. She told him about the Campbell Range and the Robbins Range south of her ranch on the horizon, and the Ducks Range further east of the Holmwood Ranch. She saw that when it came time to pay her for the milk, Edwards withdrew from his pocket a small purse that opened with a fastener in the centre. The two men left on foot, making their way in the direction of upper Campbell Creek. Edwards and Dunn were checking the lay of the land above Furrer Siding on the CPR main line.[38][39]

As Edwards and Dunn were scouting around on foot, Colquhoun was having his problems back at the camp in the hills above Ducks.

McFadden's mean bay with the white face and one white hind leg had broken away from its lead, and Colquhoun, mounted on a dark bay, was trying to round him up. He found himself about a mile south of the Barnes place near Upper Campbell Creek when he left the tree line and found Lizzie Dupuis mounted on her own horse and trying to find one of the Barnes' stray horses. Lizzie stayed at the Barnes Ranch and also worked in the Upper Campbell Creek Post Office. Colquhoun tipped his hat to her and told her he was looking for his horse, which he described. He then asked Lizzie whether there might be a corral nearby where he could put the straying horse if and when he captured it. Lizzie told him that there was not any available close by and rode away from him.[40]

The Kamloops Standard reported on the City Council meeting of May 3RD. Warden John Vicars of the Provincial Gaol at Kamloops applied for a hookup to the city's water system. The hot and dry weather so early in the year had caused the normal irrigation supply from nearby Peterson Creek to run dry and the prisoner maintained grounds to suffer. Council agreed to the connection, and Alderman Brown asserted that the gaol had to be metered, just as the CPR connection was metered. Council agreed. A letter from a disgruntled taxpayer, one Mr. C. Stevens, was read out in open council by City Clerk J.J. Carment. The irate Mr. Stevens accused some members of Council and the City Clerk of corruption in dealings with hotel licences and wished the issue to be redressed. He charged two or three council members and the City Clerk with "crookedness" and the balance of council with "not having enough brains to know what was going on." It was recommended that the letter be received and filed, and this was passed. This was the last heard of the incident.

It was also noted at the council meeting that Attorney General and Kamloops provincial government representative Frederick J. Fulton was responsible for getting a grant of $15,000 from the government for a new school, to be followed the next year by a like amount.[41][42]

On May 4TH, Billy Dunn left Colquhoun behind minding the camp, telling him he was going to Kamloops for provisions. Edwards rode down the hill to visit with Billy Plumm, the station agent at

Ducks. Dunn rode across the little wagon bridge at Upper Campbell Creek and past the Post Office. He rode down out of the high country through the narrow draw on the Vernon Road and into the main valley of the South Thompson River. He followed the good wagon road beside the CPR main line into Kamloops and checked into the Dominion Hotel under the name of Jack Mitchell. He stayed in the hotel overnight and the next day had a meeting with a man in the hotel bar. After the meeting he spent a few hours having drinks in the many hotels in downtown Kamloops. About five o'clock in the afternoon he went to the store of Ramsay and Phillips at the corner of Second Avenue and Victoria Street. William Phillips and his partner A.E. Ramsay were the town's leading grocery proprietorship. While clerk Marshall did up the order, owner Phillips packed the items in a large walnut sack marked "R&P". Dunn paid for groceries totalling $4.05 and left the store. He mounted up with the bag in a white pack over his shoulders and headed east.[43][44]

At Bostock's store at Ducks Station the day was winding down for bookkeeper and clerk William Adams when a customer came through the door. A short, dark, swarthy man, he had many days' growth of beard on his face. He wore a light coloured slouch hat and dark clothes and had a white pack over his shoulders. To Adams' confused eyes, the man, Shorty Dunn, acted deaf and dumb and unable to communicate vocally. He greeted Adams with a wave, then pointed at the twenty-five cent tobacco plugs as if he wanted them. Finally, after much gesturing and facial expressions, Adams was able to determine that the deaf and dumb man wanted two of the plugs. He passed them to the little man, and he in turn gave him two quarters. The man turned on his heel, left the store, mounted up and headed into the hills to the south. Adams walked out the door behind him and watched him ride into the distance. George Hazelhurst, a local cowboy, was leaning back in a chair on the store's porch in the early evening light, and Adams pointed out the receding rider to him as a deaf mute. Adams thought he heard a laugh drifting in from the distance.[45]

Sometime after setting up their camp near the Ducks Ranch at

Holmwood, the three itinerant prospectors set up another camp close by the Buse Ranch and near Campbell Creek. It was almost due south of Furrer Siding on the CPR main line. There they cached some of their prospecting gear, packs and also some of their excess groceries.

On the 7TH of May, Edwards and Dunn again headed in to Kamloops, taking all three horses. Colquhoun was left behind to tend to the camp. They told him they would not be back that night, or perhaps for as long as two nights, and for him to make his way to the camp closer to Campbell Creek where they would meet.

In the east end of Kamloops, Mrs. Rosie Love was busy doing her Monday washing, scrubbing up in the tubs in the sunshine outside her house on Lorne Street. At 10:30 in the morning she squinted into the sun to see Shorty Dunn mounted on one of the bays and leading the white faced bay with the one white rear leg. He skirted the north side of the cemetery on River Street and crossed the tracks heading into town. Behind him, mounted on a roan pinto, was an elderly man wearing a well worn, dark, flat brimmed Stetson and sporting moustaches and a week's growth of beard. Edwards followed Dunn by the north side of the cemetery and halted at the northwest corner, looking around at the view across the South Thompson River, and then he too rode across the tracks into Kamloops.[46]

Edwards rode down the main street of Kamloops and dismounted at the store of F.E. Burns, a dry goods merchant. He bought a pair of woolen socks from Burns and paid him twenty-five cents for them. Dunn had one of the horses shod at a local livery, and then the two of them headed out of town in the late afternoon.[47]

The two travelled east along the wagon road beside the railway almost to Campbell's Crossing of the CPR main line. Close to where Campbell Creek empties into the South Thompson, they made a rough camp near the stream. When it was almost dusk, they went down to the big concrete box culvert under the railway west of the crossing and there they met up with a third man. All three returned to the makeshift camp beside the creek and went to sleep. Early the next morning, the third man took the three horses and his own and left, going into the hills to the south. Edwards and Dunn lay around most of the day, keeping out of sight of the Campbell Ranch hands until late afternoon.[48] [49]

During that day, Paul Stevens left his house near Little Fish Lake and led three horses, one shod and two unshod, to the camp near Buse's and hobbled them out. He hobbled two of them American style, one hind foot to one fore foot. The third was tied up Siwash style with the two front feet together.[50]

The third man, on foot, joined Dunn and Edwards close to dusk. The three of them set off in the early spring twilight, heading east towards Ducks Station. After they had travelled a mile from their camp at Campbell Creek, the third man stopped and stayed behind. Edwards and Dunn continued on to Ducks Station and their fateful meeting with the Imperial Limited.[51] [52]

XII

THE DUCKS ROBBERY

As THE CPR's IMPERIAL LIMITED passenger train pounded through the night between Revelstoke and Kamloops, the Reverend Doctor James S. Woodsworth of Winnipeg finally fell asleep in his berth in the Pullman somewhere east of Notch Hill. With the superintendent of the Methodist missions in Western Canada were many of the leading Methodist church ministers from British Columbia, heading for a conference in Victoria. In the Pullman and in the regular cars the lamps were dimmed down, and the passengers jostled sleepily from side to side as train No. 97 left Shuswap and approached Ducks Station. With Woodsworth were the Reverends Balderson of Summerland, Wright of Vernon, Magee of Golden, Dean of Nelson with his two daughters, Thomas of Hedley City, Knox of Rossland and Henderson of Kelowna. Most had boarded at Sicamous Junction and had just nicely got to sleep. Doctor Woodsworth was in the early stages of thinking through his socialistic ideas, born of his Christian faith and the inequities he felt existed in Canadian society at that time. In the future, the thoughts of this founding father of socialism in Canada would develop and mature. He would play a formative role in forming the Cooperative Commonwealth Federation, the forerunner to Canada's New Democratic Party. This night he would come close to meeting another professed and aspiring socialist.[12]

Late on that warm spring evening of Tuesday, 8 May 1906, Engineer Joseph Callin of Revelstoke was approaching the little flag stop of Ducks Station driving the compound locomotive #941. He was right on schedule, 23:09 CPR time, and the trip had been

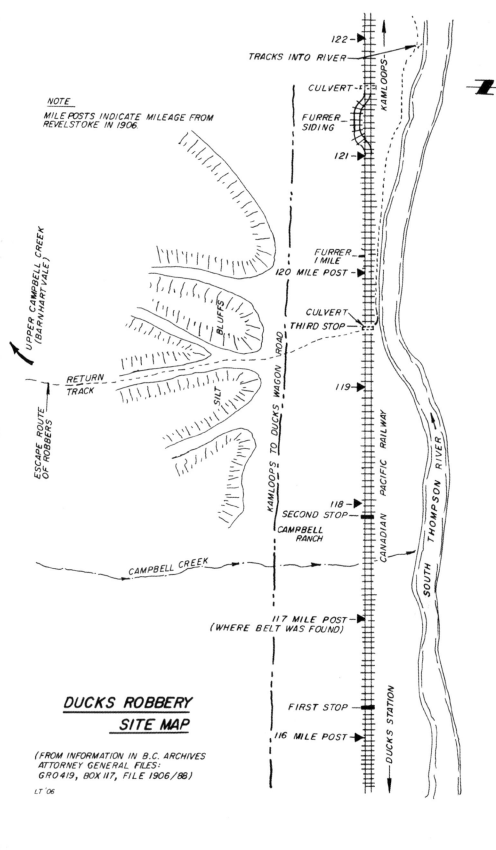

NOTE
MILE POSTS INDICATE MILEAGE FROM
REVELSTOKE IN 1906.

122 →
TRACKS INTO RIVER

CULVERT
FURRER
SIDING

121 →

KAMLOOPS

UPPER CAMPBELL CREEK
(BARNHARTVALE)

BLUFFS

FURRER
1 MILE
120 MILE POST →

CULVERT
THIRD STOP →

RETURN
TRACK

119 →

SILT

ESCAPE ROUTE
OF ROBBERS

KAMLOOPS TO DUCKS WAGON ROAD

CANADIAN PACIFIC RAILWAY

SOUTH THOMPSON RIVER

118 →
SECOND STOP

CAMPBELL
RANCH

CAMPBELL CREEK

117 MILE POST →
(WHERE BELT WAS FOUND)

DUCKS STATION

DUCKS ROBBERY
SITE MAP

FIRST STOP →

116 MILE POST →

(FROM INFORMATION IN B.C. ARCHIVES
ATTORNEY GENERAL FILES:
GRO 419, BOX 117, FILE 1906/88)

LT '06

uneventful. A full moon bathed the valley of the South Thompson River in a stark white light, reflecting off the bare silt bluffs on each side of the valley. Shadows cast were ink black blots devoid of contrast.[3]

The CPR's station at Ducks was a railroad passenger, mail and water stop. There was a siding there, and corrals and well built chutes loaded cattle from the many ranches surrounding the railroad stop. Behind the station, and closer to the south bank of the South Thompson River, sat Bostock's store where Shorty Dunn had played the deaf mute. Not a light glimmered from any of the windows on the main or second floors at that late hour. Normally the Imperial Limited didn't stop at Ducks, but that night Callin received a signal from the conductor to be prepared for a short stop. Slowing down on his way into the station, the engineer clearly saw the Ducks station agent and telegrapher William Plumm standing on the platform in the light of a yellow lantern and the full moon. Callin noticed the rail yards and siding were empty, and he had no sooner come to a halt, than he received the signal to proceed. He slowly pulled the throttle towards him, and the train pulled out of the station, gaining speed quickly.[4]

As the train pulled out, two dark figures trotted alongside the front end of the old-style combination express and mail car on the side opposite the station and climbed onto the cars. The train was crewed at the head end by the unsuspecting engineer Callin, a twenty year CPR employee, and fireman Herbert Radcliffe, a five year employee. Both of them were from the railway divisional point at Revelstoke. The train consisted of steam engine #941 with its tender carrying water and coal, a combined express and mail car, an express car, a baggage car, dining car and a number of passenger cars, including a Pullman sleeper. The conductor in charge of the train was Samuel Elliott of Kamloops.[5][6][7]

Engine #941 was a North British compound ten wheeler of a 2-8-0

The robbery at Ducks, 8 May 1906.

Ducks circa 1906, showing station, water tower, cattle-loading chutes and Bostock's store to the right and behind the station.
COURTESY OF VAL AND SANDI PRINGLE COLLECTION, WESTWOLD.

configuration built in Glasgow, Scotland. It was typical of the type of engine running between Revelstoke and Kamloops for the CPR during the first decade of the 20TH century.[8][9]

At 23:15 CPR time, and about half a mile west of Ducks Station, the two masked men, George Edwards and Shorty Dunn, made their way up the ladder of the engine tender, their way lit by the bright moonlight. Behind them in the express-mail car, the Dominion Express Company mail clerk Alexander McQuarrie of New Westminster had just finished making out the mail for the next stop, Kamloops. The hissing of the swaying acetylene lanterns in the car and the clack of the steel wheels on the rail joints covered any outside noises.[10][11]

The stooped, indistinct figures slowly and carefully made their way over the sealed water tank and the coal in the open tender. The coal was low and needed to be stocked up in Kamloops. The bright moon from the south threw dark shadows into the tender, hiding the intruders from the train crew. Then, out of the corner of his eye, Engineer Callin spotted them crouched behind the lower boards that held back the coal. They stepped over the boards and onto the gangway. Each held pistols in both hands, levelled at the two trainmen.[12] [13]

"What the mischief are you fellows doing there?" Callin laughingly called over the working noises of the engine. Radcliffe heard Callin's voice and turned from watching the track ahead of him. The two intruders stood with their legs spread apart to maintain their balance. Callin at first suspected that it was some kind of joke and had spoken to them in a jovial manner.

Both men simultaneously responded, "We are going to rob this train."

The two were dressed in dark clothes, and the leader, George Edwards, wore a black, flat brimmed, felt Stetson with a four-corner pinch, a black handkerchief mask across his nose and below his eyes, and a long black overcoat that reached below his knees. His feet were enclosed in smooth soled, slim boots. His sinister aspect was made even more bizarre with silver wire rimmed and green tinted prospector's goggles covering his eyes. Fireman Radcliffe would later describe the leader as "an elderly fellow about 40 years old, 5 feet 7 inches high, slim build and tattoo marked on back of hand."[14]

The two intruders stepped off the gangway between the engine and tender. Callin tried to joke and laughed at the two masked men, but they were in all seriousness, and the leader quickly set Callin straight. "Hands up. This is no joke, we are going to rob this train. We will tell you where to stop."[15]

"The duce you are," said Callin. "How are you going to do it?" Callin thought he heard an American accent when he heard the bandit leader talk.

The robber responded, "Yes, we are going to rob this train, and we want you to stop a mile past 116."

Callin continued to make light of them, and laughed. However, when the two stepped forward from the platform into the engine cab and held their revolvers closely under the chins of Callin and his fireman, he quickly assumed they were in earnest.[16]

Callin would remember vividly the details of the pistol Edwards pointed at his head.

"I remember as I looked down the muzzle of the revolver in the hands of the leader, making a mental calculation that it was about .38 calibre—not any larger anyway. The gun was of the short bulldog pattern, and was loaded alright, for I could see the ends of the cartridges in all the chambers."[17]

Fireman Radcliffe was covered by the other bandit in the same manner. Callin would later describe this second robber, Shorty Dunn, as short, about 5 feet 6 inches, and dark haired with his face masked with a white spotted, red handkerchief tied beneath his eyes. He wore a ragged sweater of faded blue and heavy hobnailed shoes or boots, and held a heavy calibre revolver on Radcliffe all the time. Radcliffe listened to Dunn talk and mistakenly thought he had a "very clear, distinct voice and a slight Cockney accent."[18]

The older bandit motioned with his pistol for Callin to stand up off his seat.

"Have you got a gun on you? Raise up until I see." Edwards quickly patted him down and searched in the numerous hiding places around his engine seat for any concealed weapons.

The engineer assured him. "I have no gun. You aren't joking, are you?"

"No, we mean it, we are going to rob this train. We want you to stop at the 116 mile board. When we stop we'll cut the coaches off and run ahead a piece. Remember, we wish no harm to you fellows. You are alright, the conductor and everyone on the train, but the CPR is not."[19]

Callin quickly remembered reading that the same comments had been made by the leader of the gang that robbed the CPR train near Mission Junction in September of 1904.

The goggled leader went on issuing orders to Callin. "I want you to stop the train at the 116 mile board."

While Dunn, the shorter one, leaned out the window of the engine to look for the mile board, Callin looked over at Radcliffe and asked him to shut off the steam heat to the cars. Radcliffe hesitated and looked at the goggled bandit leader.

Edwards, covering Callin, asked him why he ordered the steam to be cut off, and Callin replied that it was necessary to cut it off so that the uncoupling of the passenger cars could take place.[20]

Glancing over at Radcliffe, the American agreed. "All right, cut it off. On reaching the spot you have got to cut the coach off and go ahead a distance."

They came up on the 116 mile post fast. Shorty Dunn, leaning out the side of the engine window, called out, "Here's the board, stop."

Dunn suddenly got extremely agitated and stepped towards Callin, pointing his pistol in the engineer's face.

"This is where we stop. Stop, stop, stop!" Dunn was almost frantic as this spot was where they had agreed beforehand to pick up the third bandit, and they were overshooting it.[21]

He moved closer with his pistol and tapped Callin with it, raising his voice with each word, impatient for him to bring the train to a full stop. The train finally came to a full stop about one mile east of the Campbell Ranch. The two bandits were somewhat agitated that they were some distance past where they had wanted to stop.[22]

Dunn ordered the fireman to light his torch from the firebox and climb down onto the ballast grade on the south side of the engine. When the firebox door was opened, Callin could see the reflection of the fire glancing off the leader's goggles. It made a bizarre and sinister picture; the masked bandit, in broad brimmed Stetson, was standing with his feet apart, a pistol in each hand and his long dark rider's coat reaching below his knees. On the ground beside the tracks Dunn had a large calibre revolver in one hand and the shiny new Luger in the other. At gunpoint he escorted Radcliffe to the back end of the first car, the express-mail car. As Dunn and the fireman were making the cut, a third bandit came running out of the brush from the east where the train had overshot his rendezvous point. He had a pistol in one hand and a sack over his back. He joined Dunn, put the sack down, and filled his empty hand with another pistol. He soon jumped to the other side of the train over the coupling to control activities on that side.[23]

While the uncoupling was taking place, CPR Conductor Samuel

Elliott of Kamloops, baggageman H. W. Martin of Vancouver behind him, stood at the open door of the baggage car silhouetted against the glare of the acetylene lanterns. Elliott called out to the men outside. "What's the matter? Has a hose burst out there?"

Shorty Dunn's reply was quick in coming back. "This is not a hose burst, but a holdup. Send a man back to flag any train that may be following. Get your head in or I will blow it off!"[24]

Elliott lost no time in following these orders, which were emphasized with plenty of oaths and cursing by Dunn and the Third Man. The conductor and baggageman could see there was a robber on both sides of the train, each with pistols in both hands .

Elliott, keeping a cool head and remembering his railroad emergency procedures, proceeded to walk back through the cars to get the rear brakeman out on the track behind the rear end to flag any following train. Baggageman Martin followed Elliott to ensure he was not intercepted in his activities by any of the robbers, as a precaution to ensure a collision did not occur. There was no way to know how long the section of train would be stalled on the main line. As they were walking through the cars, they heard the sounds of the car brakes tightening up, indicating to the two that the engine and forward cars had been cut off from the following train. Elliott made a decision not to awaken those passengers that were still sleeping in their berths. As he made his way through the cars, he announced to those passengers that were awake that the train was being robbed and the robbers were cutting off the forward part of the train. Immediately, those passengers not in berths woke their neighbours, and all began scrambling to hide their money and valuables in various and novel places before the bandits could board and enter the passenger cars.[25]

The good Reverend Doctor James Shaver Woodsworth slept the sleep of the just, secure in his berth in the Pullman car and oblivious to the drama taking place around him. He was not to know that a robbery had taken place until after it was all over. It is one of history's small ironies that Canada's premier socialist by conviction should find himself, on that warm spring moonlit night in 1906, not 50 yards away from a notorious western bandit who professed to be an ardent socialist, if only for convenience. It was a coincidence that would be forgotten for 100 years.

George Woods of Vernon, in the forward passenger car, expected the robbers to come storming through the car door, guns in hand, at any minute. Woods commented later that he and the other passengers "were very happily disappointed, as they did not come."[26]

In the passenger car Melbourne next to the dining car, Mr. G. Henderson awoke from a doze and was puzzled as he thought the train had stopped at Kamloops, but he couldn't recognize the

J.S. Woodsworth, founding member of Canada's C.C.F. party. Courtesy of Saskatchewan NDP photo archives.

landscape outside. Henderson, who worked for the Victoria Public Works department, was not to know a robbery had occurred until the next morning at breakfast in the dining car.[27]

Back at the head end, Edwards was standing in the right-hand gangway, the same side as Callin, and trying to see what Shorty and the fireman were doing behind the combination car.

Callin said to him, "You are looking out this side?" Callin continued, "I will have to go to the other side to get the fireman's signal."

Edwards said, "Alright, step over," and Callin made his way to the south side of the cab, covered all the while by the bandit's pistol.

Callin knew in the confusion and pressure that both he and Radcliffe were under, it would be necessary to watch both sides to see the fireman's signal. Callin saw Dunn and the fireman with his torch at the back end of the first car making the cut as he had assumed. The engine was blowing off steam and Callin could hear nothing from the outside. As he sat in the fireman's seat looking back to the tail end, Callin noticed a third figure 40 or 50 yards away, carrying an angular sack, quickly emerging into the bright moonlight from the sagebrush and trees. He ran across the field at the south side of the train and made his way toward Dunn and Radcliffe at the rear of the first car. It was the Third Man catching up to his compatriots on the stopped train. Mail clerk McQuarrie, peering out of the mail car and puzzled over the unscheduled stop, also spotted the Third Man as he ran across the field. He didn't think anything more of it and assumed it was a broken hose or something else had gone wrong with the train. He retired to his bunk to try to get a few minutes sleep before arriving in Kamloops.[28][29]

Edwards, from his viewpoint at the other engine window on the north side, called across to Callin loudly, "They are giving the signal on this side."

Callin stepped back to his seat and saw the signal from Radcliffe to slack back to release the tension on the coupling. Passing a glance over the bandit leader, Callin saw from the light of the firebox a tattoo at the base of the robber's thumb.[30]

After successfully uncoupling the express-mail car from the express car, the fireman and Dunn, joined now by the Third Man, went back to the waiting engine and climbed aboard.[31]

As the last member of the robber trio, the Third Man climbed onto the engine gangway and threw his sack onto the engine deck. The dull orange light from the engine's firebox, left open when Radcliffe had lighted his torch, reflected for an instant full on the uncovered portion of the Third Man's face, and then he too drew a pistol to hold on the crewmen. He had ineptly attempted to cover his features by having the neck of his sweater pulled up and tethered with strings tied over his head, and the makeshift disguise had slipped. A slouch hat was jammed over his head. However, his eyes, nose, moustache and beard had been exposed. Callin saw a man of about thirty years of age, about 5 feet 10 inches tall with a light reddish moustache and a slight reddish beard on a thin, ruddy face. Radcliffe thought he was about forty years old. He wore heavy leather hobnailed boots covered with the dust of the dry soils of the surrounding countryside. During the rest of the robbery, Callin would notice that the Third Man would carry two pistols, one in each hand. Callin and Radcliffe watched the robbers going about their business, noticing how cool all three gunmen were and how they seemed to know exactly what they were doing. While they seemed to act as old hands at this type of work with plenty of experience, they also noticed that Dunn and the Third Man were obviously in the command of Edwards and waited on his every word.[32][33]

However, the perceived experience displayed by the train robbers would not save them from turning a well planned train robbery into a debacle. When Fireman Radcliffe had uncoupled the first car behind the tender, a fatal error on the part of the robbers had occurred. The car directly behind the tender was an older style combined mail and express car. This car, complete with the engine and tender, had been uncoupled from the rest of the train, which included the main express car. Unbeknownst to the robbers, the combined express-mail car was only carrying mails, and they had mistakenly identified it as the express car. The CPR had experienced a heavy run of mail for the Pacific and had added on the old car specifically to handle it. The express car was the next in line, but it would inadvertently be left behind.

After the return of the robbers to the engine with the fireman, the leader ordered Callin to continue west in the direction of Kamloops, leaving the uncoupled cars, passengers and the rest of the crew behind. The three bandits crowded into the engine cab with Callin and Radcliffe, and Dunn kept an eye out the south side of engine.

"I want you to stop at that flume alongside the track," said Dunn, referring to a flume on the Campbell Ranch used for distributing water to the various fields around the main ranch. Dunn moved close behind the fireman, and Edwards took up a position behind Callin. The Third Man stayed back on the gangway.

"Just beyond the rancher's crossing?" asked Callin.

Engine # 907, similar to Ducks robbery engine # 941. No photo has yet been found of the robbery locomotive. COURTESY OF B.C. ARCHIVES.

"Yes, that is the place."

Edwards continued to reassure the nervous head end crew. "Remember, we wish no harm to you fellows, all we want is what is in that mail car."

After about two miles, and two to three hundred yards west of Campbell's Crossing, the short train stopped again. It was just west of the Campbell's ranch house. Dunn ordered Radcliffe to light his torch again from the firebox. [34]

"Get a light and both of you come down with us."

Callin queried, "We had better have the brakes set!"

Edwards agreed. "Yes, set her tight."

The two crewmen jumped down onto the ballast of the railway

grade on the north side of the engine, joining Edwards and the Third Man. The Third Man was carrying his angular sack over his shoulder, a pistol in his other hand, and his face was now covered with a handkerchief mask. The Third Man walked around to the other side of the engine to keep a watch on the side nearest the riverbank. Shorty Dunn, keeping the crew covered with his two pistols as they left the engine, followed them out. The four of them then made their way back past the engine tender.[35]

The bandit leader stopped them at the back of the tender tank and said to Radcliffe, "You go to the door and tell those fellows to get out, tell them if they don't get out we have dynamite enough here to blow them out."[36]

Radcliffe and Callin knocked at the slightly open door at the head end of the mail car, all the while calling to the clerks to tell them someone was outside that wanted to see them. The mail clerks, Alexander McQuarrie and Walter Willis of Vancouver, both worked for the Dominion Express Company, a subsidiary of the CPR. The two clerks were on their way through from Calgary, and Willis was the registration clerk in charge of the car. However, Willis was sound asleep at the time and was unaware of the dramatic events which had transpired over the past few minutes. McQuarrie quietly woke him to tell him they were in trouble. McQuarrie and Willis stayed quiet in the car, Willis in his nightclothes. Radcliffe hammered at the door which was open a bit, but got no answer.[37][38]

"Every man come out!" yelled Shorty Dunn.[39]

"Never mind, I heard a voice in here," announced one of the robbers, pointing to the door at the mail end of the car, farther back towards the tail end. They moved back, and that door started to open.

When Mail Clerk McQuarrie opened the side door of the car, the three robbers and the train crew were plainly visible to his left in the clear light of the moon. McQuarrie cautiously asked them what they wanted.[40]

The masked bandit in the long black overcoat and the flat Stetson barked at the two clerks, "Hands up, and climb down out of that and be quick about it! If there is anyone else in the car, tell him to come out."[41]

Both McQuarrie and his dazed partner, with their arms straight over their heads, awkwardly made their way down from the car. Willis, in his nightclothes, started to shiver in the cool night air of early spring as a slight breeze came down off the hills to the southwest.

Edwards watched the unfortunate Willis and extended his concern to him. "I am sorry to have to keep you out in this condition, but we won't hold you long." [42]

Dunn asked the two clerks, "Have you got a gun on you?"

The robbers then searched the mail clerks for weapons and found none. They didn't realize that the CPR armed only their express clerks, not the mail clerks.[43]

Dunn then said to the two clerks, "Boys, you can put your hands down. We don't want you to fly away just yet."[44]

The Third Man, hanging back at the south side of the car, called, "Are they all out?"

Dunn replied, "Yes, all out."

The Third Man walked around the end of the car and joined Edwards and Dunn, Callin and Radcliffe, and Willis and McQuarrie. He dropped his sack at their feet, then reached into a pocket and pulled out another revolver, pointing both pistols at the hapless train crew.

The robbers soon determined that while Willis was the mail clerk in charge, McQuarrie was the clerk responsible for the registered mail and any valuables in shipment.[45]

Edwards ordered McQuarrie to precede him back into the mail car which was brightly lit by three of the four acetylene lamps. He demanded McQuarrie show him the pouches with the red stripes. This struck McQuarrie as significant. As only American registered mail was carried in red-striped pouches, McQuarrie quickly reached the conclusion that at least this robber was probably an American. At gunpoint he pulled some five sacks of mail into the middle of the car floor. McQuarrie closely watched the man, noting his quick movements and distinct voice tones. He was able to take long and detailed looks at the bandit leader while being covered by the snub

Ducks station shortly after the robbery, and the name has been changed to Monte Creek. Courtesy of Val and Sandi Pringle Collection, Westwold.

nosed pistol in his unwavering hand. He held the pistol in his left hand and seemed to be trying to cover up something below the knuckle on his left thumb. Afterwards, McQuarrie was to learn of the distinct tattoo in that location. He noticed that, as the bandit swept his gaze around the interior of the car, his head struck a highly individualistic pose, assumed when he was deep in thought. The bandit wore a long black or blue-black overcoat, tight across the chest, and a black, felt, flat brimmed hat, and McQuarrie judged he was about 55 years of age and 135 pounds. His thin hands were heavily sunburnt as if he spent considerable time outdoors, and he wore a black woollen mask over his lower face which only partially contained his moustaches. The mask was topped with prospector's goggles. Standing at the mail sorting table, McQuarrie was surprised to see the bandit's mask slip down his face to below his chin. From about 18 inches away, McQuarrie noticed his cavalry style moustache, appearing somewhat of an amber colour, as if being stained by pipe tobacco. His thin face was heavily tanned, marked and weather-beaten, and sported a growth of whiskers. The robber quickly shielded his face with his arm while he adjusted his mask, but this action displaced the goggles, and McQuarrie saw that his eyes were a watery blue. The robber acted in a very cool and collected manner, as if robbing trains was a well-rehearsed affair, and did not let the lapse in his disguise faze him. His pistol was a short bulldog type six shot revolver with a metal coloured barrel.[46]

Quickly McQuarrie's mind went back to descriptions he had seen given by the Dominion Express mail clerk who had been robbed during the Mission Junction robbery two years previously, on the 10TH of September in 1904. Mail clerk William Thorburn's description of the leader of the Mission Junction robbers was very similar to that of the man standing in front of McQuarrie, his features well defined in the stark white light of the hissing acetylene lamps. McQuarrie remembered that rumour had it at that time that the Mission Junction bandit leader was old Bill Miner.

"Where is the box?" barked the robber, holding his pistol to the clerk's head.

"What box?" replied McQuarrie.

"The express box. Haven't we got the express car?"

"There is no box, this is the mail car," replied McQuarrie.

"Have you an express car?" the bandit repeated.

McQuarrie asked him how many cars had been cut off.

"One."

"Well, the express car is not on and we have left it behind."

"Then give me the registered parcels and be damn quick about it."

McQuarrie made sure he gave the bandit only those pouches that were readily visible and piled them on the sorting table in the middle of the car. The robber ordered McQuarrie to assist him, and they opened all the registered mail sacks and dumped out the registered mail.[47]

In a disappointed voice he asked, "Is that all the registered mail stuff there is?"

"Yes, I guess that is all there is. The mail is light today."

Edwards stuck his pistol in McQuarrie's face and told him that he didn't want any fooling. McQuarrie replied that was all he knew of.

The robber took four registered letter packages, three addressed to Victoria, and stuffed them in his right coat pocket.

He held his pistol to McQuarrie's face and threatened, "I don't want any fooling."[48]

He asked McQuarrie if there weren't any money packages on board, and McQuarrie said that there might be, he really didn't know.

"Where is the Frisco mail?"

"We never carry the San Francisco mail. It does not go around this way anyway."

McQuarrie went on to tell the robber that he was not the express clerk, and again that the express car had been left behind.

"Which way would the Frisco mail go, then?" questioned the bandit.

"It would either go via Portal or by Mission and Newport," replied McQuarrie.[49]

"Mission Junction?"

"Yes."

This reference to San Francisco mail probably refers to the relief funds collected by Canadian charities for the victims of the devastating earthquake on 18 April 1906. These collections had been well publicized, and considerable funds had been collected from rich and poor alike. Edwards had been informed of the disaster by Albert Duck, and he had read of the funds being collected all across Canada.

The leader forced McQuarrie to open a sealed package about the size of a gold brick and which, to his expressed disappointment, held small boxes containing medicine bottles filled with Catarrh Cure.

He took one, exclaiming, "This may come in handy," and put it in his left-hand pocket.[50]

Edwards, clearly frustrated with the lack of success so far, swept his gaze around the car. He saw the letter filing case at the far end of the mail section of the car and asked the mail clerk what was in the pigeonholes. McQuarrie told him it was only ordinary regular mail of no value whatsoever. As Edwards turned his attention away, McQuarrie breathed a silent sigh of relief as the registered letters in the filing pigeonholes contained between $35,000 and $45,000 worth of cash.[51]

He then asked McQuarrie whether there was anyone or anything at the other end of the car but was told it was empty except for some "dead head paper mail." Swearing profusely, the robber forced the clerk to open up that section anyway, only to find it as McQuarrie had told him.[52]

Clerk Willis was then ordered to follow the bandit leader back into the mail car to verify McQuarrie's statements. As Willis had not heard the conversations between McQuarrie and the bandit, he found himself in a bit of a quandary.

Gesturing at the registered mail sacks strewn about the floor, the bandit asked, "Is that all the registered mail?"

Willis took a chance and answered, "I guess that is all there is," satisfying the robber as to the truthfulness of McQuarrie and giving Willis relief from his anxiety.

Keeping his pistol hard on Willis, the bandit strode around the car looking for further loot and spotted a bulging red-striped sack at the back of the car. He ordered Willis to fetch it and open it. Willis informed him that it only contained more empty sacks, and when it was opened, the robber was disgusted to see a number of empty red-striped bags tumble out.

The robber then demanded of Willis that he be shown the express safe and other express items being shipped. Willis then informed him that this combination mail and express car did not carry any express on this trip and that the express items were in the car that had been left behind when the train had been uncoupled.

"Oh, hell!" cursed the bandit.

Edwards stood for a moment in the centre of the car, his stance reflecting considerable annoyance, frustration and disappointment. Then he went to the open door of the car and said something to the other two bandits standing outside with the train crew, all the while keeping his eye on Willis. However, it was only a short time later that Willis and McQuarrie saw the leader regain his former confident manner, and he became even cheerful and, at times, sarcastic. The bandit leader had quickly reached the conclusion that they had made a blunder and had indeed left the express car behind. From overhearing conversations between the bandits, the clerks were able to determine that the robbers had expected to find both the mail and the express in one car, and that a "big haul" was believed to have been on board.

Once a month, two gold bars from the Daly Reduction Mill at the Nickel Plate Mine above Hedley were shipped by freight wagon and special escort the 50 miles to Penticton. The security of the bars was the responsibility of the Dominion Express Company, and through them, the CPR itself. Each gold bar was worth at least $30,000 to $40,000 in 1906 dollars and constituted a considerable haul if intercepted and captured by bandits. Edwards and Dunn had both spent considerable time in Hedley City and were well acquainted with the routine used to ship the gold.[53]

Although no evidence has been found to substantiate it, it is possible that the two gold bars were either in the express car left behind or on the second section of train No. 97.[54]

While the leader and the mail clerks were involved within the mail car, Callin had noticed the angular sack that the Third Man had been carrying. He asked Shorty Dunn what was in the sack.

The robber responded, "Dynamite. We have enough here to blow this car and the train to Hell!"[55]

The robber went on, "Aren't you running ahead of time tonight?" Dunn was referring to the fact that the train had been perceived by the bandits as being ahead of schedule.

Callin replied, "No, right on time."

Dunn reiterated again. "You are earlier than usual."

"Yes," responded Callin, "That is owing to this train having run somewhat late for the past several days; from one to four hours late."

Dunn went on. "They are running all kinds of trains. What does it mean?"

Callin explained that a double service was now running with two trains making up what was formerly only one. [56]

Shorty Dunn, acting in a jocular, impatient manner, called to

Edwards up in the car, "Come, come, Shorty, you are a long time in there."

Edwards jumped down out of the car after Willis and walked over to the two mail clerks. He told them he hoped they wouldn't lose their jobs over this incident and made some additional remarks to them indicating his concern. No doubt Edwards was remembering the unfortunate Express Clerk Herbert Mitchell who was fired by the CPR's Dominion Express Company after the Mission robbery.[57]

Having obtained all he felt was available to them, Edwards called "All aboard," and ordered Willis and McQuarrie back aboard the combination car. The three robbers and the two head end crew walked back along the ballast to the engine. As they climbed aboard, Edwards was the last man, and he picked up the sack of "Giant" dynamite to pass to Dunn. Dunn told him to leave it there as it was no longer necessary to take it along with them. He cautioned him to set it on the ground easy.[58]

With all back aboard, Callin released the brakes and with a hiss of steam, the engine, tender and combination car slowly started west again.

Alone in the combination car, McQuarrie and Willis expressed their relief and congratulated each other. They had prevented the robbers from obtaining a great deal of loot from the registered mail in the pigeonholes, as well as other valuable registered mail in lock bags that were not readily visible to the bandit leader. Unlike the unfortunate Dominion Express clerk Mitchell on the Mission Junction robbery, McQuarrie and Willis would keep their jobs. However, the next few weeks would find them doing more travelling and meeting more people than either ever expected.

Ahead in the engine, Callin asked the dark clad leader, "How far do you want to go?"

Edwards responded, "I will tell you when to stop."

The train crew took the engine and tender further west on the line about a mile and a half. Dunn saw a small fire burning on the beach.[59]

"That will do," said Shorty, and they pulled to a stop between the 119 and 120 mile boards just west of the Campbell Ranch railway crossing and one and a half miles east of the Furrer siding. At the turn of the last century, the Furrer siding was the first one east of Kamloops.

The train crew commented later that the point where the bandits took their leave was a spot where it would be difficult to determine just exactly where and how the robbers' escape route was taken. They could have taken their choice of two roads to the south and east. The first led back to Ducks and Shuswap Station near what is now Chase, and the second made its way to the Upper Campbell Creek-Grande Prairie road. They also could have crossed the South Thompson River, now shallow before the spring freshet, and made their way north in a circle to Kamloops or Chase. The option to head west towards Kamloops was not open as that was the way from which any pursuit would emanate.

The robbers disembarked and stood at the north side of the railway grade between the tracks and the river with the moonlight full on them and waved to the train crew.

The leader sang out over the sounds of the standing engine, "Well, so long, young fellow," looking full at Callin in the engineer's seat, "Take care of yourselves. Goodnight, boys."

Callin called back, "We certainly will. Goodbye!"[60]

And with that, they climbed over the fence and made their way on foot in the moonlight into the brush, poplars and ponderosa pines bordering the riverbank. It was only 18 minutes after Edwards and Dunn had held their pistols at Callin and Radcliffe just west of Ducks. They had obtained $15.50 in cash from the registered letters and a bottle of Catarrh Cure for their efforts of the past four weeks.

Safely after the robbers had made their escape, the crew backed the train up to re-connect with the stranded cars and passengers. When passing by the site of the second stop, they stopped to retrieve the sack containing the dynamite. It contained four or five large 40% Giant dynamite sticks with caps and fuses attached. In a smaller sack within the large one, five short sticks of Burleigh dynamite were found. They too had caps and fuses attached and were ready to go.[61 62]

The crew quickly had the rest of the train coupled together, and after waiting to build up air in the brake lines through the train, they made their way without delay towards Kamloops. Walter Campbell, with his cowboys feeling no pain and with his father's delinquent herd of cattle, watched the train rushing through the night and passing them by between the wagon road and the river. One of the cowboys remarked that No. 97 seemed to be a bit late. The train finally pulled in to Kamloops at 0:30 hours, CPR time.[63]

XIII
B.C. PROVINCIAL POLICE PURSUIT

EARLY MORNING, WEDNESDAY, 9 MAY 1906

Constable William Fernie had married a local girl, Mary Isabel Lyle, in Kamloops in September, 1905. Less than one year after their marriage, Mary was to find her husband embroiled in the first of what were to be many spectacular manhunts he was to confront during his long career in the B.C. Provincial Police. They were both asleep when after midnight on May 9TH they were awakened by a CPR call boy banging on their door. Breathless, the boy stammered out to Fernie that the CPR train had been robbed east of town and that he was to come quickly down to the CPR station. Fernie dressed and buckled on his Boer War Sam Browne belt and holster holding his five shot .38 calibre Smith and Wesson revolver. He slung a bandolier of rifle cartridges across his shoulders and placed his woollen cavalry cloak over his shoulders and a flat brimmed Stetson on his head. He picked up the satisfying weight of his Winchester carbine as he went out the door. Saddling his thoroughbred cross with a western style saddle, he quickly rode down to the station. He discussed the happenings to the east with the agitated station agent Frank Hayden and then rode over to the house of his commanding officer, Chief Constable Ernest T.W. Pearse.[1]

Earlier, Pearse had been rudely aroused from his slumbers by the same call boy pounding on his door. When Pearse opened the door, the call boy blurted out his message. "Mr. Hayden says #97 has been held up near Furrer and wants to know what you're going to do about it."

Pearse asked the boy a few more questions, then hurried into his clothes and went off to the station. He hadn't gone thirty yards from his gate when he met Fernie riding toward him. Fernie told Pearse that station agent Hayden had told him a light engine and caboose were waiting at the yards in Kamloops to take Pearse and the crew of the robbed train back to the robbery scene. The Imperial Limited had changed crews in Kamloops, and the Revelstoke crew would normally have been staying over in Kamloops until called for another eastbound train.[2]

Fernie and Pearse had some discussion on the spot about how they should commence pursuit of the bandits. It was decided that Fernie would immediately go over to the Kamloops Indian Reserve on the north side of the South Thompson and recruit some of the trackers that Fernie had used so effectively in his previous law enforcement activities. Fernie rode over the Red Bridge and roused two of his most trusted trackers. Michelle Le Camp and Alec Ignace were well known to Fernie, and he had a close relationship with both. They were known as excellent hunters and trackers and were dependable and dogged in following sign. Both spoke only Shuswap, but Fernie easily communicated with them in a mixture of Shuswap, English and Chinook Jargon. As he rode out with them, he left word with others on the reserve that he wished to have four more join him out at Campbell's Ranch as soon as possible. The vague possibility of a reward was mentioned.[3]

Immediately Pearse arrived at the station, he started to take charge. He greeted station agent Hayden and commenced to take a first statement from engineer Callin. He questioned Callin closely on the appearances of the three bandits, and the descriptions and statements were typed up in the station by one of the employees on night shift. Pearse gave a copy of the description to Hayden and had the incident and the description telegraphed to his superior in Victoria, Superintendent F. S. Hussey. Callin passed over to Pearse the sack of dynamite picked up beside the tracks, and Pearse immediately passed it on to Hayden for safekeeping. By 1:30 A.M. Pearse had finished his priority tasks, boarded the engine with the Revelstoke crew, and by 2:25 A.M. they had arrived just east of the Furrer siding. At about half a mile east of the Furrer mile board, Callin pointed out to Pearse where he had seen the robbers for the last time. He described to Pearse how the robbers had got off the north side of the locomotive, climbed the fence, and run off into the brush beside the river. The Chief Constable and the train crew got down off the engine on the north side of the tracks. The moon was still shining brightly, and it was too early for lamps to be seen at the Campbell ranch house or bunkhouses a couple of miles to the east. The engine softly hissed and clanked beside them, and the quietness and tranquility of the scene betrayed no recollection of the drama that had played out just a few hours previously. But even to the untrained eyes of Pearse and the crew, the bright moonlight made it easy to discern the tracks walking a trail running between the railroad fence and the brush beside the river. Pearse and Conductor Lawson looked around the brush and the large culvert close by, but could find nothing else. Pearse instructed everyone to stay away from the tracks and walk about as little as possible until Fernie and his trackers arrived.[4]

Pearse then ordered everyone aboard again, and they steamed back to the spot where the train had been stopped the second time. It was only a few hundred yards from Lew Campbell's house and close to Campbell's Crossing of the main line where the rancher accessed the river. The light was still not good enough to look for tracks, so Pearse took Conductor Lawson with him and went over to Lew Campbell's stables to check on his horses. In the stable Pearse found five horses. The two heavy drafts were cool and dry, but the three saddle horses were hot and sweaty, and two saddles were thrown carelessly and apparently hurriedly on the floor beside the door. The boys had been impatient to hit the sack. Pearse went over to the ranch house and woke up rancher Lew Campbell. After being questioned, the patriarch told Pearse that his son Walter, Alvy Shaeffer, Lou Fox and George Hughes had gone into town the night before to retrieve a wayward herd of his cows. With the rancher, Pearse went to the bunkhouse and woke up the sleeping partiers, dazed and confused. The cowboys, a bit sick to the stomach and with their heads spinning, tried to make some sense out of the confrontation they found themselves in. Alvy told them they had not been back long, and George told them they had been to the Montreal Hotel and had not reached home until 2:00 or 2:30 A.M. They had met #97 steaming by them as they passed the W.W. Shaw house east of Kamloops. Pearse questioned them whether they had run into anything suspicious along the wagon road, but the cowboys told them they had seen nothing and met no one. Pearse left them, leaving the cowboys a little the worse for wear, and questioning what had really happened to them early that morning. Lew Campbell's son Walter, dead to the world in his mother's house further up the creek, slept the sleep of the blissfully ignorant. Pearse and the conductor walked back to the waiting engine and crew and took the locomotive west up the track to where they had first stopped and where they hoped Fernie had arrived with his native trackers.[5]

Fernie and his two Indian trackers had made their way down the south side of the river on the wagon road alongside the railway. They watched the dust in the road for strange sign. Whenever something was spotted, Fernie and the Indians dismounted and knelt in the dust to check it out. All they saw were the hoofprints of a herd of cattle and the tracks of the shod horses of the cowboys driving them. As they rode along in the moonlight, the silhouettes of the disparate trio reflected a contrast of cultures. Fernie rode erect and cavalry style on his tall and high-stepping thoroughbred cross, his cavalry cloak flapping out behind him when a light breeze came along, brass cartridges across his chest glinting in the white light. The trackers rode closer to their mounts, hunched over with their legs hanging far down the sides of their short, stocky Indian ponies. The single commonality was their flat brimmed Stetsons with the four-cornered Montana Pinch. The south Thompson slid silently by beside them, flashes of moonlight reflecting in its current.

As they approached Furrer, they could see the dim tail end lights of the engine tender. Shuswap tracker Phillip Toma had caught up to Fernie, and together they dismounted and hitched their horses to the fence separating them from the rail line. Fernie walked over to the engine and met with Chief Constable Pearse. Pearse and the train crew with him pointed out to Fernie and his trackers the spoor of the three men beside the fence. They saw the sign of two men in hobnailed boots and one in a pair of smaller, slim, smooth soled boots. Fernie and his trackers followed the movements of the three bandits back and forth along the right-of-way, tracing their movements. There was a large culvert nearby that went under the main line and down to the river nearby, and the robbers had made their way back and forth through this culvert. Pearse showed them the remains of a small fire, still hot and smoldering, north of the railway and on the beach beside the river. The fire was close to the culvert that went under the tracks, and the prints of three men were visible around it. Fernie and the trackers cast about in circles, but could not pick up any spoor leading away from the spot. Pearse and the crew got back aboard and went back to Campbell's place again. Fernie and the Indians rode up the wagon road to meet them. They met at the 118 mile board, but could make no sense of the tracks spread about in the ballast and hard gravel of the rail bed. On the north side of the track and close to the rail, Pearse picked up a package of Munyon's Kidney Cure which contained a bottle of small white pills. Pearse and the engine crew then went on to Ducks Station to pick up orders, while Constable Fernie and his Indian trackers went to the Campbell Ranch bunkhouse for breakfast.[6]

As Fernie and the trackers had ridden to meet Pearse at the 118 Mile board, Fernie had noticed tracks coming down and crossing the road from a large gulley to the south. The tracks were of hobnailed boots, and they were heading towards the railway. Fernie and the Indians dismounted and studied them closely. They cautiously backtracked them a distance up the gulley, all the while trying to get Pearse's attention. Finally they left the tracks for later followup and returned to meet the rest of the party at the crossing. The train crew had picked up a boat at Ducks Station. Fernie and two trackers left their horses behind, and the engine took him and two trackers west towards Furrer Siding. They took the little rowboat across the river to check for tracks. They walked the banks for about a mile east and west and were able to eliminate any escape to the north across the river. They returned to the south bank to find the rest of the party had moved back to Campbell's place. Fernie and the two natives walked east along the rails, and Le Camp pointed out to Fernie the marks of hobnailed boots in the ties on the south side of the rails. Ignace pointed out hobnailed tracks on the north side of the ties also, and they followed them all the way to Campbell's Crossing.[7]

Fernie and Pearse conferred at the crossing. Pearse told him that he had taken tracker Philip Toma east with him on the engine to close to mile board 116 to see what they could pick up there. Phillip Toma found the tracks of the Third Man, running to catch up to the train as it passed the 116 Mile board, but could make no sense of any of the other sign they found as the ground was too hard and gravelly. Fernie told Pearse of the tracks his party had found, and Pearse agreed that Fernie should follow up on them.

Fernie, with Ignace and Le Camp, retrieved their horses and went to the spot at the bottom of the gulley where they had seen the tracks heading to the railway. They dismounted and led their horses as they backtracked on this sign for about a mile to the south towards Barnes Flats near Upper Campbell Creek. The steep sides of the clay cliffs beside them were turning a dull grey as dawn started to break, and the pines on the close horizon to the east started to take on features against the lightening sky. All of a sudden they saw tracks coming in from the side and heading south, away from the railroad. They followed them carefully until they came to the Kamloops to Vernon wagon road. Fernie and his trackers were elated. They had intercepted the escape route of the robbers and had made the first breakthrough in pursuing the bandits.[8]

During the time Fernie and the Indians were backtracking up the gulley, Pearse was kept busy running the crew and engine up and down the line between Ducks Station and the Furrer siding, picking up orders and letting freights go by. He and his party parked the engine at the siding at Furrer and picked up CPR Divisional Superintendent Thomas Kilpatrick from Revelstoke as he and his car were dropped off. He had been telegraphed from the Kamloops station about the robbery, and he had left on the first freight west with his private car on the tail end. Leaving Kilpatrick's car in the siding, Pearse ran up to Ducks station for more orders, then back to Furrer siding to let a freight through. When he was in Ducks that time, he picked up trainmaster W. Elson from Revelstoke who had come in on the freight following Kilpatrick. Back at the Furrer siding again, Pearse and his party checked out the riverbanks on both sides, finding nothing. He directed the trackman to take the boat down river to Kamloops, checking all the while for signs of a party having landed on the banks. Pearse then ordered the engine and crew, with Kilpatrick's car behind, to head back to Kamloops. When Pearse pulled into town, "hot, tired, dirty and hungry" at 11:30 A.M., he attended to telegrams and other business in his Provincial Police office and then went home where he had a hot bath. He was just having some lunch when he got a message from Fernie that he and his Indians were hot on "their tracks sure" and to send some help out to Valentine Curry's market garden and nursery near Upper Campbell Creek on the Kamloops to Vernon wagon road.[9]

Fernie, Le Camp and Ignace were halted at the edge of that wagon road, having lost the spoor. They walked back and forth along both sides of the dusty road, casting about for sign or track, and could not find where the robbers had crossed the road. They spent three hours there trying to see some sign. Ignace squatted beside the dusty road. He lay down and peered across the road into the midday sun. He suddenly started to laugh and spouted off a string of Shuswap, Chinook and sign language. He frantically waved Fernie over to him, saying, "Nail shoes!" He pointed out to Fernie little crescents in the dust. With a huge grin of satisfaction, he mimicked how the robbers managed to cross the road with little or no sign. He squatted on his heels with his back to the road. Maintaining his balance, he duck-walked on his heels across the road to the other side. His tracks were only small crescents in the dust, resembling nothing like the track of a human shoe or boot. He got Fernie down on his knees to peer closely at the crescents that the robbers had made, and there in the dust, just visible at the top of the dirt crescents, were the small marks made by the hobnails. On the other side of the road, after careful study in the grass and dirt, they found the sign they were looking for. There were the two pairs of hobnailed boots and a pair of smaller, slimmer, smooth soled boots. In the heel of one of the hobnailed boots were four shorter nails in the form of a cross. The nails in one pair were set all over the soles, and the nails in the other pair were fewer and tacked in lines. The tracks crossed other roads, and the same method was used by the bandits to cross, or they jumped from one side to the other. The trackers would lose the trail then pick it up again when circling ahead.[10]

They alternately found and lost the tracks all across the flats above the South Thompson valley around by Upper Campbell Creek. They crossed Curry's creek and skirted by Valentine Curry's nursery and market garden. They tracked them through fields on Curry's farm and across Curry's Flat. Fernie was confident they were hot on the trail and sent word to Pearse in Kamloops to come quickly with additional manpower and supplies. They saw where the bandits had jumped and duck-walked across the roads and pack trails. The suspects had set up dummy trails and blind trails, cut false blazes, stuck to hard ground, and split up and came back together. Fernie, Michelle Le Camp and Alex Ignace doggedly stuck to their trail, losing it, casting ever widening circles to pick them up again, and through persistence and skill, always managed to find the spoor again. All the while the robbers were heading due south into the high country on the horizon. It was a lonely area of increasingly heavy timber, high and steep hills and sparse population. Near Buse's ranch the posse found a camp that had been used by the robbers. The camp was in a secluded place and had been used for some time.[11][12]

They followed the trail of the three robbers alongside a little lake to "Dalton's Cabin," which was not being used at the time. It was boarded up and locked. As the tracks leading up to this point had been indistinct and blurred, the posse couldn't make a guess as to the probable sequence of events that may have taken place. They had to remain ignorant of any intent on the part of the robbers, and they worked their way cautiously and quietly towards the cabin. Fernie made his way around the back to see if there was any exit or window at that side and was just coming back around to the front when he saw Ignace frantically signalling him to be cautious. They crept up to the front door and found the new padlock had been broken off and was lying on the ground. Fernie drew his pistol, signed to Ignace and Le Camp to stand on either side of the door, and Fernie kicked open the door, fully expecting the robbers to come rushing out. However, the dark interior of the cabin was quiet. Fernie entered with his revolver held out in front of him, and they found everything inside had been disturbed and thrown around. Clothing had been scattered about as if the robbers had been looking for a change of apparel. They were reassured that the robbers had been there and quickly mounted up again. The trio easily found the tracks of the robbers leaving the cabin and crossing the road going up to Campbell's Meadows. Fernie called a halt at that time, and they went into Buse's ranch to get some food and rest.[13]

In Kamloops, Pearse had received Fernie's message that he was hot on the trail of the bandits. He immediately took the opportunity to send a wire.

Canadian Pacific Railway Company's Telegraph
Kamloops, B.C. May 9th, 1906

F.S. Hussey, Sup't Prov'l Police, Victoria
Just returned think we are on track.
Every effort being expected.

Pearse.
3:52 p.m.[14]

Pearse telephoned Kilpatrick at the CPR station, asking if he wished to accompany him and his men east onto the trail of the train robbers. Superintendent Kilpatrick agreed at once. Pearse put a party together, grabbed his pistol, and with Fred Coke driving, left in a buggy to pick up Kilpatrick and Trainmaster Elson. Together with mounted riders Sheriff Wentworth Wood, two cowboys from the Campbell Ranch, Special Constables F. E. Carter and R. Blair, and Shuswap Indian tracker Phillip Toma, they started off to Curry's place. Arriving there, they found Fernie had moved on and finally caught up to him at the Buse's ranch. The two officers brought each other up to date on progress both in Kamloops and on the trail. Pearse made arrangements with the Buses for a hot meal and advised Fernie of the three rewards offered totalling $11,500. Fernie passed this bit of news along to his trackers and the Specials and cowboys in the posses. They were now doubly motivated to stick with their search and to capture the escaping bandits. Pearse also told Fernie that many Special Constables had been sworn in and were leading posses of cowpunchers and trackers throughout the area, watching roads and trails and patrolling in the hills. Pearse sent Dick Blair with his double rig full of grub around the hills to the west and told him to take the main wagon road up into Campbell's Meadows. As the track of the robbers seemed to veer constantly south, he was confident they would eventually end up in Campbell's Meadows in the high plateau country above them.[15]

Near Buse's the posse found the camp close to Campbell Creek that the robbers used for the few days immediately prior to the robbery. It was in a secluded area and free from casual observation. The ashes of the fire were cold. The searchers could see that three horses had been held at that location for some time, as the ground had been packed down hard. Several wooden stakes were found driven into the ground for picketing out the horses. The trail leaving the camp headed straight for the horizon and the Campbell Range.[16]

From Buse's, the combined posse, on foot and leading their horses in the steep terrain, picked up the trail again and followed it south up to the top of the rocky escarpment above the valley at the edge of the high country. About four miles north of Campbell's Meadows, they found a small camp at a spring just below the summit. They could see that horses had been used by the suspects from that point, and they continued to follow the trail of the robbers south up onto the plateau of the high country until it was too dark to see. Their horses were exhausted and needed feed and water. Fernie and his two trackers found an empty cabin once owned by a Short in Campbell's Meadows, and there they spent their first night out on the trail. Pearse and his men stayed at Joe Greaves' place.[17 18]

THURSDAY, 10 MAY 1906

When Fernie and Ignace got up the next morning, they saw that Michelle Le Camp had already left the camp and was out making his own reconnaissance. They left the rest of the search party behind and went ahead to catch up to Le Camp. They soon ran into him carrying news of fresh tracks, and Fernie and Ignace followed him to where he had found the trail of three men leading a horse. They followed the tracks for about 200 yards or so, still in a southerly direction, and then the tracks seemed to split up and the sign became confusing to follow. Looking to the south through the morning haze, the men could see the looming heights of the Monte Hills rising in the distance. They circled around for a few hours trying to pick up the spoor again, but were ultimately unsuccessful. The heat was starting to build up on another hot day that climbed steadily into the high 80s. By mid-morning both riders and horses were suffering from a lack of water, so Fernie sent Ignace and Le Camp out to find some water. Suddenly one of the trackers came running back, loudly shouting in Chinook that they had found a cache of equipment hidden in the bush. With hand gestures, the Indian told Fernie to bring his rifle and to approach the spot carefully. Through the heavy brush Fernie and the two trackers could see a mound covered with a large wagon tarp and fir branches hiding a pile of equipment and gear. Leaving Ignace hiding in the bush a short distance from the cache, Fernie and Le Camp rode quickly back to where Pearse and the rest of the posse were camped near Short's cabin at Campbell's Meadows.[19]

When Fernie and his trackers had left camp that morning, and as breakfast was being cooked up, Pearse wrote out a series of messages and a telegram and sent Blair and his double rig into town with Trainmaster Elson for more supplies. In Kamloops, Trainmaster Elson contacted Government Agent George Tunstall to send a telegram for

Pearse to Superintendent Hussey.

Canadian Pacific Railway Company's Telegraph.
Kamloops, B.C. May 10th 1906.

Sup't Police, Victoria.
Pearse still away, expected back
tonight latest report still on trail.

G.C. Tunstall.
11:25 a.m.[20]

Pearse sent cowboys Reid Campbell and Lee Moxley off to notify all the settlers in the surrounding area to watch out for strangers and to sharply monitor all the wagon roads and pack trails leading into the Grande Prairie and Chapperon Lake country. While he and Kilpatrick were conferring to the east of the camp, a messenger came up from Mrs. Greaves at the Joe Greaves' ranch house that she had spotted two hobbled bay horses straying about near their place. Pearse had heard other news about these horses and concluded that they must belong to the robbers. With a view towards commandeering these horses for posse use, he ordered Lew Campbell Jr. and Joe Greaves to head out and round them up.[21]

Besides Fernie, Ignace and Le Camp who were predominantly in the lead at all times and riding point for the posse, the party now included quite a few members. Pearse was in charge of the main group, which included Kilpatrick, Sheriff Wood, Special Constable F.E. Carter, cowboys Lew Campbell and Joe Greaves, and tracker Phillip Toma. Dick Blair and a teamster named Coke were kept busy running the wagons and rigs back and forth to Kamloops with messages and supplies. Fernie and Le Camp led the posse in a cautious approach to Ignace and the site of the equipment cache they had found. They set men at strategic hiding places around the cache to catch the robbers if they should decide to return to pick up their gear. Fernie and his trackers continued ahead across Woodland Creek

Mary Spencer photo, The Ducks Robbery pursuit posse.
L to R, Tracker Alex Ignace, Constable William Fernie, Chief Constable
Ernest T.W. Pearse, Tracker Michelle Le Camp, Special Constable F.E.
Carter, Constable Young of Nelson, Tracker Eli La Roux, Joe Greaves Jr.,
Lew Campbell Jr., and Tracker Phillip Toma.
Courtesy Kamloops Museum and Archives.

and towards Woodland Hill to check for tracks. When Fernie and his trackers, unsuccessful, came riding back down to the hidden group in the early afternoon, they decided the robbers would not return. They dismantled the cache which had been hidden with extreme care, packed up all the robbers' gear, and returned with it to their camp area in the Campbell Meadows where they had a hot lunch.[22]

In the cache was found a variety of equipment and gear:

1 red leather saddle worth $30, saddle blanket and sweater

1 good heavy grey blanket

1 pair drawers marked C. W.

1 waistcoat, 2 pack cinches, 2 side pack bags (heavy canvas)

1 double bitted axe, a small piece of bacon, about 10 lbs. of flour, some salt, about ten .32 calibre pistol cartridges, a box of black pills,

part of a tent, 3 knives, 3 forks, 4 plates, 2 kettles, 3 fry pans, 1 new shovel that had never seen dirt, and a new gold pan which had never seen water or gravel.[23]

While all the confiscated gear was being loaded into a wagon for the trip into Kamloops, Lew Campbell Jr. and Joe Greaves came riding in. They had picked up the two bays about four miles west of Joe Greaves' place in Campbell's Meadows. Greaves reported that one of the horses had been side hobbled American style and the other hobbled in front, Siwash style. Both were branded with an "M", but one was made with a branding iron, the other with a running iron. One bay had a blaze on its face and one white hind leg. Pearse made sure the news of the capture of the robbers' equipment; provision and horses was announced to the proper authorities and to reporters. Superintendent Kilpatrick went into town with the wagon and teamster Coke to the comfort of his private car and a bath. Kilpatrick delivered another message to George Tunstall in Kamloops to wire to Hussey.[24]

Canadian Pacific Railway Company's Telegraph
Kamloops, B.C, May 10th, 1906

F.S. Hussey, Sup't of Police, Victoria.
Cache of robbers found somewhere
Near Campbell's meadows their horses
Captured. The men are supposed
To be surrounded.

G.C. Tunstall.
4:35 p.m.[25]

Fernie and the rest of the posse spent the afternoon making sweeps around Woodland Creek, Scuitto Creek and White Lake to try to pick up any sign of the men. All members of the posse were out on the search, their remuda complemented by the captured horses. Pearse took one of the stray mounts for himself and cinched on the red leather saddle found in the cache. He soon decided it was quite to his liking. They came into camp at supper with nothing accomplished for their efforts. The fleeing robbers continued to set blind trails, backtrack, separate, and set false blazes in many directions. The searchers could plainly see that the blazes had been cut some days previously, intimating the robbers had planned their getaway meticulously. It was conceded that at least one of them was an accomplished bushman and hunter, aware of all the tricks used by human and animal prey to throw hunters off the scent. The robbers had used every subterfuge in their arsenal of tricks to disguise their track and trail. After supper, Pearse sent Michelle Le Camp into town to bring out more Indian trackers and to give a message to Kilpatrick, asking him to contact a Constable Young in Nelson and have him bring his bloodhounds to Kamloops. Teamster Coke drove into camp from town with a full load of grub and other supplies, as well as the news that Superintendent Hussey was now in Kamloops and in charge of the B.C. Provincial Police efforts. Pearse and Fernie sat down to discuss the next day's operations. It was decided to make a thorough search of the Woodland Hill area to the east of where the cache was found. Fernie, Ignace and Michelle Le Camp when he returned were to take the point and scout for sign, while the rest of the posse were close by so they could close in if the robbers were found. Fernie and the trackers knew the robbers were leading them higher and higher into the jack pine timber and blow down, swamps, deep ravines and steep flanks of the Monte Hills.[26]

Friday, 11 May 1906

In the morning, Michelle Le Camp came riding in with three more trackers to add to the swelling complement of riders and trackers in the posse. Francis Basil, Eli La Roux and one known only as Peters pulled in at daybreak, and after breakfast, the trackers and searchers all made for the area around the cache. They found more sign heading in a southerly direction past Archie McGillivray's farm, and Fernie and his trackers stuck to that trail through the soft forest duff. As they got into heavier and heavier spruce timber in the bottom land, the Indians pointed out to Fernie the plain marks of the hob nails on the forest floor. They also saw the tracks of one shod horse leading them into a timbered valley below Woodland Hill and followed these tracks for another two miles into the hills, climbing steadily. They made their way up Woodland Hill above where the cache had been found, following the three sets of tracks as best they could in the difficult terrain. A heavy rain started and temperatures started to go down. The rain did not let up until evening. In one of the highest spots, on a crag overlooking the valley and Wolf Lake in the west, they found a small camp. It was a natural lookout, and the movements of the posse would have been plain to see for the past two days. In the camp they found a handkerchief, pieces of two candles, a scrap of a letter, a small sack marked "Ramsay and Phillips" and "25 LBS. Walnuts," and a piece of the Manitoba Free Press. One of the candles had been stuck in the crevice of a rock, and burned pieces of paper were scattered about. The tracks of hobnailed boots were plain to see. It was suspected by the searchers that one of the robbers had stayed behind to determine how close the trackers were to the fleeing bandits. Fernie sent these items back down to Pearse and his men, then he, Ignace and Le Camp continued on for another half mile or so before turning back and making their way down to camp. Pearse had moved camp from Campbell's Meadows to south of Archie McGillivray's place where the men enjoyed a well deserved supper. It was not a good site as feed was scarce for the horses and they had to be moved throughout the night.

Saturday, 12 May 1906

Early on Saturday morning in a rain that was to continue all day, Reid Campbell rode into camp after travelling throughout the district rousing settlers and ranchers. He reported to Pearse that he had been told the tracks of three men had been seen at Batchelor's Meadows a few days previously and that perhaps the men they were following were headed in that direction. Chief Constable Pearse then rode into Kamloops to report to Superintendent Hussey. He told Hussey he was confident they were on the right track and that the bandits would be captured within a very short time. He requested that Hussey send out more men so that more roads and trails could be covered. When in Kamloops, Pearse learned that Constable Young and three of his bloodhounds had left Nelson for Kamloops and were expected to arrive anytime. While in town, he saw a squad of Royal North West Mounted Police get off the train from Calgary, and by the time Pearse headed out of town that afternoon, the Mounties were on their way west and south into the Nicola Valley. Pearse quickly made his way back out to his men in the field who were tracking through wet and sopping brush in increasingly cold and miserable conditions.

Pearse caught up to Fernie and the main posse as they made their way south, following tracks, from McGillivray's up Woodland Hill. Fernie, Pearse and their men finally reached the top of the escarpment that formed the long southeast-trending summit of the Monte Hills. Drenching rains fell throughout the day. They followed the tracks of the three men for eight to ten miles, past the headwaters of Teakettle Creek and Monte Creek, pushing through deadfalls and immature jack pine forests. Because of the rain the tracks were blurred and indistinct, and they finally lost them. They had met a trapper who professed to be able to sort out the myriad of criss-crossing pack trails and trappers' trails they were continually being confronted with. They wasted considerable time only to determine that the man really did not know what he was about, and for all anyone knew, he had been up in this country for years and had not been able to find his way out. They left him behind and continued south, heading for a high knoll in the distance at the south end of the long ridge. Not having the benefit of prior reconnoitering as the robbers had done, the posse soon found themselves in difficult and dangerous country. The brush became very thick with alder and willow underbrush, and they often had to use an axe to cut through it. Almost at the peak, they found their way barred by a seemingly impenetrable swamp. Despite the best efforts of the Indian trackers, it was too deep to find a way across and seemed to stretch in every direction. They made a big circle back to the north and east and finally made it to the knoll they had been trying for. It was the highest point for miles in every direction. Men and riders were exhausted, and they set up camp in the rain, tired and wet. They looked to their mounts which appeared to be so done in that the men wondered if they could continue in the morning. Their mounts would go without feed that night. The posse turned in on the hard ground, rolled in their blankets. That night it snowed two inches on sleeping men, horses, saddles and gear.[27][28]

SUNDAY, 13 MAY 1906

By 5:30 the next morning, the posse was mounted and following a light trail down into the valley of Little Fish Lake and the cabin and small stump ranch of Paul Stevens and his wife Margaret. At 10:30 they saw Stevens and his wife coming round the east side of the lake. Pearse and Fernie asked Stevens and his wife if they had seen any strangers over the past few days. Stevens replied that they had seen none lately, then Mrs. Stevens said she recognized Pearse's mount and its red saddle. She said she remembered it being with one of the two men she had seen about three weeks previously.[29]

With Stevens and his wife riding alongside, the posse had made its way to Stevens' one room cabin and meadow by 11:30, and Pearse immediately ordered the mobile kitchen to be unpacked from the pack horse and set up for cooking the noon meal. The horses were rubbed down and given a good feed and a rest. Stevens told Pearse that he knew of some trails that the strangers had blazed in the vicinity, and Pearse decided to investigate. Leaving Alec Ignace manning the kitchen and Mrs. Stevens in the cabin, the posse made its way west along the road to investigate the blazes Stevens had seen. After about four miles in a southerly direction, Stevens pointed out a tree with three blazed notches, and further on a blazed track that took off in a southerly direction across the Okanagan Trail (Douglas Lake—Grande Prairie Road). They examined these signs and blazes for some time, and then Pearse decided to order the posse and trackers to search the mountains above them, the Monte Hills, for fresh tracks. He directed that a camp be set up at Stevens' place, and searches would be sent out from this location. He also wished to wait for the bloodhounds, which were expected at any hour.[30]

Fernie disagreed with Pearse at this point, saying that all the indications pointed to the men they were following heading in a southwesterly direction. Fernie and Pearse had some words of disagreement with each other at this point on how the pursuit should progress. Pearse was actually contemplating taking the posse back to Kamloops to join up with the Mounted Police. Fernie formally requested of his commanding officer if he might go on himself towards Fish Lake and Chapperon Lake, checking along the way. Pearse agreed, and Fernie rode on by himself south towards Fish Lake and Chapperon Lake.[31]

Shortly after Fernie had left, Constable Basil Gardom from Enderby and Special Constables Percy Cotton and Dick Smith from Grande Prairie strode up the rough track to the Stevens cabin on foot, packing rifles and their pistols, and with packs on their backs carrying their supplies. They conferred with Pearse and Carter and advised them that their investigations around the Grande Prairie area led them to believe that Paul Stevens may have been one of the Ducks train robbers. At the very least, they were certain that he was an accomplice. They all camped at the Stevens place that night. Some of the posse took advantage of the small one room cabin while others slept outside.

That afternoon, Fernie had soon hit the main wagon road from Douglas Lake to Grande Prairie. He cut the road near Batchelor's Meadows and immediately proceeded to head south towards Fish Lake. He called in at Alfred Goodwin's Norfolk Ranch, but they had not seen any strangers. After making fruitless inquiries there, he went on and close to dusk stopped at Brush Camp, a satellite of the Douglas Lake Ranch. The Welshman Tom Jones was in charge of the crew developing the meadows and fields at the camp to better suit the raising of hay and the grazing of the ranch's cattle. Fernie met Jones and his men and was told at the camp bunkhouse of a mysterious incident that had happened the past evening. Jones and his crew were quietly sitting around the fire in the bunkhouse, enjoying the warmth while the snow swirled outside. The Chinese cook glanced out the door and saw a stranger looking in from the shadows. The cook shouted and the cowboys jumped up to have a look, but no one was around. They went out to check the stables, but none of the horses had been disturbed. Fernie told them it sounded like these were the men he was after and that the cook's sudden reaction had scared them off. Fernie took advantage of being in a warm, dry bunkhouse that night and relished the lumpy cot in comparison with the discomforts he had suffered in the snow the night previous.[32][33]

MONDAY, 14 MAY 1906

After breakfast, Pearse sent Carter and the Indian trackers to search the hills above Stevens' place and also along the Douglas Lake to Grande Prairie wagon road and points east. He waited behind at the Stevens place in case any messages or additional manpower came from Kamloops that he would have to deal with. The rain had finally stopped, and temperatures again started to rise into the low 70s. About 10:30 that morning, a thoroughly worn out Constable Young from Nelson and his equally dejected single bloodhound made their way into camp with Joe Greaves of Campbell's Meadows as a guide. Young had left Kamloops with three hounds, but two had been lost in the fastness and difficult terrain of the Monte Hills.

The three mounted up, and with the lone bloodhound trailing, they set off to catch up to Special Constable Carter and the rest of the posse and trackers. Constable Gardom and his Specials, left behind at the little cabin, arrested Paul Stevens when Pearse had left and escorted him to a cell in Vernon. When Pearse caught up to Carter, a disappointed Carter reported no success in finding any tracks. The complete posse, trackers, cowboys and police officers, camped for the afternoon beside the Salmon River to see if Fernie might turn up. Pearse and his men had been continually on the trail of the robbers for five days, from daylight to dark. They had pushed themselves and their horses through extreme conditions of weather, terrain and vegetation. Some had almost reached the end of their tether, and Pearse took this time to give his men and horses some time to recuperate and re-gather their strength.[34]

Fernie, meanwhile, had only himself to be concerned about, and he was not about to give up the initiative he felt he and his trackers had obtained by pressing the robbers at every turn, literally stepping on their heels as they tried to escape. Throughout his past career as a cowboy in the Chilcotin and as a cavalryman in South Africa, he displayed personal characteristics that would remain with him for a lifetime. He would advance into a challenging future in the decades ahead of him and would conduct the dispatch of his duties with a tenacity of will and strong sense of personal duty to the new country he had adopted just a few years previously.

When Fernie saddled his horse at the Brush Camp that morning, he could see that five days of constant riding under adverse conditions was taking its toll on the animal. The weather was improving, so he left his heavy woollen cavalry cloak behind. He also left his Winchester and his bandolier of cartridges with Tom Jones, hoping to reduce the weight his mount would have to carry. His only firearm was his five shot .38 calibre Smith and Wesson revolver. Fernie rode on an off-road route through to the main ranch at Douglas Lake, travelling close to the line of timber high above the valley so as to intercept any tracks that may have exited the timber. At the ranch he found just a few men around the main ranch buildings. He asked after Greaves, the manager. Greaves was not there at the time, and neither was anyone in authority. He waited until Greaves finally showed up, and the ranch manager told him that the Mounted Police had left there that morning and would be stopping for lunch and to round up some pack horses at Chapperon Lake. Somehow Fernie had passed the troop without spotting them as he had made that high ride close to the timber. Fernie fed and watered his horse, had an early lunch at the cookhouse, and by eleven o'clock he headed out on a borrowed cow pony to catch up with the Mounties at Chapperon.[35]

He had only gone about two miles from the home ranch and was passing through a gate when he spotted three white men, two with white packs on their backs, walking up the road towards him. Although Fernie had no photographs to help him with identifying the three men, he had seen the detailed descriptions and was positive they were the robbers. He had no chance to turn off without alerting their suspicions, so he kept heading towards them. He saw the shortest one, Billy Dunn, was on his right, and the older man, Edwards, was in the middle. A youngish red-headed man, Colquhoun, was to Fernie's left. Dunn and Colquhoun were carrying canvas packs.[36]

Fernie reined up in front of them, plumb in the middle of the road. "Hello," he greeted them in his broadest English accent.

The older one, Edwards, seemed to be the spokesman for the trio, and he hailed Fernie and asked him the way to Quilchena. Fernie swung in his saddle and pointed to the west behind him. He spoke about the weather and inquired whether they had seen any game about, trying to be as nonchalant as possible about their meeting. He tried to study the three without being obvious, noting that all three were carrying pistols in their pockets, and there was a long gun sticking out of the pack carried by Shorty Dunn. He saw that Dunn kept his hand in his coat pocket where the bulge and butt of a semi-automatic German Luger were visible to Fernie's knowledgeable eye. He kept his hand in that pocket throughout the time Fernie talked to them. On a belt strapped around Dunn's waist, Fernie saw a heavy calibre revolver in a holster. The Constable tried to keep the conversation amiable, and through his broad English accent impress upon them that he was just an eccentric Englishman a bit out of his depth in the wilds of British Columbia's back country. He hoped to sooth the fears of the trio that he might be one of the posse looking for them. He asked them where they were from.[37]

Edwards answered, "Oh, we're prospectors. We've been to Grande Prairie."

Fernie asked, "Am I on the right road to Chapperon?" They agreed he was and they pointed behind them to the east, the direction from which they had come, as the direction he was to take.

"Well," said Fernie, "I am off to Chapperon then."

And with that, Fernie gently kicked his horse ahead, reined his way around them and rode forward down the wagon road. The hair stood up on the back of his neck, and his back seemed five feet wide as he felt their eyes following him down the road.[38 39]

He rode slowly away from them, all the while keeping his eyes down on the road, looking for tracks. He topped a small rise, and as he did so, he glanced back towards the three men. They were continuing in the direction of Quilchena and did not look back to see what he was doing. He rode over the crest of the rise and down the other side until he was hidden from view. He rode a short distance, then pulled into a grove of aspen until he was sure they had passed out of site.[40]

Fernie rode back to where he had seen the men, dismounted and knelt to examine the tracks. He could see the two pairs of hobnailed boots plain in the hard soil, but he could see no sign of a slender, smaller pair of smooth soled boots. However, the sign was enough to convince him that the men were the ones he was after. He remounted and pushed his mount as much as he dared, heading towards Chapperon Lake and the troop of Mounties he heard were there.[41]

Fernie arrived at the Mountie camp just as they were having lunch. He identified himself to them and told them of his encounter. Their horses had been unsaddled earlier in the morning and set out in an orderly picket line. The Mounties now hurriedly commenced to put the saddles back on their mounts. It took them all of three minutes. The troop was soon mounted up, headed back west towards Douglas Lake. On the way, the Indian tracker supplied to the Mounties by ranch manager Greaves found the spot west of Chapperon Lake where tracks showed where the three men came out of the high hills and timber to the north, across the grassed fields of the grazing lands, and started walking down the road towards Quilchena. Fernie and the seven Mounted Police pressed on as quickly as possible to the spot where Fernie had seen the men. Together Fernie and the Indian scouted around that spot and found more tracks in softer ground. Fernie dismounted and knelt by the tracks. He pointed out to the Mounties standing beside him the recognizable signs of the placement of the nails in each pair of boots and how the heels had distinctively worn down on the sides of the slender, smooth soled pair. He told them he was convinced that these three sets of tracks were the same ones he and his Indian trackers, Ignace and Le Camp, had been following since early in the darkness of the previous Tuesday, only hours after the robbery. Fernie drove in wooden pegs around where he had found the prints and told the Mounties he would go to the main ranch and enlist the aid of more cowboys and Indian trackers there. Sergeant Wilson said they would do a search patrol in a line across the valley and see if they might flush the bandits from cover.[42]

Fernie rode west down the road and across English bridge over the Nicola River. He kept a wary watch out for any sign of the suspects, but it was as if they had been swallowed up by the land around them. He trotted his tired horse into the cluster of buildings making up the main Douglas Lake Ranch. He sat in the cookhouse and wrote out a message to Pearse, advising him and the posse to come as quick as possible. He was writing another to send to Quilchena for bloodhounds, when he heard a horse gallop into the yard. He looked up to see Slim Jim Benyon on a lathered horse slide to a halt. The guide shouted in an excited voice to Fernie that there had been a shooting and to come quick. It had been six days since the train was robbed at Ducks.[43]

XIV

GRANDE PRAIRIE COUNTRY

IN 1905 THE LITTLE COMMUNITY OF ENDERBY at the head of the Okanagan Valley was incorporated as a city. With all the accoutrements of a city came the posting of the town's first Provincial Police Constable. Basil Gardom was born in England in 1875 and came to Canada in 1892 at the tender age of 17. He homesteaded at Deep Creek near Enderby, but after seven unproductive years, he sold his farm for a paltry sum and moved into Enderby. Like his contemporary William Fernie in Kamloops, Gardom had joined the Lord Strathcona's Horse in 1900 and was shipped to South Africa to fight in the Boer War. During his service he contracted malaria near Losberg in the Transvaal and was treated for the disease in a tent hospital in Potchefstroom.[1][2]

By 1 March 1905, property owners in Enderby had approved incorporation, and it finally became official. Elections were held and Mr. George Bell became mayor. Basil Gardom had returned from South Africa relatively unscathed and applied for the position of Provincial Police constable in Enderby. He was sworn in as a police officer by the local Justice of the Peace who administered the Oath of Office. The young policeman reported to the Chief Constable in Vernon, Edgar C. Simmons. Gardom received his .38 calibre Smith and Wesson revolver, holster and badge on the 22ND of August in 1905 and quickly took up his duties. Life seemed filled with a bright future for the young policeman who was courting a local girl, Helen Monroe, an admired and talented amateur singer.[3][4]

Adelphi Hotel with grocery store to the left, Grande Prairie.
The man and woman in the foreground would eventually marry.

TUESDAY, 9 MAY 1906

Less than a year after he had assumed his police duties, Constable Gardom was confronted with one of his more challenging investigations. The morning after the robbers had held up the CPR at Ducks, Divisional Superintendent Kilpatrick had telegraphed Gardom about the robbery, suggesting that the robbers might be headed into his jurisdiction. Gardom wired Simmons in Vernon to tell him he was heading out to "look after the country between the Salmon River Bridges" north of Schweb's Bridge and including the communities of Glen Emma and Grande Prairie. The Salmon River flowed out of Salmon Lake in the

Douglas Lake ranch country, making its way through Grande Prairie and past many farm hamlets to eventually empty into Shuswap Lake near Salmon Arm. Gardom told Simmons he could be reached by leaving a message at the first house west of Schweb's Bridge. Bidding his sweetheart goodbye, Gardom hitched his saddle horse to the back of his cart and headed due west from Enderby over the low range of hills that separated Enderby from the Salmon River Valley. As he passed by the Salmon River Indian Reserve, he notified the Indians he met of the robbery near Kamloops and advised them to be on the lookout for strangers. The first man he met west of Schweb's Bridge was a rather confused individual named McEwan. McEwan told Gardom he had been camping up by the next bridge about nine miles further up the road. McEwan said he had seen no one all night. When questioned by Gardom, McEwan confessed he had not slept all night as he was getting over the ill effects of a glorious drinking bout, and would have seen anyone who passed by. However, McEwan went on to tell Gardom that the previous day, May 8TH, two men had passed him heading to Princeton. A short young man rode a gray horse, and the older, taller one with a red moustache, rode a bay with a blazed face. Gardom was later to identify the second man as James Mohr, a friend of Paul Stevens.[5]

Mrs. Smith, at whose place Gardom stopped next, also remembered seeing the two riders the day before. She remembered that the bay the older man had been riding looked as though it had been ridden hard and was all sweated up.

Gardom continued on past the second bridge over the river and ran into Frank Gordon of Grande Prairie. Gordon, the manager of the Pylewell Ranch in Grande Prairie for the absentee owner Colonel G. Cecil Whittaker, was a polo playing friend of Constable William Fernie in Kamloops. Upon being questioned, Gordon told Gardom that a short young man on a gray was in Grande Prairie as they spoke, and Gordon thought that he had slept in the Adelphi Hotel that night. As Gardom and Gordon were talking, that same short young man on the gray horse came riding up towards them, heading south. Gardom greeted him and started to ask him about the train robbery.

The young man, to Gardom's reckoning, pretended not to have heard of the holdup the previous evening. He did admit that he had met and ridden for a distance the day previous with a man on a bay with a blazed up face. The young man said that he never did learn the other rider's name. Then he asked Gardom as to whether the red moustached man was wanted for horse stealing, as rustling was a problem in the Grande Prairie area. Gardom eventually let the man ride on his way.

Together Frank Gordon and the police constable rode past H. Guernsey's store and George Wright's blacksmith's shop by the bridge over the Salmon River and on into the prosperous little farming and ranching community of Grande Prairie. Situated in a huge bowl surrounded by high crags, the unincorporated village sported the Adelphi Hotel, containing the Post Office and a small grocery store beside it, a school, St. Luke's Anglican Church, and grocery stores. The Methodist and Episcopal Missions ran churches in homes on special Sundays. The fertile soils across the broad valley were irrigated by the Salmon River, Ingram Creek and Pringle Creek and supported productive farms and cattle ranches. Despite the rumoured predation of rustlers, life in the valley was idyllic, with all the standard civic celebrations throughout the year. Social life was very active, and everyone in the community knew each other and looked after their own. The Grande Prairie Assembly Hall held eight dances a year, and Grande Prairie's polo team had won the Roper Cup from 1901 to 1905 and would do so again in 1906.[67]

Gardom and Gordon pulled up at the Adelphi Hotel where Gordon dismounted and hitched his horse to the rail outside the hotel. Gardom halted his trap and saddle horse in front at the side of the road. The Adelphi Hotel was owned by Walter Homfray who had built it in 1895. Albert Duck of the Holmwood Ranch had been his first hotel manager. Constable Gardom, with Gordon following, strode into the sudden shade of the lobby and greeted the clerk, Gerry Talbot. The dim, cool interior provided a welcome respite as the temperatures outside were approaching 90° F, the hottest day of the year so far. Bertie Butler, whose father George worked at the Holmwood Ranch, was in the lobby at the same time. Gardom started asking questions of the two young men, and they were eager to help. They told the Enderby constable that they had noticed a man known as Mohr had been acting suspiciously around town. He had left Grande Prairie earlier that day, telling them at the hotel that he was heading to Summit Lake (Monte Lake). But when they watched him through the hotel windows as he departed, he immediately headed in the opposite direction towards Vernon. Frank Gordon told

B.C. Provincial Police Constable Basil Gardom, Enderby. COURTESY OF ENDERBY AND DISTRICT MUSEUM.

Gardom that this was very strange, as Mohr would have had to have hidden in the brush for Gordon not to have seen him when he passed on the same road heading in the opposite direction. Gardom requested that Butler keep his eye open for Mohr again, as the constable would like to question him. Clerk Talbot then told Gardom that everyone in Grande Prairie was suspicious of the activities of Paul Stevens and a Tommy Graham. They said that Stevens lived miles back in the hills behind Summit Lake and Graham lived on a farm at the west end of the lake, at the bottom of the road leading through the bush to Stevens' place. They had seen Stevens leading three horses towards Ducks just the day previously, the day of the robbery.

Gardom left his horse and trap at the hotel and took his saddle horse to investigate around the Grande Prairie area. He went to the Kirkpatrick Ranch where he knew fellow Englishman Percy Cotton was working. Cotton was often hired as a part time "Special Constable" by the Provincial Police whenever it was required for him to act in an official police capacity in the Grande Prairie country. After Cotton had come over from England, he married Martha Jane (Jennie) Kirkpatrick and they had a young daughter, Dorothy. Cotton had heard of the robbery at Ducks from the locals around Grande Prairie. Gardom discussed the robbery and his subsequent investigations further with Constable Cotton, and told him of the suspicions held locally about Paul Stevens, James Mohr and Tommy Graham. Cotton was well acquainted with Mohr, as just that day Mohr had come to Cotton to try to buy a horse and saddle. Mohr had been asking around the Grande Prairie area who the local constable was as he had heard he had some tack and a horse for sale. He had been referred to Cotton, and while haggling over price, they discussed the robbery at Ducks. As they were standing around the granary, Cotton thought it strange when Mohr said, referring to the robbers, "It will be a case of shooting when they get them." Cotton told Gardom that it was about one in the afternoon when Mohr left his place, and Mohr had mentioned to him that he was heading to Summit Lake and would be heading up to see Stevens that day.

The afternoon was growing late when Gardom decided to head back to Enderby for the night. The provincial police constable made his way south and east through the valley of the Salmon River, bright and green with new spring growth. As the late afternoon rays of the sun cast long shadows across the meadows and fields, Gardom's horse confidently made its own way along the lonely wagon road. At the first bridge north of Falkland on the Grande Prairie side, Gardom again stopped at Mrs. Steenson's house. This time Mrs. Steenson was being visited by a Mrs. Volrath, and Gardom asked questions about any suspicious strangers they may have seen. When he brought up the name of James Christie, Mrs. Volrath said, "Mr. Christie went away over the mountain at the back of my house just a week ago. I know because he had dinner with us. He had a rifle and a revolver." The Volrath place was just above Moffat Creek near Schweb's Bridge. Mrs. Volrath went on to tell Gardom that her neighbour McBrian was a friend of Christie's and that he lived alone up on the mountain near her place. Upon Gardom's further questioning, she couldn't say whether he had been home lately. Then Mrs. Steenson broke into the conversation to say that McBrian usually bought milk from her but he had not been near their place since the previous day. Gardom continued on his way and finally returned to Enderby in the dark, dozing on the seat of his trap as his horse guided him home, his saddle horse trailing behind.

THURSDAY, 10 MAY 1906

The next day found Gardom in his trap, with his saddle horse trailing, on his way back to Grande Prairie. Making inquiries along the way, he met a Dr. Bentley travelling along the road who told him of strangers he had seen in the area. In Grande Prairie, Gardom picked up Special Constable Cotton who travelled alongside him in the trap, his saddle horse also hitched behind. They continued investigations in Grande Prairie and worked their way south into the Falkland area, accumulating information all the while. Along the way they picked up a guide familiar with the area named Indian Scotty, and he rode with them. It was late in the afternoon when they headed south from Schweb's Bridge for Siwash Creek on the west side of Okanagan Lake to meet up with Chief Constable Simmons from Vernon who was working that area. At dusk the two constables saw firelight flashing on the opposite side of Round Lake. At Indian Scotty's suggestion, and before investigating the fire on the other side of the lake, they left the trap behind and led their horses to a camp and tent in the bush just off the side of the road. Two men identifying themselves as Bruce Moxley and Charlie Wilson came out of their tent to greet the policemen. They told Gardom and Cotton that they had had some grub stolen that day and volunteered to go with them to see who had the fire on the other side of the lake. Gardom was suspicious of the duo as they met the descriptions of two men who had broken jail in Vernon some days previously. He cautioned the men to be sure they made themselves available for future questioning, and Gardom and Cotton moved out into the dark.

It was 8:30 when they led their horses around the north end of Round Lake, heading towards the unknown campfire. The moon had yet to rise, and with the dark and the heavy brush, they found the going difficult. When they were within 100 yards of the campfire, a dog started to bark. They saw a man sitting beside the fire, with a rack of fish drying nearby. When the dog started to bark, he jumped up with a rifle in his hands, swinging it towards the two policemen. Gardom had his rifle bearing on the man and shouted to him that he was a provincial policeman and to throw up his hands. The man said something Gardom couldn't understand, and he again called for the man to throw up his hands, again describing himself as a British Columbia policeman. The crackling of the fire made Gardom's words indistinct, and the man again called out that he couldn't understand what was being said. Gardom walked into the firelight and again identified himself, requesting the man to throw down his rifle. The man did so and identified himself to Gardom as James Christie, a prospector and explorer. Gardom told Christie he was looking for the men who had held up the train at Ducks. Christie explained that when he first heard the dog bark, he thought Gardom and Cotton were a bear or a cow. Gardom watched him closely and saw he was dressed in brown pants and wore a jersey. A pair of hobnailed boots lay nearby. Gardom noticed that Christie did not appear to be all that interested in the story of the holdup, merely asking how much loot had been obtained. He also noted that Christie bore a resemblance to one of the descriptions of the three robbers that he had received via telegraph. Christie asked if they had a description of the men, and as Gardom and Cotton prepared to take their leave, Christie showed them an easier trail to get back to Wilson and Moxley's camp and Gardom's trap. Back at the camp of the two men, Wilson asked Gardom if he could get work as a special constable. Gardom referred him to the police offices in Vernon. Percy Cotton took his leave of Gardom, mounted his saddle horse, and made his way back to Grande Prairie.

Gardom drove on to Jimmy Logan's place at the head of Okanagan Lake, and as he made his way down the long hill from the high country, he thought about the men he had confronted that night. He was convinced that Wilson and Moxley were bad characters. He would investigate them further to determine if they were the escaped prisoners from the jail at Vernon and whether they were part of the horse rustling fraternity active around Grande Prairie, if nothing else. Christie also caused Gardom concern. His explanations of his movements and actions, his resemblance to the description of one of the robbers, and his general demeanour of disinterest raised Gardom's suspicions. At Jimmy Logan's, he left his cart and horses and took a fresh mount down to Siwash Creek to confer with Chief Constable Simmons. Simmons was directing a coterie of Special Constables who were monitoring the roads and trails coming out of the Kamloops country all along Okanagan Lake from the O'Keefe Ranch south. Gardom camped with Simmons that night, and they discussed Gardom's suspicions and concerns about Stevens, Mohr, Wilson and Christie. The Enderby constable also related rumours he had heard of the rustling activities prevalent in the Grande Prairie area and said that Butler's Meadows west of Little Bouleau Lake was a suspected horse thief camp.[8]

Friday, 11 May 1906

The next day Gardom and Simmons returned to Vernon to clean up police duties, and pick up telegrams. On their way they passed Wilson riding from Vernon back to his camp near Round Lake, having spent some time in town. At about 3:30 that afternoon in Vernon, Gardom was surprised to see Wilson again, coming in the door of the downtown police office. Wilson came up to Gardom and said he wanted to make a report. He reported that he had just come down from their camp as Moxley had been badly scared by two men who had come to their camp that day demanding grub and firearms. They stated that they were provincial policemen that had been held up and had their arms and grub stolen. When Wilson left to head back to his camp, Gardom and Simmons had a discussion about the likelihood of Wilson, Mohr and Christie being involved with the robbery or, at the very least, in collusion with Paul Stevens in rustling activities around Grande Prairie. The two policemen decided to take pre-emptive and discretionary action. As a result, Gardom left to investigate the incidents at Round

Lake and soon overtook Wilson on the trail as his horse had worn out. He advised Wilson to head back to see Chief Constable Simmons, and when Wilson did so, Simmons promptly arrested him and placed him in a cell. When Gardom got to the camp of the two men at Round Lake, he found Moxley and James Christie sitting around the fire outside the tent. Gardom questioned Moxley closely. Contrary to Wilson's report to Gardom, Moxley stated he knew nothing about two men coming to the camp and that Wilson had not been back to the Round Lake camp all day. Gardom decided to put Christie into custody and escorted him back to Vernon. In Vernon, James Christie was placed in a cell in the same jail as Wilson.

During this time, Gardom was able to determine that the red moustached man on the blaze faced bay was the Mohr he had been looking for. Mohr, who was currently in jail in Vernon, had been described to Gardom by Grande Prairie residents as almost certainly a horse thief, and Gardom's own investigations had determined Mohr was most likely associated with the Ducks robbery. Three suspects were now in custody in the little town. A Vancouver newspaper, commenting on the arrests, stated that, "The accounts they gave of themselves and their movements were contradictory and conflicting and have proved to be untrue." [9]

The manager of the Thiel Detective Agency, Captain Seavey, had arrested Mohr. The elusive Mohr was reported to have lived around Vernon for two years or more. The Province reported, "There is a supposition that he is a man who was a sailor on the Abbey Palmer when she was in collision with the CPR years ago in the Strait of Juan de Fuca. When the collision occurred a sailor on the Abbey Palmer whose name was Mohr was thrown bodily from the mark to the deck of the liner. He was brought to Vancouver, and afterward went to Vernon to live."[10]

SATURDAY, 12 MAY 1906

Gardom did an extensive interview with Wilson in the police office in Vernon. Wilson told the constable that he was a friend of Paul Stevens who lived up in the hills above Monte Lake. He said to Gardom that his partner's name in the camp at Round Lake was Cameron Bruce Moxley and that he lived at Campbell Creek, near where the robbery took place. He admitted to Gardom that he and Stevens had spent considerable time together. Late that April they been riding together up in the Monte Hills about five miles from Stevens' cabin at Little Fish Lake when they ran into two men who said they were looking for mowich (deer). Wilson described one of the men, Shorty Dunn, as "a little fellow, short, had brown whiskers, black hat and boots with heavy nails." He had a rifle with a bandolier full of cartridges strung across his chest. The rifle "was a very long one and had wood to the end of the barrel." The other, Lewis Colquhoun, "was a tall fellow, he was young, had a light cap and overalls, had a vest, shirt and no coat." Wilson talked to them further and they said they had another partner who was looking after their horses back in the bush. Later on Wilson said he and Stevens had looked for their tracks in the bush above Stevens' place but could not find any. Wilson said that he had stayed with Stevens all last winter and had only just come out after meeting those two men on the trail two weeks previously at the end of April. Wilson added that Moxley had stayed with the Stevens for two months before winter set in. Wilson kept one saddle horse over the winter at the Stevens' place, and he said that Paul Stevens himself had two saddle horses and a pack horse. During that winter they had gone into Nicola through Douglas Lake. Under questioning, Wilson admitted he knew James Mohr, confirming in Gardom's mind a connection with horse rustling around Grande Prairie. Wilson said that the first time he had met Paul Stevens was in Penticton. When asked for a description of Stevens, Wilson said that the last time he saw Stevens he rode a shod, blaze faced sorrel with an unshod pack horse trailing. He was wearing riding boots and was carrying a .45 calibre Colt's revolver.

At five o'clock that afternoon, Gardom, in the company of town of Vernon police officer Edwards, headed back for Grande Prairie. The two ran into Indian Scotty as they were approaching Round Lake. Indian Scotty told them he had seen two strangers going into the bush that morning near where Christie had been camped. Gardom sent Scotty back to the Indian Reserve to see if he could find out anything new there from any hunting parties that had been out over the past few days. Gardom and Edwards rode into Bruce Moxley's camp, where Gardom proceeded to question him about Paul Stevens. Moxley stated that it had been sixteen days since he had seen Paul Stevens. They were on the old trail between Graves' gate at the west end of Monte Lake and Stevens' gate in the Monte Hills. Moxley remembered Stevens had three horses with him that day, only one of which was shod. Together they saw two strangers approaching.

"One (Shorty Dunn) was 35 or 40 and had a growth of whiskers. He looked as if he had not shaved for a month. He was short 5 ft. 7 or 8. He had hobnailed boots on. He wore a black hat. He had a gun and cartridge belt. Further on we picked up an empty cartridge calibre 44-40. The other man (Colquhoun) was 5 ft. 6 or 7, slim, wore a light coloured cap and had blue overalls on that looked new. He had a very small moustache, was very red faced and had a long nose. The older man (Dunn) talked like an American."

"Paul asked them where they were camped and one of the men pointed to nowhere in particular. They said they had come down from the Chapperon Lake country, and asked where the trail they were on led to. Stevens told them it led to Summit Lake. They asked Stevens where he lived, how many cattle he fed, and where his ranch was. The older one told them they were going up Woods Creek (Adelphi Creek) prospecting."

Gardom questioned Moxley further about Wilson. Moxley said that Wilson was a foot race runner. He ran in Vernon under the name of Cameron and in Tacoma, Washington, under the name of Wilson. Moxley readily admitted that Wilson was with him and Stevens when they met the two strangers. Gardom was only too aware that Wilson had neglected to tell him that Moxley had been with him and Paul Stevens when they had seen Dunn and Colquhoun that day.

After their interview with Moxley, Indian Scotty and another Indian named Madeline rode up to talk to them. Together they discussed Christie, Mohr and Wilson and any other itinerant prospectors and potential horse rustlers and robbers in the country between Round Lake and the Monte Hills. Scotty and Madeline returned to the reserve, and because it was too dark to travel, Constable Gardom and Police Officer Edwards stayed at the Smith place west of Schweb's Bridge that night.

At the Steenson Place Gardom found Richard Volrath visiting. Volrath said his father and little brother had seen two men at 6:30 A.M. going into the brush close to Round Lake, near where Christie had been camped.

Mrs. Steenson told Gardom that McBrian had called there the day before and asked what Constable Gardom had been doing around there. When Christie's name was mentioned, "he hung his head and said that if the police come again tell them he has gone to the Kootenay."

SUNDAY, 13 MAY 1906

Early in the morning, Gardom left for Grande Prairie while Edwards made his way back to Vernon. Gardom got into Grande Prairie by 6:30, and there he met up with Owen Batchelor, a well known mining promoter from Kamloops. He had previously owned a piece of property near the Douglas Lake ranch known as Batchelor's Meadows. Batchelor was driving a buggy and team about and escorting W.S. Seavey of the Thiel Detective Agency in Seattle. Seavey was conducting investigations on behalf of the CPR, hoping that as a result of these investigations his company might realize more business from the big railway monopoly. Gardom brought them up to date with his investigations. From Batchelor he learned that the man with the red moustache riding the bay with the blaze on its face on the 8TH, the night of the robbery, was a good friend of Paul Stevens. This man had gone on towards Douglas Lake from Grande Prairie and would have crossed the trail to Stevens' place.

Gardom rounded up Special Constable Percy Cotton and enlisted the aid of another Grande Prairie "Special" by the name of Smith (probably Richard C. [Dick] Smith of Grande Prairie). The three, mounted on saddle horses, made their way to the northwest, heading for Paul Stevens' place at Little Fish Lake. At the north end of Summit Lake they passed the Fred Westrup farm. It was from here

Special Constable Percy Cotton,
Grande Prairie (Westwold.)

that a trail left the main Kamloops to Grande Prairie Road and headed into the Monte Hills. At the end of the lake they ran into Captain George Graves, who had more news on the activities of Paul Stevens. Graves had previously run into Edwards and Dunn on the wagon road west of Upper Campbell Creek before the robbery. He and a Mr. Montgomery were driving a rig east towards Grand Prairie when they ran into the two men. Captain Graves told Gardom that two of Stevens' horses were in his corral at 8:00 P.M. the night of the robbery. Graves said he and others in the vicinity at different times saw Stevens and Tommy Graham returning from the direction of Ducks in their wagons the next day after the robbery. Tommy Graham was described as a "bad character." Graham and Stevens met and conferred near Fred Westrup's place in the afternoon, then Graham went to his own place nearby, and Stevens went into the hills to the south.

Gardom, Cotton and Smith rode their horses up the rudimentary wagon trail to Stevens' place near Little Fish Lake. Steep and heavily forested canyon walls loomed up on both sides of them as they followed the course of Monte Creek steadily southwards. The trail became increasingly rough and rocky, and the men became fearful that their mounts might end up lame. They decided to save their horses and staked them in a clearing in the bush where there was plenty of feed and water, and set off on foot. They took their rifles and pistols, and with blankets and basic camp gear in packs, they continued on. Making their way up the trail, they suddenly came upon Lewis Campbell Jr., a cowboy from Campbell's Ranch, a son of the owner, and a member of the posse headed by Chief Constable Pearse from Kamloops. Pearse's posse was working its way east from Ducks over the Campbell Range and were now scouting the Monte Hills above Stevens' place. The cowboy told the men Pearse and part of his posse were at the Stevens' place, and the officers continued on, climbing steadily higher into the mountains. They eventually arrived close to the Stevens' place, and it was there they met Chief Constable Pearse and his right-hand man, Special Constable Fred Carter, on the trail. Pearse and Carter were riding the two horses that had been captured near Joe Greaves' place in the Campbell Meadows. Paul Stevens was in his cabin. Introductions were made and Gardom asked Chief Constable Pearse if he might speak to him in confidence. Pearse refused, saying anything Gardom might have to say to him he could say in front of Special Constable Carter. Gardom proceeded then to tell Pearse all the information he had with regards to the activities of Christie, Wilson and Mohr, and that he was convinced that Paul Stevens was one of the men who had held up the train. Pearse was shocked, and vehemently disagreed, stating that Stevens had been assisting them since they had arrived in this part of the country. He did agree, though, that his Indian trackers had followed the robbers' trail to within a short distance of Stevens' place. Then he brought Gardom up to date with the investigation as it was unfolding at the Kamloops end, including Mrs. Stevens' meeting with Shorty Dunn three weeks previously in late April. When the two law enforcement officers had finished briefing each other, Pearse and Carter, along with Stevens, headed south along the trail towards the Douglas Lake Road.[11]

Gardom cast his eyes about the rudimentary buildings constituting Paul and Margaret Stevens' painfully simple domestic world. Outside the Stevens' cabin, fish were hanging, drying in the warm spring sunshine. Gardom reflected that he had seen Christie drying his fish in the same manner.

Gardom spent some time talking to Margaret Stevens. She told the Constable that she and her husband were out looking for cows when Pearse and his posse had arrived. When Gardom asked her about her sudden meeting with Shorty Dunn, she said, "He called here three weeks ago tomorrow. That was the day before Paul saw the two men on the old trail. I have not heard of anyone else having seen them."

Gardom and his two "Specials" continued along the trail past the Stevens' cabin, where Margaret was busy attending to her domestic responsibilities. After walking some time, they met Stevens riding towards them. Gardom took the opportunity to question him on the spot. Making sure Percy Cotton was there to hear the questions and answers, he asked him about the two men, Colquhoun and Dunn, that he had seen on the old trail. Stevens said it was about three weeks ago. Gardom made sure he asked Stevens clearly and distinctly in Cotton's presence whether anyone else had seen those men besides himself and Mrs. Stevens. Stevens quickly answered that no one else had, and Gardom remembered that both Wilson and Moxley had stated to him that they had been with Stevens when the two men had showed up on the trail. Gardom's suspicions with regards to Stevens seemed to be confirmed by Stevens' evasiveness and uncooperative manner.

Together with Stevens, the three constables made their way back to the man's cabin. Gardom dismissed Special Constable Smith, requesting that he look to their horses on the way down. He and Cotton decided to stay the night at the Stevens cabin with its rudimentary facilities. Pearse and Carter returned from their fruitless search for the tracks of the robbers to the south, and together they questioned Stevens about his activities. The closest they could come to a slip-up by the now alerted suspect was when he stated that Bruce Moxley may have been with them when he saw Dunn and Colquhoun that day in April.

The small one room cabin inhabited by Paul and Margaret Stevens had only the barest of necessities or comforts. Stevens insisted that the officers use his and his wife's sleeping area and beds. The man and his spouse then delicately walled themselves off with a sheet of sheer muslin for a modicum of privacy. Pearse and Carter took the double bed, and Gardom and Cotton slept beside each other on the floor. Gardom was anxious about Stevens, having heard about the suspicions that area farmers and ranchers had about his horse thieving activities, as well as the fact Gardom viewed him as a prime suspect in the Ducks robbery. The Enderby constable slipped his revolver under his pillow, a rolled up jacket, and his Winchester was leaning against the wall beside him within easy reach. He dozed off into a fitful sleep. He was suddenly awakened with the feeling he had had the light of an electric torch shone in his face. As he awoke he saw the flash of a light on the ceiling coming from where the Stevens were sleeping. It was quickly extinguished. Gardom was convinced Stevens was on the prowl.

He drew his pistol from under his pillow and quietly awoke Cotton. Gardom whispered to him about the flash of light and told him to get his revolver and have it ready. Cotton whispered back that it was on the other side of the room. Gardom handed him his rifle, and cautioned him not to go to sleep the rest of the night. Pearse and Carter slept on.

Gardom feared falling asleep. Later he thought he felt a draft as if the door was opened. Later still a mighty bang and thump were heard from the other side of the muslin barrier. The flimsy stretcher type bed Stevens and his wife were sleeping on had given way. The rotten sacking could not support the weight of two, and the couple had broken through and slammed into the board floor. Gardom remembered having seen the cot folded up outside the cabin when he had arrived earlier that day. He was convinced that Pearse was the only one in the tiny cabin who had any sleep that night.

Monday, 14 May 1906

Early the next morning Carter and Stevens went to round up the horses, including the two captured earlier in the week. They had difficulty with the two strange horses as they continually tried to turn off and follow a blazed trail marked by trees with three notches on them. It was now well known that the men suspected of being the train robbers had blazed escape trails throughout the hills and mountains in the heavily timbered areas. The unusual part was that some of Paul Stevens' horses also wanted to break away to follow the same blazed trails. Both he and Carter remarked about the fact in a laughing manner. Carter and Pearse left Stevens with Gardom and Cotton, and they headed south towards the Douglas Lake Road where the rest of their posse was waiting for them.

When the earliest opportunity arose, Gardom approached Stevens and told him he suspected him of at least being an accomplice of the men who had held up the train. Cotton stood back at a distance with a watchful eye. Gardom told Stevens that his friend Mohr had been inquiring about him down in Grande Prairie during the day before the robbery took place, and other information Gardom had gathered led him to believe Stevens was one of the robbers. When Stevens gave his alibi and said he had been staying with his relatives the Pratts at Upper Campbell Creek, Gardom agreed that they should ride over there so that Stevens could clear his name. Stevens said flippantly, "I will lend you a horse and you can go yourself." Gardom refused and told Stevens he would have to come with him. Stevens went into the cabin to say goodbye to his wife and made preparations to leave. All the while he kept passing by Gardom's rifle leaning against the wall. Gardom decided not to make an issue of it and to play a disinterested role. He left the rifle leaning against the wall until he could unobtrusively recover it.

Gardom and Cotton gathered up their gear and packs, and with their rifles under their arms, they proceeded down the trail with Stevens leading his horse in front of them. Stevens volunteered to carry their rifles for them, but Gardom laughed and thanked him anyway. The two constables and their prisoner made good time down the trail, and soon had retrieved their horses. With Stevens between them, they rode down out of the Monte Hills.[12]

When the three mounted men got out of the Monte Hills, instead of turning left to head towards his relatives the Pratts, Stevens found himself covered by the rifles of the two constables and on his way to the lock-up in Vernon. Stevens was much agitated and ever on the alert to make his escape. He finally made his attempt to escape on the way to Vernon, but was thwarted by the actions of the two vigilant constables bringing him in. After Stevens had been placed in the Vernon jail, Chief Constable Simmons was ordered to withdraw any special constables he might have out on investigations, as he had received a wire that three men had been arrested near Douglas Lake. Later Simmons would escort Paul Stevens to the Kamloops Gaol, where he was locked up with the other robbery suspects.[13]

XV
ROYAL NORTH WEST MOUNTED POLICE

March in late winter 1906 was typically bright and sunny. But it was still cold in the heart of the Rocky Mountains of Alberta. Spring had not yet arrived in the high country or around the barracks of the Royal North West Mounted Police (R.N.W.M.P.) in Banff. Mounted Police Constable John "Jack" Browning (Reg. No. 2858) was usually stationed at Morley on the Stoney Mountain Indian Reservation, 20 miles west of Calgary. However, today he was sitting in the office of his friend and fellow member Sergeant T. M. "Shoey" Shoebotham (Reg. No. 3561). Shoey was the member in charge of the Banff detachment. The two were enjoying each other's company, comfortable in the heat from the wood-burning stove. It was a time when activities around Banff were slow, before the mountain climbing season brought in the tourists by rail from around the world. Shoey was thumbing through the latest edition of the American police magazine "The Detective."

"Say, Jack, how would you like this?" Shoey exclaimed.

"What is it?" returned Jack.

"The Americans are offering twenty thousand dollars in reward for the capture of Bill Miner, the notorious train robber."

Shoey continued with a description of Miner, which noted that Miner had a tattoo at the base of his left thumb and a dancing girl on his arm.

"Well, Shoey," said Browning, "if he did come over this way, we could not collect an American reward. It's against our Rules and Regulations."

Shoebotham and Browning's leisurely conversation that day would soon prove eerily coincidental just two months later in the heart of the cattle country of British Columbia.[1]

WEDNESDAY, 9 MAY 1906

Constable Browning was on mounted patrol in the foothills of the Rockies near Cochrane, Alberta. He rode up to the CPR station to visit his friend the station agent. The agent had been reading the telegrams as they went through, and he told Browning that the CPR had been robbed near Kamloops and that the top CPR officials were trying to get the R.N.W.M.P. sent to B.C. Browning thought to himself that this was highly unlikely as the B.C. Provincial Police had authority in British Columbia. It would require special authority for the federal police force to operate in B.C. as it was outside the force's territory.[2]

In Vancouver that same day, the General Superintendent of the CPR's western division, Richard Marpole, was applying himself to just that problem. The top management of the CPR had not been impressed with the B.C. Provincial Police force after the robbery near Mission two years previously. Their lack of success in apprehending the perpetrators convinced CPR management that other methods should be utilized. Marpole wired his supervisor in Winnipeg, Vice President William Whyte, news of the latest robbery at Ducks east of Kamloops. Whyte quickly made application through company lawyers and lobbyists to the Department of Justice in Ottawa to have a detail of Royal North West Mounted Police dispatched to Kamloops. It was normal government procedure that when the CPR, the largest business enterprise in the Dominion, made a request of government, it be implemented if at all possible and with a minimum of delay.[3]

Later that same afternoon, Acting Sergeant John Jackson Wilson (Reg. No. 2566) in "E" Division, R.N.W.M.P. headquarters in Calgary, received a wire notifying the detachment of the robbery at Kamloops. Wilson requested descriptions of the robbers and received a wire giving them early the next morning. He wired Mounted Police posts west of Calgary on the CPR main line to watch out for suspicious characters and to stand by for further orders.[4]

Thursday, 10 May 1906

On the morning of the 10TH of May, the officer commanding "E" Division, Inspector A.W. Duffus, received a wire from the Commissioner of the Mounted Police A. Bowen-Perry (O. 44) in Fort Macleod. Perry had received word from the Justice Department in Ottawa to assist in the investigations at Kamloops. He ordered that a detail of Mounties, and he listed them by name, be made ready for travel to Kamloops. They were to be in plain clothes and have rations and forage for 20 days. Perry advised that he would be in Calgary to assume command of the detail and would be leaving for Calgary on the morning train.[5]

Perry also wired Constable Jack Browning at Morley to get three good Indian trackers from the nearby Stony Indian reservation with pack ponies and to wire him back as to how much they would cost. Browning made some inquiries and found that the cost would be prohibitive, advising Perry of that fact by return wire.

Friday, 11 May 1906

On Friday afternoon, Browning received another wire from Commissioner Perry cancelling the Indian trackers. He ordered Browning, with civilian clothes, sidearms, rifle and tack, boots and Stetson, to join the detail that would be travelling on the next train to Kamloops.[6]

Before Bowen-Perry left Fort Macleod, he took the opportunity to send out a necessary diplomatic telegram.

By the time the telegram was received in Victoria, Hussey was already in Kamloops acting as his own Officer In Charge. Sergeant T.R. Murray in the head office of the Provincial Police in Victoria passed the wire along to Hussey in Kamloops.

By the time Commissioner Perry had arrived in Calgary at noon on the 11TH, arrangements for the trip to Kamloops had been completed. The detail, with all their arms, tack and gear, gathered at the station in Calgary that evening in preparation for departure. Included with their equipment was a sack containing seven sharp iron picket pins about three feet long. The enterprising individual who packed their gear obviously had no idea of the country and vegetation to be encountered in British Columbia, and envisioned a bald flat prairie devoid of trees as the type of terrain they would have to navigate over. The officious baggageman saw the vicious points sticking through the sack and walked away, saying that he would not check "that stuff" in as baggage. Wilson confronted the baggageman and asked him why he wouldn't check them in.

The railway worker smirked and, pointing to the sharp pickets, said, "That is not baggage, and in any event you are too late to have your baggage checked to go on this train. You should have been here half an hour ago."

Wilson retorted, "I think you will have to check this baggage, alright."

The baggageman raised his voice, "I'll be damned if I do."

Sergeant Wilson spun on his heel and went to the station phone. He called CPR General Superintendent Jamieson at his office and said to him, "Your baggageman here refuses to check our baggage, and if the Canadian Pacific Railway chooses to put obstacles in our way like this, we may as well stay at home."

Jamieson, thrown off guard, asked, "Where are you now?"

"At the station."

"Alright, I will be down in a minute."

Shortly the General Superintendent arrived, along with Divisional Superintendent Niblick, both with furrowed brows and determined step. Wilson apprised them of the problem with the picket pins.

Taking command, Jamieson asked, "Where is the man that refuses to put it on the train?"

Wilson pointed straight at the baggageman, who now had a worried look on his face at all the brass suddenly appearing. "There he is!"

Jamieson called the hapless baggageman before him and slowly and quietly addressed him. "You see that baggage? That is the property of the Mounted Police and it is to go on this train, and Mr. Niblick," he turned towards the General Superintendent, "you see that it gets on this train without fail, and I do not want any more fooling about it either."

Before Wilson could make a comment, the sack of picket pins was hoisted up and loaded into the baggage car. They were never to leave downtown Kamloops until it was time to return to Calgary. The baggageman was never reprimanded, and Wilson was sure that he was probably adhering to rules and procedures. If it had not been in the CPR's best interests, the pins would have stayed behind in Calgary.[8]

With Commissioner Perry and Sergeant Wilson when the train pulled out of Calgary were Sergeant Percy Thomas (Reg. No. 3186),

Corporals C.R. Peters (Reg. No. 3429) and James Stewart (Reg. No. 3754), and Constable James Tabuteau (Reg. No. 4287).

Constable Jack Browning boarded the train at Morley, and as he did not have enough time to check his baggage, he made his way into the day coach and deposited his saddle, tack, rifle and duffle bag on the nearest empty seat. He was about to sit down and make himself comfortable when he heard a voice beside him, "Good evening, Corporal." Browning looked over and saw Commissioner Perry. Then he noticed other saddles and duffel bags, and in the dim light of the coach, he saw a number of familiar faces. He walked along the aisle greeting the various other members, realizing that the best of the force in that part of Alberta had been chosen for the task to be presented to them in Kamloops.[9]

The seven member detail was complete when Sergeant T.M. "Shoey" Shoebotham got on board at Banff.

SATURDAY, 12 MAY 1906

The train carrying the Mounties pulled into Kamloops on a dreary overcast Saturday morning with rain showers coming down off the surrounding hills and with the fresh scent of sage in the air. After making introductions to Provincial Police Superintendent Frederick Hussey, Commissioner Perry met with his detail in a local hotel. Perry had obtained an old Hudson's Bay Company map of the country to the south of the railroad, and he told his men that it appeared that the robbers were heading for the Douglas Lake country in an attempt to get across the American border. He showed the men the area that the Provincial Police and their Indian trackers and posses had covered south of the Campbell Range and the Monte Hills. He then told the officers that he wanted them to set up a line of men acting as pickets from Douglas Lake east, and to start immediately. An experienced guide from the Douglas Lake ranch, "Slim" Jim Benyon, was made available to the detail to guide them through the hills and grasslands into the Douglas Lake country.

The seven Mounties had lunch, then gathered up their saddles and tack and make their way down to the corrals beside the tracks where their horses were being held. Supplied by John Roper Hull in the Edith Lake country, the green broke horses were straight in off the range after a winter by themselves. The detail saw the dust being raised by circling and agitated horses and realized they had a bit of a challenge in front of them.

"Each man picked the horse he wanted, and they started to saddle and mount them. The horses were straight out of the bush, and it did not appear that they had ever been ridden. The whole town of Kamloops turned out to see the free show and enjoyed themselves immensely. Some would buck straight up, another would try to stand on his head, another would sit down and refuse to budge, another would be trying his best to get his head where his tail ought to be, and when you have seven performing all at once and the same time you can imagine that there are no dull moments for the spectators ... As every man in this party had been picked for his riding as well as other police qualities, in a short time the horses were all subdued."[10]

They mounted up, their recently issued .45 calibre, six round, Colt New Service revolvers in Sam Browne style holsters strapped around their waists. Slung across their shoulders were the latest rifles issued to the force. They were .303 calibre, five round, Ross Mark I carbines. Weighing over seven pounds, the rifles, while very accurate, would in the future acquire an unenviable reputation for jamming in dirty conditions and the bolt "blowing out." They were dressed in civilian clothes and appeared as ordinary cowboys with their four cornered Stetsons and spurred boots. To make the picture complete, one of the riders wore chaps. In company with their guide and leading two gentler pack horses with their gear aboard, they made their way down the main street of Kamloops to where the Nicola Road led up into the hills. To the delight of downtown onlookers, the horses bucked and snorted and farted and danced all over the wooden sidewalks as the frustrated "Riders of the Plains" struggled to keep them under control.[11]

"The party disappeared over the mountains just at dusk, amid the cheers and good wishes of the good people of Kamloops."[12]

Sergeant Wilson's last instructions from Commissioner Perry rang loud in his ears: "Spare neither men, money or horses, but keep careful account of all expenditures."[13]

Darkness soon fell, and the detail was grateful that Benyon lived up to his reputation of being "able to make his way through the mountains on the darkest night that ever existed." The riders could see little or nothing in front of them as any starlight or moonlight was obscured by the heavy overcast. In the darkness and single file, the riders periodically called out their regimental number to each other, making sure none was left behind. If one did not sing out, the line was halted until the stray rider caught up. As none of the horses were especially fond of each other, the riders had to maintain at least a few yards of separation to prevent kicking and biting. After about five or six hours of travelling, it started to rain. It picked up in tempo and turned into a downpour. The heavy rain and the ink black darkness, coupled with heavy brush and unfamiliar terrain, made for a difficult time for the prairie boys. In the heavy rain they attempted to put on their waterproof slickers., Some of the more skittish, temperamental mounts bucked and protested vehemently at the flapping garments, so they decided it was best to just put up with the discomfort rather than have to walk.

Wilson had planned to try to make it to Rockford that night, about 33 miles from Kamloops. However, they started to notice their mounts were giving out. A diet of bunch grass all winter had failed to build them up enough to carry a rider any distance. Wilson conferred with Benyon who said that there was a ranch about eight miles away and they should be able to make that before too long. Slim Benyon had some reservations as to whether they could find it as it was some distance off the road, but Wilson could see each horse starting to lag. The fight had gone out of them, and they only wanted to reach some shelter and fodder. Wilson decided to try for it.

He soon questioned his decision. One after another, riders and mounts stumbled into flood irrigation cross ditches hidden in the dark, and the riders somersaulted out of their saddles. Fortunately no one was hurt, and each thrown rider shook off most of the mud clinging to him and remounted. It was 3:00 A.M. when they pulled into the ranch of a Mr. Blackburn just off the Nicola Road. They roused the sleeping and surprised occupants and were quickly given stabling and feed for their horses and hot coffee for themselves. They snatched a few hours sleep on the floor of the ranch house, thankful the sound of the rain on the roof did not mean they or their mounts were suffering. At the top of the Monte Hills miles to the east, Provincial Police Constable Fernie and his trackers tried to get some sleep under their thin blankets as they lay on the hard ground beside a dying fire. They would wake before first light with two inches of snow covering them and their gear and horses.

SUNDAY, 13 MAY 1906

The detail was up the next morning at first light at 6:00 A.M. They rubbed down their rested horses and gave them each a good feed of grain. The rancher and his wife and daughter made them a fine breakfast. Shoebotham's mount seemed to have suffered the most from the previous day's exertions, and Wilson attempted to get another from the rancher, but he had none available. So the detail left the rancher and his family, and made sure they only went as fast as Shoebotham's horse was capable. Whenever they had the chance, they continued to feed the horses grain throughout the morning, and as noon drew near, they started to see the energy return to the animals. The detail stopped at every ranch house along the way and made inquiries about any strangers that may have been seen.

In Kamloops, Commissioner Perry was busy sending telegrams to "E" Division Commanding Officer Dufus. Perry ordered Dufus to send Inspector Church, who was standing by in Calgary, and a detail of ten men and horses immediately to Vernon and points south. They were to take their field service kit and a minimum of bedding. Camp equipment, rations and forage would be obtained in the field. Church and his detail left for the Okanagan on the next available train.[14]

By 11:00 A.M., Wilson and the troopers were at Rockford. Located just south of Stump Lake, it was a small community with a roadhouse owned by Robert Scott. Together with his family, he ran the local post office that served the 150 people, ranchers, miners and their

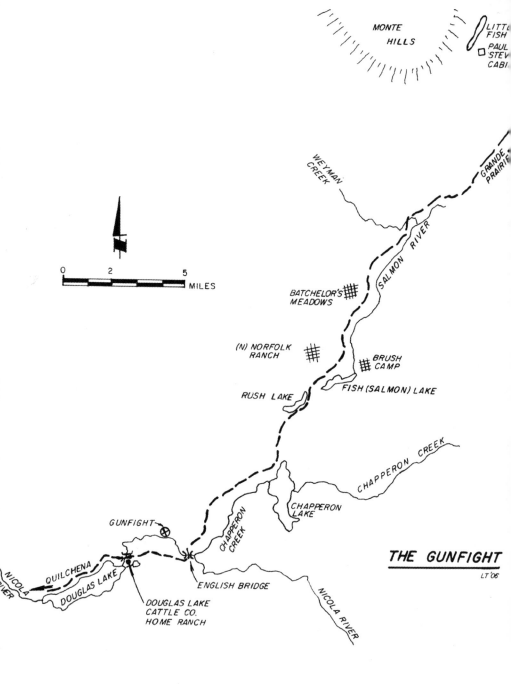

MONTE
HILLS

LITTL
FISH
PAUL
STEV
CABI

WEYMAN
CREEK

GRANDE
PRAIRIE

SALMON RIVER

BATCHELOR'S
MEADOWS

(N) NORFOLK
RANCH

BRUSH
CAMP

RUSH LAKE

FISH (SALMON) LAKE

CHAPPERON CREEK

CHAPPERON
LAKE

GUNFIGHT

CHAPPERON
CREEK

THE GUNFIGHT

LT '06

NICOLA
RIVER

QUILCHENA

DOUGLAS LAKE

ENGLISH BRIDGE

NICOLA RIVER

DOUGLAS LAKE
CATTLE CO.
HOME RANCH

0   2   5
MILES

The Gunfight and Capture near Douglas Lake, B.C. 14 May 1906 families, from the surrounding area. Scott and his wife Mary Ann put together a fine meal for the policemen, and Wilson obtained some more grain and feed for their horses. After a satisfying meal, and with their clothes finally drying out after the last night's downpour, Wilson conferred with his men. They all agreed that the load carried by their mounts was too much. Besides the rider and some personal gear, the pistol, rifle and a full complement of ammunition that were issued to each trooper added considerable weight to the load each horse was expected to carry. In addition, the heavy rifle slung over the shoulder of each trooper caused the rider to weaken and to constantly shift his balance and "when a man does not ride nice and free it is bad for the horse." In order to relieve that load somewhat, it was decided to leave the Ross rifles and ammunition behind at Rockford. They justified this by believing that pistols would probably be the most valuable when it came to any shooting, as any altercation was bound to be at close range.

When the Mounted Police left Rockford, they felt a spring in the step of their well fed horses now that some of their burden had been left behind, and the grain was giving them additional stores of energy. They made good time the rest of the day on the trails through the rolling grasslands of the Nicola Valley. The rain continued, but it was not as intense as the previous evening. They pulled east up into the high interior plateau country, and Wilson thought to himself that the country was easier to get lost in than any parts of Alberta or Saskatchewan. Despite being guided by the skillful Benyon, the Sergeant kept referring to the hand-drawn map given him before he left Kamloops. Finally they rode through Spaxomin, a community of the Okanagan nation, and pulled into the Douglas Lake home ranch early on the evening of Sunday the 13TH. Joseph Greaves, the manager of the ranch, greeted them warmly and fixed them up with "first class accommodation for both men and horses." Wilson described Greaves "as fine a type of old settler as ever went west." The Sergeant explained the detail's mission to the ranch manager, and Greaves put the full resources of the ranch at Wilson's disposal. Greaves told Wilson that they had several ranches throughout the Nicola section, and if Wilson or any of his detail should need anything, they had just to ask. Greaves issued them with a letter to that effect to present to any of the cow camp foremen. Wilson asked if they might have their pack horses replaced and a cooking outfit to borrow. The ranch also supplied an Indian tracker and cook for the detail.[15]

Greaves replied, "We have the cooking outfit here but the pack horses and saddles are at Fish Lake about ten miles further down the trail. But that is where the Hudson's Bay Trail leaves the Grande Prairie Trail, so you can call in there and get them before starting out."[16]

The Mounties took full advantage of Mr. Greaves' hospitality and dropped their personal gear in the bunkhouse. The Chinese ranch cook set them up a fine supper. Some of the troopers went to the ranch store and stocked up on tobacco and other sundries. Their wet gear and clothing steamed as they dried beside the bunkhouse stoves.

Monday, 14 May 1906

At daylight the next morning all the men were up and the horses were given a good feed again. They had a hearty breakfast and were soon mounted and on their way to Fish Lake to pick up their pack horses and begin their search north towards Campbell's Meadows. They travelled east along the wagon road which wound through the valley of Chapperon Creek on the north bank. Grasslands stretched out on both sides of the valley until they were met by the heavier timber of fir and pine in the higher elevations. Some of the fields they passed were flood irrigated by Chinese workers. The detail spread out so as to search the open gulleys and the creek bottom, searching through the dense stands of cottonwoods, willow and black birch clumps. By noon they could see the tranquil surface of Chapperon Lake shining and stretching into the distance. The spring sun was shining brightly and temperatures were climbing into the low 70s. The grass in the high country was turning green, and the fat white-faced heifers stood with their ears erect and facing forward, staring at the passing riders. Their spring calves gambolled at their sides. The leaves were budding out on all the trees and brush in the creek bottom. It was difficult for the senses of the riders not to get lulled by warm spring air and the bucolic surroundings, but they did their best to stay alert and, spreading out, kept a sharp lookout. They arrived at the shores of Chapperon Lake shortly before noon and decided to have an early lunch. They unsaddled and picketed and fed and watered their horses, then enjoyed a hot meal cooked up on the mobile kitchen supplied by the ranch. As they were cleaning up after their meal, Provincial Police Constable Fernie came riding up from the direction of the home ranch on an almost exhausted horse. Fernie introduced himself and reported that he had seen three men on the road with packs on their backs about five or six miles back towards the ranch. Fernie and the Mounties galloped back to where he had spotted the suspects. They started searching the road for tracks that Fernie could identify. The tracker found plenty of sign, but soon told the Mounties, "China boy work here."[17]

Fernie finally found a set of tracks with the tell-tale distinctive hobnailed pattern and a pair of slim smooth soled boots. Satisfied that they were now on the track of the robbers, Wilson sent Sergeant Thomas up a nearby hill to scan the country with his glasses, and sent Constable Tabuteau and Slim Jim Benyon back towards Chapperon Lake to see if they could pick up more tracks where the robbers had come out of the bush to the north. Fernie rode back to the ranch to see if he could get the bloodhounds that were supposed to be on their way. Wilson dispersed his remaining five men in a screen across the north slope of the valley between Chapperon Creek and the high country to see if they could catch up to the robbers. They slowly made their way south-west towards the home ranch located on the opposite side of the creek. Corporal Stewart drew close to where Chapperon Creek emptied into the Nicola River. Squinting into the early afternoon sun, he saw a curl of smoke drifting over the willow clumps and stubby birches in the creek bottom. He took off his Stetson and waved it at the two members who were closest to him. They, in turn, silently gained the attention of Wilson, and he and Shoebotham, Peters and Browning quickly but quietly joined Corporal Stewart. They walked their horses across the open field

Typical terrain and vegetation near where gunfight occurred beside the banks of the Nicola River, Douglas Lake, B.C. 14 May 1906. Chapperon Creek is in the foreground. PHOTO BY AUTHOR.

to the edge of the brush in the creek bottom. The gentle swish of the horses' hoofs muffled in the bunch grass and the creak of saddle leather were the only sounds they made in the soft spring air. The gurgle and splash of the stream in the midst of the spring freshet blurred any sound they might make. They were about a mile as the crow flies from the home ranch and on the north side of the Nicola River opposite the house.[18]

They dismounted, and as they approached what looked like an impenetrable thicket, they noticed a small entrance leading into the brush. The Mounties unfastened their holster flaps, but left their Colts still holstered. They walked into a small clearing with the broad dry bed of a creek wandering through it and hailed anyone who could be about. They heard an answering shout, and down in the grass of the dry creek bed almost hidden from their view, they saw two men seated around a canvas wagon tarp and another lying on his side. As they approached, they could see the almost smokeless small fire burning beside them where they were boiling up a pot of Tetley's tea. On the plates in front of them they had a meal of boiled rice and cooked beef strips. A Winchester 44:40 lay wrapped in a sack beside them in full view, and the butts of pistols stuck out from under the tarp in front of Edwards and Colquhoun.[19][20]

Wilson waited until all the officers had drawn up to the clearing, Shoebotham standing a short distance off to the side. The officers saw that two of the men were wearing hobnailed boots, and the older man was wearing a smooth soled lighter pair. Wilson asked the three men where they were from. The older one, Edwards, answered that they were from Batchelor's Meadows, over Grande Prairie way. "That would be north," he coolly added.

Wilson asked him what they had been doing there.

"Prospecting a little," said Edwards.

Wilson asked him how long it had been since they had left there.

"About two days," replied Edwards.

Wilson then confronted the men with his suspicions. "Well, we are looking for the fellows who held up the CPR and you had better give a good account of yourselves."

Edwards scoffed and asked the Mounties how they could think he was a train robber when he looked so much more like a prospector.

"No you do not," disagreed Wilson, "and if it is found you are not the men, you will be brought back again to where you want to go, but just now the description given agrees with you, and you can consider yourselves under arrest for that offence."

Dunn, to whom Wilson had not been paying much attention, suddenly threw his teacup aside and sprang to his feet. "Look out boys, it's all up," he shouted and darted off to the nearest willow clump, reaching behind him to the holster he had pushed around behind his back when he was lying on his side. He pulled a

.44 Colt's revolver from this belt holster and palmed his Luger from his shoulder holster. As he ran, weaving behind the willow clumps, he fired two quick shots back at the Mounties from his automatic before they could react. Wilson saw Dunn's movement as if in slow motion, and saw and heard one of the shots fired at him almost point blank. Shoebotham, Browning and Stewart drew their revolvers immediately and ran after Dunn, firing their double action Colts as fast as they could. Dunn made a difficult target, dodging behind the clumps of willow and birch, all the while firing his Luger back at them as fast as he could pull the trigger. The rapid rate of fire of Dunn's pistols surprised the officers, and they were careful to take advantage of any cover that presented itself.[21]

Fifteen to twenty shots were fired by Dunn and the officers in a very short time, and the smoke from the gunpowder drifted in the air. Peters and Wilson covered Edwards and Colquhoun as they sat by the tarp, and the sound of shots continued from the brush close by where Dunn was putting up a desperate attempt to escape.

Edwards moved his hand towards the butt of the .38 Smith and Wesson he had captured from express clerk Mitchell two years before, grasped it, and started to pull it out from under the tarp. Corporal Peters, watching him closely, leaned over, and putting his hand on the pistol, he looked Edwards in the eye and said in a low, threatening voice, "If you draw that I will blow your brains out."

Peters, well over six feet in height and the possessor of an intimidating demeanour, held his service revolver point blank on the old man. Edwards quickly made some mental calculations and decided he should hold his hands straight up in the air.[22]

From the corner of his eye, Peters caught glimpses of Shorty Dunn dodging behind clumps of brush, firing as fast as he could. He drew Edwards' .38 with his right hand and, with his own Colt in his left hand, keeping his eye on Edwards all the while, he snapped off three quick shots at Dunn with the Smith and Wesson.[23]

Back in the brush, it was so thick Browning could hardly make Dunn out as he ran back and forth between the willows. The three Mounties shot through the willow clumps and in the direction they thought the robber's shots were coming from. Browning ran around the side of a willow clump and saw Dunn swing his pistol towards him. Browning fired, and Dunn fired back. Browning thought he had missed and fired quickly again. Dunn fell to the side and crashed through the brush, falling into a long ditch full of soft mud and water. Browning ran around to the edge of the drop, and saw Dunn on his back in the mud and the water, his hands in the air, still clutching his two pistols.

He looked up and saw Browning coming towards him, pistol extended at arm's length. "Don't," he yelled, "I am all in. I've been hit. I'm shot."

Shoebotham had been running around in a half circle sweep in an attempt to cut off the fleeing Dunn. He heard the shots cease and Dunn's shouting and headed towards his partner. He bolted through the underbrush and with a shout sailed through the air to land in the same ditch as Shorty Dunn. Browning, covering Dunn, heard the shout and thought that another of the suspects had made a break for it. Crouching, he swung and covered the struggling figure and almost fired at Shoebotham until he noticed the arm and hand of his friend Shoebotham sticking up out of the mud and water holding a New Service revolver. They heard Sergeant Wilson shouting loudly to them from where he was covering the other prisoners, "Don't cease firing until he throws out his guns."[24][25]

When Wilson heard Shoebotham give his startled shout as he went over the bank, Wilson looked at Peters and said, "I'm afraid Shoebotham has got winged." Browning removed the pistols from Dunn's hands, and made his way back to Wilson to get help to extricate Shoebotham and Dunn from the mud. Dunn was up to his waist in mud and water, and Shoebotham had fallen headlong into the murky mess. As Browning approached Wilson and Peters covering Edwards and Colquhoun, Wilson said to Browning, "You had better see about Shoebotham. I'm afraid he has got winged." Browning reassured him that the only injury Shoebotham had suffered was to his dignity. He retrieved a rope from one of their horses and tied it around Shoebotham's waist to pull him out. The same was done to

Dunn, and together, the Mountie and the bandit looked "more like mud turtles than human beings, however outside of having his eyes, ears, hair etc. filled with slimy mud, Shoebotham was entirely unhurt." The mud was soon washed off both the Mountie and the outlaw.[26]

Stewart covered Dunn with his revolver and told him to walk ahead of him back to the tarp. As Dunn painfully limped over the uneven ground, he surprised the policeman by laughing out loud and saying, "I know I am all done in."

Browning approached Dunn as he made his way towards the rest of the group. He said, "I'm sorry I had to wing you, but you asked for it."

Dunn replied, "I wish you had put it through my guts."

The Mounties sat Dunn down in the new green grass up against a cottonwood, and Browning tore a strip off the bottom of his own shirt to bind up Dunn's wound as best he could. It was plain to see that the bullet had penetrated right through the fleshy part of Dunn's calf, making a serious and painful wound. Wilson told Dunn he had done a very foolish thing for starting the shootout and that he very well could have been shot in the head rather than the leg. Dunn laughed and said, "I wish to Christ you had put it through my head, but (then) you couldn't blame me, could you?"[27]

Wilson asked the gunman, "Why did you start firing when you saw you were surrounded like that?"

Dunn quickly answered, "I thought I would stampede the outfit, and give the boys a chance to get their guns."[28]

Thomas and Tabuteau, the Mounties who had been scouting the back trail , had returned at the sound of the gunfire, along with the guide, Slim Jim Benyon. Wilson sent Benyon to the home ranch to advise Fernie of the shooting and then to proceed on to Quilchena where the guide was instructed to telephone Commissioner Bowen-Perry in Kamloops and advise him of the happenings. Shorty Dunn had been asking for a doctor, so Wilson instructed Benyon to telephone for Dr. Tuthill in Nicola Lake and have him start up the road to the ranch and meet them on their way down to Quilchena. Wilson wanted Dunn attended to as he didn't know how much of the gunman's old and well-used long red underwear had gone into the wound along the trajectory of the bullet. Such a likelihood could cause a serious and life-threatening infection.[29]

Peters and Stewart covered Edwards and Colquhoun while Browning and Shoebotham searched them. Suddenly Shoebotham, who was working on Edwards, excitedly called out to Browning, "Jack, come here a moment."

Browning left Colquhoun and walked over behind his friend. "What is it, Shoey?"

"Jack, we have something more than the Kamloops train robbers. This is Bill Miner. You remember, we saw him in the detective magazine when we were in Banff."

"I can tell you in a minute," said Browning, and he walked around behind Edwards and told the old man to put his hands behind him. The Mounties had no handcuffs or shackles so they had to tie up their prisoners with wire and rope. As Browning cinched up Edwards' wrists, the man called out, "Hold on, don't cut a man's hands off."

Browning slacked off a bit, and while he finished tying the man's hands he saw the telltale tattoo mark at the base of his thumb. "All right, Bill, but you won't get away from us the same way as you did from Guthren." Browning was referring to the escapades Miner had pulled off that were detailed in that spring's magazine article.[30]

The Constable called over to Shoey, "You're right, Shoey." It then dawned on the seven officers just who they had captured that day, and they proceeded to search Miner more thoroughly.

Wilson sent Stewart to the home ranch to fetch a wagon and team to transport the prisoners. The rest of the officers assembled all the firearms taken from the three suspects and placed them on the tarp. Besides the 44:40 Winchester lever action rifle, Dunn's Luger and .44 Colt's revolver, Miner's .38 Smith and Wesson revolver and an automatic .32 Colt, Colquhoun's Iver-Johnson .38 revolver, and another .32 Colt automatic made an impressive arsenal. There was a large supply of ammunition for the Winchester and the revolvers, as well as several loaded magazines of automatic pistol cartridges for the Luger and the .32 Colts.[31] [32]

Wilson turned to Edwards, as he seemed to be the spokesman

for the trio. He asked the old man why they had to carry such an impressive array of armaments with them. Edwards replied that he didn't think that they carried too many, besides prospectors usually carried firearms. The old man went on to say that they could easily prove their alibi that they were prospectors and stressed that they should not be condemned before being allowed to be heard. Wilson thought to himself that the old fellow was rather pleasant to talk to, with his soft American accent.[33]

Shorty Dunn, sitting in the grass with his back against the tree, looked at the spread of pistols on the tarp and the Winchester, now out of its cloth covering, leaning against a nearby cottonwood. "I would like to have had that rifle a few minutes, there would be a hot country around here then."[34]

Browning picked up Shorty's semi-automatic Luger and passed it around to the other admiring officers. When they passed it to Wilson, who was sitting close to Dunn, Wilson attempted to remove the magazine. He fumbled with the unfamiliar firearm which still contained an unfired cartridge. Shorty watched the officer trying to figure out the mechanism and laughed.

Wilson asked his fellow officers, "Do any of you fellows know how to unload this damned Luger?"

Shorty volunteered, "I will unload it for you, Sergeant."

"Nothing doing, Shorty," replied Wilson. "We have already had an exhibition of your kind of unloading and do not want any more just now, thank you very kindly." At this Dunn, despite the pain of his wound, laughed heartily and loudly.[35]

The Mounties watched the antics of Shorty Dunn with some amazement. He appeared to be extremely excited, his eyes wide open and darting about. He was given to frequent outbursts of laughter and generally gave the impression that he found the whole affair a lark. It was easy to determine that he was an accomplished hunter and trapper and used to the hardships those occupations could impart. He would joke and make light of his wound, even though he was unable to walk. As time went by the shock and pain he was suffering must have started to exert its influence, but it did not affect his jocular good-natured manner.[36]

While the searching of the prisoners was underway, the officers took time to learn more about their new charges. Bill Miner, the old man in the broad brimmed Stetson and long rider's coat, still maintained that his name was George Edwards, he was 62 years old, and was born in Fulton County, Ohio. The red-headed man gave his name as Lewis Colquhoun, age 27, having been born in Clifford, Ontario. He told the officers he was from Phoenix in the Boundary country and said that he had only been in the Similkameen section a few months. Dunn gave his first name as William, age 42, and declared that he really had no name at all, came from nowhere, and wasn't born.[37][38]

From inside Bill Miner's long coat, Browning took a bottle of catarrh pills for a runny nose, a pen, some postage stamps, two loaded .32 Colt's automatic pistol magazines, some prospector's goggles, and Edna's letter returned undelivered from Phoenix. The bottle was wrapped in a Catarrhozone wrapper, was labelled cathartic pills, but actually contained a liquid, probably opium. Edwards had one ten dollar gold piece, one five dollar bill, one ten dollar bill, and two fifty cent pieces. From Billy Dunn were taken an electric flash lamp, a black match safe, and two magazines for his automatic 9 mm Luger. Personal items taken from Colquhoun included a pen, a metal match safe, a small locked pocket book, and a circular pocket mirror with a picture of the Cunliffe House in San Francisco on the back. In his pocket was a receipt for his membership fee to an eastern Canadian branch of the Y.W.C.A. Together, Dunn and Colquhoun had only a few pieces of silver on them.[39][40]

When Stewart rode up he was followed by Provincial Police Constable Fernie and a Douglas Lake Indian cowboy driving a wagon and team. As the wagon took a long swing around to face in the direction they had come, Stewart saw that the three men had been moved out of the thick brush and into the open grassy meadow. Dunn was seated on the ground, his back against a tree and his leg elevated on a log. Stewart watched Browning gathering all the pistols and the Winchester and wrapping them in blankets. Then some of the personal effects were gathered, placed in the tarp, and the whole was bundled together and tied up with ropes for transport in the back of the wagon. Dunn was lifted into the back of the wagon so that he could lie flat, and they rolled Miner's long coat up and placed it beneath his head.[41]

The party started off for the ranch, and as the brush was too thick, the banks too high and the Nicola River too deep to ford, they hauled their prisoners back to English Bridge and around to the home ranch, a distance of some two miles. They pulled into the main yard in front of the ranch house and were greeted by ranch manager Greaves. Greaves told the Sergeant that a Seattle detective by the name of William Seavey, representing the Thiel Detective Service, had been looking for the detail of Mounted Police. Sergeant Wilson brought Greaves up to date with events and told him that one of the men they had captured was Bill Miner. Greaves frowned and disagreed with Wilson saying that he must be mistaken as he knew George Edwards well and that he was a rancher in the Aspen Grove country and he had personally sold him horses. Wilson assured him of the man's identity, and Greaves made the bunkhouse available to the officers and their prisoners. Everyone was given a meal brought over from the cookhouse, and Greaves made a light Democrat and team available to transport the prisoners to Quilchena. The Mounties washed Shorty's leg in hot water, and the manager gave them some camphor ice, a mixture of camphor oil and wax, to sooth the pain of the wound. They then bandaged it up as best they could, using what rudimentary medical knowledge they had acquired during their service.[42 43]

Late in the afternoon they left the ranch for the hamlet of Quilchena, 18 miles distant. Wilson had hired an Okanagan Indian teamster to drive the sprung Democrat with their prisoners aboard. The detail, with Fernie and Slim Jim Benyon joining them, made their way down out of the fertile grasslands in the high country of the Douglas Lake Ranch and through Spaxomin and the reserve of the Upper Nicola Indian Band. The late afternoon sun was dropping behind the hills as the silver sheen of Nicola Lake appeared in the distance. The scent of new grass, road dust and sagebrush imprinted in the memories of the riders as they sat back in their saddles for the long downhill stretch. Little conversation passed between them as their mounts lulled their senses with an easy gait. Each man, officer, prisoner, guide or teamster, thought his own private thoughts. Every one of those men that rode down out of that country that day would carry his own memories, sights and sounds of that afternoon with him. The faces and voices of Miner, Dunn and Colquhoun, the crack of the pistol shots, the smoke drifting in the air, the quiet calmness of the cattle watching with uncomprehending interest, and the steady, quiet flow of Chapperon Creek and the Nicola River sat on the shoulders of their memories. That sunny spring day in the high grasslands and the men who shared it with them would reside in their mind's eye until each and every one of them was dead and gone.

The caravan finally reached the floor of the valley, passed through the Indian village at Quilchena, and made their way south towards Joseph Guichon's hotel a few miles down the road. Before they had proceeded too far along the shores of Nicola Lake, Dr. George Tuthill of the town of Nicola drove up in his buggy. Dr. Tuthill had just recently married Miss Grace Douglas in Nicola, and he had considerably increased his responsibilities and income by taking on the contract as medical officer to the construction camps working on the new railway line from Spence's Bridge. He was responsible for that section between 22 Mile and Nicola Lake. Sergeant Wilson and Dr. Tuthill had a brief consultation, and then the doctor got up on the Democrat to examine Shorty's wound. Tuthill agreed that the wound should be probed to ensure no foreign materials such as his red woolen longjohns had entered beneath the flesh. Wilson asked Dunn whether he wanted the doctor to probe the wound right there on the side of the road.

Shorty laughed ironically and said, "I am having the time of my life now, so I'll wait till we get to Quilchena to be cut up by the sawbones."[44]

When the party arrived at the little road stop with its hotel and a few outbuildings, it was 9:30 in the evening and fully dark. The night had grown chilly after a warm spring day. The sky was overcast and threatening more rain. Only the windows of the hotel and the hall they were heading toward showed any light in their windows. The troopers and their prisoners entered the hall, a wood frame structure about thirty feet wide by forty feet long, with a small twelve by fourteen room attached to it. When they entered the hall, Wilson ordered that more lamps be lighted and the stove started up to boil water. The prisoners were untied and allowed to arrange some blankets for the night. The Sergeant set up a guard system whereby two guards were to be alert for a period of two hours each, and then they were to be relieved by another two. All the officers, including Fernie, were ordered by Wilson to ensure no one was allowed to talk to the prisoners without his express authority.[45]

Once the water was boiling, Dr. Tuthill commenced sterilizing Shorty Dunn's wounds and his tools. With lanterns circling doctor and patient, Tuthill probed the wound. He commented on the seriousness of it and Dunn, laughing, said, "It should have gone through my head, it would have saved a lot of trouble."

Dunn laughed and joked with the surrounding men and continued to do so throughout the procedures. He kept up a banter with the Mounties and Fernie as they watched the bloody procedures. The good doctor admonished him to cease his frivolity as it was doing him no good, but the warning had no effect on the garrulous bandit. Dr. Tuthill found that the bullet had passed cleanly through the fleshy part of Dunn's right calf and no bones were broken. His examinations proved the wound to be a "puncture about four inches below the right knee passing through the upper part of the calf from behind, running forward and outward carrying pieces of garment." He carefully probed and investigated and tried to remove as much foreign material as possible as he was concerned "there may be a danger of blood poisoning for a few days on account of infection carried into the wound by the clothing."[46]

The doctor reflected on the other bullet wound he had treated just two years previously. Smoky Chisholm's injured leg, shot through and smashed with a large calibre Winchester, was much more serious than Dunn's and had left that gunman with a permanent limp. Shorty's wound would have no lasting effects other than a dimpled scar.[47]

While the medical procedures were underway and the police officers were getting their bedding ready for an overnight sleep in the hall, two strangers dressed in city clothes entered and introduced themselves to Sergeant Wilson. The first introduced himself as Detective W.L. McLaws, a Special Services agent of the CPR Police. McLaws, lately arrived from Winnipeg, was in charge of all the CPR police and special agents working on the robbery investigation, as well as the private detectives hired by the CPR. He had been busy with administrative duties during the past days in Kamloops, coordinating activities and attending to an agitated and demanding Superintendent Marpole. Even so, he still took time to conduct some of his own investigations and worked closely with Superintendent Hussey and Commissioner Bowen-Perry. The other man was the same Detective Seavey out of Seattle who had previously met with Constable Gardom out by Grande Prairie and who earlier at the Douglas Lake Ranch inquired to Manager Greaves about the location of the Mounted Police in that country. Seavey, hired to assist in the investigations by the CPR, was madly dashing around about the country on his own investigations. Whenever he could get to a phone or telegraph office, he kept the Vancouver Province informed of all the latest news, with himself identified as the principal and most successful investigator. He was accompanied in Quilchena by one Taylor from Spokane who had his bloodhounds with him. Taylor was fresh from shooting and killing the outlaw Smith in Oregon just a few days previously. Seavey's activities in Quilchena would be used tellingly by defence lawyers at the trial soon to be held in Kamloops.[48]

Some of the other members noted the presence of the town-dressed strangers in the hall and assumed they were there with permission of Sergeant Wilson. They watched McLaws questioning Miner and Dunn, but could see that any questioning bore no fruit from them. Seavey informed Wilson that he had been instructed by the CPR's Superintendent Marpole to pursue certain investigations, particularly with regard to the dynamite that had been found beside the tracks and whether or not the three captured men were, in fact, the wanted men. Earlier, Wilson had been handed a telegraph message relayed from the hotel. Commissioner Bowen-Perry in Kamloops instructed Wilson to extend all co-operation to Detectives Seavey and McLaws while they were in Quilchena. Wilson was personally very much against this as it was outside normal procedures; however, his Commissioner's orders were clear, and Wilson acquiesced. The tall and dark American detective had studied the prisoners intently from the side, then requested of Wilson to make Colquhoun available to him for questioning. He had perhaps seen something about Colquhoun that indicated he might be able to extract information from this suspect, who appeared to be somewhat overwhelmed and confused by the events that had overtaken him.[49]

Together with Seavey, Wilson got a lamp and escorted Colquhoun into the little room at the back of the main hall. Throughout the time Seavey interrogated Colquhoun, Wilson was in attendance. Wilson made sure Seavey told Colquhoun that he was a private detective, and Wilson told Colquhoun that he did not have to answer any of Seavey's questions if he did not want to. Wilson stayed nearby to ensure no undue coercion took place, and he could see that Colquhoun was reluctant to answer any of the detective's questions. Colquhoun responded to Seavey's questioning by stating that he did not wish to say anything at that time, and Seavey reluctantly did not press him. Wilson escorted Colquhoun back to his sleeping spot. The interview had lasted all of three minutes.[50]

It was now close to midnight and the lights in the Quilchena Hotel, just a short walk from the hall, were still burning brightly. Angry and loud voices drifted out into the dark night air. It was past the mandated closing hour for any liquor establishments, but business was good and the customers were demanding. Inside was a large group of cowboys and miners whose bravado was being fuelled by copious amounts of booze supplied by the willing hotel bartender. Many professional and experienced drinkers had been in the area of the Quilchena Ranch and the town of Nicola that day and had heard about the capture of Miner, Dunn and Colquhoun. Word

The original Quilchena Hotel, circa 1906.
Courtesy of Nicola Valley Museum and Archives.

had quickly spread up and down the valley before the Mounties had even come down out of the Douglas Lake country. As George Edwards, Miner was well known to many of the rowdies and toughs throughout the Nicola. Though they were well aware of his suspected rustling activities with Jack Budd, sympathies were running high to storm the hall and effect the release of the supposed train robbers. Leading this well lubricated faction of rootless ne'er-do-wells was the limping, black-moustached gunman, Smoky Chisholm. Smoky hadn't learned any lessons after his losing argument with a Winchester in Manning's roadhouse in April of 1904, or if he had, they had now been forgotten.[51]

Chisholm bragged to those around him that if he could get some fireworks going, he "could take those boys away from those Mounties." Well fortified with liquor and convinced by his own rhetoric, Chisholm limped across to the hall and tried to make his way inside to see his friend, now known as Bill Miner. He was confronted by Corporal Stewart, who barred his entrance and told him to return to the hotel. Smoky returned to the hotel to stock up on more courage and then, feeling confident of his true badness and intimidating qualities, made another attempt to get into the now quiet hall. Stewart by this time was losing his patience and quietly said to the weaving Chisholm at the foot of the stoop, "You have asked twice, ask again and I will let you in, but you will not come out." Even in his confused mind, Smoky must have determined that discretion was the better part of valour, and he spun on his heel and made his uncertain way back to the hotel.[52][53][54]

Corporal Stewart by now was getting fed up with Chisholm's implied threats and the noises coming from the hotel and reported the matter to his superior. Sergeant Wilson, with Constable Browning and Constable Fernie to enforce a provincial regulation, strode purposefully over to the hotel. Soon dark figures could be seen leaving the premises, silhouetted against the yellow lamplight from the windows and doors. The boys were soon mounting their horses, and with shouts and curses they made their way into the gloom. Finally the lamps were turned down in the hotel, and the three officers returned to the hall to try to get some sleep during the balance of the night.

TUESDAY, 15 MAY 1906

The next morning, as the police and prisoners in the hall were cleaning up after the breakfast catered by the nearby hotel, a reporter from the fledgling Nicola Herald was allowed the opportunity to interview Bill Miner. Ric Fraser, a former staff member of the Kamloops Inland Sentinel, had started the newspaper just a year previously to give coverage to the Nicola country. The subscription rate was $2 per year, and as the town of Nicola declined in future years at the expense of the upstart community of Merritt just a few miles down the road, the paper moved to the larger community and changed its name to the Merritt Herald. Fraser approached Miner, who assured him his name was George Edwards and that neither he nor his companions had anything to do with the robbery. He said they had started out from Pothole Lake near Aspen Grove and intended to prospect eastward in the Armstrong and Grande Prairie areas, and when returning to Nicola, they came through Batchelor's Meadows and along the Douglas Lake Trail, where they were captured.[55]

With a fresh team hitched to the wagon transporting the prisoners, the party started off north on their journey to the Provincial Gaol at Kamloops. Jerry Desire Mellin of Mamit Lake was the teamster. They reached Rockford, 35 miles from Kamloops, at noon and had lunch served by Robert Scott and his wife Mary Ann at their Rockford House stopping station. Robert Scott knew Miner as George Edwards quite well, as he had stopped at his road house many times on his trips to Kamloops. He was surprised to see that he had come to this sad end. It was at Rockford that the R.N.W.M.P. were met by an officious Superintendent Hussey of the Provincial Police who pulled up with another man in a buggy driving a team. Hussey confronted Wilson, introduced himself, and informed him that he had received instructions from Superintendent Marpole of the CPR to take custody of the prisoners.[56]

"You can hand over the prisoners to me and go back and look some more."

Wilson, taken aback and instantly wary, retorted, "Back where?"

"Oh, in case these are not the right men," replied Hussey.

Wilson confidently replied, "Mr. Hussey, I wish I was as sure of heaven as I am that these are the train robbers, in which case I would think that I had no cause for worry. Further, you have no escort, and in case of a rescue what could you do with a little pea shooter like you have?"

Wilson pointed to the little .22 calibre revolver in a shoulder holster strapped around Hussey just below his shoulders.

Wilson informed him, "I have arrested these men, and I am responsible for their delivery to the Provincial Gaol to be tried for the offence as charged, and it is my intention to so deliver them, and after I have obtained the Gaoler's receipt for them, my responsibility at that time will be ended."

Mary Spencer photo of prisoners and escort in hills directly south of
Kamloops. Dunn is sitting wrapped in blankets on the seat beside the
teamster Gerry Desire Mellin. Colquhoun can be seen also under blankets,
but Miner is obscured behind Mellin. In the buggy at the left of the photo
is CPR General Superintendent Marpole on the right of the front seat with
his socialite friend Captain C. Gardiner-Johnston beside him. Revelstoke
Division Superintendent Kilpatrick is in the rear seat. Constable Fernie
is riding directly behind the rear wheel of the wagon, and typically in the
background. The bundle of wrapped personal effects and the confiscated
weapons of the prisoners can be seen on the deck of the wagon beside and
below Colquhoun. The horses ridden by the Mounties now seem quite
docile in comparison to just a few days previous.

<small>Courtesy of Kamloops Museum and Archives.</small>

Wilson continued, "We are not taking our orders from anyone except our own Commissioner. If you are Sup't. Hussey, go back to Kamloops and I will hand over the prisoners to you in the Provincial Gaol."[57]

Mr. Hussey, attempting to save some face for his organization and to be seen to be at least partially responsible for the arrest, then attempted to convince Wilson to allow Colquhoun to be taken in his rig, but Wilson also refused to allow this. Hussey had to be satisfied with trailing behind the squad as it wound its way towards Kamloops. Fernie's reaction to the humiliation of his superior is not known.[58]

Wilson and his detail carried on to Kamloops, with rain getting progressively steadier as they made their way. This time when they put their yellow oilskins on, the maverick broncs that had farted and skipped out of Kamloops three days before had been magically transformed into docile and polite mounts fit for a parade ground. They had covered 185 miles through the roughest of terrain, often up to their knees in mud, and their memories of their days of freedom over the past winter were but vague, little-understood fantasies in their little horse brains.

Frederick Young's weekly Standard newspaper in Kamloops made full and innovative use of the newly strung telephone line to Hedley that had been installed in 1905. The reporters received a report from Quilchena phoned in by detective Seavey at 11:00 A.M. stating that the party had left early that morning for Kamloops and that George Edwards was in reality the notorious American bandit Bill Miner. A call from Robert Scott's roadhouse in Rockford at 12:24 P.M. ventured that the party would be in Kamloops about 4:00 P.M., and an even later report from MacDonald's at Napier Lake predicted they would be in Kamloops between four and five o'clock. The Standard's edition of that day had the very latest news for its readers and enabled the townspeople to turn out to view the prisoners as they made their ignominious way into town.[59]

About 15 miles from town, they were met by a buggy containing Superintendent Marpole and his friend Captain Charles Gardiner-Johnson. In the rear of the buggy was Revelstoke superintendent

Kilpatrick. After exchanging congratulations, they continued on. When only two miles from Kamloops and up on the flat bench above the valley, the astounded officers could scarcely believe their eyes when they "were met by practically the whole town, and in spite of the rain and mud ... photographers were along and succeeded in taking several pictures of the outfit."

One of those enterprising photographers on hand that damp day was Mary Spencer. Miss Spencer was the proprietor of the only photographic studio in Kamloops and was a skilled practitioner and portrait photographer. When the police officers and their prisoners paused in front of the crowds that day in the hills above Kamloops, Mary took the first of a series of photographs that would be reproduced constantly over the next hundred years. They were to cause a sensation all across Canada as newspapers from British Columbia through Manitoba, Ontario and Quebec and into the United States threatened, begged and cajoled to obtain copies of her photographs.

The wagon with its load of prisoners and the mounted escort of federal and provincial police officers resumed its journey down the Nicola Road into Kamloops from the west, followed by a parade of buggies filled with railway officials and townspeople. Two Mounties preceded the wagon, and the rest of the yellow-clad horsemen, including Constable Fernie, surrounded the vehicle. They made their way through the west end of the town, picking up curious onlookers and children along the way. The Kamloops Standard estimated one thousand townspeople watched the parade of Mounted Police and prisoners into town. They finally pulled up in front of the Kamloops Gaol at 4:30 P.M. in a pouring rain, having taken twelve hours to get from Quilchena to Kamloops. The harness on the wagon jingled and snapped as the team shook the rain from their backs and manes. The prisoners were a miserable and dishevelled looking trio, far from the press's perception of a dangerous gang of desperados. Miner and Colquhoun were hunched over in the back of the wagon with wet blankets trying to keep some of the rain off them. Dunn had a sopping blanket draped over his head and shoulders as he sat on the

MISS M SPENCER
KAMLOOPS, B.C.

Mary Spencer photo, Arrival at the Kamloops Gaol. Shorty Dunn is shrouded in blankets against the rain, and Bill Miner, with his distinctive four-cornered Stetson and dark full-length duster, prudently has his back to the camera. Colquhoun's distinctive hat can just be seen over Miner's head. The two figures conferring at the far right of the photo may be Constable Fernie and Superintendent Hussey.

Courtesy of Kamloops Museum and Archives.

front seat of the wagon beside the driver, his injured leg thrust out in front of him.

Standing in the excited crowd watching the prisoners come in that afternoon was the mail clerk, Alex McQuarrie, standing beside the CPR's Special Services detective Bullick and engineer Joseph Callin. When word of the capture of the suspects had been received at CPR offices in Vancouver, McQuarrie was placed on the next train to Kamloops to aid in identifying the prisoners. When he saw

Miner sitting in the back of the wagon, he immediately recognized him as the robber whose mask had fallen down in the mail car the week before.[60] [61] [62]

McQuarrie later told a Province reporter of his feelings. "It was no task at all to recognize him. I picked him out in the wagon among the officers when he was several hundred feet off when they were bringing him in."[63]

The quiet crowd watched the three prisoners helped to the ground and escorted through the doors of the prison, their hands bound behind them. Miner walked in with a nonchalant air. Shorty Dunn had to be carried. Colquhoun trailed the other two. As one of those prisoners took his first steps across the threshold of the Kamloops Gaol out of the scattered light of the overhead clouds and into the gloom of the prison, he was mercifully not to know that he would never enjoy freedom again, away from the shadows of prison walls.

The prisoners were booked in and once again searched, given dry clothes, and placed in separate cells. Dr. John Stanley Burris was summoned to administer to Shorty Dunn's leg, and after Wilson had obtained a receipt for the prisoners, the Mounties retired to their hotel for a bath, supper and a good night's sleep.[64]

XVI
AFTER THE DUCKS ROBBERY

THE NEWS OF THE ROBBERY at Ducks flashed through the telegraph lines to Vancouver at the speed of light. It was in the early morning hours after the robbery when Fernie and his trackers were making their way to Furrer Siding that Superintendent J. O. McLeod of the federal government's railway mail service in Vancouver was roused from his sleep by a telegraph boy banging on his door. Lighting a nearby lamp, he read the telegram from Chief Constable Colin Campbell of the B.C. Provincial Police in Vancouver. The Imperial Limited had been robbed east of Kamloops and presently was on its way through the Fraser Canyon. The government official immediately thought back to the robbery near Mission that he had been involved with not two years previously. McLeod dressed, and by catching an eastbound freight, he was able to meet and board the Imperial Limited at Agassiz. In the mail car he took comprehensive statements from Willis and McQuarrie, two more in a seeming unending line of statements and interviews they would give over the next few days. When No. 97 finally pulled into Vancouver at 10:45 A.M., an inquiring reporter from the Vancouver Province was waiting to interview McLeod.[1]

To the reporter, McLeod praised the coolness and courage with which McQuarrie and Willis handled themselves in a stressful situation. He credited them with the fact that the robbers did not discover the additional cash available in the mail car. From the descriptions Willis and McQuarrie had given him, McLeod told the reporter that he was convinced that the leader of the robbers was the same man who held up the train near Mission Junction, almost certainly the notorious American bandit, old Bill Miner. The official went on to reassure customers and users of the mail that little or no mail had been taken and that the railway's service was still secure. McLeod advised the Province that he took it upon himself to announce that the Dominion government would give a $1,000 reward for the apprehension of the robbers.[2]

The first issue of the Province headlining the robbery at Ducks hit the newsstands to enlighten the citizens of British Columbia the day after the robbery, May 9TH. Columns of information under the front page headline, "Train Robbers Overlooked $35,000 In Hard Cash," enlightened the readers as to the courage of the mail clerks and the ineptness of the robbers. Interviews with law enforcement and railway officials gave the details of the story, and interviews with passengers added human interest. Reverend James Woodsworth spoke for his fellow ministers travelling to the Methodist convention in Victoria when questioned about their reaction.

"I was sound asleep, so I couldn't know very much about it, could I?"

"And you weren't frightened when you learned you had been held up?" asked the Province reporter.

"Not in the least because the danger was past."

CPR General Superintendent Richard Marpole was also contacted by the hard working reporter. Marpole summarized the events east of Kamloops and expressed optimism that the perpetrators would soon be captured. He listed the substantial rewards already offered by various agencies. He noted that the CPR had offered a reward of $5,000 for the capture of the three robbers, dead or alive. If only one robber should be captured, $1,000 would be paid. The Dominion government likewise offered a $5,000 reward under the same conditions. The Provincial government offered a reward of $1,500 for their capture. The Province concluded its front page story by saying that a number of private detectives had arrived in Vancouver that day, and they and a number of CPR Special Service police were on their way to Kamloops.[3]

In Kamloops, Frederick Young's Kamloops Standard newspaper produced a special edition on Wednesday, the same day as the

Province. The fledgling weekly paper, in direct competition with its larger biweekly competition, the Kamloops Inland Sentinel, beat its rival to the punch and was the first paper to tell eager Kamloops readers about the events of the past evening. Both Kamloops papers excelled themselves in wealth of detail and investigative reporting. Most of the information gathered by the Standard at this early period of the investigation was as a result of interviews with engineer Callin and fireman Radcliffe. The Standard was even able to pen an editorial in this first edition describing the robbers as experienced "Knights of the Road." The Sentinel did not get its first issue out until two days later. Not only would the local media keep its Kamloops readers well informed of events over the next month, both would send "special" reporting to newspapers throughout Western Canada and even to Winnipeg and Montreal. The Victoria Daily Colonist and the New Westminster Columbian and small weekly publications throughout the province would avail themselves of the stellar reporting emanating from the small town in the heart of B.C.'s cattle country. Only the Province would send a reporter to Kamloops to monitor all of the action over the next weeks. In order to meet the voracious appetite of readers for news of the robbery at Kamloops, the Province's reporter would sometimes revert to manufacturing his own version of events. Desperate for first-hand news the day the bandits were booked into the jail in Kamloops, the paper presented an in-depth story covering the adventures of Constable Fernie as he tracked the robbers and met them on the road to Douglas Lake. It was plain to see that the reporting had been made up, but as the only criticism came from the local Kamloops papers, the rest of the Province's readers were in no way the wiser. Irate cries of "yellow journalism" from the Kamloops papers quickly erupted as a result of the article, but generally all the papers did stellar work ferreting out news and background throughout the interior over the duration of the affair.[4]

The Province, founded by a Kamloops pioneer rancher, Senator Hewitt Bostock, covered the events in Kamloops from start to finish. Its front pages carried columns of news on the unfolding events in the interior, directly alongside columns of more local interest. Province readers on the Saturday morning following the robbery woke to an interesting column beside that of the news of the posse's progress. One hundred and twenty Chinese laundrymen in Vancouver threatened to go out on a general strike to have their hours reduced. Their regular shifts went from seven in the morning to well after midnight, seven days a week. They wished to have their hours reduced to working from seven in the morning to only ten at night, a reduction of two hours, and with Sundays off. They were enlisting the help of several local white men in assisting them to draw up a constitution for their new Oriental Laundryman's Union.[5]

Kamloops newspaper reporters did not have to wait long before fresh news started to come in from the posse on the trail of the robbers. Chief Constable Pearse of Kamloops arrived at noon that first day on an engine and caboose to send a telegram in code to Superintendent Hussey in Victoria giving the full particulars of the incident and to round up additional posse members and trackers. He took the opportunity to advise CPR officials at the station of the progress being made and also gave an interview to the local papers. He noted the dynamite that had been left behind by the robbers and brought back to Kamloops was wrapped in a portion of the Kamloops Standard newspaper with a label affixed to it of an Aspen Grove subscriber. He added that the CPR section foreman at Furrer Siding, Valentine Ross, had found a distinctive leather belt beside the ties at Mile Board 117, and it was being held as evidence. The interview was interrupted by an urgent message from Fernie and his trackers that they were on the trail of the robbers, making good progress, and to come quickly with more men and supplies. So the supplies were loaded into the caboose and the additional men were soon aboard for the trip to Furrer Siding to meet the wagons. Back into the hills to the south went Pearse, and the newspaper reporters were off to send their telegrams or to prepare their local copy. Investigators, newspaper reporters and CPR officials would be kept up to date with the posse's progress throughout the week as Pearse, Special Constables, cowboys and trackers came into town to get supplies, send messages and telegrams, or obtain more assistance. Each member of the posse pulling into town on horseback or by wagon was greeted with a barrage of questions and requests for news.[67]

Soon after being notified of the robbery, the B.C. Provincial Police force's Superintendent Frederick Hussey arrived in Kamloops from Victoria. Checking into a local hotel close beside the station and the telegraph, he immediately set it up as his local command post. He took charge of all the activities of his force and stayed in Kamloops until the affair had ended. He would have a daunting task, as his provincial officers' efforts would be assisted by members of the CPR's Special Service police, the Pinkerton and Thiel Agency detectives, the Royal North West Mounted Police, and a host of civilian posse members and amateur detectives.

The Province of the 10TH of May tried to give some perspective on how comprehensive the search for the robbers had become and the seriousness with which the pursuit was followed. "Every man who owns or can beg, borrow or hire a saddle horse is out on the range in pursuit of the holdup men. The majority of the pursuers are sworn in as specials (special constables), but many are on their own hook, urged by the off chance of receiving a slice of the reward of $11,500. Through Nicola and to the south of it as far as Princeton the Provincial Police are watching every avenue of escape, and each lonely mountain trail is patrolled by a minion of the law."[8]

As the week progressed, tensions increased as word continued to come in from the posse. Pearse requested that bloodhounds at Nelson and at Spokane be sent for, and he speculated that the police were closing in on the robbers. The posse, after following the robbers' tracks for a ten mile stretch, now suspected they were making for Chapperon Lake in the Douglas Lake country. Pearse requested Superintendent Hussey to send out more men and supplies and to speed up the arrival of the bloodhounds.[9]

The activities of Enderby's Constable Gardom received considerable attention in the Province. The circumstances of the arrest of James Christie at Round Lake were reported in detail. Christie's description bore a close resemblance to one of the robbers, as he had a red moustache and a short beard. While Christie denied any connection with the crime, it was felt that he was at least an accessory. Christie said that while it was true he had reached for his rifle when the Constables appeared, he thought they were in fact a bear, and when he saw that it was the police, he didn't raise his gun up.[10]

The arrests of suspects Christie, Mohr and Wilson were felt to be of dubious warrant despite some rumours of horse rustling by the latter two, but the incarceration of Stevens in Vernon was viewed with more justification. It was reported that Paul Stevens, who lived "near the Salmon River Road in a sparsely settled and very rough country" had been under suspicion since the day after the robbery. The fact that the bandits had been tracked very near to the front door of his cabin and indications of his possible rustling connections and disreputable character weighed against him.[11]

The activities around Princeton in the Similkameen country to possibly intercept the fleeing train robbers were typical of events in many areas of the southern interior such as the Okanagan. Hugh Hunter, senior constable and mining recorder in Princeton, was in charge of ensuring Constable Ronald Hewat and a team of special constables were out watching and patrolling the trails north of the Similkameen to thwart any chance the bandits might be making their way into that country. Hunter was fresh from his welcome exoneration after a provincial commission had been held into his activities as a mining recorder and the irregularities perceived by mining promoter E. Voight. The investigation of the Ducks robbery would keep him and his new constable busy over the next months.[12]

Hunter placed one man on the Coldwater near the west fork of Otter Creek, three men on One Mile Creek at a point where it was possible to observe any passersby without being seen, three men at the foot of Otter Valley near Tulameen City, and three men at Five Mile Creek where the Penticton Trail crosses.

Jack Budd was observed by the locals to be acting in a peculiar manner in the Aspen Grove country. He spent days leading saddle horses around the area on pack trails and wagon roads as if he were expecting someone to meet him. Uncharacteristically, he dropped into William Dodds' store and post office at Aspen Grove just before the stage came as if he were waiting for someone, and stood around for its arrival. When the stage arrived and discharged no passengers or mail for Budd, he nonchalantly said to Dodds that he guessed he might as well go back to his claim, and he left towards Missezula Lake. Dodds was hired as a special constable by Hugh Hunter in Princeton, and together with another special, Jack Murray from Nicola, he was assigned to guard a remote trail some miles away from Aspen Grove and to be on the lookout for suspicious persons. The two kept hidden in the brush beside the trail so as not to be seen by passersby. Over the course of the next few days, they were surprised to see Jack Budd unknowingly pass them a number of times. Each time he was leading saddle horses and seeming to comb the countryside looking for someone.[13]

After the capture of the robbers, Hunter rode up to Budd's cabin on Bald Mountain above Princeton to determine for himself the whereabouts of the reclusive American. There he found, acting as caretaker in Budd's absence, Tom Arnold. Another American, Arnold had a poor reputation around Princeton. Constable Hewat would later write that his "character is not very good and when he is drunk … he is very quarrelsome. His reputation when he was in the Boundary was not good and he was continually in trouble. He has a very quick, cross grained temper."[14]

The official police description of Arnold noted that he was a well-built six feet in height, about forty years of age, and sported red moustaches. He was going bald at the front, but wore his hair quite long at the back. He wore a white felt, flat-brimmed Stetson, a long riding coat and high riding boots. He had a harsh tone of voice and was rather abrupt in his mannerisms.[15]

Answering Hunter's questions, he told him he was a rancher and a miner and that Budd had left his horse ranch in his care until he arrived back. Hunter searched the cabin thoroughly in Arnold's presence but could find nothing incriminating. Hanging on the wall above a bed, he saw a Winchester rifle that Arnold said belonged to

George Edwards and some clothes that had also apparently belonged to him. In a corner he saw a large empty trunk which he was told belonged to Colquhoun. Outside, leaning against the cabin wall, were some branding irons. Hunter was later to learn that one of them, said by Arnold to be his own personal brand, matched a brand displayed on one of the captured horses, but when Hunter returned to retrieve it, it had disappeared.[16]

The events unfolding around the good citizens of Kamloops were somewhat overwhelming. Never before in its short existence had Kamloops been such a centre of attention in the province, the country or indeed, with its large neighbour to the south. Newspapers from all over the continent were clamouring for news, and the telegraph wires and the rudimentary telephone systems were kept humming. Casual visitors from Kamloops to the major metropolitan cities at the coast such as Vancouver, Victoria and New Westminster were met by inquiring reporters as they stepped off their trains or steamers. The reporters were after any news of the events in the interior no matter how mundane or innocuous.

All the citizens of Kamloops and the surrounding district were on edge, and frequently much consternation was raised over unimportant or innocent events. At the weekly Thursday meeting of City Council, deliberations were suddenly interrupted by a local Indian, Francis Basil. He came galloping up on his horse and came to a dusty halt just outside the door to council chambers. He yelled for someone's attention. Council in its wisdom dispatched the City Clerk outside to see what all the commotion was about. Basil said that some Indians had seen some men coming west along the CPR tracks from the direction of the robbery. As soon as these men realized that they had been seen, they ran to the river and got into a boat. Basil got many willing helpers to assist, and by 9:00 P.M. Indians and whites with firearms were stationed along both sides of the river and on both bridges to keep a lookout for the boat. Even Superintendent Hussey and the CPR's Kilpatrick were there. At about 10:00 o'clock, one of the riflemen on the north shore of the river saw a boat emerge from the shadows of the trees close to shore into the clear moonlight.

He hailed the boat, which contained three men and a boy, but could get no response. Instead they seemed to be making for the opposite shore. The citizen fired at them three times, fortunately without hitting either them or the boat. A search was made of all that side of the river, but no one was found. The Kamloops Standard attributed the whole affair to overwrought imaginations. Francis Basil's enthusiasm was harnessed by his being recruited by Pearse as a tracker, and he would be off with Michelle LeCamp in short order to take up the chase of the bandits.[17]

The citizens of Kamloops could perhaps be forgiven for believing that time would stand still in the rest of the province while such riveting events were taking place in their town's back yard. But time moved inexorably on. For instance, in Victoria the Methodist convention was proceeding apace. Reverend Woodsworth and the good ministers attending felt they too were making earth shattering decisions. A former minister in Revelstoke, the Reverend Samuel Thompson, was elected President of the conference. The Victoria Colonist went on in painstaking detail, column after column, on the less than newsworthy events taking place at the convention. The only relief for readers was the juicy revelation that the Reverend W. W. Baer of Nelson, a well-known person in Victoria, Vancouver and Nanaimo, was accused, convicted and suspended from the ministry for six months for the unpardonable sin of intemperance. Reverend Baer appealed the suspension, and his appeal was upheld as it was determined that the West Kootenay court had proceeded irregularly. "Mr. Baer then filed his resignation, which was accepted with regret."[18 19 20]

Senior officials of the Canadian Pacific Railway lost no time in taking a lead and influential role in the investigations. Superintendent Kilpatrick from Revelstoke dropped off his private railway car at a siding in Kamloops and, together with Trainmaster Elson from Revelstoke, would actively participate in the actual pursuit of the bandits with the Provincial Police. They would expedite valuable logistical support with transportation, messaging, and provision of supplies. By the evening of the day after the robbery, two of the CPR's senior Special Service detectives, Inspector R.E. Bullick and Inspector W.L. McLaws, arrived in Kamloops to coordinate the CPR's response to the robbery. McLaws, with his offices in Winnipeg, would act as the coordinating officer in charge. Together the two were to play an important role in the CPR's response to the robbery. Besides conducting their own investigations, they managed and coordinated the detectives and secret agents from the Pinkerton and Thiel Detective Agencies in Seattle. Added to this responsibility was supervising the efforts of the CPR's own Special Service police force with its company team of undercover agents and detectives. Bullick and McLaws were soon joined by other agents, including William McLeod from Montreal and J.J. Brown of the Thiel detective Agency's Winnipeg office. The press watched the influx of police, secret agents and detectives into the small town "to aid in running the robbers to earth" with some awe.[21]

Within days, General Superintendent Richard Marpole of the CPR's Western Region left Vancouver in his private car No. 10 and arrived in Kamloops. Accompanying him was his friend, the Vancouver shipping magnate Captain Charles Gardiner-Johnson. Marpole had his car dropped off in the siding alongside Kilpatrick's. He would remain in Kamloops, his personal railway lodgings an object of awe, until he was satisfied with the results of the investigation. Kamloops held no strangeness for Marpole for he had held the position of Superintendent there only eight years before. He reacquainted himself with old friends and visited familiar haunts while he stayed in Kamloops. Marpole was to exert all the authority of one of the world's most powerful monopolies on the governments, organizations and people involved with the hunt for the train robbers. He, in turn, would report on a timely basis to his own superiors. Vice-President William Whyte in Winnipeg, the manager of all the CPR lines in the West, waited for Marpole's daily telegrams on the progress in Kamloops so he could telegraph the stern President of the CPR in Montreal, Lord Thomas Shaughnessy.[22]

Superintendent Marpole had not been very impressed with the results obtained by the B.C. Provincial Police after the robbery of the CPR train near Mission Junction in September of 1904. His first instincts when hearing of the robbery at Ducks were to take steps to ensure a more successful outcome to the investigation. To that end he wired his superior, Vice-President Whyte in Winnipeg, to obtain the services of the federal police to assist in the capture of the bandits. Vice-President Whyte contacted the CPR's lawyers in Montreal to pressure the Justice Minister to send a troop of Royal North West Mounted Police to Kamloops to assist in the investigation. Soon Commissioner Bowen-Perry and his seven man squad were on their way from Alberta to Kamloops. They arrived in Kamloops three days after the robbery, and watched by the bemused local citizenry, they made their rather ignominious departure into the hills toward the Nicola Valley. Commissioner Bowen-Perry would maintain a rather detached management role as he was content to leave the field investigations in the hands of his competent and experienced officers. He attended the daily meetings held with CPR officials, private detective agencies and Superintendent Hussey, but would exert no influence upon his own members other than to pass and receive messages from them in Quilchena and the Douglas Lake Ranch.

While he was in Kamloops, Bowen-Perry did handle the disbursement of another R.N.W.M.P. detachment to a specific critical location in B.C.. He had wired the Commanding Officer of "E" Division in Calgary to dispatch Inspector Frank Church with ten men to the Penticton country to try to intercept the bandits before they crossed the American border. They duly left Calgary on the 13TH, and after they had arrived in Penticton, they received another wire from the Commissioner to return to Calgary as the robbers had been captured. Inspector Church diverted to Kamloops to observe the events as they unfolded there and to assist the seven members in their future testimony at trial.[23]

One of the members of Church's troop was K.G. Murison. He had the opportunity to observe the prisoners in the Kamloops Gaol and described them in rather unflattering terms. "A more non-descript trio I had never seen nor have I since. They were everything bad men should not be. Dunn, happy go lucky, fat, wounded, and full of stories; Colquhoun, a former school teacher, tall, stooped and taciturn; and finally the redoubtable Bill Miner, a quiet little man who said nothing."[24]

It was during this first week of the investigation that we see step onto the stage one of those inevitable opportunists that seek to take advantage of any crisis that befalls organizations or societies. W.S. Seavey was the Detective Superintendent in charge of the Thiel Detective Agency in Seattle. Since 1905 he had been attempting to curry favour and business with both the CPR Special Service section and B.C.'s Provincial Police. The Pinkertons had a long history of successful dealings with both organizations, and Seavey was attempting to usurp some of that business for his own company. The Thiel Detective Agency had been started by a former Pinkerton Detective Superintendent named Gus Thiel, and in 1906 they had agents across the U.S., with head offices in Chicago. Seavey had been cultivating William McLeod of the CPR police in Vancouver and Superintendent Hussey of the provincial police since 1905, but without much success. The robbery at Ducks seemed to him to be the ticket to obtaining increased business for his employer. He was to utilize questionable methods, including manipulation of the media and private individuals, to try to achieve success and increase his employer's business.

He had arrived in Kamloops with the CPR's Bullick and other detectives soon after the robbery. He wasted no time in assuming, in his own mind at least, the leadership role in the manhunt. Hiring Owen Batchelor and his buggy and team, a rancher and prospector familiar with the country, Seavey started his investigations south of Ducks in the Grande Prairie area and points west of that. He had run into Constable Basil Gardom from Enderby at Grande Prairie, and the unsuspecting Gardom had shared the results of his investigations with him. Gardom told Seavey about his arrest of James Mohr and two others and jailing them in Vernon. When Seavey arrived back in Kamloops, he telegraphed the Province to tell them that he had ordered the arrest of one James Mohr and other undesirables in the Grande Prairie country, and that he was following leads that would soon see an end to the pursuit. He had also learned from Gardom about the suspicions against Paul Stevens, so Seavey told the paper that he was closing in on another suspect near Fish Lake, and he would take credit for Stevens' arrest when it happened. There was no limit to his self promotion, and he even told the press that he had been on hand when the capture had taken place on the banks of the Nicola River.

Once the prisoners entered Warden John Vicar's office, the process of checking them into the jail was underway. Vicars was acting under the supervision of Superintendent Hussey during all the booking procedures, and Hussey ensured all the proper rules and regulations were followed to the letter. A receipt for the prisoners was issued to Sergeant Wilson, and he and his troop quickly retired to their hotel. Each prisoner was thoroughly searched from head to toe, and their extremities were measured exactly for the Bertillon method of identification. They took this indignity coolly, surrounded as they were by police, reporters and CPR officials. Dunn and Colquhoun's hobnailed boots and Miner's smooth soled ones were taken away and entered as evidence. A black bandana was taken from Miner, and a red and white checked one was taken from Dunn. Both were entered as evidence.

The prisoners' statements were obtained and filed.

Statements of the Prisoners, Kamloops Gaol, May 16, 1906
The statement of the prisoner George Edwards.

He states: Myself, Dunn and Colquhoun have been together on a prospecting trip for the past three or four weeks at Aspen Grove and through the mountains. We were at the back of Graves' [sic] Ranch at Douglas Lake and have camped there and at different other places for the past month. We were prospecting together. We all left our tools at Batchelor's Meadows sometime last week about two days before our arrest. We had some Giant powder with us and it is in the camp at Batchelor's Meadows now. Have had it in my possession for about one year. It was kept in a box.

Louis Colquhoun states as follows:

I have been on a prospecting trip tour with Edwards and Dunn for the past three weeks. We were prospecting in the vicinity of Batchelor's Meadows. Our tools were left in the locality of Batchelor's Meadows. We left them in the woods. I formerly lived at Clifford, Wellington Co., Ontario.

Wm. Dunn states as follows:

Edwards, Colquhoun and myself have been together for the past month. We have been prospecting together near Batchelor's Meadows. I threw away our tools near our camp at Batchelor's Meadows. There was a small pick and shovel. The other two men also threw away their tools. I have a friend at Aspen Colorado named T.E. Wood. He is one of the owners of the Emma Mine at Aspen. When I last heard of Wood he was running and managing a mine near Kingston or Wardner, Idaho, for the St. Paul and Idaho Mining and Milling Company. This was his last address but he can be heard of at Aspen, Colorado. My proper name is John Grell, and I am a Milwaukee Dutchman. I was born in Milwaukee, Wisconsin. I am known in Princeton as Billy Dunn. I have worked on a ranch for Mrs. Ellison [sic] near Princeton but I am by occupation a trapper and prospector. Edwards lives at Princeton and he has an interest in a ranch there and lived on it part of the time. He has been living on his ranch at Princeton during most of the past year.

The above statements were made and taken by F.S. Hussey, Superintendent of Provincial Police, at Kamloops Gaol, May 16TH, 1906, in the presence of Mr. J.J. Brown of Winnipeg, and Warden Vicars.[25]

Hussey employed the services of Mary Spencer to take photographs of the prisoners as their questioning was completed. To his regret, he failed to ask her for the negatives, or to caution her not to use them in any unauthorized way. It was at this time that Miss Spencer took her famous photos of the three bandit suspects, placing the prisoners one by one up against the outside wall of the gaol to get full daylight on their features. The photo of Miner would enter the history books as one of the most instantly recognizable portraits ever taken in Western Canada. His weathered face and silver-grey moustaches, the flat brimmed four cornered Stetson, and the sharp penetrating eyes presented an individual that riveted the attention of the newspaper readers of the day, and it would be a required photo for any illustrated history of British Columbia for decades into the future.

Mary Spencer photo of Bill Miner, 16 May 1906. Courtesy of Kamloops Museum and Archives.

Miner was the first prisoner to be processed, and treated the whole affair as rather a light hearted affair. He was described as a "rather striking looking fellow, grizzled hair and moustache, erect and active, and does not seem to be within 10 years of his claimed age of 62. Looks like 50, and moves like he was 30. Answers all questions coolly, sometimes hesitatingly, considering his remarks well." Miner continued to assert that they were prospectors working the country between Aspen Grove and Nicola. He was placed in a special cell reserved for condemned prisoners, and a special guard was placed outside the cell door. His reputation for attempting to escape had preceded him to Kamloops.[26]

One of the railway officials asked him point blank whether or not he was Bill Miner. He answered in his soft American accent, "Can't be, seeing that I never heard of the man."[27]

After being photographed, Miner was led away to his cell. The next

Mary Spencer photo of Lewis Colquhoun, 16 May 1906.

to be processed was Lewis Colquhoun. His demeanour and mannerisms immediately struck all those present as being of a character unlike the other two. He was invariably described by the press as reticent and from his outward appearance unlikely to be a member of a holdup gang. He was "… a young man, refined and intelligent looking, who in a quiet voice gave his name as Lewis Colquhoun, his nationality as Canadian, and his occupation as book-keeper. He was very reticent and said nothing except in answer to the official questions, and replied to them in monosyllables. This is the man supposed to have come from Phoenix. His demeanour created some sympathy among those present at the examination, so uniformly quiet and courteous did he appear. Although perfectly self-collected, he seemed to feel his position keenly."[28]

This was in direct contrast to Shorty Dunn, who sat in a nearby chair with his wounded and bandaged leg propped up on another chair in front of him. He was typically described by the press as a "savage looking little man," "insolent and defiant," who "alternately glared at the officials or smiled grimly at some of the others present. This was 'Shorty' Thomas [sic] Dunn, one of the bandits who put up the fight when the arrest was made, and received a bullet hole in his anatomy for his pains. He was silently suffering from his wound and bore the pain with stoicism, merely gritting his teeth when his leg gave an unusually severe twinge." When Doctor Burris checked and re-bandaged his wound, he continued his practice of laughing all the while in the face of pain or adversity, making offhand remarks about his infirmity. "He gave the officials more trouble when they were filling up his record. His nationality he said he didn't know, 'Put it down (as) anything' and when asked for his residence it was 'Anywhere, everywhere.'"[29]

Finally tiring of the questioning, he admitted that his real name was John Grell, and that he was known in the States as the Milwaukee Dutchman.[30]

As Doctor Burris was dressing Shorty Dunn's leg a small boy,

Mary Spencer photo of William "Shorty" Dunn, 16 May 1906.
Courtesy of Kamloops Museum and Archives.

the Warden's son Desmond Vicars, was watching through the window. The youngster would have many opportunities to be with his father when the Warden was talking to Miner, and he remembered Miner telling him one time, "When you grow up, lad, go to Mexico, the grass there is all up to a horse's bellies; a great place."[31]

Alexander G. Brown had been a guard at the Kamloops Gaol since 1897, and he was normally in charge of the prison labour that maintained the grounds around the Old Men's Home. When it came time for Dunn's photo to be taken out in the prison yard, Brown carried Dunn on his back to where Mary Spencer had her equipment set up. He was placed in a chair conveniently left there just for him, and he scowled suitably into the camera. After the photographer was through with him, he was again mounted onto Brown's back and carried to his cell. As he was dropped off in his new abode, Brown asked the prisoner how it felt to be shot.

Shorty answered wryly, "Well, have you ever had a tooth pulled? It's just like that."[32]

Brown would later strike up conversations with Miner, and the bandit told Brown he had a son as old as he was.

Later that evening when the prisoners were washing up, CPR Special Services detective Bullick watched Bill Miner as he was lathering his hands and forearms. Hoping to see signs of any tattoos, he asked Miner to turn his hands over. Miner turned his hands over, but not quite enough to enable Bullick to see whether he was carrying any marks. Bullick didn't press it at the time, but when Miner was drying up with a towel, he asked him again if he could see the inside of his hands. Miner refused and Bullick grabbed his arm and turned it over. There on Miner's forearm was the telltale tattoo of the dancing girl.

Bullick was satisfied that they had Bill Miner in their clutches, but he wanted further confirmation. The Pinkertons had provided detailed descriptions of identifying features on their posters, and they were all available to the Kamloops investigators. Miner was stripped down in the presence of the prison personnel, CPR detectives, Commissioner Bowen-Perry and Superintendent Hussey. They examined him from head to toe and minutely matched every measurement, scar and blemish, tattoos and other characteristics that had been gathered so conscientiously over time and publicized on the Pinkerton wanted posters. Even though he continued to maintain that he was George Edwards, all present were convinced they had Bill Miner, the train robber so many law enforcement agencies had been chasing for so long.[33]

Bullick was interviewed by the Province reporter R.H. Hill the next day. "I have not the slightest doubt that the old man in custody is Bill Miner. I am well acquainted with Miner's sisters, and can recognize the family likeness even if I had not other proofs."

He assured the reporter that he had seen all the distinguishing marks the Pinkertons had listed. He also added that Miner's eyes were of an "unmistakable blue and piercing."

When asked why he thought Miner did not put up a fight, Bullick replied that he had never been "a desperate kind of robber but has always been quiet, even when arrested the last time. He has a characteristic turn of the head, and his eyes are crafty as if always looking for a loophole of escape."[34]

The next day after the successful incarceration of the robbers in the Kamloops Gaol, Chief Constable Pearse and his posse of specials, cowboys and Shuswap Indian trackers finally made it back into Kamloops. They had journeyed in heavy rain from Douglas Lake all that day and had arrived cold, wet, tired, hungry, unheralded and disappointed at their failure to capture the bandits after expending so much effort and being so close on their heels.

Mary Spencer, her sister Isabel on the right, and their mother.
Courtesy of Kamloops Museum and Archives.

Hussey immediately set up security and handling procedures for the prisoners in his charge. He instructed Warden Vicars that the prisoners were to be kept in separate cells and under close surveillance. He had heard the rumours bandied about Kamloops that plans were afoot to rescue the prisoners, and he had also heard of Smoky Chisholm's abortive attempts to free his friend in Quilchena. He instructed that the prisoners could confer with their counsel whenever they wished, but only one at a time. He advised Vicars as to how witnesses and detectives were to be handled when attending the jail to identify the prisoners. Well aware of his responsibilities to ensure a successful prosecution of the criminals at a future trial, and acting on prior instructions from Attorney General Frederick Fulton,

Hussey wired Deputy Attorney General Hugh Archibald Mclean in Victoria and advised him the robbers had been captured.

```
Canadian Pacific Railway's Telegraph
Rush
Kamloops B.C. May 14th. 1906


H.A. McLean, Deputy Atty General, Victoria,
B.C.


Three men supposed to be the robbers arrested
near Douglas Lake
By provincial constable Fernie and a posse of
Mounted Police.
One of the supposed robbers was shot in the
leg. Am leaving for
Quilchena tonight with two secret service men
to investigate and bring prisoners to
Kamloops.


F.S. Hussey
8:12 p.m.[35]
```

Hussey for some reason did not leave to meet the prisoners until the next day, and when he did, his plans to take over the prisoners went somewhat astray. McLean arrived in Kamloops the next day and checked in to the Grand Pacific Hotel. He was to stay there until early June, acting and operating under the watchful eye of Attorney General Frederick Fulton.

The major newspapers in British Columbia and those in Kamloops had had their front pages blanketed with news of the robbery and the capture of the bandits for over a week. Every detail and facet of the story were explored, but it is doubtful whether any rose to the rarified heights as did the Vancouver World soon after the robbers' capture.

The World decided to wax eloquent in one of its editions after the capture and incarceration of the three prisoners. A six stanza poem was printed for the edification of its readers and to celebrate the capture of the bandits. At the time, the paper believed that Shorty Dunn had given up because the magazine to his Luger was empty. The reference to Teddy is probably to King Edward.

> Bill Miner was a bandit neat
> And used to posse alarms,
> But Fernie tracked him by his feet,
> So Bill threw up his arms.
> "Shorty" to the dry belt's gone,
> In Kamloops jail you'll find him;
> This is the burden of his song—
> "'E left his magazine behind him."
> In nineteen six we chased old Bill
> Right into the Quilcheena;
> 'Is day is done, 'e's 'ad his fill,
> For Bill is an 'asbeener.
> Lives of bandits all remind us
> That the mail car's not the express;
> They'll remain sadly beside us
> For twenty years, or something less.
> Lives there a man with soul so dead
> Who has not all the extras read,
> Nor wiped the sweat from off his brow?
> For Bill's the guest of Teddy now.
> The tale is told, Bill's had his day,
> But Fernie's in an awful stew
> Counting the quid the papers say
> Is coming to him as his due.[36]

On the afternoon of the 16TH of May, one day after the prisoners entered the Kamloops Gaol, the robbers came before stipendiary magistrate George C. Tunstall. They were quickly remanded until the next day for a Grand Jury hearing to determine whether there was enough evidence to warrant a trial. All three prisoners as a group were represented by lawyer Alex Mcintyre. Mcintyre was the same defence lawyer that had so impressed Miner at the Smoky Chisholm trial during the 1905 fall assizes. Miner had at some time prior been able to convince his two partners that they should utilize the services of Mcintyre to defend them. The three would later come to regret this decision, as they eventually became aware that the lawyer was concerned not only with their best interests, but also his own.[37]

To ensure a proper case was assembled and witness statements obtained, Hussey ordered his Provincial Police force members to fan out in the Similkameen and Kamloops districts to interview witnesses and prepare evidence. The CPR put the full resources of its own force as well as the detective agencies the company's deep pockets had hired at Hussey's disposal. CPR detectives would send out operatives throughout the Fraser Valley at the same time to determine whether any information on the Mission Junction robbery might now be available.

Early in the investigation, an undercover agent of the Thiel Detective Agency in Seattle, acting for the CPR, followed up on evidence that had been obtained on the suspicious activities of Paul Stevens. The secret operative, identified in the Attorney General's files only as Agent #30, rented a rig in Kamloops and made his way east into the Upper Campbell Creek area. Only afterwards was he identified as a "P.H." or "L." Calhoun out of Seattle. He called in at the farm of James Todd near Campbell Creek. James Todd, now 71, was the first settler along Upper Campbell Creek, and Todd Lake was named after him. In 1869 he had owned and then sold what was later to become the Harper Ranch on the north side of the South Thompson River, a few miles downstream from Louis Campbell's. One of his daughters, Margaret, had married Paul Stevens. The other had been married to Reignford Knapp who had died at a young age, and she had been left widowed with three young children. She eventually remarried to Robert Pratt, another pioneer farmer in Upper Campbell Creek and a neighbour of Robert Todd's. One of the sons they had together was Toddy Pratt who had seen and met the robber trio at Campbell Creek below the schoolhouse.[38]

At the Todd farm, the agent pulled into the yard and was met by one of Todd's sons. Posing as a land buyer, he talked to the boy about the ranch and asked whether it was for sale. The boy answered that it was, but as it belonged to his father, the agent would have to discuss it with him. He told the agent that his father was right next door, indicating the next house down the road. The operative then talked to the boy about the train robbery, and the boy responded, "Yes, the robbers had a camp right over there," and the boy pointed towards the hills on the opposite side of Campbell Creek. The agent then led the boy on, and mentioned that the posse had tracked the robbers to a point close to Paul Stevens' place. Did the boy know Stevens? "Yes," he answered, "I know where the man lives; about twenty miles from here." The boy made no mention that Stevens was married to his sister Margaret. Calhoun then left the boy and drove his rig down the Kamloops to Vernon wagon road next door to the farm of Robert Pratt, the son-in-law of Robert Todd.[39]

Robert Pratt and his family had a successful farm and orchard near Campbell Creek, and Pratt's apples would eventually win him a gold medal in an international fair in England. The undercover operative drove up beside Pratt's log house, where Todd, Pratt and a young boy watched him turn in. Standing down from his rig, he introduced himself as being interested in real estate in the Upper Campbell Creek area, and he jokingly told Robert Todd that he had been trying to buy his ranch from his son.[40]

"Well, why didn't you buy it?" the old man quickly replied.

The operative replied that the boy would not give him a firm price for it.

"Well," said Todd, "$10,000 will take it."

The men and the boy then stood about in the cool spring air and talked about the ranch and others that might be for sale in the area. The agent finally brought the conversation around to the train robbery, mentioning that the posse had tracked the robbers to Stevens' place in the Monte Hills. He asked the old man whether he knew Stevens.

Immediately the rancher was quick to defend his son-in-law. "I reckon I do, he is my son-in-law. Paul Stevens had no more to do with that holdup than I did. Why Paul Stevens stayed right here in this house that night." Todd referred to the log house beside them, the home of Robert Pratt and his wife Helena, the sister of Paul Stevens' wife Margaret.

The undercover agent agreed that it was very fortunate for Paul Stevens if that were the case, as it would then give him a good alibi if he should ever need it and the family was willing to swear to it. Young 16 year-old David Knapp, Robert Pratt's stepson, had been listening to the conversation between the adults with interest. Eager to join in the conversation, he told the operative, "Yes, I can swear he came in here about 1 o'clock that night and got into bed ...."

Slyly, the operative cautioned the boy to remember that fact, noting that if Paul Stevens should be arrested that statement could very well prove valuable in obtaining his freedom. All three told the investigator about how they had been at the robbers' camp even before the robbery and had seen that they had blazed new trails up over the hills towards the highlands to the south.[41]

As Calhoun drove his rig east across Campbell Creek, he thought about the fact that Paul Stevens would have had plenty of time to get from the site of the robbery to the Pratt place by one o'clock in the morning.

The agent called in at the ranch of Samuel Bice about two miles from Todd's and managed to arrange supper for himself and a place to sleep overnight. At a table lit by an oil lamp, Bice told the detective that Paul Stevens had a bad reputation all through the area, and that he would not be surprised if Stevens should be found to have been mixed up in the robbery of the CPR. Mrs. Bice told the operative that the three men had been asking her for milk and that the older one had spoken most pleasantly to her.

Back in Kamloops, agent Calhoun interviewed Samuel Brooks, the proprietor of the grocery store across the tracks from the station. Brooks and his clerk told him of Stevens buying an expensive load of groceries, which included Tetley tea of the same type and wrapped in the same wrapper as was found in the robbers' camp. They told him of their suspicions about Stevens and that the Kamloops Police Chief had mentioned to them that he was not to be trusted or to be extended credit.[42]

At the same time his operative was busy in Kamloops, detective Seavey was busy in the Nicola Valley and the northern Similkameen. He interviewed Mr. A. Jackson, who was the Postmaster and owned the general store in Quilchena. He told Seavey that he had often seen George Edwards riding through Quilchena, once or twice in the company of Bob Tilton. One time he had a bunch of horses he said he was taking to the Tilton Ranch at Kamloops. He understood Edwards was a partner with Jack Budd in a ranch near Princeton and also had some mining property near Aspen Grove.[43]

Next, Seavey drove just a few miles south down the road to the busy little town of Nicola. There he met with the town's Provincial Police Constable Walter Clark. Clark repeated much of what Jackson had told Seavey. He too had seen Edwards often in company with Jack Budd around Quilchena and Nicola. He added that Edwards and Budd did not have very good reputations in the area with local ranchers as they were suspected of being involved with the loss of quite a few horses that had been stolen over the years. It was thought that the rustled horses had either been driven over the line into the States or sent to the auctions at the Coast. Both Edwards and Budd were thought to have interests in mining claims with Alonzo Roberts of Aspen Grove.[44]

While he was in Nicola Lake, Seavey also interviewed Jack Murray, the son of the local Government Agent and Justice of the Peace George Murray. Jack Murray worked in a local general store in Nicola and had acted as a Special Provincial Police Constable assisting William Dodds to monitor the trails around Aspen Grove. Murray told Seavey that he and his brother met Billy Dunn often when they were in the Hedley and Princeton areas and also knew George Edwards as well as any person living in the area. Murray could add little more than that to Seavey's inquiries.[45]

To get to Aspen Grove from Nicola, Seavey took the Nicola Road along the south side of the Nicola River, climbing the slopes of the grassy hills and into the highlands. He pulled his buggy to a stop in front of William Dodds' unprepossessing store and interviewed the proprietor. He showed Dodds the dynamite and fuses found at the side of the tracks at Furrer Siding. The Maltese Cross 7/8 diameter sticks were the same as those purchased by Jack Budd earlier that spring. He told Seavey he had seen Edwards at his store many times over the past year. He noted that he was a partner with Jack Budd in a horse ranch near Princeton and also had interests in mining claims near Aspen Grove with Budd and Alonzo Roberts. He told Seavey of the suspicions that local ranchers and farmers had of Budd and Edwards being mixed up in a rustling ring, and suspicions were held of their illegal handling and dealing with horses.

When Seavey had completed his interviews, most with signed statements, he turned his rig around and headed back to Kamloops. Five miles north of Nicola Lake, he stopped off at Robert Scott's roadhouse at Rockford to have a meal, and Scott told him how Edwards had often used his roadhouse as a stopping place on his way through to Kamloops from Princeton and Aspen Grove. Seavey continued on to Kamloops and made his reports to CPR Detective McLaws.[46]

In Kamloops, locomotive engineer Joseph Callin could feel the pressure on him to make sure his identification of the three prisoners was solid. Through the actions and words of Superintendents Marpole and Kilpatrick, he knew that the onus was on him to positively identify the bandits. Before the robbers were even captured, he was called on to visit Marpole in his private car on a Saturday evening. For a CPR employee at that time to even enter a divisional Superintendent's private car was almost unheard of. However, being invited to the car of the Western Region Superintendent of the CPR was an even rarer event. Kilpatrick and Marpole had him repeat his eyewitness statement and attempt to convince them he would be able to recognize the perpetrators again. In the presence of CPR detectives Bullick and McLaws and in the august surroundings of the powerful official's private car, the twenty year employee assured them all that he would do his best.[47]

The day after the prisoners had been locked up in the Kamloops Gaol, a parade of witnesses were brought up to the prison to view and identify the prisoners. In a bare room just off the warden's offices, the three prisoners were seated in chairs against the wall. Individually, and in the presence of Provincial Police Superintendent Hussey, CPR Superintendent Kilpatrick, Deputy Attorney General McLean, Prison Warden John Vicars and CPR Chief Special Agent McLaws, the witnesses were brought in singly to observe the prisoners. Dunn alternately glared and grinned at each witness as he stepped into the unfamiliar and intimidating surroundings. Rancher Albert Duck, engineer Callin and fireman Radcliffe each trooped in and made their identifications. Alex McQuarrie positively identified the man he now knew as Bill Miner as the man who was in his mail car that night.[48]

After viewing and identifying the prisoners, and being aware now of their names from newspaper reports, Callin gave another witness statement. In this newest statement he would use the names of each of the prisoners when describing the events of the night of the 8TH of May, even though the prisoners should only have been considered as suspects. In his statement he noted that he only saw someone dressed like George Edwards and not his face, and the other, Callin called him Shorty, had heavy coarse boots on and a dark sweater pulled up over his nose. Radcliffe's statement said Shorty Dunn was wearing a red and white checkered bandana mask and that the Third Man had the sweater drawn up over his face with strings tied over his head. Callin stated that he only saw the face of the Third Man in the light of the engine firebox for an instant, but was sure that was the man in the jail, Colquhoun. Both statements were very confusing and contradicted each other in many critical areas, especially when it came to describing the Third Man.[49]

McQuarrie later gave an interview to the Province reporter. "There is no possible room for doubt in my mind .... He (Edwards) wore the same clothes, has the same tones and quick movements, and there is no mistaking the moustache and features of which I had a brief glimpse while his mask was disarranged. One of the guns taken from him was of the same size as the one he waved so gracefully before my face."

"Bill Miner, or Edwards, as he calls himself, has a characteristic pose of the head when deeply interested that once seen, is impossible to mistake again. He assumed that pose for a minute in the car while he was looking around for the registered mail sack on the night of the holdup."[50]

That same day Superintendent Marpole decided he might celebrate what he considered the successful capture of the guilty train robbers. With his socialite friend Captain Gardiner-Johnson and R.N.W.M.P. Commissioner Bowen-Perry, he took a buggy and team and went fly-fishing at one of the many lakes around the area stocked with fighting Kamloops trout. When they returned, Marpole was interviewed by a reporter. He commented that some excellent fishing was to be had around Kamloops and that he and his party had been successful in landing a few. He also expressed his pleasure to the reporter that he was sure the perpetrators of the robbery had been caught, so much so that he would be returning to Vancouver shortly, convinced of a job well done. That evening, as the Imperial Limited went through Kamloops, it coupled up to Marpole's car and, at the tail end of the train, the top official of the CPR in Western Canada returned to his home and offices in Vancouver.[51]

Hussey and his constables were busily preparing for the first courtroom appearance of the robbers, the Grand Jury hearing. He wired Chief Constable Simmons in Vernon to release Mohr, Wilson and Christie due to a lack of evidence. Even though there was considerable suspicion that Mohr and Wilson were involved in horse rustling in the Grande Prairie area, no proof existed for their involvement in the robbery. However, the case against Paul Stevens was considered somewhat more damning, and Simmons was ordered to escort him to Kamloops where he was to be incarcerated in the Kamloops Gaol. Stevens was duly placed in a Kamloops cell in the same facility as the other three train robber suspects.[52 53]

On the 16TH of May, Neil McFadden in Princeton sat down and

painfully penned a letter to Hussey in Kamloops.

Princeton B.C. May 16th 1906

*"is there a horse among the horses taken from the train robbers
answering the following descriptions One bay horse weigh about 900
lbs Branded M on Right Sholdr and one White hind leg if so Kindly
let me no as i Loaned Dunn this horse about the last of march to go
on a prospecting trip for about three weeks and this is the first i have
heard of either since if the horse is there What steps must i take to
Recover him"*

"Kindly Oblidg
NB McFadden
Princeton B.C."

Hussey investigated and soon determined that the gelding belonged to
McFadden and arranged to have it shipped back to him in Princeton
after the trial.[54]

The last step Hussey took Wednesday evening before the Grand
Jury started the next day was to set out all the prisoners' effects on
a large table in the jail office. One by one he asked the prisoners to
pick out their items so they could be either returned or safeguarded.
When it came Miner's turn, he picked up the fancy belt lying on the
table. Hussey asked him if it was his, and Miner replied that yes, it
was. Hussey had placed the belt that Valentine Ross had found beside
the tracks at Furrer Siding on the table, and Miner had just identified
that he had been at that location sometime previous to when the
section foreman found it. The green tinted prospector's goggles were
also on the table. Hussey asked who owned the goggles. Miner said
he did not wear goggles, then thought about it for a minute, then he
claimed the goggles as his also.[55]

XVII
THE PRELIMINARY HEARING

WEDNESDAY, 16 MAY 1906

On the day before the Grand Jury preliminary hearings were to take place, the CPR's Superintendent Marpole released an editorial to all the newspapers in British Columbia, including the two Kamloops publications. The Vancouver Province had a wide and growing readership throughout B.C. and was on the newsstands that evening with the railway official's comments. The jurors picked for the Grand Jury in Kamloops could read the Marpole editorial in its entirety before proceedings even got underway the next day.

Looked at from today's perspective, we can now recognize what can only be described as a display of corporate arrogance presented by a senior employee of Canada's giant railway monopoly. The editorial reflected a management culture within the organization itself that seemed to hold as its due all those trappings and the power of a government unto itself. The potential was there that the influence that the organization had accumulated into its hands over the past twenty years could, when mishandled by a conceited bureaucracy, potentially affect the administration of justice and the workings of government. Some of this corporate influence would affect the administration of justice in Kamloops in May of 1906.

In the first paragraph of the editorial, Marpole expressed his conviction that the three prisoners in the Kamloops Gaol were guilty of the robbery at Ducks. He stated that he was under no doubt that George Edwards was in reality Bill Miner, and that he and his two compatriots from the Similkameen had also held up the train at

Mission. This statement was made even before a preliminary hearing had been held to determine whether there was enough evidence to hold a trial. There is no doubt but that this statement would have had an effect on the jurors and witnesses that would shortly be appearing at the hearing and the future trial. To go against a respected and powerful entity such as the CPR, which held the power of individual employment and civic and provincial prosperity, potentially compromised every individual involved with the administration of justice in Kamloops that May.

Marpole continued his editorial with a veiled criticism of the provincial government and the Provincial Police. He deplored the lack of attention paid to that area in the Boundary and Similkameen country that enabled people to move about so freely without being held accountable. "There appears to be a number of tough characters in the country south of Kamloops whose antecedents should be looked into. Some of them, like Edwards, have been allowed to roam around that section of the Province without any questions or surveillance. This is not creditable to the province and there must be some radical change to prevent such desperados making our country a harbour of refuge. We shall make representations in this connection to the executive of the provincial government."[1]

Marpole was making obvious reference to such perceived undesirables as Bill Miner, Shorty Dunn, Jack Budd, Tom Arnold and Paul Stevens. All had crossed the diaphanous border with the United States into southern British Columbia with ease and had committed or were suspected of committing crimes in the young province. However, with the exception of Miner's holdups of the trains in Mission and Ducks, one could hardly determine that a crime wave was in progress in the southern part of B.C.

The B.C. Provincial Police, while spread thinly throughout the area, managed through skilled and respected police officers like Constable John Kirkup, formerly of Revelstoke, and a fair and unelected judicial system, to keep crime to a minimum. The wife of a former Governor General, Lady Aberdeen, wrote a pertinent comment in her diary just a few years previous to these 1906 events.

She and her husband were on a tour through southern British Columbia, and she took the opportunity to write down her thoughts on the rambunctious American miners at work in the Kootenays.

"These people, belonging as they do to a wild and lawless class, are accustomed to cut a gash and shoot at one another without let or hindrance. But the moment they come into British Territory they realize that 'Aunt Peggy's laws' (Queen Victoria) are made to be obeyed—they drop their revolvers and are willing to be kept in order by one constable."[2]

Indeed, it was American capital, labour, enterprise and commitment that were opening up the West and East Kootenays to a mineral extraction economy that persists to the present day. The natural north-south corridor between the mountain ranges encouraged rail and steamship transportation between the mines in southern B.C. and the smelters in Washington and Idaho, and it was only later that the CPR saw the potential of the area and moved in with their subsidies, freight rates and capital.

To further ensure the CPR's profits were not affected by American "desperados," Marpole recommended that troops of Royal North West Mounted Police be stationed at critical points along the CPR's main line and at a strategic point in the south Okanagan or Kootenays. At the expense of the B.C. Provincial Police, his editorial described the Mounties as "a magnificent body of men" that Alberta and Saskatchewan were lucky to have to maintain law and order in those provinces. Marpole also was not averse to incorporating American law enforcement techniques into Canada. "I am strongly in favour of keeping bloodhounds at certain points in this province," he wrote. He went on to praise the handlers of the dogs that had come up from Spokane as "men of experience as hunters of outlaws."

The railway Superintendent summarized the role organizations and individuals had played in the success of the manhunt. Mention of the B.C. Provincial Police was conspicuous by its absence; however, Hussey and Fernie were singled out as being responsible for a successful outcome.

Not to miss an opportunity, Marpole approached the end of his editorial by mentioning the insight of his direct boss, Vice-President William Whyte. He described it as a "happy inspiration of Mr. Whyte's to ask for the services of the Mounted Police."[3]

Altogether it was an extraordinary example of the effect the CPR felt it could exert on public opinion. It highlighted the ability of the railway to pressure the outcome of events to its favour and to mould public reaction to its own ends. That the editorial could severely compromise or prejudice the trials of the suspect defendants was duly ignored.

The sole voice found which was raised against any portion of Marpole's demands was a quiet editorial raised three days later by editor Freeman Harding of the Kamloops Standard. He wrote that B.C. was quite capable of providing for its own mounted force through the provincial police organization. "There are plenty of men in British Columbia who can ride as hard, stand as much, and do as well as any one of the men from the plains."

So as not to step too far away from the CPR's perceived desires and their advertising revenue, he agreed with Marpole that the use of bloodhounds should perhaps be contemplated as "sentiment should not be allowed to interfere with any means of bringing train robbers to earth."[4]

The Victoria Colonist echoed the need for more police protection in the province now that the railways had opened up so much country that had previously been inaccessible. The editorial went on to point out that with the exception of the train robbery at Mission, no need had been identified that required an expanded semi-military force to be raised.

"We all remember how efficiently Mr. John Kirkup, with his strong right arm and his effective right boot, kept the peace in West Kootenay, almost unaided, during the stirring times of early mining development. When he knocked the heads of disturbers of the peace together or administered a 'swift kick' to the suspicious camp follower and told him to 'travel,' he emphasized the power of the law to deal with wrong-doers in such a way that they kept very quiet or kept far aloof."[5]

The editorial ended in a flurry of obscure language and phrasing. The Colonist admitted that the province had matured beyond Kirkup's elementary form of justice and that a more comprehensive administration of law enforcement had to be enacted. But since the coming of the railways had placed more responsibilities on the province, it behooved the federal government to pass on increased subsidies to the province to "enable

Frederick Fulton. Courtesy of Kamloops Museum and Archives.

us to adequately perform the duties incumbent upon us in this and other respects, which with our present responsibilities and local sources of revenue, we are obviously unable to perform without seriously increasing the burdens upon the people." The federal government could have been forgiven if they had not read the editorial to its tedious end, or ever to have acted upon the request for increased subsidies.[6]

The lawyers involved in the Grand Jury hearing reflected some of the most prominent in Kamloops. The prosecuting attorney for the Crown was the Attorney General of the province and the Chief Commissioner of Lands and Works, Frederick Fulton. He would be assisted in his endeavours by the Deputy Attorney General, Hugh Archibald McLean. Deputy Attorney General McLean was to do most of the preliminary investigations, interviews and leg work for the prosecution, while Fulton undertook the examinations in the court room. With a law practice in Kamloops, Fulton was also the representative for the city and region in the provincial legislative assembly in Victoria and no doubt felt it was a good political move to act for the Crown in such a high profile case in front of

*Defence lawyer Alex Mcintyre,
circa 1900.* Courtesy of
Kamloops Museum and Archives.

his constituents.

The defence was led by Fulton's old adversary, Alex Mcintyre. Mcintyre was a controversial but able Kamloops lawyer and had a reputation for skilled defence arguments and creative manipulations of the law. An ardent Liberal, he also variously held the positions of Yale County Administrator and City Solicitor. He was not popular with either his fellow lawyers or the general public and was described as having as his only purpose not the pursuit of justice, but the bending of the court to his will.[7]

Mcintyre had embarrassed a frustrated Fulton with his successful defence tactics during the trial of Smoky Chisholm's shooter in 1904. During that confrontation, an impressed Bill Miner had sat in the gallery of the Kamloops courthouse watching the defence lawyer's antics with interest. Mcintyre had convinced the three train robbery suspects to be defended by him as a group, and he was assisted by lawyers John D. Swanson and J.M. Murphy, a former federal Member of Parliament. Swanson was a well-respected Kamloops lawyer and had been hired to assist Mcintyre and act for Colquhoun's friends and relatives back in Ontario.

Thursday, 17 May 1906

The Marpole editorial was not the only potential prejudicial event that took place before the Grand Jury met on Thursday. That day the Vancouver Province newspaper arrived in Kamloops with the photos of Miner, Dunn and Colquhoun splashed across the front page. The publication had retained Mary Spencer as their photographer in Kamloops, and as she had taken the photos for Hussey at the jail as well as those of the prisoners coming into town, and no restrictions had been put on their use, she sold them to the Province. Other newspapers across Canada were clamouring for copies, and she willingly provided them until Hussey put an end to her entrepreneurship.

The Province made sure that its photos gained the maximum attention of its readers under the front page headline "First Pictures Of Train Robbers." It was this issue, on the same front page, that featured the largely fictional exploits of Constable Fernie. It was submitted by a desperate reporter, R.H. Hill, on an otherwise slow news day. The cries of "yellow journalism" from Kamloops papers went largely unheard in the rest of the province.

The captions under each photograph left no doubt as to the character of the defendants or the possibility of their guilt. Shorty Dunn was described as "insolent and defiant" and was incorrectly accused of being an ex-convict from Washington State named Lewis Cavaneas who had served time in 1902 for forgery and counterfeiting.

The two photos of Miner, one taken as he left San Quentin in 1901, and the other of George Edwards taken by Mary Spencer, were used to show that the defendant indeed was Bill Miner. "A comparison will convince anyone that the arrested man is Miner." In the Mary Spencer photo he is described as being the leader of the train robbers and fitting the Pinkerton's descriptions in every way.

Colquhoun escaped the prejudices of the Province. The caption under his photo described him as the most "genteel" of the robbers and having a "frank, open face and a quiet manner."[8]

With the attention of the media of British Columbia and the ordinary citizens of Kamloops focused on them, the shackled and manacled prisoners were loaded onto a wagon at the Kamloops Gaol. Escorted by Superintendent Hussey and armed guards, they made their way onto Seymour Street and along to the combination courthouse and municipal hall at the corner of First Avenue and Seymour Street. A large crowd was already in attendance both outside and inside the courthouse. Inside the old building there was

Kamloops Mayor and Justice of the Peace Marshall Pollock Gordon.

COURTESY OF KAMLOOPS MUSEUM AND ARCHIVES.

standing room only. The Mayor of Kamloops, Marshall Gordon, was a local furniture merchant as well as Justice of the Peace, and the Grand Jury proceedings were held under his authority.

The proceedings were delayed while police officers carried the wounded Shorty Dunn into the courtroom. He found the whole exercise extremely humorous, laughing all the while until they finally placed him in a chair beside the prisoner's dock which held his two compatriots. Colquhoun and Miner were coupled together with leg irons while they were in the dock. The Kamloops Sentinel reporter commented that "cleaned up they looked quite respectable and no one would take them for anything but quiet, ordinary citizens." Colquhoun seemed visibly distressed to one reporter; however, the other two seemed almost nonchalant. Dunn smirked and laughed throughout the proceedings, but paid close attention and did not seem to miss anything that was presented. Colquhoun appeared to another reporter to be "self-possessed and cool, and looked quite respectable after (his) cleaning up in the gaol."[9][10]

Mcintyre immediately asked the Court for a remand as he had not had the time nor the opportunity to prepare adequately for the case, had not been able to confer adequately with the accused, and could not assemble his evidence as the prisoners were not residents of the district. He had had only half an hour's interview with the prisoners and had no time to prepare a defence. He told the court that to proceed at this time would not be fair to the prisoners and that they would not be able to obtain a fair trial. He asked for a remand of eight days, noting that he had no objection to the evidence of the Mounted Police being taken so as to permit their departure for other duties. Mcintyre was attempting to delay the hearing and possible trial until after the spring assizes in Kamloops, which were to commence a week from the following Monday.[11]

Mr. Fulton responded that he certainly would not want to deny the prisoners a fair trial, but felt that the onus was on the prosecution rather than the defence to overcome the difficulties presented by a speedy trial. He went on to argue that there was no necessity for delay. Mcintyre strongly objected to any other evidence being taken and requested that he be given more time to prepare the defence. Mr. Fulton went on to add that a preliminary hearing did not necessarily call for a full defence to be made; however, Mcintyre objected to this also, stating that evidence taken at a preliminary hearing often prejudiced the case for the accused when a trial took place.

When these preliminaries were over, Justice of the Peace Pollock ruled that the charges against the prisoners were to be read.

Mr. Fulton opened the case by briefly recapitulating the details of the events of the holdup, pursuit, gunfight and capture. He then called upon Royal North West Mounted Police Sergeant Wilson to give his testimony.

Wilson testified as to his actions from leaving Calgary through to the capture and deposition of the prisoners at the Kamloops Gaol. He identified the prisoners and several exhibits such as their packs, a bottle of liquid he called catarrh cure wrapped in a wrapper noted as Catarrhozone, and the hobnailed boots taken from Dunn and Colquhoun. He could not identify Shorty Dunn's semi-automatic Luger as belonging to him as he did not take part in gathering up the pistols after the shootout.

Mr. Fulton attempted to query the witness as to what the prisoners had said subsequent to the gunfight; however, Mcintyre objected on the grounds that the men were then under arrest. Fulton insisted, and was able to get Wilson's testimony as to Dunn's offhanded comments after the shooting into the court record.

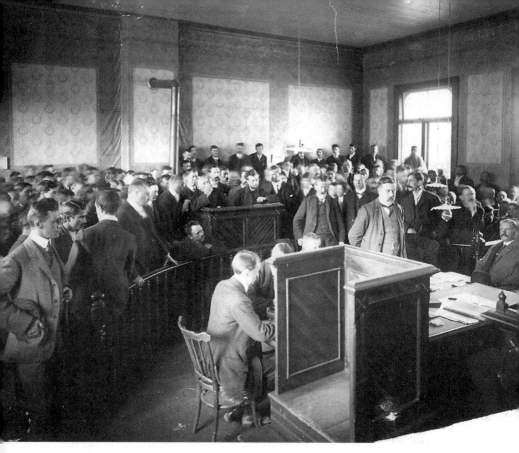

Mary Spencer photo, *The Grand Jury Hearing in the Kamloops Courthouse, 17 May 1906.* Attorney General and Crown prosecutor Frederick Fulton is addressing the court directly behind the witness box. Over his left shoulder is Chief Constable E.T.W. Pearse, and seated to Fulton's left is Superintendent Hussey. CPR Detective Inspector R.E. Bullick has not strayed far from Shorty Dunn's side. Only the eyes and the top of the head of McIntyre are visible above the edge of the witness box.

Mcintyre then cross-examined the Mounted Police Sergeant. Knowing that B.C. was policed by the Provincial Police, he attempted to assert that the Royal North West Mounted Police had no jurisdiction in B.C. When questioned about whether they had been sworn in as Special Constables, Sgt. Wilson answered that they had not, but that he had been a member of the Provincial force prior to joining the Mounted Police. They had received their instructions from Commissioner Bowen-Perry before they had left the Northwest, and upon arriving in Kamloops, they took instructions from Commissioner Bowen-Perry and Provincial Police Superintendent Hussey. Wilson commented that Dunn had been laughing after he was shot, laughed when Dr. Tuthill had probed for the bullet in his leg, and that he had been laughing ever since. When Wilson gave this testimony, Dunn, in the chair beside the prisoner's box, grinned broadly.

Mcintyre then questioned Wilson about the supposed "hot house" tactics allowed by the Mounted Police on the prisoners when they were kept overnight in the hall in Quilchena. He referred to the questioning of Colquhoun by Seavey of the Thiel Detective Agency. Commissioner Bowen-Perry had telegraphed to Quilchena instructing Wilson to let Seavey question Colquhoun.

The transcript of Wilson's Grand Jury testimony shows Mcintyre's tenacious questioning on the propriety of allowing Seavey to question Colquhoun while he was a prisoner under the protection of the Mounted Police.

Q: Did you get any instructions from Mr. Perry as to how you should meet Mr. Seavey?
A: I got a telegram on Sunday to try to see him.
Q: Have you got the telegram here?
A: Yes.
Wilson produced the telegram, and it was entered as an exhibit.
Mr. Mcintyre: At the time Colonel Perry sent this message to you, did he know that you had captured three men?
A: No.

Q: Up to that time Mr. Seavey was a stranger to you?

A: Yes.

Q: Where did he introduce himself to you?

A: At Quilchena, outside of the hotel.

Q: He told you that he was sent by Colonel Perry?

A: No.

Q: He told you who he was?

A: Yes.

Q: At the time he introduced himself, you had
Colonel Perry's message?

A: Yes.

Q: Had you any instructions from Colonel Perry as to Seavey?

A: No.

Q: You knew nothing about Seavey until you got that message?

A: No. I am wrong, Mr. Greaves told me that Seavey had
been there.

Q: Mr. Greaves had previously told you that Seavey had
been there?

A: Yes.

Q: Then when you met Seavey at Quilchena, you knew that
he was a detective?

A: Yes.

Q: Was it you who asked him in to see Colquhoun?

A: Yes. I asked Colquhoun to go into the room with him.

Q: You went personally into this hall?

A: Yes.

Q: What took place? You took Colquhoun, one of the
prisoners, out?

A: Yes.

Q: Where?

A: Into a little room opening off the hall. The hall is a fair sized
room, 30 by 40.

Q: And how large is this room?

A: I should think about 18 by 14.

Q: Is Seavey a tall dark man?

A: Yes.

Q: Then you ordered Colquhoun to go into this room?

A: I did not order him.

Mr. Mcintyre: He was your prisoner at the time and any instruction from you is an order or command.

Q: You directed Colquhoun to go into the small room?

A: Yes.

Q: Did you go in with him?

A: Yes.

Q: Did Seavey go in with him?

A: Yes.

Q: Did anyone else go in with you?

A: No.

Q: Why did you take him into that room?

A: Mr. Seavey said he had orders from Mr. Marpole to get certain information.

Q: And after what he told you, you placed the prisoner at his disposal?

A: For a little while. We very seldom do.

Mr Mcintyre: I should rather say so.

Q: You objected at first, did you?

A: Yes.

Q: How long have you been in the Mounted Police?

A: Altogether 13 years.

Q: And in that time did you ever know a similar proceedings by any person in charge of prisoners?

A: It is very often done.

Mr. Mcintyre: By whom?

(No response in the transcript.)

Q: Did Seavey tell him he was a lawyer from Kamloops?

A: No.

Mr. Mcintyre: This man says he did tell him so.

Mcintyre referred to George Edwards.

A: He was wrong there. He did not take any unfair advantage of him in that way. Colquhoun did not seem to want to tell anything and he did not press him.

Mcintyre: You took one of the prisoners under your charge and put him under sweat box conditions, unlike regular Canadian practices on this side of the border.[12]

Q: You were probably a little mistaken about the fact that Mr. Seavey told him he was a detective.

A: No, I was not mistaken.[13]

Mcintyre told Wilson that the prisoners Colquhoun and Edwards had told him that Seavey, in the presence of witnesses around the stove in the Quilchena Hall, had identified himself as a lawyer from Kamloops. Wilson answered that he was positive that Seavey did not say this.

Mcintyre then went on to question Wilson more about Seavey. "Is he here?"

Wilson looked around the crowded courtroom, trying to spot the detective. Superintendent Hussey jumped to his feet and in a loud voice advised the defence lawyer that Seavey was not in attendance in the courtroom.

"Where is he?" asked Mcintyre.

"Never mind," replied Hussey impatiently. "He is not here."

This is the first, but not the last, indication that Hussey may not have been that impressed with the recent actions of Mr. Seavey.[14]

Mr. Fulton then queried the witness again as to the demeanour of Shorty Dunn during the capture. "He was serious enough during the time the shooting was taking place," answered Wilson, "but hasn't stopped laughing since."

Mcintyre contemptuously replied that perhaps the shot in the leg that he received enabled him to see the joke.

Mcintyre asked Wilson, "And there was a good deal of excitement on both sides?"

Wilson replied, "No excitement on our side."

This finished the examination of Sgt. Wilson, and the hearing was adjourned until two o'clock.

When the proceedings resumed, Corporal Stewart gave his testimony without incident, corroborating the testimony given by

Mary Spencer photo, *The Grand Jury Hearing in the Kamloops Courthouse, 17 May 1906. Miner and Colquhoun are in the prisoner's box, Dunn is sitting in a chair on the floor to their right. CPR Special Service Detective Inspector R.E. Bullick is to Dunn's right, and defence lawyer Alex Mcintyre leans towards the witness box. Sheriff Wentworth Wood is directly behind Mcintyre, provincial government clerk Edward Fisher is to Wood's direct left, and Chief Constable Pearse is standing to Fisher's left. Superintendent Hussey leans on the table directly in front of the witness box.*

Wilson. Shoebotham followed Stewart to the stand and gave his testimony. Mcintyre cross-examined him closely and tried to insert doubt about who was instructing the Mounted Police, that Dunn was carrying a cup in his hand when he leaped to his feet, and that he only returned fire in self-defence after the Mounties opened fire first. Mcintyre said that the Royal North West Mounted Police had a world-wide reputation for policing excellence, and noted that it seemed very queer that the Mounted Police allowed Shorty Dunn to get the drop on them and get off two shots before the Mounties even had their revolvers out of their holsters.

Shoebotham testified that the standing orders at Quilchena were that no strangers were to address the prisoners. In response to Mcintyre's question, he advised that while he did know CPR detective McLaws to see him, he did not see him in Quilchena.

When Corporal Peters testified, he corroborated all the previous testimony by the Royal North West Mounted Police members. He also identified a number of the exhibits taken from the prisoners.

After Constable Browning gave his testimony, he was adamant in response to Mcintyre at cross-examination that Dunn had started shooting first. Mcintyre tried his best to bait Browning into confusing his testimony, however, with no success. With all his cross-examinations of the Mounted Police officers, Mcintyre hammered on facts that would influence the jury's decisions. He tried to insert doubt into the jury's minds as to the legitimacy of the federal police acting in British Columbia without warrants, without being sworn in as Special Constables, and wearing civilian clothes. He tried to intimate that the officers fired first and that subterfuge and coercion were used by Seavey in the back room at Quilchena. He tried to implant in the jury's minds that the detective had told the prisoners he was a lawyer, thus enabling him to get privileged information from them. However, Mcintyre found it difficult to sway the officers' testimony as they were experienced at testifying and often answered questions in a vague way or merely that they didn't know the answer to a particularly leading question. Their testimony to the actual events of the capture matched without any glaring discrepancies.

While Dunn grinned and smirked throughout the testimony, Colquhoun was seen to frequently prompt his counsel and pass on advice. He seemed to be very alert as all the testimony was given and continually, perhaps unconsciously, wore a half smile on his face. Miner sat back quietly, observant and watchful. Viewers in the gallery saw that his right eyelid drooped slightly.[15]

B.C. Provincial Police Constable Fernie then took the stand and gave a long and detailed description of the role he and his trackers played in tracking down the bandits. He started from when he was awakened by the call boy and ended at the banks of the Nicola River when the robbers were run to earth. When cross-examined by Mcintyre, he testified that he had been introduced to detective Seavey at Quilchena, and while he had seen him in the guard room, he had not seen him speak to the prisoners, nor did he know what he was there for.

Mcintyre then recalled Sergeant Wilson to the stand. He answered in response to Mcintyre's probing that Seavey had told Colquhoun while he was a prisoner in Quilchena that he was a detective from the Thiel Detective Agency in Seattle. Mcintyre sarcastically retorted that Wilson probably shut his ears to any other things said by Seavey.

J.P. Gordon then called an adjournment until 10:00 o'clock the next morning.[16]

FRIDAY, 18 MAY 1906

When the court was reassembled Friday morning at 10:00 o'clock and the prisoners settled in the dock, Defence Attorney Mcintyre again pleaded with the court for an adjournment to the 25TH of the month, one week later. He protested against going into the preliminary hearing any further as it had not been possible for him to receive adequate or proper instructions from the prisoners. As he was defending three men on the most serious of charges, he protested against the Attorney General going on with the proceedings.

Attorney General Fulton for the prosecution noted that he had no objections to an adjournment until that afternoon, "But I cannot see that my friend would be any better prepared for the preliminary in a week than he could this afternoon."

In his own defence, Mcintyre noted that preparation for a preliminary trial such as this one requires as much as it would for a first trial.

"It is customary in an important case to ask for one week of a remand, and I have not known a case where it was not granted. If forced to go on I will withdraw and give up the case so as not to prejudice the prisoners."[17]

A harried Mr. Gordon granted an adjournment until 2:00 P.M. that afternoon. Upon resumption of the preliminary hearing after the morning adjournment, Mr. Fulton called CPR locomotive engineer Joseph Callin to the stand.

CPR engineer Joseph Callin of Revelstoke was sworn and examined by prosecutor Fulton. Callin testified that at first he thought the holdup was a joke; however, his opinion was soon changed when he was confronted with the pistols in the hands of the robbers.

A brief pause occurred in the engineer's testimony as a stir rose in the courtroom. The reporter for the Kamloops Sentinel had to make his way out of the courtroom to meet his paper's afternoon deadline.[18]

Callin went on to testify to the numerous stops made by the train, the actions, demeanour and descriptions of the robbers, and the escape of the robbers that took place between Campbell's Crossing and the Furrer Siding. He described the bandit leader and his distinctive long black overcoat, and went on to positively identify Colquhoun in the prisoner's box as the third bandit whose face he had seen clearly by the light of the open door of the engine firebox. However, later in his testimony, he became confused as to the identity of the third man.

Fulton: Now could you identify the third man?
A: I could with respect to his height.
Q: His appearance?
A: The sweater he had on that night I have not seen on him since.
Q: Have you seen him since?

A: I could not say positively I have seen a man what I would judge to be exactly the same height.

Callin then identified the dynamite in the sack on the exhibit table that had been carried by Colquhoun and later found on the rail bed.

Defence lawyer Mcintyre proceeded to cross-examine Callin. He went over the numerous descriptions of the bandits given by Callin to various persons investigating the robbery. Callin recited a long list of interviews, including those with Deputy Attorney General McLean, Superintendent Hussey, CPR Special Service detective and Chief Special Agent W. L. McLaws, Superintendent Kilpatrick of the CPR, and CPR Station Agent Hayden and Chief Constable Pearse. He admitted that he had seen the photos of the suspected robbers in the Vancouver Province this same day. Mcintyre attempted to establish that Callin's identification of the bandits and the fact that he could name the individuals was a result of the prejudicial Province newspaper coverage. The Province had identified George Edwards as Bill Miner in that same day's edition and stated that Colquhoun and Dunn were the other two bandits. Upon questioning by Mcintyre, Callin admitted that when he had gone to the Kamloops Gaol to identify the three prisoners, the three of them were stood in a line by themselves, and Callin was told that they were the three men who had robbed his train. In his descriptions, he referred to Dunn and Edwards by name, not because he could identify them, but because their photos had appeared in the paper. Upon Mcintyre's questioning, Callin testified that Deputy Attorney General McLean, CPR Revelstoke Division Superintendent Kilpatrick, and CPR Special Service detective McLaws were in attendance at the time. Mcintyre went on to question the discrepancies in Callin's original descriptions of the bandits, and it seemed likely that he was probably able to generate some doubt about Callin's testimony in the minds of the jury and the gallery.[19]

The Dominion Express Co. mail clerk Alex McQuarrie was then called to the stand, sworn, and examined by prosecutor Fulton. He described the events as they unfolded around him and how he had seen the face of Edwards, the bandit leader, in the light of the three acetylene lamps burning in the combination mail and express car. He identified the man he had seen as Edwards in the prisoner's box. Upon cross-examination, Mcintyre brought up the fact that McQuarrie also had seen the photos of the suspected robbers in the Vancouver Province after he viewed the suspects at the Kamloops Gaol with Callin and Radcliffe, hoping thereby to create additional doubt as to the identification of the prisoners by the witness. McQuarrie also testified that he had met Deputy Attorney General McLean in the Grand Pacific Hotel where they were both staying, and they had spoken together about the case. Also, he told the court he had met with Superintendent Marpole and discussed the case. Marpole told him that the men that met his description had been captured and that he should go up to the Gaol to identify them.[20]

Alec Ignace, the Shuswap Indian tracker, was then called to the stand. As Ignace only spoke Shuswap and Chinook Jargon, an interpreter was provided to him. Both Ignace and the interpreter were sworn in. Ignace stated that he lived on the Kamloops reserve and was a good hunter and tracker. Fulton soon narrowed his questioning down to the three sets of tracks made by the robbers. Ignace's response to questions put to him through the interpreter caused some moments of frustration to Fulton as he attempted to extract relevant testimony and overcome the culture gap.

Q: How many tracks did you see?
A: Two or three tracks.
Q: Now what kind were those three tracks?
A: Peoples' tracks.
Q: What were they like?
A: The two of them hobnailed shoes and the other smooth bottom.
Q: Was there any difference between the hobnailed shoes?
A: I did not exactly know, they are not exactly the same kind, one is a little different.

Q: Can you tell how it is different?

A: The one tacked all over and one not so many tacks in it, tacked in rows.

Q: How were the heels tacked?

A: There were not many tacks in the heels.

Q: Were they both alike?

A: Yes.

Ignace related how the tracks were lost close to Curry's ranch, and how, after back-tracking and circling around, he had finally spotted the heel marks in the dust of the wagon road where the robbers had crossed backwards in a duck squat.

"When I seen these tracks, I called to Mr. Fernie and told him."

He then proceeded to respond to the Fulton's questions on tracking events as they unfolded. The gap in cultures became somewhat humorously apparent when Fulton attempted to determine compass directions from the witness.

Q: Where was the camp where you saw the tracks?

A: Lou Campbell's Meadow, and so we camped there. There is a little creek there.

Q: Which side of Lou Campbell's Meadow?

A: Below the meadow.

Q: Which side?

A: This side.

Q: Which side of Joseph Greaves?

A: This side.

Q: Which side of the wagon road from Lou Campbell's meadows?

A: It was below the wagon road.

Fulton then moved on to other questions, as he could see that this line of questioning was not going to be fruitful. Compass directions had no meaning to Ignace. "What side" of Campbell's Meadow was the side he was presently sitting on in the courtroom. Ignace's continuing testimony revealed the skill and tenacity displayed by the Indian trackers, and it was apparent to all in the courtroom the valuable contribution they and Fernie had made to the eventual apprehension of the robbers. When the tracks were lost on occasion, they described how they circled around in ever increasing circles until they picked them up again.

> Q: Where did you see these tracks last?
> A: The last time we seen the tracks first alongside Lou Campbell's Meadow, the lower side.
> Q: Which side of the lake?
> A: The lower side of the lake.
> Q: How far from Joe Greaves' house?
> A: I do not know exactly how far. On the same side of the lake as Joe Greaves' house.
> Q: How far from the lake?
> A: I do not know exactly how far.

Ignace, when presented with the exhibits, identified the three pairs of boots: two hobnailed and the other smooth soled.

> Q: Look at the boots there and see if any of these boots would make the same tracks as you saw.
> A: I seen two shoes they were hobnailed shoes and the other was smooth shoe. The smooth shoes had small heels.
> Ignace examined the smooth soled shoes and said, "These heels are the same as the tracks made."

As the witness was examining the boots, he stated through the interpreter that one of the boots should have something attached to the heel that was somewhat larger than a tack or nail. He turned one hobnailed boot over, and there for everyone in the courtroom to see was a small copper heel plate embedded in the heel. The boot was Shorty Dunn's, and he had attached the plate to prevent wear to the heel.[21]

Mcintyre then started his cross-examination of Ignace and concentrated on Ignace's identification of the tracks. He tried to get Ignace to admit that the tracks he had seen beside the rail line at the stops the train had made could have been those of CPR section men; however, Ignace was unwavering in his testimony. Ignace testified that either he or Fernie would spot the tracks first, and they would get down off their horses and onto their knees to examine them closely. He went on to state that while Fernie found it difficult to see the tracks through the grass in fields and meadows, he had no problems in other terrain.[22]

Phillip Toma, the second Indian tracker, was then called to the stand. He gave his full name and said that he too lived on the Kamloops reserve. He admitted that he was a good hunter and tracker and had been called out to assist B.C. Provincial Police constables Fernie and Pearse in tracking the train robbers. Fulton's questioning of Toma was not as detailed as that of Ignace; however, Fulton attempted to confirm that the three sets of boots in exhibit were the same as those the trackers were following. Mcintyre's cross-examination of Toma was brief, and in response to his question whether he had seen the boots prior to that day, Toma replied that he had not.[23]

After Toma had given his testimony, Superintendent Hussey was called. Attorney General Fulton drew out testimony from Hussey that described the Superintendent's entrapment of Miner to identify the belt found on the tracks at the 117 Mile board. Hussey noted that the personal effects of all the prisoners were laid out on a table and that Edwards had picked out the green tinted prospectors goggles and the belt found by the tracks as his. This effectively put the prisoner at the location of the train robbery sometime previous to the day after it took place.

This was the first time Miner learned that he had left the belt behind at the location of the robbery and that he had inadvertently placed himself at the site of the crime. Although the revelation must have disturbed him, he gave no sign that it had.[24]

Valentine Ross, the section foreman who found the belt, was also called to testify, and he identified the belt by a special mark that was on it. This brought the Grand Jury proceedings to an end.

Mr. Gordon then proceeded to read the charges.

"George Edwards, having heard the evidence, do you wish to say anything in answer to the charge? You are not obliged to say anything unless you wish to do so."

Miner replied, "I reserve my defence."

The same charge was read to Colquhoun, who responded the same way Miner did. When the charges were read to Dunn, he responded, "My answer is the same as the other boys."[25]

Mayor Gordon then committed them to stand trial "at the next court of competent jurisdiction, which will be the assizes which open here on (a week) Monday next."[26]

Shorty Dunn's Bill of Indictment, as a result of his shooting affray, was the most serious, and included charges over and above those faced by the other two defendants. A partial rendering of the official document makes for some rather painful reading.

IN THE SUPREME COURT OF BRITISH COLUMBIA
OYER AND TERMINER & GENERAL GAOL DELIVERY
Canada;
Province of British Columbia:
County of Yale
City of Kamloops:

The Jurors of our Lord the King present that on the fourteenth day of May in the year of our Lord one thousand nine hundred and six at Douglas Lake, in the County of Yale in the Province of British Columbia, William J. Dunn a certain firearm, to wit a revolver then loaded with gunpowder and divers leaden shot at and against one John J. Wilson unlawfully did shoot with intent thereby then unlawfully the said John J. Wilson to kill and murder against the form of the Statute in such case made and provided, and against the peace of our said Lord the King, his Crown and dignity.[27]

Signed by Attorney General Frederick Fulton, the indictment against William Dunn went on in the same language to charge "that he did shoot with intent thereby … to do some grievous bodily harm" to police officer Wilson, and that he did "shoot with intent thereby to prevent the lawful apprehension of him." The same charges were levelled against Dunn for shooting at Browning. All three, George Edwards, Lewis Colquhoun and William Dunn, were charged with "Stopping the Mail and Stealing certain Post letters."

That evening, in the same room court had been held, the weekly Thursday meeting of the Kamloops City Council took place. Mayor Gordon was presiding and thankful to be finishing off a rather busy schedule for that day. The mundane business of council was hardly as exciting for him as the events that had taken place in front of him in the same room over the past day.

Eight accounts totalling some $590 were reviewed by Council and recommended for payment, and it was moved and seconded to acquire the services of a competent engineer to draft plans and specifications for the City's first sewerage system. The Board of Trade applied for $500 for advertising, and it was so moved and seconded; Alderman Robinson gave notice that he would be introducing a bylaw to exempt the new St. Ann's Convent building from taxation. The "erection of an electric light on an iron standard" in front of Council Chambers was laid over for one week, but it was successfully moved and carried that picture moulding be installed in the living rooms at the volunteer Fire Hall on Victoria Street. At the end of the meeting, council instructed the City Clerk to send a letter to Chief of Police McGill to enforce the bylaws and curtail the wanton racing of horses on the City's main streets.[28]

When Hussey returned to his hotel room after the hearing ended, a telegram was waiting for him.

Mary Spencer group portrait of R.N.W.M.P. Sitting, left to right,
Constable James H. Tabuteau, Sergeant John J. Wilson, and Corporal
C.R. Peters. Standing, left to right, Sergeant Percy G. Thomas, Guide
Samuel "Slim Jim" Benyon, Sergeant T.M. "Shoey" Shoebotham,
Corporal James C. Stewart and Constable John T. Browning.

COURTESY OF KAMLOOPS MUSEUM AND ARCHIVES.

He filed it on top of one of his fast growing piles of paper.

After a busy day, some of the citizens of Kamloops were entertained by the Williams' Original Dixie Jubilee Singers. Regular Chautauqua circuit performers, the black American vocal group consisted of four men and three women. Manager Charles P. Williams and his accomplished singers performed everything from opera to ragtime and spirituals with a piano accompanist.[30]

One group that had to miss out on the evening's entertainment were the R.N.W.M.P. Wilson and his six officers boarded the eastbound train out of Kamloops at 6:00 P.M. that same evening bound for Calgary. Joining them were Commissioner Bowen-Perry and Inspector Church. Wilson and the other four members that testified at the preliminary hearing would not have to return until the start of the spring assizes on Monday, the 28TH.

Before the squad of Mounted Police left Kamloops, they, along with their Guide Slim Jim Benyon, dropped into Mary Spencer's photography studios to have a group portrait taken. After the prisoners had been returned to the Kamloops Gaol that afternoon, Wilson and his officers paid a last visit to the suspects. When they met with Shorty Dunn, the prisoner was in good spirits, and he asked Wilson to "tell all members of the R.N.W.M.P. that he had no grievance against any of them, they had done their duty well and he was thankful for the kind attention which he received after being wounded, and he said, you may think it funny coming from me, but

I certainly admire the way you boys do your work." Dunn then shook hands with each of the Mounties in turn and said, "Goodbye, boys, write me when you get home."[31]

On the train trip back to Calgary, Wilson sat next to a young man from Ontario named C.J. Hawes. Hawes had recognized the photo of Colquhoun in all the Canadian papers, and told Wilson he had gone to teacher's college with him. It is probable they discussed the concerns felt by some as to the guilt of the former schoolteacher. The young man intimated to Wilson that he might be able to do something with Colquhoun as to getting the truth out of him. Wilson gave Hawes a signed note from him introducing Hawes to the lead CPR investigator, Inspector McLaws. Wilson told Hawes that McLaws was acting with the Attorney General.

After Wilson arrived in Calgary, he took a welcome Sunday off. The next day he wrote up a seven page report on his activities in British Columbia. In good bureaucratic style, both he and the Officer-In-Command of "E" Division, Inspector A.W. Duffus, signed the document.

XVIII
THE INVESTIGATION

THE DAY AFTER THE GRAND JURY hearing had come to an end, publisher Frederick Young's Kamloops Standard was on the streets bringing local readers up to date on the latest events. The Saturday edition reviewed the complete story of the posse and R.N.W.M.P. pursuit, the gunfight and capture of the bandits, and the results of the Grand Jury trial. Mary Spencer's soon to be famous photos of the three suspected train robbers were presented two columns wide. Shorty Dunn gave his best scowl, Miner's eyes drilled through the reader, and Colquhoun looked calm and accepting of his fate. Another Spencer photo showed the group as they were crossing the plateau to the west of town on the Nicola Road. The seven Mounted Police and Constable Fernie surround the three prisoners and the driver in the wagon, and CPR Superintendents Marpole and Kilpatrick with Marpole's socialite friend Captain Gardiner-Johnson hanging back in their buggy are seen in the three-column-wide photo. The last photo caught the group as they pulled to a halt in front of the Kamloops Gaol, Dunn wrapped in his blanket, and Miner in his distinctive Stetson in the back of the rig. A formal photo of William Fernie completed the photographic array.

The paper gave extensive coverage to an interview with Constable Fernie, with a short biography of his accomplishments and his service in the Boer War. The editor, Freeman Harding, praised the tenacity and skill which Fernie, Pearse, the trackers and the rest of the posse displayed in putting up with adverse weather conditions and a skilled and knowledgeable quarry.[1]

Superintendent Hussey fulfilled a number of responsibilities during this period of investigation and preparation for trial. He was at the service of the Deputy Attorney General who was not reluctant to utilize Hussey and his constables for whatever he needed to assist him in trial preparation. The Superintendent also had constables like Fernie and Pearse out issuing subpoenas and following up on investigations as each day went by.

Hussey was constantly being requested to send copies of Mary Spencer's photos to newspapers across the continent. The Winnipeg Telegram in Manitoba wired him soon after the robbers were captured.

Canadian Pacific Railway's Telegrams
Winnipeg, Man. 16 May 1906

To Chief Constable Kamloops

Please have photographer who made pictures of robbers
rush us copies, as we will pay well, wire answer.

Daily Telegram

Before he had a chance to respond, the telegraph boy handed him another wire.

Canadian Pacific Railway's Telegrams
Winnipeg, Man. 16 May 1906
To Chief Constable Kamloops

Please ask photographer what train he will express bandit pictures on.

Telegram

B.C. Provincial Police Superintendent Frederick Hussey.
Courtesy of Kamloops Museum and Archives.

It is not known today whether Mary Spencer was paid well, but it is hoped that she managed to gain some monetary reward for her efforts before Hussey stopped further dissemination of the photographs until after the trial.[2]

On the Saturday night following the end of the preliminary hearing, and after the Friday night presentation of the Jubilee singers, Kamloops was treated to the travelling tour group of the great Madame Albani. It was the 54 year old diva's last concert tour, and the audiences in Victoria and Vancouver had been enthralled with the performance of her large ensemble. The impressive vocal section was supported by violinists and a pianist, and no doubt the crowd of local Kamloops citizenry in the local church hall was well supplemented by the many investigators and other individuals in town as a result of the upcoming trial.

Hussey did not soon stray far from his responsibilities as he requested Constable Hunter in Princeton to submit a more detailed report on the activities of the three bandits and Jack Budd in the Similkameen section. Hunter's handwritten reply details all the rumour and stories associated with the mysterious American. Hunter personally saw little of Miner except on mail days when he would come down from Budd's place to pick up his frequent correspondence. Hunter remembered him attending a number of dances in the Princeton area. He had heard that Miner "was supposed to have an interest in the ranch with Budd, but as it was only a pre-emption his title would not be recorded. In the fall of 1904 he left for South America, that was the report given out, and returned in the spring of 1905." No comment was made by Hunter that this was the very time that the CPR at Mission Junction was robbed. Hunter went on to check on Tom Arnold at Budd's place, who still was not home, and found that all the branding irons with the exception of one were now missing. He canvassed Aspen Grove for witnesses and interviewed William Dodds at his store. He reported that Billy Dunn had done some work for Mrs. Allison on an off and on basis over the years and had spent most of the spring trapping with a man named Tilton. Colquhoun had only showed up in the area from Phoenix early this spring and had stayed for a few days in the Princeton Hotel where the bartender got to know him. Colquhoun had not, to any of the locals' knowledge, spent any time previous to this in the Similkameen.[3]

Hussey had mailed photos of Miner to an ex-convict from San Quentin asking for a positive identification of the robber held in the Kamloops Gaol. It is probable that the Pinkertons provided the identity of this individual. Soon after the preliminary hearing, he received a telegram from his second-in-command in Victoria,

Sergeant T.R. Murray. Murray had received a communication from the former inmate of San Quentin, and he passed the information along to Hussey.

Canadian Pacific Railway Company Telegram
Victoria B.C. May 19, 06.

F.S. Hussey, Supt. Prov. Police, Ka.

Photos received party positively identifies
Miner served five year term San Junentin [sic]
prison time Miner there. Would go
Kamloops to identify but unwilling to appear
in court.

T.R. Murray
21:40[4]

When Chief Constable Edgar Simmons of Vernon delivered Paul Stevens to the jail in Kamloops on the 14TH of May, he was ordered by Hussey to assist in the investigations around Kamloops. His first rather delicate task was to go out by buggy to the Stevens' remote cabin in the Monte Hills and escort Paul Stevens' wife Margaret to the Kamloops Gaol to determine whether she could identify William Dunn. No record survives as to the thoughts that must have been going through her mind when she stepped into the prison knowing her husband was incarcerated in one of the cells. It is also not known whether she took the opportunity to visit him when she was there. However, we do know that she saw Shorty Dunn in prison that day and identified him as the man she had seen riding the bay horse with the white blaze on its face and white hind leg. She also remembered Edwards' distinctive red leather saddle on the horse. She told Simmons Dunn had told her he was sick and asked the way to Grande Prairie and other questions about the trails in the area. Simmons showed her the red saddle in the room with all the other exhibits, and she thought that it was the same saddle she had seen under Dunn that day. Simmons then drove the wife of the robbery suspect to the Kamloops corrals, where she identified the horse that Dunn was riding that day. She added to Simmons that the next time she had seen that same horse and saddle was the previous Sunday when Chief Constable Pearse came riding up to her cabin with his posse. He was riding that same bay horse with the red saddle.

Margaret Stevens also told Simmons that on a day shortly after the robbery, and at the Stevens' cabin at Little Fish Lake, she and an Indian woman named Julia were preparing and drying fish outside the cabin about mid-morning. Julia was camped nearby at the lake with her family. It was the warmest day of the year so far, and they were air drying the fish on racks outside the cabin with smoke smudges to keep the flies away. Suddenly through the clear air from the mountain above them to the west they could hear the sounds of whistles. They then heard answering ones from a different direction. The two women waited for people to show up as they thought some Indians might be coming over the hills to fish, but no one showed up. She didn't think anything more about it until after she had heard about the robbery, when she thought that perhaps it was the robbers she was hearing, signalling to each other through the dense forest.[5]

At the beginning of the next week, George Bromley, the rancher from just outside Princeton, was in Kamloops. He visited the offices of the Provincial Police when he was in town, and he was given to Simmons to be interviewed. It was Bromley's good-looking daughter Eliza who had befriended Budd and Edwards up on the mountain northeast of Princeton. Bromley volunteered that he had known Edwards for some time as he and Budd had a spread not too far from his own. The last time he had seen him was about two months ago. Edwards had always acted as a gentleman around him; he dressed well, always rode a good horse, and constantly seemed to have plenty of money to pay his way. Bromley had never known him to work at any real job. He went on to state that he had known Billy Dunn for about six or seven years. He had worked quite a bit for Mrs. Susan Allison at her ranch and at odd jobs around Hedley. Most winters he hunted and trapped in the heart of the Ashnola country and had a number of mineral claims. The last time Bromley had seen Dunn was this spring when he had stopped at his ranch for lunch. At that time Dunn took with him a "well put up small bay" with a white spot in the centre of the forehead and a white back leg. It had a heavy, shaggy mane and was known to be a little mean if the wrangler did not keep ahead of him. Dunn used him as a pack horse on his expeditions. He was branded with an "M" which belonged to Dan McCurdy of Keremeos, and Neil McFadden had bought him from McCurdy. Simmons took the rancher up to the jail where he readily identified Edwards and Dunn and then to the city corrals where he recognized the bay used by Dunn as a pack horse. After Bromley continued on his way, Simmons wrote up his report to Hussey on the interview and sent a letter to McCurdy in Keremeos for an impression of his brand.[6]

There is no record of the reaction of the prisoners to the parade of witnesses brought up to identify them, but it certainly must have caused them some consternation. Colquhoun's visitors were few and far between as he had only been in the Similkameen since early spring. Dunn especially would have felt somewhat awkward and embarrassed having people he considered as friends visiting the prison and seeing him in irons while they identified him. To Miner it was most assuredly old hat and most likely didn't cause him to turn a hair. He was a master of cynicism and used to betraying friendships, and this chapter of his career would have been no different than all the others preceding his short visit to Canada.

Before the Grand Jury proceedings were even over, two undercover agents known to us today only as "H." and "G.H." conducted investigations and interviews along the Kamloops to Vernon wagon road and also at Grande Prairie. The first place they stopped was at the Holmwood Ranch where Albert and Edith Duck would be subjected to another in a long list of interviews they would give to all manner and types of investigators over the period leading up to the trial. They questioned Edith and hired hand Cecil Russell, and later on they talked to F.C. Barnard and his wife who lived three or four miles down the road. The Barnards couldn't give the agents any specific information, nor could Mr. Westrup. But they thought they remembered the man in the photo of Miner from somewhere around the area.

The operatives continued on and canvassed throughout the Grande Prairie area. They interviewed Thomas Graham, W.M. Homfray and George Butler. Butler remembered meeting the old man when he and Cecil Russell were riding together. Most of the interviewees recognized the old man in the photo as being around Grande Prairie at one time or another. Mrs. Tom Smith, F.J. Clemitson, H. Guernsey and Mr. Woods identified Miner as riding by in the past couple of years as well as within the last three weeks. Back in Kamloops, the private detectives typed up their report and presented it to CPR Special Services Agent McLaws.[7]

That same Friday, CPR detective R.E. Bullick hired Owen Batchelor and his rig to drive him to the ranch of William McLeod on the Nicola Road. In the bed of the buggy was the distinctive red leather saddle found in the cache near Campbell's Meadows. Bullick introduced himself to the father, William McLeod, and then interviewed sons Evander and William Jr. He showed them the red saddle, and each of the two boys readily identified it as belonging to their friend George Edwards, now revealed as Bill Miner. The boys told Bullick of the various times Miner had stayed at their place, how he had eaten meals, discussed desperados of the old west and the notorious train robber Bill Miner, and treated them as equals and as friends. Bullick then went east into the Rose Hill country and interviewed Cyrus Tilton and Angus MacKay. Tilton told the detective of the $1,000 bill Edwards had cashed at the local bank, how Edwards had attended the Smoky Chisholm trial a year ago this past fall, and that he always stayed at the Colonial Hotel when in Kamloops. If Tilton remembered correctly, he said Edwards had stayed there at least nine times. When the Rose Hill interviews were finished, Batchelor drove Bullick down the Rose Hill Road into Kamloops, where the detective continued his interviews of that day. He met with an Al Johnson of Princeton who remembered Shorty Dunn as an accomplished teamster in the Cariboo and bronco buster in Princeton. Bullick then accompanied a Mr. Martin of Princeton to the city corrals, where Martin identified the brands on the captured horses found at Campbell's Meadows as belonging to the Princeton district.[8]

CPR detective William McLeod was probably the busiest of all the investigators in Kamloops, with the exception of Superintendent Hussey. He was tireless in his travels to interview witnesses and obtain statements. On top of that, he was kept busy by Deputy Attorney General McLean vetting potential jurors for the prosecution and assisting McLaws with his investigations.

Armed with Mary Spencer's photographs, he went to Ducks to interview many of the residents of that area. He spoke to Adams, the clerk in Bostock's store that had served Shorty Dunn playing the deaf mute earlier that month, and obtained a statement from him. He interviewed George Hazelhurst, the cowhand outside the store when Dunn left. He also tracked down Valentine Ross, the CPR section foreman. Ross told him about the leather belt he had found beside the ties at Mile Board 117 at 2:30 in the afternoon after the robbery and signed a statement to that effect. He was told by others he spoke to that Mrs. Bice and Mrs. Duck could both give him information of value.

He drove his rig up to Holmwood and interviewed Albert and Edith and their hired hand Cecil Russell. Russell had passed the old man on his horse, a bottle of milk in each hand. McLeod obtained signed statements from each of them. He interviewed nineteen other people in the Ducks and Monte Creek areas that day, but could get no further information.

The next day found him back out at the Campbell Creek Post Office where he interviewed Mr. and Mrs. Barnes and Lizzie Dupuis, who lived with them. He finally made contact with Mrs. Buse who described Miner's gold ring and watch to the agent. He interviewed Montgomery and Graves who, in their wagon, had passed Miner and Dunn on the Grande Prairie road west of Campbell Creek.

When he was in the Campbell Creek country, he had asked Lizzie Dupuis to call him the next time she was in town. When she finally did so, McLeod took her to see the two horses that had been captured out on the Campbell Range. She easily identified them as the ones she had seen with Colquhoun, and when McLeod took her to the jail, she readily identified the ex-schoolteacher.[9]

Staying in town one day, McLeod interviewed Mrs. Rosie Love down on Lorne Street beside the cemetery. After seeing the photos of the three suspects, she told McLeod she had watched two of the men ride by when she was scrubbing clothes in the sunshine outside her house earlier that month. She told him she saw Dunn first, riding a horse and leading another, heading across the tracks and into town. The second man, whom she identified as Miner by his photo, came along some distance behind, and appeared to be elderly, with about a week's growth of beard. McLeod drove Mrs. Love in his buggy up to the Gaol, and there she identified Dunn and Miner as being the two men she had seen. After he returned her to her home, McLeod made additional inquiries in the neighbourhood, but could get no further response. He returned to his hotel room where he wrote his report to McLaws.[10]

Thiel detective L. Calhoun and CPR Special Services Agent McFoy of Calgary, guided by Fred Carter and driven by Richard Blair, made an investigation of the two camps found by the posse early in the chase. Blair and Carter, as former posse members, were familiar with the locations. The first camp they checked out was about two miles from the Holmwood Ranch along the Grande Prairie Road and beside Robbins Creek. The well-used road down to the CPR station at Ducks was a stone's throw from this spot. From all the signs it was obvious the three had been camped there some days. They found grass trampled flat where a tent had been erected, and up on the hillside they found four stakes that had been used to tie up the horses on long ropes so they could graze. Scattered about they found the detritus of three weeks camping by three men, including an empty one gallon honey tin, one undershirt, assorted scraps of rags, a copy of Cassel's magazine, and the cover of a Polson's magazine. In their detailed report, they even listed scraps of the Montana newspaper "The Butte Intermountain" with the dateline 19 March 1906. Fortunately the thorough detectives did not bring this evidence back to town as the scraps had been used for toilet paper.

The second camp used by the bandits was closer to Campbell Creek by Buse's place and had only been used a couple of days. There they found a long-handled shovel with about two feet of its handle cut off. The handle had been removed from the metal shovel, cut off and then re-riveted. Also included were a prospector's gold pan, a Royal baking powder can with dried beans in it, a pocket key chain, a small tobacco sack with table salt in it, and a 110 pound empty cloth sugar bag on which was stamped "R & P, KAM" in block letters.

On their way back to town, they stopped at Dalton's cabin which had been broken into and found the lock had been replaced. The four then returned to Kamloops where Calhoun typed up his report and presented it to McLaws.[11]

CPR Special Services detective R.E. Bullick continued his investigations around Kamloops. He interviewed all the dry goods merchants in Kamloops with regards to whether any of the suspects had purchased any clothing during their stay in the area. After checking with almost all those particular merchants in Kamloops, he finally was successful when he talked to proprietor F.E. Burns. This storeowner was the only one who remembered serving any of the three. He had sold a pair of woollen socks to Bill Miner for 25 cents.

He went into the Ramsay and Phillips grocery store at the southwest corner of Second Avenue and Victoria Street to interview Mr. Phillips and his clerk Marshall. He showed them the photos of the suspects, and both identified William Dunn as the fellow they had sold groceries to earlier that month. Bullick showed them the walnut sack discovered at one of the campsites marked "R&P Kamloops," and they identified it as coming from their store.

With the captured roan pinto thought to be Miner's horse trailing behind him, the detective inspector then canvassed all the livery stables and blacksmith shops in Kamloops. He had been informed that Miner or Dunn had his horse shod in Kamloops, but met with little success. None of them recognized the photos as previous customers. He went into William Hargraves' shop which dealt in Deering harvesting machinery, farm implements, buggies, wagons and bicycles.

He also provided blacksmith and farrier services. Bullick asked him to look at the paint's shoes, and Hargraves told him that the horse had never been shod in Kamloops as he would have recognized the work. In addition, he said that the shoes had been on the horse for a considerable period of time. Bullick returned to his room at the hotel and wrote his report to McLaws.[12]

CPR detective W.A. McFoy drove his buggy east out of Kamloops to interview potential witnesses. He went up out of the lower valley on the Kamloops to Vernon wagon road and crossed Upper Campbell Creek. The CPR detective first stopped at William Buse's ranch, where the owner and his hired hands were working. Buse informed McFoy that he remembered when Mrs. Buse had seen the three men, but he was so far away he could not identify the photos shown him. The others didn't see the three men that day.

At Herbert Taite's ranch, Taite told the detective he had seen three men passing by his place earlier and tried to hire them to help fix his irrigation flume, but they refused. When the photos of the three men were presented to him, he identified them and told McFoy that he thought the story they told him was a bit crooked. He added that the old man was riding a roan pinto shod all around. McFoy then went to Hickson's place, but though the rancher and his son saw the men passing, they did not pay any particular attention to them. Before McFoy went back to Kamloops, he tried to see if anyone was home at the Dupeau place, but it was deserted. When he returned to Kamloops, he wrote his report to chief detective W.L. McLaws.[13]

The same day McFoy was working the potential witnesses east of Kamloops, CPR detective C. Gouch from Nelson re-interviewed Adams and Hazelhurst out at Bostock's store, but this time he obtained some further information. George Hazelhurst stated that he and his friend Alf Goodwin were riding in the hills above the Douglas Lake Road south of Grande Prairie, about ten miles north of where the shootout had occurred. They found where the robbery suspects had shot a calf with a high-powered rifle and butchered it. At a nearby camp, some cooked rice was found, as well as footprints of two men shod in hobnailed boots and one in smooth soled boots.

Alfred Goodwin was the owner of the Fish Lake Ranch, later to be named the Norfolk Ranch. Goodwin was himself to be charged within a year by Constable Fernie for rustling cattle and horses from the Douglas Lake Cattle Company.[14]

On the Monday following the Grand Jury hearing, a private detective in the employ of the Thiel Detective Service out of Seattle, known to us now only as Operative #38, climbed on the Great Northern for Vancouver. He arrived at 10:15 that night and took a room in a downtown hotel. At nine the next morning he arrived at the offices of CPR Western Region Superintendent Marpole. Marpole didn't arrive until 9:15, and as he swept in, he called the operative into his offices. Marpole showed the agent a telegram he had recently received.

Canadian Pacific Railway's Telegram
Harrison, B.C. 18 May 1906

Sup't Marpole

Jeff Harrison of Chilliwack can show you
where you can get evidence that old man
Edwards was in vicinity of Chilliwack at the
time of train hold-up at Mission. His horses
were kept at livery barn there and other good
proof can be had.

Geo. Hunt

Jeff Harrison was the purser on the CPR steamer Minto out of Chilliwack, and George Hunt was the station agent at Harrison. The photographs that had appeared in provincial papers were having a marked effect on the investigation. Marpole supplied the agent with a map of the Chilliwack area showing the towns, roads and trails off the railway in that vicinity and with copies of Mary Spencer's photos of the robbery suspects. He was given a pass to travel on the line and instructed to take the 5:15 P.M. train for Harrison, B.C. When he arrived later that evening, the undercover agent contacted Hunt, who arranged for him to meet Harrison. The Minto ran between Harrison Mills and Chilliwack Landing and was just pulling out when the agent arrived. He and Harrison made arrangements to meet later that evening, and the agent went back to Chilliwack and got a room at the Dominion Hotel. When Harrison got off the steamer later, he met the agent in his hotel room. Harrison was shown the photos of the men in jail in Kamloops, and he unhesitatingly picked out Bill Miner's picture as the man who had been in Chilliwack in the fall of 1904 after the Mission robbery.

He told the undercover detective all about Miner's stay in Chilliwack, about Marriott's pool room and the McKenzies of the Dominion Hotel, and all the stories that had accumulated over that time. He told him how Miner would pass CPR detectives on the street with nary a turn and sit across the poker table from other undercover CPR detectives. He told the agent that at the time he had mentioned to the captain of the Minto that he suspected the old man of holding up the train at Mission.

The agent followed up all the leads Harrison had given him and generated more as he conducted his interviews. He interviewed Rowatt of the Chilliwack Livery, another liveryman named Reese, Chadsey of the barbershop, and Mr. and Mrs. McKenzie of the Dominion Hotel. Dundas of the Commercial Hotel told him of Miner meeting Budd and how George Aldous had partnered with Miner to drive horses to New Westminster. Satisfied with his results, the agent retired for the evening in his hotel room, and the next day he left on the CPR for Vancouver.

He called upon Marpole in his offices, and even though Marpole said he was extremely busy, he made time for the agent and directed him into his private offices. Marpole listened to an outline of the investigation and then took the agent to the offices of the corporate attorney. This individual was also very busy, and his staff asked that the agent return at 6:00 P.M. The agent did so, and was then asked to return at 8:00 P.M. He then finally got to lay out the fruits of his investigation in detail to the lawyer whose private secretary took shorthand notes as he talked. When he was done, the lawyer dismissed him, and after he had left the maps and photographs in Marpole's offices, he returned the next morning to Seattle. He went straight to the offices of the Thiel Detective Agency in the New York Block in downtown Seattle. The branch manager of the agency in Washington was the now familiar William Seavey, and the agent gave his detailed report to him also. Seavey's secretary took notes, and on the 28TH of May, Seavey mailed a detailed report on his operative's activities to Marpole in Vancouver. The branch was no doubt well paid for its efforts of the last few days.[15]

Four days after he was placed in a cell in Kamloops on suspicion of being an accessory to the robbery, Paul Stevens was released back into society for lack of evidence. The preliminary hearing was over, and it was plain to the prosecution that they had enough evidence to make a good case against Edwards, Dunn and Colquhoun. The investigators were now more interested in concentrating on making a case against the three prisoners they already had in the Kamloops Gaol. The authorities were sure they had the culprits who held up the train at Ducks in custody, and while they also knew that the bandits most assuredly had assistance from others such as Stevens and Jack Budd and others in their horse rustling fraternity, adequate proof for a conviction was probably not forthcoming without the expenditure of a lot of energy and monies. Besides, Mr. Marpole of the CPR was confident that the three perpetrators were behind bars, and he was the one that most needed pleasing. However, the American Stevens would not escape the long arm of the people's justice for too much longer, as fate would finally catch up to him and end his suspected horse rustling and train robbing activities for good.[16]

Interest in Hussey's prisoners from other police agencies was high as Miner had an international reputation and had been the focus of a number of true crime magazine features and newspaper articles across America. The Pinkertons had been chasing Miner for almost two generations and had assembled the most comprehensive collection of data of anyone on the bandit's activities. They were, of course, most interested in successfully resolving the two train robberies in the U.S.; the one at Ballard, Washington, and the other near Corbett, Oregon. As information was being assembled for the trial in Kamloops, Hussey received a communication on the letterhead of the Pinkerton's National Detective Agency in the Bailey Block in downtown Seattle. P.K. Ahern was the Superintendent of the detective agency, and he requested that Hussey forward to him copies of Mary Spencer's photos of the suspects as well as their full Bertillon Signaletic System descriptions. He also asked for a listing of the firearms that were captured and their serial numbers. Hussey assembled the information, complete with some newspaper clippings, and sent it off to Ahern by return mail.[17]

Ahern later wrote Hussey thanking him for his information and mentioned to him his office subscribed to the Vancouver Province and Daily News Advertiser. Ahern noted that William Seavey of the Thiel Detective Agency, Ahern's competition, was trying to gather to himself and his operatives "a great deal of the glory" for the capture of the robbers. He sympathized with Hussey, telling him he was aware that it was Hussey's men who, along with the R.N.W.M.P., had been responsible for their capture. He assured Hussey that anyone familiar with the case knew the real facts and that "Seavey had nothing to do with the matter." Ahern was taking the opportunity to ensure the Thiel detective agency would not be first on the list when Hussey required investigative assistance in the future.[18]

John R. Greenfield was the federal government's Post Office Inspector based in Vancouver. From the time of the robbery he was kept busy trying to trace the amount and extent of the registered letters and monies stolen from the mail car. Throughout his investigations, he kept CPR Superintendent Marpole informed of his progress with frequent letters itemizing the senders and intended recipients and the money orders and cash included. His investigations required letters to be sent to fellow postal inspectors across Canada, and he received positive responses from Calgary, Winnipeg, Ottawa, and Montreal advising that customers from those locations had been affected by the robbery. By the 21ST of May he was able to provide to B.C.'s Attorney General a comprehensive list of registered items stolen from His Majesty's mails.

The final tally reflected a record of commerce activities normal in a fledgling industrial society. Coupons, express orders, cheques and refund claims constituted non-negotiable items, and $15 in cash was also listed. A ten dollar and a five dollar bill were found on Miner after the robbery, along with other currency. Mrs. L. Petrie of Victoria was expecting $5 in cash and a $50 money order which she was never to receive, and the Kam Yung Ling Company of Victoria was out $10 in cash. In later correspondence to Mr. Greenfield, Mr. Sing Tai tried to make claim on the $10 bill found on Miner by describing it as a Canadian Bank of Commerce bill, and Mrs. Petrie was to claim her $5 bill was from either the Bank of Ottawa or the Imperial Bank of Canada. Neither was successful in retrieving the money. Other Chinese merchants in Victoria who lost letters or money orders were the Chong Lung and the Chon Lun companies.[19][20]

Deputy Attorney General Hugh Archibald McLean had been allocated the responsibility of prosecuting the three robbery suspects by the chief of his ministry, Attorney General Frederick Fulton. McLean was an astute lawyer in his own right with a record of successful prosecutions behind him. He waded with gusto into the mass of evidence and the scope of the investigations required to convict the suspects. He sent investigators throughout the region and utilized Frederick Hussey of the Provincial Police and William McLeod of the CPR Special Service section to coordinate these activities. He had linen-backed pen and ink maps drawn up detailing the site of the robbery and the gunfight. He closely reviewed and annotated the newspaper accounts of the preliminary hearing as well as the transcript of the Grand Jury hearing. At times, the newspaper accounts were more adept in identifying the subtle nuances of the defence attorney's arguments and thinking processes than were the bland and colourless hearing records produced by the court stenographer. Copious detailed witness statements were obtained from anyone found to have been in contact with the suspects during the weeks leading up to the robbery, as well as those in the Nicola and Similkameen country that knew Miner and Dunn. Witness statements on Colquhoun were few and far between. They referred only to that time period since he arrived from Phoenix in the early spring. In the three weeks leading up to the robbery in Kamloops, the contacts witnesses had experienced with the former schoolteacher were confined to the Upper Campbell Creek and Holmwood Ranch areas. All witnesses interviewed had reports typed up on their potential testimony, and often the statements were signed.

With the assistance of Hussey, McLean prepared a list of exhibits to be presented at trial. The twenty-five items included spare magazines for the semi-automatic pistols, the red leather saddle, the firearms, Munyon's Kidney Cure pills, and the walnut sack from Ramsay and Phillip's store.[21]

To spur McLean's efforts on, a letter was received in the Attorney General's ministry from the federal justice minister in Ottawa. In it he expressed his satisfaction with the energy the Provincial Police provided the federal force in trailing and capturing the suspected train robbers. He assured the Attorney General the "Dominion Government will regard with strong approval the meting out of the severest punishment to anyone found guilty of this crime." He went on to state that, "It is of the highest importance in a country situated as Canada is, that those border ruffians should be taught that the Dominion is no place of safety for them."[22]

Spearheaded by the inquisitive talents of detective William McLeod, a comprehensive list of sixty of the male taxpayers of Kamloops and the surrounding district was assembled to provide the pool of jurors that were to be picked for that spring's assizes. They consisted of labourers, miners, merchants, ranchers, dredge engineers and clerks. They lived in Kamloops, Coal Hill, Cherry Creek, Grande Prairie and Monte Creek. McLean had McLeod investigate thirty-six of them to determine their suitability to the prosecution. On that annotated list, McLeod's comments on each individual are enlightening. They included "flighty," "inclined to be wild," "fair minded," "won't stand for crooks," "wants to nip it in the bud," "poor reputation," "perfect gentleman," "no interest in country," "shaky," "soft-brained," and finally, somewhat tellingly, "low grade formation." John Freemont Smith, the black Kamloops city councillor described by McLeod as a journalist, was noted by the Montreal detective as being "OK and straight." An interesting comment was noted beside that of Richard Blair, the teamster who worked with the posse from Ducks to Stevens' Meadows. McLeod penned the comment, "Inclined to sympathy" beside the driver's name. Blair perhaps reflected an empathy common among some in the community, in that the CPR held no place of special esteem in their hearts. Consequently, anyone who attempted to thwart the best interests of the capitalist monopoly was deserving of support rather than censure. Miner's socialistic self aggrandizement to specific individuals he knew, and through them to the community at large, would cloud his real motivations for decades. It would be lost on this minority of sympathizers that on the whole, the railroad was enhancing the life of most individuals and businesses in the communities and districts it passed through. As well as urban manufacturers and businesses, even ranchers and farmers in the rural areas found markets for the fruits of their labours across Canada.[23]

On May 22ND, Deputy Attorney General McLean wrote a formal letter to the defence lawyer. In it he advised Mcintyre that evidence in addition to that presented at the preliminary hearing would be introduced by the Crown. This evidence would chiefly consist of witness testimony tracing the movements of the accused prior to the commission of the robbery. McFadden of Princeton, Lizzie Dupuis of the Campbell Creek Post Office, rancher Buse and his wife, Albert and Edith Duck, their hired hands Cecil Russell and George Butler and CPR fireman Radcliffe were all listed as perhaps testifying.

McLean went on to note that it may also be necessary to introduce the testimony of select witnesses who would be able to identify exhibits pertinent to the case. He ended with a commitment that if anything else material to the case should arrive before the trial, he would make sure Mcintyre was advised.[24]

Albert and Edith Duck's testimony on their meeting with George Edwards at Holmwood before the robbery was deemed most important to the prosecution's case. Their evidence would show that the suspects were in the area and familiarizing themselves with the country around Ducks station in the weeks prior to the robbery. When Constable Fernie went to issue a subpoena for them to appear at the assizes at the end of May to testify at the robbers' trial, he found that they had left for a holiday in Victoria. The children had been left in the care of the hired hand and friend of the family, Cecil Russell.[25]

Fernie informed Hussey about this, who immediately took steps for his trusty Sergeant Murray in Victoria to advise the Ducks to return to Kamloops for the trial. Albert Duck, after submitting to numerous interviews and witness statements, was now in no mood to have his life interrupted once again due to the requirements of the trial soon to take place in Kamloops. The Attorney General's office held out no promise of restitution for the travel expenses of either him or his wife, and he refused to voluntarily return to Kamloops. Hussey in turn was not about to go to McLean to advise him that he could not get one of the Deputy Attorney General's important witnesses to return to Kamloops. He instructed Sergeant Murray accordingly.

Canadian Pacific Railway's Telegram
Kamloops, B.C. May 26, 1906

Sargeant [sic] Murray.
Provincial Police
Victoria B.C.

Rex V Edwards, Dunn and Colquhoun. Subpoena
as witnesses for the prosecution to
appear at Kamloops next Monday Albert
Duck and Mrs Albert Duck of
Ducks Station now at Victoria, probably
Dominion Hotel. Inquire there. Wire reply.

FS Hussey
11:35am[26]

The Ducks duly reported back to Kamloops for the trial.

Albert later submitted a letter to obtain compensation for his travel expenses after the trial was over. It included return fare from Victoria to Kamloops, a berth on the boat across the strait and a sleeper in the railway car. Chief Constable Pearse in Kamloops recommended that it be paid, but Albert was only to get travel costs for himself, not for Edith. Having met Bill Miner did not turn out to be an altogether pleasurable experience for the Albert Ducks.[27]

By the spring of 1906, Maisie Campbell-Johnston and her mother and mining consultant father had moved from Aspen Grove to Lower Nicola. Word of the arrest of the three suspected robbers had spread through the Nicola and Similkameen country like wildfire, and the young girl was confused and heartbroken to hear her good friend was now in prison. Knowing the young girl's fondness for old George Edwards, "Dad" Allen rode down from his mining claims at Aspen Grove to visit the young girl. They sat outside in the warm late spring sunshine, and the old frontiersman cautioned the girl not to judge their friend too harshly.

"Because, 'Little 'Un', he never killed anyone, nor robbed the poor. He was just one of those socialist fellows, who took from the rich and gave to the poor." Allen went on to plant the seeds of the future legend in a young and impressionable mind. Maisie would not soon forget Allen's words. She would become an influential lady of letters in her own right during her lifetime, becoming editor of the important magazine "The Native Voice." Her thoughts and reminiscences of those early days in the Nicola would be shared with future generations. "Dad" told her that Bill Miner "had educated eighteen girls and boys; putting them through college." Although it is almost certain that Bill Miner was not such an altruistic philanthropist, Maisie Campbell-Johnston's memories would help perpetuate the myth of the socialistic Robin Hood bandit. Bill Miner never was above taking from the poor when the occasion demanded, but he also never gave up the opportunity to be his own best press agent, whether it be with a young girl or a jaded reporter.[28]

XIX

THE TRIAL

ON THE SUNDAY BEFORE THE TRIAL started, an official of the San Quentin prison in San Francisco, Warden Kelly, stepped off the train in Kamloops and was met by an unidentified member of the investigative team. Kelly had been a warden at the notorious prison at the time Bill Miner had been incarcerated there and knew him well. The detective greeted the prison official and put him up in a local hotel. The next day when the trial started, a large and curious crowd had gathered to watch the prisoners being brought in. Standing back in the crowd in civilian clothes was the San Quentin Warden Kelly. He watched the prisoners shuffling into the courthouse and recognized Miner as one of the three suspects. He turned to the detective and told him that the individual he had just seen was the former convict from California, Bill Miner. The detective thanked him and asked him to be in the same spot tomorrow morning when the prisoners were brought to court again.[1]

The twenty year old, wooden clapboard courthouse building at the corner of First Avenue and Seymour Street had seen better days. Part of the Grand Jury's responsibilities that May was to report on the state of provincial facilities in Kamloops. The description of the courthouse was not flattering. It was reported as being in "a bad state of repair especially as regards ventilation and sanitary arrangements and inadequate for conducting the largely increased civil and departmental business which has and is increasing very rapidly."[2]

Justice Paulus Aemilius E. Irving of the Supreme Court of British Columbia was the son of a knighted and distinguished treasurer of the Law Society of Upper Canada. He had formerly been a Deputy Attorney General and founded the "British Columbia Reports," a legal publication. In that position he had worked long and hard at the extradition of the notorious American bandit and murderer known as "Bulldog" Kelly. He was president of the Victoria Bar Association and had a reputation as a formidable cricketer. He was described in a contemporary Victoria Colonist article as driving "a very handsome equipage of the Tally Ho type, which the learned justice drives four in hand."[3][4]

Alexander Duntroon Mcintyre was the chief defence lawyer for the three robbers. He was assisted by his law partner, James Murphy. J.D. Swanson again sat close by the defence looking after Lewis Colquhoun's interests for his family.

Deputy Attorney General Hugh Archibald McLean was the sole prosecuting attorney.

MONDAY, 28 MAY 1906

On the morning of the 28TH of May 1906, the trial of the train robbers began. The courtroom was crowded with sitting and standing observers, and not another body could be fitted in. The gallery included witnesses, some of Edwards' many friends in the area, and curious onlookers. The spectators wound down the stairs and across the hall, out onto the porch and into the street. It was remarked at how many ladies were attending, and their splashes of colour would be added to when Sergeant Wilson and his fellow officers in red serge arrived to testify.[5]

The proceedings began with Chief Justice Irving giving the case to the Grand Jury, and less than a half hour later a true bill was found. The prisoners were led into the courtroom, their shackles and leg irons removed throughout the time they would spend in the courtroom. The prisoners pleaded not guilty, and the trial began. Mr. Mcintyre immediately proceeded with a request for an adjournment to the fall assizes and supported his request with affidavits from the prisoners requesting an extension so that they could obtain more witnesses favourable to their case. Mcintyre also presented an affidavit from himself in which he referred to the sensational coverage of the case in the Vancouver Province complete with photos identifying George Edwards as the notorious American Bandit "Bill Miner." He read out excerpts of the photo captions as describing all three suspects as train robbers and comments about their certain guilt. He read parts of several of the articles to further illustrate his points. He referred to the high state of excitement in the town of Kamloops after the robbery and during the chase and apprehension of the suspects. He alleged that an impartial jury would be impossible to obtain in Kamloops and quoted precedence in several English cases to back up his assertions. He reminded His Lordship of his previous admonitions to juries for absolute fairness in criminal trials and also pointed out the compromising role one of Canada's largest corporations played in the investigation and the undue pressures it could initiate.[6]

Prosecution attorney McLean voiced an objection to these arguments, and his objections were sustained by His Lordship. Justice Irving, while severely criticizing the "yellow journalism" practiced by the Vancouver Province, noted that three things must be shown in advance of an adjournment due to an absence of witnesses. The court must be presented with their names, the court should be satisfied that the witnesses will be on hand after the adjournment, and the evidence would be material to the case. He continued that it should be shown that some effort had been extended by these potential witnesses to attend the trial now in session. He also noted that he did not feel that the newspaper coverage would have any adverse effect on the jury.[7]

Mcintyre continued and asserted that it would be utterly impossible to find twelve jurors in Kamloops who would be able to render an impartial verdict, and if the trial was proceeded with, it would be a farce as the case had been severely prejudiced. He went on to state that all potential jurors in Kamloops were capable of reading and would have been exposed to the blatant sensationalism of the newspapers and the suspects most likely had already been prejudged.

Deputy Attorney General McLean argued against any postponement, saying that ten days had passed since the arrest of the suspects and this should be ample time to prepare a defence.

He pointed out that the jury panel was obtained from throughout the district, not just in Kamloops.

Justice Irving then refused the applications as there was nothing in the affidavits to warrant granting it. He did somewhat agree with Mr. Mcintyre's contention about prejudicial newspaper reports, but went on to state that newspapers no longer carry the authority they once did. His Lordship then adjourned the proceedings until two o'clock.[8]

The Hedley Gazette's reporter had some unfavourable comments to make about defence lawyer Mcintyre. "Mcintyre wanted the case postponed, the venue changed and incidentally the earth. He gratuitously insulted Kamloops by contending that a fair trial could not be procured there."[9]

Promptly at two o'clock Justice Irving again took his seat, and the process of selecting a jury began. A role call of early Kamloops pioneers was called; some were challenged and some were requested to step aside by the Crown. After thirty candidates had been called forward, the desired twelve were obtained. The twelve were the jury foreman D.J. Morrill, D.J. Kinnear, Charles Tucker, J.S. Howie, D.J. Manson, W.H. Alcock, George Clapperton, E. Cooney, D.J. Johnson, F.J. Bradwin, J.M. Menzies and C.E. Leighton.[10]

Deputy Attorney General McLean then launched into his address outlining the prosecution's case. He noted that it was usually the case that crimes such as the robbery of trains were not carried out by petty thieves. "The crime which is now under consideration," he said, "had been well and carefully planned. Those who committed the crime must have considered every detail." He went on to state that such undertakings are usually carried out by experienced and clever criminals who take extreme care and planning to ensure success. He noted that the prosecution would give evidence of that same care and planning taken by the three "land pirates" before the jury now. He went on to praise the efforts of the B.C. Provincial Police and the Royal North West Mounted that saw the apprehension of the suspects within a reasonable length of time.[11]

Albert Duck was called as the first prosecution witness, the first of a list that had not been heard at the preliminary hearing. The court heard Mr. Duck's testimony of Edwards buying groceries from the Ducks, and a brief flurry took place when Mr. Duck was escorted to a window in the courthouse looking out into the courthouse yard. There he saw two horses sleeping at the rail in the yard. He identified one of them as the horse Edwards had been riding. Mrs. Duck supported her husband's evidence with regard to the visit from the old man.

As McLean called the many witnesses forward, the defendant Edwards was watched closely, and while he put on an air of nonchalance, he was seen to closely watch "all that goes on from beneath drooping lids and out of the tail of his eyes."[12]

H.B. Taite was the next witness, and he also identified the horse in the yard seen from the courthouse window as the one Edwards was riding when Taite saw the three prisoners near his place on the 29TH of April. Miss Lizzie Dupuis, who lived at the Barnes' place and the local post office, identified Lewis Colquhoun as the man she saw chasing a horse in the bush on May 4TH. Mrs. Bice, who lived close to Campbell Creek and not far from Mr. Barnes, recognized both Dunn and Edwards as the two men asking for milk one day before the robbery.

Mcintyre cross-examined each of the witnesses and elicited the information that each of their homes was close beside the main highway to Grande Prairie and the prisoners had made no attempt at concealment from the residents.

Joe Greaves identified the two horses in the courthouse yard as the two he had captured near Campbell's Meadows soon after the robbery. He testified one was side-hobbled "American style" and the other hobbled in front "Siwash style." Both were branded with an "M"; however, one had a running brand tracing the "M" on it while the other brand was stamped on.

William Phillips of Ramsay and Phillips, General Merchants, testified to William Dunn coming into his store to buy groceries. He noted that the groceries were placed in one sugar bag labelled "R&P KAM" and another labelled "25 LBS. walnuts." The prosecutor produced an empty soap box that formerly held oatmeal toilet soap and two lead wrappers from package tea. Phillips identified the tea wrappers as Tetleys and Hoonda, both of which were sold by his firm. Dunn had purchased one half-pound packet and a one-pound packet with his groceries.[13]

F.E. Carter identified the "R&P KAM" bag as the one he found at the suspect's camp five miles south of Furrer on the 11th. He also recognized the tea wrappers as being found at another camp nearer the railroad.

All of these witnesses presented new testimony and had not appeared at the preliminary hearing. Engineer Callin was then called to the stand. During his testimony, the sacks of dynamite complete with sticks and fuses were entered in as evidence. "The entire court including His Lordship was nervous when the sack was being identified and breathed more freely when the sack was out of the way."[14]

Joseph Callin testified until 5:30 P.M., when the Chief Justice adjourned the court until ten o'clock the next morning. His Lordship cautioned the jury to remain aloof from any discussion of the trial proceedings. He added that under normal circumstances the Crown would provide proper accommodation and a place to sequester the jury, but local conditions precluded that. He hoped that new courthouse facilities in Kamloops would soon address that lack.

That day Sergeant Wilson, with his fellow members Shoebotham, Peters, Stewart and Browning, returned to Kamloops in preparation for giving evidence the next day. The group were to be conspicuous in their red serge in the courtroom until the trial was over.

Tuesday, 29 May 1906

Tuesday dawned as only a late spring, clear day in Kamloops can unfold. The sky was a bright blue fading to hazy white on the horizon, and a skiff of dust rose up from horses' hoofs and wagon wheels. The promise of midday heat hung in the air, and the scent of sagebrush slipped down from the hills on the morning breeze. Young men and boys on bicycles escorted the wagons transporting the prisoners down from the Kamloops Gaol. As the crowd gathered in front of the courthouse to watch the prisoners brought in that morning, Warden Kelly was again in attendance, but this time he was closer to the front. Hussey was standing directly beside him. The two stood outside on the porch of the old courthouse, as did many other curious onlookers and potential jurors, waiting for the arrival of the wagons. Escorted by Provincial Police Constables Pearse and Fernie, the wagons finally halted in front of the old courthouse. The prisoners awkwardly stepped off the wagons, encumbered by manacles and leg irons, and slowly made their way towards the entrance. Colquhoun and Miner were cuffed together, making movement difficult, and Dunn limped along, supported by a constable.

As they approached the entrance to the courthouse, Warden Kelly quickly stepped forward and thrust his hand out at George Edwards, exclaiming, "Hello Bill, old pal, how are you?"

Miner, thrown off balance at first, quickly recovered and retorted, "I'll shake hands with you all right, but I don't know who you are."[15]

Nearby reporters would write about the meeting with glee.

When court resumed that morning, Mcintyre recalled Mr. Taite to the stand. Under questioning, Mr. Taite agreed that the horse he saw Miner riding the day he saw him was not the roan pinto, but a much darker one. McIntyre also brought Albert Duck back to the stand, and he too said he had looked closer at the horses since yesterday's proceedings and was now convinced that the horse he saw was not the one Edwards had been riding. Duck turned to McLean and told him that the horse in the yard was a bay, and that the horse Miner was riding was definitely a roan pinto.

When McLean attempted to continue with the testimony of the engineer Callin, he started to show the witness a linen map of the area around Furrer Siding and Campbell's Crossing. Defence lawyer Mcintyre objected on the grounds that it contained other information as well as that pertinent to the robbery, and the map was withdrawn. Mcintyre attempted to present evidence that Callin was unduly intimidated by the number of authority figures present when he attended the Kamloops Gaol to attempt an identification of the prisoners. Mcintyre went on to list them, including Superintendent

Hussey, CPR Superintendent Kilpatrick, CPR Special Services agents McLaws and Brown, Sheriff Wentworth Wood and Government Agent Tunstall.

Mcintyre baited Callin, "So you went up with a regular bodyguard?"

Mr. McLean leapt to his feet and retorted, "He said they were there when he got to the jail."[16]

Callin's testimony concluded without further incident, and he did not vary his testimony despite Mcintyre's efforts to compromise his somewhat contradictory and vague descriptions of the bandits, especially Colquhoun.[17]

Neil McFadden of Princeton was a new witness, and when he went to the window in the courthouse to peer down at the horses in the yard, he readily identified one as his. "That's my horse," he exclaimed as the shaggy-maned bay with the white blaze on its face and one white hind leg was pointed out to him. He went on to tell the court he had known Dunn and Edwards for some time and that Dunn often borrowed his horse for prospecting trips. Joe Greaves was again called and verified that the horse identified by McFadden was one of the two he had captured at Campbell's Meadows.

Fireman Albert Radcliffe took the stand, and after giving his testimony, he was aggressively cross-examined by Mcintyre. When the defence lawyer's tactics were considered as going too far, His Lordship called a halt to the proceedings and admonished Mcintyre.

"That is not cross-examination. Let's understand what we are speaking about. For the life of me, I don't know."[18]

The temperature within the courthouse, especially in the top floor courtroom, had been steadily rising since early morning. The late spring sun was beating down on an uninsulated roof and walls, heating the top floor of a building that had not had time to cool off from the previous day's temperatures. Adding to the heat was the congestion of bodies jammed into the courtroom to witness the proceedings. It can only be imagined the discomfort caused by the wool suits of the lawyers and the red serge of the Mounted Police. It was described as "insufferably hot," and "an air of languidness pervaded the whole room." "The jury listened to dry evidence, while counsel would turn and gaze refreshedly out of the window to where the North Thompson lazily flowed." Sheriff Wentworth Wood made sure copious supplies of ice and water were available to counsel, judge and jury. It was the first heat wave of a typical Kamloops summer.

"Edwards sat leaning back in the prisoner's box, his long thin fingers idly drumming on the wooden ledge. He looks much more haggard and worn than at the time of his arrest, and often appears listless, but some important point brought out in the evidence sees him straighten up, his eyes—those dark, searching eyes—glancing piercingly at counsel and greedily searching jurors' faces."

"Colquhoun sits well back in the box, a healthy red flush on his cheek. A beard that was but a few days lack of shave has now become formed, giving him a gentle appearance. Now and then as evidence swings round in his direction, his blue eyes brightened and he follows the questioning of a witness closely."[19]

Mail clerks McQuarrie and Willis gave similar evidence to what they volunteered at the preliminary hearing. Defence counsel tried desperately to shake their testimony, especially McQuarrie's.

Q: When the prisoners arrived at the gaol they were unshaven and unkempt, were they not?

A: Yes, they looked just as if they had come down from the mountains.

Q: And yet you say, with them in that condition, you can identify them in that condition, you can identify that prisoner with the man in the car?

A: Yes.[20]

McQuarrie testified of how he had seen the bandit leader's face when his mask slipped down. He described his face as "thin and brown."

Mr. McLean: Do you see him here?

A: Yes, that is the old man.

McQuarrie pointed at the prisoner Edwards.

Chief Constable Pearse was called to the stand. Under questioning from the Deputy Attorney General, he went into minute detail on the pursuit of the bandits and the acquiring of each individual piece of evidence. The gallery was starting to fidget in their seats when McLean finally brought the questioning of Pearse to an end.

Alec Ignace was called to the stand with his interpreter. Mr. McLean had learned from Mr. Fulton's questioning of Ignace at the Grand Jury proceedings not to go into the details of compass bearings, and he managed to extract some positive testimony from the expert tracker. The gallery listened spellbound as Ignace described the tracking of the fugitives in his native tongue, aided by sign language and the interpreter. Mcintyre had no questions for Ignace.

Constable Fernie was called to the stand. He retold his evidence from the preliminary hearing and related his lonely meeting with the three men. Mcintyre aggressively cross-examined him, but Fernie's testimony remained unshaken.

Sergeant Wilson in his red serge was called to the stand. He related the events as they unfolded from when the detail had left Calgary until they handed the prisoners over to Warden Vicars and Superintendent Hussey. Under Mcintyre's cross-examination, he reiterated testimony that they were dressed in civilian clothes. One officer, Wilson stated, was even dressed in chaps. He admitted they looked like cowboys and carried Colt .45's. Mcintyre questioned him closely about the night they held the prisoners in the hall in Quilchena and why he had let Seavey interrogate Colquhoun. Wilson stated that Seavey wanted information about the dynamite. Mcintyre focused on why Seavey wanted to question Colquhoun.

Q: You know very well, Wilson, you are not as simple as you look. He wouldn't have got anything from Edwards, would he?
A: I don't think so.
Q: You did not hear the detective say he was a lawyer from Kamloops?
A: No.

Mcintyre asked Wilson, "Did Dunn fire at you?"

"Well," laughed the Sergeant, and looking in Dunn's direction he added, "it came in my direction."

Dunn squirmed in his seat with a big grin spread across his face and almost laughed out loud.[21]

Corporal Browning was called to the stand and repeated similar evidence. At the end of his evidence, the court was adjourned until the next morning.

R.N.W.M.P. Sergeant Wilson had been watching the proceedings closely and would later write, "As Mr. McLean and Mr. Mcintyre are both clever lawyers as well as witty and able speakers, it is needless to say there were no dull moments during the trial; sarcasm and repartee flowed like a river at times, but withal in a good natured manner. The newspapers commenting on the trial drew attention to the fact that many a man coming home expecting to find a hot supper, instead found that his wife was still at the courthouse where standing room was at a premium, sometimes for half a block at the courthouse."[22]

In Tuesday's Vancouver Province additional information was given to the paper's readers that could be construed to compromise a fair trial for the accused, particularly Edwards. One of the exhibits taken from Edwards after the shooting incident at Douglas Lake was a fine .38 calibre Smith and Wesson revolver. That day mail clerk William Mungo Thorburn had arrived in Kamloops. He was the clerk on the train that was stopped and robbed at Silverdale west of Mission in 1904. The express clerk, Herbert Mitchell, had been fired as a result of the incident, and Thorburn was the only employee left who was part of the incident in the express car. The leader of the bandits had taken the Smith and Wesson revolver from the clerks that night and it had never been seen again. Edwards' pistol was presented to Thorburn for identification, and he recognized it right away. The Province put this incident under the headline "Accuse Miner Of Mission Holdup" on page one.[23]

The trial resumed at 10:30 Wednesday morning, the third day of proceedings. Almost half the overflow crowd of spectators were women. Many of them had brought along their needlework and sewing. Some even went so far as to bring a small lunch and drinks so that they could be assured of having their seats after the noon adjournment.[24]

The three defendants made their way into the courtroom and took their places. Dunn limped in, handcuffed and smiling all the while. Mcintyre again applied for postponement of the trial until the fall assizes and called on the court to discharge the jury on the grounds that nearly all the jury had been in attendance when the defendant Edwards was confronted and greeted as Bill Miner by the warden of the San Quentin Penitentiary. This had been allowed to happen right on the portico of the entrance to the courthouse, and Superintendent Hussey had been standing nearby. The lawyer maintained that this incident could not help but prejudice Mr. Edwards' case by trying to meld the identity of the bandit Bill Miner with his client Edwards. He dramatically emphasized the perceived injury to his client by loudly slapping a copy of the Vancouver Province that detailed the event on the exhibit table. Mcintyre went on to state that his client denied in the strongest terms the accusation that he was, in fact, Bill Miner.[25]

Mcintyre submitted an affidavit, signed by George Edwards, that outlined the defendants' grievances.

In the affidavit, Edwards described the events he felt aggrieved him. As the prisoners in their wagons were arriving in front of the courthouse, he observed that most of the jury was present in the large crowd gathered there to observe the prisoners enter the building.

"After I had stepped from the said conveyance in company with my fellow-accused, to one of whom I was handcuffed, a large man with a grey moustache, whom I am informed claims to be Warden Kelly of a Penitentiary in the United States of America in company with Superintendent Hussey, the Superintendent of the Provincial Police, and who was in custody and charge of me and my fellow accused, came up to me and while the said Superintendent Hussey was standing close to me and evidently with his approval, said to me in a loud tone of voice, so that the same could be heard by all those in the neighbourhood including the said jurymen, "Hello, Bill, old pal, how are you?" or words to that effect, implying and giving the impression as I am informed and believe that I was and am (which I deny) Bill Miner, an alleged well-known criminal on the American side of the line."

Edwards' affidavit went on to point out that at no time did Superintendent Hussey attempt to protest or halt the actions of Warden Kelly, whom Edwards did not recognize. The affidavit also included references to the Vancouver Province and that paper's coverage of the Warden Kelly event. It was the view of the defendant that the interview with Warden Kelly and the remarks in the Province newspaper attributed to Kelly "were brought about and made with a view to prejudicing my case before the jury called for the present assizes."

"It is my belief that the continuous references in the said Province and other papers to me as Bill Miner has [sic] prejudiced the trial of my case and of my fellow accused."[26]

Justice Irving reviewed the document and gave it due consideration. He then retorted that it was a very unusual occurrence to postpone a trial. He added that any injury that Mr. Edwards might suffer had already been done, and the proper course for Mr. Mcintyre to pursue was to charge Mr. Kelly with interfering with the administration of justice. He refused the application for postponement.

Mail clerk McQuarrie was recalled by the Crown to the stand. He testified that he had travelled to Vernon to see if he could identify the three men held there, but he could not. McLean advised the court he had recalled McQuarrie to allow the defence to question him further. At cross-examination the day previous, Mcintyre had objected to McQuarrie's exceptionally detailed statement taken down by the stenographer of the Superintendent of the railway mail service in Vancouver, J.O. McLeod. So McLean had instructed the stenographer to attend the court, and he was prepared to now put the report into evidence and the stenographer in the witness box to give his honoured colleague the opportunity of gaining more information. Mcintyre continued to object to the report going into evidence, and the matter was closed. However Mcintyre was not finished with the mail clerk quite yet. He had McQuarrie repeat that the bandit leader's coat fitted tightly across his chest. Mcintyre got Edwards down in front of the jury and witnesses and put the long riding coat on.

"Now, close your coat," he instructed the prisoner.

The prisoner did so, and the coat overlapped on his chest by several inches.

"That will do," said Mcintyre, and Edwards went back to the prisoner's box.

The Crown then called R.N.W.M.P. officer Corporal Stewart to the stand, and he repeated his Grand Jury testimony with hardly any change. When Mcintyre confronted him, he drew from the witness that the federal police had no warrant for British Columbia, they were not wearing their regulation uniform with the exception of hats, boots and spurs, weapons and tack. Mcintyre had the officer agree that they looked like ordinary cowboys and not persons in authority. Sergeant Shoebotham was also severely cross-examined, but defence counsel could not shake his testimony either.

The Crown then called Superintendent Hussey to the stand. Mcintyre subjected Hussey to severe cross-examination. He attempted to show that there was collusion between Hussey and the CPR and to determine whether or not he and McLean had rehearsed his testimony. Hussey told the court that he had come to Kamloops at the request of the Deputy Attorney General and to render him what assistance he might desire. He stated he had not requested the assistance of the Mounted Police or private detectives and that Pearse and Fernie had acted without direction from him to start the pursuit of the robbers. He testified that he knew who Detective Seavey was, but had not asked him to attend or assist in Kamloops. He had little to say to him, did not know who had brought him to Kamloops, and had had no private conversations with him. He questioned Hussey about whether he had gone out to Rockford to meet the prisoners.

Q: Did the police refuse to deliver up the prisoners?
A: Yes, at Rockford.
Q: Did you have the prisoners photographed at the jail?
A: Yes.
Q: What in the name of common sense was that for?
A: It was part of my business.

Hussey testified that he had ordered that the prisoners be photographed at the jail, and Mcintyre tried to get him to admit that it had been a mistake. He asked Hussey if this was standard procedure, and he responded it was. When asked where the negatives were, he said they were in the hands of the photographer. The photos themselves were in the witness's possession. Hussey testified he only learned later that the single local photographer had been previously retained by the Province newspaper, and he had been obliged to get permission from a representative of the paper before he had the photos taken. He had not told the photographer she could use the negatives for her own use. When he found that the photos were for sale, he had it stopped.

Mcintyre then focused on the Warden Kelly incident. Hussey admitted that he had met Kelley previously, but did not know he was coming to Kamloops and did not send for him. He admitted he stood beside him when the warden shook hands with Edwards. When queried by Mcintyre, he admitted that he was not in charge of running the case against the suspects.

"Then nobody is managing it, it runs itself?" Mcintyre questioned facetiously.

"It is in the hands of the Crown," replied Hussey, adding that the Crown makes up his own case.

Hussey had heard on the streets that Kelly was coming and had supposed that the reason was to identify Edwards as Bill Miner. He had first met Kelly in the government offices of the very building they now found themselves in at the trial. He did not have social contact with him. Under further questioning, Hussey said that he did know the CPR chief of detectives, W.L. McLaws, but he did not know whether McLaws went to Quilchena or not. If he did, Hussey did not know about it. Mcintyre continued with his questioning, hoping to open a tiny crack in his composure.

Q: Is it usual to keep prisoners in separate cells and under close surveillance?
A: When I think necessary.
Q: You took precautions that were never taken here before even in the case of a murderer.
A: I did what I thought necessary.

Hussey revealed to the defence that he had heard rumours that some of the prisoners' friends were planning to break them out of jail. Mcintyre asked whether there was considerable excitement around town after the arrests, and Hussey answered that there did not appear to be any excitement, it was more curiosity than anything.

Q: Was the machinery of justice under the control of the CPR?
A: No, the CPR have no control over me whatever. ·

Hussey went on in his testimony that a young man had come to see Colquhoun, and he had permitted him to converse with him. He was present but did not hear what passed between them. He was apparently an old school fellow of Colquhoun's from his boyhood days and he had asked permission of Hussey whether he might converse with his old friend. He intimated to Hussey that he might assist in employing counsel for Colquhoun.[27]

Hussey voluntarily stated that there had been no attempt on his part to get a confession. Mcintyre snapped back at him. "Why do you say that?"

Hussey replied that he did not know what the prisoners may have said and had made no attempt to learn. It was a matter of indifference to him. Mcintyre announced that he had completed his questioning of the witness, and Hussey was allowed to step down.

McLean told the court that the case was closed for the Crown, and Mcintyre called no witnesses for the defence.

The case was adjourned for lunch, and immediately after the adjournment, McLean began presenting the case for the Crown. His presentation was described by the Kamloops Inland Sentinel as being perfectly fair to the prisoners. He summarized the case with "great ability" and itemized each fact with "dispassionate clarity." His presentation lasted for over an hour and also included glowing praise for the actions of the Provincial Police officers and the Mounted Police. He referred to the Mounties as that "gallant little band who so nobly made the arrest" and reiterated his assertion that the federal force had jurisdiction in any province in Canada.[28 29]

J.D. Swanson then made a separate plea on behalf of Colquhoun. He made an appeal for the acquittal of Colquhoun on the basis of unreliable circumstantial evidence and the fact that he was descended from a good and hard working Canadian family in Ontario. When counsel went on to describe Colquhoun's boyhood days in Ontario and the testaments of his high school and university friends, the Colonist reporter thought he noticed tears come to the defendant's eyes.[30]

Mcintyre then presented on behalf of all the accused and assailed the critical evidence of McQuarrie as being "absolutely untrue so far as his alleged identification of Edwards was concerned." He further stated that the actions of Dunn were not those of a guilty man, but actually were acts of mere impulse.

"If one spoke seriously to any schoolboy about an orchard, he would take to his heels and run ... Shorty had probably been connected sometime or other with the robbery of hen roosts. I am sorry, gentlemen, that Shorty is not better looking, it would help my case considerably." At that Shorty joined in the laughter as heartily as did the jury and the gallery.[31]

He deemed the Indian trackers as unreliable witnesses even though they might be good hunters. The tracks could have been made by any passing trappers or miners. He attempted to throw discredit on all the evidence submitted by the Crown. All the while defence counsel was speaking, the prisoner Edwards kept his eyes constantly on the jury, trying to determine the effects of his lawyer's comments. Even Shorty

Dunn was observed to be taking more of a serious interest in the case in contrast to his constant grinning and laughing of previous days.[32]

Before he concluded his remarks, Mcintyre attempted to smooth over some ruffled feelings and complimented the Mounted Police "for the fair evidence given by them." "The prisoners and myself have every reason to feel grateful to the mounted police and we have nothing to say except as in the many kindnesses we have received from them."[33]

It was pushing on 5 o'clock when Justice Irving finally began his charge to the jury and his summing up of the case. He carefully and painstakingly pointed out to the jury their responsibilities. He referred also to the perceived certain identification of Edwards by McQuarrie and Colquhoun by Callin. When it came time to address the identification of Shorty Dunn, the judge was quite adamant.

"The actions of Shorty at the time he was arrested agreed so minutely with the actions of the short dark man at the train robbery, or the actions of the short dark man at the train robbery was so similar to those of Shorty when he was arrested, that it was a very curious coincidence to say the least."

Referring to the train robbery, His Lordship described, "A short dark man who acts in a good natured manner, he flourishes his revolver around and boasts of how he is going to hold up the train. He seems to want to put everyone in a good humour and to treat the whole business as a joke."

Then he described the altercation at Douglas Lake. "You have a short dark man who fires off his revolver at the least provocation, he is continually joking and laughing, and indeed he is laughing now." The jury and the gallery turn their eyes to Dunn, sitting in his chair beside the prisoner's box. He is slapping his knees and almost bursting with pent up laughter.[34]

When His Lordship had finished his review of the evidence and the exhibits, it was near six o'clock, and the jury retired to its deliberations.

After His Lordship had completed his comments, Edwards was heard to say, "I want to go see my little bed."

Dunn complained they were being asked to work overtime.[35]

Four hours later the jury came into the courtroom to have some questions answered. At that point they stood at seven for conviction and five for acquittal. Among the clarifications sought were with regard to identification of clothing and the location of the camps. It was obvious by the questions asked that there was considerable confusion in the minds of the jury as to the description and sizes of the robbers and the suspects. The jury retired again to deliberate.

One hour later they again traipsed into the courtroom, and hopes rose that a verdict finally had been reached. But it was to no avail, as they asked more questions. The court stenographer's notes were read back to them, and the exhibits were taken into the jury room.

It was approaching one A.M. when the prisoners, counsel, the judge and jury again took their places, and anticipation ran high that a verdict would finally be realized.

But hopes were dashed when at 15 minutes before 1:00 A.M., the jury was addressed by a visibly irritated Justice Irving.

"I understand, gentlemen, you cannot agree on a verdict."
"No, my Lord," replied the jury foreman Morrill.
"Are there any further questions you would like to ask,
any information on points that would help you?"
"The disagreement is on all points," replied a juror.
"Is there no possibility of your arriving at an agreement?"
"No, my Lord."
"It's an awful thing to have to go through this again."
"It is, my Lord," sighed Deputy Attorney General McLean.
"There is nothing for it, the jury is discharged, the prisoners are remanded," ordered the disappointed Chief Justice.

Justice Irving asked McLean, "At what time tomorrow morning, ten o'clock?"

McLean agreed, and the second trial was scheduled to start the next morning.

It was rumoured that the sole holdout for acquittal was the

jury foreman, J. Morrill, and he had stated to his fellow jurors his "willingness to stay there for as long as they liked." He was also heard to comment that no poor man should be sent to prison.[36][37]

THURSDAY, 31 MAY 1906

Court resumed at 10:00 A.M., and Mcintyre again applied for postponement to the fall assizes, submitting the same affidavits as previously, and they were again refused. However, he had other avenues to pursue that had not yet been explored.

Mcintyre had submitted to the court before it had resumed that the prisoners had to be arraigned again. McLean countered with an affidavit to the court maintaining it was unnecessary for the prisoners to be arraigned again. The indictment of the three robbers had been found by the Grand Jury on the 28TH of May, the accused were arraigned on the same day and pleaded "Not Guilty," the trial proceeded and resulted in a disagreement of the jury, and on the 31ST of May a new trial on the said indictment took place.

"As the accused had already been arraigned and pleaded 'Not Guilty' at the former trial, I submit it was unnecessary that they should be arraigned and plead again at the new trial on the same indictment."[38]

Mcintyre then asked for a change of venue. To support his application for a change of venue, Mcintyre referred the court to the Ponton case in Napanee, where a change of venue request was made by the Crown.

Court: If they are meant for my consideration I shall be very glad to have them.

Mr. Mcintyre: Yes, My Lord—Regina v. Ponton, number 2, 1899—2 Canadian Criminal cases, page 417, and other cases My Lord. I refer you to Crankshaw, 2ND addition [sic], at page 615.

Court: Well, won't you tell me about them?

Mr. Mcintyre: Yes, My Lord—the point I am quoting is that although the jurors swore they were in no way influenced by the demonstration, it took place in their hearing.

Court: If you will get the book I will be very glad to look at it.

During his presentation for the change of venue with the bench, Mcintyre tried desperately to equate the present circumstance with rather bizarre and serious events in other jurisdictions and times.

"What I mean to say, My Lord, is that the affidavits put in do go to show that the circumstances surrounding the arrest and afterwards the actions, whether on behalf of the prosecution or not, of this man Kelly, are sufficient to show that a fair trial would not be had here by reason of the preconceived opinions of all the inhabitants from the surrounding circumstances."

Judge Irving reviewed the highlighted references and then advised defence counsel that in the particular case quoted, the life of the presiding Judge had been threatened and mob rule was feared a possibility. Ponton had been a very popular man in that neighbourhood, and some of the defendant's friends had physically attacked the judge. He had no fear of that happening in Kamloops; as a matter of fact, he could see no signs of excitement whatsoever, and he was confident the suspects could have a fair trial in Kamloops. His Lordship therefore refused the application, saying Mcintyre had not made a telling case.[39]

McLean told the court that the original jury panel summoned totalled thirty-six, twelve of whom had served on the previous trial. As Mr. Mcintyre could possibly challenge a total of thirty-six names, twelve for each suspect, he asked the court for permission to gather twenty-four more names to the panel. This was agreed to, and a short adjournment was made until such time as Sheriff Wood rounded up the new jurors. This took until 11:40 A.M., and then the court reassembled.

Once more Mcintyre requested a change of venue to either Revelstoke, Clinton or a coastal community. He produced cases to support his request and submitted reports to the bench requiring the Chief Justice to read aloud lengthy extracts.

Justice Irving declined the defence's request.

Court: The strongest ground that the prisoners or that you have for making this application is the—the strongest ground I think is the fact that some of the newspapers have published sensational anticipations of the evidence. Well, now, those papers circulate in any other part of British Columbia just as much as they do here, and the injury is done, and probably there is less excitement or probably any excitement that did exist must have been very much allayed by the trial that has taken place, and after all is said and done the jury will be told that they are to try it according to the evidence being brought before them. You have hardly made out a case to convince me that it is my duty to change the venue, and it is for you to make out that case. The Act says a change of venue shall be made if it shall appear in the interests of justice, and I am not satisfied that this is an occasion that it is necessary to change [40]

The selection of the jury then commenced, with fifty-eight names being called. A. McGregor was the foreman, and the rest consisted of A.T. Ball, D. Bath, E. Sanbrook, Frank Newsam, J.C. Byrne, R. Blair, J.A. Scott, R.R. Smith, W. Hargraves Jr., J.W. Morris and Thomas Newman.

While waiting in the prisoner's holding room for the jury to be formed, the normally jovial and cocky Shorty Dunn "broke down with hysteria." The facade he had maintained since the time of the shooting at Douglas Lake had finally given way as he realized that his days of freedom prospecting, hunting and trapping in the Ashnola country were rapidly coming to an end. His poet's soul found it difficult to cope with the fate he knew was approaching, and his bravado had deteriorated into a sudden realization of the difficult and intimidating days ahead.

He told his minders that confinement to a prison cell would either kill him or drive him mad. He became so irrational and incoherent that Superintendent Hussey summoned Doctor J.S. Burris to attend to the panic-stricken prisoner. Dr. Burris mixed him up a concoction of laudanum, an opium derivative, to calm him down. "Throughout the tedious afternoon and evening, Dunn sat with his head between his hands, leaning on the rail, completely broken." He appeared to be almost asleep for the rest of the afternoon, and his former perpetual smile was never again seen. Billy Dunn saw the daunting spectre of "hard time" in his future, and he did not relish his countenance.[41][42]

The Vancouver Province reporter watched the actions and demeanour of the three prisoners closely and reported that Colquhoun appeared to be handling the strain of the trial better than the other two.

The jury was sworn in by half past twelve, and after a brief address to the jury by His Lordship, witnesses were called.

Prosecutor McLean opened the proceedings with a short concise summary of the case, now for the second time. The first witness called was the hapless Albert Duck, now thoroughly familiar with the entire case and wishing it were finally over. He was followed by his wife Edith, and the parade of witnesses continued all that afternoon and into the evening.

When Callin's testimony touched on his identification of Colquhoun, strong objections were made by defence counsel, but they were overruled by the Chief Justice. [43]

Testimony was heard throughout the whole of the afternoon and evening, and the court finally adjourned at about ten o'clock, having made considerable progress. It was plain to see that Justice Irving was not going to tolerate any unnecessary delays, and some pressure was being insinuated to the jury to come to a speedy verdict.

At the close of his cross-examination of mail clerk McQuarrie, Mcintyre apologized to the witness and to the jury for using phrases in the previous trial such as "deliberately untrue" to describe the clerk's testimony when addressing the jury, and he withdrew those comments. Perhaps some of the public's criticism of his aggressive tactics had come to his attention. The apology did not curtail the Hedley Gazette's editor from recommending that Mcintyre's "language towards mail clerk McQuarrie made him a meritorious candidate for cowhide." There is no doubt others in the gallery also felt that a horse whipping was in order as the defence lawyer's machinations did not sit well with most observers, reporters or trial participants. One hundred years later the same sympathies are sometimes prevalent.[44]

Storekeeper William Phillips was called for the second time that morning, but failed to appear. Justice Irving shared his frustrations with the court and suggested that some penalties should perhaps be in order in order to get subpoenaed Crown witnesses to appear.[45]

It was getting late in the day and Mcintyre suggested that it might not be prudent to start on Mr. Fernie and perhaps an adjournment might be the best way to proceed. Justice Irving queried the jury as to their desire to work into the evening, and the response was totally in the affirmative. The jury, too, wanted the trial over with as soon as possible.[46]

Constable Fernie testified in perhaps even greater detail than in the previous trial. He was still testifying when the court was adjourned until later. After supper, Mrs. Bice was called to the stand, and then the now subdued and repentant Mr. Phillips, the wayward grocer. Tracker Ignace and Sergeant Wilson gave their testimony, and the court was finally adjourned at 10:00 P.M.

For this trial Justice Irving would tolerate no compromising of the jury to interfere with a speedy verdict. He had ensured suitable accommodation was available for them when he called for sequestering of the jury. The Y.M.C.A. Hall was turned into a temporary dormitory to accommodate the jurors. The jurors now had a personal vested interest in seeing a speedy end to the trial.

FRIDAY, 1 JUNE 1906

At the request of the jury, the court resumed as early as possible, at 9:30 A.M. They were anxious to get back to their normal lives. Some of the public interest had subsided, and the members of the court found they could make their way about without forcing a path through crowds in the corridors and the courtroom.[47]

By 11 o'clock all the evidence was in, and the same witnesses had given the same testimony as in the previous trial. At 11:30, Prosecutor McLean gave his same summary of the evidence to the jury, but in a briefer form. Swanson made the same presentation on behalf of Colquhoun, but this time went back to the Magna Carta and argued that the "principals of that ancient and honourable document had been grossly violated in this case." Court was adjourned until two o'clock.[48]

Upon resumption of the proceedings, the word was out that things were coming to a head in this second trial, and the courthouse was again jammed with citizens and onlookers. Mr. Mcintyre made a powerful defence, summarizing the same items as the previous trial. His Lordship once more went over the evidence, presenting all the facts and informing the jury of their duty. The jury retired at 4:20 P.M., and after half an hour they were back with a verdict.

The ominous knocking on the jury room door announced a verdict had been arrived at. A now sombre crowd jostled into the courtroom. The prisoners were returned from the holding room to the dock, the lawyers took their appointed places, and the jury filed in and answered to their names.

"What is your verdict, gentlemen?" asked the Registrar.
The courtroom was dead quiet on that late sunny afternoon in early June.
The foreman's voice cut through the warm air, clear and distinct "Guilty."
"Are you all agreed?"
"We are," replied the foreman.
Chief Justice Irving turned to the prisoners and asked, "Have you anything to say, prisoner Edwards?"
"No, Sir."
"And you, Colquhoun?"
"No, Sir."
"You?" nodding at Dunn.
"Nothing whatever," said Dunn.

Justice Irving turned to the court. "The jury has found you guilty. The case against you was very clear. I agree with the verdict. You, Edwards, I sentence to the penitentiary for life. You, Dunn, for life, and Lewis Colquhoun to imprisonment for twenty-five years."

It was the end of a long and sometimes lighthearted story, now dampened by the reality of harsh justice. The concrete cells and high wooden walls of the federal facility in New Westminster, the B.C. Penitentiary, formed a maximum security prison for long-term offenders throughout British Columbia. Here the convicted train robbers would experience a life remote from the care and concern of regular folk, and the fate of the three settled like a dark blanket over the prisoners and gallery alike. Silence greeted the Chief Justice's sentences, broken only by the sobs of a few women in the gallery.[49]

The Judge called the next case in the spring assizes, and the prisoners were led way, manacled and subdued. "The cult of train robbers has been taught a salutory [sic] lesson as to the strong arm of British Columbia justice."[50]

At 5:00 P.M. the wagons carrying the prisoners left the Kamloops courthouse bound for the prison for the last time. Edwards was manacled to Colquhoun as they made their way into the wagon and took their seats. Edwards turned to the crowd standing around watching the condemned prisoners, lifted his Stetson and addressed the curious and partially sympathetic citizens of Kamloops, "Well, goodbye boys," and he flourished his hat in a circle.

In the other wagon sat Dunn. Still feeling his wound, still under the effects of the laudanum, and weighed down with the knowledge that the years ahead of him would be difficult, he remained defiant to the end. Although he no longer had the laugh and smile that characterized his presence over most of the trial, he made sure that his countenance wore a scowl that the reporter could gleefully describe in the most sinister terms.

Fernie and Pearse took their places on horseback alongside the wagons, and the party made its way up Third Avenue to the prison.

Soon afterwards, Hussey was in the CPR's telegraph office.

Canadian Pacific Railway Company's Telegraph
Kamloops, B.C. June 1 1906

Sergt Murray, Prov Police Victoria

Second trial. Edwards life. Dunn life.
Colquhoun twenty-five years. Returning
Victoria.

FS Hussey
6 04 pm[51]

SATURDAY, 2 JUNE 1906

On the Saturday after the trial, the Kamloops Standard printed an editorial comparing the sentences the three Kamloops train robbers had received with that given to a particularly odious character named Desire Brothier. The "unspeakable vileness of the crimes (of Brothier) appears almost incredible." His crimes were concerned with selling women into prostitution, and the paper described him as a "moral leper, an outlaw in the sight of God and one whose very presence should make any man with a spark of manhood in him shrink with loathing." The Minister of Justice for some reason had pardoned Mr. Brothier despite him being sentenced to a prison term of several years. The Standard's editor said that this loathsome creature should not even be mentioned in the same breath with the three who were sentenced to life in Kamloops and who were at least "real men."[52]

During the trial of the three robbers, Justice Irving had criticized the amount of drunkenness and carousing he had seen on Kamloops streets during the trial. The Standard continued in its editorial and took umbrage with the Chief Justice. The editor noted that at the time the trial was taking place, the town was in some state of repressed excitement. There were plenty of strangers, posse members, private detectives and curious onlookers from throughout the interior gathered in Kamloops and staying at the many local hotels. Also Queen Victoria's birthday was celebrated on the 24TH of May, and this added to the celebratory atmosphere. The paper quoted local Chief of Police Neil McGill as saying that under normal circumstances Kamloops is a very orderly and law-abiding town and had lost its reputation as a hard drinking town long ago. In fact, when a Kamloopsian on his travels refuses an invitation to share a drink, it no longer causes amazement.

The Standard concluded its editorial with a criticism of the first jury's inability to obtain a verdict, thereby costing the province $500. It inconvenienced a great many people over a number of days and greatly set back the schedule and efficiency of the spring assizes. "It is almost enough to make one wonder whether the jury system is all that it is supposed to be."[53]

The editorial of the Victoria Colonist for that weekend commented that the sentences, while they might seem overly harsh, were required to set an example and provide deterrence to others contemplating similar future crimes. "The prisoners are, nevertheless, to be greatly commiserated on their lot. Even Miner, who was the leader of the gang, though a hardened offender, seems to have been well liked by those who knew him, and, from certain things that are related of him, under other circumstances might have found an entirely different ending for his career. It is often a case of starting off with the wrong foot first. As has often been remarked, the dividing line between a good man and a bad man is usually very thin."[54]

XX

The Journey to New Westminster

The evening before the prisoners were to leave for New Westminster, Dr. Burris gave them each physical checkups to ensure they were fit to be transferred. He certified that the prisoners were "free from any putrid, infectious or cutaneous disease, and (they) are fit to be removed." He signed J.S. Burris as the Gaol Surgeon, and it was counter-signed by Warden John Vicars.[1]

On Saturday the 2nd of June, the temperature in Kamloops soared into the high 80s f. The two wagons with their prisoners aboard, escorted by Chief Constable Pearse and Constable Fernie, slowly made their way down to the CPR depot. There were groups of the curious and the well-wishers all along Third Avenue calling out to the prisoners, Miner in particular. Boys and young men on bicycles darted along and circled the party, trying to slow their pace to that of the wagons. Rumours of an attempt to free the prisoners kept the two Provincial Policemen nervous and aware, and their charges were heavily manacled to each other.

At the depot, the prisoners were unloaded and assisted in boarding the train. They were surrounded by numerous law enforcement officials seizing the opportunity to ride down to the coast with the notorious prisoners. In addition to Constables Pearse and Fernie, about fifteen persons accompanied the prisoners. They included Superintendent Hussey, CPR Special Service agent William McLeod, Thiel Detective Agency undercover operative L. Calhoun, and several other Thiel Detective Agency and CPR Special Service detectives. Warden Kelly from San Quentin was also there, as was Post Office Inspector John R. Greenfield.[2]

Dunn was shackled to a recently convicted horse thief named Canning who was also on his way to the federal penitentiary in New Westminster. This did not sit well with Dunn, as horse rustlers were considered to be the lowest form of criminal. He would ignore the rustler throughout his journey and tried to keep his back to him at all times. When Shorty saw the crowd gathered at the CPR depot, he felt it was an occasion that warranted a few words. Before boarding the waiting train, and trying to ignore the horse thief handcuffed to him, he addressed the milling crowd.

"Good-bye, ladies and gentlemen. You have treated me very kindly since my stay in the city. Next time I pass through, I will stay off and visit you."[3]

As Miner, shackled to Colquhoun, made his way towards the passenger car, Fernie and Pearse allowed a man to approach the prisoner with a box of fine cigars and his well wishes for a pleasant journey. Settling in their seats, the prisoners enjoyed the cigars all the way to Westminster Junction.[4]

The moustached warden from San Quentin, Kelly, took the opportunity to talk to Miner on the way down. Miner now made no effort to conceal his identity from the prison official, and they spoke quite freely together. Miner, with a smile, said to Kelly, "You know how I am situated, Kelly; I couldn't recognize you."[5]

As the train rocked and clattered on its way through the Fraser Canyon, Miner was asked to explain his obsession with robbing stagecoaches and trains. He answered with a cocky smile that he was a "college man who had graduated with first-class honours in draw poker, and had found halting cannonball expresses with a revolver easy compared with holding on a pair of deuces."[6]

Dunn was watching the rugged snow-capped mountains slide by as the train made its way down the Fraser Canyon and through the Fraser Valley. Chief Constable Pearse saw him daydreaming and asked Shorty how he would like to have to hike over them. Dunn was quick to reply. "You only give me a chance and you'll see whether I can get over them or not."[7]

Fernie and Pearse remembered the trip to the coast and that the prisoners acted and talked very calmly on their way to the prison at New Westminster. Miner said to the two officers that he did not have that long to live anyways, and it was just as well to put in his time in the penitentiary as anywhere. Miner was already putting preliminary plans into effect that would assist him in escaping from the prison, intimating that he was resigned to his fate and that he would probably die in prison.[8]

At Agassiz crowds had gathered. One excited woman declared aloud as she saw Miner through the car window that she recognized him as a man who had once sat down to dinner in her house and spent the night there.[9]

At Mission some of the people gathered at the depot spotted Miner through the car window and recognized him from Mary Spencer's photos. They called out to him in greeting, "Hello, Bill, here you are again." Miner turned to Hussey and said, "At Kamloops I was called Mr. Edwards, but down here even the dogs seem to take me for Bill Miner." The prisoners seemed to enjoy the trip down from the upper country and seeing the people turn out to wave and call to them as they slid by the stations. However, none of the people or reporters were allowed too close to the train because of security concerns.

The stories that the police were hearing had much credence attached to them. They had been told that an attempt would be made to set the prisoners free, so the prisoners were heavily shackled to each other and well guarded by the large contingent of law enforcement officials.[10][11]

With the exception of a delay of an hour and three-quarters caused by a mishap at Port Hammond, the train arrived uneventfully at Westminster Junction at 9:00 P.M.

At Westminster Junction station, as they were waiting for the short line train to take them from the junction to the penitentiary, the prisoners remained shackled together and encircled by officials. Surrounding the party was a large crowd of onlookers, calling out greetings. Colquhoun was shackled hand and foot to Miner and the two were sitting on a box in deep conversation. Shorty Dunn, humiliated and scowling, was shackled to the horse thief Canning and leaning against a wall, his back to the ostracized horse thief. The escort from Kamloops had been added to by officials and law enforcement from the Lower Mainland. Provincial Police Chief Constable Stanley Spain of New Westminster was there to see the man upon whom he had expended so much unsuccessful effort to capture after the Mission Junction robbery. New Westminster Chief of Police McIntosh came and confirmed his suspicions that Miner was the man he had seen staying at the Lytton Hotel in New Westminster in the fall of 1905. Miner had been in town after successfully selling a remuda of horses that he had driven to Ladner from the upper country. New Westminster detective Bradshaw and Vancouver detectives Waddell and Jackson were curious to see what manner of man they had been chasing after the Mission robbery. A reporter from the New Westminster Columbian newspaper attached himself unobtrusively to the assemblage and would the next day give his readers some detailed descriptions of the robbers as they waited in the darkness outside the depot, lit by the dim yellow gleamings of scattered electric bulbs.[12]

CPR engineer Nathaniel Scott had found out the schedule of the train that would be carrying Miner to New Westminster and was there when the train from Kamloops pulled in. He introduced himself to Fernie and Pearse as the engineer of the train that had been robbed near Mission Junction and asked permission if he might approach prisoner Bill Miner. Permission was granted, and he went up to Miner as he was sitting on a box. He saw Miner recognized him, and Scott greeted him. "Well, Billy, when are you going to have a ride on my train again?"

Miner cockily replied, "Don't worry, my boy, I may be along sooner than you think."[13]

The New Westminster Columbian reporter took good advantage of his enviable access to the prisoners. He studied the three men closely and first described Miner as he sat there. "The strenuous days of the two trials at Kamloops had told on him to a great extent, and while he was still alert of eye and ruddy of cheek, he walked with stooped shoulders, a weary carriage and an almost halting gait that told of nerve-racking nights and days since his capture a short time ago. His hat, a cowboy Stetson, he wore with a jaunty tilt. A light-weight grey overcoat, faded to a dull green, hung to below his knees, while a soft dark shirt, worn dark trousers and coarse, travel-stained cowhide boots completed his costume. Except for an occasional glance, he paid not the slightest attention to the crowd around him at the Junction station, while he conversed in low tones with Colquhoun, occasionally stopping to take a fresh chew of tobacco or to light another cigar from his box, one of a large box the prisoners had consumed on the short trip down from Kamloops. His face was a very interesting one, rather long and thin with a nose to match. A drooping, yellow-white moustache hid his upper lip and the corners of his mouth and short shaggy eyebrows hung well out over his bright eyes. With his old, broad-brimmed hat pushed well back from his forehead, and the toe of his cowhide boots beating a tattoo on the station platform, one would never think that justice had ordained that he should spend the remainder of his days behind bars."[14]

The reporter's description of Shorty Dunn was not quite so favourable. "He looked an all-round bad egg. Since the life sentence imposed on him, he had regained his jaunty bearing. Evidently the surly … Canning to whom Shorty was manacled, was poor company for the gay crook, and with his back turned to this forced companionship, his battered, soft, brown hat well down over his forehead, the man who had put up the fight the morning of his capture, leaned against the station wall and surveyed the throng around him with a half-contemptuous smile. Dunn still limps with his bullet wound, received in his vain dash for liberty. His costume, to say the least, was not elaborate. An old brown hat, that had faded to a light something-or-another, threw a shadow over his shifty, keen, dark eyes. He wore a soft shirt, a dark coat, a handkerchief about his neck and a pair of very light and very old fawn trousers."[15]

Colquhoun he found more non-descript. "Colquhoun would have

liked those who saw him to believe he was a very good man, in an entirely false position .... Colquhoun does not seem to have any individuality at all."

"Lewis Colquhoun was by far the best dressed one of the three. He wore a fairly new, dark brown suit and soft hat to match. His small, well-shaped feet were encased in a neat pair of light black boots. His bearing (is) altogether too retiring to inspire the beholder with any confidence in him."[16]

The reporter's description of the deterioration of Bill Miner, the "stooped shoulders, a weary carriage and an almost halting gait" was naively attributed by the journalist to the pressures and tribulations of the trials recently undergone by the elderly bandit leader. However, Bill Miner had gone through similar events often in the past, and it is unlikely the one suffered through in Kamloops would have caused such a debilitating effect. Rather, it is more likely that the wily criminal was setting the scene and characterization for his future escape from the penitentiary before he had even been officially entered into its rolls.

When the train was ready to leave from the depot at Sapperton, Hussey called out, "Well boys, I guess we'll get aboard." The prisoners, accompanied by the Columbian reporter, shuffled their way into the railway car, Miner pulling on his cigar the whole while. Dunn's leg was still weak, and he needed assistance to climb the metal stairs into the car. Once aboard and on the last leg of their journey to the penitentiary, the prisoners were handed a silver flask full of whiskey by one of the escorting officials so they could have their last swallows before the iron gates slammed shut behind them. Miner talked freely and easily to those around him and commented that the Kamloops House, who had apparently prepared some of the food for the prisoners during their incarceration in the Kamloops Gaol, prepared an excellent meal and that if he should ever find himself back in that country he would ensure "that hostelry would most certainly have his patronage." Colquhoun sat quiet and still beside him, starting bleakly at the floor. Shorty Dunn, sitting further back in the car with the ignored horse

B.C. Penitentiary circa late 1890s, with CPR locomotive #374 passing by.

thief, wore the familiar sneering smile "that has characterized him ever since his capture." When the conductor came round taking tickets, Dunn said to him that "he didn't think he would be needing a return ticket for any time soon."[17]

The canny Hussey had anticipated that a large and boisterous crowd would be on hand at the New Westminster train depot, and so he had organized the meet with the road transportation to take place at Sapperton, a suburb of New Westminster a short carriage ride north of the penitentiary.[18]

As Hussey had expected, a large crowd had gathered at the New Westminster location, but they were to be sadly disappointed. The prisoners were transferred to horse-drawn cabs at the Sapperton depot, and from there they were to be driven the short distance to the penitentiary. Still, there were about two hundred people at the Sapperton depot, and there was a crush around the prisoners and their escorts as the crowd attempted to catch a glimpse of the three desperados. A large squad of police and detectives surrounded the prisoners as they wedged their way through the clamouring throng.

The escort had their hands full piloting their charges through the press of people to the waiting carriages, and all the while Miner was greeted with shouts of "Hello, Bill!" and "How are you, Bill?" Miner, with one arm shackled to Colquhoun and the other resting on the shoulder of an escort, heard many goodbyes and wishes of good luck from the people gathered about.[19][20]

Once loaded, the vehicles lost no time in starting out for the penitentiary, passing the Brunette Sawmill with the Fraser River and the Brunette River slipping darkly by on the other side of the CP railway tracks. They soon reached the penitentiary gates, and as they were expected, the gates opened upon their arrival and the carriages rumbled through into the prison grounds and up to the main penitentiary building. There the prisoners were assisted out of the carriages and escorted into the forbidding stone and brick prison block. There they were confronted by the warden, Lieutenant Colonel John Connal Whyte, and they were formally booked into the facility.[21]

The Vancouver Daily News Advertiser, commenting upon the incarceration of the three bandits, expressed what was probably held to be the prevailing opinion of its readers as to the fate of the prisoners. "The three ... have probably seen their last of life and liberty as free men and citizens of either country on the North American continent." It was expected that the three prisoners would be serving literal life sentences and that they would die within the prison walls. In fact, that was to be the actual grisly fate of only one of the trio, but it would almost be the perceived personal spiritual death of a second. For the third, it would be considered just a temporary stumble on his life's journey towards fulfilling some unknown but premeditated goal.[22]

In that same issue, the News Advertiser unwittingly fanned the flames of consternation and retribution by interviewing a Thiel Detective Agency agent that had accompanied the escorting party down from Kamloops. The paper's reporter had repeated the claims made by the boasting agency operative. The undercover agent, undoubtedly reflecting his supervisor Seavey's desires, embellished the accomplishments of the Pinkerton rivals. In the process he gave more credit to his agency than was warranted and thereby earned the wrath of an irate Provincial Police Superintendent.

"Great credit is given Detective L. Calhoun of the Seattle office of the Thiel Detective Agency." The paper repeated the agent's claims that it was he and his men that had put together a "masterly case" and had consequently been highly complimented by CPR officials. On his way back to his head office in Seattle, Calhoun was quoted as saying that it was a pleasure to work with such fine organizations of men as the provincial and R.N.W.M. Police.[23]

The Vancouver Province took great glee in presenting Superintendent Hussey with the attributions the Thiel Detective Agency had made on the front page of their rival daily, the News Advertiser. The Province's reporter pointed out that the article conveys the impression that Seattle detectives had assisted in the capture of the train robbers near Douglas Lake. The enterprising reporter contacted Hussey in his Victoria offices, and he denied either Seavey or Calhoun had assisted the Provincial Police in any way. The paper went on to provide a verbatim quote on Hussey's comments.

"Calhoun or Seavey never did any work under my instructions in Kamloops. I never saw the former until he was just leaving for Vancouver. The interview conveys a grossly unfair impression and, in view of the arduous work done by other detectives in gathering up all the threads that led to the conviction of the robbers, should be denied in the press."

"Besides Provincial Constables Fernie, Pearse and Simmons, the men who were working on the case were W.L. McLaws, the Special Agent of the CPR who assisted me in every possible way; Detectives R.E. Bullick of Vancouver, W.H. Foy [sic] of Calgary and C. Gooch of Nelson, also in the CPR service; W. McLeod of the Montreal office ... and J.J. Brown of the Winnipeg office also rendered valuable assistance. I did not see Calhoun until just as he was leaving for Vancouver, and he was certainly not working in co-operation with the authorities."[24]

Hussey's comments may be a bit unfair, because Calhoun

did undertake some investigations in Kamloops such as witness interviews and investigations at the various camps east of Campbell Creek. But as a result of Mr. Calhoun's inopportune interview with the reporter, it is safe to assume that the Seattle office of the Thiel Detective Agency would not be hired by the B.C. Provincial Police anytime soon after the Ducks robbery investigation.

Many years after the events in the last chapter had taken place and many of the participants were dead and gone, Staff Sergeant John J. Wilson wrote down his memories and thoughts of those events of May and June in 1906.

"Now the question has often been asked of me, 'Why did you not have your revolvers drawn when you went into the bush?' For my answer I have two reasons, in the first place there was nothing to show that these men were train robbers. Let us suppose that these men had been prospectors as they claimed to be. If we had gone in there with revolvers drawn, would they not be justified in shooting every one of us thinking that we were hold-up men, as we were not dressed in uniform, and after two days and nights in the rain and mud we were anything but smart looking officers, unshaved, unwashed and clothing torn and covered with mud. In the second place, it is not the code of the R.N.W.M.P. to shoot first. He is given firearms and taught how to use them, but he is also told to let the other fellow start the fireworks if any has to be started; and with I believe two exceptions, these instructions have succeeded beyond all expectations. The two exceptions being the case of Sergeant Colebrook shot by the Indian Almighty Voice, and of Sergeant Wylde shot by the Indian Charcoal. In neither of these cases did the officers attempt to draw their firearms, in all other cases, although the police were the last to draw they eventually got the upper hand, but this is the chance a policeman has to take in following his vocation. He must first have ample evidence of the other's intention to shoot, before having recourse to his own firearms."[25]

Wilson went on to state that if Shorty Dunn had not lost his nerve, jumped up and started firing, "it is very doubtful in my mind if these men would ever have been convicted as there was nothing taken from the CPR train that could positively be identified, and the identification of the men by the train crew was none too strong; especially the fireman." The Sergeant went on to state his belief that there would have been no conviction of train robbery. Wilson praised the efforts of Fernie and his trackers, and admitted that if it were not for them the outcome may have been a very great deal different. He also stated that Fernie showed good instincts in not trying to arrest the three men when he first came onto them along the Douglas Lake Road. "He was heavily outgunned and I think he displayed great tact and wisdom in pursuing the course he did, and as I mentioned before, I think Constable Fernie is entitled to a great deal of the credit for his part in the affair."[26]

XXI
SERVING THEIR SENTENCE

THE B.C. PENITENTIARY IN NEW WESTMINSTER had accepted its first convicts in the fall of 1878. The grounds of the federal institution on the north bank of the Fraser River were located on the former campsite of the Royal Engineers, who had played such an important role in the formation of the province. It was considered an excellent and progressive penal facility in the early 1900s and would serve as a federal prison for Western Canada for over one hundred years.[1]

Lieutenant Colonel John Connal Whyte, born in Scotland, had been the Warden of the B.C. Penitentiary since 1897. Commanding officer of the Sixth Regiment in New Westminster, the respected civil servant had come to British Columbia from Ontario in 1877. After arriving in the province, he had been actively involved in the machinery business. He had also been superintendent of construction on the Revelstoke to Arrowhead and Nakusp and Slocan railways before taking the position of Warden. He and his wife Margaret, with their six children, made their home on Columbia Street in New Westminster. A staunch Presbyterian, he was considered one of the foremost sportsmen in B.C. in his day and was an excellent lacrosse player. As was normal, he received his position as a result of patronage, and he had no previous experience at prison administration. Before the turn of the century he had purchased a brick making machine, and through convict labour, many of the new facilities required as the prison expanded had been built.[2]

The Deputy Warden was David Dominick Bourke, an Irish Catholic who had come over from Ireland to New Brunswick when

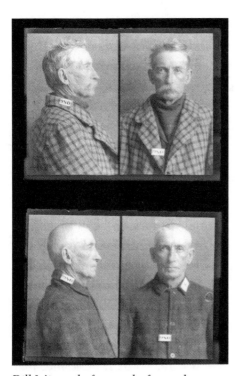

Bill Miner, before and after a shave and a haircut. Courtesy of Anthony Martin Collection.

he was quite young. He joined the public service as a hospital overseer at the Manitoba Penitentiary in 1886, and in 1895 at the instigation of Sir Charles Tupper, the federal Minister of Justice, he transferred to the B.C. Penitentiary. Bourke and his wife Jessie were strict practicing Catholics within a civil service culture predominantly made up of English and Scottish Protestants. They had twelve children in total, and nine were surviving at the time the Ducks robbers were interned in the prison. Most of the children still living with their parents at this time were daughters. One daughter, Katherine, would play an interesting role over the next few months.[3]

The relationship between the Warden and the Deputy Warden at this time was rather unique. The warden had very little to do with the day-to-day running of the prison, the movement of convicts within the system, or the administration of discipline. It was common to appoint men untrained in penal administration, but with the proper connections, to the position of Warden provided the Deputy Warden had the proper background. In this case, by 1906 Bourke had twenty years of experience as a prison official, eleven as Deputy Warden at the B.C. Penitentiary.[4]

When the prisoners from Kamloops went through the normal check-in procedures, they were again given a physical examination by the prison surgeon. He checked the trio over on the 2ND of

June 1906 and processed his report on the 4TH. In the case of Edwards, he found that he had not been vaccinated and was free from any "contagious, cutaneous or putrid disease." He was found to be in sound bodily health with the exception that he had volunteered that he had contracted smallpox in the past. The results of the surgeon's examinations of the other two are not known, but he undoubtedly learned at that time that Colquhoun had active tuberculosis.[5]

The prison Chaplain, Albert Edward Verk, interviewed Edwards that same day and found that he declared he was a practicing Methodist.[6]

Lewis Colquhoun, before and after a shave and a haircut. COURTESY OF ANTHONY MARTIN COLLECTION.

By the second week of June, the warden had received numerous requests for copies of the prison photos taken of the three prisoners. Pictures and Bertillon measurement solicitations came in from Superintendent Ahern of the Pinkertons, Superintendent Hussey, Superintendent Marpole, Commissioner and Lieutenant Colonel Sherwood of the Dominion Police in Ottawa, Chief Constable Colin Campbell of Vancouver, and CPR Inspector William McLeod. The photos were taken by the prison photographer, a guard skilled in the procedures. Using glass plate negatives, the photos showed the convicts as they looked when they arrived, then after they were shaven and had their hair cut. The Bertillon descriptions were on the reverse of the shaven depictions only. Whyte advised the requestors that he had used up the last of the glass plates taking the

William "Shorty" Dunn, after a shave and a haircut. COURTESY OF ANTHONY MARTIN COLLECTION.

photos of these prisoners, and it is supposed that negative film was to be used for future procedures. He cautioned the recipients that they were not to be given out for publication under any circumstances without contacting the warden of the B.C. Penitentiary. Requests were to continue to come in over the following months from law enforcement officials and institutions interested in cleaning up old cases and updating their records. Such was the case with the San Quentin State Prison identification section and Messrs. Conley and McTague from the Montana State Penitentiary in Deer Lodge, Montana. Persistent rumours that Miner may have operated in the Montana territory had continued to surface over the years.[7]

A return letter from the Director of the Criminal Bureau of Identification at the San Quentin prison offers his sincerest thanks for the photos, and comments, "The old fellow has aged considerably since I saw him last but is still easily identified as Billy Miner." He noted to Whyte that he was still searching the records to see if he could find anything on Billy Dunn.[8]

By July the new prisoners had settled into the regimented prison routine. Miner was put to work in the prison's cobbler shop where the trade he had learned in San Quentin was put to good use. Dunn was placed on a construction gang where he acted as a carpenter building a new wing on the main prison building, and later he would work on the erection of a new kiln for the brick factory. Colquhoun found himself in the carpentry shop, where he was kept out of the elements in deference to his disease. However, the humid climate of the west coast and the proximity of the wide Fraser River just outside the gates of the prison must have aggravated the symptoms of his tuberculosis.[9][10]

The week of July 9TH, 1906, saw a visitor from Oregon to see Miner. It was George Hoben, the older brother of the 15 year old who was captured after the ill-fated robbery of the Oregon Railway and Navigation Company train on the 23RD of September in 1903 at Corbett, Oregon. The youth was serving ten years for his part in the holdup.

"Hoben claims that his connection with the robbery was solely due to Miner's persuasive abilities. He would never have been near the place but for the glowing get rich quick stories told by Miner."

The boy's brother attempted to persuade Miner that he had exerted undue influence on the lad so that the authorities would then reduce his sentence. However, Miner callously would not admit to being the bandit in case his conviction was successfully appealed by defence lawyer Mcintyre, and the downcast brother left the prison unsuccessful in his quest.[11]

In June of 1906, Alex Mcintyre visited his three clients in the penitentiary. Ten days after the conviction in Kamloops, he had made application to the court for a reversed case, but the application had been refused. He met with his clients separately, and the discussions he had with them were for the provision of funds to carry out an appeal against their convictions. Some discussion was also held with regard to alleged alibis held by Miner and Colquhoun near Penticton and Grand Forks, but nothing came of these. After he left them that June, Mcintyre was never to see the three prisoners again.[12]

In September, Mcintyre wrote Warden Whyte requesting a private interview with Miner out of earshot of penitentiary officials. Mcintyre wanted to discuss funding for the appeal with Miner and wanted absolute privacy for the discussions. The Kamloops lawyer had heard the stories about the bonds that were supposedly taken from the train at Mission, and there is no doubt that he wanted to get his hands on some of those securities. Warden Whyte wrote back to him, refusing the application as it was against prison security rules. Mcintyre wasn't about to accept that and launched a letter writing campaign against the prison official with his federal superiors in Ottawa. The federal justice minister finally wrote Mcintyre back and advised that he could meet with his client any time he wished, however, never without a prison official present. Mcintyre had expected the appeal to be launched in the fall of 1906, but as no funds were forthcoming from either the prisoners or their friends, he allowed the appeal to drop. Mcintyre received his last letter from Miner in 1906, and then he never heard from him again.

Communications with the outside world were strictly regulated through the prison offices, but clandestine methods were common and relatively easy. Convicts on release would smuggle messages out, and visitors would smuggle in messages and contraband. Spots along the prison fences were identified where drops could be made to outside confederates and former prison mates, and they could do the same in turn. Newspapers, letters, whiskey and tobacco were the most frequently traded smuggled goods. For those like Miner who had ready sources of cash outside the prison walls and many friends faithful to them, it was relatively simple to keep abreast of the latest news, arrange meets at the prison walls, organize visits, and get tobacco and other necessities not available to regular prisoners. The ability to get this contraband from the outside world conferred considerable status on those with the proper connections, and their life was made considerably more acceptable.

The future testimony of a convict by the name of Campbell serves to give us some idea of the covert world existing in the little known or understood life that existed behind the normal prison routine and administrative security.

Convict Campbell testified that the convicts "Toole, Mason and Jones were the prison postmasters. Ex-convicts and others got into the yard at night and planted letters, opium, tobacco, matches and maybe other things in the woodshed near the laundry. Toole and Mason and sometimes Jones would get these letters and things and distribute them when the convicts were brought to the laundry to be washed and shaved. When Toole got out he sent things in. I have seen and heard Mason posting Bill Miner when Miner was taking his bath. One plan they had was for pals to come in at night, overpower the yard patrol, use him as a shield and enter the prison by force. They would let all the Americans out. This plan never came to a head. They could not work it right."[13]

Bill Miner's previous thirty-four years of incarceration at San Quentin had taught him all the tricks known to long-term offenders about surreptitious prison activities and how to bypass official rules and regulations.

"They got letters right along that didn't come through the Warden's office. I saw Miner with a copy of the Portland Oregonian newspaper, and a letter written by one Thurston of Bozeman, Montana. Thurston I think was with Miner when he robbed the train at Mission. Miner got the paper and the letter in the brickyard where outsiders had planted them. Miner got several letters that I know about."[14]

The prisoners' smuggling activities were encouraged by the fact that no sentries were posted around the perimeter of the prison where the brickyard was located after the convicts had been locked in their cells for the night. Any breaches in the prison security initiated from the outside had the cloaking advantage of darkness to aid them in their activities, and full advantage was taken of this lapse in security. [15]

Miner kept up a relationship with the guards who perceived the old man as a harmless lifer with no threat to anyone and who was fond of telling stories. He told one that he had two cousins and a sister in Vancouver and an uncle who was a farmer in Delta. He told trades instructor Doyle that he had recently inherited $5,000 from an aunt who had died in New York shortly after he had entered the penitentiary. If he had inherited the money, it hadn't made it inside the walls in any official way. Later it was speculated in the press that this money could have gone towards funding Miner's future escape plans.[16]

In late May Miner received a visit from a curious Provincial Police Sergeant G.R. Murray from Superintendent Hussey's offices in Victoria. Murray wanted to see just what the elderly man who had caused such consternation over the past three years looked and sounded like. Keeper Stewart was present during the entire interview in the warden's office, and Murray asked Miner whether he had any news of a new trial. Miner answered in the negative, and after a few more words, Murray left.[17]

Soon after the prisoners arrived, a lengthy correspondence began in the best traditions of practicing government bureaucrats. Post Office Inspector John Greenfield of Vancouver was still trying to retrieve the cash stolen from the mail car at Ducks. Mrs. Petrie of Victoria had been expecting a $5 bill from Mrs. John Burns of Ottawa, and a $10 bill addressed to the Kam Yung Ling Company in Victoria was also missing. When Edwards had been captured, he had a total of $50.10 in his possession, including a five and a ten dollar bill. Greenfield wanted those bills used to reimburse his client's losses, and on 8 June 1906 he requested that Warden Whyte furnish a description of the bills. Whyte wrote him back and recommended that Greenfield supply the descriptions and he will see if they fit the ones in his possession. Greenfield didn't feel he was getting any satisfaction in dealing with the warden, so he sent off another letter requesting the same thing from the Attorney General, Frederick Fulton. He gave a vague description of the bills. The $5 bill was either a Bank of Ottawa or an Imperial Bank of Canada bill, and the $10 bill was a Canadian Bank of Commerce bill. Greenfield did not get any satisfaction from Mr. Fulton either, so in the manner of all good bureaucrats, he filed the matter away. Almost six months later, Whyte was feeling some amount of frustration with the Postal Inspector. On 21 November 1906, he wrote to Greenfield requesting notification of the outcome to the post office official's inquiries because, as he wrote, convict Edwards wanted to settle some outstanding debts he had on the outside. By the end of the month, Greenfield had written back to Whyte and advised him that the Attorney General, in his wisdom, had decided that the money cannot be used for the reimbursement of the persons sustaining the losses as none of the bills could definitely be identified as part of the ill-fated robbery loot. Greenfield did not mention to Whyte as to how he could utilize Miner's funds; however, it is expected that the old man finally ended up with access to his ill-gotten gains for whatever purposes he required it for.[18][19]

After the successful prosecution of the Ducks robbers and the safe cloistering of the convicted felons behind the walls of the penitentiary, the CPR was feeling smug and satisfied with how their efforts had been rewarded. Early in June, Vice President William Whyte in Winnipeg passed on to Superintendent Marpole in Vancouver a congratulatory letter he had received from the President and General Manager of the Dominion Express Co., E.W. Stout. "Marpole is to be highly congratulated on having successfully located, captured and convicted Bill Miner," he wrote. He singled out Miner and commented that it was a "very great satisfaction" to him that he finally is behind bars as the bandit had been "unsuccessfully sought for by practically all the transportation interests on the Pacific Coast for many years and on whose capture we have spent much labour and a very large sum of money since the Mission hold up." He went on to say how "exceedingly glad" he was that Miner had been fully identified and that he was so clearly associated with the Mission holdup. He ended the letter by stating his conviction that the sentences handed out will discourage others from preying upon the Dominion Express or the CPR. Ironically, and a bit incestuously, the Dominion Express Company was a subsidiary of the CPR, and anything that affected the one affected the other.[20]

Later that month, Marpole received a letter from detective William Seavey in Seattle. The Thiel Detective Agency was still on the CPR's payroll and trying to justify its billings. Seavey stated that Miner and Jack Budd's mutual friend Tom Arnold was still hanging around Princeton and in the hills around Budd's ranch. He reminded Marpole that Arnold is suspected of being one of Miner's cohorts when holding up the train west of Mission Junction. But then, Seavey writes gratuitously, Marpole probably knew those facts already.[21]

The interest of the CPR in activities in the Similkameen continued into July. Dominion Express President Stout wrote to Marpole expressing his gratification and congratulating Marpole "most heartily on your success." In the letter he notes the conviction now held by the CPR that Miner was also "interested in" the Mission holdup. He goes on to surmise that Budd will no longer cause any problems without the presence of Miner around, but that it would be worthwhile "to look after him and put him safely away if possible and I hope you may succeed in doing so." The memory of the CPR was not soon to forget about Bill Miner's "boys" in the Similkameen Valley.[22]

In early July, CPR detective Bullick wrote to Marpole to inform him that Warden Whyte at the B.C. Penitentiary had written him to advise that the prison office had intercepted a letter from Bill Miner to his friend Tom Arnold in Princeton. In the letter he requests that Arnold sell off some of his horses that were being kept at Budd's ranch and to use some of the funds to settle some outstanding accounts in Princeton. He also asked that Arnold pass on his best regards to the boys around Princeton in general. Bullick reminded Marpole that there was a close connection between Miner and Budd and that perhaps it should be investigated further. He advised further that Warden Whyte would hold the letter if Marpole wished to see it, but if not it would be forwarded to Arnold.[23]

Marpole was not about to slack off on attempting to investigate and convict more of the American desperados close to the border. He wrote to Hussey about the CPR's convictions with regards to Budd and Arnold and enclosed copies of Bullick's and Seavey's letters to him. He requested that the Provincial Police constables in the Princeton area be candidly ordered to covertly investigate suspicious friends of Miner around Princeton and Hedley.[24]

Princeton's fresh new constable was having troubles of his own. Ronald Hewat wrote to Chief Constable Pearse in Kamloops on the 13 June 1906 and advised him that he had contracted typhoid fever that spring, however, had now recovered. Hewat had a most pressing problem in that he had no reliable mount to enable him to fulfill his duties in the district surrounding Princeton. The Provincial Police budget allocated from Victoria was noted for its meanness, and officers frequently had to supply many of their own needs from their own pockets if they wished to be effective enforcers of the law. He wrote to his superior expressing his concerns and hoped that he might receive a sympathetic response.

"I write to ask if you would get the government to supply me with a horse and forage during the construction of the railway through here as I will have to do a lot of riding. The railway is now graded to Keremeos and they will soon be to Hedley, which is only 25 miles from here. You see if I wanted a saddle horse in a hurry I could not get one in Princeton. I have a good stable and saddle etc. and I would like a horse that would be handy. If they would supply me with one I would get you to buy one in Kamloops and sent out to me by stage for a saddle horse can be purchased in Kamloops for half the price a person could buy one in here. Mr. Hunter has an old white horse that is a government animal but he is too old and no good. He must be about twenty years old and can not stand long journeys."

"Yours obediently,
Constable R. Hewat."[25]

It is hoped that Superintendent Hussey's concerns, pressed by the CPR's Marpole, ended up expediting Constable Hewat's transportation needs, as he had much ground to cover over the next few months.

Hussey lost no time in writing to Constables Hunter and Hewat in Princeton and instructing them to discreetly start to assemble information on Arnold and Budd and any other refugees from across the line that might be worthy of attention in the area. Constable Ronald Hewat accordingly saddled and mounted his newly acquired horse and casually dropped in on the Budd ranch in the hills above Princeton. It was only a few miles from the town, and he acted as if he were just passing by. The new constable dutifully reported to Hussey that he had seen that Arnold was presently looking after Budd's horse ranch and that Budd had been up at his cabin near Aspen Grove since before the robbery. He intimated that while he knew Arnold to see him, they were not on intimate terms. The constable added the comment that Arnold had a poor reputation and was known to be very mean when he was drunk. He had an inflammatory temper and was very quick to take offence. Arnold had been involved in the periphery of the mining industry in the Boundary country. There his reputation was not very good, and it was reported that he was constantly in trouble.[26]

When Hussey received Hewat's short report, he immediately passed it on to Marpole. Marpole in turn initiated discussion with Vice President Whyte in Winnipeg as to the value of pursuing these characters on the fringe of the law close to the border. While Whyte seemed to demure, Marpole was for pressing on with the secret investigation. Marpole stated he was reluctant to "let well alone" and was of the opinion that they should pursue putting Budd behind bars as soon as possible. Marpole agreed with the Vice President's stipulation that the evidence for Budd's arrest should be beyond doubt, and that the investigation into Budd's connivance in criminal matters should be done in strict secrecy.

Marpole referred Whyte to interviews he had held in his private car when in Kamloops. There he had held talks with Sheriff Wentworth Wood of Kamloops and CPR Special Services detective W.L. McLaws with regards to their suspicions regarding the supposed confederates of Miner—Stevens, Budd and Arnold. Also discussed were a mysterious "man and woman in a new wagon" that had proceeded east from Kamloops the day previous to the holdup.

Marpole went on to disparagingly refer to Mr. Hussey's replies and Hewat's reports in response to his letters requesting further investigation of Budd and Arnold. He noted, "You will see how little interest the provincial Authorities as a whole take in the desperado element of the residents of Yale and Kootenay Districts." Marpole ended with noting his intention "to have a quiet talk with the Executive as to this peculiar feature of careless indifferent espionage and treatment of the criminals of other Countries by our Constabulary." Marpole enjoyed ready access to Premier McBride's offices and was not reluctant to press the CPR's concerns on the most senior of government representatives.[27]

Constable Hewat meanwhile continued with his covert investigations in the Similkameen, blissfully ignorant of the pressures exerted upon Superintendent Hussey by the CPR. He conscientiously kept track of Budd and Arnold and kept his activities under cover so as not to let them become aware of law enforcement's interests. He had been keeping a close eye out for Budd and Arnold ever since Hussey's order had arrived, but matters continued much as before. Towards the end of July, Budd was still in the bush up around Aspen Grove, and Arnold was still looking after Budd's ranch. Hewat told Hussey that he knew them both well. He had often seen Arnold in town lately, but he still planned on riding out towards Osprey Lake and would pay a visit to Arnold again at that time. Hewat agreed that Jack Budd was worth watching as he was a great friend of Edwards, having spent time with him in the United States before they came to Princeton. He had observed in the past that besides their similar American accent, Budd's actions and methods were much like those of Edwards. Both carried revolvers on their persons at all times, and both acted as if they were afraid of meeting someone they did not want to meet. Hewat had noticed that characteristic of Edwards the first time he met him.[28]

It took Hewat until almost the end of August before he gained an opportunity to meet and speak to Tom Arnold again without raising his suspicions. He told Hussey that he had just been talking to him the day previously, and as a result of that meeting, Hewat had prepared a detailed Bertillon description of Arnold on the official Provincial Police form. Budd still had not shown his face around Princeton, but the constable assured Hussey he would send Budd's description as soon as he showed up. He added that he knew both Budd and Arnold well, he had even worked alongside Arnold before he had been accepted as a provincial constable. He stressed to Hussey that he was keeping all the investigations very secret, and would ensure that no one suspected investigations were taking place. From the tone and wording of his report, it is easy to feel the constable's enthusiasm with the task he had been presented with and the thrill he experienced acting as an undercover agent.[29]

It wasn't until almost the end of October before Jack Budd finally showed up back in the Princeton country. Hewat had been talking to him just the past Sunday, and Budd had told him that he had not been to Princeton in some while. He had been attending to his claims in the Aspen Grove area and had only now returned to his ranch. Hewat sent off a report and another Bertillon description done on Budd to Hussey. As he was such a frequent correspondent with the Superintendent, the young constable thought it pertinent to make a request of the remote official in Victoria. He requested that Hussey send him a set of lightweight "police nippers" as the regular issue cuffs were too cumbersome to carry about easily.

Hewat's October communication with Hussey was the last to take place with regard to Arnold and Budd until an event in 1907 would refocus attention on the Similkameen.

The saga of the final distribution of the $11,500 reward warrants special attention as a splendid early twentieth century example of foot dragging and government and corporate lack of empathy in meeting publicly-expressed obligations. Now that the bandits were captured and safely behind bars, there was no need for haste in compensating those most responsible for the successful final outcome. The needs of the CPR had been met, and that giant corporate citizen had refocused its attentions again on the business of business—expansion and profits. The feelings and anxieties of those expecting at least some word of the eventual disposition of the monies were now of secondary importance.

But to those ordinary citizens in the heartland, whether they had been posse members or not, it was a matter of primary importance. The annual salaries of workers of what would today be considered the average middle class rarely exceeded one thousand dollars, and most businessmen held more than one job so as to bolster their earnings. The prospects of acquiring a portion of the five figure award loomed large in many households.

One such household was that of Percy Cotton, the Special Constable from Grande Prairie who had assisted Constable Basil Gardom of Enderby in Grande Prairie and in the Monte Hills. He wrote to Superintendent Hussey on 30 May 1906, before the trial of the robbers was yet over. He requested that Hussey remember him when it came time to apportion the reward as he had been working the trails near where the bandits had been captured and had assisted in investigating and arresting Paul Stevens.[30]

By early June a tribunal had been set up to evaluate and fairly distribute the rewards. Superintendent Hussey in Victoria was to represent the provincial government's interests, Post Office Inspector John R. Greenfield of Vancouver was to represent the federal government, and Assistant Solicitor J.E. McMullen would represent the CPR.

Shortly after the appointment of the triumvirate, Hussey wrote Pearse in Kamloops requesting that he send to him by return mail the names of all the members of Pearse's posse, the length of time they were engaged, the service they provided to the effort, and those who displayed the most value to the enterprise. He wanted to know the number of miles each had travelled and instructed him to include the Indian trackers.[31]

Pearse replied, listing Constable Fernie, F.E. Carter, Sheriff Wood, Joseph Greaves of the Campbell Range, Lewis Campbell Jr., and the trackers Phillip Toma, Alex Ignace and Michelle LeCamp. He appended some comments about the individuals in his posse. He noted that the Indian trackers stayed with him from the first day until eight days later when they finally rode into Kamloops, wet and tired.

Of the trackers, he wrote, "The work done by these men certainly deserves special mention and recognition as without it there would have been great difficulty in determining which course the robbers had taken and in securing a conviction against them. They are all equally good."

Speaking of the posse members as a whole, he praised them all equally. "Every man on the party proved himself to be capable and willing and those who went right over the trail with me had to endure more than ordinary hardships."

Pearse added a postscript to recognize the valuable efforts of CPR Superintendent Kilpatrick of Revelstoke at the scene of the robbery that first day and up in the Campbell Range on the two days following.[32]

Three days later he added the list of R.N.W.M.P. members who took part in the actual arrest of the robbers. They included Sergeant

John J. Wilson, Sergeant Thomas E. Shoebotham, Corporal Joseph C. Stewart, Corporal Christopher E. Peters and Constable John T. Browning. He went on to note that while Sergeant Thomas and Constable Tabuteau were with the party from the beginning, they were patrolling at another location and did not take part in the arrest. Samuel "Slim Jim" Benyon was hired by the provincial government as the Mounted Police's guide, and he had been paid as such.[33]

After that brief flurry of paper activity, Pearse and his posse members would hear no more of the matter for almost six months. In early August he wrote Hussey to inquire as to the status of the reward monies. Pearse passed his concerns on to his Superintendent that a great many rumours were circulating around Kamloops and throughout the district. People were grumbling that the government and the CPR were about to renege on their promises, and the initial distrust of the populace was not alleviated by the delay. The trackers in particular were cynical about receiving any compensation even though they had initially been promised a portion of the reward to entice them to assist in the apprehension of the bandits. There is no record that Pearse would hear anything more about the reward until early that winter.[34]

Despite no word being passed out to the public, interest in the reward had not waned. In late September, mining promoter Owen Batchelor wrote Hussey advising him he should receive some share of the reward for the capture of the train robbers as he had been driving detectives around throughout the period from the robbery up to the trial. He had been out all that time, and he felt that it was owing to his knowledge of the trails and wagon roads in the area that the Mounted Police were dispatched to the Douglas Lake area.[35]

Not to be outdone, the CPR station agent for Ducks Station, William Plumm, took the opportunity to inform Hussey that he had "contributed greatly to the cause of justice" by gathering information around Ducks and the Holmwood country and passing it on to detectives. Because of the valuable services he had contributed, he stressed that he should not be forgotten when the time eventually came for the dispersion of the reward.[36]

The wheels of the business of the bureaucracies continued to grind exceedingly slowly, but exceedingly fine. By October, five months after the arrest, Hussey had received the $1,500 cheque from the provincial government, endorsed it, and sent it on to CPR lawyer McMullen. By mid-November, three copies of the joint decision report to be issued by the three panel members were chasing Hussey around the province as he bounced from the Lower Mainland to Fernie, to Midway, and back to Victoria. Finally they arrived in front of him for his signature, but not before he was to receive one more veiled solicitation for reward recognition.[37]

CPR Special Service detective W.A. McFoy in Calgary wrote to Hussey expressing his confidence the reward "will be distributed fairly to all entitled to have a share." He went on to note that R.N.W.M.P. members in Calgary had expressed their concerns that they might be left out. McFoy also noted that he had heard that other CPR employees had submitted claims. The detective modestly did not include himself on the list of those deserving of a reward, but his very communication with Hussey ensured that his name was brought forward to the superintendent's attention.[38]

McFoy continued to communicate with Hussey that fall, advising Hussey that Dunn had authorized him to have one of his pistols, and Colquhoun had said he could have his gold cufflinks. Hussey put him off, saying that the appeal had not yet been filed, but it has to be assumed that sometime later McFoy may have collected on his souvenirs.[39]

Finally Hussey and his two bureaucratic companions had completed their report recommending the reward distribution and released it to the public at the end of November. The distribution of the $11,500 would ultimately be deemed fair and equitable, although there would have certainly been some disappointment.[40]

Constable Fernie and R.N.W.M.P. members Wilson, Shoebotham, Peters, Stewart and Browning were each to receive $1,350; Chief Constable E.T.W. Pearse of Kamloops, $800; Special Constable F.E. Carter, Kamloops, $500; and the three Indian trackers, Alex Ignace, Michel LeCamp and Phillip Toma, were each to receive $700.[41]

The three made comments about the contribution made by the individuals noted. The R.N.W.M.P. were described as being deserving of first rate consideration in the final assessment of the rewards. Pearse, Carter and the three trackers were also deserving of recognition and should be so recognized. "The three Indians proved to be expert trackers and their assistance was, therefore, of considerable value." Referring to Pearse, Carter and the trackers together, the adjudicators went on to note that they "stayed together and worked continuously until after the capture took place." The five posse members "contributed to the capture, and we think they deserve to be recognized."

Constable Fernie was also singled out for his contributions. The three stated that Fernie, "seems to deserve special consideration." They went on to describe Fernie's actions from when he left Kamloops and added, "We think that Constable Fernie displayed bravery in accosting the three men as he did and that the information which as a result he was able to give lead [sic] to the location of the robbers."[42]

Constable Fernie's annual salary in the period 1 July 1905 to 30 June 1906 was $840 per year. His $1,350 share of the $11,500 reward amounted to over one and a half times his yearly salary. He had been married less than a year previously to Mary Lyle of Kamloops, and he would use the reward money to build his first house at the far west end of Kamloops.[43][44]

Despite the spectacular lack of success experienced by the bloodhounds brought in to hunt down the Ducks robbers, Hussey was getting pressure from some of his constables in the Kootenays to authorize the use of the hounds in their regular work. On 20 June 1906, Hussey wrote Attorney General Fulton on the topic. He noted that some Provincial Police members kept their own bloodhounds and wished to be able to use them at their discretion without checking with Victoria first. Constable Young in Nelson, who had such a pitiful lack of success with his dogs south of Ducks, owned six, and Constable Darraugh of Midway had one or more. Other officers had solicited him for permission to be able to own and use such animals.

Hussey advised the Attorney General that in his judgment the dogs were almost useless unless they had been highly and competently trained in man hunting and were in the hands of exceedingly skilled handlers. It is under only the most favourable circumstances that these animals could be successful and do useful work.

He noted also that there exists a strong feeling from the general public against such use of bloodhounds excepting perhaps in the most extreme cases. Hussey recommended to Fulton that under no conditions should the use of bloodhounds be authorized except under the direct permission of the Superintendent's office in Victoria.

He requested instructions from Fulton so that he might advise the constables in the field, and Fulton agreed that they should not be used in B.C. unless under emergency conditions.[45]

During the hunt for the train robbers, Constable Gardom had arrested James Christie south of Glen Emma near Round Lake. The reasons for the apprehension are vague, but probably were based on the fact that his description coincided with that given of the Third Man and that he could give no good accounting for his whereabouts and actions over the previous days. He had been locked in a cell in Vernon on May 12TH and had been released along with Mohr and Wilson on a lack of evidence six days later. CPR mail clerk McQuarrie had been in Vernon that day and did not identify either Mohr or Wilson as suspects, but he noted that Christie did look like the Third Man. However, as the supposed real bandits had been captured earlier that week, Christie was set free.[46]

Christie was born in Speyside, Scotland, in 1852 and immigrated to Canada as a teenager. He joined the Canadian Artillery, B Battery, in Quebec, and by 1870 he was in command of a gun crew at Fort Garry. In 1876 he joined the North West Mounted Police and was one of the police who met with Sitting Bull and his bands of Sioux after the battle of the Little Big Horn. After a series of adventures in the North West Territories of Canada and the North West United States, he pre-empted two parcels of land on the west side of the Shuswap River at the south end of Mabel Lake. By 1905 he had discovered coal near Shorts Creek, close to Fintry.[47]

The Armstrong Advance issue of the week Christie was released gave further details of Christie which served to alleviate all suspicions about the man.

"James Christie was in town this week, having been freed of suspicion as having been connected with the train robbery. The following, taken from a Rossland dispatch, conveys an idea of Christie's past life:

"Christie has resided in and about Rossland for the past 10 years, being a rancher, prospector and timber cruiser and has coal, timber and mineral interests in different sections of the province. Twenty-five years ago he was a scout in the Northwest Territories and has always been a typical frontiersman and knows the remote portions of the continent perhaps as well as any man. In 1889 he, in company with several others, explored the Olympic Mountains in the interests of the Seattle press, and he and the party with him were the first men, white or red, to explore the wild vastness of that range. He was one of a party that climbed Mount Elias in Alaska. In his wanderings he has visited the Peace River country and has been as far north in Canada as where the surf of the cold Atlantic [sic] beats against the northern shores. It is thought here by men who have known him for two decades and who have never known him to commit a dishonest or unlawful act that the police have made a mistake in arresting him."[48]

Christie was alternately outraged and humiliated by his experience of being incarcerated in a jail in Vernon with the two other robbery and horse thieving suspects, Wilson and Mohr. He took pen in hand in June of 1906 and started a correspondence with the Provincial Police which would last for three months, and demanded an explanation for their actions. His handwritten letters portray a well educated man, comfortable in dealing with inert bureaucracies.

Glen Emma Post Office, Armstrong, B.C.
26 June 1906
To Superintendent Hussey,
Dear Sir,
    Would you kindly furnish me with a copy of any report made to
you by any party which led up to or was the cause of my arrest as
a suspected person in connection with the late train robbery near
Kamloops. Also a copy of the report made to your department by
any person connected with my arrest, the person actually responsible
for the arrest and any reasons given for same or should this letter of
inquiry be sent to any other department? Kindly advise.
    Yours Truly,
    J.H. Christie, lately under arrest at Vernon, B.C.[49]

Christie obviously had his vengeful eye on Constable Gardom in
Enderby. He also sent a letter in the same vein to Chief Constable
Simmons in Vernon requesting an explanation and received a typically
vague reply.

Chief Constable's Office, Vernon, B.C.
15 Aug 1906
To J.H. Christie, Glen Emma
    I have the honour to acknowledge the receipt of your letter of
the 6th. If Mr. Hussey, my Superintendent, or the Honourable
the Attorney General, wish to know on what grounds the order
was given for your arrest, I should be pleased to furnish them with
the information. Regarding the public statements I am supposed to
have made, I can only say that I can not hold myself responsible for
anything the press may say.
    E.C. Simmons, Chief Constable[50]

This was in no way satisfactory to Christie, who painstakingly made a handwritten copy of Simmons' reply to him and included it with another letter to Hussey.

> *Glen Emma Post Office, Armstrong, B.C.*
> *21 Aug 1906*
> *To Superintendent Hussey,*
> *Dear Sir,*
> *In accordance with your position I have written the Chief*
> *Constable here in Vernon, E.C. Simmons, re my arrest. In his first*
> *communication he simply informed me that I was arrested by his*
> *order. I requested him to give me reason or cause for same. I enclose*
> *you a copy of his answer. I would infer from the Constable's answer*
> *that he has not given, as is expected, a report to your office or that of*
> *the Attorney General's office regarding the unwarrantable arrest. It*
> *is surely not possible that any such authority is held as given to any*
> *mere policeman in B.C. Kindly advise me if such is the case.*
> *Would you kindly demand from Mr. Simmons a report giving his*
> *whole reasons on cause of reasonable suspicion for his order for my*
> *late arrest.*
> *Remaining yours respectfully,*
> *J.H. Christie* [51]

The harried Hussey sent off another letter to Simmons, and as the Chief Constable was away on leave, Constable Gardom from Enderby was looking after his affairs at Vernon. Gardom, now well aware of the ire of Christie, replied in a suitably vague and non-committal manner to Hussey.

28 Aug 06
Chief Constable's office in Vernon
To Superintendent F.S. Hussey.
Dear Sir,
Re Train Robbery. Mr. Simmons has instructed me to
acknowledge receipt of your letter to him of Aug. 25th making
inquiries as to arrest of J. H. Christie and he wishes me to say that
he will get you full particulars on his return this office next week. I
arrested this man but I am unable to give a detailed report until I
have seen my notes on the matter which are at Enderby.
The honour to be Sir,
Your Obedient Servant,
Basil Gardom,
Provincial Constable.[52]

After some weeks in the bush, Christie returned to Glen Emma and
received a letter from Hussey promising a full explanation. Christie
expressed his appreciation and anticipation in a return letter.

Glen Emma Post Office, Armstrong, B.C.
17 Sept 1906
To Superintendent Hussey,
Dear Sir,
My absence in the mountains for the last three weeks account for
my not acknowledging yours of the 25th of August sooner. This I
found awaiting me here on return and desire to thank you for your
prompt consideration of my request. I look forward to reading the
copy of Mr. Simmons' report with some pardonable curiosity.
Remaining Yours Truly,
J.H. Christie[53]

Unfortunately no copy exists of the Chief Constable's explanation
for Christie's arrest; however, no further correspondence is found

pertaining to the matter. The incident must have been resolved amicably and to Mr. Christie's satisfaction.

Christie would continue his explorations of the interior and filed claims and started mines in other areas. In 1907 he moved to Clint Hill, four miles east of Armstrong. There he took up with Amelia Duteau of Lavington whose mother was an Okanagan Indian. Together they would have a son named after the British Prime Minister, Lloyd George Christie. Over the years Christie would competently take up the cause of the Okanagan Indians in their disagreements with Indian Affairs and on unauthorized sales of their lands at the northern end of Long (Kalamalka) Lake. He was to act as an advocate for many of the Okanagan bands over the years, and the memory of his brief spell in the Vernon jail was gratefully lost in the passage of time. [54]

In February of 1907, tragedy struck Warden Whyte and his family. A particularly aggressive form of tuberculosis struck him, and the symptoms were at first pronounced to be "inflammatory rheumatism." However, soon the disturbing diagnosis was made and Whyte began a progressive decline. He made a trip to the Harrison Hot Springs in April during a brief period of respite to see if the sulphur baths might alleviate his condition, but it was to no avail. He continued to deteriorate and soon was confined to his bed. He turned his penitentiary duties over to Bourke, who assumed the title of Acting Warden. Bourke, in turn, appointed guard and hospital overseer F. Stewart to the position of Acting Deputy Warden. [55]

More than a year after the three prisoners had started their sentences, in July of 1907, R.N.W.M.P. Sergeant Jack Wilson was at the coast on official business. He had renewed old acquaintances while he was there, including the New Westminster Chief of Police McIntosh and CPR Special Services detective Waddell. McIntosh and Vancouver detective Waddell had both been part of the manhunt for Miner after the Mission robbery, and together with Wilson, they had more than a passing interest in the old bandit.

The three met with the Deputy Warden in his offices, and Bourke greeted Chief McIntosh warmly, as they were personal friends. Bourke gave the three visitors permission to tour the facility in the company of Acting Deputy Warden F. Stewart. Wilson asked Bourke if he might have a word with Miner while they were on their tour. Bourke agreed, advising it should only be for a minute or two.

The three officers went through the prison in the company of their guide, Stewart, and when they approached the brickyard, Wilson saw Miner working with a group of other prisoners. Miner recognized the officer immediately, and after receiving permission from Stewart to approach and speak, he took Wilson's hand in both of his and shook it warmly. Miner then proceeded to shake the hands of each of the visitors. Wilson could see that Miner had put on weight since he had seen him last and was apparently resigned to spending the rest of his life in prison.

Miner expressed his sincere pleasure in renewing old acquaintances, telling Wilson he was being well treated and that he had "no outside engagements at present." He went on to intimate to the visitors that "he was getting old and remarked with a smile that he had now settled down for life." He told the visitors his age, sixty-one years, and one of the visitors remarked that he looked as though he was good for another twenty years yet.[56]

Wilson hoped that Miner would bear him no grudge for sending him to prison.

The old man answered, "I am glad to see you my boy, you know this is no personal matter between you and me, it is your business to catch me and if I am not smart enough to get out of your way, well I deserve to be caught, but this is too big a question for us to talk about. I was glad to hear you boys got the reward, you know if I can't get the money myself I always like to hear of someone getting it, and we were all so glad at the way your boys treated us, and at the straightforward and truthful way in which they acted at our trial that we were all very much pleased when we learned that the Boys had got the reward, and I will say with all my heart, much good may it do them and may they live long to enjoy it."

He laughed and joked with Wilson about his ill-fated robbery attempt and intimated that there was no reason why a man in his position shouldn't become a practical philosopher, even though he was serving a life term.

"You know I am getting out a petition for parole, will you sign it? I mean when I am too old to rob a train. You know I may rob a train or stage coach but I never killed anyone, and I never robbed a poor man in my life, you know these big corporations and express companies never miss a few thousand and I always try and do some good when I get a haul."

He asked Wilson, "Did you get any of our effects, I mean as a souvenir?"

Wilson replied that he had not.

"Well I will give you an order to get my Luger Automatic, she is a dandy and I can shoot a coyote at 400 yards with her, and I don't suppose I will want her again."

Wilson turned to Stewart and asked him if there would be any objections to the prisoner issuing him the order for the firearm that was in the custody of the jailer in Kamloops. Stewart gave his permission, and with that, Chief McIntosh supplied a leaf from his notebook, and Miner wrote out an order to hand the pistol over to Wilson.[57][58]

"I guess I will sign this 'Edwards'," he said with a grin, and passed the page to the Sergeant.

Before the party said their goodbyes, Chief McIntosh said to Miner that he thought he recognized him from the fall of 1905 at the Lytton Hotel in New Westminster. Miner agreed that he had been there for two or three days while bringing horses down from the Similkameen to Ladner.[59]

Wilson was then taken to the shops where Dunn was working, and they shook hands. A few words of greeting passed between them, and as they were standing there talking, the tailor's gang came out of one of the buildings for their daily exercise. Wilson spotted Colquhoun and greeted him with, "How are you, Colquhoun?" Colquhoun replied with, "Alright," and the officer and the ex-schoolteacher shook hands.[60][61]

A few days after the visit, Bourke had occasion to meet with the prison doctor DeWolf-Smith. The doctor mentioned an interview he had read in the Vancouver Province with Sergeant Wilson about his meeting with the felon Bill Miner. Bourke sent for the paper and was dismayed when he saw the content of the article and the interview with Wilson. He was especially shocked when he read that a note had been exchanged between the prisoner and the visitor. Bourke's concerns were well-founded as before the month was out, he was ordered to submit a report on the whole incident to the federal bureaucrat responsible for penitentiaries. The Inspector of Prisons was Inspector G.W. Dawson, and he was at the Stony Mountain Penitentiary in Manitoba when Bourke sent his explanatory report to him. Bourke gave an outline of the events leading up to the Province's article and told the inspector how humiliated he felt that his professional courtesy had been so abused. He advised his management superior that he had interviewed Acting Deputy Warden Stewart as to his actions, and Stewart had expressed his apologies and intimated that he didn't think anything had been untoward in the transaction as permission had been given for Wilson to converse with the convict. Bourke advised Dawson that the transaction with the convict was without his own personal knowledge or consent. He had no further comments to make to assuage the federal inspector, and it was left at that.[62]

Inspector Dawson would eventually become Bourke's relentless nemesis, as the wily Bill Miner, "resigned to his fate," was to escape before a month had passed after Wilson's visit.

XXII
ESCAPE PLANNING

BEFORE THE HEAVY DOORS of the B.C. Penitentiary had closed behind him, Bill Miner was planning his eventual flight from the institution. The British Columbia prison had rarely, if ever, enjoyed the visit of a convict so experienced in serving hard time with a minimum of inconvenience and a maximum of opportunity. Their approach to Miner's tenure at the penitentiary would reflect some naivety and laxity in comparison with that practiced by the San Quentin Penitentiary in California. His plan was to pose as the elderly and non-threatening old man, incapable of mounting a challenge to good prison discipline and routine. On the trip down to New Westminster from Kamloops contemporary witnesses described Miner's resignation to his fate. He told Fernie and Pearse that he had not much longer to live anyway, and he might as well serve it in a prison. The reporter from the Columbian described his "stooped shoulders," "weary carriage" and "halting gait." It is doubtful these physical characteristics reflected the actual state of Miner's health at the time, as he had undergone trials and convictions to San Quentin at least three times previously, as well as prison tribunals for attempted escapes and disciplinary problems. So his disposition was well inured to the rigours of a trial. All contemporary descriptions up to and during the Ducks trial described a man of alert disposition, keen wit and having the physical attributes of a man a decade less than his actual sixty years. That a man of that age managed to elude a mounted posse on foot for over five days through some of the toughest terrain in the interior reflects a physical stamina and strength of will belying any infirmities or resignation to his fate.

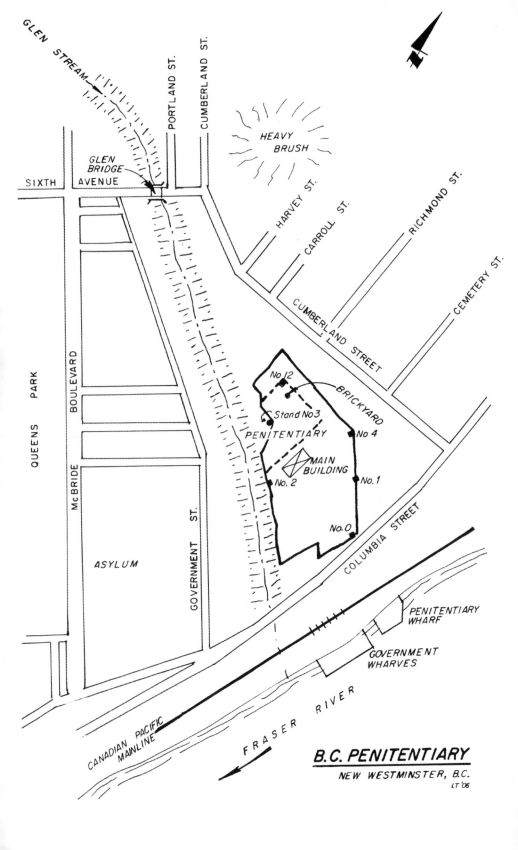

B.C. PENITENTIARY

NEW WESTMINSTER, B.C.

LT '06

Miner was already acting out his façade of the elderly criminal waiting to die in an institution and who did not pose a threat to the facility's security or administration. Miner depended upon the press releases and personal observances being passed to the prison administration, thereby providing a solid and long-term foundation upon which to build his escape attempt.

One of the ruses Miner would employ was to create the impression that he had undergone a newfound respect for religion, and he cultivated the thought with as many in the prison administration as possible. He had a solid Christian background imparted to him by his mother, and he used keen communications skills and a quick mind to be able to preach sermons when called upon and to quote biblical text when the occasion demanded. Never at a loss for words, he found a sympathetic figure in the impressionable young daughter of the Acting Warden. Katherine Bourke was raised in a deeply religious Catholic family, and she had been allowed some freedoms within the institution to cultivate the religious aspirations of some of the convicts considered less dangerous than others. Miner had laid his groundwork well and was one of the fervent young girl's fondest confidants. Katherine was drawn to the elderly but notorious bandit and felt she could make a better man of him through Christ. The old convict made sure that he presented the very image of a repentant criminal compelled to mend the ways of an errant life, and whose now frail health was being impacted by infirmities and an increasingly frail constitution. He asked for religious works that he could read and frequently joined the young girl in prayer. Katherine would fondly remember those times spent with the old man. "Bill said he was resigned to his fate, was satisfied, did not care to get away, and would do everything to merit a happier home in the other world."[1]

Miner attempted to address every contingency that could compromise a successful escape. One of those barriers to success was the appearance every convict presented to the normal outside population. Each prisoner was shaved and had his hair cut as close

---

B.C. Penitentiary and surroundings in 1906.

to the skull as possible, and was kept that way by regular visits to the prison barber. If Miner was to be able to blend into the outside world after an escape, he had to do something about his appearance. Once the prison administration's wariness had been somewhat mollified by his supposedly genuine approach to religion and the success of his non-threatening and resigned behaviour, he started to institute those procedures affecting his appearance.

In December of 1906, Miner requested of the prison surgeon that his upper lip not be shaved as it hurt his eyes. Despite any reasonable person's difficulty in determining a cause and effect between the two situations, he was successful in having a major prison rule set aside just for him. The surgeon, W.A. De Wolf Smith, felt that it might have this effect, so he ordered that the convict's lip be clipped rather than shaved. He instructed the prison barber "to keep such a length as one week's growth would obtain." Miner would spend the next weeks and months building on that little crack he had opened in the prison's security.[2]

During that winter a controversial incident took place in a prisoner interview room in the B.C. Penitentiary. The catalyst for the controversy began in September of 1904 when the CPR train was robbed west of Mission Junction.

When the robbers made their escape, the official statement given to the press was that $7,000 in gold dust and cash had been stolen. Also included in the loot were the contents of the registered mail package.[3]

Soon after the robbery, the Pinkerton's National Detective Agency issued a two page reward circular listing the complete amount of the materials, cash and gold dust stolen in the robbery.

"The robbers secured one canvas sack in which was a tin can containing $4,000 in gold dust, and a canvas sack containing two boxes of gold dust amounting to $2,000. This gold dust was consigned from Ashcroft, B.C., having originally come from the Cariboo Mining District."

The circular went on to describe packages of cash and cheques stolen amounting to $911.30. It also gave a complete list of the contents of the registered mail sack, which mostly consisted of letters. Only four packages were listed: the contents of one being a magazine; the second, two tax notices; and the third, a "Blank P.O. Bill". One package is listed whose content is noted as "Not Known". It is described as "Registered Package No. 625". It had been shipped from Winnipeg and was addressed merely to Victoria. All of the other contents of the registered mail had more detail as to the sender's particulars, giving at least the names and addresses. In all other instances of letters or packages, either the names of the recipients were given or the contents listed, or both.[4]

Cell typical of those that housed Miner, Dunn and Colquhoun during their incarceration. COURTESY OF ANTHONY MARTIN COLLECTION.

Further investigation as to the contents of this vaguely described registered mail package with the CPR Archives by the author have proved fruitless, and staff advised that this particular information would have been in Lord Shaughnessy's personal papers which were destroyed after his death.

Speculation as to the contents of the registered mail package had started to circulate in 1905, and a Bellingham paper had first mentioned publicly that year that the package contained bonds variously described as Australian or American and worth widely differing amounts. Their value was noted as being as little as $50,000 to "several hundred thousand dollars" and everything in between. All the primary source material from the time indicates that Bill Miner and his pals had started the rumour. CPR Special

Alternate view of typical cell in the B.C. Penitentiary. Courtesy of Anthony Martin Collection.

Services detective Bullick, under oath in 1909, swore that, "The story of the missing bonds was a fake invented on behalf of the train robber by Miner himself or his friends." Still under oath, Bullick stated that positively no bonds or securities had ever been stolen from any CPR train.[5]

Other events would add fuel to the rumours about the fictitious stolen bonds. In the summer of 1905 and after the rumours of the stolen bonds had started to circulate, "Cowboy" Jake Terry approached the CPR in Vancouver with an offer to work as an undercover agent for the railway company to help them in the return of the stolen securities.[6]

Cowboy Jake Terry was a smuggler and counterfeiter from the Bellingham and Sumas areas of Washington state. He and Miner had met while each was serving a stretch in San Quentin, and it was rumoured that Terry was one of Miner's partners during the holdup at Mission.[7]

Terry had a number of clandestine meetings with CPR detectives, and he advised them that he was a personal friend and partner of Miner's and had personal knowledge of the whereabouts of the bonds and other valuables stolen from the CPR at Mission. He told them that in return for monetary payments he would pursue retrieving their lost items. He acted in a very devious manner with the officials, and for a while they thought there may be something to his statements. While the detectives knew that no bonds existed, they were intrigued by his stories and had him shadowed for a period of five weeks.[8]

Furthering their follow-up with Terry, CPR detective Bullick decided to test Jake Terry's declared friendship with Bill Miner. On 9 February 1907, Bullick arranged an interview with Miner and Jake Terry in the Warden's office at the penitentiary to test Terry's veracity. In the presence of Warden Whyte, now in the first stages of his battle with tuberculosis, Bullick and Terry met with the old train robber who had been brought up from the prison shoe repair shop. For some reason, prison rules were either waived or overlooked, and the detective and Terry's visit was not entered into the prison daybook that day. Future events and inquiries would make much of this bureaucratic error. While Bullick himself did not exchange but a few words with Miner, Terry did hold discussion with him over a few minutes.[9]

Terry went straight up to Miner, extended his hand and said, "Hello, Bill."

Miner, unperturbed, extended his hand in return and stated, "I don't know you but I will shake hands with you."

A short conversation of no great interest took place between the two, then Terry said, "You never knew me to lie, did you, Bill?"

Miner replied, "No, Jake, I never did," revealing that he did, indeed, know Terry.[10]

Bullick, later testifying under oath about the interview, stated that at no time was the loot stolen at the Mission robbery or the fictitious bonds discussed or referred to.[11]

The CPR terminated their relationship with Terry soon after their visit with Miner as they concluded that the outlaw and informer was "romancing," that the bonds were a fictitious story concocted by Miner and his pals, and the railway company refused to have anything further to do with him.[12]

When Miner returned to the shoe repair shop from his interview with Bullick and Terry, he approached guard and instructor George McKenzie and asked permission to speak.

The conversation that followed would later echo through the halls of the House of Commons in Ottawa. It is unlikely that either of the two principals was quite aware of the potential impact of what was said, but there is no doubt that Miner was continuing his plan of sowing seeds of distrust and suspicion against the CPR. Anyone else running afoul of his plans against the railway giant was expendable. A reading of the guard's testimony without taking into consideration the devious and designing mind and intentions of Miner would result in conspiracy theories cropping up over the years attempting to explain the unexplainable. Miner's reasons for reciting his mixture of truths and untruths to the unsuspecting McKenzie will forever remain in the realm of speculation.

When the prison guard and instructor saw Miner return from his visit to the Warden's office after an hour's absence, he was struck but the obvious state of excitement Miner displayed. McKenzie asked him what was on his mind. McKenzie's subsequent recall of the conversation was given under oath.

"He told me Detective Bullick, who was in the service of the Canadian Pacific Railway company, and his lawyer from up-country had come to see him. He said Mr. Bullick told him he had been empowered by the CPR company to say that the company had the promise of the government that Miner would be pardoned if he would surrender to the company certain Australian bonds valued at fifty thousand pounds sterling, which the company believed Miner had taken from the express car when he had robbed the train near Mission two or three years ago, or prove to the satisfaction of the company that the bonds had been destroyed.

"Miner quite frankly admitted that he was the leader of the gang who held up and robbed the CPR train near Mission. I asked him if he had kept the bonds, and he said he had but he did not know their value or whether they were negotiable. He said they emptied the contents of the express safe into sacks, and did not look to see what they had secured until they were camped for the night. They did not light a fire. The only light they had was that given by matches which they burned. By the light of the matches they examined the contents of the sacks of plunder, and found the bonds. At first they thought they were American bonds, and if so they believed they could negotiate them. When they found they were Australian bonds with King Edward's name on them Miner concluded that it would be too dangerous to attempt to realize on them. He proposed to send them back, but his confederates would not agree. They feared it might get them into trouble. Finally they decided to bury them, and they did so, under a log within four miles of Linden (WA). Their rifles they buried near the bonds.

"Miner asked me to go and examine the bonds, and see if they were the bonds the detective wanted. He said I could ask for a leave of absence for four days, to go shooting. He would give me a map which would enable me to find the bonds. He had not had time to examine them himself. I was to return and tell him exactly what the bonds were, and he would then know just how to negotiate with the detective.

"At this time I told Miner to stop. I said to him I was too old in the service to be caught in a trap like that. I would be as guilty as he is if I failed to give up the bonds to the rightful owners when I found them. I advised him to go at once to the warden and tell him all about it. I told him he would be safer to trust the warden to do what is right than to make any bargain with detectives.

"I then went to the warden and told him what Miner had said about the detectives offering to secure his pardon if he would tell them where the bonds were. The warden said he knew about it, so I said no more.

"Miner said that if he was in an American prison he would be liberated within twenty-four hours with so powerful a corporation as the CPR at his back. He said such a company in any of the states would get him out in twenty-four hours in exchange for the bonds. He said he thought the lieutenant governor of the province could order his release the same as the governor of a state could. I told him it was different here, and that the minister of justice alone had the power to secure his pardon.

"I asked him how much money he had secured when he robbed the express car near Mission. He told me thirty to forty thousand dollars. I asked him what he had done with it, and he said he had a good many mouths to seal between the Fraser River and Montana, and that he had not much left. He said that it was all gone within nine months.

"Miner said he was alone with the lawyer and the detective. He said another man was with these two but not present at the interview. He said nobody was present but the lawyer and the detective. Neither the warden nor any other officer was present. He said they were coming back in a week. He wanted to know about the bonds before they came back. I heard later that the third man was Jake Terry, who was killed not long ago in a row at Sumas, Washington. Terry was supposed to be one of Miner's partners in the Mission robbery. He is said to have served a term in San Quentin penitentiary with Miner."[13]

The guard's recollections of the conversation he had with Miner and the events subsequent in the warden's office raise more questions than they answer, which was probably Miner's intent. Many complicated, romantic and interesting conspiracy theories can be assembled from pieces of this conversation, the earlier press reports that mention the bonds, and the reporting feeding frenzy that would take place in detailing Miner's future escape. However, the fact remains that there is no direct primary evidence of any kind existing for any bonds being on the train that September night, and much of Miner's conversation with McKenzie would be proven to be lies and half-truths under oath at a subsequent libel action.

Miner's perceived resignation to his fate and his new-found religious piety demanded that he have regular access to the prison chaplain. This ensured that his performances portraying contriteness and repentance were repeated to the warden and, after his confinement, to Acting Warden Bourke.

In mid-June of 1907, the Reverend A.D. Owen, the rector of St. Paul's Reformed Episcopal Church in New Westminster, relieved for the regular penitentiary chaplain Albert E. Vert while he was absent for a month on leave. On the first of July, the Reverend Owen came to the penitentiary to see the convict Bill Miner at the prisoner's request. Owen remembered the date well as it was Dominion Day, and the prison was closed up with no work gangs out. Before meeting with Miner, the clergyman saw Acting Warden Bourke, informing him that he had come to the prison to see Miner, and he and Bourke had a conversation about the convict.

Bourke told him that he felt sorry for the old man as he was getting old and sick. He asked Owen to inform Miner that he, the warden, was treating him as well as possible because of his advanced age and deteriorating health, and that he hoped the convict would do nothing to cause the warden to regret his lenience in some matters. Owen thought to himself that Bourke was acting in a commendable and compassionate manner towards the prisoner.

Owen waited for the prisoner in the library, and Miner was eventually escorted to him by a guard. During their time together, Owen told Miner of Deputy Warden Bourke's concerns, counselled him to behave and to show his appreciation for the liberties and kindnesses extended by the deputy warden.

"Bill," Owen asked outright, "are you going to try to get away?"

Miner, aware of Owen's confidentiality responsibilities, responded to the question truthfully. "I shall not stop here a moment longer than I can help."

"Would you hurt anyone to get away?"

"No, Mr. Owen, I would not hurt anyone to get away."

Owen then queried the convict on his past crimes.

Miner adopted his best socialistic stance and said, as if by rote, "I do not consider it a crime to lift money from rich corporations. It is not a crime, it is not a sin, it is neither immoral nor wrong. On the contrary, I feel it to be my duty to lift money from rich corporations and give it to the poor. Many a mortgage on a poor man's home have I helped to pay with money I have taken from corporations. I am what I am, and I have done what I have done, but I can look God and man in the face unashamed."[14][15]

After Owen had finished his session with Miner, he again saw Bourke and discussed the convict's state of mind. Bourke asked what Miner's response to his concerns was. Without betraying any confidences and advising Bourke of his responsibilities, Owen advised him that it would probably be best to not give Miner too much liberty.

"Bill is well worth watching; a wink is as good as a nod, Mr. Bourke."[16]

In this surreptitious manner, Owen obviously hoped to advise the deputy warden that Miner had not changed his ways and that escape was probably in his future plans. However, Bourke neglected to take the veiled words of advice from the chaplain, and preferred to trust his own instincts about the unoffending and pious old man.

As the summer of 1907 progressed, Miner's plans for escape accelerated. Suitable funds were required to bribe fellow convicts and to purchase needed materials for the escape. Miner's plans almost went awry when a letter to him that was smuggled into the prison containing money was intercepted by prison officials. A subsequent investigation was able to determine that clandestine communications between convicts and the outside world were common, but the prison officials were unable to determine methods or to whom the money was destined.[17]

In June, G.W. Dawson arrived in New Westminster and registered at the Guichon Hotel. Dawson had been the Inspector of Penitentiaries for the federal government in Ottawa for a number of years and was to review procedures and systems at the B.C. Penitentiary. The former Liberal Member of Parliament in Laurier's government expressed his satisfaction at the way things were being run at the institution in his report to the justice ministry in Ottawa.[18][19]

Active measures to put his escape into motion were taken by Miner when, in late July, he asked for and was given an interview with Acting Warden Bourke. He confided to Bourke that his health was breaking down and his feet, which had suffered from the application of the Oregon Boot when in San Quentin, were giving him trouble. He displayed swollen and sore feet to the prison administrator to prove his deteriorating condition. He asked that he be transferred outside to work in the brickyard so that the outside air might be able to extend its benefits to his condition. Before he left Bourke, he

Deputy Warden Bourke and his family. Which daughter in the photo is Catherine Bourke is not known. Courtesy of Anthony Martin Collection.

jokingly said to him, "Warden, I think sometimes I shall go crazy if I can't get a little tobacco." Knowing it was against prison regulations, Miner was attempting to show the Acting Warden that he was adhering to prison rules. Little did Bourke know but that Miner was able to get all the tobacco he could ever need by having it smuggled in through, under and over the prison walls.[20][21]

Miner supplemented his request to the Acting Warden by appealing to the Christian charity of Bourke's daughter Katherine, hoping her sympathy towards him would be passed along to her father. He complained to her about the trouble with his feet while he worked in the shoe shop and told her he thought it could be cleared up by working in the outside air, possibly the brickyard. Katherine passed on her concerns about the old man to her father, and at the beginning of August, Miner was transferred outside to work in the brickyard. It is not known how Miner was able to have feet in such poor condition, and then two weeks later display no infirmity whatsoever in making his way about. The next step in his eventual escape had been taken.[22][23]

In the brickyard Miner was given the relatively non-taxing job of repairing pallets used to stack bricks on. He was given a combination hammer and hatchet and happily worked alongside the other prisoners. Shorty Dunn, who had been working with outside construction crews all along, was working at building the new brick kilns under the direction of the guard Walsh. There is no record of any interaction between the two, and it was unlikely that Shorty would have initiated it as his previous relationship with Miner had been none too successful.[24]

The very day Miner was assigned to the brickyard, his friends on the outside were told just where he would be working. A letter informing them of the moves underway putting Miner's plans in motion had been left for them in the prison woodshed, and Miner's pals had covertly accessed the prison yard from outside and picked the message up at the pre-determined drop.[25]

On August 2ND, the prison guard Sampson was shortly to leave on his annual vacation. Normally in charge of the laundry, change room, bath and barbering activities, he had the opportunity to observe the convict Miner before taking his leave. He noticed that Miner had not had his hair cut for some time, and it was almost as long as it had been in photographs taken before Miner had been shaved after entering the prison just over a year previously. He thought to himself that it was at least as long as people wore it on the outside. Miner's moustache also seemed somewhat longer than the clipped one recommended by the prison doctor in December. He did not mention his observations to anyone.[26]

It appears likely that Miner might have had a number of fallback plans underway if one should be compromised. On August 5TH, a stranger rode into Vancouver and was put up in a good hotel where Miner was known to have many friends and admirers. During his short stay, he let it be known to select individuals that $5,000 was available to anyone that helped him in getting his friend Miner out of the penitentiary. This was the equivalent of five years wages to an ordinary working man and would have been a tempting offer. The stranger was believed to have left town the next day, and his identity remained a mystery.[27]

Despite the precautions for secrecy taken by Miner and his compatriots, both inside and out, the total prison convict population was well aware of the upcoming escape attempt days before it took place. The prison administration was completely unaware of any impending escape plans, and conditions and security precautions continued as normal.[28]

On the night of August 7TH as the prisoners were locked away in their cells, shadowy figures scaled the west outer fence and confronted the new board fence directly behind the brickyard machinery building. Confident from the success of past entries and prisoner reports that no sentries were posted at night, the figures moved quickly and efficiently. At the wooden barrier, they stooped to the ground, and with shovels brought with them, they scooped out a hole under the fence large enough to pass a man through. Because the fence penetrated into the soil six to ten inches, the men could not access far into the inner side of the fence, but that portion directly under the fence was removed. Enough of the rest of the opening to pass a man through could easily be excavated in a few minutes. They covered the opening on their side with boards, dirt and handfuls of grass and spread the excavated materials about so it would be inconspicuous to a glancing eye. Then they scaled the outer fence again and faded into the gloom to the west.[29] [30] [31]

XXIII

THE ESCAPE

THE BRICKYARD OF THE B.C. PENITENTIARY was considered a model of enlightened prison administration. Surrounded by a twelve foot fence erected to ensure security for the activities, the yard was spread about with buildings, drying racks and machinery. The prisoners were trained and put to work making the rust red bricks with "B.C.P." stamped on them to provide building materials for future building expansion. The prison administration was fond of telling the public and the press that, as well as cutting construction costs prisoners acquired valuable training and work ethics, thereby better preparing them for the outside world after their sentences were served.

On 8 August 1907, the convicts assigned to the brickyard were performing their regularly assigned duties under the eyes of three guards. The prisoners were confined to their areas of responsibility and were not supposed to wander freely through the yard. However, as years had passed since the brickyard was started and no security incidents had taken place, discipline was allowed to relax. Shorty Dunn was with the crew assembling the new wood-fired brick kiln, and Miner was working with his hatchet at the pile of broken pallets, repairing those that had been damaged. The strongest prisoners worked with wheelbarrows moving sand, cement, clay and wet bricks. Another crew loaded the clay for the bricks into the pug mill to prepare it for moulding. A gang worked at firing the old kiln with wood, drying the wet bricks on racks, and then baking the bricks. A few wheeled the cooled, baked bricks to the lines of pallets and stacked them neatly. The long rows of bricks drying on the pallets

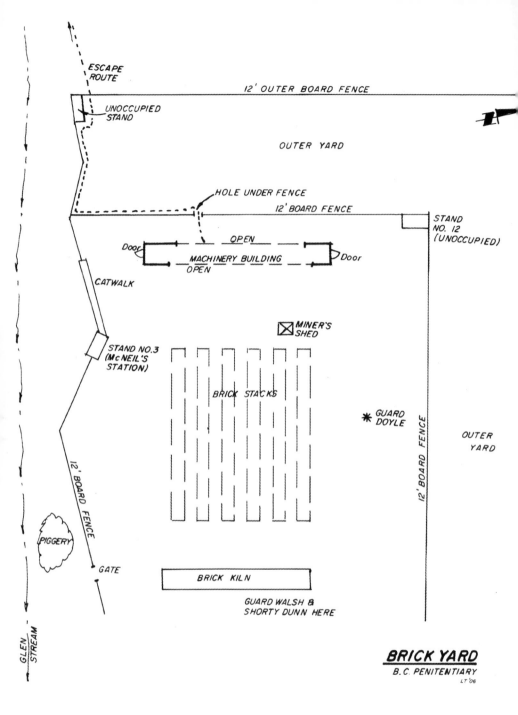

ESCAPE
ROUTE

12' OUTER BOARD FENCE

UNOCCUPIED
STAND

OUTER YARD

HOLE UNDER FENCE

12' BOARD FENCE

STAND
NO. 12
(UNOCCUPIED)

OPEN

Door

MACHINERY BUILDING

Door

OPEN

CATWALK

MINER'S
SHED

STAND NO.3
(McNEIL'S
STATION)

BRICK STACKS

GUARD
DOYLE

OUTER
YARD

12' BOARD FENCE

12' BOARD FENCE

PIGGERY

GATE

BRICK KILN

GUARD WALSH &
SHORTY DUNN HERE

GLEN STREAM

BRICK YARD
B.C. PENITENTIARY
LT '06

Detail of Brickyard and Miner's escape route, 8 August 1907 were higher than a man's head, and convicts could easily duck down out of site of the guards between the rows. The convict Thomas Young piled wood to fire the old kiln close to Guard Stand #3. In Guard Stand #3 above where Young was working was guard J. McNeil, a thirteen year employee.[1]

Guard McNeil had a number of duties that he was charged with undertaking on Guard Stand #3 that day. He had been assigned to the stand fourteen feet above the yard three months previously. His primary duty was to keep his eye on the twenty-seven convicts working in the brickyard, and that morning he had noted Miner working around the broken pallets. Although McNeil had not been instructed to keep a close eye on Miner, he did know that the convict was considered "a dangerous man and a clever one, a man of nerve and resource."[2]

The duties of the guards on the walls, in the stands and patrolling the yards were to observe the actions of the convicts on a continual basis. They were issued instructions on how to undertake their assigned duties by Acting Warden Bourke, and they were to adhere to those rules without fail. In the event of an incident or an attempt to escape, the guards were under no specific orders to shoot to kill. They were told that they were to shoot with intent to wound or maim first, and if the prisoner refused to halt, they were then ordered to shoot to kill.[3]

To the south of his Guard Stand, outside the wall and close to the ravine, Guard McNeil was to periodically give a visual check to the area around the prison's piggery and the gate leading to it. It was through this gate where the prison cows and horses were led out every morning by a trusted convict to graze in the ravine and then returned to the yard and the stables before evening. From his stand, which was about fifteen feet long, he was to watch the gate where kitchen refuse was removed by convicts and keep an eye on Guard Stand #2, as well as the fence between Guard Stand #3 and Stand #2. Lastly, and most importantly, he was to regularly patrol the 100 foot long walkway along the top of the fence to the west of his stand. This would enable him to see to the unmanned Guard Stand #12 to the north, behind the machinery building and including the rest of the west wall stretching to the west of the prison yard. When he did patrol out to the end of the walkway, he could see into the outer prison yard west of the new board fence and also enclosed by the high wooden fence. Only when he was at the extreme west end of his catwalk could he have seen where the hole had been dug if the planks, dirt and grass covering it did not disguise it so well.[4]

McNeil and the convict Young were familiar with each other, and each was aware of the other's underground activities in the prison culture. It was after the noon meal and the two talked easily with one another as no one was near where they were working. McNeil had a view over the whole brickyard area, and when he walked his catwalk to the west, he could see the fence behind the machinery building and the rest of the south wall as it formed the barrier to meet the west wall. Young, however, had his own duties with McNeil that day, and they didn't just involve piling wood at the woodpile below the guard's Stand. He did his best to interest the guard in his conversation so as to concentrate his attention away from the north end of the yard and the machinery building.[5]

McNeil had, in the past, smuggled items into the prison for Young. In return for an I.O.U for $10, McNeil had just recently brought in for the convict some tobacco, a pipe and some fruit. That afternoon they talked idly of nothing of real importance, and Young could easily attend to his wood piling duties while talking to McNeil. They talked about their mutual love for horses, when Young expected to be released, and the convict's hopes of acquiring a "Ticket of Leave." "Tickets of Leave" were granted to those prisoners who had exemplary behaviour while in prison and who had friends and relatives on the outside who would vouch for their good conduct. McNeil noted to Young that Bill Miner would probably have paid a great deal to have a Ticket of Leave granted to him. They laughed together at the thought.[6]

The convict and the guard continued to banter back and forth to each other for about two hours. Young was a secret informer in the prison hierarchy, and today he related to McNeil how he had heard that some of the convicts were planning to manufacture duplicate keys for an escape, but McNeil scoffed at him and treated the information as just idle and wishful thinking on the part of the convicts involved. He assured Young that the convicts would be severely taxed to determine how the locking systems and procedures operated in the prison.[7]

With that, McNeil's conversation with the prison informant took on a more serious tone and content. McNeil adopted a stern attitude and spoke in a low but threatening tone to Young. With periodic glances over toward the pallets of bricks and the men working in the brickyard, McNeil quietly warned Young that he had heard that Acting Warden Bourke had discretely called him to his office for an unscheduled interview in the past few days. McNeil looked Young straight in the eye and said that if Bill Miner had been the subject of discussion, Young had better keep his mouth shut. Shaken, Young took the warning seriously as Miner had told him previously that he had one of the guards on his side and that the guard would help him to escape as far as he dared without it becoming obvious. While Miner did not mention a name to Young at the time, the informant understood him to mean that it was McNeil that would be assisting him to escape.[8]

During the time the conversation between the guard and the convict took place, McNeil would periodically pace to the end of the fifteen foot stand, but since the lunch hour had ended, he had not walked the thirty paces along the gangway at the top of the fence heading west. Most of the time McNeil spent leaning his arms on the rail of the stand, his hips cocked, and one knee bent. His rifle was leaning beside him as he carried on his talk with convict Young. His back was toward the south and west fences and the area behind the machinery building. McNeil periodically glanced at the main prison building in the distance and the grey Fraser silently flowing by on the other side of the CP railway tracks.[9]

The interior of the machinery building where the pug mill was located was unobserved by the guards much of the time. While the south and north exposures were open to allow direct access to the pug mill, the old kiln and furnace, walls and other obstructions enabled the convicts to watch Instructor Doyle in the yard, Guard Walsh by the new kiln, and Guard McNeil in his stand. Convicts passed in and out of the machinery building during the normal course of their work, and most of the activities undertaken in there were not readily seen by any of the guards. A door in the wall of the south end of the building was always left open, and a convict standing back in the shadows inside the building could watch the guard in Stand #3 and warn anyone working at the hole under the fence directly behind the machinery building.[10]

Instructor and guard James Doyle had overall responsibility for supervising the prisoners working in the brickyard. "The convicts were trained by Doyle to temper the brick clay, mould the brick, air dry them, build a kiln and to burn the bricks in the kiln to harden them." Miner was directed by Doyle to repair the wooden pallets upon which the clay bricks were air dried. Miner was sitting by himself under a shed in full view of Stand #3, about midway between the machinery building and the drying racks. At about 3:00 P.M., instructor Doyle walked down the north side of the yard to the kiln, passing the prisoner Clark who was wheeling broken pallets from the drying racks to where Bill Miner was repairing them. At the kiln, Doyle stopped to show the convicts working there under Guard Walsh's direction how to place the bricks in one of the fire arches.[11]

During the few days he had spent working in the brickyard, Miner had been busy with his getaway plans. He quickly was able to identify the convicts he needed to recruit to assist him in his escape. The ones committed to his endeavour were all relatively short-time convicts, and none had any distinguishing characteristics or special skills. One common trait they enjoyed together was the respect and admiration they held for the old lifer who held such status in prison society, told so many interesting stories, and was so knowledgeable about prison life. Bank and train robbers held the highest status of all prisoners in the penitentiary, and Miner used this advantage to his own benefit. He would use his partners to undertake the tasks required to initiate his escape, then after success had been realized, abandon them to their own devices. With the exception of Miner, all the men were close shaved with hair cut close to their heads. Miner sported the fine beginnings of his trademark moustache and a good crop of grey hair, thanks to his planning efforts over many months. He wore a wide brimmed straw hat when he worked in the brickyard, stating that it was to keep the sun and rain off him, but it also served the added advantage that it covered his growing hair from prying eyes. At this time he was described as "of slight build, tall and straight, sharp featured and grey hair." Miner had earned 49.5 days remission in his sentence for good behaviour.[12] [13]

Albert F. McCluskey, alias Angus Grey and alias Frank Mull, was the first of four who would join Miner in the escape. He was a petty thief from Vancouver who was serving four concurrent terms of seven years each for stealing and shoplifting. He had served four years. He had a lengthy record, and in his last caper he had broken into a store and been confronted with a night watchman with a revolver for his troubles. The twenty-seven year old McCluskey was described as "a man of medium build, with dark complexion and a sour expression of face." At the time of the escape he had a clean record at the prison and had earned 110.5 days remission of his sentence.[14] [15]

John W. Clark was a twenty year-old ex-policeman who had served eight months of a three year sentence for passing bad checks in Nanaimo and had earned 7 days off his sentence for good behaviour. He had previously violated Prison Rule #1 in December of 1906 and had served a sentence of twenty-one meals consisting of bread and water. He was about five feet ten inches tall, of slight build, fair hair and a light complexion.[16] [17]

Convict John Woods had been sentenced to three years for theft in Victoria. He had served one year of his sentence and was "of stout build, about five feet nine in height and of dark complexion." In December of 1906 he had been served five meals of bread and water for throwing one meal and dish down his latrine. Thirty years of age, he had only earned 9 days remission since his previous default. Woods had the added distinction of being described as a man who would not hesitate to kill someone and would "stoop low enough to rob a woman or child." The local New Westminster Columbian noted that this was in direct contrast to Bill Miner, who "would never think of doing such an act."[18]

The scene had been set, and Miner and his new-found partners were ready to make their moves. Miner had unobtrusively made his way back and forth from his little pallet repair shed to the machinery building all morning to confer with his three temporary associates and direct the planned escape. Other convicts were assigned to their places and responsibilities for watching the three guards. McCluskey, Clark and Wood were working at the rear of the machinery building around the pug mill and close to the fence. Picks and shovels were close at hand.[19]

Eyes watched the guard McNeil as he leaned on the railing, talking to Young. Even if he had stood up and walked to the end of his stand, he wouldn't have been able to see the spot which had been dug out the night before. If he did venture out on the catwalk, his view would have been obstructed by the machinery building itself, the old kiln, the furnace and the smokestack.[20]

Guard Walsh's attention was consumed by the activities of the six men assigned to him and the erection of the new kiln. Two of the men were lifers, including Shorty Dunn. Shorty knew what was going to go down that day, but did not take part in any way.[21]

At the pug mill, the convict Campbell was in charge of the machinery, and that afternoon the mill equipment had been shut down for a short period for maintenance. The convicts Woods and McCluskey were assisting Campbell, cleaning the machinery and repairing drive belts. The convict Clark helped them at times and also wheeled broken pallets to Miner sitting in his little shed.[22]

Throughout the early part of the afternoon as spotters watched the guards, McCluskey, spelled off by Woods, took a shovel and started enlarging the hole under the fence. Careful to do only a few shovels at a time, the convicts paid close attention to the habits of the guards. When the two were done, they had excavated a hole that went down under the fence, below where it projected down into the surrounding soil. It was about eighteen inches wide and two feet deep. In length it probably ran to four feet. After they were satisfied, the hole was covered with pallet planks, which in turn were covered with soil and grass to disguise it. Everything was ready for the signal to go.[23]

Clark was wheeling pallets over to Miner's work station. Miner had left his work station on the pretext of having his axe sharpened at the machinery building. Convict Campbell took the axe and proceeded to work on it with a stone. Miner conferred quietly with McCluskey and Woods. After his axe was sharpened, Miner went back to his pallets and Woods was sent to speak to Guard Doyle and tell him that some direction was needed at the new kiln. The placing of bricks in the fire arches required some skill, and the request for assistance would effectively remove Doyle and Walsh from observing the actions behind the pug mill section of the machinery building. When Woods returned to the pug mill area, he brought Clark with him. Miner's three partners arranged themselves around the pug mill, out of sight from Doyle, Walsh and McNeil.[24]

The guard Doyle started moving from Miner's pallet repair area towards the kiln at about 3:00 P.M. He walked slowly down the east side of the yard towards the machinery building. Miner, pretending to use his axe on his pallets, watched Doyle and McNeil closely. In his stand, McNeil alternately stood comfortably, leaning his arms on the rail while talking to Young, or strolled very slowly to the other end of the stand. He did not once attempt to walk on the catwalk. Everything was in readiness, and the convicts waited for Miner's signal.[25]

Outside the west fence of the prison, a solitary figure made its way on a cow trail through the bush. The figure was clothed in a nun's habit and appeared to be carrying a bundle of men's clothing. The bundle was cached at the base of a tall burnt out snag near the corner of Cumberland and Eighth Avenue. The figure continued on and was lost in the dense vegetation.[26]

In the brickyard, the late afternoon of a warm summer seemed quiet and lazy, waiting for the end of a normal shift. It was approaching four o'clock. Miner looked from McNeil in his stand to Doyle and Walsh at the kiln. Shorty Dunn was watching him and the other three from the far end of the yard, but he gave no sign of assistance or of joining them. The three convicts' eyes were glued to Miner's figure, he gave them a signal, and they started moving toward the fence. They quickly drew back the camouflage, and Woods quickly darted down the hole and up the other side. Clark followed him, and McCluskey turned towards Miner at his station and softly called for him to come, motioning with his arm. Miner saw him, and nonchalantly made his way towards the machinery building, carrying his hatchet. Down through the hole went Miner, quickly followed by McCluskey. The convicts watching the guards gave the escapees the all clear, and they made their way towards the west fence.[27]

The four escaping convicts were still not free of their prison. They quickly made their way directly south along the fence until they came to the south wall. They turned and headed west towards the southwest corner of the outside yard. Only a few yards from the first west boundary fence that they had gone under was a second wooden wall about twelve feet high. In the corner was an unoccupied guard stand and a ladder leaning against the stand that was used to access the tower. The ladder was chained to the stand, and McCluskey took Miner's hatchet and smashed the lock off. They placed the ladder against the outside wall and had no difficulty in scaling it and jumping down on the other side. Miner was the last over, and they broke his fall as he dropped down. Ahead of them a few blocks were the city limits of New Westminster, and after they crossed a few wagon roads, miles of bush and forest extended almost all the way to Burrard Inlet.[28]

As the convicts quickly made their way northwest and away from the prison, they skirted the ravine that held Glen Stream. The weather had been warm, and two young boys were splashing and wading and enjoying themselves in the cool water. Fifteen year old Hamilton Sclater with his thirteen year old brother James were playing in the creek at the bottom of the ravine near the brick clay pit close to the Glen bridge. Looking up to the top edge of the ravine, Hamilton Sclater saw four men dressed in convict's clothes walking quickly along the level ground beside the drop-off and towards

1930s aerial photo looking west of B.C. Penitentiary showing location of Glen Stream on the left, Cumberland Street on the right and Sixth Avenue and Glen Bridge in the background. COURTESY OF B.C. ARCHIVES.

Sixth Avenue. The moment he saw the escaped prisoners, Hamilton recognized a serious situation. He hurriedly put his boots on. He knew something critical had happened, and he needed to see what was going on.[29]

Further along, Mrs. Milton and her children, who lived on Sixth Avenue, saw four men running down the road shortly after four o'clock. Her children called her attention to them as in their convict clothing they seemed to be wearing funny looking clothes and they were travelling so fast.[30]

Miner and his three companions travelled together as far as where they crossed Thorn Road, north of Gunn Road. They were less than a mile from the penitentiary and heading towards Gunn's milk ranch on Thorne Road when Miner bid his partners goodbye and left them to make their own way. He travelled on alone and any tales or reports of his travels in British Columbia after leaving his partners are pure speculation. His escape was so successful that it appeared as if he had disappeared into thin air, frustrating Canadian law enforcement and the politicians in Laurier's government for the next two years. No reliable report of him surfacing in British Columbia has ever came forward.[31][32]

Back inside the penitentiary, everything was proceeding as normal, with the exception of some flurry of activity near the fence behind the machinery building. After the prisoners had escaped, some of those convicts left behind started to fill the hole under the fence with broken brick, debris and soil. The guard Doyle, after contributing his expertise to Walsh and the crew building the kiln, walked back to where his normal station was near Miner's pallet shed. After about six minutes had passed, he started to feel that something was wrong. Miner had not returned to his work station, and it seemed other prisoners were also missing. With a sudden awful realization, he ran over to McNeil's stand and shouted at him that some prisoners seemed to have escaped. He told McNeil to sound the alarm, and he checked around the back of the machinery building. He soon saw the signs of their escape, but could not extract the debris from the hole under the fence with his bare hands. He ran back to McNeil and told him he needed the key for the gate in the west fence. He told McNeil to fire two shots as an alarm that there had been an escape, and then quickly ran back to the gate. He unlocked the gate and started running across the outside yard towards the outside perimeter fence. He saw the ladder leaning against the wall, and climbed up and over to continue his pursuit across the field. As he cleared the fence, two shots sounded through the still summer air. McNeil seemed to have taken his time in announcing news of the escape.[33]

As James Sclater was struggling to tug his boots onto his wet feet, he heard two shots fired from the direction of the prison. He hurriedly followed his brother Hamilton who was also running up the side of the ravine to where the convicts had passed. When the two brothers reached the top of the ravine, they were met by the agitated and panting prison guard Doyle. Doyle said he was in hot pursuit of the escapees, who at the moment were nowhere in sight. The boys told Doyle that the convicts had passed not five minutes before he arrived, and Doyle quickly left them and ran across the field towards Sixth Avenue.[34]

New Westminster Police Constable Grey was on a picnic with his wife and family on the Glen Bridge that afternoon, and upon hearing two shots from the direction of the prison, he looked up to see instructor Doyle coming over the fence on the ladder and crossing the field in the corner between Sixth and Cumberland Avenues. He saw him stop and talk to the two boys at the edge of the ravine, and when Doyle ran towards Sixth Avenue, Grey met him there. Doyle hurriedly explained about the prison break, and Grey informed him that he had been on or near the bridge all afternoon. While they were talking, the two ton brass prison bell sounded, announcing a prison break. Grey told Doyle that he had seen no one pass by in his direction, and that the prisoners had probably seen him and kept to the north to avoid him. Grey watched Doyle return towards the prison, and then he looked for tracks between the bridge and Cumberland Avenue, but found none.[35]

When Doyle left the two Sclater boys, they watched him run across the field towards Sixth Avenue. They started walking to their home on Cumberland for their supper, and at about 4:20 P.M., they heard the huge prison bell ring, giving the general alarm announcing the prison breakout.

Doyle quickly made his way back to the prison to assist in putting a search party together. There he found that his fellow guards had followed the established procedures. They had assembled the convicts, marched them into their cells, and put the penitentiary in lockdown mode. Doyle, with some of his fellow guards, examined the hole dug under the fence, and all were agreed that as much as possible had been dug from outside. The guards then all reported to Acting Warden Bourke for assignment in pursuit of the four convicts.[36]

XXIV

PURSUIT OF THE CONVICTS

IMMEDIATELY HE HEARD OF THE PRISON BREAK, Acting Warden Bourke swung into action. He had twenty-one years of experience behind him in the administration of prisons, and this was not the first escape he had had to deal with. Past prison breaks under his tenure had resulted in the eventual recapture of every convict that it had been his experience to pursue.

Directly the convicts had been marched back into their cells after the break for freedom of Miner and his three compatriots, Bourke issued orders that all prisoners were to remain locked in their cells for a period of at least one week or until the escapees were captured, whichever came first.[1]

Later, having the opportunity to contemplate the actual facts of the escape as they became obvious, Bourke changed his tune to lengthen the period of lockdown the convicts would suffer.

"Until the men are caught we'll keep the prison closed, and I don't care how much the industries may suffer. I figure that these prisoners are given into our keeping to expiate their crimes, and they should be made to do it. They will, if we have anything to say."[2]

Bourke "kept the wires hot giving descriptions of the convicts to the police departments of all the cities and towns," including Vancouver, Mission, Steveston and Blaine and all surrounding points, asking them to be on the lookout for the convicts. He also telegraphed the Department of Justice in Ottawa advising them of the escape.[3]

```
Canadian Pacific Railway Company's Telegraph
New Westminster, B.C., Aug.8.1907


Inspector of Penitentiaries, Ottawa.


Four convicts escaped from Brickyard this
afternoon.


D.D. Bourke
7:53 p.m.[4]
```

Hoping that the convicts would only be gone a short time, Bourke just could not at that moment bring himself to add to the officials in Ottawa that the notorious train robber Bill Miner, sentenced to life imprisonment only just a over a year previously, was included in the four. Inspector of Penitentiaries G.W. Dawson, who had inspected the more than adequate administration of the penitentiary only a month before, would not receive the telegrams for many days as he was on holiday. The delay would exacerbate Acting Warden Bourke's mounting problems and the criticisms of his actions.

Prison guard Walsh was escorting his and guard Doyle's convicts from the brickyard to the main prison building after the escape when he heard the two shots being fired by McNeil. As he and his crew continued on their way, they ran into Deputy Acting Warden Stewart. Walsh asked Stewart if he would take Doyle's convicts back to their cells for him. Stewart agreed, and told Walsh to continue on and take his own crew back to their cells. On the way to lock up his six man crew, including Shorty Dunn, Walsh ran into the guard Cameron, and he told Cameron to ring the penitentiary's huge brass bell to announce the escape and then to advise Acting Warden Bourke of the escape.[5]

Immediately upon hearing the prison alarm bell stridently clamouring out the news of the break-out, the rest of the guards and instructors escorted their convict crews back to the main prison building where the convicts were all locked up in their cells. Individually the staff reported to Acting Warden Bourke, and he and Acting Deputy Warden Stewart allocated the search responsibilities to the guards. Each drew a rifle from the armaments store and quickly left to follow up on the pursuit of the escapees. Most were immediately dispatched to the area behind and to the north of the prison. The guards were instructed to concentrate on the area north and west of Sapperton. Some were mounted on prison horses, and others had taken the prison horse and rig. They were directed to go to the Thorne Road and Cumberland Street area and fan out from there, making inquiries as they went along. They searched around the Glen Bridge, along Sixth, Eighth and Tenth Avenues and as far back as Twelfth and Thirteenth Avenues, the areas around the city reservoirs and the Sapperton Cemetery, Sherbrooke Street and Columbia Street, Distillery Road and Pitt River Road. The guards found the underbrush that had grown up since the area had been logged to be so dense as to make it impossible to see any tracks or sign even if they stumbled across it. By 8:00 P.M. no progress had been made in apprehending the convicts, and the disappointed searchers were ordered to return to the prison for further orders.[6]

Bourke and Stewart, now with seventeen penitentiary guards and instructors at hand, widened the net. They realized that enough time had passed to enable the convicts to put more distance between them and their former prison. The guard Disney was allocated responsibility for operating the gasoline powered government launch, the "Viking." By 7:00 P.M., he and guard George McKenzie had checked out the bridges at Eburne, then motored up the river to past New Westminster. They then drifted down the Fraser again with the current, all the while watching and searching the shoreline. After reaching the Eburne bridges again, they returned to the penitentiary by 9:00 P.M.[7]

Other guards were dispatched in the evening throughout the area. The Burnett sawmill was visited, and the foreman requested to instruct his night watchman to remove all the oars and oarlocks from any boats near the mill. Railway bridges up and down the

Fraser would have guards stationed on them twenty-four hours a day throughout the search, as would the major road crossings. At Port Moody, guards patrolled the roads and railroad all night. Guards Atkins and Henderson took the short line train to Westminster Junction and walked down the tracks in the dusk to patrol the Pitt River Bridge all night.[8]

The harried and concerned Deputy Warden Bourke had taken all the steps he could and thought necessary to intercept and capture the escaped convicts. He had used the "telephone, telegraph, pigeon post, horses and steamer" to throw a cordon of searchers around "the entire country between the Fraser River, the Pitt River, Westminster Junction, Burrard Inlet, Central Park and Lulu Island. Chief Constable Spain of the Provincial Police joined forces with the Warden and over twenty sentries and patrol men" were stationed throughout the country.[9]

New Westminster's senior Provincial Police representatives were Chief Constable Colin Campbell and Constable Stanley Spain. Both had spent weeks chasing the elusive Bill Miner after the Mission Junction train robbery, with no success. The country south of the Fraser River, west to Vancouver and east to Hope, and into Washington state had seen both constables expending much time, energy and anxiety to catch the train robbers, all to no avail. In June of 1906 they had both eagerly met the train at Westminster Junction to see for themselves what the elderly bandit looked like, and then they had escorted the party to the Sapperton Depot. They both watched as the three train robbers and the horse thief entered the buggies for the short ride to the penitentiary, thinking that this would be the last they would see of the American bandit. Now, just over a year later, their days would be consumed with chasing the same felon all over again.

Chief Constable Campbell had been eagerly anticipating an emergency situation to make use of the services of a local bloodhound and its trainer, Bradford Nanton of Vancouver. Despite Hussey's reluctance to utilize the animals, the rule was initiated that under special circumstances they might be employed. As soon as Campbell

B.C. Penitentiary Guards and officials some time after the prison break. Many of the individuals in this photograph took part in the pursuit of Bill Miner and his confederates. Instructor George McKenzie is second from the left in the front row, and Instructor James Doyle is third from the left in the third row, slightly behind the others in that row. Deputy Warden F. Stewart is in the officer's cap at the right of the last row. Warden J.C. Brown, fourth from the right in the front row, replaced the late Warden Whyte and Acting Warden Bourke.

<small>Courtesy of Anthony Martin Collection.</small>

received the call from Bourke about the prison breakout, he assigned Constable Spain that evening to escort the hound and handler to the penitentiary.[10]

When Campbell and Spain, the handler and his hound arrived at the prison, they were met by some prison guards. The guards escorted the party to the brickyard, where the hound was given Miner's scent from the straw hat he had left behind. Immediately the hound picked up the scent in the brickyard, and after circling the compound a few times, it tracked the scent to the hole under the fence.

Moving into the outer yard, the hound picked up the scent again which led the party to the door in the perimeter wooden wall. Here it was determined by the dog's actions that Miner had tried the latch on the door before leaning the ladder on the fence and clambering over. The hound sat down and whined at the base of the ladder that was still leaning against the wall. Outside the prison walls, the dog led them alongside the ravine that held Glen Stream and into the brush to the north. As it was too dark to be thrashing about in the thick underbrush and risking destroying the scent, the handler and his hound, Spain and the guards called off the search until daylight.[11]

Daybreak at 5:30 A.M. found the previous night's bloodhound party joined by two newspaper reporters. The guards included Keeper W.A. Patchell, Instructor Doyle and guards Devine and McLure. Years later Patchell would become the first warden of the B.C. Penitentiary to be promoted from the ranks. The handler led the hound to where they halted the search in the dark the previous night, and again presented the animal with Miner's scent. The trail was picked up once more, and the party was led through the brush about a mile and a half from the penitentiary wall. The dog was able to show the guards and the trackers that Miner had separated from the other convicts at a location close to Thorne Road and the city boundary. Here the dog inexplicably seemed to have a change of heart, and the newspaper reporter described the animal's antics in a scathing paragraph.

"The bloodhound chase was a total failure, the animal seemingly being out of whack, and its owner out of sorts. The animal, a highly bred English hound, seemed to be primed for work, but after a few whiffs of the damp alfalfa, he apparently lost courage, and could not pick up the scent. He ... sulked fearfully Friday morning."[12]

Patchell also described the hound as "sulky," and after the searchers had wandered through the brush for two hours, he reported that the seemingly moody and sensitive animal refused to work any more. The fruitless search with the dubious aid of the emotionally challenged canine and his handler was abruptly terminated.[13]

Colin Campbell's expectations that the hound would be able to enhance the search efforts proved groundless, and it was to be some time before the Chief Constable, later to inherit Superintendent Hussey's mantle, would again cast his eyes towards a dog to aid in the apprehension of criminals.

FRIDAY, 9 AUGUST 1907

Searching began early the day after the escape for all the guards and constables. Some were dispatched to their locations by 4:00 A.M. Reports that the convict McCluskey had been spotted at the Gladstone Hotel in South Vancouver raised a brief flurry of excitement. Dressed in civilian clothes, he had apparently asked for a drink even though he had no money. Guards Devine and Doyle were dispatched to check out the rumour. Attorney General Bowser issued orders to Hussey and the Provincial Police "to do all within their powers to recapture the convicts." Chief Constable Campbell was short of officers for the New Westminster jurisdiction, so he used an existing list to hire special constables from the general population. With penitentiary guards and under the direction of Constable Spain, the special constables were distributed throughout the Lower Mainland to patrol roads and railway lines.[14]

The penitentiary guards were working on little sleep, but in the morning morale was good and expectations high that their searches would be successful. The government launch was working throughout the day and night, ferrying guards to railway bridge crossings and ferry crossings. The search difficulty was exacerbated by the many logging camps and railway building camps on both sides of the Fraser. The searchers knew that if a man wished to, he could hide in one of those locations as even the camp occupants wouldn't know a stranger was in their midst. That night, guards were posted on the Eburne Bridges, the Diamond Crossing on the V.W. and Y and B.C.E railways. The Pitt River Bridge and the Fraser River Bridge would be patrolled every night as long as the search was underway. The guards were starting to become somewhat troubled and feeling a bit isolated as during their inquiries with the general population, they were consistently told direct to their faces that the majority wanted Bill Miner's escape to be successful. The predominant reaction experienced by the guards was that no one was about to inform the authorities if they should see Miner passing through their backyard, but would assist him on his way.[15]

Bourke wanted to help counteract the support from the public that the former train robber was experiencing by requesting a reward be issued for the apprehension of the escapees.

Canadian Pacific Railway Company's Telegraph
New Westminster, B.C., Aug. 9, 1907

George Dawson, Via Ottawa,
Inspector of Pens, Kingston.

Will I offer reward if so how much bill miner among those gone.

D.D. Bourke
Acting Warden
8:12 p.m.[16]

Bourke now realized that over twenty-four hours had passed since the escape, and the likelihood of quickly recapturing the convicts was becoming more remote as each hour passed. He had to swallow the bitter pill and finally brought himself to advise his superiors in Ottawa that the high profile Miner was among the escaped prisoners. He no doubt knew that his actions both before and after the escape would now be subjected to intense scrutiny and criticism, and the possibility of his termination loomed on the horizon. However, the personality of the Acting Warden was such that his subsequent actions would ensure the inevitability of his future replacement. His struggle to retain some modicum of his own professional and personal pride would embarrass him and his family, the federal penitentiary organization, and finally the government of the country.

In the evening of the first day after the escape, the morale of the guards started its slow deterioration when the acting warden suspended the guard McNeil pending an inquiry into the escape to be held by officials from Ottawa.

SATURDAY, 10 AUGUST 1907
The next day, Saturday, Bourke sent a terse wire to Ottawa.

Canadian Pacific Railway Company's Telegraph
New Westminster, B.C., Aug. 10, 1907

Inspector of Penitentiaries, Ottawa.

Suspended guard McNeil yesterday afternoon.

D.D. Bourke
Acting Warden
3:05 p.m.[17]

By now, thirty-five armed penitentiary guards, Provincial Police officers and special constables had been dispersed throughout the Lower Mainland in the hunt for the convicts. Six guards including Keeper Patchell were transported to Eburne by Disney on the Viking. Word had come to search headquarters at the penitentiary that Woods and Clark had been seen near Magee Station and had taken the road to Point Grey from there. They had begged some breakfast as they had no money, and an alert member of the public had phoned in their description. The guards stopped at the Indian Reserve on the North Arm and asked the residents to keep a watch out for the escapees and to keep an eye on their boats. They asked all the salmon canneries to remove their oars and oarlocks from twenty to thirty boats. They searched and made inquiries at Woodward's Landing and Steveston. They were discouraged to hear so many people wish that Bill Miner would successfully get away. The party spent the night in the rain patrolling the bridges at Eburne.[18]

Criticism of the way the guards had been dispatched had started to appear in press reports. Guards were described as being conspicuous in full uniform with prison issue topcoats and recognizable as representatives of the penitentiary to anyone with the least knowledge of recent events. They were easily spotted around Vancouver, Burnaby and New Westminster and "it could hardly be figured out what chances they posed of getting their men unless the hunted ones should decide to give themselves up and should walk right into their arms."[19]

Bourke and Stewart visited the terminally ill Warden Whyte as he lay in his sickbed to inform him of the escape. The head of the penitentiary staff was reported to have wept like a child upon hearing of the incident. He tried to leave his sickbed to re-assume his duties; however, his physician was called and was able to calm and persuade the dying man that he was in no condition to carry out his duties. Throughout that night he would call on his wife for news of the pursuit and repeatedly sent his son to the penitentiary over the next days to seek out news of their progress. Orders were issued that no further contact with penitentiary officials was to be entertained by the Warden as the news was too trying for him.[20]

SUNDAY, 11 AUGUST 1907

By Sunday the press furor was starting to die down, and the reporters moved on to more current events. The search for the escapees would continue until the 17TH of August, a full nine days after the event, before it was finally terminated. The search quadrants spread out to North Vancouver and around Burnaby Lake, Ladner's Landing and Port Guichon, English Bay and Point Grey, Westham Island and Port Moody, Woodward's Slough and the Great Northern "Y" at Port Kells. London's Landing and canneries as far as the Scottish Canadian

Cannery on the North Arm, Elgin, Mud Bay, Point Roberts and the bridge over the Nicomekl River all saw penitentiary guards and special constables visiting and patrolling in the vain hope that they might intercept the escaped criminals. The long nights of dark boredom and rain guarding bridges and crossings, and the indifference of the public to the capture of Miner, weighed the guards down, and by the time the exhausted penitentiary employees were finally called in, they too felt the capture of Miner a matter of indifference.

R.N.W.M.P. Staff Sergeant Wilson's comments to a Vancouver paper summed up the thoughts of many of the readers. From Calgary he stated that he "did not think Miner would be retaken owing to his having so many friends all through that section of the country."[21]

By a week after the escape, only nine penitentiary guards were sent out to man stations at the farthest lookout posts. Mounted Provincial Police Special Constables continued to patrol lightly forested areas in hopes of flushing out their quarry, while others on foot searched the heavily timbered tracts, but hope was rapidly fading. McCluskey's convict socks were found on Lulu Island with his penitentiary number, 142, marked on them. This caused some excitement which soon died down as all trace of him had vanished. Bourke had heard no word from Ottawa authorizing any reward, and this tardiness by the federal government added to the regular sense of abandonment that many already harboured. British Columbians would, as was commonly felt, be left to muddle through the best they could without the assistance of the senior government.[22]

A brief hustle of activity again fanned the dying embers of the search when it was reported that a farmer, George DeRoche, had reported sighting Miner east of Mission on Nicomen Island. The French-Canadian rancher stated that an elderly man, "tired and footsore," appeared at his door asking for food. He told the rancher that he worked for a logging camp and was looking for a stray horse. De Roche gave him a meal and described him as ravenous, and the old man disposed of one loaf of bread, three pounds of meat, five cups of coffee and one quart of strawberry preserves. The generous rancher heard nothing of the jailbreak until he came to New Westminster on

$500 Reward

The above reward will be paid for the arrest and detention of WILLIAM (Bill) MINER, alias Edwards, who escaped from the New Westminster Penitentiary, at New Westminster, British Columbia, on the 8th August, 1907, where he was serving a life sentence for train robbery.

DESCRIPTION:

Age 65 years; 138 pounds; 5 feet 8½ inches; dark complexion; brown eyes; grey hair; slight build; face spotted; tattoo base of left thumb, star and ballet girl right forearm; wrist joint-bones large; moles centre of breast, 1 under left breast, 1 on right shoulder, 1 on left shoulder-blade; discoloration left buttock; scars on left shin, right leg, inside, at knee, 2 on neck.

Communicate with

LT.-COL. A. P. SHERWOOD,

Commissioner Dominion Police,
Ottawa, Canada.

Monday the 16TH of August, and when he saw the pictures of Miner, he immediately recognized him as the sore footed old man he had fed almost a week earlier." Newspapers speculated that Miner then would probably have made his way south of Chilliwack and into the mountains towards the Similkameen. Despite the good rancher's positive description, it is much more likely that by that time Miner was well on his way over the mountains into the Similkameen in the company of old friends.[23]

Constable W.W. Lane was the Provincial Police officer in charge in Mission, and he, with a posse of Special Constables, rode east on horseback and conducted a thorough search around Nicomen and Nicomen Island. No trace of the elderly stranger was found, and the press speculated that Miner knew the country around that area very well, being familiar with all the trails and roads.[24]

Finally, after more than eight days had passed since the escape, the federal government got around to offering a reward for the capture of Miner. The other three convicts were conspicuous by the absence of reference to them in the reward circular. Over the signature of Lieutenant Colonel A.P. Sherwood, the Commissioner of the Dominion Police in Ottawa, photos of Miner shaven and unshaven were prominent with a detailed description of his scars, tattoos and other physical characteristics. The reward posters were sent to "all police departments of importance in the United States, Mexico, Canada, South America, South Africa and elsewhere and to all important police publications and private detective agencies." Criticism was immediately levelled at the federal government for the miserly amount it had offered for the bandit's capture. Five hundred dollars was considered woefully inadequate to entice any of Miner's friends to even contemplate giving him up to the authorities. The senior government would suffer continual criticism in the future over its lack of motivation in encouraging the capture of Miner. However, it was probably considered by the federal bureaucrats

Reward Poster eventually issued by the Dominion Police in Ottawa.
COURTESY OF ANTHONY MARTIN COLLECTION.

to be in Canada's and the government's best interests if Bill Miner were quickly forgotten about and that he would hopefully return to his former haunts in the United States. If that indeed was the government's rationale, they would be most upset to realize that the conniving bandit over the next few years would cause consternation at the highest levels of the Canadian government and severely impact Prime Minister Laurier and his ruling Liberal party.[25]

In his interview with a Winnipeg paper, R.N.W.M.P. Sergeant Wilson, never at a loss for words, made his thoughts known on the escape and the paltry reward offered. He pointed out that the convicts would certainly had to have had help from the outside to make such a successful escape, and the paltry reward of $500 certainly appeared to most that the government really wanted to be sure he was not recaptured. "The reward offered is not large enough to get him, as he has too many friends in B.C. Bill is one of the smoothest fellows you ever saw, when he's not robbing trains, always willing to spend his money, and making friends with women and children. He makes a point of never taking anything from a man who works for wages, but believes that corporations are not to be pitied, and has no compunction about taking a toll on them …. Only a few days before his escape he gave me an order for his automatic gun—and it was the wickedest-looking one I ever saw—saying he did not expect to have any more use for it."[26]

Bourke received telegrams and letters from across Canada and the United States requesting descriptions and photographs of the convicts, particularly Miner. The Assistant Commissioner of the R.N.W.M.P. in Dawson in the Yukon Territories, Provincial Police Chief Constable Campbell, the Chief of the Metropolitan Police Department in Butte, Montana, and Superintendent Ahern of the Pinkertons were included on the list.[27]

An intriguing letter causing some furrowing of brows and wild speculation in the warden's office was received on the 26TH of August. From a Mrs. A.E. Miner with a street address of a town in eastern Washington near Spokane, it was addressed to the Warden. In a very legible and fine hand, Mrs. Miner asked how old the escapee was and requested that the Warden's office send her his photo. "Where did he hail from?" she asked. "I would very much like to see his picture; hoping you will comply to my request." This letter lends one to believe that perhaps Bill Miner went on trips from the Similkameen to eastern Washington for more reasons than to visit soiled doves and to rob the Great Northern.[28]

The first glimmers of problems from Ottawa were starting to be felt by Acting Warden Bourke. He had conscientiously, he thought, ensured that his superiors were kept up to date and abreast of all events and activities since the escape. He would be somewhat concerned when he received a wire from Ottawa.

Canadian Pacific Railway Company's Telegraph
Ottawa, August 17/07

The Warden,
The Penitentiary,
New Westminster, B.C.

Anxiously awaiting detailed reports re
escape. When were
They forwarded?

Douglas Stewart
Collect[29]

Quickly Bourke responded to Stewart, the head of the penitentiary inspectors in Ottawa.

Canadian Pacific Railway Company's Telegraph
New Westminster, B.C., August 18 1907

Insprs of Penitentiary
Ottawa

Report re escape forwarded Monday
twelfth inst.

D.D. Bourke
Actg Warden
8:29[30]

Continuing to feel a nagging unease, Bourke attempted to thwart any further apprehension in the national capital by anticipating any possible communications foul-ups.

Canadian Pacific Railway Company's Telegraph
New Westminster, B.C., August 20th- 1907

Inspectors of Penitentiaries
Ottawa, Ont.

Have wired you on eighth re escape on ninth
re reward and re McNeil.
On seventeenth a reply have you received
these telegrams.

D.D. Bourke
Acting Warden[31]

Unfortunately for Acting Warden Bourke, his burden of problems was about to be considerably added to, and the whole question of the legitimacy of the Penitentiary Service was to be brought into question by an event farther up the Fraser Valley.

On the 21ST of August at nine in the evening, two First Nations convicts, spurred on by the success of Miner and his cohorts, made a break for freedom. They successfully made their escape from the woodcutting gang stationed at Wright's Island in the middle of Pitt Lake by breaking the lock with an axe and stealing the only boat available to the guards and convicts. The escapees planned their escape carefully and also took with them the homing pigeons which were the only means of communication from the camp to the outside world. Bourke would only find out the next morning, and he hastily dispatched his exhausted and demoralized guards to watch out for the convicts. This incident severely compromised Bourke's already questioned credibility and competence. The print media and his superiors in Ottawa would view this latest incident from differing points of view. The media could sense with delight future juicy headlines while the mandarins in Ottawa foresaw the need for a sacrificial head to roll.[32]

The press continued to play an important role in reporting to British Columbians the details of the escape and the attempted recapture of Miner and his three partners. Vivid reporting and insightful background investigations held readers spellbound, kept advertisers paying for their exposure, and virtually guaranteed sales increases surpassing those of former years. Bill Miner was a marketable media commodity that ensured profits and employment for newspaper owners, reporters, printers and delivery boys. Also, the lurid reporting of the press played a vital role in ensuring the story of Bill Miner would live on for years into the future as his supposed exploits captured the imagination of the readers.

The public readership had an inherent sympathy for Miner that had built up since his capture and trial in Kamloops the previous year. Every common worker and businessman had felt the boot of CPR freight rates on their necks, and the federal government in Ottawa was a nebulous entity that only represented the large metropolitan cities and big business corporations of central and eastern Canada. It was perceived as being just plain inefficient, ignorant and incompetent in its dealings with the West. The benefits of federalism were not any too visible to the ordinary British Columbian, and any potential champion that jousted with the CPR and the Canadian government had the public's support. If Miner could fleece some money off them, or thumb his nose at them and embarrass them, so much the better. The press, as it would do with many misfits and social outcasts in the future, fastened onto Miner and exploited the feelings of readers for financial gain and parochial and political self-interests. Fortunately, most future attempts to manipulate the readership would be thwarted by a discerning public, but not in the case of Bill Miner. Whether he deserved it or not, readers thought they saw a reflection of themselves in the indomitable spirit of the old man, and they snatched up copies of local and provincial newspapers across Western Canada. The reporters and editors rose to the occasion and penned prose not readily found in today's politically correct and legally inhibited dry purveyors of sanitized news.

The normally staid Victoria Colonist led off the admiring press coverage of the escaped train robber with the blatantly anti-establishment headline, "Miner's Escape Worthy The Man."

"Did you ever meet Bill either in his days of adversity or affluence? He is a smooth individual whose wits have been taxed to their capacity in order to permit him to mingle with men. He knows his business – that of the fellow who cares not whether honesty is proper or not, provided it yields him revenue." Little did the paper realize that its musings over Miner's motivations had probably exposed the most logical reasons for the old bandit's robbing ways.[33]

"Not the least remarkable feature of the escape is the sympathy being extended to the aged robber leader by the general public. Five out of six people you meet on the street in Vancouver, for instance, openly express the hope that Bill will get away and are not afraid of injuring the feelings of anyone when they declare the sincere wish that he will remain a free man for the rest of his life. Not only is this true in Vancouver and New Westminster, but it is particularly the fact ... in the Similkameen and Nicola districts, where Miner bought land and horse-traded back and forth for years between the occasions of his hold ups of the finest trains of the unfriendly railway companies."

A Vancouver man who had recently arrived in Vancouver from Spence's Bridge was quoted as saying, "Not only would nine-tenths of the people of the Nicola and Similkameen not betray Miner were he there, but they are proud of the fact that there is a wide open welcome for him, good at any time and under all circumstances, with what amounts to practical protection from the police. The people up there rejoice that he got away, and hope that he will succeed in eluding the police."[34]

He went on to tell the reporter that on Saturday afternoon, half the population of Spence's Bridge gathered around the CPR depot waiting for the late train. The impression he received from those gathered there was that if Bill Miner should show up in Spence's Bridge, he should have to go no further, for all assistance he required to elude the authorities would be offered to him. The paper went on to speculate that the reasons for this sympathy included Miner's advancing age and the cleverness of his exploits.[35]

The Vancouver daily newspaper "The World" was the first paper to report the escape the day it happened with a front page exclusive. It continued its escape coverage with some dramatic irony. The World was speculating, sometimes tongue in cheek, that Miner would not be caught.

"There is little doubt that Miner has got clear and is now working east along the flanks of the mountains, most likely taking the ease that becomes his age and quite prepared to do a month's summer camping until the chase shall have quieted down and time stalled the keenness of the officials."

In the same issue, the World contributed its part in ensuring the legend of Miner would continue through the years. "Perhaps the most peculiar feature of the escape is the very general sympathy expressed with Miner and the large number of people who proclaim their wish to see the old highwayman get off altogether. The abstract principle that life and property must be safe if a country is to qualify for a claim to high civilization does not affect these people half so much as the plea that Miner always preyed on large corporations and never touched a poor man. Instead of ascribing this to Bill Miner's mental qualities, for it is obvious that there is not much to be made out of robbing poor men, these people regard his methods as showing the excellent qualities of the bandit's heart and admire him accordingly."

"In fact his position in the opinion of many people today is almost exactly that occupied by Robin Hood in the Yorkshire mind a few hundred years ago."[36]

The New Westminster Columbian quoted many of the good women of the Royal City as saying, "If Bill Miner should come to my house and ask for a meal he would get it and welcome." The men were quoted in the same vein. "I hope he not captured [sic], he never did a mean thing in his life". Many of the newspapers of the day were not afraid to skirt with "yellow journalism" and would make up fictitious interviews when they felt the urge or necessity to enhance a good story.

"At all events Bill Miner the hold up man, whose record in outlawry is probably unsurpassed in the whole of the great west and in the marked contrast the picture of an old man of nearly seventy making a last attempt to retain liberty in his old age the while pursued by armed posses intent on ending that dearly bought liberty appeals to the imagination of the average man and woman and causes the sympathetic remarks that are heard on every hand."[37]

The Vancouver News Advertiser continued in the same vein. "The general remarks one hears on the street are not likely to assist the hunters, as nine out of ten people will say that they hope Bill Miner will get away clear. 'If he wants grub and comes to my house, he will get it,' is a remark often heard on the street ...."[38]

As the time passed and Miner was not recaptured, the editor of the Victoria Colonist thought he should perhaps lead the way in showing how wantonly partisan on the part of a career criminal the newspapers in Vancouver were. The editor lamented the fact that Canadians were extending anything like sympathy for a notorious criminal like Miner. He called it a stain on the good name of British Columbia throughout the Dominion. The editor remarked that if there were one thing that held B.C. in good reputation for frontier settlement, it was the respect for the majesty of the law, not only by its administration, but by the people of B.C. at large. "There has hitherto been no need in Canada for the law of the shotgun."

"Public sympathy with criminals ... is one of the most fruitful causes of crime in the western part of the United States. Criminals are converted into heroes. The newspapers exploit their crimes; every word they say is published."

"To meet the public taste a new vocabulary has been invented. Thieves have become larcenists, convicts are men who do time, then the man who has done time has squared himself with the community." Political correctness was just beginning to rear its ugly head. The editorial concluded by hoping that the correspondents of the various other papers were incorrect in describing the sympathies of the general populace to be with Bill Miner, and that instead the citizens of B.C. would tender every assistance to the forces of law and order that was required. The provincial capital's newspaper of record had conveniently forgotten its very own partisanship of a few days previously.[39]

The next day the Colonist showed its dependence upon the limited attention span of its readers. After editorially criticizing their competition for their embracing of Miner as a sympathetic figure, the paper this day outdid all others with their positive depiction of last of the Western bandits.

Of his friends in the Similkameen, the Colonist wrote, "Some of Miner's confederates of past years are still in the Nicola and Similkameen countries, and to them the intelligence of their old associate's escape was carried from the centres of population to the secluded localities in which they live, with all the swiftness with which good and bad news can be conveyed, and undoubtedly there will be many a man on the outlook for old Bill with fleet horses and supplies to speed him on his way to safety."

"This feeling, so prevalent in the interior, must not be regarded as an evidence of sympathy with wrong doing. None of Miner's confederates share with him the goodwill of the population. Miner is looked upon here as anything but the cold-blooded life-taking desperado that train robbers usually are. He is spoken of by all who knew him as a most amiable, open-hearted, kindly old fellow, who would go far out of his way to do a good turn to a fellow man, and it is recalled that in all his escapes he left no trail of blood behind him. Then his courage and resourcefulness are themes which have cheered many firesides since the people came to know he was and what his career has been [sic]. He is regarded as a Robin Hood of these later days of steam railways, and indeed if all that is said of him is true, he has some of the qualities which endeared to the public the old highway robber of Sherwood Forest."

Even Jack Budd, hoping he would soon be forgotten about and hiding in his cabin near Aspen Grove, didn't escape the scrutiny of the press.

"In Chilliwack alone he (Miner) is well known and well thought of by a number of people. Further east, down through the Similkameen Valley, he has friends, one of whom, Budd, has been corresponding with him regularly since his incarceration, and it is unlikely that Budd represents only himself. Miner is too wise to allow the authorities to know who all his friends are, and he is also too wise to have left the penitentiary without a good idea of how he would reach safety."[40]

As for the other three convicts, it was surmised by the World that they did not have such an intimate knowledge of the Fraser Valley as did Miner and that they would probably have hoped to escape across the river in a stolen boat and make for the border across the delta.

The World criticized the pursuit to date as being "loosely organized" and "not very thorough" as one of its reporters travelled most of the roads, calling at many houses and asking questions of many of the travellers he met, only to be advised that not one of these individuals had seen a guard, officer or patrol boat looking for the prisoners. The reporter went on to comment that "Bill Miner could have done nothing safer than hire a horse and rig and drive all over the very country in which the authorities supposed the fugitives to be lurking."

Only at Port Moody did he find any sign of the manhunt, and there the two guards were sarcastically described as being "stationed and stationary."[41]

A week after the escape, the Victoria Colonist related the story of the bonds that had supposedly been stolen from the CPR during the Mission robbery. This is the first mention of the bonds in a Canadian newspaper, and while many of the facts are blatantly sensationalistic and factually incorrect, the basic information conformed to the story that eventually would be accepted as the truth. The yarn repeated incidents and details that would never appear in print again as they were proved to be so transparently fictitious. Unfortunately, the legend would end up feeding upon itself, and it grew beyond any reality. The article erroneously noted that Pinkerton detectives had followed the trail of the bonds halfway across the continent, but the securities had never been recovered. Miner's sister was purportedly keeping them safe for him, and they followed her to Minneapolis and then to Kansas City, where they lost her trail. Jake Terry, who had been shot dead just a few months prior to Miner's escape, had supposedly been having confidential discussions with the CPR as to the location of the bonds, but the CPR's conclusion was that Terry had just been trying to lead them on, and the railway company cut off all further dealings with him. This mixture of half-truths and absolute fiction would perpetuate the myth of the bonds for over one hundred years. In reality the tale was just the product of the errant dreamings of reporters eager to seize on the next anecdote about Bill Miner.[42]

The press in British Columbia was always quick to criticize the federal government. It sold newspapers, and Ottawa was almost always viewed as deserving of the criticism. When it became known that no reply had been returned to Bourke from Ottawa on his request for the posting of a reward, the newspapers fastened onto the sloth of the federal bureaucracy with delight.

"The one thing that is causing a lot of talk is the total inaction of the Dominion Government. On Friday morning the Deputy Warden telegraphed the Department of Justice, asking for instructions as to the offering of a reward for their capture, and has not received any orders from this department. It seems rather a slur on the reputation of the Dominion, when the department is so slow to act."[43]

"The fact that the Dominion authorities have up to the present time offered no reward for the recapture of the jail breakers would go to show that they intend to delay the offering of a reward until the convicts are clear away from the comparatively confined circle in which they still must be." The report went on to speculate that despite considerable support for Miner on the outside, this could be offset by the offering of a substantial reward."[44]

Acting Warden Bourke made himself readily available to reporters on demand and did not hesitate to start his own campaign of foisting the blame for the fiasco of two escapes from his institution within one month's time onto others. However, his familiarity with the press would not sit well with Ottawa, and he would find that his public statements would be tossed up in front of him again at the federal inquiry now being contemplated into the escape.

Bourke told the Victoria Colonist that the escape was due to negligence on the part of the guard whose duty it was to patrol the brickyard, and especially his failure to keep an eye on the spot behind the machine building and the smokestack. He also blamed the miserliness of the federal government for the fact that he had insufficient staff to adequately man the stands or patrol the yard. He went on to speculate that the escape had been engineered from the outside, as it was common knowledge that Miner had considerable sums of money available to him cached in various locations. Bourke hypothesized that clothing, food and transportation were waiting for Miner as soon as he had escaped the prison and shed himself of his three cohorts. Bourke boasted to the reporter that during his many years of service in Manitoba and in B.C., no prisoner under his care had retained his liberty after escaping. "I will have Miner and his three companions behind prison walls within twenty-four hours," he trumpeted. The reporter wryly speculated that this recent jailbreak would probably shatter his record.

In another quote Bourke stated, "I figure that Miner stands no show in the world of getting away unless he is already in the hands of friends, and that is improbable, and my reasons for figuring that way are that Bill is too old to go any kind of a pace in making his getaway and also that his friends could not have been there without our perceiving them. I would not be at all surprised should he die in the woods rather than give himself up, providing he does not commit suicide."

Bourke declared that he had examined Miner's feet a few days previously and found them to be in such poor condition that he could not fathom how such an old man could go more than a few miles without dropping from exhaustion. The paper called this a rather startling statement in light of the fact that there had been no sign of the prisoners for the past three days, and the likelihood of the capture was fast receding.[47]

Bourke seems to have issued letters in the form of press releases to the print media to bring them abreast of the latest developments in the pursuit, as many of them repeated the same facts as contained in all the other sources. He stated that he was positive Miner had help from friends on the outside for the initial breakout, and that additionally, help in the form of money, clothing, food and transportation was available to him once he was freed. Bourke mentioned some of the names that had come to his attention, including that of Bob Tilton of Kamloops.[48]

Despite the plight of the Acting Warden becoming more serious as time went on, his situation was not enhanced in the view of discerning readers and the gnomes in Ottawa when Bourke allowed his daughter Katherine to be interviewed by the Victoria Colonist.

"It was by the clever ruse of shielding behind a mask of piety, a craving for religious literature, and illness that Bill Miner enjoys liberty, according to Miss Katherine Bourke, daughter of deputy warden Bourke. The charming young girl, who has on more than one occasion displayed interest in tending to the welfare of the convicts, is one of the most disappointed of all concerned in the wholesale escape, because it shattered hopes which she had entertained that her efforts would eventually lead to making a better man of the notorious bandit.

"'Why, only last week Bill said he was resigned to his fate ....' said Miss Bourke. 'Bill complained of trouble with his feet while he worked in the shoe shop, and he asked to be given some occupation in the outer air. It was then that papa decided to place him in the brick yard. This was ten days ago, and Bill was very happy.'

"'We all felt sorry for Bill when we realized he had to spend all of his life in prison, and we took much interest in him. He pretended to have become highly interested in religion, and asked for religious works, and he had been so good lately that he could be regarded as a model prisoner. But my, it's different now.'

"'If he is again brought to prison, will you try to reform him by again giving him nice books?' Miss Bourke was asked.

"'When he is brought back', replied the demure miss in a confident tone, 'he will have to demonstrate first that he is not shamming before I will do anything tending to make his life more pleasant. I think it was horrid of him to escape after we had done so much to make life easier for him.'"[49]

When Miner had made his hasty and unexpected departure from the bosom of the B.C. Penitentiary, he left some valuables behind. Besides $149 in cash, a gold watch and chain valued at $190 were left to reside in the vault. Prison rules stated that any valuables belonging to individual prisoners were only to be returned to them when their sentences had been served. The value of the watch exceeded two months' salary for an ordinary working man, and it would remain in the penitentiary's vault for many years. It would be lost or stolen sometime before the penitentiary finally closed its doors for the last time in 1980. No report was ever made on the heavy gold ring with the snake's head on it that Miner had been wearing before the robbery in Kamloops. Both the watch and the snake's head ring may still be in some family's collection of heirlooms, waiting for exposure to the British Columbia public again. Miner, however, would never make a documented appearance in Canada again.[50]

XXV

THE INQUIRY

THE PRIVATELY HELD ANTHONY MARTIN COLLECTION of B.C. Penitentiary documents contains the complete records of the official federal government inquiry into the escape of Bill Miner. Starting in the late summer of 1907, the sources document the activities of the inquiry principal, Inspector George Dawson from Ottawa. Letters and reports highlight the vain attempts of Acting Warden Bourke to slip out of any responsibility for the escape and detail the situation control exerted from Ottawa by the chief Inspector of Prisons, Stewart, and the Minister of Justice.

Acting Warden Bourke sent his first report east to Ottawa by the 12TH of August. He notes that he would have needed to have had on hand a regiment of guards on duty that day to prevent the escape. As he did not have enough, the brickyard was undermanned. Still, if guard McNeil had followed his instructions to patrol the walkway, he would certainly have been able to spot the escapees. Consequently, Bourke informed Stewart, he had temporarily suspended guard McNeil pending the outcome of the forthcoming inquiry. Bourke stated that he had had the walkway built especially for that reason and added that McNeil had been issued a disciplinary warning a year previously. The worried deputy warden ended his report by noting that there was a clear indication that outside forces aided in the successful escape.[1]

Two days later Bourke again wrote Ottawa to advise that Miner had now been suspected of retreating to the "upper country" of the Similkameen and suspected he planned to meet up with his friends Jack Budd, Tom Arnold and Bob Tilton. He added that Sheriff

Wentworth Wood in Kamloops also agreed that Miner was heading into the interior.[2]

Meanwhile, Bourke had his prison guards busy submitting their own reports to him on their pursuit activities since the day of the escape. Thirteen harried guards submitted reports varying from half a page in length to multi-page reports over the period from August 8TH to August 19TH. Prompt replies were made to his letters to Ottawa from Inspector Stewart. The Ottawa mandarin started right off by questioning Bourke as to why five officers were assigned to the ten convicts unloading wood at the dock, while only three guards were assigned to provide security to a brickyard with twenty convicts and more . He requested Bourke send him a detailed sketch of the penitentiary, in particular the brickyard, so as "to decide (the) matter intelligently." He agreed that guard McNeil's suspension was probably apt and would be settled upon further investigation.[3]

In Ottawa, Inspector Stewart wrote to the junior Inspector of Prisons, George Dawson. He advised Dawson that the Minister of Justice had received all copies of reports and letters pertaining to the escape in British Columbia and was of the opinion a thorough investigation should be made on the spot. The Minister suggested that Dawson should cut his visit of inspection at the prison at Dorchester short and return to Ottawa without visiting St. Vincent de Paul this trip. Stewart confided in Dawson that he thought it was the Minister's intention that Dawson himself conduct the investigation. The Minister told Stewart that in his opinion, it should not be delayed in view of the adverse comments and criticisms evoked in the West. Stewart ordered Dawson to wire him when he was ready to return to Ottawa.[4]

On the 22ND of August, Bourke's world started to collapse on itself, and the possibility of his termination loomed. The two convicts had escaped from the woodcutting crew on Wright's Island the day previous and were well on their way into the hinterland before word came to Bourke in New Westminster. Bourke reluctantly sat down and composed a telegram to his superiors in Ottawa. He told them about this additional embarrassment to the department and advised there was little hope of recapturing the escapees.

In a letter to Stewart on the same day, Bourke admitted to his supervisor that little had changed since his last report other than the fresh escape. The search for Miner and his accomplices was shut down on the 19TH, and Bourke stated that he found it difficult to believe that the three had escaped so handily, making him sure that help from the outside was provided. He enclosed a sketch of the penitentiary and pointed out to Stewart that if McNeil had followed orders, he would have been able to shoot the convicts as they escaped. Bourke hoped that McNeil was not colluding with the convicts. Knowing that he would face criticism for allowing Miner outside access, Bourke went on to describe the poor condition of Miner's feet and how he had inspected the brickyard not two days before the escape, checking Miner's feet at that time. He said he watched as McNeil conscientiously patrolled the catwalk in his presence. He added that there were four lifers in the brickyard that day, and Miner was least suspected to escape due to his age and physical condition.

Bourke complained that his officers informed him on a constant basis that there was considerable public sympathy for Miner, and this made recapture more difficult. However, the officers were conscientious in the discharge of their duties. He ended his letter requesting that he would like to make future recommendations as to the prison security.[5]

Mr. Dawson in New Brunswick wired Stewart in Ottawa that he would soon be back in the capital to discuss the future inquiry.

```
The Great North Western Telegraph Company of
Canada
Dorchester NB Aug 23.,


Douglas Stewart Esq.
Dept Justice,
Ottawa Ont.,


Letter received leave tonight see you office two
oclock Sunday afternoon.


GW Dawson[6]
```

On the 23RD of August, Bourke sent another letter to Stewart. This one contained the first hints of mental deterioration that Bourke was starting to suffer. This letter no doubt initiated some worry in the Ottawa mandarins in charge of penitentiaries, if the litany of escapes had not.

Bourke thanked Stewart for allowing him to discontinue sending convict crews to Wright Island to cut wood. He told Stewart that he was now "relieved of very much uneasiness." The Deputy Warden went on to list the recommendations he thought should be implemented to enhance security and intimated to Stewart that they had not previously been undertaken as when they had been presented to Warden Whyte, he had ignored them. Improvements included modifications to the exterior fencing and modifications necessary to enhance the guards' view of the yard.

Bourke then went on to complain that some initiatives had been undertaken by the warden without consulting him and that the failure to include him in discussions was "part of a systematic plan" to discredit him. He criticized that, "Discipline and safety of the prison were becoming secondary to industrial pursuits," and that even though he had "experience of a disciplinary character which no other officer here possessed," his experience was not valued.

Bourke started disparaging the work of the Warden Whyte, intimating that he "never told me anything of importance ... which I should know." However, despite this Bourke stated that he was always loyal to the warden.

"The struggle I have had for the past two weeks has been a strain on the mind." He knew that the use of Wright Island as a woodcutting endeavour for the convicts was a poor move, but had held his tongue as his "motives would be misconstrued."

Bourke concluded this letter by accusing the guard McNeil with the single and total blame for the escape, no one else.

When Inspector Stewart received this letter, he immediately forwarded a copy to Dawson so that he would be aware of the future difficulties he might be faced with.[7]

Towards the end of the month, Stewart received another report from Bourke, and also in the same package, a private letter to him. In the report, Bourke tried to outline his reasons for allowing Miner to be placed on outside work, but none of his excuses can be seen to bear any weight.

The Acting Warden explained to Stewart that he never kept long-term prisoners continually at the tailor or shoe shops as the repetitive work tended to "mean a breaking down of the convict's constitution and probably death. Some months before, I saw Dunn's health failing rapidly, and he gave me the impression of showing a tendency to insanity. I placed him outside."

"On 31ST July, Miner showed me his feet which were slightly swollen and his toes badly blistered. He said it was through want of exercise. I intended to let him out anyway."

This was the only part of the report focusing on the reasons for putting Miner in the outside yard, and it did not answer the basic questions asked by the senior inspector in Ottawa. All five pages of the report went on in a rather rambling and disjointed way. It appeared Bourke was becoming increasingly unstable.

The private letter to Stewart enclosed with the report removed all doubt Stewart may have had about Bourke's mental stability. Bourke's paranoid delusions spoke of warnings from friends that he had received after he had assumed the Acting Warden position upon the confinement of Whyte. He was advised by these friends to "keep a sharp lookout, that a certain clique would endeavour to make my temporary management a failure and thus destroy any chance I might have for promotion." He noted in this private letter to Stewart that he was now convinced the escapes were orchestrated to defame him.

It must be assumed that his supervisor in Ottawa looked on this letter with a critical and concerned eye. It would have been plain even to him that something was seriously wrong in New Westminster.[8]

On Tuesday the 3RD of September, Inspector George W. Dawson arrived in New Westminster to start his inquiry. The next morning he inspected the brickyard and fences where the escapes had taken place and watched how the guards and prisoners worked on the inside of the institution.

The reporter for the Columbian was told that the investigation would be far-reaching, and would include the smuggling rumoured to have taken place, as well as the escapes from Wright Island. He told the reporter that the CPR had told the Department of Justice it did not feel like offering any more rewards as after offering and paying out the last reward, the main perpetrator took flight just over a year later.

Dawson went on to tell the reporter that all the guards and pertinent convicts would be interviewed, and all would be under oath. He expected that the inquiry might take about a week.

The paper speculated that the resignation of certain officials was rumoured.[9]

In his letter to Stewart, his supervisor in Ottawa, Dawson advised that he was right now "going over the mass of correspondence, newspaper clippings and other reports" in the files and listening to "long statements of the deputy warden as to how the convicts got away." He hoped to start the investigation the next day.[10]

When Dawson arrived at the penitentiary, a sealed confidential letter was waiting for him. From Dominion Police Commissioner Sherwood in Ottawa, it enlightened the inspector as to some facts that had come to the Commissioner's attention. Sherwood had learned that Bourke had been warned by the acting prison chaplain about Miner's attempt to escape some days before it actually occurred. He mentioned that he had heard that the prisoners had escaped through the open piggery gate, that McNeil was complicit in the escape, and Miner's hair and moustache had been allowed to grow considerably before he escaped.[11]

The Vancouver Province of September 5TH had a scathing editorial sharply critical of the penitentiary management in New Westminster. "Col. Whyte was a good officer. It would appear from what has taken place since his active superintendency ceased that his deputies do not come under the same category of good officers. The condition of things at the penitentiary has been such to arouse grave questionings."

It went on to state that Miner had been allowed to let his hair and moustache grow long enough that he would not be recognized as a convict. The Province recommended, with the advantage of hindsight, that the government should have had an inspector at the penitentiary days after the escape to take charge of running the institution. "Straws show which way the winds blow. It is time for a change in Ottawa." It would appear that the Province was a partisan Conservative paper. Minister of Justice Aylesworth in Ottawa had the Province in hand when he circled the section on Miner's hair and moustache and sent a clipping on to Stewart and Dawson.[12]

As a result of intensive questioning as to his actions by Dawson, Bourke sent a rambling nine page report to the investigator. In the report, Bourke attempts to answer the Inspector's questions with regard to the Acting Warden's concerns with how the penitentiary was being run. Bourke managed to discuss each item, but each was answered in such a way as to cast criticism on the bedridden Warden Whyte. When the acting Warden finally got to the last pages of his almost incoherent, poorly handwritten report, the real reason for his delusional paranoia came to the fore. While his fears probably had some basis in fact, his response to them by advising the federal investigator of his suspicions was inappropriate and denied him any sympathy from the management of his department. Bourke was a good practising Irish Catholic, and he was surrounded by a sea of Protestants. In the past, he had had occasion to discuss a sermon he had read in the press spoken by a compatriot of the Protestant clergyman Reverend Owen. He had mentioned to Owen how heartening it was to hear of his fellow reverend's sermon in the press and how his address to Orangemen expounded "such high ideas." Owen responded to Bourke that his partner's thoughts and words might be high-minded when it came to Catholics in politics, but he personally would strongly oppose a Catholic Premier. Bourke took a personal affront to these remarks of Owen and was now convinced that Owen was one of those responsible for the conspiracy now underway to destroy him. He went on to advise Dawson that he had applied for a smaller "Wardenship" position some years previously, and it was only much later that he found out it was due to his Catholicism that a top management position had been denied him.

Bourke concluded his remarks to Dawson by saying, "I may say to you, Mr. Inspector, that the connection is growing stronger in my mind that this trouble has been planned for my downfall .... I hope most sincerely you will be fortunate enough through the help of a Just God to get so much light as will enable you to see through the dark cloud that now hangs over me, and which I think the Reverend Owen has taken no small part in forming."[13]

Dawson was not yet into his inquiry more than a day when he was faced with this disturbing missive from the Acting Warden. No doubt one of his inquiry recommendations would already have formed in the investigator's mind. Whether Bourke's suspicions warranted investigation will never be known, but in retrospect it is doubtful that it was his Catholicism that held him back, but rather his convoluted thinking processes. However, there should be no doubt that religious prejudices played a role in the predominantly Protestant society in which Bourke found himself. The question is, how much?

The inquiry made interesting news, and interesting news sold newspapers. Local papers speculated with glee that "official wrath will be visited upon everyone connected with the affair in the most remote degree. In anticipation of official action the dispensers of federal patronage are making appointments already." A reporter wondered aloud as to who the individuals were that might pick the plum of the position of warden, and names the unfortunates so identified. Bourke's impending doom was also a subject for public discussion as it was noted that he was slated for superannuation.

The Columbian got on the spicy subject of the stolen securities and stated that "a very influential quarter" desired the release of Miner because he was knowledgeable about a package of Australian bonds taken at the Mission Junction holdup. Some of the information that the newspapers appear privy to lends one to believe that selective leaking of information was taking place, most to Bourke's discredit. Much was written, tongue in cheek, about the controversial subject of Bill Miner's hair. "The absence of his moustache affected his eyesight. Bill it seems being of peculiar physical makeup and when his eyes were tested his head commenced to experience the most intense pains for lack of his natural covering. So Bill's hair was allowed to sprout, and then the trouble shifted to his feet, which commenced to itch against the hard floors of the institution and to be attracted irresistibly to Mother Earth. So Bill worked his way out to the brickyard, moustache, hair and all."

Ottawa was continually criticized for being totally uninterested in the escape as over a week had been allowed to pass before inquiries were answered and action initiated. Miner was thought to be probably a thousand miles away by then. And then the Dominion government had offered a paltry $500 which would have enticed no one to turn "Old Bill" in. The Columbian, partisan as always against a Liberal government, thought that Ottawa would make heads roll in B.C., and what was really needed was some attention paid to senior members of the department in Ottawa itself for allowing "slackness of regulations" and the "singular apathy of those in high quarters."[14]

By the 19TH of September, Dawson sent a report to Stewart in Ottawa summarizing his investigation. The guard McNeil was found negligent, but there was no evidence of collusion. He had simply failed to patrol his beat as instructed. Testimony was used from a number of sources against McNeil, including the convict Young who had engaged him in conversation that day. Convict Young had been rewarded for his co-operation with the investigation and was now out on a "Ticket of Leave."

Dawson criticized Bourke for not posting a guard on Stand #12. Bourke's excuse that he had none to spare was nullified by the presence that day of a substantial number at the dock guarding a small number of convicts unloading wood from the scow.

Bourke had been warned by the Reverend Owen just a month before that Miner should not be given too much liberty, but he transferred him to the brickyard regardless. Bourke did not utilize the services of the prison surgeon to assess Miner's complaints of sore feet. Bourke did not make changes to stands and fences he felt should be made as he did not want to antagonize the Warden. Deputy Warden Bourke was not faring well in the report's apportionment of blame.

The controversial subject of Miner's hair was addressed and suitably dismissed. "Miner's hair was not long when he escaped. His moustache was clipped. It appeared about as it would be with three weeks growth after shaving," and Dawson referred to the testimony of the guard Atkins.

Bourke stated in evidence to Dawson that he was convinced that the escape was engineered to ensure his downfall. Dawson stated in his report, "Need I say there is not a shadow of evidence to support his belief."

Dawson continued, referring to the fact that he was not allowed to interview Warden Whyte due to his condition. Dawson had wished to talk to him about the visit of Mcintyre, Bullick and Jake Terry that was revealed in guard McKenzie's testimony.

With his report, Dawson included a copy of Guard McNeil's resignation letter and recommended that it be accepted. Also included was a letter from Deputy Warden Bourke stating that he desired to retire from the service "if his retiring allowance can be arranged satisfactorily." Dawson recommended that Bourke be retired and granted such entitlements as were his due.[15]

Near the end of September an event took place that would have a profound effect in the House of Commons in two years. J.D. Taylor, the editor of the New Westminster Columbian, was elected to stand for the Conservative Party in the New Westminster district. He beat out five other candidates including Charles Hibbert Tupper, the son of former Prime Minister Charles Tupper. The paper described the tone of the rally and echoed the remarks of the candidate who stated that the electors of the province will no longer allow the federal authorities in Ottawa to ignore the claims of B.C. with impunity. The people will send representatives to parliament "who will have the interests of the province at heart and to whom subservience to party is a minor consideration." Taylor would be elected as a Conservative opposition M.P in the October, 1908, federal election, won by Laurier and his Liberals. Taylor and his paper would be a thorn in the government's side in 1909 when the Bill Miner case went to Ottawa.[16]

The New Westminster Columbian was reluctant to give up on reporting on the trials at the B.C. Penitentiary. It cheerfully printed the details of another juicy case of attempted escape from the B.C. Penitentiary. It seems that earlier in 1907 on 21 April, before Miner and his compatriots escaped, one George Stone, convict, was thwarted from trying to burrow out through the rocks and mortar of his cell and cut his way through expanded wire mesh under the roof. He had only removed two bricks when he was observed by the guard Patchell to be acting strangely. When the convicts were at Sunday service, Patchell took the opportunity to check Stone's cell and found the loose bricks hidden behind a hanging towel. Patchell testified he thought that the convict was attempting to escape into the ventilation system and up through the roof. He was cross-examined by the prisoner who made it very clear to the court that it would have been impossible for him to have escaped that way. Stone took the stand in his own defence and testified that he was only loosening two bricks so as to have a secure spot where he could stash his tobacco, as every prisoner did at one time or another. He was asked by the jury if he considered it possible to escape the prison by cutting through the walls, and Stone responded that it wasn't worth the trouble, time and energy as there was lots of opportunity to escape from the prison any time a convict wished. He referred to the recent escapees and stated that all the convicts knew the plans of the escape long before it went down. The paper ironically stated that Stone's testimony gave "the impression that it was only a matter of accommodation on the part of the convicts to stay there at all." The jury returned from their deliberations with a verdict of "Not Guilty." Inspector Dawson sat in the gallery, listening to the testimony with a critical ear.[17]

On the 9TH of October, Warden and Lieutenant-Colonel J.C. Whyte died of his illness. He had been the warden of the B.C. Penitentiary for eleven years, and during his tenure he had been "responsible for initiating numerous reforms in penal administration and implemented a vocational training regime at the New Westminster institution."[18]

Stewart wrote to Dawson on the 15TH of October and asked him to make security changes to the piggery gate and the ladders used to gain access to the guard stands. Also, and more importantly, he and the justice minister wished to get to the bottom of Bullick's visit to Miner.

"The Minister is anxious to have more information with reference to the mysterious visit of McIntyre [sic], Bullock [sic], and the unknown, who were apparently allowed to interview the convict without supervision eight or nine months ago. It is not likely that McIntyre will give any information, but perhaps if you can obtain the address of Bullock, [sic] it will be possible to have on file his statement of what their business was and also whether they were allowed to interview the convict without official supervision. The matter was quite fully referred to in instructor McKenzie's evidence."[19]

It is obvious Mcintyre's reputation had preceded him to Ottawa, as it was naturally assumed that he would be uncooperative. Dawson wrote to Bullick requesting he explain his visit to the prison to visit Miner.

"A Mr. McIntyre, [sic] another man, and you visited convict Edwards alias Bill Miner in this penitentiary. Minister of Justice requests that you state the nature of business discussed with convict and whether warden or any other pen officer was present during the whole time the interview lasted."[20]

By early November, Dawson had received a reply from the Inspector of the CPR's Special Service Department which he forwarded to Stewart in Ottawa. Written in a garish green ink, Bullick's statements in his letter to Dawson, later to be repeated under oath in different circumstances, dispel any notions that a conspiracy was taking place in the Warden's offices that day in February.

CANADIAN PACIFIC RAILWAY COMPANY
Special Service Department
Vancouver B.C   Nov 5 1907
2398

G.W. Dawson, Esq.,
Inspector in control
New Westminster Penitentiary.

Dear Sir:-
I am in receipt of your letter of the 29th ult.
I think you have been wrongly informed as to me visiting
Convict Edwards at the Penitentiary in company with
Mr. McIntyre.
I might say the only time I visited Edwards
in the Penitentiary was on the 9th day of February last
in company with Jake Terry. The late warden, Colonel Whyte,
was present all the time. The visit was merely to see if
Terry and Edwards knew each other, as they were both in the
San Quentin Penitentiary together. There was a short
conversation between Terry and Edwards in reference to the
Mission hold-up Sept 1904.
Yours truly,
Signed "R E Bullick
Inspector [21]

Bullick's letter, given in its entirety above, and his subsequent repeating of the substance of the letter under oath, should dispel any lingering thoughts of a conspiracy between the CPR and Bill Miner. The preponderance of the evidence shows that the whole question of stolen bonds was most likely promulgated by a sensationalist press and an opportunistic career criminal.

Before October was out, the hapless Deputy Warden Bourke had resigned from his position to take retirement. He advised the local reporter for the Columbian that he had resigned, not through fear of consequences as a result of the inquiry, but for personal reasons. Bourke confided to the reporter that throughout his career he had been the victim of broken promises and conspiracies. He told a long and rambling story, reminiscing about stories when he was a schoolteacher during the Riel Rebellion. He ended the interview by announcing he would enter superannuation of $1,000 per annum and planned to spend the remainder of his days in New Westminster. However, the federal government was not yet finished with Mr. Bourke and would ensure his dissatisfaction and vengefulness by backing out on its perceived promises to him. To rectify his supposed wrongs, he would ensure the government squirmed in Ottawa as long as he could have any influence on it.[22]

In early November, some of Bourke's injured feelings were relieved when the guards at the penitentiary held a retirement party in the guard room for him. After the prison was closed and locked for the night, Bourke was invited to the guard room where speeches were given and a gold chain and locket were presented to the former Deputy Warden. It was inscribed "Presented to D.D. Bourke, D.W., by the officers of B.C.P, 1.11.'07."[23]

XXVI

THE HOUSE OF COMMONS DEBATES

IN JANUARY OF 1909, almost a year and a half since the escape of Bill Miner, retired Deputy Warden D. D. Bourke started on his journey to attain self-vindication. The amount of superannuation he was receiving from Ottawa was considerably less than he had been led to expect, and a letter writing campaign undertaken with the pension section to rectify this had not been satisfactory. Frustrated with the inflexible bureaucracy in Ottawa, he decided to use an only too obliging press to attempt to embarrass into action his former employers in the Penitentiary Service and the government of Prime Minister Wilfrid Laurier. The tool Bourke used to hammer the government with was the ideally located and partisan Conservative newspaper, the New Westminster Columbian. The publisher, Conservative Member of Parliament James Davis Taylor, had been elected to Ottawa in the October 1908 election, ultimately won by Laurier's Liberals.

Bourke started his campaign by hinting in the Columbian that he had startling new information about Bill Miner's escape that would be divulged over future issues of the paper.

Penitentiary Inspector George Dawson in Ontario, knowing Bourke's rather unstable personality, wrote him after reading about the planned exposé. He requested Bourke to advise the department and the Minister with a "statement of any information you may possess regarding the matter that you have not already disclosed."[1]

Bourke, couching his reply in vague and indirect language,

answered Dawson and told him that he had given him in his previous reports during the inquiry all the information and facts that were in his possession. But Bourke had plans for the other information that he knew was in Dawson's inquiry files, like the Miner statement to guard McKenzie of the stolen bonds from the Mission robbery.[2]

On the evening of the 11TH of February, 1909, in the House of Commons, New Westminster M.P. J.D. Taylor confronted the government when the penitentiary service budget was up for review. He opened fire by criticizing the department for the inordinate number of escapes that had taken place in 1907.

Solicitor General Bureau stated that he had nothing to report; they were just normal escapes.

Taylor wanted it put on record that the federal authorities had failed to act in the Bill Miner escape until after more than a week had passed. Taylor read from a government report that discipline was slack, and he asked the minister if he had a response.

There was no answer from the government benches.

Mr. Taylor then proceeded to enlighten the House. He quoted a letter from D. Bourke that Bill Miner "was handed out" of the penitentiary and that sensational disclosures were coming. He told the House Miner had been let out by the arrangement of a large corporation to disclose the location of stolen bonds from the Mission robbery. Taylor demanded that an investigation be launched from outside the government. The trap Bill Miner had set for the government and the CPR was about to be sprung.

Minister of Justice Aylesworth responded and advised that he believed implicitly in the report of Inspector Dawson and did not know of any irregularities in it or the investigation.

The Honourable Mr. Bureau verbally abused the member for New Westminster and held the member's accusations up to ridicule. In reviewing the member from New Westminster's statements, the Solicitor General did admit, however, certain points raised by Taylor were correct.

Mr. Taylor demanded that the Minister be further apprised of the circumstances of his charges so that that he might deal with

Taylor's request for more information on the charges of collusion with the bandit Bill Miner. Taylor intimated that Dawson may have more information about Miner's escape than had been given to the Minister. Behind the scenes, Bourke's hand was at work attempting to get even with his old nemesis, Dawson.[3]

In the same issue the news of Taylor's actions in the House of Commons was printed with the accusations of collusion with Miner and the stolen bonds, the Columbian interviewed Bourke. He smugly told the paper he had information for the upcoming inquiry in Ottawa, but would hold onto it for a while. Bourke hoped Mr. Taylor would keep the matter before the public until everything had been cleared up. Bourke wanted to enjoy his anticipated pound of flesh.[4]

Overnight the minions of the federal government in Ottawa worked overtime to find and prepare information on the Miner affair for Minister of Justice Aylesworth.

The Minister listed for the House the visits the convict Miner had experienced during his brief stay at the penitentiary. They included Mcintyre on 12 June 1906, the visit of Detective John Stanton of Portland, Oregon, and that of Bullick and Terry on 9 February 1907. He also enumerated the visits of Sergeant Murray of the Provincial Police on 29 May 1907, and R.N.W.M.P. Sergeant Wilson, New Westminster Chief of Police McIntosh with detective Waddell that had occurred on 27 June 1907. The minister noted that there was no record of the visit of Mcintyre, Bullick and Terry entered in the daybook, but the fact of the visit was admitted. Aylesworth told the house that a guard named McKenzie had repeated to Inspector Dawson during the escape inquiry the story of the CPR negotiations for Miner's release in return for Miner giving up the bonds. The Minister also repeated the letter from Bullick to Dawson that the only time he, Bullick, had visited Miner in the B.C. Penitentiary was when Jake Terry was with him and the warden was present throughout. Aylesworth continued to maintain that the department had no further information on any bonds.

On the west coast, the minister's words were misunderstood by the Vancouver News Advertiser reporter who read the wire of the

House's proceeding. The paper mixed up the statement of guard McKenzie, who had related the Miner story of the bonds, with the New Westminster Chief of Police McIntosh, stating it was McIntosh who had informed the warden of Miner's story of the bonds. The New Westminster Columbian ran with the News Advertiser's story, to the eventual embarrassment of their editor and Member of Parliament, J.D. Taylor.[56]

The New Westminster Columbian, sensing a good lead column on its front page, quickly brought a copy of the News Advertiser's erroneous reporting on the House proceedings to the attention of New Westminster Chief of Police McIntosh. McIntosh, realizing his professional reputation could be severely compromised, vehemently denied the paper's reporting of the information coming out of Ottawa and credited to the Minister of Justice. The Chief noted that the only time he had seen Miner was in the company of Staff Sergeant Wilson in June of 1907. He had never heard of any bonds missing from the Mission robbery until after Miner's escape from the penitentiary.[7]

In Vancouver, CPR Inspector Bullick irately reacted to the stories of his meeting with Miner in a press statement. He issued a specific denial in the local papers to the charges made on the floor of the House of Commons that he and the CPR had assisted the train robber to escape in return for the return of several hundred thousands of dollars worth of bonds said to have been stolen in the train robbery at Mission. Bullick stated that "not only did he not discuss any plan for Miner's liberation, but he knows that the story of the missing bonds was a fake invented on behalf of the train robbers by Miner himself or his friends." Bullick was adamant that no bonds or securities of any type had been stolen.[8]

On the evening of February the 19TH, the business of the Commons was held up for three hours when the penitentiaries branch of the Department of Justice was held to account again over the Bill Miner affair. Taylor, the Leader of the Opposition, and others on the Conservative side of the House took part in the questioning of the governments. Taylor opened with a series of questions for Minister of Justice Aylesworth, but as the Minister was so hard of hearing, they were answered by Solicitor General Bureau.

The first question Taylor brought before the House was the meagrely retiring allowance of $279.22 dealt out to former Deputy Warden D.D. Bourke. This little item of information goes a long way towards explaining how and why the subject of Miner's escape arose in the Canadian House of Commons a year and a half after the incident took place. Bourke, having guard McKenzie's confidential testimony of his interview with Miner about the CPR bonds in the back of his mind, was about to determine how the flavour of revenge tasted for his perceived ill treatment at the hands of Dawson, Stewart and the penitentiary branch of the Ministry of Justice.

Taylor criticized the government for being so niggardly with the retirement of a long-term and faithful employee. He then questioned the accounts of the penitentiary service that had been placed before the House. He pointed the government's attention to an expenditure in 1907 of $2,485.85 to the Canadian Detective Bureau, itemized as "searching for escaped convicts," and asked whether the federal agency had had any success for such an excessive expenditure.

Bureau advised the line item was for chasing Bill Miner and the other convicts after their escape. They had no success to speak of; however, he was assured by staff that news of success was forthcoming.

Then followed a classic parry and thrust between Taylor and Solicitor General Bureau. It reached no conclusions, enlightened no one, and did not reflect well on either the government or the opposition other than to confirm pre-existing impressions of normal actions in the House.

Mr. Taylor (Conservative): In the annual report of the minister we read charges of general insubordination and neglect of duty or worse in the B.C. Penitentiary. I submit that when we are called upon to pass the estimates for the support of that institution we are entitled to have a serious explanation from the minister in charge of it and I ask him now to make a fuller explanation than has been made respecting the condition of affairs shown by this report to have existed in this institution.

Mr. Bureau (Liberal): I understand that at the time of the escape of

Bill Miner, Bourke, the Deputy Warden, was acting as warden and did not keep the discipline he ought to have kept and allowed an escape, and it was for that reason that the unflattering references were made. Now Mr. Bourke has disappeared, a new warden has been appointed, and the reorganization is complete.

Mr. Burrell (Conservative): I do not think that is exactly a satisfactory explanation. The case of Bill Miner was a specially notorious one in British Columbia, and indeed in the whole of Western Canada. The man has held up trains, his exploits had attracted unusual attention on the other side of the line, and flattering references were made to the expeditious way in which justice was meted out to this man. Yet he escaped on the 8TH of August and the department responsible for the penitentiary did not know until the 13TH of August that he had escaped, and did not take steps to recapture him until a week afterwards when it was practically impossible to catch him.

Taylor went on at length to describe the conspiracy to enable Miner to escape and that the other three were just a cover for the deed. He referred to the public statement Mr. Bourke had made advising that he had some sensational and far-reaching disclosures to make. Taylor went on to refer to Dawson's letter to Bourke requesting him to reveal those disclosures. Taylor noted that Dawson was the very man that Bourke had charged knew something about the circumstances of the conspiracy and had not communicated these to the penitentiary department. Taylor read from one of the Columbian's interviews with Bourke and the statements he had made.

Mr. Gordon (Liberal): Who is the editor of that paper you are quoting from?

Mr. Taylor: For the information of the honourable gentleman I may tell him that I, when I am at home, am the editor of that paper, and that I am not ashamed of it.

Much laughter is heard from the government benches, and cries of "Shame" and "Fiction" were heard.

Mr. Hughes (laughing): And it is Bourke's own statement you are reading?

Mr. Taylor: Certainly they are Mr. Bourke's statements, and I think the merriment of the honourable gentleman opposite is very much out of place in the midst of an indictment like this.

Taylor again went on to describe the conspiracy to enable Miner's escape, charging that the penitentiary service not only knew about it, but assisted in its success by not moving on the escape until many days after it had happened. Much was made of the fact that Bourke had telegraphed Ottawa the day the escape took place, but Ottawa had no reaction for days afterward. He followed up his initial telegram with one requesting permission to offer a reward, and when the government finally did respond they offered only the paltry sum of $500. Taylor continued to describe a litany of offences committed by the federal government.

The government, secure in its majority, did not take Mr. Taylor's accusations and demands seriously.

Mr. Talbot (Liberal): And his moustache was so grown that you would not recognize him.

The government benches erupted in laughter.

Mr. Taylor: Apparently the honourable gentleman responsible for the justice department sees nothing but a subject for a slim joke in the circumstances I have raised.

The member from New Westminster continued at length to describe the collusion of the penitentiary service, the government and certain guards that had also contributed to the escape. Before the escape, a guard was caught passing letters and money to Miner, was subsequently found guilty, and retired from the service. Apparently Inspector Dawson was at the penitentiary for his June inspection at the same time, and Taylor had previously asked the ministry whether the department had any knowledge of any communications from outside the penitentiary with Miner before the escape. He had received a reply in the negative, showing that the department was not aware of the troubles at the penitentiary.

Taylor went on to call for an inquiry of some sort. "I think the Minister of Justice cannot afford to let an incident like this be dismissed with a laugh on the part of his supporters." Taylor advised the government that it was not in receipt of all the facts from the ministry employees on the Miner affair. Taylor was referring to Bourke's literal interpretation of Miner's interview with the guard McKenzie and the fictitious bonds.

Taylor: Therefore I ask that the minister, as the responsible head of the department, to take steps to make a full inquiry and to see that the inquiry is conducted by some other person than the inspector who is now writing to Mr. Bourke, and who stands arraigned on the grave statement of Mr. Bourke to the public press.

Mr. Aylesworth told the House that while he had not been able to hear Mr. Taylor, he wished to make a statement outlining the circumstances of the escape. He reviewed the incidents of August 1907 and charged that the department acted with the utmost alacrity to put the wheels in motion to issue a reward and take steps to recapture the escaped convicts. He went on to praise the efforts of Inspector Dawson, who took charge of the institution as soon as he arrived. There he remained until the following December, attempting to restore discipline, undertaking reorganization and a lengthy and in-depth inquiry. Inspector Dawson also was able to determine that senior management of the institution had not met its obligations in a professional manner; however, Mr. Bourke's resignation was not demanded. "He was the man in charge, the responsibility rested primarily and to a greater extent upon him than upon anyone else .... It was his duty, his business, his power and right to assign the different gangs of convicts to the different guards around the institution. However, Mr. Bourke was not dismissed. Mr. Bourke was allowed to retire and was given his retiring allowance calculated upon the full basis of his service."[9]

The minister focused on the main reason for the debate: Mr. Bourke's perceived dissatisfaction with his superannuation. He pointed out that Bourke had gone to the press to appeal to public opinion in the matter to right his case and would hold the government to task if his demands were not acceded to. The articulate Aylesworth, despite his hearing challenges, was able to outline what really were the true facts of the case.

"Allusions are made, hints are thrown out, I do not know but statements have been made, it may be that it has been in so many words charged that this was no real escape on the part of the malefactor Miner, that this was something connived at, something assisted and furnished by someone in connection with the institution, or someone of the authorities. I can say nothing in that respect except what I know."

He went on to state that "there is not one word, not one breath of foundation" to the rumour that there had been a conspiracy to wink at the escape of Miner if he should give up the secret location of the stolen bonds. "It was investigated so far as was possible to investigate such a shadowy, vague and unsubstantial rumour, and it was found to be exactly as I described, absolutely unfounded. If Mr. Bourke has information in regard to the existence of any such understanding I wish certainly that he would make it known."

Taylor, however, was not about to give up on this vulnerable spot in the government's armour. He called on the Justice Minister to give the Opposition positive assurance that the department never did give permission to any person to enter the penitentiary to interview Miner, and again repeated the Opposition's call for a full inquiry.

The Leader of the Opposition, R.L. Borden, then entered the fray. He stated that perhaps, "Mr. Bourke has said either too much or too little," and recommended that the Minister of Justice and the Solicitor General should determine whether "they should take at once into their grave and serious consideration whether this man should not be brought before a committee of this House and the statements which he has made so frequently in the public press tested by a thorough and strict and stern examination of him under oath in order that he either withdraw or make good."

Mr. Bureau advised Mr. Borden that his suggestion would have careful consideration. Mr. Borden would never know how lucky he was to have that particular wish, of bringing Bourke to Ottawa to testify in front of the House, not fulfilled. Taylor and Borden and other opposition members continued to bring up concerns with regard to the penitentiary service. Bullick's visit with Jake

Terry to see Miner and to talk about the Mission robbery also came up, but the government ended the evening debate by indicating that considerable discussion of the point was still needed, and that the item should be left to stand as had been agreed and move on to discussion of penitentiary affairs in Alberta. The House would return to it at the next sitting.[10]

During the lull between sittings, Bourke kept up a letter writing campaign to the New Westminster Columbian, providing the fuel that their publisher and M.P. needed in Ottawa.

On the 22ND of February, Bourke wrote that it had been his intent by now to give the first of a series of letters regarding the escape of Bill Miner. However, he had read in Hansard that he might be summoned to Ottawa to give evidence before a committee, and his release of any letters before that time would be imprudent. In this, his first letter, he admits that his going public was partly due to the meagrely retirement allowance he received. He filled the rest of his letter with the pompous platitudes of a frustrated former civil servant. "The stabs that I have received have been at the hands of grafters or their friends who felt I was in the way, and, looking back at the group, I see Conservatives as well as Liberals, Catholics as well as Protestants, Irishmen as well as Englishmen, Scotchmen and Frenchmen. My appeal therefore is not to politics, or to religion, or to race, but to the good and true men of both great parties, of both great churches and of the four great races from which our Canadian citizenship springs."[11]

On the 24TH, Bourke followed with another diatribe detailing the mix-up in telegrams delaying notification of the escape in Ottawa and continuing to attempt to accuse Dawson of collusion in the cover-up to Miner's escape.[12]

The next day another letter appeared, and Bourke continued to enlighten readers with regard to the elusive telegrams in Ottawa. He also disagreed with the Hansard record which stated that he was not dismissed nor was he requested for his resignation. He recalled a conversation with Inspector Dawson during the inquiry where Dawson advised the former Deputy Warden that if he were Bourke, he would resign, for if he did not he would fare worse. Bourke asked what he had done to warrant resignation or dismissal.

Bourke quoted the conversation verbatim. Dawson replied, "It is not what you have done, it is what you did not do."

"What is it I should have done that I did not do?"

"You should not have let these men go from Wright Island."

Bourke retorted, "There were better precautions taken this summer under my management than last summer under the warden's management."

Dawson was blunt, "That is nothing, the men went, the country is excited and a victim is necessary."

Bourke wrote in his letter that nothing he could say to Dawson could dissuade him from deciding Bourke should go, so Bourke drafted him a letter of resignation in pencil for his review. In his draft letter he stated his conviction that he was sure that a conspiracy existed against him and as he did not want to embarrass the government, he would resign. He included some superannuation requests in the document, and the document was written up and formally submitted, and to all intents and purposes Bourke was under the impression that his pension requests had been granted. The conditional resignation called for $1,000 per year, and when his pension started to arrive, Bourke was horrified to see that he was to receive $450 per year. He at once entered a protest, and there the matter sat, as he wrote in his letter that he was sure that "justice would be done." But he was to finally realize that he was not to see justice, and this had prompted him to pursue the course now set upon.[13]

That same month, the escaped convict John Clark was captured near Burlington, Washington. Canadian authorities immediately took steps to extradite him, and he was kept in the jail at Mt. Vernon until they arrived. The twenty-three year old Clark had told his relatives around Burlington the story of his escape with Bill Miner. It confirmed what investigators had already determined. Miner had arranged all the details of the escape, and near the time of the breakout, he had asked Clark if he wished to join the group. They had gone through a hole under the first fence and scaled the second. The hole had been pre-dug and loosely covered. After they had cleared the wall, they went straight into the bush, later splitting up and Miner going his own way. Clark had said that the three had hidden out for about a week in the heavy bush with almost nothing to eat. Clark and Woods had headed south together, and Woods had hidden out near Anacortes in Washington.[14]

Bourke continued his letter writing campaign with missives on the 1ST and 2ND of March, 1909. By now the Columbian's readership must have been tiring of his boring and self-serving epistles, but they definitely served the purposes of the newspaper's publisher and Opposition M.P. Taylor. In these communications, Bourke advised all his readers on how he had taken a penitentiary that was "more like a lumber camp than a disciplinary institution" in 1895 and turned it into a modern example of enlightened prison administration. He also advised the readership about all the good deeds he had done over the years in looking after penitentiary employees and their families.[15]

On March 2ND, sparks were jumping between the benches of the House of Commons in Ottawa. "The stormiest and most exciting scene of the session occurred this afternoon, and for a while the House almost got beyond the control of the Speaker."[16]

Opposition M.P. Taylor challenged the government on a motion of supply for having allowed three weeks to pass before taking any action on the B.C. Penitentiary affairs. He quoted from Bourke's voluminous supply of letters published in his paper and how Inspector Dawson had concealed from his department in Ottawa information that he should have passed on. He also questioned a letter he had in his possession signed by CPR detective Bullick in which he denies meeting with Miner to discuss the bonds, and describes the story of the hidden bonds an invention concocted by Miner and his friends. Taylor quickly pointed out that this flew directly in the face of the government's statement that Miner had indeed stated to prison officials that he had talked to Bullick about the bonds.[17]

When Taylor had completed his questions for the Minister of Justice, Mr. Aylesworth rose and made a scathing attack on the New Westminster M.P. Aylesworth verbally thrashed Taylor for the erroneous reporting of his paper with regard to Chief McIntosh and for conducting a trial by newspaper. The opposition benches commenced to hiss the Minister for his mean-spirited attack. Several members of the opposition were quick to "roast" Aylesworth "for his picayune attack on the member for New Westminster and his dodging of the grave indictment against the honour of the Department of Justice."[18]

Aylesworth's accusations caused "a loud uproar, the Opposition crying 'take it back' and the Liberals cheering."[19]

Mr. Taylor attempted to correct the record; however, the Liberals howled him down. The Speaker had to intervene to ensure he obtained a hearing. Taylor told the House that the report had not been telegraphed to his paper, but had been picked up from the Vancouver News Advertiser.[20]

Mr. Taylor rose to a point of order, but was howled down by the Liberals. He "stuck to his guns," and the Speaker ruled in his favour.[21]

Mr. Aylesworth continued to criticize Taylor for using his paper for his own political ends and accused the member of wilfully changing the name from McKenzie to McIntosh. The harried Mr. Taylor tried to correct this, but the Liberals behind the Minister shouted him down. Aylesworth added fuel to the fire by noting that every other newspaper in British Columbia had got the name right. Mr. Taylor finally got the Speaker to put a stop to Aylesworth's attacks. Shouting continued back and forth, and Mr. Taylor tried to advise the House that the article had been taken word for word from the News Advertiser.[22]

"Mr. Aylesworth continued his speech without paying any attention to the point of order raised by Mr. Taylor, whereupon the latter somewhat heatedly asked the Speaker if Mr. Aylesworth was privileged to insult him in the House. This brought another burst of jeers from the government benches and applause from the Opposition. The Speaker ruled that allusions to a newspaper could hardly be regarded as an insult to a Member of the House."[23]

"Mr. Aylesworth said that he was not able to penetrate into the secrets of Mr. Taylor's sanctum, and went on to speak with great sarcasm of 'this remarkable piece of enterprise.' Mr. Taylor again protested at these repeated insults, but the Speaker ruled that Mr. Aylesworth's references to the newspaper did not infringe on the rights of the member who happened to be its owner. Mr. Aylesworth went on to speak of the Columbian as having, by copying the dispatch, defrauded the paper which paid for it, and also accused the west coast editor of forgery. He described the dispatch as it appeared in the Columbian as 'unaccountably erroneous' and went on to refer to McIntosh's repudiation of the statement ascribed to him."[24]

With his sails now full, the Minister told the House that all questions with regards to Opposition's concerns had been satisfactorily answered, and it was plain for all to see that the department had "left no stone unturned to recapture Miner." Mr. Aylesworth then sat down to the applause of his fellow Liberals.[25]

Opposition Leader Borden then rose with a copy of the February 18 issue of the Vancouver News Advertiser in his hand. He addressed Minster Aylesworth and asked if he adhered to the charge against Mr. Taylor of forgery or wished to withdraw it. Aylesworth had a hasty discussion with Solicitor General Bureau sitting beside him, rose, and said that his authority for repeating the charges was not him personally but gained from statements that had been made to him.[26]

The Conservatives hooted with disdain, and one of the members shouted, "Slandering by proxy."

Mr. Borden then referred to the News Advertiser in his hand and conclusively proved that it was that paper that had caused the reporting muddle and substituted "McIntosh" for "McKenzie."

Mr. Aylesworth made no apology or retraction.

Prime Minister Laurier supported Aylesworth in declaring that there was no necessity for an inquiry or an investigation. He lectured Mr. Taylor "for not giving notice of his intention of bringing the matter up, and an observation that a good deal of irrelevant matter had been brought into the discussion, the premier remarked that the only question in which the country was interested was whether there had been connivance in Miner's escape."[27]

The Prime Minister "said vague rumours were not sufficient

grounds for an investigation."

It was 10 P.M. before the House got into committee of supply, and the furor finally ended without a vote and nothing settled after five hours of debate.[28]

In the same issue of the Columbian which detailed the debates of that day was the inevitable letter from Bourke. In it he was to go a step too far in his accusations, and he would find himself in court for libel. In this letter, Bourke quoted the story that Miner had told to penitentiary guard and instructor McKenzie. Bourke directly connected lawyer Alec Mcintyre in Kamloops with Bullick and Terry when they had their interview with Miner. He directly stated in his letter that "Mr. Mcintyre ... came to the prison with Mr. Bullick and an old pal of Miner's, Terry." The Columbian had been given a secret copy of McKenzie's statement of his meeting with Miner, probably provided by Bourke, and proceeded to summarize the intent of the document. The paper repeated the story that Miner told the guard of his meeting with Mcintyre, Bullick and Terry, and how Warden Whyte had left the room. Miner said that Bullick had offered him a pardon if he would reveal the location of the bonds. For anyone unaware of the background to this statement, it was a damning piece of information, and the Conservative Opposition would use it tellingly for its own political ends. However, Bourke would come to regret the remarks he had made in print that day, probably never realizing that he was being used as a tool and dupe by political forces beyond his ken.[29]

Bourke's interminable letters to the editor of the Columbian continued uninterrupted throughout March. Five letters were received between March 6TH and 15TH. Finally on the 18TH of March, the last of this series of letters from the disaffected Bourke appeared on the front page of the New Westminster paper. In this last missive, in rambling, self-serving, self-pitying, endless paragraphs, he admits to his readers that he had two goals in mind when he started his campaign. The first was to ensure the "moral improvement of the penitentiary service," and the second, to achieve the superannuation allowance which he felt had been promised him. He felt that he had partially achieved the first task; however, the second seemed to have continued to elude him. In his frustration and disappointment, he lashed out again at the government and penitentiary department. He felt deceived and manipulated, and concluded his last letter with a scathing rebuke and criticism of his nemesis and the architect of his destruction, Inspector Dawson. In typical overstatement, he wrote how, from the beginning of the inquiry, Dawson had his knife all ready for Bourke's official decapitation and accused the Inspector of graft, corruption and exploitation of prison labour for his own uses.[30]

The ex-deputy warden, through his letter writing campaign and interviews, had managed to ensure numerous pages of ink had been spent in newspapers all across Canada and that Bill Miner's name, if not formerly well known across the country, now certainly was. However, his goals and those of the Opposition would continue to be frustrated for some time. The Conservative Opposition would have to wait until 1911 to take its revenge on Laurier and his Liberals when its use of Bourke and his allegations had been long forgotten. The penitentiary service continued on into the future, with philosophical and disciplinary changes, escapes, riots and scandals systematically appearing through the years. The B.C. Penitentiary at New Westminster would finally close its doors for the last time in 1980.

On March 22, the matter of funding for the B.C. Penitentiary again came before the House, and again M.P. Taylor called for supplementary information relative to the "untimely departure of Bill Miner." This time the government was ready and released all the details of Inspector Dawson's report to the House. It included Dawson's final report and recommendations and all the interviews of guards and convicts, including McKenzie's on his interview with Miner about the bonds. It also included a copy of CPR Inspector Bullick's letter of denial with regard to visiting Miner in the company of lawyer Mcintyre or discussing stolen bonds with Miner. The Opposition was overwhelmed with the amount and detail of material, and debate was finally halted to allow study of the Inspector's report. In May Mr. Taylor attempted to resurrect the Miner affair, but to no avail, and it finally died a quiet death. For years the affair rested in the obscurity of Hansard and the crumbling pages of a few partisan and sensationalist west coast newspapers. It would be rudely awakened only by prying and inquisitive eyes almost 100 years after the events took place.

In April of 1909, Mr. Bourke was to be confronted by the litigious lawyer Alex Mcintyre from Kamloops. Mcintyre had not been impressed to see his name bandied about on the front pages of Canadian newspapers. The accusations that he had attended meetings with Bill Miner which he knew were entirely fictitious caused him to proceed with legal actions against the letter-writing Bourke.

The action of Mr. Mcintyre against Bourke for defamatory libel was based on a letter sent by Bourke to the New Westminster Columbian newspaper on the 3RD of March in 1909. The preliminary hearing commenced in police court in Vancouver before Magistrate Corbould. J.E. Bird of Vancouver acted for Mr. Mcintyre, and W.A. McDonald acted for Mr. Bourke. The news editor of the New Westminster Columbian Stewart was called to testify, and he produced the particular letter Mr. Bourke had sent to the Columbian that contained the libellous statements. The original letter was entered as an exhibit. The editor was questioned extensively by the counsel for the complainant as to what Bourke had said in conversation to him regarding the letters.

Counsel for the defendant referred to references to Miner and Mcintyre and the alleged visits and whether they were available. The witness didn't know.

"Did Mr. Bourke tell you that he had been told by instructor McKenzie that Mcintyre had visited the penitentiary with Mr. Bullick?"

The news editor responded, "Yes, I think he did."

Mr. Mcintyre was then called to the stand. He advised that he was a barrister practicing in Kamloops and had acted for Bill Miner in May and June of 1906. After the convictions, he had seen his three clients privately in Kamloops. Ten days later he made application to the court for a reserved case, but the application had been refused.

In June 1906, he saw his client Miner and the two others separately, in the presence of a prison officer, in the penitentiary to discuss procuring funds to carry on an appeal against the conviction. The complainant's counsel then read references from various newspapers as to further meetings Mcintyre was supposed to have had with Miner and asked the witness when he had next seen Miner.

Mcintyre responded that he had never seen him again, but had had some correspondence with him. Mcintyre also noted that he and Warden Whyte were on the best of terms, and any indication that the Warden had been rapped on the knuckles at Mcintyre's instigation was incorrect. He had asked Whyte for a private interview with Miner, but this had been refused. He had then written the penitentiary department in Ottawa asking the Minister of Justice for that privilege. The Minister had advised Mcintyre that he could meet with his client any time, but not privately.

Mcintyre said he had expected to launch the appeal of the three convicted robbers early in the fall of 1906, but as funds were not forthcoming, the matter was allowed to lapse. It had died a natural death.

Mcintyre said it was not true that he had visited Miner in the company of Bullick and Jake Terry, and he had lost no time in bringing the matter to court. He said he had no idea he had been mentioned as being at the meeting until the publication of the Columbian had detailed instructor McKenzie's testimony to the inquiry. Mcintyre further stated he had no reason to assume Burke had a grudge against him. Mcintyre admitted he had attempted to get an interview with his client Miner out of earshot of penitentiary officials, and had requested it. He had wanted to talk to Miner about funds for the appeal of his case. Mcintyre admitted that there had been mention made of the stolen bonds since shortly after the trial in Kamloops. He had received letters from Miner, but not since December of 1906.

CPR detective Inspector R.E. Bullick next took the stand and went under oath. He testified he knew nothing of the escape and had not been at the prison with Mcintyre at any time. He described his meeting with Miner and Jake Terry that took place in February of 1907. Bullick stated that the warden was present throughout the interview, which had been initiated to determine whether Terry knew Miner. Bullick had met Terry in Vancouver, and they had gone to the B.C. Penitentiary together to see if Terry had been truthful in his statements.

Defendant's counsel warned Bullick, "Let out with it, you went there with reference to the bonds."

"What bonds?" replied Bullick, and went on to add that he had never known of any lost or stolen bonds. He added that Terry had been working for him for about five weeks previous to the Miner visit, and Bullick had been attempting to get some information from Miner about some items stolen at the Mission robbery that had never been recovered. During this visit to Miner he, Bullick, had only said a few words to the prisoner, and the lost property was not discussed. He did note that Terry had satisfied him that he knew Miner. The penitentiary's visitors register was then produced and it was determined that Bullick and Terry's visit had not been entered, although it was the prison rule that all visitors be registered.

Bullick went on to testify that he had first heard the story of the stolen bonds in 1905. He stated that he knew the story had started in a Bellingham paper and there was no truth to it. Bullick told the court that Miner probably told the story to instructor McKenzie on the chance of working up some kind of scheme in the future.

In the afternoon, Instructor McKenzie, ex-guard McNeil, guard Doyle and New Westminster Chief of Police McIntosh were called as witnesses for the defendant.[31]

Later that same afternoon, the case came to an abrupt halt, and Bourke undertook to withdraw the objectionable reference to Mcintyre contained in his letter to the Columbian. Bourke's defence lawyer MacDonald read a statement that as sworn statements in testimony revealed Mr. Mcintyre was not in attendance at any meetings with Miner and Bullock, his client "feels it is his duty in an open manner to withdraw any reference to Mr. Mcintyre made in the letter referred to, and wishes to apologize to Mr. Mcintyre for any such reference made to him under this misapprehension and desires that the papers shall give the utmost publicity to this statement."[32]

Fortunately for Mr. Bourke, with this apology his dealings with Mr. Mcintyre came to an end.

Mr. Mcintyre, though, was not finished with the Bill Miner affair. That same year he had launched an action that would not reflect generously upon his character to future generations. The Kamloops lawyer, almost three years after the trial, felt more monies were due him for defending the three Ducks train robbers. In County Court he claimed that the three bandits still owed him $500 for his services in 1906. Miner still had approximately $150 and his gold watch in the penitentiary safe, and Mcintyre wanted access to it, as well as to any monies in the accounts of Dunn and Colquhoun. In May the new Warden Brown of the B.C. Penitentiary was served with a garnishee order against the two convicts and the absent Bill Miner.

In a letter to his supervisor, Inspector Stewart in Ottawa, Warden Brown notified him that the order instructed to pay into the court all the "debts, obligations and liabilities, owing, payable or accruing due" from Mcintyre to the defendants. The amount of the claim was $522.35, including legal and processing costs.

"Both Dunn and Colquhoun have seen me since they were served with the summonses yesterday, and protested against the action. Dunn telling me that he transferred to Mcintyre mining property of value considerably exceeding the amount of Mcintyre's charge for defending the prisoners. And that the said transfer was accepted by Mcintyre in full settlement.

"Colquhoun had a little money sent him by his people some time ago for the purposes of having his teeth, which were in a very bad condition, attended to by a dentist, and he very naturally objects to have this small amount, sent to him for a special purpose, taken from him. He tells me that he thoroughly understood at the time of the trial that the lawyer's fees were provided for, and that further when Mr. Mcintyre saw these men in the interview referred to by Mr. D.D. Bourke, nothing was said, so far as Colquhoun could recollect, about any payment being due on account of the trial. The whole talk was as to raising money, $300 is Colquhoun's recollection, to pay the charges of an appeal for a new trial .... Both Dunn and Colquhoun have given notice that they propose to defend the action, and I therefore refer the matter to you for instructions."[33]

When Warden Brown's letter was received in Ottawa, Inspector George Dawson wired Brown the next day, ordering him to adhere to the garnishee order.[34]

Dunn and Colquhoun lost what little amount of funds they had in their accounts to the avaricious nature of the Kamloops lawyer. It is not known whether Miner's funds and gold watch and chain were also claimed by Mcintyre, as all records of them have been lost.

XXVII
THE TRAGEDY OF
LEWIS COLQUHOUN

LEWIS COLQUHOUN'S STORY is one of mystery and of tragedy, full of
unanswered questions and unfulfilled family expectations.

Lewis Colquhoun was born 27 April 1877 in the little community
of Clifford on the Niagara Peninsula of Ontario. Clifford was an
agricultural town in Minto Township, Wellington County, about
70 kilometres northwest of Guelph. His father Robert was born in
Dunbartonshire, Scotland, and came to Canada in 1842. He married
Jessie Grant in 1860, and together they settled down on their farm in
Minto to raise a large family. Robert and Jessie were a hard working,
thrifty and energetic couple who gradually accumulated over 300
acres of farmland in the area. He became a well-known and respected
Liberal who took a great interest in the questions of the day. Robert
and Jessie had four daughters: Margaret, Marion, Mary and Jessie; and
five sons: Peter, Alexander. Robert Jr., John and the youngest, Lewis.
Lewis's older brothers Peter, Alexander and Robert Jr., had their own
farms by 1906 and were "counted amongst the most substantial and
progressive citizens of Minto."[1]

A close friend of Colquhoun's has left us a detailed description
of Lewis's early childhood in Ontario. Robert H. Rea grew up in a
farmhouse about a mile away from where Lewis was raised and knew
Lewis and his many brothers and sisters well. Living about three miles
from Clifford, Ontario, Rea and Colquhoun attended Clifford Public
School together. They also attended Harriston High School and

frequently walked or rode their horses back and forth to classes.

"His people are industrious, and are well thought of by all in the community, both in business and socially. I have never known anything reflecting discredit or dishonour on any of the family .... Lewis was given a better education than others of the family. He was a good-looking young man, intelligent.

"At high school he did not make very fast progress with his studies although he gained a measure of efficiency. He always paid some attention to his work, but never worked very hard at it. He was at this time about eighteen or twenty years. He was of a good-natured, jovial easy-going temperament. His manner was quiet rather than boisterous, and not very self-assertive. He was not at all given to be wild or ill-at-ease in conduct or conversation, but always behaved himself well.

"Indeed, so far as I knew Lewis, I could not see anything in him that would lead me to suspect that he would ever have to face a charge as is brought against him. I have not seen him since about 1900, but have heard through correspondence that he came out west to Alberta, and afterwards located in Phoenix, B.C. I do not know him to have been in any way implicated in any offence before."

Rea speculated that in the case of the train robbery, he could only imagine that Lewis must have been led astray by a manipulative and adept leader as the man he knew would never have had the "moral nature and training" necessary or the tendency and inclination to be involved in anything so criminally inclined. He noted that neither Colquhoun's family nor Lewis himself ever exhibited any criminal tendencies.[2]

Lewis graduated from a teacher's college in Ontario and taught school near Clifton for a few years. When he contracted tuberculosis is not known, but by 1904 he had moved out to western Canada to get away from southern Ontario's high humidity and to take advantage of the dry climate near Calgary and the southeast corner of British Columbia near Phoenix and Greenwood. It must have been devastating for the young man, recently graduated and with a respected career ahead of him, to hear the diagnosis of tuberculosis, a virtual death sentence. A future with a wife, children and a home was now lost to him, and he could only watch his brothers and sisters with envy, sadness and regret as they married and ventured out on their own to raise families and become productive members of their community. Lewis chose the path which did not remind him of his mortality, and one where he would not pass on the disease to children in his charge.[3]

After the capture of the three suspected train robbers, reporters watched the prisoners closely so that they could describe the manners and characters of the men to their readers. Colquhoun was universally described in all the papers as restrained, quiet, taciturn, courteous and an "educated man with more genteel training" than either Edwards or Dunn. The Vancouver News Advertiser stated that Colquhoun looked like "the last man who would be suspected of being in a hold up." He was "very reticent, and evidently feels his position." The Province reported that Colquhoun "was very reticent and said nothing except in answer to official questions, and replied to them in monosyllables." His demeanour "created some sympathy among those at the examination, so uniformly quiet and courteous did he appear. Although perfectly self collected, he seemed to feel his position keenly." "With a frank and open face and a quiet manner" he was an "easy going young fellow" of "good character" that "no one thought … would have been connected with a train robbery, as he seemed to lack grit and get up enough for such an undertaking."[4]

What we hear described by the reporters was a young man, well educated and respectful of society and its institutions, with no great chip on his shoulder or blatant criminal intent obvious to the casual observer. We see a man somewhat confused by the position he finds himself in, but who is prepared to leave his fate in the hands of a trained purveyor of the law and of those responsible for Canadian justice. He received bad advice both from his short-term friend Edwards and from defence lawyer Mcintyre. He would come to regret deeply his association with them both.

Mcintyre's decision to defend all three suspects himself would be a fateful decision. This severely compromised each of the defendants, especially Colquhoun. Colquhoun, as an educated man, was perhaps too willing to put his fate in the hands of the Kamloops lawyer, probably upon the advice of Miner. Miner had seen Mcintyre in action at the trial of Smoky Chisholm's shooter, and most likely advised the ex-schoolteacher that he was a skilled lawyer that would probably be successful in getting the three of them off. Miner's recognized ability to impress and guide young men is well documented, and Dunn and Colquhoun both readily accepted his advice as that of a man wise in the ways of the courts and lawyers. Unfortunately for them, they didn't realize that Miner, following his own advice, had spent most of his adult life behind the bars of San Quentin.

While Swanson valiantly tried to assist Mcintyre to represent Colquhoun and his family's interests, the lawyer had nothing to work with, and there is no record anywhere of Colquhoun's reaction to his twenty year sentence or any communications he might have had from his family at any time.

During the trial, Provincial Police Superintendent Hussey had seen an isolated news report of Colquhoun having served time for petty theft in Walla Walla State Penitentiary in Washington state. This would prove prior criminal activity and could be used as evidence during the trial proceedings at Kamloops. He pursued the rumour, and in July of 1906 he received a letter from the Superintendent of the Penitentiary H.F. Kees. Hussey had sent Colquhoun's photo and description to the penitentiary official, requesting that a search of the institution's files be made to determine if Colquhoun had spent time there. Kees wrote him back and advised him that they did not have anyone in their files or photo gallery with that name or who matched the photo and description provided. He included the photos, descriptions and rewards offered of convicts that had escaped from his institution, and asked Hussey to have his organization be on the lookout for them. The report of serving time at Walla Walla was determined to have been the product of "yellow journalism" and was probably manufactured news.[5]

Not much is known of the time Colquhoun spent in the B.C.

Penitentiary. His files were sent to Ottawa upon his death, and access there is difficult. What is known is that he spent most of his time inside, working in the carpentry shop and other trade locations. The west coast marine climate that he encountered at New Westminster directly adjacent to the Fraser River and not far from the influence of the Pacific Ocean must have compromised the symptoms of his tuberculosis, as the humidity was extremely high. Heavy rains for much of the year and primitive conditions in the cells added to his misery. His relatives in Ontario continued to press for his release, but to unheeding and uninterested ears.[6]

In 1909, the avaricious lawyer Mcintyre launched his garnishee action against Dunn and Colquhoun and Bill Miner's effects left behind after he escaped. As it was to Dunn, it was a low blow to Colquhoun also, as they were convinced that the lawyer's defence fees had been looked after, especially with the mining claims and properties turned over to Mcintyre by Dunn. These values were said to exceed by far the amount needed for their mutual defence. Mcintyre had mentioned nothing to them about monies owing on his visit in June soon after their incarceration, confining his discussions with them on the need to obtain additional funds for their appeal. No money was available, so the appeal was dropped, and the two convicts assumed that was the end of the story. However, Mcintyre had heard the stories about the stolen bonds, excess cash Miner had supposedly received from the proceeds of a relative's estate in New York, and funds contributed by relatives and friends of the two unfortunate remaining convicts.[7]

Like Dunn, Colquhoun protested against the action, stating that what little he did have in his prison account was provided to him by his relatives for rehabilitation of his teeth by a dentist. His progressive disease and the rigid prison conditions and food had severely affected his dental health, and he was sorely in need of attention.

However, all their protests were to no avail, and the accounts were forfeited to the lawyer in Kamloops. This example of powerlessness on the part of Dunn and Colquhoun contributed greatly to their difficulty in facing their prison existence, and Colquhoun's health started to decline further.[8]

By 1911, Colquhoun's disease had caught up to him, and his condition worsened rapidly. Shorty Dunn stuck by his fair and foul weather friend and "fought hard to secure him better treatment, being to some extent successful."[9]

But on the 22ND of September, 1911, Lewis Colquhoun's agony came to an end and he died in the penitentiary hospital. He was thirty-four years old. Cause of death was attributed to phthisis, defined as the wasting away or atrophy of the body. It was an unscientific way of describing tuberculosis early in the twentieth century. A short obituary appeared in the Vancouver Province which described him as a schoolteacher, bookkeeper and train robber.[10]

His family in Clifford claimed his body, and it was shipped by rail in a plain coffin to the Ontario town where he was born. Ironically the baggageman that accompanied Colquhoun on his last journey to the east was Theo Michell, one of the CPR employees on the train crew which had suffered under Bill Miner's depredations west of the Mission Junction in 1904. Colquhoun's relatives interred him in the Clifford Public Cemetery in Howick Township, Huron County, Ontario, marking his resting place with a fine, tall and imposing red granite marker. Other than his name and the dates of his birth and death, no other inscription describes the ex-schoolteacher who died such a lonely death.[11] [12]

After the doors of the penitentiary closed behind him, we only have one document composed by Colquhoun himself, and most of the controversial facts in it are supported from other sources. The document, along with similar ones written by both Miner and Dunn after their incarceration in December of 1906, makes for chilling reading as it indicates a dire miscarriage of justice may inadvertently have occurred in a Kamloops courtroom one hundred years ago. Copies of the documents were sent to Warden Whyte of the B.C. Penitentiary, the Vancouver offices of the CPR, and Superintendent Hussey of the Provincial Police in Victoria. None were ever answered or acted upon in any way.

The documents themselves were found in the British Columbia

Archives' Provincial Police files of "Correspondence Inwards to the Superintendent." The statements of Colquhoun, Dunn and George Edwards were found together, and included with them was a covering letter from Inspector R.E. Bullick of the CPR's Special Service police to Superintendent Hussey. Bullick refers Hussey to the copies of the statements of the three robbers enclosed and makes no further comments. The actual documents are on 8½ by 14 inch carbon flimsies. No other information is known about the documents, other than an identical copy of the George Edwards' statement is found in the "George Edwards (Bill Miner) Correspondence" file saved by Anthony Martin from destruction at the B.C. Penitentiary in 1980, and now in his collection. Presumably copies of Dunn and Colquhoun's statements and other valuable information would have been in their own personal penitentiary files, but these are now either lost or squirrelled away in archives in eastern Canada and unavailable for research by western Canadians.

The documents purport to maintain that Colquhoun was innocent of taking any part in the robbery at Ducks and that he had no idea Miner and Dunn had criminal plans underway. He had maintained the camps, cooked the meals, and looked after the horses, unaware of the plans set in motion by Dunn and Edwards. He had not even had the chance to go into Kamloops until after the capture of the three robbers. The document was typed, presumably copied from the individual convict's handwritten copy by the warden's secretary.

Statement of Colquhoun

Got employment in Vancouver early in the fall of 1904 work on construction CPR telegraph line on Lake Slocan. After finishing that helped repair line from Rossland to Trail. Went from Trail to Grand Forks. Only stayed there for perhaps a day or two before going to Phoenix where I got work at the Granby Mine, worked until I got hurt and was laid off. Afterwards, worked at what odd jobs I could get such as helping to build the cribbing on the Great Northern in town, and odd days for Hunter Kendrick Company. Only got about 5 days more of work at Granby towards spring, than got book keeping for P. Burns, and then afterwards book keeping and time keeping for Great Northern construction works at Rock Creek. Was laid off and afterwards got work at Brooklyn Mine where I worked until the time of leaving Phoenix in latter part of winter 1906. In winter of 1906 Dr. Gordon performed an operation on me. After going through the operation went to Spokane in March of 1906. Stayed 2 days. Consulted Doctor there. Office on the main street but name forgotten. In Spokane I bought a pistol intending to go hunting. Came back to Midway and stayed a day or so there and then on to Princeton by stage. First met Edwards in the fall of 1906 (1905, PRG) at Phoenix. He invited me if I was in his section of the country to call on him. When I went to Princeton I met Edwards and went out with him to his ranch. Stayed there about 2 weeks. There I met Budd, Guy Main Price. Some days afterwards Dunn arrived. The time would be late in March. He came and went once or twice. I told him I would like to go hunting. We agreed to go together. Started out from Budd's ranch early in April. Edwards spoke of catching up on us in the neighbourhood of Aspen Grove. He met us there in about 2 weeks. That would be about the end of the third week in April. He came on horseback. We had a pack horse. We started out north shortly after Edwards arrived. Stopped sometime at a place called Batchelor's Meadows perhaps a week. We then came right along to Kamloops, reaching there not later than the 2ND of May. These days and times are only approximate. Would go with Dunn hunting occasionally. Some days before the holding up of the train Dunn went to Kamloops on horseback. He told me he was going for provisions. He was riding. Neither Dunn nor Edwards slept in the camp the night of the robbery or the night before. They left sometime in the day previous. They took their horses with them. I was not left in charge of them. As I did not see the horses afterwards, I concluded that they had taken them. When they returned to camp on the morning after the robbery they must have brought the horses back for the horses were used to take the stuff to the cache. At the cache I made a fire to which Dunn objected as he said the water was not good. The horses were then turned loose. They spoke of hunting in the woods and coming back for the horses. We were in the woods about 5 days. Wondered why we were not getting out of the woods. Thought we were lost. Then came to camp where we were arrested. I never had the smallest suspicion of what Dunn and Edwards were after.[13]

Shorty Dunn's statement chillingly reveals the self-serving reason why Colquhoun was allowed to come on Dunn and Edwards' expedition to Kamloops. Shorty does not in any way dispute his own personal guilt in the Ducks robbery. The reader should also be aware that the Third Man mentioned in Dunn's statement had never been positively identified, and both Dunn and Edwards would be careful to lay a false trail in both their statements that would conceal the Third Man's identity.

STATEMENT OF DUNN

I first met Colquhoun in the spring of 1906 at Budd's ranch. This would be about the end of March. Never saw him before. In the fall of 1905 had been planning with Edwards to hold up CPR train. About the first week of April started out with Colquhoun with one pack horse. Started for Aspen Grove to prospect and hunt. Edwards picked us up in about two weeks, say in about the second or third week of April. From Aspen to Kamloops Camp took some time say about two weeks as we were prospecting and hunting etc. At Batchelor's Meadows we must have stayed about one week. When Edwards met us at Aspen Grove he said to me, "We had better be moving on. We'll have to catch that train before they change the time of it." He told me that he had arranged for one of us to meet a third party in Kamloops who had been in Vancouver to obtain information. Kamloops Camp was about 10 or 11 miles from Kamloops. Stayed there about a week. About three or four days before the holdup, left in the morning for Kamloops to see third party referred to. Registered at the Dominion Hotel under the name of Jack Mitchell. Stayed there all night. Saw third party. Came out next day to camp where Colquhoun and Edwards were. Got back about 4:00 pm. Told Edwards where third party could be met. Had fixed date before. Was camped on creek on Thompson River day previous to the robbery, and there met the third man at the culvert that day. We three were all together in the camp that night. Colquhoun was not there. Slept most of the next day. At dusk, Edwards and I went to Ducks, left third party at the point where the train was first stopped, about a mile east of our camp. That night we held up the train as was arranged. Before parting with the third man we agreed to meet at a certain point and if third party couldn't make it, was to write and let us know where he was and where he could be met. Left for Colquhoun's camp, arrived early in the morning, just breaking day. Brought the two horses up to the camp, broke up the camp, took everything about a mile up the hill, and taking some provisions, cached the remainder. Hobbled the horses and turned them loose. One saddle we hung on a tree, the other we cached.

In any conversation regarding the robbery which Edwards and I had, Colquhoun was not a party and was not present. Colquhoun came with the party greatly against my personal wish, and at the suggestion of the third party, his idea being that the presence of a respectable party with us would have a tendency of allaying suspicion from us.

This statement is made of my own free will and had been read to me and is with the probable exception of dates and days correct.[14]

The statement attributed to George Edwards alias Bill Miner is the first document ever found in which the notorious American stagecoach and train robber confesses to a crime, and we can only assume that it was motivated by a genuine sense of empathy and justice. For once, the base facts he would relate probably related to the truth; however, the details of the Third Man were an obvious fiction. It should be noted that his first meeting with Colquhoun in Phoenix would have taken place shortly after Miner had robbed the Great Northern north of Seattle and absconded with a rumoured $36,000. His visit to Phoenix was no doubt fuelled by a goodly supply of cash, and young Colquhoun would have been impressed by the successful mining entrepreneur.

STATEMENT OF EDWARDS

I met Colquhoun first in the hotel in Phoenix, I think it was Blacks hotel on my return from Spokane. This would be on or about October of 1905. I believe he was time keeper in the railway construction work at that time. Met him casually. Was about a week there, and met him two or three times. Told him that I lived at Princeton, and was interested in mining and stock raising. If he came to Princeton would be pleased to see him. About three weeks after I made another trip to Spokane, and on my return I think I saw Colquhoun at Phoenix. Did not stay there long, and then went west on to Princeton. Next spring, about April of 1906, while in the barber's shop at Princeton, my attention was called to a young man who was said to be a stranger. I recognized him as Colquhoun, and went out to the hotel to meet him there. Asked him what he had come out there for. Said he had been hunting and prospecting. Invited him to come out to the ranch. It is known as Budd's ranch. He then came with me to the ranch, he walking and I riding. Jack Budd, Tom Arnold, Deafie the barber, Guy Main Price were at the ranch sometime during Colquhoun's stay there. I am not sure if Dunn was present when Colquhoun first came, but in a day or so he arrived from a trapping expedition. Colquhoun stayed for about a couple of weeks assisting me in the work. Three or four months before this, Dunn, another party and I had talked over the holding up of a train. I had mentioned the idea to two or three men in the vicinity. Dunn, self, and another party had arrived at an understanding in regards to holding up a C.P.R. train in the vicinity of Kamloops. Colquhoun and Dunn went down to the neighbourhood of Aspen Grove, prospecting, hunting and trapping. The plan was that I should meet Dunn after in the vicinity of Aspen Grove. They left the ranch the first week in April. This was about a fortnight before I left the ranch. In the meantime the third man came down on the train to Vancouver. Third man left from I think Armstrong. I rode from Princeton to Aspen. They at Aspen had pack horse and tent. I then told Dunn that I was ready for the job, the third man had gone to Vancouver, would be back at Kamloops, and I wanted to get to Kamloops to see him on the week of the tenth of May. I arranged to meet him at either the Dominion or the Grand Pacific hotel in Kamloops. Left Aspen, went through by way of Bachelors Meadows and the main road to about seven or eight miles from the river, between Ducks and Kamloops, south of the railroad. This would be about fifteen miles from Kamloops. We were about five or six days at this camp. Before train was robbed Dunn and I went toward Kamloops, passing Campbell Creek P.O. I then left Dunn, examined the track, Dunn riding into Kamloops alone, to meet the third party, with whom I had made the arrangement. I then went back to the camp where Colquhoun was, and Dunn came from Kamloops that night, between six and eight P.M. He stayed all night at our camp. He reported to me that third man had been seen and was ready. He was down by the track. In the morning Dunn and I went to the third man. Stayed together till dusk, then Dunn and I went to Ducks, and the third man stayed beside the track. The third man was held at the track so that when Colquhoun heard of the robbery he would not associate us with it. That night Dunn, and I, and a third man carried out our plans, and held up the C.P.R. train between Ducks and Kamloops. Before daylight we reached camp, broke camp same morning, and started south with packs on our backs, after looking for about two hours for pack horses which had strayed. Cached balance of provisions, including riding saddle and pack saddle. From beginning to end Colquhoun had no suspicion of our mission, and had no part whatsoever in the holding up of the train. I am making this statement of my own free will.[15]

Miner had thought that after the robbery Colquhoun would have heard that three bandits held up the train, and he naturally would have assumed that Shorty Dunn and George Edwards could not have done it as there were only the two of them that he was aware of.

After Colquhoun had died and before Shorty Dunn had been released from prison, Dunn wrote to his friend George Winkler in Victoria and told him about Lewis Colquhoun and his innocence of having taken any part in the robbery. He again repeated that Colquhoun was not the mysterious Third Man, but Dunn would not tell his mining friend who the guilty individual was.[16]

The innocence of Lewis Colquhoun seems certain, but if this is so, who could the mysterious Third Man have been?

Paul Stevens was born to John and Clara Stevens in LaGrande, Oregon, on the 12TH of January, 1872.[17] By June of 1880, Paul, his two sisters Clara 13, and Hattie 2, and their parents were in the vicinity of Lewiston, Nez Perce County, in Idaho Territory. His father must have been somewhat successful as the census for that year notes that two workers were resident in the Stevens household. One was a 28 year old seamstress named Mary Struck from Kentucky, and the other an older farm labourer of 49 years named John Bofinger from Wurtenburg, Germany.

The father, John, was born in Michigan, mother Clara in Maine, sister Clara in Oregon, and little sister Hattie in Idaho. All the children, even little Hattie, were noted as having attended school in the past year. A strange coincidence to this census record is that Shorty Dunn claimed that before he came into Canada he came from a town in the States called "Lewiston." Lewiston, Idaho, is right on the border between the states of Idaho and Washington, on the banks of the Snake River.

On the 20TH of March, 1895, Paul Stevens married Rosie Aldrich in Idaho. Rosie was from Juliaetta, Latah County, in Idaho, and Paul is noted as being from Genesee in Latah County. Both Julietta and

Gensee are within twenty miles of Lewiston and about 120 miles south of the Canadian border.[18]

By 1900, Paul (28) and Rose (22) Stevens, living in Stuart Township, Idaho County, had a son, Ray, of four years, and a daughter, Ruth, of two years. Paul worked as a stagecoach driver, he could read and write, and rented a house for his young family. Shortly after this census, Paul Stevens gave everything up and left for Canada. To our knowledge, he was never to return to the States and virtually abandoned his wife and two children.

What precipitated Paul Stevens' flight to Canada is not known, but some information indicates that some sort of incident happened in either Oregon, Idaho or Montana that convinced him that he should light out for parts unknown. The area he eventually found himself in near Little Fish Lake in the Monte Hills is even today isolated and far from public roads. One hundred years ago it was even more remote, inaccessible and secluded. He did not pre-empt the land he built his cabin on and where he and Margaret Todd would spend only a few years. He supported himself and "Maggie" by raising a few cattle and horses, hunting deer in the hills, and selling the meat to willing businesses in Kamloops. He supplemented his income with a good deal of horse rustling, preying on local ranchers and farmers and driving his slicks and branded horses south to the border. He did not have many friends around the area, but one was Tommy Graham who lived at the north end of Monte Lake, and at the bottom of the trail that led up to Stevens' virtual hideout.

There are substantial reasons to believe that horse thief Paul Stevens was the mysterious Third Man, based on contemporary evidence from the time, and also in the memories of the descendants of the Todd and Pratt families, of whom Stevens' wife Maggie was a relative.

The writer had numerous conversations and interviews with Edward Cecil "Toddy" Pratt during the decades prior to his death in 1993, many specifically about the Bill Miner affair. Toddy Pratt was the son of Robert Pratt and Helena (Ellen) Todd, the widow of Reignford Knapp and sister to Paul Steven's wife Margaret. Born in 1900, Toddy was a half-brother to David Knapp, and they lived together in a log house that still stands today. Besides other facts, stories and anecdotes, before his death in 1993 Toddy mentioned to the writer that the Pratt and Todd families had always suspected Paul Stevens of being mixed up in the Ducks train robbery. Toddy Pratt's nephew, James Pratt, also admitted to the writer that his father Bob Pratt and his uncle Toddy told him that Paul Stevens was a known horse thief and rustler and had close connections with the robbery at Ducks.[19][20]

Paul Stevens' complicity in the robbery is also referenced in the files of the Attorney General's Crown Prosecutor. In one of the boxes of files are details of the investigations conducted by the various detectives and law enforcement officers around the Kamloops area after the robbery. Assembling the information against the three train robbers for the trial to be held in Kamloops was intensive and far-reaching. One of the investigators was an undercover agent known only as "Operator #30," but it has been determined by the writer that it was probably the Thiel detective Calhoun. Numerous witness statements were included in the documents with a covering letter from Captain W.L. Seavey of the Thiel Detective Agency to the head of the CPR Special Service police investigators in Kamloops, W.L. McLaws.

Working for the Pinkerton's rival detective agency, and under the direct control of Seavey, Calhoun interviewed James Todd and his son-in-law Robert Pratt at the latter's log house in Upper Campbell Creek. Standing beside them was Toddy Pratt's older half-brother David Knapp. When James Todd told the detective that Paul Stevens had spent the night right there in Robert Pratt's home, young David jumped right in and destroyed Paul Stevens' alibi.

"Yes, I can swear he came in here about 1 o'clock that night and got into bed …."[21]

In his covering letter to McLaws, Seavey brings McLaws' attention to the young boy's statement and notes that Stevens climbed into bed at the Pratt house a full two hours after the train robbery which had occurred just down over the silt bluffs from the Pratts' farm.

Other activities of Stevens, while not as incriminating by themselves, taken together add to the circumstantial evidence for his involvement in the robbery. Ranchers and farmers like Sam Bice told detectives that Paul had a poor reputation around the Kamloops country, and it was known that he was a horse thief, but no one could prove it. He was perpetually short of cash and had ruined his credit with Kamloops merchants. He had probably been given money by Miner to pick up the groceries for the three at Brooks' grocery store in Kamloops. On the 20TH of April, while Miner and his two companions were at their campsite east of Kamloops, his conspicuous and uncharacteristic buying of groceries and other goods with a ready supply of cash had brought him to the attention of the store clerk and the Kamloops Chief of Police, and finally to robbery investigators.

The strange activities that took place at the Stevens cabin in the Monte Hills, the attempts by the captured horses to follow the trail to Stevens' cabin, and the arrest of the known horse thief by Constable Gardom, taken together with the other information, are strong indications that Paul Stevens was the mysterious Third Man that assisted Shorty Dunn and Bill Miner at Ducks that night. The fact that Stevens, the morning of the day of the Ducks robbery, was observed leading three horses meeting the description of those of the robbers, cross country towards Campbell Creek from his cabin at Little Fish Lake, one shod and two unshod, is another piece of purely circumstantial but intriguing evidence. His desperate attempt to escape from his Provincial Police captors Gardom, Smith and Cotton on his way to a jail cell in Vernon also did not reflect the actions of an innocent man.[22][23]

Bill Miner had most likely made the acquaintance of Stevens during mutual horse rustling activities that Miner and Budd were

---

Taken in the late 1930s in the east Kootenays, in the foreground is the future Senator Syd Smith of Kamloops. Behind him, holding a rifle, is his guide Paul Stevens. This is the only known photograph of the elusive Stevens, and has been identified with 90% certainty by a Pratt descendant who knew him personally. COURTESY OF JO-ANNE PORTMAN COLLECTION, MERRITT, B.C..

involved with around the Grande Prairie and Douglas Lake country in the months and years preceding the Ducks robbery. Predation by rustlers was prevalent throughout the area, including the Nicola Valley, and known temporary collection and holding spots for rustled livestock were located in isolated valley spots such as Butler Meadows southeast of Paul Stevens' cabin. North-south transport routes to the States were well known and used by skilled drovers far from prying eyes.

After his arrest by Constable Gardom, Paul Stevens was to spend only a few days in jail in Vernon, then was transported by Chief Constable Simmons to the Kamloops Gaol. He was ultimately released for lack of evidence. The CPR and the Provincial Police already had three train robbers in custody in Kamloops, so they were not interested in trying to make a case against a fourth, when there was no indication four robbers were involved. Paul Stevens scuttled back to his cabin in the Monte Hills, secure in his isolation and remoteness.

However, Paul Stevens would not escape unscathed. Official law enforcement may have been satisfied that they had the train robbery perpetrators in custody, but the good ranchers and farmers of Grande Prairie were not so sure. They were convinced Stevens had been preying on their stock for years. Perhaps by consulting beforehand with former Special Constables Percy Cotton and Dick Smith in Grande Prairie, they were able to increase their certainty that Stevens was also involved in the train robbery. Tired of his nefarious antics, a group of farmers and ranchers from Grande Prairie rode up to Paul Stevens' cabin shortly after the robbery, made sure no one was home, and burnt it to the ground. They hoped to convince the American horse thief to leave the country by burning him out and forcing him to leave the area, away from the temptations of their horses and cattle.[24][25]

The suspected thief and train robber must have counted his blessings that he could escape with his hide intact, for he soon left the Kamloops country for a while and took up hunting and guiding in the Kootenays. However, after a few years had passed and the heat had died down, he was drawn back to his old haunts. There is no future reference to his being involved in any other law-breaking activities. He and Maggie continued to live around Monte Lake and Kamloops for many years, still close to their Todd and Pratt relatives who were so loyal to Maggie. Stevens was a very accomplished hunter and would again take up hunting deer in the Monte Hills. He would wait at known water holes, shoot the deer, dress them out on the spot, then haul them to Kamloops and sell them to local restaurants. James Pratt told the writer he remembers Stevens talking about Tea Kettle Creek in the Monte Hills as where Miner was to have hidden his stolen bonds. Stevens used his exceptional hunting and tracking abilities to make a living as a big game guide and would take parties to the Kootenays to get elk and bear. It was in the Kootenays where Kamloops Senator Syd Smith would use him as a game guide on his hunting expeditions. Paul Stevens and Maggie lived together until they died. Towards the end of their lives, they lived with relatives at 12TH Avenue and Battle Street, near the railway tracks in Kamloops. When he could and when he was able, Stevens would head back out to Monte Lake on a summer's day and sit in front of the store there and swap lies with the other old-timers, watching the traffic going by on its way to Westwold and Vernon.[26][27]

On the 29TH of March in 1950, Margaret Stevens died in Kamloops at the age of 72. On the 8TH of November that same year, Paul Stevens followed his faithful Maggie and passed away at age 78 in the Royal Inland Hospital in Kamloops. To the knowledge of the writer, no word had ever been sent or received from his family in the United States, nor were any of his relatives in Canada even aware of them. Paul and Maggie had no children.[28]

XXVIII
THE REDEMPTION OF
SHORTY DUNN

Billy Dunn was born John William Grell in Milwaukee, Wisconsin, on the 15th of April, 1869. His mother and father were German-American Catholics and U.S. citizens. Young Grell's parents died when he was a child, but the circumstances surrounding their death are not known. He was raised by a man named Dunn, referred to by Grell as his stepfather. He was to more than once state to Canadians that he was from Lewiston, Idaho, on the banks of the Snake River, directly across the river from Clarkston, Washington.[1][2]

Shorty Dunn's pervading sense of humour and jovial attitude towards life served him well all his life, maintaining a positive attitude through his mining, hunting and trapping adversities and challenges. This light-hearted characteristic enabled him to weather the physical trauma of a serious and painful gunshot wound, as well as the stress of a trial which would see him be sentenced to serve a life term. It was only at the end of that trial, final sentencing looming on the horizon and the verdict of guilty almost assured, that Shorty Dunn's composure finally broke and he became hysterical. The happy days of wandering through the trails, across the streams, and over the mountain passes of the Similkameen country were all seen to rapidly shrink into a nebulous past, and he could see the grey doors of the penitentiary opening before him. For a man who had spent so much of his life in the freedom of the outdoors, indulging in the highly individualistic professions of hunting, trapping and prospecting, confinement within the stark yard and prison walls of the B.C. Penitentiary would assuredly be a gruelling and debilitating experience. It was only the liberal dosage of laudanum administered by Dr. Burris that enabled him to get through the final stages of the trial. It was in that somnambulant state that he watched the final sentences passed. He made a brave front of it, addressing the crowds at the station in Kamloops and joking with his escorts in the train going to New Westminster, but a dire sense of foreboding and apprehension was overwhelming him. Perhaps more so for Shorty than Colquhoun and Miner, the sense of loss, parted from his beloved wilderness and the freedom it engendered, sat like a heavy weight on his shoulders. It did not bode well for his ability to survive a twenty-five year sentence.

Lifers like Dunn and Bill Miner were normally kept inside secure shops and buildings in the B.C. Penitentiary. They were not allowed to work in the outside prison area until such time had passed to assure the guards and the prison administration that the particular inmate was capable of being trusted not to attempt to escape.

It was only months after his initial incarceration that Shorty Dunn found himself succumbing to prison regimen, and visible signs of deterioration appeared. It was common for prison officials see the repetitive work pressed on some men confined to the prison workshops contribute to a breaking down of the individual's constitution, and sometimes even to their death. The guards brought the Deputy Warden's attention to Dunn, and Bourke could see the convict was starting to weaken physically and "he gave me the impression of showing a tendency to insanity." Bourke transferred Shorty outside to work on construction projects with the rest of the general prison population, and his descent into mental instability seemed to be somewhat halted for a time. Outside, he was at least able to see the Fraser River drifting by outside the walls of the prison, and on a rare clear day, the forest clad and snow-capped peaks of the Coast Range to the east, beckoning cruelly from afar.[3]

The day-to-day regularity of prison life was difficult for Shorty Dunn to get used to or accept. All his adult life of 38 years had been spent in unrestricted freedom, away from the rules of society and government, only indulging in personal contacts when they suited him. Now his whole life was governed by a mentally stultifying routine, mind-numbing and desiccating in its endless interminability. He was assigned to the carpentry crew, and under the guidance of instructors and the watchful eyes of the guards, he worked on the erection of buildings and facilities for the prison. It was while working on a project in the brickyard that he watched his former partner Miner make his break for freedom and leave him behind. It is not known if Miner asked Dunn to join him, but by now Dunn had probably realized that venturing into another of the old bandit's schemes was not a good idea.

Letter writing was only permitted every two months; only under special circumstances was this rule waived, and then it was only temporary. All letters were heavily censored by a trained guard before they were posted. Shorty Dunn had a quick and active mind, and this restriction was doubly onerous to him. He was forced to use the underground smuggling route, using convicts going out on release and, on the rare occasions when necessity demanded, the clandestine methods over, under or through the fences. The letters were headed with the initials "B.C.P." for British Columbia Penitentiary, and the mailing address was the nondescript "Box M, New Westminster, B.C." Shorty's hand was neat and distinct, and his grammar and composition readable and vivid, reflecting an educated, active and sensitive mind.[4]

One friend that remained true to Shorty Dunn after his train robbery conviction was George Winkler, the mining promoter and poet. He remained faithful to Shorty after his imprisonment, and they exchanged numerous letters with each other. In one letter, Shorty Dunn described to Winkler his version of the train robbery at Ducks. This is as close as one will ever get to what happened that night from the robber's perspective. Dunn refused to say who his mysterious Third Man was.[5]

Shorty Dunn first knew Bill Miner as George Edwards. He did not know his real name until the old bandit told him shortly before the robbery in Kamloops. They were riding together on their way into town to pick up some supplies, leaving Colquhoun behind to tend to the camp near Holmwood.

"We, that is Bill Miner and I, some days later got aboard the train at Ducks by way of the back end of the tender while the train stopped for water. Directly after it started again we climbed over the coal and covered the crew, Bill covering the engineer and I the fireman. When I got time to look at the landscape I noticed we were directly at the spot where we had agreed to stop the train, and as I rather insisted on the immediate stopping of the train, the engineer said I got excited. As the train had pulled by the intended stopping place, No. 3, who was waiting at this point, could not take care of the fireman, so I got down with him and had him uncouple what I took to be the mail and express car.

"While doing this the conductor started to come toward us, and I said to him, 'This is a holdup. Send a man back to flag any train that may be following.'

"After the uncoupling, the fireman and I and No. 3, who came up in the meantime, went back to our places on the engine, and we pulled away from the train about a mile and a half or so and stopped again. Then all hands got off the engine, No. 3 on our side and the rest of us on the other side of the car, and Bill ordered the engineer to go to the car door and ask the clerk to open the door.

"There was some short delay but finally two clerks came out and Bill took one of the clerks back in the car while I took care of the three men on my side of the car."

Dunn recounts that he told the clerks from the mail car at this time, "Boys, you can put your hands down. You look like a bunch of birds trying to fly."

"After a while No. 3 also came over to me and we all stayed on one side of the car. After Bill got through he ordered everyone back to their places and we pulled up opposite our camp, where I again gave the signal to stop. Bill was the last man to get back on the engine when he boarded her the last time, and he wanted me to take the Giant Powder aboard. But I told him to leave it, but set it on the ground easy. That is all I can tell you, except I destroyed all the checks and other written matter by fire."[6]

By 1909 Shorty Dunn's true friends in the Interior felt that he had served enough time to pay for his crimes as they were aware of the deleterious effect his imprisonment was having on his sanity and health. They started to petition the federal government to parole Shorty into their care and custody. It is a testament to the true effect that he had on these good citizens and the regard they held for him personally that they continued over the years of his captivity to write to him to attempt to keep his spirits up, all the while unceasingly pressing for his release. The petitioners included individuals in the highest strata of the societies in the towns and districts where Shorty had left his mark.

The petitioners included the Reverend Edward Ernest Hardwicke of Princeton. A Methodist minister, Hardwicke was formerly from Victoria and Revelstoke. It was in Revelstoke that he had married Margaret Masefield in 1898, and he knew Dunn as basically a good man, holding no threat to society. George E. Winkler had been a friend of Dunn's for all the time Shorty had spent in the Similkameen and had grubstaked him often on his forays into the bush. He would stand by the skilled trapper and prospector for years into the future. Together with a Mr. W. Knight, Mrs. Susan Allison of Princeton kept her faith with Shorty and continued the letter writing and petitioning to a distant federal government year after year. Archie McKinley was a rancher and hotelier at 115 Mile House, near Lac la Hache. Shorty Dunn had worked for him in the Cariboo before he had made his fateful move to the Similkameen. McKinley would not soon forget the skilled horseman and adept bartender that had won the friendship of the people of the area, and petitioned from the Cariboo for his friend's release.

Two years after his imprisonment, Shorty wrote to his friend Winkler, severely criticizing the treatment he was suffering. The theme that he repeated time and again was the ignorance of the justice system in keeping a man behind bars after he has realized the error of his ways, as continued imprisonment ensures that the

"Shorty" Expresses Ironical Opinion

Gent, with key: "Your physical test is satisfactory and you may report for duty at once; and now, sir, if you have a mind of your own let me have it and I'll lock it in the safe for you 'til you call for it again."

This is the only known example of Shorty Dunn's cartoon drawing and art expertise. Completed while he was in the B.C. Penitentiary, it reflects his cynicism and unquenchable sense of humour.

Upgraded from a poor microfilm reproduction of a 16 December 1923 edition of the Victoria Colonist, by Kirsten Grauer.

individual will have to revert to criminal activities to survive in that milieu. No doubt the letter found its way out of the institution in an irregular way.

"When a man has made up his mind to keep out of deviltry, he is no longer a menace to society and it is folly to keep him longer locked up, just as much as it is in folly to lock a drunkard in a liquor outlet and expect him to keep sober in there. I admit that I have placed myself within reach of the law, a law which simply aims to punish a man for a crime committed, without regard to the moral condition of that man in consequence of the punishment inflicted, but I do not admit that I brought myself in range of a sentence having a tendency to make a man a maniac in this life and damn his soul in the next. I am perfectly willing to do what is right if given a show to do so, but no man may blame another for going wrong when labouring under the stress of a life sentence or its equivalent, a long term."

Many of the prisoners, hidden from the guards, tried to keep their sanity by making models, small works of art and carvings that could be smuggled out in return for money, tobacco, a letter or a visit. Shorty Dunn made a small leather and horsehair quirt about four inches long and sent it to an acquaintance. Accompanying the little souvenir was a poem composed by the convict.

This slight token of remembrance
(Whose intrinsic value's nil)
Shows the silent dogged patience
Of imprisoned mortal's skills,
Tells of secret occupation
Guarded against a guard's surprise
Where Hope dens with Desolation
In a grim grey house of sighs.[7]

In 1909, after a friend from the Similkameen had paid him a welcome visit, Shorty Dunn wrote to him that night to tell him of his pleasure at seeing him and hearing the news from the upper country.

"You people in the Similkameen all know that I am not as bad a criminal as those notoriety-seeking policemen and the daily papers made me out to be. There were a few odds and ends of honesty about me and an average good suit of principle covered my soul. If I had received a reasonable sentence I believe I would have pulled around OK and have more honestly principle and respect for the law than I have today. Now, I don't want to be a criminal any more than you do, but I tell you honestly and sincerely that a long term in the pen has a decided tendency to make a man a criminal and a life sentence a murderer, in spite of himself. What I fear mostly is that I may turn loose some day while labouring under the strain of my sentence and do something dirty that will undo all my friends have done for me. An overloaded mule may be able to pack his load for quite a while, but if that load is not removed before his strength fails, he will go down and stay down. May it not be so with me? I have staggered several times. I'll be forty years old in April, and I know it will be but a few years more under existing conditions ere I'll be dried up and useless."[8]

From the perspective we find ourselves at now, what Shorty Dunn doesn't say, and what is left to the imagination, is the most chilling of a convicts experiences in prison. In our mind's eye we can see the predation and intimidation practiced by fellow convicts and guards, the inadequate meals, heavy workload, and the lack of creature comforts, all beating down on the ability of an individual to survive.

"When a man, after serving a long term in the pen, is turned loose upon the world with the questionable congratulations of the pen officials, a cheap and conspicuous suit of clothes to advertise him as an ex-convict, and the usual five dollars in his pocket, to start life anew, what has he to face? Broken in health and spirit, he cannot compete with men of his trade (if he has one). If no other objection might arise, infirmity of age alone will bar him, and infirmity in an ex-con means far more than is usually meant by that word. It means the loss of physical and mental energy, coupled with general degeneracy of all sound principles he may have had before he entered the pen. Do you think, after seeing me and noting the change in me, that I'll hold out the time you mentioned? I do not think I am asking too much when I ask the chance not to become a criminal."[9]

Dunn was so moved by his friend's visit to see him inside the grey penitentiary, and rendered so emotional and morose, that the night after the visit he composed a poem to try to impart to his friend his feelings at the visit.

Sympathy
When hand clasps hand of sympathetic friend,
A golden current, clear and unalloyed,
Quickens the blood and makes the heart extend
A silent tribute to the hand employed.
A soothing solace allays sorrow's pain,
And man is richer, stronger to defend,
Convinced his hand is not held out in vain,
When hand clasps hand of sympathetic friend.[10]

In his anguish, Shorty rails against the CPR as well as the Canadian justice system in another letter to George Winkler. It was dated after the third robbery of the CPR, east of Kamloops. In 1909 the Haney brothers had held up a CPR train, and during their escape, one of the brothers and a provincial Special Constable had been killed.

"I have been repeatedly told that my sentence was made severe so that it could be advertised as British Columbia's punishment for train robbers, to deter others from working along the CPR. Has it acted as a deterrent? I question if it is as good a deterrent as the one I once told you I had. They cannot stop train robbery by punishment any more than they can stop burglary or petit larceny by punishment. It can only be stopped by proper precautions being taken by railway officials or by finding some other means for transporting money across the continent. For my part, I think airships will some day carry the valuable express. That will put train robbery out of business the same as trains put stage robbery on the blacklist."[11]

The lonely prisoner described his feelings about the hypocrisy displayed by those people and institutions of the day that professed to be Christian.

"This atmosphere leaves no room for faith in the teachings of Christianity. It leads man to challenge the sincerity of people who call themselves Christians, see the evil and say they deplore it, yet make no effort to change the existing disorder of things that cause the evil."[12]

Shorty's faith in his fellow man was severely tested by his former defence lawyer Mcintyre. He had garnisheed what little funds Dunn had in his prison account. He had been given a few dollars for necessities by people like Mrs. Allison, Reverend Hardwick's parishioners and George Winkler. The prisoner was adamant that there were no funds owing. He had turned over to the Kamloops lawyer all of the mining claims and properties he had accumulated over years of prospecting and exploration. The value of the properties greatly exceeded the costs of the three train robbers' defence, but protestations were to no avail, and the court acceded to Mcintyre's petty and small-minded demands.

King George V's coronation as Emperor of India was to take place in 1911. It was traditional that some prisoners were extended clemency to celebrate the occasion, and Shorty Dunn's friends were not about to let the occasion go by without attempting to free their favourite convict. Early in the new year, they circulated petitions throughout the Similkameen and the Cariboo asking for Dunn's pardon, suggesting that the poet and former bushman could be no finer example of a reformed train robber. Shorty, while maintaining a pessimistic frame of mind, also spurred on the efforts of the petitioners and hoped for clemency on Coronation Day.

"I am well satisfied," he wrote New Year's Day as he sat at the small table in his cell, "that if I am forgotten that day I'll be damned forever. Snowed last night; can see it through the bars of the window. As this is a holiday, will not go to work."[13]

The dampness and the cold in the prison condemned him to a state of continually declining health. His former physique, toned and honed by packing and hiking through the mountains and canyons of the upper country, was wasting away from a poor diet and heavy workload.

"I was entirely free of a cold for about nine days a couple of weeks ago. This was the longest time my head was not plugged up with a cold in about two years. It is plugged up now and though it is afternoon I guess I'll get back to bed as I am getting cold. Have been in bed all day except long enough to eat dinner and go to church."[14]

"Perhaps you think all my letters are short. They are, considering that two months elapse between them. The same old routine, doing my work under protest day by day, does not give material for long letters. Locked in a cell from about five o'clock in the evening to about eight in the morning and all day on Sundays and holidays does not develop brain power nor furnish interesting literature. I do a lot of reading but I do it mostly to kill time, and in an endeavour to turn my thoughts away from my cursed condition."[15]

Coronation Day, with all the hope that it held, came and passed and no word came from Ottawa. While the failure to secure his pardon did not deter his friends, Shorty fell into a deep despair. Mrs. Allison offered to assist him with a little money so he could purchase some items to relieve his gloom, but he meanly rejected her offer, telling Winkler, "If she has more money than she knows what to do with, and she still wants to help me, let her pay an honest debt I owe to Schubert and Thomas (grocers in Princeton). That would please me, as I want to get those men off my conscience. Then forget me, I've got the knife of B.C. justice sticking in my ribs."[16]

But his friends were not about to take his self-penalizing advice. One wrote to him after the failure to secure the pardon.

"You like my letters because I have not lost faith in you. To me you are the same impulsive, warmhearted Billy Dunn that I knew and whose friendship I valued in the past and still value.

"I know that you are not criminal by nature and that your troubles are due to your companionship with a man who exerted a harmful influence over you.

"We are all creatures of our environment and the best of us do things that at other times we are heartily ashamed of. I do not think the inmates of a prison are much, if any, worse than the people outside – in fact, I think some of our greatest criminals are not only free but highly respected members of society. Their whole attitude is anti-social, anarchistic, individualistic, but owing to our chaotic ideas on many things, such men are worshipped and looked up to by a considerable portion of the very people they wrong. The time is approaching, however, when our viewpoint on these matters will change, and men who are today held up as models will be seen in their true colours; human life and happiness will be valued higher than dollars and cents, and men who have done wrong will be given a chance to do right instead of being discouraged and degraded in spirit as is too often the case under our present system."[17]

It was in 1911 that Lewis Colquhoun, the quiet and thoughtful ex-schoolteacher from Clifford, Ontario, finally succumbed to the grim terminal symptoms of tuberculosis. Dunn tried to do as much as he could to ease his companion's agonies and was successful in getting him some better treatment before he finally died in September in the penitentiary hospital. No doubt Billy Dunn looked within himself at his own mortality and was not buoyed by Colquhoun's lonely and grisly fate, far from friends and family.[18]

Billy Dunn watched his friend die, and afterwards saw many of the same conditions exhibited by his own body, leading him to fear that he had contracted tuberculosis also. He didn't trust the prison doctor, so he agitated to be examined by a physician outside the penitentiary. Again his friends on the outside rose to the occasion, and George Winkler wrote to the federal Minister of Justice.

"I have been unable to get any reply from you re Wm. Dunn's case about which I wrote you some time ago, asking you to have him examined by some physician outside of the penitentiary at New Westminster to see if his lungs were affected by tuberculosis.

"This has evidently not been done or if it has been done I have received no information of the fact through your department."

Winkler wrote that he had received nothing but printed forms from the Minister's department, and he threatened to put the matter before the public "as I am not going to let my friend rot like a dog for want of proper care, if I can prevent it."

He promised to write so many publications that the Minister's offices would be flooded with enough letters to keep a clerk hired well into retirement. "I hope, however, you are not going to drive me to this extremity, and that this case will have your immediate, careful attention."

Winkler's efforts were quickly successful. The prison administration agreed to Dunn's demands, and an independent doctor came into the penitentiary to examine him. The diagnosis was "chronic catarrh." Despite his worst fears, Billy Dunn had a persistent chest cold. Used to the dry climate of the interior, he complained in his letters that colds and fevers seemed to never leave him in that damp and humid climate beside the Fraser River.[19]

By March of 1912 the interminable slow tread of time marching drearily through the New Westminster penitentiary had not dulled Dunn's pessimism. "I am not looking forward to any good accruing to me from the result of anything you friends may try for me."

"I am realizing more and more every day the hold that is strangling every decent impulse I used to have, and that grip is becoming a death grip if I know anything about myself previous to my arrest and the present day …. I think all my friends will be disappointed, both as to the time of my release and my physical and moral condition when (if ever) I get out."[20]

The passing of time also did nothing to change his opinion of the penal system, and he couldn't help but think that if the ordinary citizens knew what was being undertaken in their name, there would be an uproar.

"When I look back on the time it has taken me to gain the little useful knowledge that I acquired in here, I cannot help but think what a rotten waste of time, what a burlesque on civilization is a penitentiary. If it were possible to bring the mass of good, honest, law-abiding people in touch with actual facts in this connection alone they might possibly see they are taxing themselves foolishly. If they would open the eyes which they so resolutely force shut, they might see how they possibly unconsciously discourage honesty. I would like to be in a position to ask the first one hundred men I met what each thinks constitutes prison life. I would like to have each write down what he thinks is proper treatment of a convict, and what moral and physical effect such treatment should produce. I should then compare my actual experience with their 'thinks' and I'll bet there would be a difference somewhere. Incidentally I think some of them would find they know absolutely no facts about something of vital importance to society."[21]

He periodically requested that his friends finally forget about him and leave him to his fate. But faithful to the end, they ignored him and continued to petition Ottawa.

"I would ask you to quit writing Ottawa in my behalf. You have quite done your share, and I appreciate it, but I am not the man to go on my knees and beg anyone to allow me to be honest, and I don't want you to do it for me. You might as well throw in the sponge, Ottawa has no intention to make anything but a criminal or a fool out of me."[22]

Despite his depression, Shorty managed to conserve his well-known sense of humour. He continued to embellish his letters with cartoons and poems satirizing the prison system, and in 1913 he created a little booklet of drawings and poems. He coloured the drawings with crayons and sent it to one of his friends. The title "Stray Thoughts, by Shorty Dunn" reflected the frustration of an active mind confined to a daily existence of boredom.

In December of 1913, his sentence was commuted to fifteen years, entitling him to be freed sometime before 1921. His response to the justice department's generosity can be imagined.

"My sentence has been reduced to fifteen years. That may look good to you as it does to some others. But I look upon it a good deal as a certain beggar looked at a coin a juggler placed in his hand. The audience praised the juggler's generosity for giving what looks to them like a bright new gold coin, but the beggar knew his fingers closed on only a penny."[23]

He did admit in the same letter that his physical condition seemed to have improved. "I have been feeling quite a bit better this Fall and Winter than at any other Fall and Winter for the last six years. But I do not eat much. I somehow never feel hungry."

Early in 1915 the disillusioned prisoner heard distant rumours that his release might be at hand. A letter came from the Justice Minister announcing he might expect his release soon. The diligent and incessantly unfailing efforts of his true friends were perhaps about to bear fruit. But, pessimistic to the end, Billy Dunn wrote to George Winkler in Victoria. Past disappointments kept his optimism in check, but he couldn't help writing and expressing his thoughts if parole should be granted.

"*I don't go much on the contents of the Minister of Justice's letter. It just shows me that there will probably be another delay after April 1st, and although I hope and expect to get out this spring, still I will not be greatly surprised if I am turned down again. However, I want you to leave me your address in case you leave the coast. My thoughts turn naturally to the mountains, and the stock-in-trade of my natural bent. I am curious to know about present game laws, miner's license, trapper's license and gun license. I understand B.C. has made some changes in these. How about cayuses and a camping outfit? Has the war made much difference in the price of these?*

"*I am in good health, but that does not say I will be able to stand much violent exertion right after I get out. It will take some time before I get in proper shape.*

"*In the hope of seeing you this spring, I remain, Yours Truly, Shorty Dunn.*"[24]

The pent up excitement in his writing is almost palpable. His beloved mountains were almost within reach, and the solitude of the forests, quiet except for the murmurs of streams and the wind, beckon to him, far away from the dull, incessant roar in the hallways of the prisoners and guards that had been his incessant and sometimes threatening companions. Dare he put his faith in a scrap of paper from the Justice Minister?

His fears were for naught, and he was released in the spring of that year to a two year parole. Nearly fifty years old, he apprehensively wrote Winkler after taking his first tentative steps outside the sterile bosom of the federal penitentiary.

"Well, the final day got here at last and I have a room at the Guichon Lodgings. Will probably stay here three or four days. At the moment of writing I have just $15.20 in my jeans to start life on .... Say, I feel completely lost. I have followed the old routine so long that I don't know how to act like a civilized man. Also dropping into a strange town makes it worse."[25]

The now ex-convict had only lived a few miles away from his rented room for the last nine years, and he felt like he was in a strange new world. It was a world of automobiles and electricity and war. Impatient to flee into the upper country, he had to stay fixed until he could regain his bearings.

"I have all kinds of invitations to call and see people, but you know how it is. I'll stay with my old standbys."

He first went to Hope for a time to do some house painting, one of the trades which he had picked up in the pen. But the mountains in the upper country were calling too loudly, and he took a train back to Princeton. There he found himself welcomed by the good people of Princeton with open arms, his past transgressions forgotten. Just the laughing, smiling and carefree Shorty Dunn was remembered.

George Winkler later wrote about his friend Billy Dunn, reflecting upon his release from prison and why he was held in high regard in the Similkameen.

"The motherly faith of Mrs. Allison of Princeton had a lot to do with the continuance of the efforts for parole in the face of refusals. She never lost her faith in Shorty's ability to make good if given another chance. Dunn was not a man to fail his friends, and when they guaranteed his good conduct he didn't throw them down."[26]

Rancher Arthur Reith had his place near Jack Budd's horse ranch northeast of Princeton. The annual destruction of his ranch fences had mysteriously ceased after the Ducks robbery, and he and the reclusive horse trader were on as good terms as could be expected. In the summer shortly after Billy Dunn got out of prison, the rancher was desperate for help with his haying. He was at the train depot when Shorty Dunn swung down onto the platform with a small box of belongings. He looked thin and frail. He heard Reith talking to some men about needing help for his haying, and he approached him about being hired on. Reith knew who Dunn was and listened as the former prison inmate told him how he was quite weak and not much good at the present, but if he could be well fed and able to rest up for a couple of days, he would try his best at being good help. Reith gave him a chance, and Dunn faithfully worked for him all that summer and fall for wages and room and board.[27]

That winter he worked as a clerk for A.J. White's general store in Princeton, reflecting the community's trust and faith in the ex-convict. Dunn was now bulking up with good food and work that was not so debilitating as that in the grim penitentiary squatting on the banks of the Fraser at New Westminster.[28]

The next summer he again worked for Arthur Reith; this time his strength had been completely regained and his efforts were much appreciated. He also worked for Jack Hanna at the Blakeburn coal mine on Granite Creek helping to build the tramway. As well, he did a stint with Bert Thomas on his ranch. For many years, on one of the ranch house walls, along with other paintings he had done, was a large canvas of the steam engine pulling the train at Ducks, the smokestack filling the front perspective of the picture, and billowing steam punching into the air.[29]

He saved his money and soon had enough to put a stake together. He wrote to his friend George Winkler to let him know what he was doing.

> "Just a word to let you know that I am off for the hills. I had to get a packhorse. Had my choice to break in a colt and buy him later for $50 or buy a gentle packhorse. Took the latter. One reason because I don't want to spend too much time looking for and chasing a colt in the hills and the other reason was because old Bill McKay's wife is sick and the doctor ordered him to take her south. So old Bill had to sell his stock and get a bit of cash to travel on, and it gave me a chance to help him out that way."[30]

Shorty Dunn was soon back in his beloved mountains, staking claims, trapping and hunting. He again displayed that uncanny ability to spot promising showings, and his skills were quickly recognized by his friend Winkler. In 1918, Winkler sent Shorty to a six week geology course at the University of British Columbia under the direction of Professor J.M. Turnbull. The $120 course included a class picture entitled "Short

Term Geology and Mineralogy, 1918" with Dunn in the photo, but a search for it at the B.C. Archives was fruitless. In George Winkler's archive files there is a class photo for the same course in 1917, but not one for Dunn's class.[31]

When Shorty Dunn was in prison, he met a fellow convict named Albert McDougal. In 1912 McDougal had shot and killed his cousin Dave McDougal at a mining camp said to have been back in the hills across the lake from Kelowna. Albert and his brothers Dan and Joe and cousin Dave had set up the camp with their father Ed. The reasons for the prospector's shooting of his cousin are lost, but considerable drinking had taken place that night around the fire. The fatal shooting was reported to the authorities, and Provincial Police Constable Tooth took Al, his rifle and shells into custody. Originally slated to hang at Kamloops, Albert received a last-minute reprieve and was transported to New Westminster to serve his life sentence there.[32]

In prison, he soon met up with Dunn, as Albert had heard of Dunn's familiarity with the country he had prospected in. They talked about potential mines and mother lodes in the Similkameen country. McDougal, knowing that the chances of him getting back into those hills were slim, told Dunn about a lost gold mine that he and his relatives had discovered. Ore samples had been found that contained a rich showing, but they had not traced it to its source when the shooting took place. When Dunn was paroled, he took the secret location of the gold mine outside the prison walls with him, planning on finding it himself when he had regained his strength. The closest he came to telling anyone about its location was in a conversation with his friend George Winkler. He and Dunn had partnered together on a prospecting trip east of Aspen Grove. The two friends were bunking in the barn of the ranch owned by butcher Chris "Kit" Summers on Summers Creek near Missezula Lake. Dunn told Winkler that McDougal had told him the mine was up Summers Creek, and that was all he told his friend.[33]

Despite the good intentions of his friends and all who knew him in the Princeton district, Shorty Dunn still felt the weight of his past transgressions on his shoulders. He remembered the anonymity of the Cariboo country and the endless vast spaces to the north and the west. He wanted to escape into that anonymity and leave Princeton, now a bustling mining, ranching and railway town, reluctantly behind.

In July of 1921, Billy Dunn held a farewell picnic for the children of all his friends in the community at the ranch of George Aldous, the well-known businessman in Princeton and a former friend and business partner of George Edwards. Shorty had met two Norwegians and hired on to help them drive a herd of cattle up into the Burns Lake area. That fall he left Princeton and its multitude of memories and good friends behind, never to return.[34][35]

On the 10 August 1921, he arrived with the herd of cattle in the Burns Lake area. By that time the ex-convict and prospector had changed his name back to that of his birth parents and would be known to everyone in the Ootsa and Eustache Lake country, south of Burns Lake and Francois Lake, as John William "Billy" Grell. Happy now, and content in his anonymity, he set his traplines and tramped the hills looking for good showings of minerals. In the winters he clerked in the store of George F. Henson. Henson, originally from North Dakota and Montana, had settled with his wife Mary and his three sons on the north shore of Ootsa Lake at a little community called Marilla. There he raised cattle and Percheron horses and opened a small store and trading post, trading with the Indians, settlers, prospectors and trappers throughout the area. Billy Grell introduced himself to Henson and told him in confidence about his criminal past. However, Henson must have been a trusting soul, or else saw something about Grell that allayed any fears, as the prospector and trapper would work for him every winter for many years. Henson was the only one in the country that knew the ex-train robber's secret.[36]

Billy Grell made sure that his friend Winkler knew how he was doing. He told him about the country he now grew to love. He told him of the little lakeside communities of Marilla, Ootsa Lake, Streatham and Wisteria and how the long narrow lakes in that

country made even the remotest areas accessible. He told him of the Henson family and the people he met, and of the mineral showings he found in the area. He built his own boat, and a visitor to Winkler from that country told him a story of Grell's life in the Ootsa Lake country. He repeated a tale told by the locals of Grell performing a formidable feat of strength and endurance packing his boat over a certain portage and that it "would reflect credit upon him." Billy was also given a camera by a friend, and he looked forward to taking some "pictures if he could get some film."[37]

Grell's letter caused Winkler to remember the Billy Dunn he had known for so long. "Dunn wasn't what you might call a bad man. I have always liked him, and when he went to jail I felt that he had just made a mistake and would go straight if allowed another chance. It was probably an impulsive, adventurous spirit which prompted him to take part in the hold up. He must have had some doubts about the venture himself, because he said goodbye to some friends in Princeton before the robbery took place. Shorty was honest enough at heart, I have always believed. When in prison he worried over money he owed."[38]

Sometime in 1925, Billy Grell felt that he should become a citizen of Canada. Despite his bad memories of past dealings with the Justice Ministry, he wanted to be a Canadian. He knew Provincial Police Constable Corporal Andrew Fairbairn (Reg. No. 33) and ran into him one day in Telkwa, near Smithers. He told Fairbairn of his desire to go into Smithers and apply to become a Canadian, and also confided in him about his previous criminal past. Fairbairn told him he would do what he could for him, and the officer put in a good word to Judge F. McB. Young at Smithers for Grell. Fairburn told Judge Young that due to the fact that Grell had put in so many years of exemplary behaviour and achieved such an unblemished record in the Ootsa Lake country, he should be given a chance to obtain

John William Grell (Shorty Dunn) in happier times. Photo taken by B.C.L.S. surveyor Frank Swannell, Ootsa Lake country, 1922.
Courtesy of B.C. Archives.

Canadian citizenship. After completing his application in his cabin at Ootsa Lake on the 20 July 1925, he sent it in to the Judge of the County Court of Prince Rupert in Smithers.[39][40]

The wheels of government started their ponderous, slow and methodical processing of Billy Grell's application. RCMP officer Maurice T. Berger (Reg. No. 7978) was on regular patrol at Grassy Plains, between Ootsa Lake and Francois Lake. One of his responsibilities was to investigate individuals who had applied for Canadian citizenship. Among the applicants he had to investigate was one William Grell, an American citizen who had filed for a pre-emption in the area.[41]

Before interviewing Grell, inquiries in the district had elicited the information that he was a hard-working and respected man, a bachelor, who minded his own business. None of the local residents interviewed had anything but good to say about him.[42]

In a secret and confidential document compiled over the signature of RCMP Corporal O.L. Hall (Reg. No. 6488) of the Telkwa detachment, the details of Grell's life in Canada are laid bare.

This document summarizes information obtained on "John William Grell alias Billy 'Shorty' Dunn." It states he is single with no children and has spent 30 years in Canada. He made his living as a trapper, prospector and farmer and "was recognized in his neighbourhood as being of good reputation and character." When the RCMP officer asked for the names of prominent persons in the community who might vouch for his character, Billy was quick to give him three. They were his employer George F. Hansen, Merchant, of Ootsa Lake; L. White, Merchant, Princeton; and George E. Winkler of Victoria.

As to why he wished to become naturalized, Grell's response was "To enjoy the privileges of a Canadian citizen." Ironically, when the subject of his loyalty to Canada during the Great War came up, he was described as a "good and loyal citizen," even though he had been in prison for much of it.[43]

The interviewing officer asked the standard questions, and Grell followed the usual pattern of answers. "He gave his age, place of birth, length of time in Canada, etc. Then we came to the well known paragraph: Police record, if any. I was just about getting ready to write Nil on this line, when Grell gave me the shock of my life by saying, 'Yes, I served 18 years [*sic*] of a life sentence in New Westminster Penitentiary and got the remainder of the sentence remitted.'"

"Well, for goodness' sake, what did you do, anyhow?" I asked.

"Did you ever hear of Bill Miner?" I replied that I had indeed.

He then said, "Well, I used to be known as Shorty Dunn."

"This was indeed Shorty Dunn. He had all the documents to prove it, but he had kept his secret to himself and none of his neighbours had any idea of his identity."[44]

Grell's police record was not publicly known in the Ootsa Lake area. The officer's inquiries about Grell in the area with prominent citizens and a number of trappers regarding his standing in the community resulted in the comment that "to a man (they) spoke very highly of him as a man of great character and a friend."

Communications were sent to Grell's references and their comments were universally positive and favourable.

George F. Hansen, the merchant with the store in Ootsa Lake, wrote that he had known Grell for about four years and that he had employed him to work for him in his store as a clerk for a considerable part of that time. Hansen described him as "a reliable, sober, industrious and conscientious man. He recently told me of his past, but notwithstanding that, I would not hesitate to keep him in my employ in a position of trust."

A.J. White, the general merchant in Princeton who had employed Shorty Dunn as a clerk after his parole, replied to the RCMP officer. "I beg to acknowledge receipt of your letter that while he was in my employ has always kept himself a respectable and very willing and a good worker. I have trusted him implicitly and never had a cause to find him at fault. I would sincerely recommend him to your service and there is no doubt whatever he will make a fine citizen able to gain to the benefit of the public at large."

"Must further state that I have been frequently in correspondence with him, especially while he was residing at Ootsa Lake, B.C.

"Hoping this will suffice for your information and that you shall transmit my best wishes to Mr. Grell for his prosperity and welfare.

"I beg to remain etc. etc."

George Winkler of Victoria also replied to the officer.

"I found your favour of the 24TH ult. awaiting upon my return from Atlin yesterday.

Concerning your inquiry as to the fitness of J. W. Grell for Naturalization, I may say that I can see no good reason why his request should not be acceded to.

"You know that he had served a term in prison for participating with Bill Miner in a train hold up, but this was his first, last and only 'break'.

"I knew him for some years before this offence and have kept in touch with him since his release. He is just as good a citizen today as a vast majority of his fellows."

During the processing of his application, Grell was requested to dictate a short biography to the County Court at Ootsa Lake on 15 July 1926.

"I came from Lewiston, Wash. under the name of William Dunn and arrived at Keremeos B.C. on horseback. I never made any report of my entry into Canada."

Q: Why did you come under the name of William Dunn?

"I was a little bit on the crooked side in those days. I had not been doing anything against the laws of the U.S. and Canada. My inclination was on the wild side of life and I was liable to jump crooked any day. I had not been in trouble since a boy when I was sent to a reform school in Pontiac, Illinois, and that is where I learned not to respect law or order. But for all that I never got into any trouble for all that up to the time I came into Canada. In Canada I was arrested for interfering with H. M. Mail. I was sentenced in Kamloops for life in 1906. This was for holding up a train near Kamloops. I served 9 years in B.C. Penitentiary. I was paroled. I then went to Princetown [sic]. That was in September 1915. I remained there until I came up to this country. I have not been in trouble since. I was with Bill Miner at the hold up. I have tried since my parole to live the life of a respectable citizen. (The applicant files a letter from Mr. Henson, a merchant-farmer residing at the lower end of Ootsa Lake.) I ran a store for him last winter and he wants me to run it again this winter. I told Mr. Henson last fall of the story of the hold up and my term in prison. I also told Constable O. L. Hall the same last fall. I have not told this to any one else in this district. I could get recommendations from reputable businessmen at Princeton, B.C. who know my story and I am perfectly satisfied they would certify that I have tried to go straight since then. The reason I do not want to ask for a certificate of character in this district is because none except Mr. Henson know my past. I cannot ask for recommendation without disclosing it, which I do not want to do because I am doing my best to live it down. If my past is generally known I would be a hero to some and a convict to others."

The same day, Billy Grell had to fill out another document, a "Petition For Naturalization," and send it to the Secretary of State in Ottawa. The petition listed basic facts about the applicant. Stating his name, address, date of birth and former citizenship, he adds further details, filling in the blanks of the standard form. Grell stated that he had previously petitioned for naturalization at Princeton; however, he never appeared at the court to petition for this decision as he was out in the hills prospecting when the court was in session.

At the time of this petition, he was 57 years old, was a height of five feet three inches, white with a dark complexion, brown eyes and brown hair. As for distinguishing marks he listed that his left thumb was stiff due to circular saw cut, also had saw scars on inside of left hand. The scars were most likely picked up during his prison years.

John William Grell's signature is attached to this document, and it is witnessed by a James E. Kirby, Clerk of the Court.[45]

In Smithers on the 4TH of January, 1927, Billy Grell took the Oath of Allegiance.

"I, John William Grell of Ootsa Lake in the District of Omenica swear by Almighty God that I will be faithful and bear true allegiance to His Majesty King George the Fifth, His heirs and successors according to law, so help me God."[46]

Within a week John William Grell, alias Shorty Dunn, received a letter stating that as of 10 January 1927 he was now a Canadian citizen.

Unfortunately the ever-smiling, newly-Canadian prospector, trapper and store clerk did not get to enjoy his new citizenship long.

Just six months later on 27 June 1927, Billy Grell died while ferrying a geologist in a canoe from Whitesail to Ootsa. The waters were in flood, and in the treacherous current the canoe was upset. Billy Grell was drowned, but his passenger managed to swim to a nearby water-covered island and pull himself into a large tree above the speeding current. There he stayed for three days until another boat, manned by George Seel, passed by and he was rescued.[47]

Grell's body wasn't discovered until a year later when a crew blasting log jams out of the river came across it, floating face down in a backwater and hung up in the willows near the Tahtsa River Forks.

The finding of the body was reported to provincial Police Constable G.A. Johnson at Burns Lake, and a few days later a police party including Constable Johnson and Edward van Tine of Ootsa Lake made its way in and identified the remains. Constable Johnson presided over a brief ceremony at the bank of the river, and in a grove of trees looking out over the valley, John William Grell's body was committed to the grave.[48]

When Billy Grell's estate was probated, it was found that all he left behind was an estate worth $82.90 and a Waltham watch that was found on his body and used to identify him. No relatives were ever located, and the fate of his family remains unknown. His body was recognized by van Tine, and it was he that processed William Grell's letters of probate in Smithers in May of 1929.[49]

The Kamloops Sentinel published Billy Grell's obituary a month after the tragic event. Even at the end he could not escape the events at Ducks Station, but at least he could rest assured that some of his better qualities were recognized by those closest to him in Princeton.

"Shorty" Dunn, Bill Miner's Pal, Loses Life in Ootsa Lake
Princeton

Recently A.J. White received a telegram from C.H. [sic] Hansen of Ootsa Lake, northern B.C., stating that J. W. Grill [sic],better known locally as "Shorty" or Billy Dunn, had met his death by drowning.

After serving a long period he was paroled, and later took up his residence here, assuming for a time the management of Mr. White's store. Prior to his leaving here in the summer of 1921, he gave all the children of Princeton a picnic at a grove on the Aldous ranch, of which those taking part will always carry glad recollection. Whatever his faults may have been, nothing but kindly recollection of him is held by people here.

It was through the untiring efforts of Mrs. Allison, Sr., that Mr. Grill's [sic] reprieve was finally accrued. The wire asked for possible information regarding relatives, but Mr. White could not supply any.[50]

The site of William Grell's grave is now covered by a great depth of water as the valley was flooded by the building of the Kenney Dam on the Nechako River in the 1950s.

XXIX
AFTERWARD

BILL MINER

After Bill Miner's escape from the B.C. Penitentiary, there would be no official sightings of the elusive escaped convict in British Columbia or anywhere else in Canada. Primary source B.C. Provincial Police files in the archives in Victoria are silent with regard to his movements after leaving the penitentiary and before arriving back in the United States. In Attorney General W.J. Bowser's correspondence file, there is a covering letter dated 24 February 1910 from police Superintendent Hussey referring to enclosed Pinkerton reports. The B.C. Provincial Police had hired the Pinkertons to undertake clandestine and covert investigations in the United States, hoping to find Bill Miner and then apply for his extradition.

Hussey had received reports that the escapee had been spotted in Spokane and also on the Flathead Indian Reservation near Kalispell, Montana. These investigations took place as a result of a tip received from an informant in Portland, Oregon. The informant, who had reported to the Chief of Police in Portland, stated that Miner was living with an Indian girl on the reservation near Kalispell.

The private Pinkerton investigator set out to follow up on these reports in early February. He visited little towns near Kalispell like Dayton, Polson, Ignatius, Arlee, Ronan, Dixon and Ravalli, and admitted he spent much time in saloons trying to pick up word of his elusive quarry.

In Spokane his investigations were concentrated near the Coeur d'Alene Indian Reservation and also in the saloons of Coeur d'Alene

City. In total, the operative sent in eighteen pages of investigative reports, all with nothing to show for what must have been a considerable expenditure of funds. Hussey, frustrated by the lack of success, cancelled the investigation by the end of February.[1]

An unsubstantiated rumour filtered out of the Princeton country after the escape, and of all the speculative reports of Miner's journeys after his escape, this one could contain some kernels of truth. Sometime after Miner's escape, a lone prospector found himself in a remote section of the Similkameen country with darkness starting to set in. He was in unfamiliar country and was thankful when he rounded a corner in the trail and spotted a cabin in the trees. Smoke was rising from the metal chimney, and yellow light from a lantern glowed from the single window in the wall beside the door. Knowing he would not be turned away, he eagerly knocked on the door. Immediately the light was turned down and the door opened just a few inches. Even in the dim light, the prospector was sure he recognized Bill Miner, whom he had known to see as George Edwards in Princeton.

Through the opened door, the familiar face demanded that he announce what he wanted.

The prospector, somewhat taken aback by Miner's appearance, asked for shelter for the night.

"You can't have it here," was the abrupt reply.

The prospector had noticed two other men, whom at first he failed to identify, in the dim glow of the lantern standing behind Miner. They interjected, and after some discussion, the prospector was allowed to stay the night. He was given a bunk with blankets and spent an unsettled night, thankful that at least he was dry and warm.

He took a closer look at the two men with Miner and later identified them as suspected accomplices of Miner in the Ducks robbery, but who had never been arrested or prosecuted due to a lack of evidence. Scattered around the cabin was what he would later describe as a veritable arsenal of rifles and pistols, as well as a box of ammunition, visible when a blanket was removed to give to the unwelcome guest.

Before the sun was even above the trees the next morning, the prospector was told to be on his way, and he was accompanied on his journey for a while by one of the men to show him the main trail that would bring him out of the isolated spot he had found himself in.

When back in civilization, he lost no time in reporting his discoveries to local law enforcement, and he cautiously guided them back to the remote cabin. They surrounded it, made a rush on it, but found it abandoned.

Some days later the Great Northern Express was robbed in the United States and a haul of $40,000 was rumoured to have been taken. The cabin was staked out off and on for a few weeks, the men eager to get any reward offered as a result of the robbery. But their diligence was in vain as no one ever did show up.[2]

There were rumours after his escape that Miner did make his way back to the Similkameen country and that his friends smuggled him across the Canadian border into the United States. One story had him disguised as a woman, and another noted that he was hidden under a load of hay that ended up in Washington state.[3]

The fact remains that no reliable information exists for where Miner went directly after his escape, nor how he got back to the United States. Boessenecker and Dugan in their definitive work, "The Grey Fox," relate unsubstantiated sightings after the escape of Miner in Oregon, Washington and Colorado. He went back to his train robbing ways, was captured, escaped again, and was recaptured.

In May of 1911, the Warden of the B.C. Penitentiary in New Westminster received a letter from the Commissioner of Roads and Revenues offices in Newton County, Georgia. A Mr. Almand of Mansfield, Georgia, advised the warden that Bill Miner was now working on their road gang and that he had requested Almand write to his former captors in British Columbia. The official asked that Miner's possessions left behind when he escaped from Canadian custody be made available to the prisoner in Georgia as he was destitute and an old man. The letter specifically mentioned that it included about $155 in cash and a gold watch and chain.[4]

In reply, the Warden at New Westminster advised the Georgia

official that any prisoner property must be held by the prison until the day of the prisoner's release. As Miner was never officially released from the Canadian penitentiary, his possessions could not be returned to him. It was the last act that would be played out directly between Miner and his former associates in Canada.[5]

Miner died in prison in Milledgeville, Georgia, on the 2 September 1913. In 1964 a fine granite tombstone was contributed by a sympathetic businessman and erected over his gravesite.[6]

WILLIAM FERNIE

With his share of the reward, William Fernie and his wife Mary built their first house west of Kamloops where they raised their three children. By September of 1906, he had been appointed Chief Constable in Kamloops after the retirement of Ernest Pearse to pursue other endeavours.

Soon after the Ducks robbery, Fernie was involved with a number of high-profile criminal incidents. There was the third holdup of a CPR train, again east of Kamloops, by the Haney brothers in 1908. This was followed by the chase and trial of Paul Spintlum and Moses Paul in 1911. In 1913, 350 men struck against Canadian National Railway construction companies near Kamloops. On three occasions matters almost got out of hand, but Fernie and ten other officers and special constables managed to keep control of the situation. Fernie later reported that this was one of the most critical incidents of his career.[7]

At the outset of the Great War, Fernie acquired a commission in the 31ST B.C. Light Horse; however, he was shortly seconded to the 172ND and went overseas with them. With Fernie was a well thumbed volume of the poetry of Robert Service. When the 172ND was broken up and the personnel appointed to various other regiments, Fernie was transferred to the 5TH Canadian Division as an Intelligence officer. After serving in this capacity for some time, he was again transferred, this time to the Assistant Provost Marshall's (APM) staff of the 3RD Division. During a period of time in this service, he acted as APM under General Lipsett. After the war, he joined the 5TH B.C. Light Horse and eventually became Officer in Command of this unit.[8]

Shortly after Fernie had joined up in 1914, he was put in command of a troop tracking down escaped German prisoners of war that had been incarcerated at the camp in Vernon. As the United States was still neutral at that time, the escapees were heading for the American border. After an intense pursuit of ten days, and utilizing all his tracking and hunting skills, Fernie and his group captured the escapees three miles from the American border.[9]

After his return from overseas, Fernie's attention was focused not just on the demands of his Provincial Police job and his family, now consisting of a son and two daughters. True to his love of the West, and the outdoor life he led hunting, fishing and riding, he assisted and was instrumental in getting the Bowron Lakes set aside as a provincial wilderness park. John Bowron was one of the Fraser River Overlanders, and it was through the Fernie family's friendship with Bowron's daughter Lottie that he became involved in the project.

On his extensive holdings west of Kamloops, Fernie operated his Kamloops horse station for the federal government for seven years. Under a grant from the Department of Agriculture in Ottawa, he and his family raised and trained thoroughbred horses. Here his knowledge of horses and their breeding ensured that the best bloodlines were acquired and incorporated into Kamloops equine stock circles. By 1920 he had been promoted to Inspector of the Provincial Police, responsible for B.C.'s southern interior, and by 1923 was making the princely sum of $2,205 per annum.10 [11]

In 1930 a tragedy struck the Fernie family a cruel blow. Their son Vacey, who was attending U.B.C. and working as a surveyor in the Cariboo during the summer months, was struck down with meningitis. He was rushed into the Royal Inland Hospital, where he succumbed to the disease at the age of 23. His sister Mary was a Registered Nurse on the same floor at the time, and she was present at his passing. As expected, both Fernie and his wife Mary, together with Daphne and Mary, never fully recovered from this blow. The next year Fernie himself was severely injured in an automobile accident.[12]

Upon the retirement of Colonel and former Kamloops Gaol Warden J.R. Vicars in 1924, Fernie became the commanding officer of the Rocky Mountain Rangers with the rank of Lieutenant Colonel. He retired from the Provincial Police force in 1934 with 33 years of service. Shortly after his retirement, he took an extended vacation by himself in the South Pacific. It was probably due to his wife Mary's asthma, somewhat assuaged by Kamloops' dry climate, that she did not accompany him. In his later years Fernie would suffer the slow and debilitating onslaught of Alzheimer's, but many of his numerous friends would make the trip from Kamloops to his house, "The Kloof," to pay their respects, to keep him company, and help his wife Mary.[13]

Fernie died in 1943 at the age of 73. His passing was noted in many B.C. newspapers, as well as many police publications across Canada. After the death of her husband, Mary Fernie joined her daughters on Vancouver Island. They purchased a house on five acres close to Metchosin where they raised vegetables, strawberries, chickens and some dairy cows. They opened an internationally famous English tea room and served tea, Devonshire cream and scones with strawberry jam made by the expert hand of Mary, until the late 1990s. They retired to live in Oak Bay, and both sisters passed away in 2005.[14]

FREDERICK FULTON

Attorney General Frederick Fulton was to cross legal swords with Alex Mcintyre many times over the years. In 1908 he was prosecuting attorney in the Alfred Goodwin trial for rustling cattle from the Douglas Lake Ranch and Mcintyre was the defence lawyer. Mr. Fulton, unlike in the Miner affair, was not so successful in this prosecution. After much legal wrangling on the part of Mcintyre, his client was deemed not guilty of a total of nine charges.

In 1909 Fulton resigned from the government of Sir Richard McBride on a point of principle. When the CPR was built through the Fraser Canyon, construction activities had destroyed much of the Cariboo Road that was hanging on the sides of the cliffs. Some sections had been rebuilt due to the lobbying efforts of Fulton, but much still needed to be done to gain access to the Lower Mainland.

*Frederick Fulton visiting William Buse and his children in
Upper Campbell Creek.* Courtesy of Kamloops Museum and Archives.

Fulton could see that the future transportation needs of the
automobile demanded better road access to the coast. Automobiles in
the interior had to be shipped by rail to get to Vancouver. Premier
McBride was actively courting the Grand Trunk Railroad, and
accusations were being flung about of cronyism and corruption. The
railroad was granted access through the canyon, effectively destroying
the road for decades into the future. Fulton resigned in disgust, despite
the high regard he and McBride held for each other.[15]

Fulton became City Solicitor in Kamloops in 1910, and in 1917
ran successfully as a Conservative. He was appointed to the wartime
coalition government as a Conservative Unionist, and when the
coalition ended in 1920, he resigned from politics. He continued to

develop his law firm in Kamloops and later turned it over to his son, E. Davie Fulton. Frederick Fulton died in 1936, two years after his old nemesis Mcintyre.[16]

ALEXANDER MCINTYRE

Alexander Duntroon Mcintyre was a highly individualistic and skilled lawyer who probably deserves more study. One book has already been written that highlights the skills of the controversial Kamloops defence attorney. "The Bootlegger's Lady" features the case of Edith Julia Frye of Albreda who, in 1922, shot her abusive and drunk husband with a lever action .303 Savage to prevent him from harming the children. Charged with murder, Mrs. Frye was originally to be tried in Prince George, but Mcintyre successfully got a change of venue to Kamloops. It was a sensation as women throughout British Columbia held bake sales and rallies to raise funds for the hapless woman's defence. Mcintyre was successful in having her acquitted.[17]

In August of 1907, Alfred Goodwin, owner of the Norfolk Ranch just east of the Douglas Lake Ranch, was arrested by Chief Constable Fernie for horse and cattle rustling and locked up in the Kamloops Gaol. Jack Budd was rumoured to have been a partner of Goodwin's in the horse rustling, but there was never enough evidence to charge him. A preliminary hearing was held in Kamloops in February of 1908 in front of former Chief Constable Ernest T.W. Pearse, now a Justice of the Peace. Mcintyre, assisted by his law partner J. Murphy, acted for the defence.[18] [19]

The Nicola Herald reporter paid close attention to the proceedings. J.B. Greaves, manager for the Douglas Lake Cattle Company, was first called to the stand and then swore to the company's Douglas Lake brand, stating that cattle raised by his company were branded on the right hip, bought cattle being branded on the left hip. Oliver Walker, cowhand for Mr. Goodwin, deposed that about April 12TH of 1907 he rounded up twenty-eight head of horses belonging to the Douglas Lake Cattle Company in the Company's Marsh Meadow. They were taken into a corral, and the brands of fourteen head were treated to the application of a certain lump-jaw and spavin cure which, acting as a blister agent, raises the hide where it was applied and causes the brand to slough off in three or four days. In this operation he was assisted by the accused, Alfred Goodwin. These animals, with others totalling twenty-five head, were removed to a field belonging to the accused who, in conversation with the witness, expressed his intention to ship them out for sale after they got over the effects of the brand treatment. Later the accused Goodwin had got into a row with a rancher named Lauder over some beef, and Lauder had told Goodwin that he had seen enough that day to put the accused in jail. Goodwin, who was unaware of what Lauder had witnessed, asked the cowboy what he thought Lauder was going to do about it. The cowboy replied that he did not know.[20]

Oliver Walker was then cross-examined by Mcintyre. The cowboy had been born in Colorado and had occasionally worked as a cowboy over the years. He testified that he was about eighteen years of age when he left that state and was about twenty-four years old now. He had come to Canada with an uncle to take up land and had not been in trouble of any sort when he left Colorado nor was he wanted there. He had not re-visited the place, and the Colorado people knew his address. The witness said he came to Kamloops by way of Calgary and Medicine Hat in November of 1904. After staying a couple of months in Kamloops, the witness went to work for the Douglas Lake Cattle Company and stayed there eighteen months before being dismissed for neglect of duty. He then went to work for Mr. Goodwin.[21]

William Lauder, Joseph Coutlee, J. McCoy and the three Lamproses also gave evidence. Goodwin was committed for trial on seven charges. They were horse stealing, disfiguring brands on horses, disfiguring brands on cows, stealing cows and calves, killing steers, theft of calves, and theft of steers. Bail was refused, and he was locked up until his next court appearance, which was to be the spring assizes in Kamloops.[22]

Mcintyre used one of his commonest ploys in his client's defence, and he was successful in getting a change of venue to the Vernon spring assizes. There Mcintyre, because of disagreements within the jury, was able to get all the charges dismissed with the exception of stealing horses and obliterating brands. These charges were held over to the fall assizes in Kamloops, and Goodwin was released on bail.[23]

In Kamloops in October, Mcintyre's colleague Fulton was the prosecuting attorney and Judge Paulus Irving was again presiding. Mcintyre was successful in getting his client off with a fine, but the experience broke Goodwin and he soon sold out. The ranch eventually became part of the Douglas Lake Cattle Company's Norfolk Ranch.

Mcintyre practiced law until the day he died on 26 January 1934. His obituary recognized in a backhanded way the successes he had in the courts throughout his career. "None can take the place in legal circles of Alex D. Mcintyre who died Wednesday night after a residence here of 35 years. He bridged the old and the new, pioneer with modern times. His practice was a criminal one and he held a remarkable number of successes due to the times." The paper went on to state that "his methods belonged to another age, they were those of an opportunist, bent on a single purpose, the carrying out of his wish in court. He was considered an able lawyer, but was not popular with other members of his profession or the public."[24]

Jack Budd

After the Ducks robbery incident and the arrest and trials of his horse rustling friend Alfred Goodwin in 1908, Jack Budd diligently kept a low profile, staying close to his horse ranch near Princeton. No records of any mining activities he may have taken part in have been found in any contemporary mining reports. No doubt feeling his 53 years, he was never known to skirt the fringes of the law again before he died in 1948 at almost 100 years of age. He had decided to become a Canadian, and in his 1940 National Registration documents, he says he was naturalized in the Nicola courthouse in 1896, but records in Ottawa state that it took place in 1909. As all of the actual source naturalization records in Ottawa between 1854 and 1917 have been destroyed, and only a card index with limited information survives, we will never know for sure the year that event took place in Nicola.[25]

Jack Budd spent the rest of his life in Princeton, raising his beloved horses and mules on his ranch in the hills above the town. He would employ many of the younger men and older boys around the town to assist him with his chores. He raised many of the best horses in the area, and it was said that anyone would be proud to own a Jack Budd horse. In the thirties he made one of his only documented trips back into the United States to ride one of his best horses in the Parade of Roses in Portland, Oregon.[26]

Jack Budd entered the Princeton Hospital in July of 1947 and passed away on the 5 April 1948. Desmond Vicars in Kamloops repeats the story he heard of the death of Budd. "When he was in hospital, one moonlight night, he said, 'Oh what a wonderful night for rustling.' Just before he died, he asked the doctor if he should give his horse away. It showed his love for horses and bringing up. So much of their life depended on their horse, and they dearly loved a good one and looked after them."[27]

In Princeton in 1948, he was thought to be 99 years old; however, documentation on the year of his birth varies greatly. In the 1940 Canadian National Registration, Jack Budd gives his birth date as 19 January 1854 in Texas. In the 1901 Census he gives the date as 1857. In either case, his age at his death was in his nineties.

Much speculation has been engendered by the finding of documents in Jack Budd's possession after his death. The papers purported to show that Budd and Bill Miner were brothers. They have never been seen by historians or researchers, and their content has never been published. Whether they still exist is doubtful, and references to them that do exist are extremely fragmentary.

The respected B.C. historian Verna Cawston, writing in the B.C. Pioneer News in 1984, gave a good summary of the circumstances of Budd's death and put together the most comprehensive reference to the mysterious documents yet found.

"On April 4, 1948, the Baldy [sic] Mountain hermit died in hospital, of old age—ninety-eight years, it was said. Letters, clippings and old receipts, land papers, etc., found in his effects gave the town something to think about for many a day. A close neighbour and the local mortician vouched for the contents. The letters began, 'Dear

Bro. Jack'... and were signed, 'Wm.' One mentioned 'our sister' and asked if their mother was still alive. Another contained an obituary notice from a southern newspaper, concerning the death of a Mrs. McDonald and mentioning two sons (Jack and George), whereabouts unknown. One statement gave Budd the Power of Attorney .... And of course at this time, Miner was long since dead, at least forty years ago. Too bad these letters are not in evidence today, with names, places and dates to prove their case. They would have settled the obvious questions, 'Were Jack and Bill brothers? half-brothers? What were their real names?'"[28]

Elisabeth Duckworth, in an article published in 1994 also speculated about the relationship of the two Americans. "According to Millie Huey, after Jack Budd's death in 1948 the undertaker gave some letters found in Budd's pocket to Mrs. Huey's brother. The letters were written by Miner to Jack Budd and in them Miner revealed that his name was neither Miner nor Edwards. His real name was McDonald and ... Bill Miner was Jack Budd's brother .... The alleged family connection between Bill Miner and Jack Budd has not been verified."[29]

Cliff Schisler, the son of one of the attendees at Budd's funeral, wrote to the writer in 2002 and expressed his thoughts with regards to the parentage of the two. "The local mortician called my Dad, Fred Clifford Schisler, and was in the above's office during the time of Jack Budd's death. My Dad read the letters there and no doubt he believed Budd and Miner were brothers. Some years before, Jack Budd (in a state of drunkenness and at Budds house) told my Dad of the following. My thoughts are the letters etc. could well be in the family of the above mortician's family. His name I believe was George Gurr."[30]

With what we know as a result of Boessenecker and Dugan's painstaking primary source research into Miner's birth in Michigan, and Budd's own statements in more than one source as to his birth in Texas, at this time the best information is that Miner and Budd were not related. This myth of their filial relationship has been accepted to such an extent that even the B.C. Archives have filed Bill Miner information under the surname "McDonald," but unless there is other information available or that comes forward, we must assume Miner and Budd were not related.

In his probate documents, Jack Budd is noted as being a widower, leaving only a daughter behind. The daughter was described as Mrs. B.L. Barron who lived at Route 1, Box 53, Chico, California. The gross value of Budd's estate was $4,055, with real estate valued at $3,800 and horses to the value of $255. However, Mr. Budd had not paid his taxes since 1919, and they were $2,118 in arrears. Also, he had run up large credit bills at the F.P. Cook Estate grocery store and another grocery account with Robert Caldwell. When medical and undertaking services and probate fees were paid, the net value of the estate was nil. The land was sold, and the unfortunate daughter, Mrs. Barron, was informed that after her father's debt had been paid, nothing was left.[31]

Some sources mention that Jack Budd's daughter had a son named Clyde Wilkinson and that he would come up to visit the old man in the summers. In Jack Budd's obituary in the Similkameen Star, it mentions that he left behind his daughter, Mrs. L. Barron, and a grandson, Clyde Wilkonson [sic].[32][33]

With the death of Jack Budd in 1948 and Paul Stevens in 1950, the personal stories of all the major players in Bill Miner's world in British Columbia came to an end. Parts of the tale of Bill Miner and his activities in British Columbia would be romanticized and given importance and effect far beyond their due. Most of the genuine facts would remain buried in the restricted Provincial Police files of the B.C. Archives, rescued B.C. Penitentiary documents, scattered community archives and private collections for 100 years. The actual facts would prove to be far more fascinating than those dreamt up by the most fertile imaginations in decades past. However, the myth and the legends still live on, and so they should. It gives all of us a chance to touch our common past, and to realize that Canadians do have a history that can fuel the popular imagination. The restaurants and the stage plays, the re-enactments and the articles, each adds to our own chronicle of good and evil, and how each must inevitably blend into the other. But the authentic account, as it always does, resides with those whose names did not live on, those whose adventures, stories and anecdotes only resided with friends, families and obscure publications down through the years. It is they who would eventually ensure this story could finally be told.

⸺•⸺

Written in Barnhartvale, east of Kamloops
in the winter of 2005–2006.

NOTICE TO THE READER

Subsequent to the publication of this book, additional information on Bill Miner and the people and places in his world in B.C. has and is expected to accumulate. The author wishes to share this new information with the reader as these original source materials, anecdotes and photographs are identified. To access this bonus section of the web site **www.billminer.ca**, type in the user name "**GEdwards**" and the password "**RedSaddle**." Readers are urged to interact with the author on their various areas of interest in the British Columbia of 100 years ago, and contribute their own comments on the people and places of those days, or on this book in general. Interest in the history and stories of early B.C. has never been higher, and it is hoped that this book and its companion website will heighten the enthusiasm for and participation in the creative documentation of our truly unique province.

Peter Grauer, Kamloops, B.C., April 2006.

ENDNOTES

I

BILL MINER

1   John Boessenecker, *"Buckshot For Bill Miner,"* True West, Vol. 35, No. 8 (August 1988), 20–24.The scarring and pock marks on Bill Miner's face were a result of being hit by a partial load of buckshot fired at him during a prison break. On 28 November 1892 in San Quentin prison in California, Bill Miner and a cellmate attempted to escape during a storm. The guards had been tipped off by a stoolie, and Miner's partner was killed instantly. Miner took part of the charge in the face, knocking him unconscious, knocking out two teeth, and putting him in the prison infirmary for a number of days. This cured him of any further attempted escapes during this term in prison.

2   Anthony Martin Collection, B.C. Penitentiary Files, George Edwards Correspondence File, 1906–1954, (Kamloops, B.C.: 1 June 1906; New Westminster, B.C.: 4 June 1906). In June of 1906 Miner was examined by prison doctors in Kamloops and New Westminster, and during the examinations he advised the attending physicians that he had had smallpox as a child. This would have added to the pockmarks visible on Miner's face.

3   Mark Dugan, Bandit Years. A Gathering of Wolves (Santa Fe, NM, Sunstone Press: 1987), 21. Back in the 1880s Miner worked in the lead mines near Leadville in Colorado. His brother-in-law, Louis Wellman, owned mines in the area. However, working for a living never did appeal to Miner, and he was soon back robbing stages. By December of 1881 he was back in San Quentin serving his third 25 year term.

4   Mark Dugan and John Boessenecker, The Grey Fox (University of Oklahoma Press: 1992), 99.

5   Verna Cawston, *"The Grey Fox Goes To Earth Again!"* 48th Annual Report of the Okanagan Historical Society (Vernon, B.C., Wayside Press: 1984), 69–75.

6   E-mail from Val Patenaude, Curator, Maple Ridge Museum. "Telephone Conversation with Ellen Paterson, 1962." Maple Ridge Historical Society, 30 Jan. 2002.

7   Harry D. Barnes, Frontier Days in British Columbia, Early History of Hedley Camp (Langley, B.C., Sunfire Publications: April 1993), 122–133.

8   Harry D. Barnes, Frontier Days in British Columbia, Early History of Hedley Camp (Langley, B.C.: Sunfire Publications, April 1993), 122–133.

9   Laurie Currie, Princeton. 100 Years. 1867 to 1967 (Princeton, B.C., Similkameen Spotlight: 1967), 12.

10 Princeton History Book Committee, Princeton. Our Valley. A History (Allison Pass, Tulameen, Sterling Creek, Aspen Grove, Osprey Lake, Copper Mtn., Darck Mtn., Allenby, Blakeburn, Coalmont), (Altona, MB, Friesens Corporation, History Book Division: 2000), 503.

11 There is some secondary source information that indicates that Bill Miner and Jack Budd were brothers. This is based on letters reviewed after Budd died; however, these letters are now lost. It does not seem likely that this is correct, as the birthplaces of both individuals, Miner in Michigan and Budd in Texas, are well documented. (For Miner see Boessenecker's *"The Grey Fox,"* and for Budd refer to the 1901 Census, Budd's 1909 naturalization papers, and his 1940 National Registration papers.) It seems more likely that Budd and Miner may have met up in California in the 1870s. However, other than undocumented hearsay, there are no original primary sources that indicate a closer relationship.

II

JACK BUDD

1   Vera B. Cawston, *"The Quick Grey Fox … Fact vs Fiction,"* Bank of British Columbia's Pioneer News, (Feb./Mar. 1984), 6. Cawston is quoting Herbert Heald (Bert) Thomas, who first met Jack Budd when they worked together at the Douglas Lake Ranch in 1892 before either of them came to Princeton.

2   Canadian Census for 1901 (http://www.collectionscanda.ca/02/0122_e.html), 2006.

3   Public Rights Administration, Naturalization Papers of John Charles Budd, File No. B-300 (Citizenship and Immigration Canada, Ottawa, ON, 1909).

4   B.C. Supreme Court, Princeton. Probate Files 1926 to 1950, B.C. Archives, GR2506, Reel B09326, 25 June 1948, Item #10.

5   Statistics Canada, National Registration File of 1940, John Charles (Jack) Budd, Census Operations Division, Ottawa ON, Canada, 19 August 1940, Card #17.

6   Clifford Schisler, Letter to author (Orillia, ON: 9 May 2002).

7   Const. R. Hewat, Letter and Description Report to B.C.PP Sup't. Hussey, "John Budd Description," GR0055, Box 56, Files 7 & 8 (B.C.PP Office, Princeton, B.C., 23 Oct 1906).

8   Charlie Shook, A Young Boy's Memories of Jack Budd, Princeton History Book Committee, Princeton. Our Valley. A History (Altona, MB, Friesens Corporation, History Book Division: 2000), 194.

⁹   Manager W.S. Seavey, Letter to CPR's SS Detective W.L. McLaws, Results of
    Investigations South of Kamloops, GR-0419, Box #117, File #1906/88 (Thiel
    Detective Agency, Seattle, WA: 22 May 1906).

¹⁰ Helen Reith, *"Memories of Pioneer Life at Princeton,"* 41st Annual Report Okanagan
    Historical Society, (Wayside Press, Vernon, B.C.: 1977), 163.

¹¹ Phyllis Miller and Verna Cawston, *"H.H. Bert Thomas. 1874–1973,"* 38th Annual
    Report Okanagan Historical Society (Wayside Press, Vernon B.C.: 1974), 94, 95.

¹² Manager W.S. Seavey, Letter to CPR's SS Detective W.L. McLaws, Results of
    Investigations South of Kamloops, GR-0419, Box #117, File #1906/88 (Thiel
    Detective Agency, Seattle, WA: 22 May 1906).

¹³ Verna Cawston, *"The Grey Fox Goes To Earth Again!"* 48th Annual Report of the
    Okanagan Historical Society (Wayside Press, Vernon B.C.: 1984), 69.

¹⁴ Frank W. Anderson, Bill Miner ... Stagecoach and Train Robber (Surrey, B.C.,
    Heritage House Publishing: 1982).

¹⁵ Henderson's British Columbia Gazetteer and Directory for 1905 (Henderson's
    Publishing Co Ltd, Vancouver, B.C., 1905).

¹⁶ Mark Dugan and John Boessenecker, The Grey Fox (University of Oklahoma Press:
    1992), 18–19, 91–92.

¹⁷ Government of British Columbia, Annual Report of the Minister of Mines for the
    Year Ending Dec. 31, 1906 (http://www.em.gov.B.C..ca/DL/GSBPubs/AnnualReports/
    AR_1906.pdf).

¹⁸ No documentary evidence has been uncovered verifying Miner's rumoured land
    and mining partnerships with Budd. All references to the investments of Miner are
    from secondary sources. It may just have been a method of covering up unexplained
    income that Miner so conspicuously flashed about.

¹⁹ M. Stoneberg, *"Unpublished pencil notes of Bill Miner and Jack Budd"* (Princeton and
    District Museum and Archives, Bill Miner Vertical Files, Date unknown).

III

SIMILKAMEEN COUNTRY

¹   Aurelia Angela Allison-McDiarmid, Meet Mr. Edwards (Princeton and District
    Museum and Archives, Unpublished Manuscript, Uncatalogued Miner Files, 1978).

²   Collections Canada, Canadian Census for 1901. http://www.collectionscanada.
    ca/archivianet/020122_e.html (19 Oct 2005).

³   D.O. Vicars, Life of Bill Miner, Train Robber. An Unfinished Narrative, Bud Walters
    Interview (Kamloops Museum and Archives, Unpublished Manuscript, Kamloops,
    B.C., 1962).

4   Nina G. Wooliams, Cattle Ranch. The Story of the Douglas Lake Cattle Company (North Vancouver, B.C.: Douglas and McIntyre, 1979), 91–97.

5   Cresse, Gillian, Exclusion or Solidarity? Vancouver Workers Confront the 'Oriental Proble' in Canadian Working Class History. Edited by Laurel Sefton MacDowell and Ian Radforth. 2nd Edition. (Toronto: Canadian Scholar's Press, 2000.), 293–319.

6   Union White Labour, Inland Sentinel (Kamloops B.C., 13 Jan. 1905).

7   M. Stoneberg, Unpublished pencil notes of Bill Miner and Jack Budd (Princeton and District Museum and Archives, Date unknown).

8   R.E. Bullick, CPR Special Service Detective, "Witness Statements of Brothers Evander and William McLeod, A Duck, McKay, etc". (Report to CPR Sup't. Kilpatrick, Revelstoke, B.C., 18 May 1906), B.C. Archives, GR55, Box 51, B.C.PP Corr.

9   Collections Canada, Canadian Census for 1891. http://www.collectionscanada. ca/archivianet/020122_e.html (19 Oct 2005).

10   Rosehill Farmers Institute, Bunchgrass to Barbed Wire (Cloverdale: Friesen & Sons, Cloverdale, 1984), 94–95, 221–223.

11   George James, "Fred and Alice James. Their Early Years on the Commonage and Rose Hill," 45th Annual Report of the Okanagan Historical Society (Vernon, B.C.: Wayside Press, 1981), 164–165.

12   Chief Constable E.C. Simmons, Witness Statement of J.H. Bromley, B.C. Archives, Box 51, File E, B.C.PP Corr. (Kamloops, B.C.: 20 May 1906), 2.

13   Doug Cox, Mines of the Eagle Country (Penticton B.C.: WeB.C.o West, 1997), 63–65.

14   Ibid.

15   Ibid.

16   Ibid.

17   "Robbers Were After $30,000 Gold Brick," Vancouver Province, 25 May 1906, 1.

18   Chief Constable E.T.W. Pearse, "Hedley Escort, letter to Sup't F.S. Hussey," B.C. Archives, GR0055, Box 66, File 7, Corr. Inward to Sup't., 1891–1910 (Kamloops, B.C.: 19 Nov. 1904).

19   Clifford Schisler, Letter to Peter Grauer, Bill Miner and Garrison's Freight Business (Orillia, ON: 30 June 2002).

[1] Map, *"Municipality of Mission"* (Mission Museum and Community Archives, circa 1900). The Gibbard quarter section was the NW Corner of Section 28 and the Solloway quarter was the NE Corner of Section 28.

[2] Rene Corbett, e-mail message to author, October 2004.

[3] Map, *"Municipality of Mission"* (Mission Museum and Community Archives, circa 1900).

[4] Malcom Turnbull, *"Miner's Major Mission,"* Vancouver Province, Vancouver, B.C., 12 Sept 1966, 9.

[5] Don Waite, The Langley Story Illustrated. An Early History of the Municipality of Langley (D.W. Friesen and Sons Ltd., MB: 1977), pp.174–178, http://www.fortlangley.ca/langley/6amodern.html#BMiner, 10 Dec 2006. The anecdotes Waite gives in his work are from taped conversations with local pioneers. Names referenced are W.J. Cornock, L Harris, and D. Cumming. These anecdotes do not appear anywhere else in reviewed sources.

[6] Willis J. West, Stagecoach and Sternwheel Days in the Cariboo and Central B.C. (Surrey, B.C.: Heritage House, 1985). Willis West, a former BX Company general manager, originally published this article in the B.C. Historical Quarterly. Willis died in 1955. He wrote about his own personal experiences, and his anecdotes about Miner are probably contemporary.

[7] Ibid.

[8] Cecil Clark, *"The Saga of Bill Miner" and "Thousands in Loot"*, in The Islander (Daily Colonist weekend magazine, Victoria, B.C.: 4 Nov. 1962 and 11 Nov. 1962), 4, 5 and 6, 7, 11. In the November 11th article, Cecil Clark gives considerable detail on the Ashcroft stories. Unfortunately some of Clark's work has to be considered suspect and cannot be taken as a good source unless confirmed from other works. None of his facts in any of his articles are sourced, but the writer has seen some of the Ashcroft related Miner articles confirmed by other sources.

[9] Don Waite, Tales of the Golden Ears Illustrated (New Westminster, B.C.: Canart Studio Ltd., 1975), 76.

[10] Don Waite, The Langley Story Illustrated. An Early History of the Municipality of Langley (D.W. Friesen and Sons Ltd., MB: 1977), 174–178.

[11] *"Pacific Express Held Up Near Mission City,"* New Westminster Daily Columbian, 12 Sept. 1904, 1.

[12] A. H. Mitchell, Notes on the Mission Robbery (Various dates, submitted to Kamloops Museum and Archives by descendant of Dominion Express clerk Mitchell, Aug. 1993).

[13] *"Robbers Cross Fraser. Escape To United States,"* Vancouver Daily Province, 12 Sept. 1904, 1.

14 Verna B. Cawston, *"The Grey Fox Goes to Earth—Again!"* 48th Annual Report of the Okanagan Historical Society (Vernon, B.C.: Wayside Press, 1984), 72.

15 *"Robbers Cross Fraser. Escape To United States,"* Vancouver Daily Province, 12 Sept. 1904, 1.

16 Ibid.

17 *"Pacific Express Held Up Near Mission City,"* New Westminster Daily Columbian, 12 Sept. 1904, 1.

18 Val Patenaude, *"Donatelli Witnesses,"* 30 Jan. 2002, e-mail to author.

19 *"A Large Reward Posted,"* New Westminster Daily Columbian, 13 Sept. 1904, 1.

20 *"Pacific Express Held Up Near Mission City,"* New Westminster Daily Columbian, 12 Sept. 1904, 2.

21 *"Robbers Cross Fraser. Escape To United States,"* Vancouver Daily Province, 12 Sept. 1904, 1.

22 *"Judge Bole Was Hero Of Hold-Up,"* New Westminster Daily Columbian, 15 Sept. 1904, 8.

23 *"Pacific Express Held Up Near Mission City,"* New Westminster Daily Columbian, 12 Sept. 1904, 2.

24 Guido Marziali, *"Last Stop For Bill Miner,"* Fraser Valley Community Record, 29 Sept. 1993: Section B.

25 A. H. Mitchell, Notes on Mission Robbery, (Various dates, submitted to Kamloops Museum and Archives by Dominion Express clerk O.H. Mitchell, Aug. 1993).

26 *"Pacific Express Held Up Near Mission City,"* New Westminster Daily Columbian, 12 Sept. 1904, 1.

27 *"A Large Reward Posted,"* New Westminster Daily Columbian, 13 Sept. 1904, 1.

28 R.N.W.M.P. Staff Sergeant John Jackson Wilson, (Ret.), *"Capture of Bill Miner,"* Unpublished and undated manuscript, R.C.M.P. Archives, Regina, SK.

29 Harold Horwood and Ed Butts, *"Bill Miner,"* in Pirates and Outlaws of Canada. 1610 – 1932 (T.H. Best Printing: 1984), 220.

30 *"Pacific Express Held Up Near Mission City,"* New Westminster Daily Columbian, 12 Sept. 1904, 1.

Pursuit and Investigation

[1] "*Pacific Express Held Up Near Mission City,*" New Westminster Daily Columbian, 12 Sept. 1904, 1.

[2] Chief Constable Colin Campbell, "*Telegram to Sergeant Murray,*" B.C. Archives, GR0065, Box 3, File C. CPR Telegrams Jan 1901 – July 1906 (Vancouver B.C.: 10 Sept. 1905).

[3] "*Pacific Express Held Up Near Mission City,*" New Westminster Daily Columbian, 12 Sept. 1904, 1.

[4] "*Robbers Cross the Fraser,*" Vancouver Daily Province, 12 Sept. 1904, 1–3. The reporting by the Province provides the best primary source material for this section of the pursuit of the train robbers. It is the sole source until the events later the next day unless otherwise noted.

[5] "*Robbers Cross the Fraser,*" Vancouver Daily Province, 12 Sept. 1904, 1–3.

[6] Chief Constable Colin Campbell, "*Telegram to Sergeant Murray in Victoria,*" B.C. Archives, GR0065, Box 3, File C, CPR telegrams, 11 Sept. 1904.

[7] "*Robbers Cross the Fraser,*" Vancouver Daily Province, 12 Sept. 1904, 1–3.

[8] Don Waite, The Langley Story Illustrated. An Early History of the Municipality of Langley (D.W. Friesen and Sons Ltd., Manitoba, 1977), 174–178.

[9] Kevin Cairns Map Collection, Map of New Westminster District, Vancouver to Matsqui (Vancouver, B.C.: London and British North America Ltd.), circa 1913.

[10] Waite, "*The Langley Story Illustrated*", 174–178.

[11] "*Robbers Cross the Fraser,*" Vancouver Daily Province, 12 Sept. 1904, 1–3

[12] "*A Large Reward Posted,*" New Westminster Daily Columbian, 13 Sept. 1904, 1.

[13] Jo-Anne Colby, CPR Archives, "*Registered mailbag, contents unknown,*" 12 Nov. 2001, e-mail to author.

[14] Collection of Anthony Martin, "*Testimony of Instructor George Mackenzie,*" B.C. Penitentiary Records, Escape Inquiry Files, 13 Sept. 1907, 46–49.

[15] "*Bandits Still At Large,*" New Westminster Daily Columbian, 15 Sept. 1904, 4.

[16] "*Scouring Woods for Train Robbers,*" Vancouver Daily Province, 13 Sept. 1904, 1.

[17] "*A Large Reward Posted,*" New Westminster Daily Columbian, 13 Sept. 1904, 1.

[18] Ibid.

[19] Ibid.

[20] Ibid.

[21] Mark Dugan and John Boessenecker, The Grey Fox (University of Oklahoma Press, 1992), 92.

[22] "*The Train Robbers,*" Vancouver Daily Province, editorial, 13 Sept. 1904, 4

23 Gordon, C.L., *"Robbers Doubled Back to Canada,"* Vancouver Daily Province, 14 Sept. 1904, 1

24 Ibid.

25 Ibid.

26 *"No Trace of Robbers,"* Victoria Daily Colonist, 15 Sept. 1904, 1.

27 *"Bandits Cornered,"* New Westminster Daily Columbian, 15 Sept. 1904, 4.

28 Gordon, C.L., *"Have Probably Escaped Across the Cascades,"* Vancouver Daily Province, 17 Sept. 1904, 1.

29 Ibid.

30 *"Search for Bandits"* and *"C.P.R. President Talks,"* New Westminster Daily Columbian, 20 Sept. 1904, 1, 4.

31 Ibid.

VI

THE GETAWAY

1 Collection of Anthony Martin, *"Testimony of Instructor George Mackenzie,"* B.C. Penitentiary Records, Escape Inquiry Files, 13 Sept. 1907, 46–49.

2 Kevin Cairns Map Collection, New Westminster District, Vancouver to Matsqui (Vancouver, B.C.: London and British North America Ltd.), circa 1913.

3 Don Waite, *"Canada's First Train Robbery"* in Tales of the Golden Ears Illustrated (New Westminster: Camart Studio Ltd., 1975), 76.

4 W.S. Seavey, Thiel Detective Service, Letter to Marpole from McLaws, and Report to CPR's McLaws, Mission Robbery Investigation in Chilliwack (Seattle, WA, 28 May 1906), Vancouver Archives, Private Record #: Add Mss 358. 550-C-5, File 9. Under a covering letter from McLaws in Winnipeg (CPR Special Services Detective) to CPR General Superintendent Marpole in Vancouver, this report is from Detective Seavey of the Seattle office of the Thiel Detective Agency and relates the investigations of "Operator #38" in the Fraser Valley at the time of the Ducks Robbery investigation in Kamloops. It is mainly concerned with tying Edwards in to the Mission Junction holdup.

5 Henderson's Gazetteer and Directory for 1905 (Vancouver, B.C.: July 1905).

6 W.S. Seavey, Thiel Detective Service, Letter to Marpole from McLaws, and Report to CPR's McLaws, Mission Robbery Investigation in Chilliwack (Seattle, WA, 28 May 1906), Vancouver Archives, Private Record #: Add Mss 358. 550-C-5, File 9.

7 Ibid.

8 Ibid.

9 Ibid.

10 Ibid.

11 V.B. Cawston, *"The Quick Grey Fox ... Fact vs Fiction,"* Bank of British Columbia's Pioneer News, (Feb/Mar 1984), 6.

12 Penny Lett, *"Grey Fox Had Chilliwack Link,"* Fraser Valley Community Record, 30 March 1983.

13 W.S. Seavey, Thiel Detective Service. Letter to CPR Sup't. Marpole from CPR Detective McLaws, and Report to CPR's McLaws, *"Mission Robbery Investigation in Chilliwack,"* Seattle, WA, 28 May 1906, Vancouver City Archives. Private Record #: Add Mss 358. 550-C-5, File 9.

14 *"Chilliwack Exhibition,"* Chilliwack Progress, 14 Sept. 1904.

15 Ibid.

16 *"Local and Personal,"* Chilliwack Progress, 21 Sept. 1904.

17 W.S. Seavey, Thiel Detective Service. Letter to CPR Sup't. Marpole from CPR Detective McLaws, and Report to CPR's McLaws, "Mission Robbery Investigation in Chilliwack," Seattle, WA, 28 May 1906, Vancouver City Archives. Private Record #: Add Mss 358. 550-C-5, File 9.

18 *"Local and Personal,"* Chilliwack Progress, 28 Sept. 1904.

19 Don Waite, *"Canada's First Train Robbery"* in Tales of the Golden Ears Illustrated (New Westminster: Camart Studio Ltd., 1975), 76.

VII

THE GUNFIGHT AT MANNING'S

1 Murphy Shewchuk, Exploring the Nicola Valley (Vancouver: Douglas and Mcintyre Ltd., 1981), 113.

2 *"Some Gunplay,"* Similkameen Star, 9 April 1904, 1.

3 Maisie A.C. Armytage-Moore, *"A New Side of Bill Miner's Character,"* Vancouver City Archives, Add. MS 54m vol. 13, File M206, Bill Miner. 8 July 1943,

4 *"Some Gunplay,"* Similkameen Star, 9 April 1904, 1.

5 *"Shooting Affray,"* Kamloops Inland Sentinel, 8 Apr. 1904, 4.

6 *"Some Gunplay,"* Similkameen Star, 9 April 1904, 1.

7 *"Shooting Affray,"* Kamloops Inland Sentinel, 8 April 1904, 4.

8 *"City and Country,"* Kamloops Standard, 30 April 1904.

9 *"The Assizes,"* Kamloops Inland Sentinel, 10 May 1904, 1.

10 *"Town and Country,"* Kamloops Standard, 27 Aug. 1904, 10 Sept. 1904.

11 R.E. Bullick, CPR Special Service Detective, "*Witness Statement of Cyrus Tilton, etc.*," B.C. Archives, GR55, Box 51, File Don-El, B.C. Provincial Police Correspondence, Oct. 1905–Jan. 1908, Report to CPR Superintendent Kilpatrick, Revelstoke, B.C., 18 May 1906, 3.

12 "*Steven Brooks Indictment,*" Report From the General Assizes Held in Kamloops, 6 Oct. 1904," B.C. Archives, GR1323, Reel B2051, B.C. Attorney General Correspondence, Letters Inward, 1902 to 1937.

13 "*Brooks Acquitted,*" Kamloops Inland Sentinel, 11 Oct. 1904, 1.

14 Ibid.

15 "*Rex vs Brooks,*" Letter From the Prosecutor Frederick Fulton to Attorney General Wilson, 18 Oct. 1904, B.C. Archives, GR1323, Reel B2051, B.C. Attorney General Correspondence, Letters Inward, 1902 to 1937.

16 "*Nicola Notes,*" Kamloops Inland Sentinel, 21 Oct. 1904, 1.

17 W.S. Seavey, Thiel Detective Service, Letter to Marpole from McLaws, and Report to CPR's McLaws, Mission Robbery Investigation in Chilliwack (Seattle, WA, 28 May 1906), Vancouver Archives, Private Record #: Add Mss 358. 550-C-5, File 9.

18 Ibid.

19 Ibid.

20 Ibid.

21 Ibid.

22 Ibid.

23 Ibid.

24 Ibid.

25 "*The Nickel Plate Gold Brick,*" Hedley Gazette, 31 May 1906, 1.

26 "*Woman In Miner Case Left The City,*" Vancouver Province, 26 May 1906, 1.

27 "*Robbers Were After $30,000 Gold Brick,*" Vancouver Province, 25 May 1906, 1.

VIII
ROSE HILL AND ANDERSON CREEK

1 Inspector W. McLeod to B.C. Provincial Police Superintendent F.S. Hussey, "*Information to the Press*" (Letter and clippings, Vancouver, B.C., 13 Jan. 1905), B.C. Archives, GR0055, Box 44, File 1. B.C. Provincial Police files, Inward to Sup't., 1891–1910.

2 Ibid.

3   Harry D. Barnes, Frontier Days in British Columbia, Early History of Hedley Camp (Ed. Garnet Basque, Sunfire Publications, Langley, B.C., April 1993), 122–133.

4   Tom Knowles, Interview with the author, Life in Hedley (Kamloops B.C., 21 Jan. 2004).

5   Doug Cox, Mines of the Eagle Country: Nickel Plate and Mascot (Penticton, B.C.: Skookum Publications, 1997), 61–66.

6   "City and Country," Kamloops Inland Sentinel, 28 Mar. 1905, 4.

7   "Nicola Railway," Kamloops Inland Sentinel, 18 Apr. 1905, 1.

8   "City and Country," Kamloops Inland Sentinel, 23 May 1905, 4.

9   Princeton History Book Committee, Princeton Our Valley (Altona, Manitoba: Friesens Corporation, 2000), 22, 553.

10 Laurie Currie, Princeton 100 Years 1867–1967 (Princeton, B.C.: Similkameen Spotlight Publishing, 1967), 13, 19.

11 Vera Cawston, "The Quick Grey Fox … Fact vs Fiction," Bank of British Columbia's Pioneer News (Feb./Mar. 1984), 5, 6.

12 Clifford Schisler to Peter Grauer, "Bill Miner and Garrison's Freight Business" (Orillia, ON, 30 June 2002).

13 Rosehill Farmers Institute, Bunchgrass to Barbed Wire (Cloverdale: Friesen & Sons, 1984), 2, 3, 82.

14 CPR Special Service Detective R.E. Bullick to CPR Superintendent T. Kilpatrick, Witness Statements of William and Evander McLeod, etc., B.C. Archives, GR0419, Box 117, File 1906/88 (Kamloops, B.C., 18 May 1906), 1, 2.

15 Ibid.

16 Ibid.

17 Mark Dugan and John Boessenecker, "The Grey Fox," (Norman OK: University of Oklahoma Press, 1992), 93.

18 CPR Special Service Detective R.E. Bullick to CPR Superintendent T. Kilpatrick, Witness Statements of William and Evander McLeod, etc., B.C. Archives, GR0419, Box 117, File 1906/88 (Kamloops, B.C., 18 May 1906), 1, 2.

19 Princeton History Book Committee, Princeton Our Valley (Altona, Manitoba: Friesens Corporation, 2000) 26.

20 "The Assizes," Kamloops Inland Sentinel, 16 May 1905, 1.

21 Ibid.

22 Thiel Detective Service Operative G.H., Witness Statements, B.C. Archives, GR0419, Box 117, File 1906/88 (Kamloops, B.C., 18 May 1906), 3.

23 Albert McKay, Interview by Jack Montieth and Don Keizer, Vancouver, B.C., 20 February 1990.

24 Ibid.

25 Ibid.

26 Ibid.

27 Ibid.

28 Ibid.

29 Ibid.

30 Rosehill Farmers Institute, Bunchgrass to Barbed Wire (Cloverdale: Friesen & Sons, 1984), Original Homesteader Maps.

31 CPR Special Service Detective R.E. Bullick to CPR Superintendent T. Kilpatrick, Witness Statements of William and Evander McLeod, etc., B.C. Archives, GR0419, Box 117, File 1906/88 (Kamloops, B.C., 18 May 1906), 3.

32 B.C. Provincial Police Constable B. Gardom to Sup't. F.S. Hussey, Receipt of Smith and Wesson, B.C. Archives, GR0055, Box 54, File 2, Provincial Police Files Corr. Inward to Sup't, 1891–1910 (Enderby: 22 Aug. 1905).

33 Robert and Joan Cowan, Enderby, an illustrated history (Vernon: Wayside Press, 2005) 20. Constable Gardom's son, Garde Gardom, would many years later become Lieutenant Governor of British Columbia.

34 Daryl Drew, "Albert Jordan Remembers The Grey Fox," Princeton and District Museum and Archives, Bill Miner Vertical Files, Unknown newspaper clipping, date unknown.

35 Ibid.

36 "The Dick Duval of the Far West," Vancouver Daily News Advertiser, 19 Feb. 2009, 1.

37 Daryl Drew, "Albert Jordan Remembers The Grey Fox," Princeton and District Museum and Archives, Bill Miner Vertical Files, Unknown newspaper clipping, date unknown.

38 Ibid.

39 Ibid.

40 Ibid.

41 Mark Dugan and John Boessenecker, "The Grey Fox" (Norman, OK: University of Oklahoma Press, 1992), 113–117.

42 "Colquhoun, Robert" in Historical Atlas of Wellington County, 1906, http://www.rootsweb.com/~canB.C./conlist.htm#5, (27 Dec. 2005).

43 "Colquhoun," Canadian Censuses for 1871, 1881 and 1891, http://www.rootsweb.com/~canB.C./conlist.htm#5, (27 Dec. 2005).

44 "Train Robber From Phoenix," Phoenix Pioneer and Boundary Mining Journal, 19 May 1906.

45   Colquhoun, Lewis. Witness Statement of Lewis Colquhoun, B.C. Archives, GR0055, Box 45, File 7, B.C. Provincial Police Corr. Inward to Sup't, 1891–1910 (circa fall 1906).

46   Edwards, George. Witness Statement of George Edwards, George Edwards Corr. File, Anthony Martin Collection, B.C. Penitentiary Files (circa Fall 1906), 1.

47   CPR Special Service Detective R.E. Bullick to CPR Superintendent T. Kilpatrick, Witness Statements of William and Evander McLeod, etc., B.C. Archives, GR0419, Box 117, File 1906/88 (Kamloops, B.C., 18 May 1906), 3.

48   Laurie Currie, Princeton. 120 Years (Princeton B.C.: Similkameen Spotlight Publishing Co., 1990), 14.

49   Edwards, George. Witness Statement of George Edwards, George Edwards Corr. File, Anthony Martin Collection, B.C. Penitentiary Files (circa fall 1906), 1.

50   Laurie Currie, Princeton 100 Years 1867–1967 (Princeton, B.C.: Similkameen Spotlight Publishing, 1967), 19.

51   Constable Ronald Hewat, "Oath of Office" (Princeton, B.C.: 9 Nov. 1905), B.C. Archives, GR0055, Box 44, File 1. B.C. Provincial Police files, Inward to Sup't., 1891–1910.

52   Chief Constable E.T.W. Pearse to Sup't F.S. Hussey, "Hewat Appointment" (Kamloops, B.C.: 13 Nov. 1905), B.C. Archives, GR0055, Box 44, File 1. B.C. Provincial Police files, Inward to Sup't., 1891–1910.

53   Constable R. Hewat to Sup't F.S. Hussey, "Revolver Receipt" (Princeton B.C.: 13 Dec. 1905), B.C. Archives, GR0055, Box 44, File 1. B.C. Provincial Police files, Inward to Sup't., 1891–1910.

54   Government of British Columbia, G.C. Tunstall, Gold Commissioner, Yale District, Nicola Mining Division, "Annual Report of the Minister of Mines for the Year Ending Dec 31, 1906." (http://www.em.gov.B.C..ca/DL/GSBPubs/AnnualReports/AR_1906.pdf)

55   M. Stoneberg, Unpublished pencil notes, "Bill Miner and Jack Budd" (Princeton, B.C.: Princeton and District Museum and Archives, Date unknown).

56   Ibid.

57   D.O. Vicars, "Life of Bill Miner, Train Robber. An Unfinished Narrative" (Kamloops, B.C.: Unpublished manuscript, Kamloops Museum and Archives, 1962).

58   Manager W.S. Seavey of Thiel Detective Service to CPR Special Service Detective McLaws, "Results of Investigations South of Kamloops" (Seattle, WA: 22 May 1906), B.C. Archives, GR-0419, Box #117, File #1906/88.

59   Gordon Heslop, Interview with author, Kamloops, B.C., 28 January 2006.

60   Maisie Campbell-Johnston, "A New Side of Bill Miner's Character," City of Vancouver Archives, Major Mathews Collection, Private Record #: Add. MSS. 54, 504-A-5, File 34, mf #AM0054.013.00678 (8 July 1943), 1–4.

[61] Ibid

[62] Ibid

[63] Ibid

[64] Ibid

IX

SHORTY DUNN

[1] Desmond O. Vicars, Life of Bill Miner, Train Robber. An Unfinished Narrative, Unpublished manuscript (Kamloops Museum and Archives, Kamloops, B.C.: 1962), 3. The writer has been unable to determine whether this is a genuine instance of Shorty Dunn's poetry or whether he was quoting something he had previously read.

[2] Hedley Gazette, 31 May 1906, 1.

[3] Victoria Daily Colonist, 16 Dec. 1923, 10.

[4] Irene Stangoe, History and Happenings in the Cariboo-Chilcotin. Pioneer Memories (Surrey B.C.: Heritage House Press, 2000), 41.

[5] Louis Lebourdais Fonds, B.C. Archives, Mss 0676, Box 6, File 8 (Unpublished 1 page manuscript with notes, Quesnel, B.C., attributed to Shorty Dunn, circa 1896).

[6] Wilfred Wright, letter to author, Shorty Dunn's Cabin (Williams Lake, B.C.: circa 20 November 2005), 1.

[7] Louis Lebourdais Fonds, B.C. Archives, Mss 0676, Box 6, File 8 (Unpublished 1 page manuscript with notes, Quesnel B.C., attributed to Shorty Dunn, circa 1896).

[8] Ibid

[9] Victoria Daily Colonist, 16 Dec. 1923, 10.

[10] Enderby Progress, 18 May 1906, 3.

[11] Victoria Daily Colonist, 16 Dec. 1923, 10.

[12] Victoria Daily Colonist, 23 Dec. 1923, 34.

[13] Margaret F. Mitchell (nee Hunter), The Movie The Grey Fox (Princeton and District Museum and Archives, Uncatalogued Miner Files, Unpublished manuscript, Aft. 1981). Margaret Mitchell was the daughter of Constable and Mining Recorder Hugh Hunter.

[14] Cecil Clark, "McDougal's Lost Mine," Victoria Colonist, The Islander Weekend Supplement, 2 October 1966, 6, 7, 8.

[15] Provincial Police Constable Hugh Hunter, Hunter Report, B.C. Archives, GR 0055, Box 51, File DON – EI (Princeton B.C.: Bfr 19 May 1906.

[16] Chief Constable Simmons, Witness Statement of J.H. Bromley, B.C. Archives, GR 0055, Box 51, File DON to EI, (Kamloops, B.C.: 20 May 1906).

[17] Laurie Currie, Princeton. 120 Years (Princeton, B.C.: Similkameen Spotlight Publishing Co. 1990), 14.

[18] William Dunn, Statement By Dunn, B.C. Archives, GR 0055, Box 45, File 7 (New Westminster Penitentiary: Circa Dec. 1906).

[19] Verna B. Cawston, *"The Quick Grey Fox ... Fact vs Fiction"* (Bank of British Columbia's Pioneer News, Feb./Mar. 1984).

[20] R.E. Bullick, CPR Special Service Detective, Witness Statements of Brothers Evander and William McLeod, A Duck, McKay, etc. B.C. Archives, GR 0055, Box 51, File DON – EI (Report to CPR Sup't. Kilpatrick, Revelstoke, B.C.: 18 May 1906).

X

KAMLOOPS COUNTRY

[1] Government of British Columbia, Annual Report of the Minister of Mines for the Year Ending Dec. 31, 1906, http://www.em.gov.B.C..ca/DL/GSBPubs/AnnualReports/AR_1906.pdf (2004).

[2] Mary Balf, Kamloops A History of the District Up To 1914 (Kamloops B.C.: Clow Printing, 1969), 126. Some of the information following this paragraph has been gleaned from this pivotal document that first summarized Kamloops' history, and the reader will not be burdened with unnecessary end notes.

[3] Robert Cail, Conversation with the author (Kamloops B.C.: 9 Dec. 2005).

[4] Gillian Creese, *"Exclusion or Solidarity? Vancouver Workers Confront the 'Oriental Problem,'"* in Canadian Working Class History, ed. Laurel Sefton MacDowell and Ian Radforth (Toronto: Canadian Scholars' Press, 2000), 296–301.

[5] James J. Clark, City of Kamloops History. 1893 to 1964. (Unpublished manuscript, ca 1990). James Clark, a former City Clerk in Kamloops, assembled an unpublished document detailing the works of the various Councils since Kamloops' incorporation. It is an invaluable tool for the researcher of the history of early Kamloops, and many of the details in this section can be attributed to his labour of love.

[6] Chief Constable Joseph W. Burr in Ashcroft to B.C. Provincial Police Superintendent F.S. Hussey in Victoria, Appointment of Walter Clark in Nicola Lake, B.C. Archives, GR0055, Box 37, File 8, B.C. Provincial Police Files, Inward to Sup't, 1891–1910. (Ashcroft, B.C.: 13 May 1905).

[7] Lynn Stonier Newman, Policing a Pioneer Province. The B.C. Provincial Police. 1858–1950 (Madiera Park, B.C.: Harbour Publishing 1991).

[8] Chief Constable E.T.W. Pearse in Kamloops to B.C. Provincial Police Acting Superintendent Bullock-Webster in Victoria, Appointment of E.T.W. Pearse as Chief Constable in Kamloops, B.C. Archives, GR0055, Box 66, File 7, B.C. Provincial Police Files, Inward to Sup't, 1891–1910. (Kamloops, B.C.: 6 Aug. 1904).

9   Col. Fernie, Real Pioneer of Great Northwest, Unknown newspaper clipping, Kamloops Museum and Archives, January 1934.

10   Peter R. Grauer, Interviews with Daphne and Mary Fernie. (Transcribed tape recorded interview, Victoria, B.C., 3 April 2001).

11   Ibid.

12   John Stewart, Kamloops Museum and Archives published article, William L. Fernie, Vol. 10, #178, Part 1 (Kamloops B.C., 4 Jan 1982).

13   James J. Clark, City of Kamloops History. 1893 to 1964. (Unpublished manuscript, ca 1990), 33.

14   Desmond O. Vicars, Life of Bill Miner, Train Robber. An Unfinished Narrative, An Interview With Lou Fox of Duck Range. Unpublished manuscript (Kamloops Museum and Archives, Kamloops, B.C.: 1962), 10. Vicars states that cowboy George Martin may also have been along with Walter Campbell and the rest of the bunch on their foray into Kamloops; however, Pearse in his official report to Sup't. Hussey does not mention him.

15   Chief Constable E.T.W. Pearse, Report Re Train Robbery of 8 May 1906, B.C. Archives, GR0419, Box 117, Attorney General Files 1906 (Kamloops, B.C.), 3

XI

PREPARATIONS

1   Michael C. Neitzel, The Valencia Tragedy (Surrey, B.C.: Heritage House 1995).

2   Colquhoun, Lewis, Statement of Colquhoun, B.C. Archives, GR0055, Box 45, File 7, B.C. Provincial Police Corr. Inward to Sup't, 1891–1910 (circa Fall 1906).

3   Ibid.

4   Ibid.

5   Constable Hugh Hunter to Sup't. F.S. Hussey, Report on Edwards and Dunn, B.C. Archives, GR0055, Box 51, File Don-El, B.C.PP Corr., Oct. 05–Jan. 08 (Princeton: 23 May 1906).

6   CPR Special Service Detective R.E. Bullick to CPR Superintendent T. Kilpatrick, Witness Statements of William and Evander McLeod, etc., B.C. Archives, GR0419, Box 117, File 1906/88 (Kamloops, B.C., 18 May 1906), 3.

7   George W. Edwards, Princeton, B.C. to Edna Moore, Phoenix, B.C., B.C. Archives, GR0055, Box 51, B.C.PP Corr., File E (22 Feb 1906).

8   George Edwards, "Letter to Bert McKay," Kamloops Museum and Archives, Vertical Bill Miner Files, (Princeton, B.C.: 4 March 1906). This letter is a photocopy of an original, and difficult to discern. The provenance of the original is unknown, but it is probably in the possession of the descendants of Bert McKay.

⁹ Constable Hugh Hunter to Sup't. F.S. Hussey, Report on Edwards and Dunn, B.C. Archives, GR0055, Box 51, File Don-El, B.C.PP Corr., Oct. 05–Jan. 08 (Princeton: 23 May 1906).

¹⁰ Sears, Roebuck Catalogue (New York: Bounty Books, Crown Publishing, 1902), 319.

¹¹ Constable Hugh Hunter to Sup't. F.S. Hussey, Report on Edwards and Dunn, B.C. Archives, GR0055, Box 51, File Don-El, B.C.PP Corr., Oct. 05–Jan. 08 (Princeton: 23 May 1906).

¹² George W. Edwards, Witness Statement of Edwards, B.C. Archives, GR0055, Box 45, File 7, B.C. Provincial Police Corr. Inward to Sup't, 1891–1910 (circa fall 1906).

¹³ Constable Hugh Hunter to Sup't. F.S. Hussey, Report on Edwards and Dunn, B.C. Archives, GR0055, Box 51, File Don-El, B.C.PP Corr., Oct. 05–Jan. 08 (Princeton: 23 May 1906).

¹⁴ Neil McFadden letter to Sup't. F.S. Hussey, B.C. Archives, GR0055, Box 51, File E, B.C.PP Corr., (Princeton, B.C.: 16 May 1906).

¹⁵ Chief Constable E.C. Simmons, Witness Statement of J.H. Bromley, B.C. Archives, Box 51, File E, B.C.PP Corr. (Kamloops, B.C.: 20 May 1906), 2.

¹⁶ George W. Edwards, Witness Statement of Edwards, B.C. Archives, GR0055, Box 45, File 7, B.C. Provincial Police Corr. Inward to Sup't., 1891–1910 (circa fall 1906).

¹⁷ Constable Hugh Hunter to Sup't. F.S. Hussey, Report on Edwards and Dunn, B.C. Archives, GR0055, Box 51, File Don-El, B.C.PP Corr., Oct. 05–Jan. 08 (Princeton: 23 May 1906).

¹⁸ Ibid.

¹⁹ Encyclopaedia Americana International Edition, 2001, s.v. "San Francisco."

²⁰ James J. Clark, City of Kamloops History. 1893 to 1964 (Unpublished manuscript, ca 1990), 75.

²¹ Chief Constable Simmons, Witness Statement of Mrs. Paul Stevens, B.C. Archives, GR0055, Box 51, File Don-El, B.C. Provincial Police Corr., Oct. 1905 – Jan. 1908 (Kamloops, B.C., 20 May 1906).

²² James J. Clark, City of Kamloops History. 1893 to 1964 (Unpublished manuscript, ca 1990), 106.

²³ The Kamloops Standard, 28 Apr. 1906.

²⁴ W.S. Seavey of Thiel Detective Service, Report to CPR Chief Special Agent W.L. McLaws, Special Service Operative #30 Witness Statements, B.C. Archives, GR0419, Box 117, File 1906/88, Attorney General Crown Prosecutor Files (Seattle, WA: 21 May 1906).

²⁵ T. Eaton Company Limited, 1901 Spring Summer Fall Winter Catalogue (Don Mills, ON: Musson Book Company, 1970), 180.

26 W.S. Seavey of Thiel Detective Service, Report to CPR Chief Special Agent W.L. McLaws, Special Service Operative #30 Witness Statements, B.C. Archives, GR0419, Box 117, File 1906/88, Attorney General Crown Prosecutor Files (Seattle, WA: 21 May 1906).

27 Ibid.

28 Operative *"L.H."* of Thiel Detective Service, Camp Investigations, B.C. Archives, GR0419, Box 117, File 1906/88, Attorney General Crown Prosecutor Files (Kamloops, B.C.: 19 May 1906).

29 CPR Special Service Detective R.E. Bullick to CPR Superintendent T. Kilpatrick, Witness Statements of William and Evander McLeod, etc., B.C. Archives, GR0419, Box 117, File 1906/88 (Kamloops, B.C., 18 May 1906), 4.

30 Canadian Census for 1901 (http://www.collectionscanada.ca/02/020122_e.html).

31 Environment Canada, Climate Gateway Query Results, Temperatures and Precipitation , Kamloops, B.C., April, May and June 1906.

32 Operative *"G.H."*, Russell and Butler Statement, B.C. Archives, GR0055, Box 51, File Don-El, B.C. Provincial Police Corr., Oct. 1905 – Jan. 1908, (Kamloops, B.C.: 18 May 1906).

33 CPR Special Services Inspector W. McLeod to CPR Chief Special Agent W.L. McLaws, H.B. Taite Statement, B.C. Archives, GR0055, Box 51, File Don-El, B.C. Provincial Police Corr., Oct. 1905 – Jan. 1908 (Kamloops, B.C.: 22 May 1906).

34 Canadian Census for 1901 (http://www.collectionscanada.ca/02/020122_e.html).

35 Verna B. Cawston, *"The Grey Fox Goes To Earth – Again,"* in Forty-Eighth Annual Report of the Okanagan Historical Society, Ed. Jean Webber (Vernon, B.C.: Wayside Press, 1984), 72.

36 Canadian Pacific Railway Co., Time Table No. 8, Shuswap Section, David Davies Collection, Kamloops, B.C. (6 May 1906).

37 CPR Special Services Inspector W. McLeod to CPR Chief Special Agent W.L. McLaws, Graves and Montgomery Statement, B.C. Archives, GR0055, Box 51, File Don-El, B.C. Provincial Police Corr., Oct. 1905 – Jan. 1908 (Kamloops, B.C.: 18 May 1906), 2.

38 Ibid.

39 Deputy Attorney General Hugh A. McLean, Notes on Prosecution's Final Arguments, B.C. Archives, GR0419, Box 117, File 1906/88 (Kamloops, B.C., circa 30 May 1906), 3.

40 CPR Special Services Inspector W. McLeod to CPR Chief Special Agent W.L. McLaws, Lizzie Dupuis Statement, B.C. Archives, GR0055, Box 51, File Don-El, B.C. Provincial Police Corr., Oct. 1905 – Jan. 1908 (Kamloops, B.C.: 18 May 1906), 2.

41 J.J. Carment, City Clerk, City of Kamloops Council Meeting Minutes, 3 May 1906, 2.

⁴² The Kamloops Standard, 5 May 1906.

⁴³ CPR Special Service Detective R.E. Bullick to CPR Chief Special Agent W.L. McLaws, William Phillips Statement, B.C. Archives, GR0055, Box 51, File Don-El, B.C. Provincial Police Corr., Oct. 1905 – Jan. 1908 (Kamloops, B.C.: 22 May 1906).

⁴⁴ William Dunn, Witness Statement of Dunn, B.C. Archives, GR0055, Box 45, File 7, B.C. Provincial Police Corr. Inward to Sup't., 1891–1910 (circa fall 1906).

⁴⁵ CPR Special Services Inspector W. McLeod to CPR Chief Special Agent W.L. McLaws, Adams and Hazelhurst Statements, B.C. Archives, GR0055, Box 51, File Don-El, B.C. Provincial Police Corr., Oct. 1905 – Jan. 1908 (Kamloops, B.C.: 18 May 1906), 1.

⁴⁶ Special Services Inspector W. McLeod to CPR Chief Special Agent W.L. McLaws, Rosie Love Statements, B.C. Archives, GR0055, Box 51, File Don-El, B.C. Provincial Police Corr., Oct. 1905 – Jan. 1908 (Kamloops, B.C.: 23 May 1906).

⁴⁷ CPR Special Service Detective R.E. Bullick to CPR Chief Special Agent W.L. McLaws, Witness Statement of F.E. Burns, B.C. Archives, GR0419, Box 117, File 1906/88 (Kamloops, B.C., 22 May 1906).

⁴⁸ William Dunn, Witness Statement of Dunn, B.C. Archives, GR0055, Box 45, File 7, B.C. Provincial Police Corr. Inward to Sup't., 1891–1910 (circa fall 1906).

⁴⁹ George W. Edwards, Witness Statement of Edwards, B.C. Archives, GR0055, Box 45, File 7, B.C. Provincial Police Corr. Inward to Sup't., 1891–1910 (circa fall 1906).

⁵⁰ "Stevens Tried To Make Escape," Vancouver Daily Province, 16 May 1906, 1.

⁵¹ William Dunn, Witness Statement of Dunn, B.C. Archives, GR0055, Box 45, File 7, B.C. Provincial Police Corr. Inward to Sup't., 1891–1910 (circa fall 1906).

⁵² George W. Edwards, Witness Statement of Edwards, B.C. Archives, GR0055, Box 45, File 7, B.C. Provincial Police Corr. Inward to Sup't., 1891–1910 (circa fall 1906).

XII

THE DUCKS ROBBERY

¹ "Clergymen Give Lighter Side," Vancouver Daily Province, 9 May 1906.

² Joanna Sanders, James Shaver Woodsworth, The Early Years, http://www.saskndp.com/history/woodsworth.htmal, (Jan. 2006).

³ Environment Canada, "Official Weather Record for April, May and June 1906 for Kamloops, B.C.," Climate Gateway Query Results (10 Dec. 2002). Environment Canada records were obtained for April, May and June of 1906. These records serve as a good verification of the contemporary reported weather throughout the time leading up to the robbery, the robbery, the pursuit and capture, and the trial in Kamloops.

⁴ "Witness Statement of Joseph Callin," May 1906. Vancouver City Archives, Major Mathews Collection, Private Record #: Add. MSS 358, 550-C-5, file 9.

5 "*Train Held Up,*" Kamloops Inland Sentinel, 11 May 1906, 1. Contemporary B.C. newspapers, including the twice weekly Kamloops Sentinel, the weekly Kamloops Standard, and the daily Vancouver Province provide usually reliable, but sometimes exaggerated or erroneous data on the robbery and pursuit of the robbers. Newspaper source data is almost always cross-checked with other records; however, they do provide a good outline of the events, and their timeline. Details of events, conversations and character descriptions are obtained from primary sources such as witness statements, unpublished manuscripts and first person articles.

6 "*Grand Jury Testimony of Joseph Callin,*" King Versus George Edwards, Lewis Colquhoun and William Dunn, Kamloops, B.C., B.C. Archives, GR0419, Box 117, File 1906/88, Attorney General files, 17, 18 May 1906.

7 "*Witness Statement of Joseph Callin,*" May 1906. Vancouver City Archives, Major Mathews Collection, Private Record #: Add. MSS 358, 550-C-5, file 9.

8 Dave Davies, Telephone interview with author, Kamloops, B.C., 29 Jan. 2002.

9 Robert D. Turner, "*West of the Great Divide,*" (Morriss Printing, Victoria, B.C., 1987), 73.

10 "*Witness Statement of William McQuarrie to Postal Inspector,*" 9 May 1906, Vancouver, B.C., B.C. Archives, File 0419, Box 117, File 1906/88, Attorney General files.

11 Joseph Callin, "*Grand Jury Testimony,*" The King vs Edwards, Dunn and Colquhoun, B.C. Archives, GR0419, Box 117, File 1906/88, Attorney General Crown Prosecutor Files, 17–18 May 1906, 54–67.

12 "*Letters of Convict Discloses Tortures of Mind Undergone,*" Daily Colonist, Victoria, B.C., 16 August 1923, 10.

13 "*Accuse Miner of Hold-Up,*" Vancouver Province, 29 May 1906, 1.

14 George Edwards (Bill Miner) was often underestimated as to his age. His demeanour and habits would contribute to this common error in assumptions made by many witnesses and friends during subsequent investigative interviews.

15 "*The Hold Up on C.P.R.,*" Kamloops Standard, 12 May 1906, 1. This quote is taken from the actual conversational recollections of Callin and Radcliffe. Radcliffe specifically refers to the use of the phrase "Hands Up" by the older leader of the bandits. This phrase lives on over the years as being attributed solely to the bandit Bill Miner, who is somewhat dubiously credited as being the first to use the phrase. It is, however, difficult to believe that previous interactions between robbers and their victims, or lawmen and their quarry, would not have utilized such a basic command as this.

16 "*Witness Statement of Joseph Callin,*" May 1906. Vancouver City Archives, Major Mathews Collection, Private Record #: Add. MSS 358, 550-C-5, file 9.

17 "*Train-Robbers Overlooked Over $35,000 in Hard Cash,*" Vancouver Daily Province, May 1906, 1.

18 *"Grand Jury Testimony of Joseph Callin,"* King Versus George Edwards, Lewis Colquhoun and William Dunn, Kamloops, B.C., B.C. Archives, GR0419, Box 117, File 1906/88, Attorney General files, 17, 18 May 1906.

19 *"Witness Statement of Joseph Callin,"* May 1906. Vancouver City Archives, Major Mathews Collection, Private Record #: Add. MSS 358, 550-C-5, file 9. The conversation that took place between Callin and the bandit leader are transcribed from the actual conversations that were reported in witness statements and other primary sources.

20 Ibid.

21 Ibid.

22 *"The Hold-Up of the CPR,"* Kamloops Standard, 12 May 1906, 1.

23 *"Grand Jury Testimony of Joseph Callin,"* King Versus George Edwards, Lewis Colquhoun and William Dunn, Kamloops, B.C., B.C. Archives, GR0419, Box 117, File 1906/88, Attorney General files, 17, 18 May 1906.

24 *"Letters of Convict Discloses Tortures of Mind Undergone,"* Victoria Daily Colonist, 16 August 1923, 10.

25 *"Train Robbers Overlooked …,"* Vancouver Daily Province, 9 May 1906, 1.

26 Ibid.

27 "Victorian Tells Of C.P.R. Train Robbery," Victoria Colonist, 12 May 1906, 3.

28 "Witness Statement of Joseph Callin," May 1906. Vancouver City Archives, Major Mathews Collection, Private Record #: Add. MSS 358, 550-C-5, file 9.

29 *"Witness Statement of William McQuarrie to Postal Inspector,"* 9 May 1906, Vancouver, B.C., B.C. Archives, File 0419, Box 117, File 1906/88, Attorney General files

30 *"Witness Statement of Joseph Callin,"* May 1906. Vancouver City Archives, Major Mathews Collection, Private Record #: Add. MSS 358, 550-C-5, file 9.

31 *"Letters of Convict Discloses Tortures of Mind Undergone,"* Victoria Daily Colonist, 16 August 1923, 10.

32 *"Grand Jury Testimony of Joseph Callin,"* King Versus George Edwards, Lewis Colquhoun and William Dunn, Kamloops, B.C., B.C. Archives, GR0419, Box 117, File 1906/88, Attorney General files, 17, 18 May 1906.

33 *"The Hold-Up of the CPR,"* Kamloops Standard, 12 May 1906, 1.

34 *"Committed For Trial,"* Kamloops Sentinel, 22 May 1906, 1.

35 *"Witness Statement of Joseph Callin,"* May 1906. Vancouver City Archives, Major Mathews Collection, Private Record #: Add. MSS 358, 550-C-5, file 9.

36 Ibid.

37 At least five previously published authoritative works have identified William Thorburn, the mail clerk who was held up during the Mission Junction robbery, as McQuarrie's fellow mail clerk during the Ducks robbery. However, trial transcripts,

witness statements and newspaper reports of the Ducks robbery show clearly that Willis was the second clerk.

38 *"Witness Statement of William McQuarrie to Postal Inspector,"* 9 May 1906, Vancouver, B.C., B.C. Archives, File 0419, Box 117, File 1906/88, Attorney General files

39 Ibid.

40 Ibid.

41 Ibid.

42 *"Hold-Up of Imperial Limited,"* Vancouver News Advertiser, 10 May 1906, 2.

43 *"Hold-Up of Imperial Limited,"* Vancouver News Advertiser, 10 May 1906, 2.

44 *"Witness Statement of Walter Willis to Postal Inspector,"* 9 May 1906, Vancouver B.C., B.C. Archives, File 0419, Box 117, File 1906/88, Attorney General files.

45 Ibid.

46 *"Witness Statement of William McQuarrie to Postal Inspector,"* 9 May 1906, Vancouver B.C., B.C. Archives, File 0419, Box 117, File 1906/88, Attorney General files.

47 Ibid.

48 Ibid.

49 Ibid.

50 Ibid.

51 *"Train-Robbers Overlooked Over $35,000 in Hard Cash,"* Vancouver Daily Province, 9 May 1906, p1.

52 *"Grand Jury Testimony of William McQuarrie,"* *"King Versus George Edwards, The Third Man and William Dunn,"* Kamloops, B.C., 17 and 18 May 1906, B.C. Archives, GR0419, Box 117, File 1906/88, Attorney General files.

53 Cox, Doug, *"Mines of the Eagle Country: Nickel Plate and Mascot"* (Penticton, B.C.: Skookum Publications, 1971), 24.

54 *"Robbers Were After $30,000 Gold Brick,"* Vancouver Daily Province, 25 May 1906, p1.

55 *"Witness Statement of Joseph Callin,"* May 1906. Vancouver City Archives, Major Mathews Collection, Private Record #: Add. MSS 358, 550-C-5, file 9.

56 Ibid.

57 *"Hold-Up of Imperial Limited,"* Vancouver News Advertiser, 10 May 1906, 2.

58 *"Robber Laughingly Tells Train Crew to Put Hands Down,"* Victoria Daily Colonist, 30 Dec. 1923, 2.

59 Chief Constable E.T.W. Pearse, *"Incident Report,"* B.C. Archives, GR0055, Box 51, File Don-Ei, B.C. Provincial Police Corr., Oct. 05–Jan. 08 (Kamloops, B.C., May 1906), 1.

60 *"Witness Statement of Joseph Callin,"* May 1906. Vancouver City Archives, Major Mathews Collection, Private Record #: Add. MSS 358, 550-C-5, file 9.

61 Ibid.

62 Ibid.

63 Ibid.

XIII

B.C. PROVINCIAL POLICE PURSUIT

1 *"Constable Fernie Grand Jury Testimony,"* King Versus George Edwards, Colquhoun and William Dunn, B.C. Archives, GR0419, Attorney General Files, Box 117, File 1906/88 (Kamloops, B.C.: 17 to 18 May, 1906), 42, 43.

2 Chief Constable E.T.W. Pearse, *"Incident Report,"* B.C. Archives, GR0055, Box 51, File Don-Ei, B.C. Provincial Police Corr., Oct. 05 – Jan. 08 (Kamloops, B.C., May 1906), 1.

3 *"Constable Fernie Grand Jury Testimony,"* King Versus George Edwards, Colquhoun and William Dunn, B.C. Archives, GR0419, Attorney General Files, Box 117, File 1906/88 (Kamloops, B.C.: 17 to 18 May, 1906), 42, 43.

4 Chief Constable E.T.W. Pearse, *"Incident Report,"* B.C. Archives, GR0055, Box 51, File Don-Ei, B.C. Provincial Police Corr., Oct. 05–Jan. 08, (Kamloops, B.C., May 1906), 1.

5 Ibid.

6 Ibid.

7 *"Constable Fernie Grand Jury Testimony,"* King Versus George Edwards, Colquhoun and William Dunn, B.C. Archives, GR0419, Attorney General Files, Box 117, File 1906/88 (Kamloops, B.C.: 17 to 18 May, 1906), 44.

8 Ibid.

9 Chief Constable E.T.W. Pearse, *"Incident Report,"* B.C. Archives, GR0055, Box 51, File Don-Ei, B.C. Provincial Police Corr., Oct. 05 – Jan. 08 (Kamloops, B.C., May 1906), 4.

10 *"Constable Fernie Grand Jury Testimony,"* King Versus George Edwards, Colquhoun and William Dunn, B.C. Archives, GR0419, Attorney General Files, Box 117, File 1906/88 (Kamloops, B.C.: 17 to 18 May, 1906), 45

11 *"Committed For Trial,"* Kamloops Inland Sentinel, 22 May 1906.

12 *"Constable Fernie Grand Jury Testimony,"* King Versus George Edwards, Colquhoun and William Dunn, B.C. Archives, GR0419, Attorney General Files, Box 117, File 1906/88 (Kamloops, B.C.: 17 to 18 May, 1906), 45.

13 *"How Fernie Tracked Robbers Many Days,"* Vancouver Province, 17 May 1906, p. 1

[14] Chief Constable E.T.W. Pearse, *"Telegram to F.S. Hussey,"* B.C. Archives, GR0065, Box 3, File O-P., CPR Telegrams, 9 May 1906.

[15] Ibid.

[16] *"The Hold Up On CPR,"* Kamloops Standard, 12 May 1906, 1.

[17] *"The Chase, Capture and the Committal,"* Kamloops Standard, 19 May 1906.

[18] *"Constable Fernie Grand Jury Testimony,"* King Versus George Edwards, Colquhoun and William Dunn, B.C. Archives, GR0419, Attorney General Files, Box 117, File 1906/88 (Kamloops, B.C.: 17 to 18 May, 1906), 45.

[19] Ibid.

[20] George Tunstall, *"Telegram to Hussey,"* B.C. Archives, GR0065, Box 3, File T, CPR Telegrams, 10 May 1906.

[21] Chief Constable E.T.W. Pearse, *"Incident Report,"* B.C. Archives, GR0055, Box 51, File Don-Ei, B.C. Provincial Police Corr., Oct. 05 – Jan. 08 (Kamloops, B.C., May 1906), 5.

[22] Ibid.

[23] Ibid.

[24] *"Tried By Jury,"* Kamloops Inland Sentinel, 29 May 1906, 1.

[25] George Tunstall, *"Telegram to FS Hussey,"* B.C. Archives, GR0065, Box 3, File T, CPR Telegrams, 10 May 1906.

[26] Chief Constable E.T.W. Pearse, *"Incident Report,"* B.C. Archives, GR0055, Box 51, File Don-Ei, B.C. Provincial Police Corr., Oct. 05 – Jan. 08, (Kamloops, B.C., May 1906), 7.

[27] *"The Chase, Capture and Committal,"* Kamloops Standard, 19 May 1906, 1.

[28] D.O. Vicars, *"Life of Bill Miner, Train Robber. An Unfinished Narrative"* (Kamloops, B.C.: Unpublished manuscript, Kamloops Museum and Archives, 1962), 5.

[29] *"The Chase, Capture and Committal,"* Kamloops Standard, 19 May 1906, 1.

[30] Chief Constable E.T.W. Pearse, *"Incident Report,"* B.C. Archives, GR0055, Box 51, File Don-Ei, B.C. Provincial Police Corr., Oct. 05 – Jan. 08 (Kamloops, B.C., May 1906), 8.

[31] D.O. Vicars, *"Life of Bill Miner, Train Robber. An Unfinished Narrative"* (Kamloops, B.C.: Unpublished manuscript, Kamloops Museum and Archives, 1962), 5.

[32] "The Chase, Capture and Committal," Kamloops Standard, 19 May 1906, 1.

[33] *"Constable Fernie Grand Jury Testimony,"* King Versus George Edwards, Colquhoun and William Dunn, B.C. Archives, GR0419, Attorney General Files, Box 117, File 1906/88 (Kamloops, B.C.: 17 to 18 May 1906), 47.

34 Chief Constable E.T.W. Pearse, *"Incident Report,"* B.C. Archives, GR0055, Box 51, File Don-Ei, B.C. Provincial Police Corr., Oct. 05 – Jan. 08 (Kamloops, B.C., May 1906), 9.

35 *"Constable Fernie Grand Jury Testimony,"* King Versus George Edwards, Colquhoun and William Dunn, B.C. Archives, GR0419, Attorney General Files, Box 117, File 1906/88 (Kamloops, B.C.: 17 to 18 May 1906), 47.

36 Ibid.

37 *"The Chase, Capture and Committal,"* Kamloops Standard, 19 May 1906, 1.

38 Ibid.

39 *"Constable Fernie Grand Jury Testimony,"* King Versus George Edwards, Colquhoun and William Dunn, B.C. Archives, GR0419, Attorney General Files, Box 117, File 1906/88 (Kamloops, B.C.: 17 to 18 May 1906), 47.

40 Ibid.

41 Ibid.

42 Ibid, 48.

43 Ibid.

XIV

GRANDE PRAIRIE COUNTRY

1 *"Gardom In Boer War,"* Enderby Commoner, 9 Feb. 1939.

2 *"Obituary of Basil Gardom,"* Enderby Commoner, 27 Jan. 1961.

3 Robert and Joan Cowan, *"Enderby an illustrated history"* (Vernon, B.C.: Wayside Press, 2005), 123.

4 Const. Basil Gardom to Sup't. F. Hussey, *"Receipt of Smith and Wesson,"* GR0055, Box 54, File 2, Gaq-Gu, B.C. Provincial Police Corr. To Sup't. (Enderby, B.C.: 22 August 1905).

5 B.C. Provincial Police Constable Basil Gardom, *"Extracts From Constable Gardom's Notes,"* Provincial Police Corr. Inwards to Sup't., B.C. Archives, GR0055, Box 54, Files Goa-GN, Goa-Gz and Fos-Gaq, (Enderby, B.C.: 9 May 1906 to 14 May 1906) The new constable left extensive, sometimes confusing, extracts from notes he made as a result of his investigations Most of his movements and actions in the country between Glenemma and the Monte Hills are based on those notes End notes in this chapter are only used to identify sources other than Gardom's notes Some of Gardom's extracts are quite confusing and require considerable interpretation and cross-referencing from other sources.

6 Margaret F. Young, *"Quelle Grande Prairie"* (Vernon, B.C.: Wayside Press, 1994), 11.

7 Sandra Pringle, *"Westwold Tidbits,"* 16 Jan. 2006, personal e-mail (17 Jan. 2006).

8   Sandra Pringle, *"Bits and Pieces,"* 11 Jan. 2006, personal e-mail, (21 Jan. 2006).

9   *"Close To The Quarry,"* Vancouver Daily News Advertiser, 13 May 1906, 1. It is here that Constable Gardom's notes become confusing as they do not reflect what other sources say about his investigations up to this point. The Vancouver Daily News Advertiser for Sunday, 13 May 1906 stated that Constable Gardom had arrested three men in the days previous to their edition and incarcerated them in Vernon. As Gardom states in his notes, and the News Advertiser confirms, W. Wilson and James Christie were arrested and were lodged in the Vernon gaol. However, the paper adds the elusive James Mohr to Gardom's arrest list. The Vancouver journal speculated that Mohr and Wilson were arrested for suspicion of being confederates of the robbers. The News Advertiser added that Christie and a few others around the Grande Prairie area warranted strong suspicion.

10 *"Bandits near Capture South Of Kamloops,"* Vancouver Province, 12 May 1906, 1.

11 *"Christie, Arrested At Vernon …,"* The World, Vancouver, B.C.: 14 May 1906, 1.

12 Constable Gardom's notes cease at this point. A final page or pages are missing from the B.C. Archive files, and a second trip down to the Archives to initiate a search of the pertinent box of files to find the missing pages was fruitless. The end of Gardom's journey with Special Constable Percy Cotton and their prisoner Paul Stevens is determined from other contemporary sources. Actions and events can also be confidently extrapolated from known facts.

13 *"Undoubtedly Are The Men,"* Vancouver Daily News Advertiser, 16 May 1906, 1.

XV

ROYAL NORTH WEST MOUNTED POLICE

1   R.N.W.M.P. Sergeant J.T. Browning (Ret.), *"Capture of Bill Miner and His Gang,"* New Westminster Columbian, 13 June 1953.

2   Ibid.

3   R.N.W.M.P. Staff Sergeant John Jackson Wilson (Ret.), *"Capture of Bill Miner,"* Unpublished and undated manuscript, RCMP Archives, Regina, SK. Wilson wrote a 13 page memoir after his retirement giving his description of the capture of Bill Miner. It is a refreshing departure from the normal bureaucratic reporting of official police reports and the transcripts of Grand Jury trials. Wilson gives a colourful description of the trials and tribulations of the detail as it made its way to Douglas Lake and the gunfight beside the Nicola River. It should be understood that most of this chapter's material is taken from Wilson's unpublished memoir, and only other sources will be end noted.

4   R.N.W.M.P. Inspector A.W. Duffus and Acting Sergeant J.J. Wilson, *"Hold Up of CPR Train No. 97 Near Kamloops,"* R.N.W.M.P "E" Division Crime Report,

5   Vancouver Archives, Major J.S. Mathews Coll., Private Record #: Add. MSS 358. 550-C-5, File 9 (Part of H.A. Price Coll.), (Calgary, AB, 21 May and 13 June 1906).

5   Ibid.

6   R.N.W.M.P. Sergeant J.T. Browning (Ret.), *"Capture of Bill Miner and His Gang,"* New Westminster Columbian, 13 June 1953.

7   R.N.W.M.P. Commissioner Bowen-Perry, *"Telegram to Hussey,"* B.C. Archives, GR0065, Box 3, File N, CPR Telegrams, 11 May 1906.

8   R.N.W.M.P. Staff Sergeant John Jackson Wilson (Ret.), *"Capture of Bill Miner,"* Unpublished and undated manuscript, RCMP Archives, Regina, SK.

9   C.G. Stephens, *"$20,000 Reward,"* Peachland-Okanagan Review, March 1971, 4.

10 R.N.W.M.P. Staff Sergeant John Jackson Wilson (Ret.), *"Capture of Bill Miner,"* Unpublished and undated manuscript, RCMP Archives, Regina, SK

11 Roger F. Phillips and Donald J. Klancher, *"Arms and Accoutrements of the Mounted Police. 1873 – 1973"* (Bloomfield, ON: Museum Restoration Service, 1982), 39–47.

12 R.N.W.M.P. Sergeant J.T. Browning (Ret.), "Capture of Bill Miner and His Gang," New Westminster Columbian, 13 June 1953.

13 R.N.W.M.P. Staff Sergeant John Jackson Wilson (Ret.), "Capture of Bill Miner," Unpublished and undated manuscript, RCMP Archives, Regina, SK.

14 R.N.W.M.P. Inspector A.W. Duffus and Acting Sergeant J.J. Wilson, *"Hold Up of CPR Train No. 97 Near Kamloops,"* R.N.W.M.P. "E" Division Crime Report, Vancouver Archives, Major J.S. Mathews Coll., Private Record #: Add. MSS 358. 550-C-5, File 9 (Part of H.A. Price Coll.), (Calgary, AB, 21 May and 13 June 1906).

15 R.N.W.M.P. Staff Sergeant John Jackson Wilson (Ret.), *"Capture of Bill Miner,"* Unpublished and undated manuscript, RCMP Archives, Regina, SK.

16 Ibid.

17 *"The Chase, Capture and Committal,"* Kamloops Standard, 19 May 1906, 1.

18 *"Grand Jury Testimony of Stewart,"* King Versus George Edwards, Colquhoun and William Dunn, 17 to 18 May, 1906. B.C. Arch, GR0419, Box 117, File 1906/88, 22.

19 R.N.W.M.P. Staff Sergeant John Jackson Wilson (Ret.), *"Capture of Bill Miner,"* Unpublished and undated manuscript, RCMP Archives, Regina, SK.

20 *"Grand Jury Testimony of Shoebotham,"* King Versus George Edwards, Colquhoun and William Dunn, 17 to 18 May, 1906. B.C. Arch, GR0419, Box 117, File 1906/88, 22.

21 *"Grand Jury Testimony of Shoebotham, Stewart, Wilson, Peters and Browning,"* King Versus George Edwards, Colquhoun and William Dunn, 17 to 18 May, 1906. B.C. Arch, GR0419, Box 117, File 1906/88, 4–42.

22 R.N.W.M.P. Staff Sergeant John Jackson Wilson (Ret.), *"Capture of Bill Miner,"* Unpublished and undated manuscript, RCMP Archives, Regina, SK.

23 *"Grand Jury Testimony of Shoebotham, Stewart, Wilson, Peters and Browning,"* King Versus George Edwards, Colquhoun and William Dunn, 17 to 18 May, 1906. B.C. Arch, GR0419, Box 117, File 1906/88, 4–42.

24 R.N.W.M.P. Staff Sergeant John Jackson Wilson (Ret.), *"Capture of Bill Miner,"* Unpublished and undated manuscript, RCMP Archives, Regina, SK.

25 R.N.W.M.P. Sergeant J.T. Browning (Ret.), *"Capture of Bill Miner and His Gang,"* New Westminster Columbian, 13 June 1953.

26 R.N.W.M.P. Staff Sergeant John Jackson Wilson (Ret.), *"Capture of Bill Miner,"* Unpublished and undated manuscript, RCMP Archives, Regina, SK.

27 R.N.W.M.P. Inspector A.W. Duffus and Acting Sergeant J.J. Wilson, *"Hold Up of CPR Train No. 97 Near Kamloops,"* R.N.W.M.P "E" Division Crime Report, Vancouver Archives, Major J.S. Mathews Coll., Private Record #: Add. MSS 358. 550-C-5, File 9 (Part of H.A. Price Coll.), (Calgary, AB, 21 May and 13 June 1906).

28 R.N.W.M.P. Staff Sergeant John Jackson Wilson (Ret.), *"Capture of Bill Miner,"* Unpublished and undated manuscript, RCMP Archives, Regina, SK.

29 Ibid.

30 R.N.W.M.P. Sergeant J.T. Browning (Ret.), *"Capture of Bill Miner and His Gang,"* New Westminster Columbian, 13 June 1953. Attempts to obtain a copy of the text of this particular magazine article have been fruitless. The Guthren Browning is referring to does not appear in any other sources on Miner, including Boessenecker and Dugan's "The Grey Fox".

31 R.N.W.M.P Staff Sergeant John Jackson Wilson (Ret.), *"Capture of Bill Miner,"* Unpublished and undated manuscript, RCMP Archives, Regina, SK.

32 R.N.W.M.P. Inspector A.W. Duffus and Acting Sergeant J.J. Wilson, "Hold Up of CPR Train No. 97 Near Kamloops," R.N.W.M.P "E" Division Crime Report, Vancouver Archives, Major J.S. Mathews Coll., Private Record #: Add. MSS 358. 550-C-5, File 9 (Part of H.A. Price Coll.), (Calgary, AB, 21 May and 13 June 1906).

33 *"Train Robbers Caught,"* Kamloops Inland Sentinel, 15 May 1906.

34 R.N.W.M.P. Staff Sergeant John Jackson Wilson (Ret.), "Capture of Bill Miner," Unpublished and undated manuscript, RCMP Archives, Regina, SK.

35 R.N.W.M.P. Sergeant J.T. Browning (Ret.), *"Capture of Bill Miner and His Gang,"* New Westminster Columbian, 13 June 1953.

36 *"Grand Jury Testimony of Shoebotham, Stewart, Wilson, Peters and Browning,"* King Versus George Edwards, Colquhoun and William Dunn, 17 to 18 May, 1906. B.C. Arch, GR0419, Box 117, File 1906/88, 4–42.

37 R.N.W.M.P. Staff Sergeant John Jackson Wilson (Ret.), "Capture of Bill Miner," Unpublished and undated manuscript, RCMP Archives, Regina, SK.

38 "Train Robbers Sentenced," Kamloops Standard, 2 June 1906, 1.

39 R.N.W.M.P. Staff Sergeant John Jackson Wilson (Ret.), *"Capture of Bill Miner,"* Unpublished and undated manuscript, RCMP Archives, Regina, SK.

40 R.N.W.M.P. Sergeant J.T. Browning (Ret.), *"Capture of Bill Miner and His Gang,"* New Westminster Columbian, 13 June 1953.

41 *"Grand Jury Testimony of Shoebotham, Stewart, Wilson, Peters and Browning,"* King Versus George Edwards, Colquhoun and William Dunn, 17 to 18 May, 1906. B.C. Arch, GR0419, Box 117, File 1906/88, 4–42.

42 R.N.W.M.P. Sergeant J.T. Browning (Ret.), *"Capture of Bill Miner and His Gang,"* New Westminster Columbian, 13 June 1953.

43 R.N.W.M.P. Inspector A.W. Duffus and Acting Sergeant J.J. Wilson, *"Hold Up of CPR Train No. 97 Near Kamloops,"* R.N.W.M.P "E" Division Crime Report, Vancouver Archives, Major J.S. Mathews Coll., Private Record #: Add. MSS 358. 550-C-5, File 9 (Part of H.A. Price Coll.), (Calgary, AB, 21 May and 13 June 1906).

44 R.N.W.M.P. Staff Sergeant John Jackson Wilson (Ret.), *"Capture of Bill Miner,"* Unpublished and undated manuscript, RCMP Archives, Regina, SK.

45 *"Grand Jury Testimony of Shoebotham, Stewart, Wilson, Peters and Browning,"* King Versus George Edwards, Colquhoun and William Dunn, 17 to 18 May, 1906. B.C. Arch, GR0419, Box 117, File 1906/88, 4–42.

46 Nicola Herald, 17 May 1906.

47 *"Train-Robbers Leader Was Old Bill Miner,"* Vancouver Daily Province, 15 May 1906, 1.

48 R.N.W.M.P. Staff Sergeant John Jackson Wilson (Ret.), *"Capture of Bill Miner,"* Unpublished and undated manuscript, RCMP Archives, Regina, SK.

49 *"Grand Jury Testimony of Shoebotham, Stewart, Wilson, Peters and Browning,"* King Versus George Edwards, Colquhoun and William Dunn, 17 to 18 May, 1906. B.C. Arch, GR0419, Box 117, File 1906/88, 4–42.

50 Ibid.

51 This original hotel was replaced by the one now in existence, which was built in 1907 and 1908 and opened on 3 July 1908.

52 D.O. Vicars, *"Life of Bill Miner, Train Robber. An Unfinished Narrative"* (Kamloops, B.C.: Unpublished manuscript, Kamloops Museum and Archives, 1962.)

53 *"Grand Jury Testimony of Shoebotham, Stewart, Wilson, Peters and Browning,"* King Versus George Edwards, Colquhoun and William Dunn, 17 to 18 May, 1906. B.C. Arch, GR0419, Box 117, File 1906/88, 4–42.

54 R.N.W.M.P. Sergeant J.T. Browning (Ret.), *"Capture of Bill Miner and His Gang,"* New Westminster Columbian, 13 June 1953.

55 Nicola Herald, 17 May 1906.

56 D.O. Vicars, *"Life of Bill Miner, Train Robber. An Unfinished Narrative,"* (Kamloops, B.C.: Unpublished manuscript, Kamloops Museum and Archives, 1962.)

57 R.N.W.M.P. Sergeant J.T. Browning (Ret.), *"Capture of Bill Miner and His Gang,"* New Westminster Columbian, 13 June 1953.

58 R.N.W.M.P. Staff Sergeant John Jackson Wilson (Ret.), *"Capture of Bill Miner,"* Unpublished and undated manuscript, RCMP Archives, Regina, SK.

59 *"Bandits Are Captured,"* Kamloops Standard, 15 May 1906, 1.

60 Ibid.

61 *"Undoubtedly Are The Men,"* Vancouver World," 16 May 1906, 1.

62 *"Grand Jury Testimony,"* The King vs Edwards, Dunn and Colquhoun, B.C. Archives, GR0419, Box 117, File 1906/88, Attorney General Crown Prosecutor Files, 17–18 May 1906, 1–86.

63 *"Is Certain Of His Identification of Bill Miner,"* Vancouver Province, 21 May 1906, 1.

64 R.N.W.M.P. Staff Sergeant John Jackson Wilson (Ret.), *"Capture of Bill Miner,"* Unpublished and undated manuscript, RCMP Archives, Regina, SK.

XVI
AFTER THE DUCKS ROBBERY

1 *"Train Robbers Overlooked $35,000 In Hard Cash,"* Vancouver Daily Province, 9 May 1906, 1.

2 Ibid.

3 Ibid.

4 *"How Fernie Tracked Robbers Many Days,"* Vancouver Province, 17 May 1906, 1.

5 *"Chinamen Will Go On Strike,"* Vancouver Daily Province, 12 May 1906, 1.

6 *"Train Held Up,"* Kamloops Inland Sentinel, 11 May 1906, 1.

7 Provincial Police Chief Constable E.T.W. Pearse, *"CPR Telegram to F.S. Hussey,"* B.C. Archives, GR2479, Box 1, File 5, Telegrams, (Kamloops, B.C.: 9 May 1906).

8 *"Find Deserted Camp Of The Robbers,"* Vancouver Province, 10 May 1906, 1.

9 *"Bandits Near Capture South Of Kamloops,"* Vancouver Province, 12 May 1906, 1.

10 *"Blood-Hounds In Hot Chase Of Bandits,"* Vancouver Province, 14 May 1906, 1.

11 *"Vernon Arrests Are Discounted,"* Vancouver Province, 14 May 1906, 1.

12 *"City and Country,"* Kamloops Inland Sentinel, 8 May 1904, 4.

13 William Dodds, *"Statement to W.S. Seavey,"* B.C. Archives, GR0419, Box 117, File 1906/88, Attorney General Crown Prosecutor Files, 16 May 1906, 36.

14 Constable Ronald Hewat, *"Tom Arnold,"* Letter to Sup't. F.S. Hussey, B.C. Archives, GR0055, Box 45, File 6, Provincial Police Corr. In, Princeton, B.C., 11 July 1906.

15 Constable Ronald Hewat, *"Description of Thomas Arnold,"* B.C. Archives, GR0055, Box 56, Files 7 & 8, Provincial Police Corr. In, Princeton, B.C., 24 Aug 1906.

16 Constable Hugh Hunter, *"Investigations in Princeton,"* Report to F.S. Hussey, B.C. Archives, Box 51, File Don-El, Provincial Police Corr. In, Princeton, B.C., 23 May 1906, 1–3.

17 *"The Hold Up On CPR,"* Kamloops Standard, 12 May 1906, 1.

18 *"Methodist Conference Honours Victoria,"* Victoria Colonist, 12 May 1906, 8.

19 *"Serious Charges Against Clergy,"* Vancouver World, 12 May 1906, 1.

20 *"Rev. Mr. Baer's Case,"* Vancouver Province, 17 May 1906, 1.

21 *"The Hold Up On CPR,"* Kamloops Standard, 9 May 1906, 1.

22 *"Bandits Near Capture South Of Kamloops,"* Vancouver Province, 12 May 1906, 1.

23 R.N.W.M.P. Inspector A.W. Duffus and Acting Sergeant J.J. Wilson, *"Hold Up of CPR Train No. 97 Near Kamloops,"* R.N.W.M.P. "E" Division Crime Report, Vancouver Archives, Major J.S. Mathews Coll., Private Record #: Add. MSS 358. 550-C-5, File 9 (Part of H.A. Price Coll.), (Calgary, AB, 21 May and 13 June 1906).

24 Sgt. K.G. Murison, Reg. No. 4385 (Ret.), *"Kamloops Train Robbery Recalled,"* RCMP Quarterly, October 1948, Vol. 14, No. 2, 89.

25 *"Prison Statements of Edwards, Dunn and Colquhoun,"* B.C. Archives, Victoria, B.C.GR-0099. Superintendent of Provincial Police correspondence inward, 1891–1910 (Kamloops, B.C.: 16 May 1906).

26 D.O. Vicars, *"Life of Bill Miner, Train Robber. An Unfinished Narrative"* (Kamloops, B.C.: Unpublished manuscript, Kamloops Museum and Archives, 1962), 8.

27 *"The Chase, Capture and the Committal,"* Kamloops Standard, 19 May 1906, 1.

28 Ibid.

29 Ibid.

30 *"How Fernie Tracked Robbers Many Days,"* Vancouver Province, 17 May 1906, 1.

31 D.O. Vicars, *"Life of Bill Miner, Train Robber. An Unfinished Narrative"* (Kamloops, B.C.: Unpublished manuscript, Kamloops Museum and Archives, 1962), 8.

32 Harold H. Forsell, *"Law Enforcement In Pioneer Days,"* Unpublished manuscript (Kamloops, B.C.: Date unknown), 84.

33 *"Dancing Girl Tattoo Identifies Miner,"* Vancouver Province, 16 May 1906, 1.

34 Ibid.

35 Provincial Police Superintendent F.S. Hussey, *"CPR telegram to Deputy Attorney General McLean,"* B.C. Archives, GR0429, Box 13, File 3, Attorney General Corr., Kamloops, B.C., 14 May 1906.

36 *"Train Robbery Case,"* Reprinted from the Vancouver World, Kamloops Standard, 18 May 1906.

37 *"Curious Crowd Greets Prisoners,"* Vancouver Province, 16 May 1906, 1.

38 John Stewart, *"The Todds and Pratts of Barnhartvale,"* Kamloops Museum and Archives Article, (Kamloops, 15 Sept. 1987). The Robert Pratt house referred to here still stands along the south side of the Barnhartvale Road east of Kamloops.

39 Thiel Agent, Operative #39, *"Investigation re Train Robbery,"* Special Service Report, B.C. Archives, GR0419, Box 117, File 1906/88, Attorney General Crown Prosecutor Files, Kamloops, B.C., 14 May 1906. 39–40.

40 John Stewart, *"The Todds and Pratts of Barnhartvale,"* Kamloops Museum and Archives Article, (Kamloops, 15 Sept. 1987).

41 Thiel Agent, Operative #39, *"Investigation re Train Robbery,"* Special Service Report, B.C. Archives, GR0419, Box 117, File 1906/88, Attorney General Crown Prosecutor Files, Kamloops, B.C., 14 May 1906. 39–40.

42 Ibid, 40–41.

43 Ibid, 33–38.

44 Ibid.

45 Thiel Detective W.S. Seavey, *"Letter and Witness Statements to CPR's W.L. McLaws,"* B.C. Archives, GR0419, Box 117, File 1906/88, Attorney General Crown Prosecutor Files, Kamloops, B.C., 14 May 1906. 33–38.

46 Ibid.

47 Joseph Callin, *"Grand Jury Testimony,"* The King vs. Edwards, Dunn and Colquhoun, B.C. Archives, GR0419, Box 117, File 1906/88, Attorney General Crown Prosecutor Files, 17–18 May 1906, 54–67.

48 *"Undoubtedly Are The Men,"* Vancouver News Advertiser, 16 May 1906, 1.

49 *"Witness Statements of Callin and Radcliffe,"* Vancouver Archives, Major J.S. Mathews Collection, Private Record #: Add. Mss. 358. 550-C-5, File 9 (Part of H.A. Price Collection), Kamloops, B.C., After 15 May 1906.

50 *"Is Certain Of Identification Of Bill Miner,"* Vancouver Province, 21 May 1906, 1.

51 *"Marpole Suggests …,"* Vancouver World, 16 May 1906, 1.

52 *"Mr. Marpole's Suggestion,"* Vancouver Daily News Advertiser, 17 May 1906, 2.

53 *"The Trial At Kamloops,"* Vancouver Daily News Advertiser, 18 May 1906, 1.

54 Neil McFadden, Letter to Sup't. F.S. Hussey, B.C. Archives, GR0055, Box 51, File Don-El, Provincial Police Corr. In, Princeton, B.C., 16 May 1906.

55 *"Committed For Trial,"* Kamloops Inland Sentinel, 22 May 1906, 1.

1 *"Mounted Police Are Required Here,"* Vancouver Province, 16 May 1906, 1.

2 Lady Aberdeen, *"The Journal of Lady Aberdeen,"* Annotated and Edited by R.M. Middleton (Victoria, B.C.: Morriss Publishing, 1986), 69.

3 *"Mounted Police Are Required Here,"* Vancouver Province, 16 May 1906, 1.

4 *"Editorial Notes,"* Kamloops Standard, 19 May 1906.

5 *"The Lesson Of The Holdup,"* Editorial, Victoria Colonist, 19 May 1906, 4.

6 Ibid.

7 Ruth Balf, *"Kamloops."* (Kamloops, B.C.: Peerless Printers, 1975), 53.

8 *"First Pictures Of Trainrobbers,"* Vancouver Province, 17 May 1906.

9 *"Train Robbery Case,"* Kamloops Sentinel, 18 May 1906, 1.

10 *"The Trial At Kamloops,"* Vancouver Daily News Advertiser, 18 May 1906, 1.

11 *"Grand Jury Testimony,"* The King vs. Edwards, Dunn and Colquhoun, B.C. Archives, GR0419, Box 117, File 1906/88, Attorney General Crown Prosecutor Files, 17–18 May 1906, 1–86. This chapter on the Grand Jury hearing is based on the original transcript of the proceedings. Newspaper reporting is used to gather background information relevant to the proceedings and to place the proceedings in the context of the events as they unfolded.

12 *"Train Robbery Case,"* Kamloops Sentinel, 18 May 1904, 1. The original content of this section of the Grand Jury transcript has been cut off by the Court Stenographer, and the content has been determined from the reporting of the Kamloops Standard for this section.

13 Grand Jury Transcript, 14.

14 *"Train Robbery Case,"* Kamloops Sentinel, 18 May 1904, 1.

15 *"If You Draw It ...,"* Vancouver World, 18 May 1906, 1.

16 Grand Jury Transcript, 53.

17 Ibid.

18 *"Train Robbery Case,"* Kamloops Sentinel, 18 May 1904, 2.

19 Grand Jury Transcript, 54–67.

20 Ibid, 67–75

21 Kamloops Sentinel, 22 May 1906, 2.

22 Grand Jury Transcript, 75–81.

23 Ibid, 81–83.

24 *"Train Robbers Sent Up For Trial At Kamloops,"* Vancouver World, 19 May 1906, 1.

25 Grand Jury Transcript, 86.

26   *"Committed For Trial,"* Kamloops Inland Sentinel, 22 May 1906, 1.

27   *"Bill of Indictment against William J. Dunn,"* B.C. Archives, GR0419, Box 117, File 1906/88, Attorney General Crown Prosecutor Files, 17–18 May 1906.

28   J.J. Carment, City Clerk, City of Kamloops Council Meeting Minutes, 17 May 1906, 1–2.

29   J. Fraser, *"Telegram to Hussey,"* B.C. Archives, GR0055, Box 51, File Don-El, B.C. Provincial Police Corr. In, 17 May 1906.

30   Kamloops Standard, 12 May 1906.

31   R.N.W.M.P. Staff Sergeant John Jackson Wilson (Ret.), *"Capture of Bill Miner,"* Unpublished and undated manuscript, R.C.M.P. Archives, Regina, SK.

XVIII
THE INVESTIGATION

1   *"The Chase, Capture and the Committal,"* Kamloops Standard, 19 May 1906, 1.

2   Winnipeg Daily Telegram, *"Request for Photos,"* B.C. Archives, GR2479, Box 1, File 5, Telegrams (Winnipeg, MN: 16 May 1906).

3   Provincial Police Constable Hugh Hunter, *"Report to Sup't. Hussey on Edwards, Dunn and Colquhoun,"* GR0055, Box 51, File Don-El, Provincial Police Corr. In, Princeton, B.C., 23 May 1906, 1–3.

4   Provincial Police Sergeant T.R. Murray, *"Wire to Sup't. Hussey,"* GR0055, Box 51, File Don-El, Provincial Police Corr. In, Victoria, B.C., 19 May 1906.

5   Provincial Police Chief Constable E.C. Simmons, *"Witness Statement of Margaret Stevens,"* GR0055, Box 51, File Don-El, Provincial Police Corr. In, Kamloops, B.C., 20 May 1906.

6   Ibid.

7   Unknown Private Detectives, *"Interviews With Ducks and Grande Prairie Residents,"* B.C. Archives, GR0419, Box 117, File 1906/88, Attorney General Crown Prosecutor Files (Kamloops, B.C., 19 May 1906), 1–2.

8   CPR Detective R.E. Bullick, *"McLeod, Tilton & McKay Interviews,"* B.C. Archives, GR0419, Box 117, File 1906/88, Attorney General Crown Prosecutor Files (Kamloops, B.C., 18 May 1906), 1–4.

9   C.P.R. Special Service Detective William McLeod, *"Investigative Report re Ducks, Dupuis, Barnes, Buses et al,"* Vancouver Archives, Major J.S. Mathews Collection, Private Record #: Add. Mss. 358. 550-C-5, File 9 (Part of H.A. Price Collection), Kamloops, B.C., 18–29 May 1906, 1–6.

10   Ibid.

11 Thiel Detective L. Calhoun, *"Robber Camp Investigations,"* B.C. Archives, GR0419, Box 117, File 1906/88, Attorney General Crown Prosecutor Files (Kamloops, B.C., 19 May 1906), 1–2.

12 C.P.R. Special Service Detective R.E. Bullick, *"Investigative Report re Kamloops Merchants,"* Vancouver Archives, Major J.S. Mathews Collection, Private Record #: Add. Mss. 358. 550-C-5, File 9 (Part of H.A. Price Collection), Kamloops, B.C., 22 May 1906.

13 C.P.R. Special Service Detective W.A. McFoy, *"Investigative Report re Buse, Taite, Hickson,"* Vancouver Archives, Major J.S. Mathews Collection, Private Record #: Add. Mss. 358. 550-C-5, File 9 (Part of H.A. Price Collection), Kamloops, B.C., 23 May 1906.

14 CPR Detective C. Gouch, *"Adams and Hazelhurst Interview,"* B.C. Archives, GR0419, Box 117, File 1906/88, Attorney General Crown Prosecutor Files (Kamloops, B.C., 19 May 1906), 1.

15 Thiel Detective Agency Manager W.S. Seavey, *"Report to Sup't. Marpole on Chilliwack Investigations,"* Vancouver Archives, Major J.S. Mathews Collection, Private Record #: Add. Mss. 358. 550-C-5, File 9 (Part of H.A. Price Collection), Seattle, WA, 28 May 1906, 1–6.

16 *"Train Robbers Sent Up For Trial At Kamloops,"* Vancouver World, 19 May 1906, 1.

17 Pinkerton Superintendent P.K. Ahern, *"Request for Information to F.S. Hussey,"* B.C. Archives, GR0055, Box 67, Files 5 & 6, Provincial Police Corr. In (Seattle, WA: 26 May 1906).

18 Ibid.

19 Post Office Inspector John R. Greenfield, *"Stolen Mail Correspondence,"* B.C. Archives, GR0419, Box 117, 1906/88, Attorney General Crown Prosecutor Files (Vancouver, B.C.: 10, 16, 17 & 21 May 1906).

20 Post Office Inspector John R. Greenfield, *"Letter re Money to Lieut. Col. J.C. Whyte, Warden,"* George Edwards Correspondence File, Anthony Martin B.C. Penitentiary Collection (Vancouver, B.C.: 9 July 1906), 1–2.

21 *"Trial Exhibits,"* B.C. Archives, GR0419, Box 117, File 1906/88, Attorney General Crown Prosecutor Files (Kamloops, B.C.: 18 May 1906).

22 Federal Minister of Justice, *"Satisfaction,"* B.C. Archives, GR0429, Box 13, File 3, Attorney General Corr. (Ottawa, ON: 22 May 1906).

23 CPR Special Service Detective W. McLeod, *"List of Potential Jurors and Comments,"* GR0055, Box 51, File Don-El, Provincial Police Corr. In (Kamloops, B.C.: May 1906). This two page unsigned document is handwritten on the stationery of the Grande Pacific Hotel, P.A. Barnhart Prop. It is known that Deputy Attorney General McLean stayed there during the time he was in Kamloops. William McLeod is the only investigator in any of the sources noted as assisting McLean to put the jury list together, and it is assumed that he was the originator of the document.

24 Deputy Attorney General H.A. McLean, *"Letter to Defence Attorney Mcintyre re Witnesses,"* B.C. Archives, GR0419, Box 117, File 1906/88, Attorney General Crown Prosecutor Files (Kamloops, B.C.:17–18 May 1906).

25 Doris (Duck) Crossley and Brenda Thompson, The Story of the Duck Family, 1881 to 1932, Unpublished manuscript, March 1986.

26 Provincial Police Superintendent F.S. Hussey, *"Subpoena Ducks,"* B.C. Archives, GR0065, Box 3, File H, CPR Telegrams (Kamloops, B.C.: 26 May 1906).

27 Chief Constable E.T.W. Pearse, *"Compensation to Mr. and Mrs. Duck,"* B.C. Archives, GR0055, Box 67, Files 5&6, Provincial Police Corr. In (Kamloops, B.C.: 9 June 1906).

28 Maisie A.C. Armytage-Moore, *"A New Side Of Bill Miner's Character,"* Vancouver Archives, Major J.S. Mathews Collection, Private Record #: Add. Mss. 358. 550-C-5, File 9, Part of H.A. Price Collection (Vancouver, B.C.: 8 July 1943), 1–4.

XIX

THE TRIAL

1 *"Warden Kelly of San Quentin …,"* Vancouver Province, 28 May 1906, 1.

2 *"Grand Jury's Presentment,"* Kamloops Standard, 2 June 1906.

3 Honourable David R. Verchere, *"A Progression of Judges, A History of the Supreme Court in British Columbia"* (Vancouver, B.C.: University of British Columbia Press, 1988), 99–100.

4 Victoria Colonist, 23 July 1903.

5 *"Miner's Party Near Kamloops Many Days,"* Vancouver Province, 29 May 1906, 1.

6 *"Warden Kelly Of San Quentin Positively Identifies Bill Miner,"* Vancouver Province, 28 May 1906, 1.

7 *"Train Robbers On Trial At Kamloops,"* Victoria Colonist," 30 May 1906, 3.

8 *"Tried By Jury,"* Kamloops Sentinel, 20 May 1906, 1. No transcript of this trial presently exists, although that of the Grand Jury proceedings are found archived in two locations, Vancouver and Victoria. Consequently most of the trial proceedings are excerpted from newspaper accounts of the day, primarily the Kamloops Inland Sentinel for 29 and 30 May and 1 June 1906. It is supplemented by the Kamloops Standard, the Vancouver Province, World and Daily News Advertiser and the Victoria Colonist. Archival sources are limited to the work file of the Deputy Attorney General in the B.C. Archives.

9 Hedley Gazette, B.C. Archives, Reel 3004, 1905 to 1908, 7 June 1906, 1.

10 *"The Jury On Robber Trial Disagree,"* Nicola Herald, 31 May 1906, 1.

11 *"Miner's Party Near Kamloops Many Days,"* Vancouver Province, 29 May 1906, 1.

[12] *"Trial Of Train Robbers Nears Its End,"* Vancouver World, 30 May 1906, 1.

[13] *"Train Robbers Sentenced,"* Kamloops Standard, 2 June 1906, 1.

[14] Ibid.

[15] *"Warden Kelly Of San Quentin Positively Identifies Bill Miner,"* Vancouver Province, 28 May 1906, 1.

[16] *"Accuse Miner Of Mission Hold-Up,"* Vancouver Province, 29 May 1906, 1.

[17] This map still exists in the B.C. Archives in Victoria. Drawn by a professional draftsman, it portrays the site of the robbery in some detail, as well as the three spots where the robbers commanded the engineer to stop the train. It is a linen-backed drawing done in India ink.

[18] *"Accuse Miner Of Mission Hold-Up,"* Vancouver Province, 29 May 1906, 1.

[19] *"Break Heat Record At Kamloops Assize,"* Vancouver Province, 30 May 1906, 1.

[20] *"Tried By Jury,"* Kamloops Sentinel, 30 May 1906, 1.

[21] *"Break Heat Record At Kamloops Assize,"* Vancouver Province, 30 May 1906, 1.

[22] R.N.W.M.P. Sergeant J.J. Wilson (Ret.), *"Capture of Bill Miner,"* Unpublished and undated manuscript, RCMP Archives (Edmonton, AB, Date Unknown), 1–13.

[23] *"Accuse Miner Of Mission Hold-Up,"* Vancouver Province, 29 May 1906, 1.

[24] *"Last Day Of C.P.R. Hold-Up Trial,"* Victoria Colonist, 31 May 1906, 1.

[25] *"Found Guilty,"* Kamloops Inland Sentinel, 1 June 1906, 1.

[26] George Edwards, *"Affidavit of Prejudice,"* Rex vs. Edwards, Dunn and Colquhoun, B.C. Archives, GR0419, Box 117, File 1906/88, Attorney General Crown Prosecutor Files (Kamloops: 30 May 1906), 1–2.

[27] There is some evidence to suggest that the individual who visited Colquhoun in the Kamloops Gaol was named McNeil.

[28] *"Found Guilty, "Kamloops Inland Sentinel,"* 1 June 1906, 1.

[29] *"Last Day Of C.P.R. Hold-Up Trial,"* Victoria Colonist, 31 May 1906, 1.

[30] Ibid.

[31] R.N.W.M.P. Sergeant J.J. Wilson (Ret.), *"Capture of Bill Miner,"* Unpublished and undated manuscript, RCMP Archives (Edmonton, AB, Date Unknown), 1–13.

[32] *"Last Day Of C.P.R. Hold-Up Trial,"* Victoria Colonist, 31 May 1906, 1.

[33] Ibid.

[34] R.N.W.M.P. Sergeant J.J. Wilson (Ret.), *"Capture of Bill Miner,"* Unpublished and undated manuscript, RCMP Archives, (Edmonton, AB, Date Unknown), 1–13.

[35] *"Jury Disagrees In The Train Robbery Case,"* Vancouver World," 31 May 1906, 1.

[36] *"Found Guilty,"* Kamloops Inland Sentinel, 1 June 1906, 1.

[37] "New Trial Starts In Train-Robbing Case," Vancouver Province, 31 May 1906, 1.

38 Deputy Attorney General H.A. McLean, *"Affidavit against Re-Arraignment,"* Rex vs. George Edwards, William Dunn and Lewis Colquhoun, B.C. Archives, GR0419, Box 117, File 1906/88, Attorney General Crown Prosecutor Files (Kamloops: June 1906), 1–2.

39 Transcript of Second Trial, *"Change of Venue,"* Rex vs. Edwards, Dunn and Colquhoun, B.C. Archives, GR0419, Box 117, File 1906/88, Attorney General Crown Prosecutor Files (Kamloops: 31 May 1906), 1–9.

40 Ibid.

41 *"Dunn Breaks Down In Kamloops Court,"* Vancouver Province, 2 June 1906, 1.

42 *"Second Trial At Kamloops,"* Vancouver Daily News Advertiser, 1 June 1906, 1.

43 *"Train Robbers Sentenced,"* Kamloops Standard, 2 June 1906, 2.

44 Hedley Gazette, B.C. Archives, Reel 3004, 1905 to 1908, 7 June 1906, 1.

45 *"Train Robbers Sentenced,"* Kamloops Standard, 2 June 1906, 2.

46 Ibid.

47 Ibid.

48 Ibid.

49 Ibid.

50 Ibid.

51 Provincial Police Superintendent F.S. Hussey, *"CPR Telegram to Sergeant T.R. Murray,"* B.C. Archives, GR0065, Box 3, File H, CPR Telegrams (Kamloops, B.C.: 1 June 1906).

52 *"Editorial Notes,"* Kamloops Standard, 2 June 1906, 2.

53 "Ibid.

54 Editorial, *"The Train Robbers,"* Victoria Colonist, 3 June 1906, 4.

XX

THE JOURNEY TO NEW WESTMINSTER

1 J.S. Burris, *"Prisoner Health Certifications,"* George Edwards Correspondence File, Anthony Martin B.C. Penitentiary Collection (Kamloops, B.C.: 1 June 1906).

2 *"Train Robbers Arrive To Serve Long Terms,"* New Westminster Daily Columbian, 4 June 1906, 1.

3 Harold H. Forsell, *"Law Enforcement In Pioneer Days,"* Unpublished manuscript (Kamloops, B.C.: Date unknown), 84.

4 *"Train Robbers Arrive To Serve Long Terms,"* New Westminster Daily Columbian, 4 June 1906, 1.

5   *"Landed In Penitentiary,"* Kamloops Standard, 9 June 1906, 1.

6   *"Bill Miner, the Notorious Train Robber,"* Victoria Colonist, 30 December 1923, 12.

7   *"Landed In Penitentiary,"* Kamloops Standard, 9 June 1906, 1.

8   Ibid.

9   Ibid.

10 *"'Even The Dogs Know Me,' Says Miner,"* Vancouver Province, 4 June 1906, 1.

11 *"Landed In Penitentiary,"* Kamloops Standard, 9 June 1906, 1.

12 *"Train Robbers Arrive To Serve Long Terms,"* New Westminster Daily Columbian, 4 June 1906, 1.

13 R.N.W.M.P. Sergeant J.J. Wilson (Ret.), *"Capture of Bill Miner,"* Unpublished and undated manuscript, RCMP Archives, Regina, SK, (Edmonton, AB, bfr 1933), 1–13.

14 *"Train Robbers Arrive To Serve Long Terms,"* New Westminster Daily Columbian, 4 June 1906, 1.

15 Ibid.

16 Ibid.

17 Ibid.

18 *"Landed In Penitentiary,"* Kamloops Standard, 9 June 1906, 1.

19 *"Train Robbers Arrive To Serve Long Terms,"* New Westminster Daily Columbian, 4 June 1906, 1.

20 *"Landed In Penitentiary,"* Kamloops Standard, 9 June 1906, 1.

21 *"Behind The Bars,"* Vancouver News Advertiser, 3 June 1906, 1

22 Ibid.

23 Ibid.

24 *"'Even The Dogs Know Me,' Says Miner,"* Vancouver Province, 4 June 1906, 1.

25 R.N.W.M.P. Sergeant J.J. Wilson (Ret.), "Capture of Bill Miner," Unpublished and undated manuscript, RCMP Archives (Edmonton, AB, bfr 1933), 1–13.

26 Ibid.

XXI
SERVING THEIR SENTENCE

1   Jack David Scott, *"Four Walls In The West,"* (New Westminster, B.C.: 1984), 1, 2.

2   *"Lieut.-Colonel J.C. Whyte Succumbs After Long Illness,"* New Westminster Columbian, 10 October 1907, 1.

3   *"Deputy Warden Bourke Resigns,"* New Westminster Columbian, 12 October 1907, 1.

4   Ibid.

5   W.A. DeWolf-Smith, *"Prisoner Health Certifications,"* George Edwards Correspondence File, Anthony Martin B.C. Penitentiary Collection, (New Westminster B.C.: 1 June 1906). Medical certification documentation for Dunn and Colquhoun is not available in the Anthony Martin collection of penitentiary documents. Normal procedures in the prison were that when the individual convict was released or had died in prison, his files were returned to the federal authorities in Ottawa. As Ottawa is too remote to visit to take the chance that the documents still exist, this avenue has been unexplored. Email inquiries at the archives in Ottawa lead the writer to believe that no records now exist.

6   Albert Edward Verk, *"Prisoner Religious Beliefs,"* George Edwards Correspondence File, Anthony Martin B.C. Penitentiary Collection, (New Westminster B.C.: 1 June 1906).

7   Warden John C. Whyte, *"Prisoner Photo Requests,"* George Edwards Correspondence File, Anthony Martin B.C. Penitentiary Collection, (New Westminster B.C.: 12 June 1906).

8   Director F.H. DePine, *"Edwards Photo,"* George Edwards Correspondence File, Anthony Martin B.C. Penitentiary Collection, (San Quentin, CA: 25 July 1906).

9   *"Visits Bill Miner,"* Kamloops Sentinel, 2 July 1906.

10 *"Break For Freedom,"* Kamloops Standard, 10 August 1907.

11 *"Miner Still Has Hope,"* Armstrong Advance, Armstrong B.C., 20 July 1906.

12 *"Mcintyre Wins Libel Suit,"* Kamloops Inland Sentinel, 13 April 1909, 1.

13 *"Convict Campbell Testimony,"* Escape Inquiry Files, Anthony Martin B.C. Penitentiary Collection, (New Westminster B.C.: 16 Sept. 1907), 55–59.

14 Ibid.

15 *"What Happened At The Pen,"* New Westminster Columbian, 12 August 1907, 1.

16 *"Bill Miner And Companions Enjoy Prolonged Liberty,"* Vancouver News Advertiser, 12 August 1907, 1.

17 Keeper Stewart, *"Inquiry Testimony,"* Inquiry Files, Anthony Martin Penitentiary Collection, (New Westminster B.C.: 16 September 1907), 52–53.

18 *"Greenfield and Whyte Correspondence, seven letters,"* George Edwards Correspondence File, Anthony Martin B.C. Penitentiary Collection, (New Westminster and Vancouver B.C.: 18 June 1906 to 30 November 1906).

19 *"Visits Bill Miner,"* Kamloops Sentinel, 2 July 1906.

20 President W.S. Stout, *"Letter to CPR VP. W. Whyte,"* Vancouver Archives, Major J.S. Mathews Coll., Private Record #: Add. Mss 358. 550-C-5, File 9 (Part of H.A. Price Coll.), (Toronto ON: 13 June 1906).

21 Manager W.S. Seavey, Thiel Detective Agency, *"Arnold in Princeton, Letter to Marpole,"* B.C. Archives, GR0055, Box 45, File 6, Provincial Police Corr. In, (Seattle WA: 25 June 1906).

22 President W.S. Stout, *"Letter to CPR Sup't Marpole,"* Vancouver Archives, Major J.S. Mathews Coll., Private Record #: Add. Mss 358. 550-C-5, File 9 (Part of H.A. Price Coll.), (Toronto ON: 4 July 1906).

23 CPR Detective R.E. Bullick, *"Miner Writes Arnold, Letter to Sup't Marpole,"* B.C. Archives, GR0055, Box 45, File 6, Provincial Police Corr. In, (Vancouver B.C.: 4 July 1906).

24 CPR Sup't R. Marpole, *"Miner and Arnold, Letter to Sup't Hussey,"* B.C. Archives, GR0055, Box 45, File 6, Provincial Police Corr. In, (Vancouver B.C.: 7 July 1906).

25 Constable Ronald Hewat, *"Horse Needed, Letter to C.C. Pearse,"* B.C. Archives, GR0055, Box 67, File 5, Provincial Police Corr. In, (Princeton B.C.: 13 June 1906).

26 Constable Ronald Hewat, *"Budd and Arnold, Report to Sup't Hussey,"* B.C. Archives, GR0055, Box 45, File 6, Provincial Police Corr. In, (Princeton B.C.: 11 July 1906).

27 CPR Superintendent R. Marpole, *"Princeton Investigations,"* Vancouver Archives, Major J.S. Mathews Coll., Private Record #: Add. Mss 358. 550-C-5, File 9 (Part of H.A. Price Coll.), (Vancouver B.C.: 19 July 1906).

28 Constable Ronald Hewat, *"Budd and Arnold, Report to Sup't Hussey,"* B.C. Archives, GR0055, Box 56, File 7&8, Provincial Police Corr. In, (Princeton B.C.: 21 July 1906).

29 Constable Ronald Hewat, *"Arnold Description, Report to Sup't Hussey,"* B.C. Archives, GR0055, Box 45, File 7&8, Provincial Police Corr. In, (Princeton B.C.: 24 Aug. 1906).

30 Special Constable Percy Cotton, *"Letter to Sup't F.S. Hussey,"* B.C. Archives, GR0055, Box 45, File 1, Provincial Police Corr. In, (Adelphi B.C.: 30 May 1906).

31 Superintendent F.S. Hussey, *"Reward Letter to Pearse,"* B.C. Archives, MF B 2579, Vol. 21 (531) to Vol. 23 (245), Provincial Police Corr. Outward, 1864–1918, (Victoria B.C.: 13 June 1906).

32 Constable E.T.W. Pearse, *"Posse Members, Letter to F.S. Hussey,"* Vancouver Archives, Major J.S. Mathews Coll., Private Record #: Add. Mss 358. 550-C-5, File 9 (Part of H.A. Price Coll.), (Kamloops B.C.: 15 June 1906).

33 Constable E.T.W. Pearse, *"R.N.W.M.P Members At Arrest, Letter to F.S. Hussey,"* Vancouver Archives, Major J.S. Mathews Coll., Private Record #: Add. Mss 358. 550-C-5, File 9 (Part of H.A. Price Coll.), (Kamloops B.C.: 15 June 1906).

34 Constable E.T.W. Pearse, *"Disposition of Reward, Letter to Sup't F.S. Hussey,"* B.C. Archives, GR0055, Box 67, Files 5 & 6, Provincial Police Corr. In, (Kamloops B.C.: 1 August 1906).

35 Owen Batchelor, *"Share of Reward, Letter to Sup't F.SD. Hussey,"* B.C. Archives, GR0055, Box 37, File 4, (Kamloops B.C.: 20 September, 1906).

36 William Plumm, *"Share of Reward, Letter to Sup't F.S. Hussey,"* Vancouver Archives, Major J.S. Mathews Coll., Private Record #: Add. Mss 358. 550-C-5, File 9 (Part of H.A. Price Coll.), (Kamloops B.C.: 28 Sept. 1906).

37 *"Reward Letters to Sup't F.S. Hussey,"* Vancouver Archives, Major J.S. Mathews Coll., Private Record #: Add. Mss 358. 550-C-5, File 9 (Part of H.A. Price Coll.), (27 Sept. to 27 Nov. 1906).

38 CPR Special Services Detective W.A. McFoy, *"Reward Distribution, Letter to Sup't F.S. Hussey,"* B.C. Archives, Box 54, Files Goa to GN, Goa to Gz and Fos to Gaq, B.C.PP Corr. In, (Calgary AB: 23 Nov. 1906).

39 CPR Special Services Detective W.A. McFoy, *"Pistol and Ring, Letter to Sup't Hussey,"* B.C. Archives, Box 54, Files Goa to GN, Goa to Gz and Fos to Gaq, B.C.PP Corr. In, (Calgary AB: 23 Nov. 1906).

40 Hussey, Greenfield and McMullen, *"Report on Distribution of Reward,"* Vancouver Archives, Major J.S. Mathews Coll., Private Record #: Add. Mss 358. 550-C-5, File 9 (Part of H.A. Price Coll.), (Vancouver B.C.: 31 Oct. 1906, backdated.).

41 "The Rewards Awarded," Kamloops Sentinel, 30 Nov. 1906.

42 Hussey, Greenfield and McMullen, "Report on Distribution of Reward," Vancouver Archives, Major J.S. Mathews Coll., Private Record #: Add. Mss 358. 550-C-5, File 9 (Part of H.A. Price Coll.), (Vancouver B.C.: 31 Oct. 1906, backdated.).

43 "Wages Paid To B.C. Provincial Police For Yearly Period," B.C. Archives, GR0055, Box 80, B.C. Provincial Police, Lists of names taken from public accounts, 1 July 1905–30 June 1906, b39.

44 "Daphne Fernie Interview with the Author," (Victoria B.C.: 3 April 2001).

45 Superintendent F.S. Hussey, "Bloodhound letter to Fulton," B.C. Archives, GR)429, Box 13, File 3, Attorney General Corr., (Victoria B.C.: 20 June 1906).

46 "Town and District Notes," Enderby Progress, 18 May 1906, 4.

47 James, H. Christie, Letters and Diaries, Okanagan Indians Non-registered. The Reason Why, Intro. Robert L. de Pfyffer, 54th Annual Report of the Okanagan Historical Society, (Wayside Press, Vernon B.C.: 1990), 77–79.

48 Armstrong Advance, 25 May 1906.

49 James H. Christie, "Letter to Sup't F.S. Hussey," B.C. Archives, GR0055, Box 45, File 1, Provincial Police Corr. In, (Glen Emma B.C.: 26June 1906).

50 Chief Constable Edgar C. Simmons, "Letter to James Christie," B.C. Archives, GR0055, Box 45, File b1, Provincial Police Corr. In, (Vernon B.C.: 15 Aug. 1906).

51 James H. Christie, "Letter to Sup't F.S. Hussey," B.C. Archives, GR0055, Box 45, File 1, Provincial Police Corr. In, (Glen Emma B.C.: 21 Aug. 1906).

[52] Constable Basil Gardom, "Letter re Christie to Hussey," GR0055, Box 54, File 2, Provincial Police Corr. In, (Vernon B.C.: 28 Aug. 1906).

[53] James H. Christie, "Letter to Sup't F.S. Hussey," B.C. Archives, GR0055, Box 45, File 1, Provincial Police Corr. In, (Glen Emma B.C.: 17 Sept. 1906).

[54] James, H. Christie, Letters and Diaries, Okanagan Indians Non-registered. The Reason Why, Intro. Robert L. de Pfyffer, 54th Annual Report of the Okanagan Historical Society, (Wayside Press, Vernon B.C.: 1990), 77–87.

[55] "Lieut.-Colonel J.C. Whyte Succumbs After Long Illness," New Westminster Columbian, 10 October 1907, 1.

[56] Keeper Stewart, "Inquiry Testimony," Inquiry Files, Anthony Martin Penitentiary Collection, (New Westminster B.C.: 16 September 1907), 52–53.

[57] Ibid.

[58] "Chief Denies Statements," New Westminster Columbian, 18 Feb. 1909, 1.

[59] "The Dick Duval Of The Far West," Vancouver News Advertiser, 19 Feb. 1909, 1.

[60] Keeper Stewart, "Inquiry Testimony," Inquiry Files, Anthony Martin Penitentiary Collection, (New Westminster B.C.: 16 September 1907), 52–53.

[61] R.N.W.M.P Sergeant J.J. Wilson, (Ret.), *Capture of Bill Miner,* Unpublished and undated manuscript, RCMP Archives, Regina SK, (Edmonton AB: bfr 1933), 1–13.

[62] Acting Warden D.D. Bourke, *Report to G.W. Dawson, Inspector of Prisons,* George Edwards Correspondence File, Anthony Martin B.C. Penitentiary Collection (New Westminster B.C.: 13 July 1907), 1–3.

XXII
ESCAPE PLANNING

[1] *Miner's Escape Worthy The Man,* Victoria Colonist, 11 August 1907, 5.

[2] *Surgeon De Wolf Smith Testimony,* Escape Inquiry Files, Anthony Martin B.C. Penitentiary Collection (New Westminster, B.C.: 5 Sept 1907), 6.

[3] *Pacific Express Held Up Near Mission,* New Westminster Columbian, 12 Sept. 1904, 1.

[4] Pinkerton's National Detective Agency, *Mission Robbery Reward Circular,* Escape Inquiry Files, Anthony Martin B.C. Penitentiary Collection (After 10 Sept. 1904), 1,2.

[5] *Bill Miner's Escape,* Victoria Colonist, 19 Feb. 09, 1.

[6] *Another Man Thinks He Entertained Miner,* Victoria Colonist, 16 Aug. 1907, 5.

[7] Mark Dugan and John Boessenecker, The Grey Fox (University of Oklahoma Press: 1992), 93, 108, 109.

8   *"Another Man Thinks He Entertained Miner,"* Victoria Colonist, 16 Aug. 1907, 5.

9   *"Sudden Termination To Bourke Libel Case,"* New Westminster Columbian, 8 April 1907, 1.

10 Ibid.

11 Ibid.

12 *"Another Man Thinks He Entertained Miner,"* Victoria Colonist, 16 Aug. 1907, 5.

13 *"Instructor George McKenzie testimony,"* Escape Inquiry Files, Anthony Martin B.C. Penitentiary Collection (New Westminster, B.C.: 13 Sept. 1907), 46–49.

14 *"Reverend A.D. Owen Testimony,"* Escape Inquiry Files, Anthony Martin B.C. Penitentiary Collection (New Westminster, B.C.: 6 Sept. 1907), 1–3.

15 *"Information On Bill Miner,"* New Westminster Columbian, 13 March 1909, 1.

16 *"Reverend A.D. Owen Testimony,"* Escape Inquiry Files, Anthony Martin B.C. Penitentiary Collection (New Westminster, B.C.: 6 Sept. 1907), 1–3.

17 *"What Happened At The Pen,"* Daily Columbian, New Westminster, B.C., 12 August 1907, 1.

18 New Westminster Columbian, 12 June 1907, 1. (Headline Unknown).

19 *"Probing Starts,"* New Westminster Columbian, 4 Sept. 1907, 1.

20 *"Acting Warden D.D. Bourke Testimony,"* Escape Inquiry Files, Anthony Martin B.C. Penitentiary Collection (New Westminster, B.C.: 6 Sept. 1907), 14.

21 *"Break For Freedom,"* Kamloops Standard, 10 Aug. 1907, 1.

22 *"Miner's Escape Worthy The Man,"* Victoria Colonist, 11 August 1907, 5.

23 *"Five Thousand Dollars To Help Bill Miner,"* Vancouver World, 10 August 1907.

24 *"Convict Campbell Testimony,"* Escape Inquiry Files, Anthony Martin B.C. Penitentiary Collection (New Westminster, B.C.: 16 Sept. 1907), 55–59.

25 Ibid.

26 *"Guard Sampson Testimony,"* Escape Inquiry Files, Anthony Martin B.C. Penitentiary Collection (New Westminster, B.C.: 5 Sept. 1907, 4–5.

27 *"Five Thousand Dollars To Help Bill Miner,"* Vancouver World, 10 August 1909, 1. The Vancouver World later reported the name of the man from the Similkameen to authorities; however, no record exists as to who the stranger was. It would only be speculation to guess that it might have been either Jack Budd or Tom Arnold. One friend of Miner's that is mentioned by Bourke in his testimony after the prison break is the known friend of Miner's, Bob Tilton.

28 *"Doors Of Pen Are Wide Open,"* New Westminster Columbian, 7 October 1907, 1.

29 *"Instructor George McKenzie testimony,"* Escape Inquiry Files, Anthony Martin B.C. Penitentiary Collection (New Westminster, B.C.: 13 Sept. 1907), 46–49.

30 *"Miner Has Not Reported As Yet,"* The World, Vancouver, B.C., 12 August 1907, 1

31 "*Bill Miner Escapes From The Penitentiary*," Vancouver World, 9 Aug. 1907, 1.

XXIII
THE ESCAPE

1 "*Convict Thomas F. Young Testimony*," Inquiry Files, Anthony Martin B.C.
   Penitentiary Records Collection (New Westminster, B.C.: 6 Sept. 1907), 24–25.
   Most of the details of the escape of Miner are obtained from the primary source
   material available in the Anthony Martin Collection of B.C. Penitentiary files. The
   inquiry into the escape included the testimony of guards and convicts alike, and
   these are invaluable in determining what actually happened that day. The local press
   coverage is also important; however, it is used to flesh out the story, not as source
   material for what actually took place. Not all the newspaper references have been
   footnoted as there is just too much and it would mesmerize the reader. The New
   Westminster Columbian, the Victoria Colonist, The Vancouver Province, World
   and News Advertiser, and both Kamloops papers were consulted and provided
   background.

2 "*Guard J. McNeil Testimony*," Inquiry Files, Anthony Martin B.C. Penitentiary
   Records Collection (New Westminster, B.C.: 6 Sept. 1907), 26–31.

3 "*Bandit Bill Miner Makes Escape With Three Convicts*," New Westminster Columbian,
   9 Aug. 1907, 2.

4 "*Guard J. McNeil Testimony*," Inquiry Files, Anthony Martin B.C. Penitentiary
   Records Collection (New Westminster, B.C.: 6 Sept. 1907), 26–31.

5 "*Convict Thomas F. Young Testimony*," Inquiry Files, Anthony Martin B.C.
   Penitentiary Records Collection (New Westminster, B.C.: 6 Sept. 1907), 24–25.

6 Ibid.

7 Ibid.

8 Ibid.

9 Ibid.

10 "*What Happened At The Pen*," New Westminster Columbian, 12 Aug. 1907, 1.

11 "*Guard Doyle Testimony*," Inquiry Files, Anthony Martin B.C. Penitentiary Records
    Collection (New Westminster, B.C.: 7 Sept. 1907), 32–35.

12 "*Bandit Bill Miner Makes Escape With Three Convicts*," New Westminster Columbian,
    9 Aug. 1907, 2.

13 Warden John C. Brown, "*Geo. W. Edwards alias Bill Miner Prison Record, sent to
    Minister of Justice, Ottawa*," Inquiry Files, Anthony Martin B.C. Penitentiary Records
    Collection (New Westminster, B.C.: 19 March 1909).

14 "Bandit Bill Miner Makes Escape With Three Convicts," New Westminster Columbian, 9 Aug. 1907, 2.

15 Warden John C. Brown, "McCluskey Prison Record, sent to Minister of Justice, Ottawa," Inquiry Files, Anthony Martin B.C. Penitentiary Records Collection (New Westminster, B.C.: 19 March 1909).

16 "Bandit Bill Miner Makes Escape With Three Convicts," New Westminster Columbian, 9 Aug. 1907, 2.

17 Warden John C. Brown, "John W. Clark Prison Record, sent to Minister of Justice, Ottawa," Inquiry Files, Anthony Martin B.C. Penitentiary Records Collection (New Westminster, B.C.: 19 March 1909).

18 "Bandit Bill Miner Makes Escape With Three Convicts," New Westminster Columbian, 9 Aug. 1907, 2.

19 "Bill Miner Escapes From Penitentiary," Vancouver World, 9 August 1907, 1.

20 "Miner's Escape Worthy The Man," Victoria Colonist, 11 August 1907, 1.

21 "Guard Walsh Testimony," Inquiry Files, Anthony Martin B.C. Penitentiary Records Collection (New Westminster, B.C.: 12 Sept. 1907), 41–42.

22 "Convict Campbell Testimony," Inquiry Files, Anthony Martin B.C. Penitentiary Records Collection (New Westminster, B.C.: 6 Sept. 1907), 55–59.

23 Ibid.

24 Ibid.

25 Ibid.

26 "Evidence That Miner Got Help From Outside," Victoria Colonist, 13 August 1907, 1.

27 "Convict Campbell Testimony," Inquiry Files, Anthony Martin B.C. Penitentiary Records Collection (New Westminster, B.C.: 6 Sept. 1907), 55–59.

28 "What Happened At The Pen?" New Westminster Columbian, 12 August 1907, 1.

29 "Hamilton and James Sclater Testimony," Inquiry Files, Anthony Martin B.C. Penitentiary Records Collection (New Westminster, B.C.: 6 Sept. 1907), 36–37.

30 "Bill Miner Still Free," Vancouver News Advertiser, 10 August 1907, 1.

31 "Miner's Escape Worthy The Man," Victoria Daily Colonist, 11 August 1907, p 5.

32 "Bill Miner and His Companions Still at Large," The World, Vancouver, B.C., 10 August 1907, 1.

33 "Guard Doyle Testimony," Inquiry Files, Anthony Martin B.C. Penitentiary Records Collection (New Westminster, B.C.: 7 Sept. 1907), 32–35.

34 "Hamilton and James Sclater Testimony," Inquiry Files, Anthony Martin B.C. Penitentiary Records Collection (New Westminster, B.C.: 6 Sept. 1907), 36–37.

35 "Constable Grey Testimony," Inquiry Files, Anthony Martin B.C. Penitentiary Records Collection (New Westminster, B.C.: 7 Sept. 1907), 38.

[36] *"Guard Doyle Testimony,"* Inquiry Files, Anthony Martin B.C. Penitentiary Records Collection (New Westminster, B.C.: 7 Sept. 1907), 32–35.

XXIV
PURSUIT OF THE CONVICTS

[1] *"Bandit Bill Miner Makes Escape With Three Convicts,"* New Westminster Columbian, 9 August 1907, 1.

[2] Victoria Daily Colonist, 11 August 1907, p. 5.

[3] *"Bandit Bill Miner Makes Escape With Three Convicts,"* New Westminster Columbian, 9 August 1907, 1.

[4] Acting Warden D.D. Bourke, *"Four Convicts Escape, telegram to Inspector of Penitentiaries, Ottawa,"* Inquiry Files, Anthony Martin B.C. Penitentiary Collection (New Westminster, B.C.: 8 August 1907).

[5] *"Guards Walsh and Tweedle Testimony,"* Inquiry Files, Anthony Martin B.C. Penitentiary Collection (New Westminster, B.C.: 19 August 1907), 1–2.

[6] *"Guard Atkins Testimony,"* Inquiry Files, Anthony Martin B.C. Penitentiary Collection (New Westminster, B.C.: 19 August 1907), 1–2.

[7] *"Guard Disney Testimony,"* Inquiry Files, Anthony Martin B.C. Penitentiary Collection (New Westminster, B.C.: 19 August 1907), 1.

[8] *"Guard Atkins Testimony,"* Inquiry Files, Anthony Martin B.C. Penitentiary Collection (New Westminster, B.C.: 19 August 1907), 1–2.

[9] *"Bill Miner Escapes From Penitentiary,"* Vancouver World, 9 August 1909, 1.

[10] *"Bill Miner Still Free,"* Vancouver News Advertiser, 10 August 1907, 1.

[11] *"Bandit Bill Miner Makes Escape With Three Convicts,"* New Westminster Columbian, 9 August 1907, 1.

[12] *"Miner's Escape Worthy The Man,"* Victoria Colonist, 11 August 1907, 5.

[13] *"Guard Patchell Testimony,"* Inquiry Files, Anthony Martin B.C. Penitentiary Collection (New Westminster, B.C.: 19 August 1907), 1–3.

[14] *"Five Thousand Dollars To Help Miner,"* Vancouver World, 10 August 1909, 1.

[15] *"Searchers Discouraged In Fruitless Pursuit,"* New Westminster Columbian, 10 August 1907, 1.

[16] Acting Warden D.D. Bourke, *"Reward? Bill Miner Gone, telegram to Inspector of Penitentiaries, Ottawa,"* Inquiry Files, Anthony Martin B.C. Penitentiary Collection (New Westminster, B.C.: 9 August 1907).

[17] Acting Warden D.D. Bourke, *"Suspended Guard McNeil, telegram to Inspector of Penitentiaries, Ottawa,"* Inquiry Files, Anthony Martin B.C. Penitentiary Collection (New Westminster, B.C.: 10 August 1907).

[18] *"Guard Testimonies,"* Inquiry Files, Anthony Martin B.C. Penitentiary Collection (New Westminster, B.C.: August 1907).

[19] *"Bill Miner Still Enjoys Freedom,"* Victoria Colonist, 14 August 1907, 5.

[20] *"Miner's Escape Worthy The Man,"* Victoria Colonist, 11 August 1907, p 5

[21] *"Miner Has Not Reported As Yet,"* Vancouver World, 12 August 1907, 2.

[22] *"Search For Fugitives Practically Abandoned,"* New Westminster Columbian, 15 August 1907, 1.

[23] *"Another Man Thinks He Entertained Miner,"* Victoria Colonist, 16 August 1907, 5.

[24] *"Fed Miner,"* New Westminster Columbian, 14 August 1907, 1.

[25] *"Five Hundred Dollars Reward For Miner,"* Victoria Colonist, 16 August 1907, 1.

[26] *"The Dick Duval Of The Far West,"* Vancouver News Advertiser, 19 Feb. 1909, 1, 4.

[27] *"Photo and Description Request letters,"* George Edwards Correspondence Files, Anthony Martin B.C. Penitentiary Collection (19 August to 9 October 1907), 70–79.

[28] Mrs. A.E. Miner, *"Photo and Description of Miner Request,"* George Edwards Correspondence Files, Anthony Martin B.C. Penitentiary Collection (19 August to 9 October 1907). 76

[29] Inspector Douglas Stewart, *"Where Are Escape Reports? telegram to D.D. Bourke, New Westminster, B.C.,"* Inquiry Files, Anthony Martin B.C. Penitentiary Collection (Ottawa, ON: 17 August 1907).

[30] Acting Warden D.D. Bourke, *"Report Sent Twelfth, telegram to Douglas Stewart, Ottawa, ON,"* Inquiry Files, Anthony Martin B.C. Penitentiary Collection (New Westminster, B.C.: 18 August 1907).

[31] Acting Warden D.D. Bourke, *"Reports Received? telegram to Douglas Stewart, Ottawa, ON,"* Inquiry Files, Anthony Martin B.C. Penitentiary Collection (New Westminster, B.C.: 20 August 1907).

[32] *"Two More Convicts Make Break For Liberty,"* New Westminster Columbian, 22 August 1907, 1.

[33] *"Miner's Escape Worthy The Man,"* Victoria Colonist, 11 August 1907, 5

[34] Ibid.

[35] *"Bill Miner Still Enjoys Freedom,"* Victoria Daily Colonist, 14 August 1907, 5

[36] *"Bill Miner and His Companions Still at Large,"* Vancouver World, 10 August 1907, 1.

[37] *"Why Does Government Not Offer Reward For Miner?"* New Westminster Columbian, 12 August 1907, 1.

[38] *"Suspicious Men Are Seen Prowling Around Park Drive,"* Vancouver News Advertiser, 13 August 1907, 1.

[39] *"Bill Miner's Case,"* Editorial, Victoria Colonist, 15 August 1907, 5.

40 "*Bill Miner and His Companions Still at Large,*" Vancouver World, 10 August 1907, 1.

41 Ibid.

42 "*Another Man Thinks He Entertained Miner,*" Daily Colonist, Victoria, B.C., 16 August 1907, 5.

43 "*Escaped Convict Seen At Hotel Near Vancouver,*" Vancouver News Advertiser, 11 August 1907, 1.

44 "*Searchers Discouraged In Fruitless Pursuit,*" New Westminster Columbian, 10 August 1907, 1.

45 "*Miner's Escape Worthy The Man,*" Victoria Colonist, 11 August 1907, 5.

46 "*Miner Has Not Reported As Yet,*" Vancouver World, 12 August 1907, 1.

47 "*Miner's Escape Worthy The Man,*" Victoria Colonist, 11 August 1907, 5.

48 "*Miner has Not Reported As Yet,*" Vancouver World, 12 august 1907, 1.

49 "*Miner's Escape Worthy The Man,*" Victoria Daily Colonist, 11 August 1907, p. 5

50 Inspector G.W. Dawson, "*Miner's Effects, letter to Inspector Douglas Stewart, Ottawa,*" Inquiry Files, Anthony Martin Penitentiary Collection (New Westminster, B.C.: 6 September 1907), 1.

XXV
THE INQUIRY

1 Acting Warden D.D. Bourke, "*Escape Report to Inspectors of Penitentiaries, Ottawa,*" Inquiry Files, Anthony Martin Penitentiary Collection (New Westminster, B.C.: 12 August 1907), 1–4.

2 Acting Warden D.D. Bourke, "*Escape Report and clipping to Inspectors of Penitentiaries, Ottawa,*" Inquiry Files, Anthony Martin Penitentiary Collection (New Westminster, B.C.: 14 August 1907), 1–2.

3 Inspector Of Penitentiaries Douglas Stewart, "*Letter To D.D. Bourke re reports and telegrams,*" Inquiry Files, Anthony Martin Penitentiary Collection (Ottawa, ON: 21 August 1907), 1–2.

4 Ibid.

5 Acting Warden D.D. Bourke, "*Report to Douglas Stewart re escape details,*" Inquiry Files, Anthony Martin Penitentiary Collection (New Westminster, B.C.: 22 August 1907), 1–5.

6 Inspector George Dawson, "*Telegram to Douglas Stewart in Ottawa re arrival,*" Inquiry Files, Anthony Martin Penitentiary Collection (Dorchester, NB: 23 August 1907), 1–2.

7 Acting Warden D.D. Bourke, "*Report to Douglas Stewart re escape recommendations,*" Inquiry Files, Anthony Martin Penitentiary Collection (New Westminster, B.C.: 23 August 1907), 1–11.

8   Acting Warden D.D. Bourke, *"Report to Douglas Stewart re Miner transfer to outside, and private letter enclosed,"* Inquiry Files, Anthony Martin Penitentiary Collection (New Westminster, B.C.: 28 August 1907), 1–5 & 1.

9   *"Probing Starts,"* New Westminster Columbian, 4 Sept. 1907, 1.

10 Inspector G.W. Dawson, *"Letter re Arrival in New Westminster, to Douglas Stewart, Ottawa,"* Inquiry Files, Anthony Martin Penitentiary Collection (New Westminster, B.C.: 4 September 1907), 1.

11 Dominion Police Commissioner Sherwood, *"Bourke Told Escape Was to Take Place, letter to Geo. Dawson New Westminster,"* Inquiry Files, Anthony Martin Penitentiary Collection (Ottawa, ON: 3 September 1907), 1.

12 W.C. Nicol, *"The Penitentiary,"* Vancouver Province, 5 Sept. 1907, clipping c/w annotations, Inquiry Files, Anthony Martin Penitentiary Collection (Ottawa, ON: 3 September 1907), 1.

13 Acting Warden D.D. Bourke, *"Questions and Answers, report to Inspector Dawson,"* Inquiry Files, Anthony Martin Penitentiary Collection (New Westminster, B.C.: 6 September 1907), 1.

14 *"Why Miner Left,"* New Westminster Columbian, 7 Sept. 1907, 1.

15 Inspector George Dawson, Report On Escape Of George Edwards Alias Bill Miner," Inquiry Files, Anthony Martin Penitentiary Collection (New Westminster, B.C.: 19 September 1907), 4.

16 *"Monster Mass Meeting,"* New Westminster Columbian, 27 Sept. 1907, 1.

17 *"Doors Of Pen Are Wide Open,"* New Westminster Columbian, 7 Oct. 1907, 1.

18 *"Lieut.-Colonel J.C. Whyte Succumbs After Long Illness,"* New Westminster Columbian, 10 Oct. 1907, 1.

19 Inspector Douglas Stewart, *"Piggery Gate, Ladder and Bullick Visit, letter to Dawson in New Westminster,"* Inquiry Files, Anthony Martin Penitentiary Collection (Ottawa, ON: 15 October 1907), 1–2.

20 Inspector G.W. Dawson, *"February Visit to Edwards, letter to Inspector R.E. Bullick, Vancouver, B.C.,"* Inquiry Files, Anthony Martin Penitentiary Collection (New Westminster, B.C.: 29 October 1907), 1.

21 Inspector R.E. Bullick, CPR Special Services, *"Meeting With Edwards, letter to Inspector Dawson, New Westminster,"* Inquiry Files, Anthony Martin Penitentiary Collection (Vancouver, B.C.: 5 November 1907), 1.

22 *"Deputy Warden Bourke Resigns,"* New Westminster Columbian, 16 Oct. 1907, 1, 2.

23 *"Deputy Warden's Tenure Closes,"* New Westminster Columbian, 4 Nov. 1907, 1.

THE HOUSE OF COMMONS DEBATES

[1] Inspector G.W. Dawson, *"Disclose Information, letter to D.D. Bourke, New Westminster,"* Inquiry Files, Anthony Martin Penitentiary Collection (Ottawa, ON: 30 Jan. 1907), 1.

[2] D.D. Bourke, *"Have No Information, letter to Inspector G.W. Dawson,"* Inquiry Files, Anthony Martin Penitentiary Collection (New Westminster, B.C.: 6 Feb. 1909), 1.

[3] *"Miner Escape Before House,"* New Westminster Columbian, 12 Feb. 1909, 1.

[4] *"Will Welcome Investigation,"* New Westminster Columbian, 12 Feb. 1909, 1.

[5] *"Department Was Unaware,"* New Westminster Columbian, 18 Feb. 1909, 1.

[6] *"Aylesworth Provokes Stormy Scene In House,"* New Westminster Columbian, 12 March 1909, 1.

[7] *"Chief Denies Statements,"* New Westminster Columbian, 18 Feb. 1909, 1.

[8] *"Bill Miner's Escape,"* Victoria Colonist, 19 Feb. 1909, 1.

[9] *"Bill Miner Holds Up Ministerial Benches,"* New Westminster Columbian, 19 Feb. 1909, 1.

[10] Ibid.

[11] *"Expects to Go Before House,"* New Westminster Columbian, 22 Feb. 1909, 1.

[12] *"Ex-Warden Writes Again,"* New Westminster Columbian, 24 Feb. 1909, 1.

[13] *"Contradicts Aylesworth,"* New Westminster Columbian, 25 Feb. 1909, 1.

[14] *"Convict Clark Silent About Bill Miner,"* New Westminster Columbian, 27 Feb. 1909, 3.

[15] *"Ex-Warden Bourke defends Record,"* New Westminster Columbian, 1 March 1909, 3.

[16] *"Miner's Escape Hotly Discussed,"* Victoria Colonist, 3 March 1909, 1.

[17] New Westminster Columbian, 12 March 1909, 1.

[18] Ibid.

[19] *"Miner's Escape Hotly Discussed,"* Victoria Colonist, 3 March 1909, 1.

[20] *"Aylesworth Provokes Stormy Scene In House,"* New Westminster Columbian, 12 March 1909, 1.

[21] *"Miner's Escape Hotly Discussed,"* Victoria Colonist, 3 March 1909, 1.

[22] *"Aylesworth Provokes Stormy Scene In House,"* New Westminster Columbian, 12 March 1909, 1.

[23] *"Miner's Escape Hotly Discussed,"* Victoria Colonist, 3 March 1909, 1.

[24] *"Aylesworth Provokes Stormy Scene In House,"* New Westminster Columbian, 12 March 1909, 1.

[25] Ibid.

26   Ibid.

27   Ibid.

28   *"Government Shirks Penitentiary Enquiry,"* New Westminster Columbian, 3 March 1909, 1.

29   *"Says Release Of Miner Promised By Detective,"* New Westminster Columbian, 1 March 1909, 1–2.

30   *"Mr. Bourke Concludes His Series Of Letters,"* New Westminster Columbian, 18 March 1909, 1, 8.

31   *"Sudden Termination To Bourke Libel Case,"* New Westminster Columbian, 8 April 1909, 1.

32   *"Mcintyre Wins Libel Suit,"* Kamloops Inland Sentinel, 13 April 1909, 1.

33   Warden J.C. Brown, *"Mcintyre Judgment, letter to Inspector Dawson, Ottawa,"* George Edwards Correspondence Files, Anthony Martin B.C. Penitentiary Collection (Sapperton, B.C.: 6 May 1909) 49, 48.

34   Inspector Geo. Dawson, *"Authorization To Let Monies Go, letter to Warden Brown, Sapperton,"* George Edwards Correspondence Files, Anthony Martin B.C. Penitentiary Collection (Ottawa, ON: 7 May 1909) 36.

XXVII
The Tragedy of Lewis Colquhoun

1   Historical Atlas of the County of Wellington, Ontario, Historical Atlas Publishing Co., Toronto, 1906. (Reprint Edition. Port Elgin, Ont., Cumming Atlas Reprints: 1972).

2   *"Engineer Tells How Robbers Acted,"* Vancouver Province, 21 May 1906, 2.

3   The writer attempted to contact the family by letter, but no answer was ever received. Contacts with non-family members in the area advise the writer that the family is still very sensitive to Lewis's conviction and prison term, and are not eager to re-visit the story of their infamous relative.

4   The British Columbia newspapers consulted with regards to their observations of Colquhoun were consistently sympathetic to his plight. The papers included the Vancouver Province, World and News Advertiser, the Victoria Colonist, the New Westminster Columbian and the Kamloops Inland Sentinel and Standard.

5   H.F. Kees, Superintendent of Walla Walla State Penitentiary, "Colquhoun," B.C. Archives, GR0055, Box 77, File 6, Provincial Police Corr. In (Walla Walla, WA: July, 1906).

6   *"Visits Bill Miner,"* Kamloops Inland Sentinel, 2 July, 1906, 1.

7 Warden J.C. Brown, *"Mcintyre Garnishee, letter to Inspector Geo. Dawson, Ottawa ON,"* Anthony Martin B.C. Penitentiary Collection, George Edwards Correspondence File (Sapperton, B.C.: 6 May 1909).

8 *"County Court of Westminster, Garnishee,"* Anthony Martin B.C. Penitentiary Collection, George Edwards Correspondence File (New Westminster, B.C.: 30 April 1909).

9 *"Frenzied, He Waits In Vain …,"* Victoria Colonist, 23 Dec. 1923, 34.

10 *"Convict Deaths In British Columbia, 1875–1916,"* 1913 Sessional Book, (http://www.rootsweb.com/~canB.C./conlist.htm#5). (28 Feb. 2006).

11 *"Old Timers Recall Miner Train Robbery,"* Vancouver Province, 11 September 1954, 10.

12 Clifford Historical Society, *"Clifford Cemetery,"* 26 January 2002, personal e-mail, cliffordhistoricalsociety@hotmail.com (27 January 2002).

13 *"Statement of Lewis Colquhoun,"* B.C. Archives, B.C. Provincial Police Corr. In, GR0055, Box 45, File 7, circa December 1906, 1, 2.

14 Ibid.

15 *"Statement of George Edwards,"* B.C. Archives, B.C. Provincial Police Corr. In, GR0055, Box 45, File 7, circa December 1906, 1, 2.

16 *"Letters Of Convict Disclose Tortures Of Mind Undergone,"* Victoria Colonist, 16 December 1923, 1.

17 Kamloops Family History Society, *"Pleasant Street Cemetery Records and Monumental Inscriptions"* (Kamloops, B.C.: 1997, Second Edition), 191.

18 Brigham Young University, *"Marriage of Paul Stevens and Rosie Aldrich, Idaho, 20 Mar. 1895,"* Western States Historical Marriage Record Index, http://abish.byui.edu/specialCollections/fhc/.

19 Edward Cecil *"Toddy"* Pratt, Interview with the author, Kamloops, B.C., 1985.

20 James Pratt, Interview with the author, Kamloops, B.C., 8 December 2005.

21 Thiel Agent, Operative #39, *"Investigation re Train Robbery,"* Special Service Report, B.C. Archives, GR0419, Box 117, File 1906/88, Attorney General Crown Prosecutor Files, Kamloops, B.C., 14 May 1906. 39–40.

22 *"Mr. Marpole's Suggestion,"* Vancouver News Advertiser, 17 May 1906, 2.

23 Ibid.

24 James Pratt, Interview with the author, Kamloops, B.C., 8 December 2005.

25 Val Pringle, Interview with the author, Kamloops, B.C., January 2005.

26 James Pratt, Interview with the author, Kamloops, B.C., 8 December 2005.

27 Sandi Pringle, *"Telephone Conversation With Donny Johnson,"* 8 January 2006, personal e-mail, val@direct.ca, (8 January 2006).

28 B.C. Archives Birth, Marriage, Death Index, (http://www.B.C.archives.gov.B.C.ca/textual/governmt/vstats/v_events.htm).

XXVII
THE REDEMPTION OF SHORTY DUNN

1 Mark Dugan and John Boessenecker, The Grey Fox (University of Oklahoma Press, 1992), 105.

2 Louis Lebourdais Fonds, B.C. Archives, Mss 0676, Box 6, File 8. (Unpublished 1 page manuscript with notes, Quesnel, B.C. Author unknown), circa 1896. Other sources mention that he could have come from the little hamlet of Loomis, Washington, on Sinlahekin Creek that flows into the Similkameen River just south of the Canadian border from Keremeos in Okanogan County.

3 Acting Warden D.D. Bourke, "Report to Douglas Stewart re Miner transfer to outside, and private letter enclosed," Inquiry Files, Anthony Martin Penitentiary Collection (New Westminster, B.C.: 28 August 1907), 1–5 & 1.

4 "Letters Of Convict Disclose Tortures Of Mind Undergone," Victoria Colonist, 16 Dec. 1923, 10.

5 The Victoria Colonist of December 16th, 23rd and 30th carried excerpts from letters that Shorty Dunn wrote while he was in prison. At this time, it is assumed that he wrote them to the respected prospector, geologist and poet George Winkler. However, this is only informed speculation until such time as the voluminous Winkler fonds at the B.C. Archives are reviewed. Much of the information in this chapter detailing Dunn's life in the penitentiary is taken from those Colonist issues.

6 "Letters Of Convict Disclose Tortures Of Mind Undergone," Victoria Colonist, 16 Dec. 1923, 10.

7 "Robber Laughingly Tells Train Crew To Put Hands Down," Victoria Colonist, 30 December 1923, 12.

8 "Letters Of Convict Disclose Tortures Of Mind Undergone," Victoria Colonist, 16 Dec. 1923, 10.

9 Ibid.

10 Ibid.

11 Ibid.

12 Ibid.

13 Ibid.

14 Ibid.

15 Ibid.

16 Ibid.

17 Ibid.

18 Ibid.

19 Ibid.

20 Ibid.

21 Ibid.

22 Ibid.

23 Ibid.

24 Ibid.

25 Ibid.

26 Ibid.

27 Helen Reith, "*Memories of Pioneer Life at Princeton,*" 41st Annual Report of the Okanagan Historical Society (Wayside Press, Vernon, B.C.: 1977), 164.

28 "*Frenzied, He Waits In Vain For Parole On Coronation Day,*" Victoria Colonist, 23 December 1923, 34.

29 Phyllis Miller and Verna Cawston, "*H.H. Bert Thomas (1874–1973),*" 38th Annual Report Okanagan Historical Society (Wayside Press, Vernon, B.C.: 1974), 94–95.

30 "*Frenzied, He Waits In Vain for Parole On Coronation Day,*" Daily Colonist, Victoria, B.C., 23 December 1923, 34.

31 Cecil Clark, "*McDougal's Lost Mine,*" Victoria Colonist, The Islander Weekend Supplement, 2 October 1966, 6, 7, 8.

32 Ibid.

33 Ibid.

34 "*Shorty Dunn, Bill Miner's Pal, Loses Life in Ootsa Lake,*" Kamloops Inland Sentinel, 27 July 1927.

35 Helen Reith, "*Memories of Pioneer Life at Princeton,*" 41st Annual Report of the Okanagan Historical Society (Wayside Press, Vernon, B.C.: 1977), 164.

36 Jean Clark Giesbrecht, "*Heritage Lost, A People's History of the Ootsa Lake Region, 1905–1955,*" (Quesnel Lake Publishing, Likely, B.C.: 1994), 31, 33.

37 "*Frenzied, He Waits In Vain for Parole On Coronation Day,*" Victoria Colonist, 23 December 1923, 34.

38 Ibid.

39 Colin Rickards, "*Bill Miner — Fifty Years a Holdup Man,*" Real West, Vol XIII, Number 86 (October 1970), 53.

40 "*Shorty Dunn,*" The Shoulder Strap, 15th Edition (Apr.–Sept. 1946), 69–70.

41 RCMP Sergeant (Ret.) J. T. Browning (Reg. No. 2858), "*A Sequel to the Capture of Bill Miner,*" Scarlet and Gold, No.32 (1950), 111.

[42] Ibid.

[43] RCMP Constable O.L. Hall (Reg. No. 6488), *"Secret and Confidential C.I.B. report,"* 29 October 1925), Public Rights Administration, Naturalization Papers of John William Grell, File No. 6515–25, Citizenship and Immigration Canada (Ottawa, ON: 1925–1927), 3.

[44] RCMP Sergeant (Ret.) J. T. Browning (Reg. No. 2858), *"A Sequel to the Capture of Bill Miner,"* Scarlet and Gold, No.32 (1950), 111.

[45] John William Grell, *"Petition For Naturalization,"* Public Rights Administration, Naturalization Papers of John William Grell, File No. 6515–25, Citizenship and Immigration Canada (Ottawa, ON: 1925–1927), 8–10.

[46] *"Oath of Allegiance of John William Grell,"* Public Rights Administration, Naturalization Papers of John William Grell, File No. 6515–25, Citizenship and Immigration Canada (Ottawa, ON: 1925–1927), 12.

[47] Alan Sandercott, *"Death of Billy Grell,"* 13 November 2004, personal e-mail, (14 November 2004).

[48] *"Shorty Dunn,"* The Shoulder Strap, 15th Edition (Apr.–Sept. 1946), 69–70.

[49] *"Probate of John William Grell,"* B.C. Archives, GR1466, Smithers Probate Estate Files, 1921 to 1953, Film Reel B09544, Item #33, 1929.

[50] *"Shorty" Dunn, Bill Miner's Pal, Loses Life in Ootsa Lake,"* Kamloops Sentinel, 29 July, 1927.

XXIX

AFTERWARD

[1] Pinkerton Detective Agency, *"Bill Miner Investigation Reports,"* B.C. Attorney General Corr. In, B.C. Archives, GR0429, Box 17, File 4 (Washington and Montana: Feb. 1910 to 24 Feb. 1910,), 1–20.

[2] *"Bill Miner At Princeton,"* Vancouver Province, aft. August 1907, undated clipping.

[3] Jim Harrison, Kamloops, Telephone Interview with the author, February 2004.

[4] *"Gold Watch and Cash Request,"* George Edwards Correspondence Files, Anthony Martin B.C. Penitentiary Collection (5 May 1911), 28.

[5] *"Gold Watch and Cash Denial,"* George Edwards Correspondence Files, Anthony Martin B.C. Penitentiary Collection (29 May 1911), 25.

[6] Mark Dugan and John Boessenecker, The Grey Fox (University of Oklahoma Press: 1992), 194–199.

[7] *"Inspector William Lewis Fernie,"* British Columbia Police Annual, 1931, 13, 15.

[8] John Stewart, William L. Fernie, Kamloops Museum and Archives manuscript, Vol. 19, N155–N194, date unknown.

9   "*Inspector William Lewis Fernie,*" British Columbia Police Annual, 1931, 13, 15.

10 John Stewart, William L. Fernie, Kamloops Museum and Archives manuscript, Vol. 19, N155–N194, date unknown.

11 "*Provincial Police Personnel and Salaries,*" B.C. Archives, GR0091, Headquarters Personnel Records, Vol. 1, 1896–1950.

12 Daphne and Mary Fernie, Interview by author, Victoria, B.C., 3 April 2001.

13 Ibid.

14 Ibid.

15 R.G. Harvey, Carving the Western Path (Surrey, B.C.: Heritage House Publishing, 1998), 71,72.

16 Ruth Balf, Kamloops, 1914 – 1945 (Kamloops, B.C.: Peerless Printers, 1975), 58.

17 Ed Sager and Mike Frye, The Bootlegger's Lady (Blaine, WA: Hancock House Publishers, 1993), 130–131, 134–139.

18 "*Bail Was Refused,*" Nicola Herald, 21 Feb. 1908, 1.

19 Campbell Carroll, Three Bar. The Story of Douglas Lake (Vancouver, B.C.: Mitchell Press, 1958), 54, 55.

20 "*Bail Was Refused,*" Nicola Herald, 21 Feb. 1908, 1.

21 Ibid.

22 Ibid.

23 Nina Wooliams, Cattle Ranch, The Story of the Douglas Lake Cattle Company (Vancouver, B.C.: Douglas and McIntyre, 1979), 101–107.

24 "*Obituary of Alexander D. Mcintyre,*" Kamloops Sentinel, 26 Jan. 1934, 4.

25 Public Rights Administration, Naturalization Index Card of John Charles Budd, File No. B-300, Citizenship and Immigration Canada (Ottawa, ON: 1909).

26 Laurie Currie, "*Princeton 100 Years, 1867 to 1967,*" (Princeton, B.C.: Similkameen Spotlight, 1967), 19.

27 D.O. Vicars, "*Life of Bill Miner, Train Robber. An Unfinished Narrative*" (Kamloops, B.C.: Unpublished manuscript, Kamloops Museum and Archives, 1962), 8.

28 V.B. Cawston, "*The Quick Grey Fox ... Fact vs. Fiction,*" Bank of British Columbia's Pioneer News, Kamloops Museum and Archives Vertical Files, photocopy, Feb./Mar. 1984, 5–7.

29 Elisabeth Duckworth, "*Another Bill Miner Story,*" Kamloops Museum and Archives manuscript (Kamloops, B.C.: 30 June 1994).

30 Clifford Schisler, Letter to the author, Kamloops, B.C., "*Jack Budd's Papers,*" (Orillia, ON: 9 May 2002).

31 "*John Charles Budd Probate,*" Probate Files 1926 to 1950, B.C. Archives, GR2506, Princeton, B.C., Reel B09326, Item #10, 1948.

32 Margaret Stoneberg, Bill Miner, Robber, Princeton and District Museum and Archives, Uncatalogued Miner Vertical Files, Unpublished hand-written manuscript (Princeton, B.C.: 30 July 1990).

33 (Obituary of Jack Budd), Similkameen Star, 1 April 1948, 1.

BIBLIOGRAPHY

BOOKS

Anderson, Frank W. *Bill Miner ... Stagecoach and Train Robber*. Surrey, B.C.: Heritage House Publishing,

Anderson, Frank W. *The Dewdney Trail. Hope to Rock Creek*. Frontier Book # 19. Aldergrove, B.C.: Frontier Publishing, 1969.

Anonymous, *British Columbia Centenary, 1858–1958, A Century to Celebrate*. Vancouver, B.C.: International Publishing, circa 1958.

Anonymous. Okanagan Roots, *A Historical Look at the South Okanagan and Similkameen*. Compiled by Doug Cox. Penticton, B.C.: Skookum Publications, 1987.

Bailey, Frank. *Nicola, Similkameen and Tulameen Valleys. The Richest Section of British Columbia*. Vancouver, B.C.: Ward, Ellwood & Pound, circa 1914.

Balf, Mary. Museum Curator. *Kamloops. A History of the District up to 1914*. Kamloops, B.C.: Clow Printing, 1969.

Balf, Ruth. and History Committee, Kamloops Museum. *Kamloops 1914–1945*. Kamloops B.C.: Peerless Printers Limited, 1975.

Barlee, N.L. *The Best of Canada West*. Langley, B.C.: Stagecoach Publishing, October 1978.

Barman, Jean. *The West Beyond The West: A History of British Columbia*. Revised Edition. Toronto: University of Toronto Press, 2001.

Barnes, Harry D. *Frontier Days in British Columbia, Early History of Hedley Camp*. Ed. Garnet Basque. Langley, B.C.: Sunfire Publications, April 1993.

Boessenecker, John. *Gold Dust and Gunsmoke. Tales of Gold Rush Outlaws, Gunfighters, Lawmen and Vigilantes*. Somerset, NJ: John Wiley and Sons, 2000.

Carroll, Campbell. III *Three Bar. The Story of Douglas Lake*. Vancouver, B.C.: Mitchell Press, 1958.

Cherrington, John A. *The Fraser Valley: A History*. Madiera Park, B.C.: Harbour Publishing, 1992.

Clark, Cecil . *B.C. Provincial Police Stories, Vol. 2*. Surrey B.C.: Heritage House Publishing, 1989.

Cobb, Myrna and Morgan, Sher. *Eight Women Photographers of British Columbia 1860–1978.* Cobb and Morgan, with the assistance of the B.C. Ministry of Labour in conjunction with Camosun College, 1978.

Cowan, Joan and Robert. *Enderby, An Illustrated History.* Vernon, B.C.: Wayside Press, 2005.

Cox, Doug. *Mines of the Eagle Country: Nickel Plate and Mascot.* Skookum Publications, Penticton, B.C.. 1997.

Creese, Gillian. *"Exclusion or Solidarity? Vancouver Workers Confront The Oriental Problem."* In Canadian WorkingClass History, Selected Readings. Edited by McDowell and Radforth. Toronto ON: Canadian Scholar's Press, 2000.

Currie, Laurie. *Princeton B.C.. 120 Years.* Princeton, B.C.: Similkameen Spotlight Publishing, 1990.

Currie, Laurie. *Princeton. 100 Years. 1867 to 1967.* Princeton, B.C.: Similkameen Spotlight Publishing, 1967.

Dugan, Mark and Boessenecker, John. *The Grey Fox.* University of Oklahoma Press, 1992.

Dugan, Mark. Bandit Years. *A Gathering of Wolves.* Santa Fe, NM: Sunstone Press, 1987.

Dunn, Joyce. *A Town Called Chase.* Penticton, B.C.: Theytus Books, Penticton, B.C., 1986.

Eagle, John A. edited by Hugh A. Dempsey. *The CPR West, The Iron Road and the Making of a Nation"*, *"Shaughnessy and Prairie Development 1899–1914.* Douglas and McIntyre, Vancouver and Toronto, by Glenbow-Alberta Institute, T. Eaton Company Limited. 1901 Spring Summer Fall Winter Catalogue. Don Mills ON: Musson Book Company, 1970.

Francis, R. Douglas and Smith, Donald B., Editors. *Readings In Canadian History, Post-Confederation.* 2nd edition. Canada: Holt, Rinehart and Winston of Canada, 1986.

Bennett, Sherry. *"Upstaging History: Outlaws as Icons."* In "The Small Cities Book. On the Cultural Future of Small Cities." Edited by W.F. Garrett-Petts. Vancouver, B.C.: New Star Books, 2005.

Giesbrecht, Jean Clark. Heritage Lost. *A People's History of the Ootsa Lake Region 1905–1955.* Likely, B.C.: Quesnel Lake Publishing, 1994.

Gray, James H. *Red Lights on the Prairies.* Toronto: MacMillan, 1971.

Harvey, R. G. *Carving the Western Path. By River, Rail and Road Through B.C.'s Southern Mountains.* Surrey, B.C.: Heritage House, 1998.

Haydon, A.L. *The Riders of the Plains.* Rutland, Vermont: Charles E. Tuttle Co., 1910.

Horwood, Harold and Butts, Ed. *Pirates and Outlaws of Canada, 1610–1932.* Toronto ON: Doubleday Canada, 1984.

Jackman, S.W. *Portraits of the Premiers. An Informal History of British Columbia.* Sidney, B.C.: Gray's Publishing, 1969.

Johnston, Hugh J.M. *The Pacific Province. A History of British Columbia.* Vancouver, B.C.: Douglas and McIntyre, 1996.

Kluckner, Michael. *Vancouver The Way It Was.* Altona, MN: D.W. Friesen and Sons, 1984.

Lady Aberdeen (Ishbel Maria Marjoribanks). *The Journal of Lady Aberdeen. The Okanagan Valley in the Nineties.* Annotated and edited by R. M. Middleton. Victoria, B.C.: Morriss Publishing, 1986.

Murphy, P.J and Jennifer, Editors. *Sentences and Paroles. A Prison Reader.* Vancouver, B.C.: New Star Books, 1998.

Neitzel, Michael C. *The Valencia Tragedy.* Surrey B.C.: Heritage House, 1995.

Newman, Lynn Stonier. *Policing a Pioneer Province. The B.C. Provincial Police. 1858–1950.* Madiera Park, B.C.: Harbour Publishing, 1991.

Nicola Valley Archives Assoc. *Merritt and the Nicola Valley: An Illustrated History.* Merritt, B.C.: Sonotek Publishing, 1989.

Norton, Wayne and Schmidt, Wilf. *Thompson Valley Histories.* Kamloops, B.C.: Plateau Press, 1994.

Ormsby, Margaret (Editor). *A Pioneer Gentlewoman in British Columbia, The Recollections of Susan Allison.* Vancouver, B.C.: UB.C.. Press, 1976, Reprinted 1991.

Paterson, T.W. *Outlaws of Western Canada.* Langley, B.C.: Stagecoach Publishing.

Pleasant Street Cemetery, Kamloops Family History Society, 1997.

Princeton History Book Committee. *"Princeton. Our Valley. A History."* (Allison Pass, Tulameen, Sterling Creek, Aspen Grove, Osprey Lake, Copper Mtn., Darck Mtn., Allenby, Blakeburn, Coalmont),. Altona, MB: Friesens Corporation, History Book Division, 2000.

Rosehill Farmers Institute. *Bunchgrass to Barbed Wire.* Cloverdale, B.C.: Friesen & Sons, 1984.

Sager, Ed and Frye, Mike, *The Bootlegger's Lady,* Blaine, WA: Hancock House Publishers, 1993.

Sanford. Barrie, *McCulloch's Wonder. The Story of the Kettle Valley Railway.* Vancouver, B.C.: Whitecap Books, 1978.

Scott, Jack David. *Four Walls in the West, The Story of the B.C. Penitentiary.* Retired Federal Prison Officer's Association of B.C.: 1984.

Sears, Roebuck Catalogue. New York: Bounty Books, Crown Publishing, 1902.

Shewchuk, Murphy. *Exploring the Nicola Valley.* Vancouver: Douglas and Mcintyre, 1981.

Siemens, Alfred H., editor. *Lower Fraser Valley. Evolution of a Cultural Landscape.* Vancouver B.C.: Tantalus Research, 1968.

Skelton, Robin. *They Call It the Cariboo*. Victoria, B.C.: Sono Nis Press, 1980.

Stangoe, Irene. *History and Happenings in the Cariboo-Chilcotin. Pioneer Memories*. Surrey, B.C.: Heritage House, 2000.

Steele, Samuel B. *Forty Years in Canada*. Toronto, ON: Ryerson Archive Series, 1915.

Turkki, Pat. *Burns Lake and District. A History*. Burns Lake, B.C.: Burns Lake Historical Society, 1973.

Turner, Robert D. *West of the Great Divide*. Victoria, B.C.: Morriss Printing, 1987.

Upper and Lower Nicola Cemeteries, Kamloops Family History Society, 2000.

Verchere, Honourable David R. *A Progression of Judges, A History of the Supreme Court in British Columbia*. Vancouver, B.C.: University of British Columbia Press, 1988.

Waite, Don. *Kwant'stan*. Self Published, 1972. B.C. Archives Call # NW 971.1F W145k v.1

Waite, Donald E. *The Langley Story Illustrated. An Early History of the Municipality of Langley*. Manitoba: D.W. Friesen and Sons, 1977.

Waite, Don. *Tales of the Golden Ears Illustrated*. New Westminster, B.C.: Canart Studio, 1975.

Ward, W. Peter and McDonald, Robert A.J., editors. *British Columbia: Historical Readings*. Vancouver, B.C.: Douglas and McIntyre, 1981.

Ward, W. Peter. *White Canada Forever*, McGill-Queens University Press, 1978.

Watson, Patrick. *The Canadians. Biographies of a Nation, Volume II*. Toronto ON: McArthur and Company, 2001.

West, Willis J. *Stagecoach and Sternwheel Days in the Cariboo and Central B.C.* Surrey, B.C.: Heritage House, 1985.

Williams, David Ricardo. *Call in the Pinkerton's. American Detectives at Work in Canada*. Toronto, ON: Dundurn Press, 1998.

Woolliams, Nina G. *Cattle Ranch. The Story of the Douglas Lake Cattle Company*, North Vancouver, B.C.: Douglas and McIntyre, 1979.

Young, Margaret F. *Quelle Grande Prairie*. Vernon B.C.: Wayside Press, 1994.

Turner, Robert D. *West of the Great Divide*. Victoria B.C.: Morriss Printing, June 1987.

CENSUSES

"*Canadian Census for 1891*." http://royal.okanagan.B.C..ca.

"*Canadian Census for 1901*." http://www.collectionscanada.ca/02/020122_e.html

COLLECTIONS

Collection of Anthony Martin, B.C. Penitentiary Records, *"Escape Inquiry Files,"*

Collection of Anthony Martin, B.C. Penitentiary Files, *"George Edwards Correspondence File,"* 1906–1954.

DIRECTORIES

"Henderson's British Columbia Gazetteer and Directory for 1904". Henderson's Publishing Co Ltd, Vancouver, B.C., 1904.

"Henderson's British Columbia Gazetteer and Directory for 1905". Henderson's Publishing Co Ltd, Vancouver, B.C., 1905.

"Henderson's British Columbia Gazetteer and Directory for 1910". Henderson's Publishing Co Ltd, Vancouver, B.C., 1910.

"Henderson's Kamloops City Directory, 1914". Henderson's Publishing Co Ltd, Vancouver, B.C., 1914.

"The Kamloops City and District Directory, 1915". W. A. Jeffries and Co. Publishers, Kamloops, B.C., 1915.

"Wrigley's British Columbia Directory 1918". Henderson's Publishing Co Ltd, Vancouver, B.C., 1918.

"Wrigley's British Columbia Directory 1925". Henderson's Publishing Co Ltd, Vancouver, B.C., 1925.

"Kamloops Directory for 1877–78".

EMAILS

Armstrong, Hugh. Shorty Dunn, Email message to the author, (25 January 2002)

Campbell, Holly. Campbell Ranch, Email message to author, (11 March 2001).

Colby, Jo-Anne. CPR Archives, Registered mailbag, contents unknown. Email message to author, (11 December 2001).

Corbett, Rene. The Solloways of Mission. Email message to the author, (11 October 2004).

Hill, Shiela. Colquhoun, Email messages to the author, (January 2002 to April 2003)

Hume, Stephen, Herb Mitchell, Email message to the author, (1 October 2004).

Kishkan, Theresa. Sisters of Grass and George Edwards. Email message to author, (29 December 2003).

Klancher, Don. Miner Documentary, Email message to the author, (6 January 2002).

Klancher, Don. Scarlet and Gold Articles, Email message to the author, (3, 7, 13 February 2001).

Martin, Anthony. B.C. Penitentiary. Email message to the author, (26 August 2004).

Moore, Heather. Librarian, Solicitor General Canada Library. B.C. Pen Records, Email message to the author, (30 January 2002).

Osborne, Fiona. Maisie Armytage-Moore and George Edwards, Email message to author, (19 February 2002).

Osborne, Fiona. Maisie Armytage-Moore, Email message to author, (8 March 2002).

Patenaude, Val. Curator, Maple Ridge Museum. Telephone Conversation with Ellen Paterson, 1962. Maple Ridge Historical Society, Email message to author, (30 Jan 2002).

Patenaude, Val. Maple Ridge Museum. Donatelli Witnesses. Email message to author, (30 Jan 2002).

Pringle, Sandra. Westwold Tidbits, Email message to author, (17 Jan 2006).

Pringle, Sandra. Bits and Pieces, Email message to author, (11 Jan 2006).

Pringle, Sandra. Telephone Conversation With Donny Johnson. 8 January 2006. Email message to author, (8 January 2006).

Sandercott, Alan. Death of Billy Grell, Email message to author, (13 November 2004).

Waddington, Margaret, Mary Spencer Postcards, Email message to author, (14 November 2004).

Waite, Don. Fraser Valley Story, Email message to the author, (3 February 2001).

Walker, Larry J. Magazine House, Email message to author, (27 December 2003).

Whalen, Jim. Alberta Report, Email message to author, (9 March 2001).

White, Jack. R.C.M.P. Personnel Files, Email message to the author, (12 March 2001).

Whittaker, Lloyd. R.C.M.P. Information. Email message to the author, (26 February, 22 December 2001).

INTERVIEWS

Robert Cail, Interview with the author, Kamloops B.C.: 9 Dec 2005.

Davies, Dave. Telephone interview with author. Kamloops, B.C.: 29 Jan 2002.

Fernie, Daphne. Interview with author. 3 April 2001, at Victoria B.C.. Transcript held by Peter Grauer; Kamloops B.C.

Heslop, Gordon. Interview by the author, Kamloops B.C.: 28 Jan Knowles, Tom. Interview with the author, Kamloops B.C.: 2004.

McKay, Albert. Interview by Jack Montieth and Don Keizer, Vancouver, B.C.: 20 February 1990.

Pratt, Edward Cecil "Toddy". Interview with the author, Kamloops B.C.: 1985.

Pratt, James. Interview with the author, Kamloops B.C.: 8 December 2005.

Pringle, Val. Interview with the author, Westwold, B.C.: January 2005.

Wright, Wilf. Interview with the author, Williams Lake, B.C.: October 2004.

JOURNALS

Nicola Valley Archives Assoc. Journal, Nicola Valley Historical Quarterly, "Doctors of the Nicola Valley." Jan 1980.

Nicola Valley Archives Assoc. Journal, Nicola Valley Historical Quarterly, "Jesus Garcia." May 1984.

38th Annual Report of the Okanagan Historical Society. "H.H. Bert Thomas. (1874–1973)." Phyllis Miller and Verna Cawston. Wayside Press, Vernon B.C., 1974.

41st Annual Report of the Okanagan Historical Society, "Memories of Pioneer Life at Princeton." Helen Reith. Wayside Press, Vernon B.C., 1977.

43rd Annual Report of the Okanagan Historical Society. "The History of Policing in Enderby." Barbara Newman. Vernon, B.C.: Wayside Press, 1979.

44th Annual Report of the Okanagan Historical Society. "Does Anyone Remember? Early Reminiscences of Princeton." Margaret Mitchell. Vernon, B.C.: Wayside Press, 1980.

45th Annual Report of the Okanagan Historical Society. "Fred and Alice James. Their Early Years on the Commonage and Rose Hill." George James. Vernon, B.C.: Wayside Press, 1981.

48th Annual Report of the Okanagan Historical Society. "The Grey Fox Goes to Earth—Again!" Verna B. Cawston. Vernon, B.C.: Wayside Press, 1984.

54th Annual Report of the Okanagan Historical Society. "Okanagan Indians Non-Registered. The Reason Why," J.H. Christie. Vernon, B.C.: Wayside Press, 1990.

56th Annual Report of the Okanagan Historical Society. "Cliff Hardwick and Bob Tilton." Vernon, B.C.: Wayside Press, 1992

60th Annual Report of the Okanagan Historical Society. "The Birthday. Brenda Thompson. (Life of Doris Crossley)." Vernon, B.C.: Wayside Press, 1996.

Balf, Mary, "Courthouse and Jail in Early Kamloops." Kamloops Museum and Archives article 33, date unknown.

Mobbs, Leslie. "Kamloops Club." Kamloops Museum and Archives article, date unknown.

Ken Favrholdt. "Lewis Campbell." Kamloops Museum and Archives article, date unknown.

Elisabeth Duckworth. "Another Bill Miner Story." Kamloops Museum and Archives article, 30 June 1994.

Stewart, John. "The Todds and Pratts of Barnhartvale." Kamloops Museum and Archives article, 15 Sep 1987.

Stewart, John. "William H. Fernie." Kamloops Museum and Archives article, 4 Jan 1982.

LETTERS

Catton, Frank R. Letter to Ken Favrholdt, Kamloops Museum and Archives. Coquitlam, B.C., 6 Apr 1987.

Montieth, J.W., Bill Miner Info Request, Letter to Armstrong Spallumcheen Museum, 27 Sept 1991.

Morton, Lottie Miner, (Mrs F.L. Morton?). Letter to Kamloops Museum and Archives, McLeod, Frisken, Graves, Miner et al. Nakusp, B.C. 31 Mar 1958.

Schisler, Clifford. Letter to author, Kamloops, B.C. Jack Budd's Papers. Orillia, ON., 9 May 2002.

Schisler, Clifford. Letter to author, Kamloops, B.C. Bill Miner and Garrison's Freight Business. Orillia, ON, 30 June 2002.

Stewart, John, Assistant Archivist. Letter to Ed McCann, Regina, Bill Miner's Pistols. Kamloops Museum and Archives, 19 Apr 1983.

Tilton, Robert, The Tilton Family. Letter in the Kamloops Museum and Archives, circa 1973.

Wilfred Wright, Letter to author, Shorty Dunn's Cabin. Lac La Hache, B.C. ca 20 November 2005.

MANUSCRIPTS

Allison-McDiarmid, Aurelia Angela. *Meet Mr. Edwards*. Unpublished manuscript, Princeton and District Museum and Archives. 1978.

Canadian Pacific Railway Co., *Time Table No. 8, Shuswap Section, 6 May 1906*. David Davies Collection, Kamloops B.C.

Clark, James J. *City of Kamloops History. 1893–1964*. Unpublished manuscript, TNRD Library, Kamloops, B.C.: late 1980s.

Duke, Miss. (Pseudonym) *Saga of Westwold*. Foreward by L.R.Pearse. circa 1954.

Fetterly, N., Kamloops, B.C. *History of the Kamloops Bar. The Pioneer Years: 1884 to 1914*. Unpublished manuscript, 1996.

Forsell, Harold. *Law Enforcement of Pioneer Days in South Central British Columbia*. Unpublished manuscript, date unknown. In collection of author.

Forsell, Harold. *The Forsell Family History*. Unpublished manuscript, circa 1970s. In collection of author, courtesy of Peggy Muir.

Kamloops City. "*Kamloops City Council Meeting Minutes*." 3 May to 31 May, 1906.

Mitchell (nee Hunter), Margaret F. *The Movie The Grey Fox*. Unpublished manuscript, Princeton and District Museum and Archives, After 1981.

Munro, J.H. *Jake of All Trades. An Autobiography*. Penticton, B.C.: 1977.

Stoneberg, M. *Bill Miner, Robber*. Unpublished manuscript, Princeton and District Museum and Archives. 30 July 1990.

Stoneberg, M. Unpublished pencil notes of Bill Miner and Jack Budd, Princeton and District Museum and Archives, Bill Miner Vertical Files, Date unknown.

Thomson, Brenda. *The Story of the Duck Family. 1881 to 1932*. (From interviews with Doris Crossely (Butler) nee Duck). March 1986. In collection of author, courtesy of Sandi Pringle.

Vicars, D.O. *Life of Bill Miner, Train Robber. An Unfinished Narrative*. Unpublished manuscript, Kamloops Museum and Archives, Kamloops, B.C., 1962.

Wilson, R.N.W.M.P. Staff Sergeant John J. (ret.). *Capture of Bill Miner*. Unpublished manuscript, RCMP Archives, Regina.

MAPS

Map, "*Municipality of Mission*," circa 1900.

Kevin Cairns Map Collection, *British Columbia*. Vancouver B.C.: London and British North America Ltd., circa 1913.

FEDERAL GOVERNMENT DOCUMENTS

Environment Canada, Climate Gateway Query Results, *Temperatures and Precipitation* , *Kamloops, B.C. April, May and June 1906.*

National Registration File of Public Rights Administration, *"Naturalization Papers of John Charles Budd,"* File No. B-300, Citizenship and Immigration Canada, Ottawa, ON, 1909.

National Registration File of Public Rights Administration, *"Naturalization Papers of John William Grell,"* File No. 6515–25, Citizenship and Immigration Canada, Ottawa, ON, 1925–1927.

PROVINCIAL GOVERNMENT DOCUMENTS – B.C. ARCHIVES

GR0055, B.C. Provincial Police, *Correspondence Inward To Superintendent. 1891–1910,* Boxes 37 to 80.

GR0061, B.C. Provincial Police, *Correspondence Outwards From Superintendent. 1864–1918,* Reels B02578 to B02580 and B02610. (Restricted.)

GR0063, B.C. Provincial Police, *Correspondence Inward To Superintendent from Attorney General, 1898–1912.,* Boxes 2 to 7.

GR0064, B.C. Provincial Police, *Correspondence from Superintendent to Attorney General, 1898–1918.*

GR0065, B.C. Provincial Police, *Telegrams to Superintendent, 1901 to 1906.*

GR0066, B.C. Provincial Police, *Correspondence Inwards To Superintendent, Private, 1891–1910.*

GR0091, B.C. Provincial Police, *Headquarters Personnel Records, Vol. 17, 18 and 19.* (Restricted)

GR0099, B.C. Provincial Police, *Misc. Correspondence, Reports and Publications, 1892–1942,* Box 1, File 1; Box 3, File 20A.

GR0104, B.C. Provincial Police, *Superintendent's Misc. Notes, Memos, Correspondence, 1900 to 1916.*

GR0419, Attorney General Crown Prosecutor Files, *Transcripts of Preliminary Hearings and Trials, 1857 to 1966,* Boxes 111–117, and reel B395.

GR0429, *Attorney General Correspondence, 1872–1937,* Boxes 13, 17 and 18. (Restricted)

GR1323, *Attorney General Files, 1902–1937,* Reels B02050 to B02081.

GR1466, *Smithers Probate/Estate Files*

GR1481, B.C. *Provincial Police, Scrapbook*

GR1738, B.C. *Provincial Police, Central Correspondence Files, 1909 to 1979,* Box 18, Files 8 to 9; Box 35, File 34; Box 33, File 11.

GR1727, Court Records, Judge's Bench Books, Vol. 521, *Judge Paulinus Irving's Bench Books*

GR2479, Rex v. *George W. Edwards, (Bill Miner), Lewis Colquhoun and William J. Dunn* for "Stopping the Mail and Stealing Certain Post Letters," Files 1, 2, 3, 4 and 5.

GR2506, *Princeton Probate/Estate Files*

B.C. ARCHIVES MANUSCRIPTS

97908–16, *George Edgar Winkler Fonds*, 512 Photographs, 1920 to 1940.

MS0323, *Thomas Kilpatrick Fonds*, 1893 to 1965.

MS0416, *Mrs. Thomas Kilpatrick Fonds*.

MS0425, B.C. Provincial Police, F.S. *Hussey Diary and Letterbook, 1890 to 1904*.

MS0672, *Frederick Stephen Hussey, Letters, 1852 to 1911*.

MS0676, *Louis LeBourdais Fonds, 1817 to 1945*.

MS2793, B.C. *Provincial Police, Veteran's Assoc. Files, 1905–1988*. (Restricted)

VANCOUVER CITY ARCHIVES MANUSCRIPTS

Add. MSS.54, *Campbell-Johnson files*, Part of Major Mathews Collection, 504-A-5, file 34, mf #AM0054.013.00678

Add. MSS. 358, *Bill Miner–Train Robber*, Part of H.A. Price Collection, 550-C-5 file 9, 1906-1907.

NEWSPAPERS

ARMSTRONG ADVANCE	KAMLOOPS STANDARD
ASHCROFT JOURNAL	NICOLA HERALD
CALGARY HERALD	PHOENIX PIONEER
CHILLIWAK PROGRESS	RICHMOND REVIEW
NEW WESTMINSTER COLUMBIAN	SALMON ARM OBSERVER
ENDERBY COMMONER	SIMILKAMEEN SPOTLIGHT
ENDERBY PROGRESS	SIMILKAMEEN STAR
FRASER VALLEY COMMUNITY RECORD	VANCOUVER PROVINCE
GUELPH MERCURY	VANCOUVER NEWS ADVERTISER
HEDLEY GAZETTE	VANCOUVER WORLD
KAMLOOPS INLAND SENTINEL	VICTORIA COLONIST

UNPUBLISHED NOTES

Mitchell, A.H. "Notes on Mission Robbery". Various dates, submitted to Kamloops Museum and Artchives, Aug 1993.

Stoneberg, M. Unpublished pencil notes of "Bill Miner and Jack Budd". Princeton and District Museum and Archives, Date unknown.

Bill Miner File, Armstrong Spallumcheen Museum.

PERIODICALS

Pawley, Eugene. "He Outrobbed Jesse James." Badman, Western Publications, Austin, TX, Vol.1 No. 1, Annual, 1971.

Cawston. V.B. "The Quick Grey Fox ... Fact vs Fiction." Bank of British Columbia's Pioneer News, Feb/Mar 1984.

Paterson,Thomas W. British Columbia. The Pioneer Years, "The Grey Fox", Vol.#1, pages 16 to 21,. Stagecoach Publishing Co. Ltd., Langley, B.C., 1980.

Author unknown. British Columbia Provincial Police Annual, "The Life of Inspector W. L. Fernie". 1931.

Chandler, Ann. "The Lost Patrol." The Beaver, December 2003, 22.

Sismey, Eric D. Canada West, "The 'Hands Up' Gentleman." Summerland, B.C., Winter 1969.

Curtis, Allan. Canadian West, "The Grey Fox." Sunfire Publications, Langley, B.C., Fall 1987.

Belyk, Robert. Canadian West, "The Grey Fox." Sunfire Publications, Langley, B.C., Winter 1987.

Milner. "To the Pioneers." Easy Living, Aug von Kreisler, Max. "The Badman From The East Who Terrorized The West." Frontier West, Reese Publishing, New York, NY, Vol. 3, No.2, April 1973.

Fraser, John A. "Bill Miner Notorious." Cariboo Digest, Quesnel, B.C., Jun, Jul, Aug, 1955.

Stephens, C.G. "True Story of One of NorthWest's Most Notorious Bandits." Peachland Okanagan Review, Mar 1971.

RCMP Quarterly, "Brief History of the Canadian Pacific Police." RCMP, Ottawa, Ont., April 1963,

Murison, K.G. RCMP Quarterly, "Tribute to ex-Sgt. P. G. Thomas." RCMP, Ottawa, Ont., October 1948.

RCMP Quarterly, Old-Timer's Column, "Late Constable Tabuteau Took Part in Search for Bill Miner Gang." RCMP, Ottawa, Ont., April 1963.

Tench, C. W. "The Gentle Bandit". *Real West*. Charlton publications, Derby, Connecticut, Vol VII, Number 34, March 1964.

Rickards, Colin. "Fifty Years A Holdup Man", Part 1. *Real West*. Charlton Publications, Derby, Connecticut, Volume XIII, Number 85, Sept 1970.

Rickards, Colin. "Bill Miner—Fifty Years A Holdup Man." Conclusion. *Real West*. Charlton Publications, Derby, Conn., Vol XIII, Number 86, October 1970.

Berger, Maurice Theodore, Reg. # 7978. *Scarlet and Gold*, "A Sequel To The Capture of Bill Miner." RCMP, Ottawa, Ont., 1950.

Editor-in Chief. *Scarlet and Gold*, "The Bill Miner Case." RCMP, Ottawa, Ont., December 1919.

Browning, Ex-Sgt. *Scarlet and Gold*, "The Bill Miner Case." RCMP, Ottawa, Ont., 1949.

Scarlet and Gold, "Robin Hood—1906 Model", "Kind Hearted Prospector." and "Bill Miner's Party Captured." RCMP, Ottawa, Ont., 1937.

The Shoulder Strap, The Old Timer, "Bill Miner, Outlaw and Stagecoach Bandit." B.C. Provincial Police, 10th Edition.

The Shoulder Strap, "Shorty Dunn," 15th Edition, Apr–Sep 1946.

Brown, George D., Kamloops. *The Shoulder Strap*, "They Knew Bill Miner." B.C. Provincial Police, Winter Edition, #7, Feb. 1942.

Clark, Cecil. *The Shoulder Strap*, "Hotter Than a Sheriff's Pistol." 24th Edition. B.C. Provincial Police.

Watts, Alfred, QC. *The Advocate*, Vol. 26, Part 3. Vancouver Bar Ass., May –June 1968.

Parsons, Chuck. "The Grey Fox's Death." Answer Man column. *True West*, Western Publications, Stillwater, OK, Vol. 37, No. 6, June 1990.

Parsons, Chuck. "Holdup King." Answer Man column. *True West*, Western Publications, Stillwater, OK, Vol. 37, No.5, May 1990.

Boessenecker, John. "Buckshot for Bill Miner." *True West*, Western Publications, Stillwater, OK, Vol. 35, No. 8, August 1988.

Wishart, Bruce. "Bill Miner: The Canadian Years." *True West*, Western Publications, Stillwater, OK, Vol. 37, No. 1, January 1990.

Western Canada Police Review, "Bill Miner, Last of the Train Robbers." Vancouver, B.C.

Williams, Jan. "Bill Miner, Gentleman." *Western Living*, (March 1975).

Boessenecker, John. "The Grey Fox: Stage and Train Robber Bill Miner." *Wild West*, Primedia Enthusiast Grp, Leesburg, VA, Vol. 15, No.1, June 2002.

Voter's Lists

Voter's List for Kamloops and Area, 1876.

From the Sessional Papers of the British Columbia Government, 1899, extracted by Hugh Armstrong, *"British Columbia's Voters List, 1898,"* http://www.rootsweb.com/~canB.C./vote1898/voters98.htm.

Province of British Columbia. *"British Columbia Voter's Lists, General Election 1907"*. 5 Nov 1906.

Web Sites

Government of British Columbia, Annual Report of the Minister of Mines for the Year Ending Dec 31, 1906. http://www.em.gov.B.C..ca/DL/GSBPubs/AnnualReports/AR_1906.pdf.

Chilliwak Museum and Archives. Chilliwak Landing. http://chilliwack.museum.B.C..ca/history/cov/chilliwack.htm. (2004).

Gold Country B.C. Portal. Early History of Ashcroft. http://www.goldcountry.B.C..ca/hist/ashhist.htm. (2005).

Early History of Coalmont. Atjeu Publishing, 2000. http://www.ghosttowns.com/canada/B.C./coalmont.html. (2005).

Fraser Valley Country Store Ltd. The Fraser Valley Guide. Highways. http://www.fraservalleyguide.com/History.html. (2005).

B.C. Archives. Birth, Marriage, Death Index. http://www.B.C.archives.gov.B.C..ca/textual/governmt/vstats/v_events.htm. (2004)

Sanders, Joanna. James Shaver Woodsworth, The Early Years. http://www.saskndp.com/history/woodsworth.html. (Jan. 2006).

SchoolNet Digital Collections Program. Brief History of Victoria. http://collections.ic.gc.ca/building/. (2005)

Brigham Young University, Western States Historical Marriage Record Index, Marriage of Paul Stevens and Rosie Aldrich, Idaho, 20 Mar 1895. http://abish.byui.edu/specialCollections/fhc/. (January 2006).

Canadian Censuses for 1871, 1881 and 1891. "Colquhoun." http://www.rootsweb.com/~canB.C./conlist.htm#5. (27 Dec. 2005).

INDEX

393, 395
Trackers xvii, xxi, 48, 124, 132, 182–186, 188, 190–204, 219, 227, 230, 233, 259, 262, 277, 305, 309, 311, 317, 355, 377, 393, 394, 395, 396, 442
Tulameen 7, 8, 14, 71, 79, 136, 264
Tunstall, George Christie 127, 191, 192, 194, 279, 346
Tuthill, George Henry 73, 74, 242, 247, 248, 299

U

Unions 19, 123
Upper Campbell Creek xvi, xxii, 147, 152, 153, 155, 186, 187, 188, 218, 222, 280, 281, 328, 334, 513, 553

V

Valencia 135, 576
Vancouver Province 47, 52, 59, 65, 67, 90, 123, 249, 259, 289, 294, 307, 308, 332, 341, 349, 350, 351, 361, 375, 405, 469, 504
Vancouver World 278
Vernon xxii, 5, 8, 25, 144, 147, 151, 152, 155, 159, 167, 186, 187, 200, 205, 206, 209, 211–217, 223, 233, 264, 270, 281, 286, 321, 323, 328, 351, 397–402, 487, 515–517, 551, 555
Vicars, Desmond 275
Vicars, Warden 277, 348
Victoria x, xvii, 5, 12, 25, 41, 45, 49, 50, 58, 60, 97, 102, 104, 118, 128, 130, 135, 150, 155, 159, 167, 175, 182, 189, 192, 194, 228, 260–263, 266, 267, 278, 291–293, 313, 320, 321, 327, 333, 336, 337, 340, 365, 366, 375, 385, 386, 388, 392, 393, 395–397, 411, 429, 454, 456, 459, 460, 461, 504, 511, 523, 524, 532, 540, 542, 547
Victoria Colonist 58, 118, 150, 267, 292, 340, 366, 454, 456, 459, 460, 461, 524

W

Waddell, Detective 52, 370, 402, 479
Walker, Oliver 554, 555
Ward, John 33, 36
Washington 2, 3, 7, 8, 22, 26, 51, 56, 86, 91, 93, 98, 100, 101, 136, 216, 291, 295, 331, 332, 412, 416, 440, 450, 451, 487, 488, 502, 511, 519, 549
Webley, E.E. 86
Wellman, Mary Jane 56

West, Willis 31
Westminster Junction 368, 369, 440
White, A.J. 535, 541, 544
Whonnock 42, 43, 46, 47, 48, 51, 52, 63
Whyte, Warden 383, 386, 388, 402, 413, 441, 446, 466, 467, 469, 472, 491, 494, 504
Whyte, William 59, 226, 268, 292, 387
Wildlife Park xv, xvi
Wilkie, Otway J.J. 55
Willis, Walter 30, 31, 171, 172, 176, 178, 259, 347
Wilson, Robert 37
Wilson, Sergeant 36, 37, 57, 69, 204, 211–216, 219, 220, 226, 228, 229, 231, 232, 233, 235–237, 239–244, 246–255, 258, 264, 271, 286, 297, 299, 302, 305, 312, 314, 315, 340, 344, 348, 349, 362, 376, 377, 394, 395, 397, 398, 402–405, 422, 447, 450, 479, 480
Winchester 35, 73, 76, 93, 151, 181, 201, 221, 239, 243, 244, 245, 248, 251, 265
Winkler, George Edgar 6, 23, 116–118, 511, 521, 523, 527–530, 532–542
Wolf Lake 196
Wood, Wentworth Fletcher 190, 298, 346, 347, 390, 464
Woods, John 429
Woodsworth, James Shaver 159, 166, 167, 260, 267
Wright, Ernie 114
Wright, Wilfred x, 113

Y

Yale wagon road 63
Young, Constable 193, 195, 197, 200, 396
Young, Frederick 255, 260, 317
Young, Thomas 425

Colophon

"Ancillon, a seventeenth-century divine
of eminence, wrote, 'The less the eye is
fatigued in reading a book, the more
at liberty the mind is to judge of it.
That, as the beauties and faults of it
are more easily perceived when it is printed
than in the manuscript,
so the same beauties and faults
are more clearly seen when it is printed in
fair character, and upon good paper,
than when it is printed on bad paper,
or with bad letter.'"
"… Beauty of the page as a whole is attained
by the use of proper types and by
taking advantage of a pause or break
in the text for the insertion
of some characteristic decoration,
an initial, or headband, or possibly
by the dignified and simple arrangement
of the types themselves …"

Frederic W. Goudy, *Typologia*;
University of California Press, 1940.

Typeset in (Adobe) Goudy Old Style,
GOUDY OLD STYLE SMALL CAPS
AND OLD STYLE FIGURES,
designed by Frederic W. Goudy,
and (Adobe) Wood Type Ornaments
designed by
Barabara Lind and Joy Redick.

This book was designed and set into type by
David J. DiFrancesco,
Digital Art and Design,
Thompson Rivers University,
Kamloops, British Columbia.